**Library of Congress Cataloging-in-Publication Data**

Living with television now: advances in cultivation theory and research / edited by Michael Morgan, James Shanahan, Nancy Signorielli.
p. cm.
Includes bibliographical references and index.
1. Communication—Social aspects—United States.
2. Television programs—Social aspects—United States.
I. Morgan, Michael. II. Shanahan, James. III. Signorielli, Nancy.
HM1206.L577 2013 303.48'330973—dc23 2012002284
ISBN 978-1-4331-1369-7 (hardcover)
ISBN 978-1-4331-1368-0 (paperback)
ISBN 978-1-4539-0764-1 (e-book)

Bibliographic information published by **Die Deutsche Nationalbibliothek**. **Die Deutsche Nationalbibliothek** lists this publication in the "Deutsche Nationalbibliografie"; detailed bibliographic data is available on the Internet at http://dnb.d-nb.de/.

The paper in this book meets the guidelines for permanence and durability of the Committee on Production Guidelines for Book Longevity of the Council of Library Resources.

29 Broadway, 18th floor, New York, NY 10006
www.peterlang.com



Printed in the United States of America

# LIVING WITH TELEVISION NOW

This book is part of the Peter Lang Media and Communication list.
Every volume is peer reviewed and meets
the highest quality standards for content and production.

PETER LANG
New York • Washington, D.C./Baltimore • Bern
Frankfurt • Berlin • Brussels • Vienna • Oxford

# LIVING WITH TELEVISION NOW

## advances in cultivation theory & research

EDITED BY
MICHAEL MORGAN,
JAMES SHANAHAN,
NANCY SIGNORIELLI

PETER LANG
New York • Washington, D.C./Baltimore • Bern
Frankfurt • Berlin • Brussels • Vienna • Oxford

To the memory of George Gerbner:
colleague, mentor, teacher, friend...

# Contents

# Foreword: George Gerbner and Cultivation Analysis

*Larry Gross*

George Gerbner played a central role in the emergence of mass communication theory and research as an important contributor to the national conversation about the power of the mass media in contemporary life. Working from the platform provided as dean of the Annenberg School at the University of Pennsylvania—a position he held for an unprecedented 25-year term (1964–1989)—and augmented by his simultaneous role as editor of the *Journal of Communication* from 1973 to 1991, Gerbner often seemed to be the public face of media research. More important, however, was his insistence on using this public visibility to challenge conventional wisdom about the influence of mass media.

I first met George Gerbner when I visited the Annenberg School in April 1968 for a somewhat informally arranged job interview—I had not applied, nor had a position been advertised (those were simpler days). A mutual colleague had suggested that they might be interested in me—an atypical social psychology student just finishing his dissertation—and that I would be intrigued by communications as a field in which to pursue interests in art and culture that were not welcomed by psychology departments. It turned out that he was right on both counts, and I ended up spending 35 years at the school.

Shortly after my arrival at the Annenberg School George and I began a series of conversations about the impact of media on culture and how this might be subjected to empirical study. These conversations lasted for nearly forty years. George enlisted my social science training in the challenge of assessing the impact of media on beliefs, attitudes, and conceptions of reality. This is an especially difficult task when one assumes, as George and I did, that the primary function of the media is to stabilize rather than to change behavior patterns, whereas most social science research aims at measuring the alterations in beliefs and behaviors induced by exposure to media messages.

Our conversations led to the design and implementation of research approaches that came to be known as *cultivation analysis*, based on George's preference for the term "cultivation" to describe the cultural function of media as the shapers of social reality. Joined by our students-turned-colleagues Michael Morgan and Nancy Signorielli, and then Michael's student James Shanahan, the "Cultural Indicators" team, which included numerous other students and colleagues over the years, produced scores of studies, provoked several notoriously heated debates—George never shied from an intellectual fight—and left an indelible mark on the field of communication research.

In an era dominated by simplified assumptions about the impact of television violence, George insisted on a broader perspective and a sharper analysis, arguing that the primary impact of the media was to reinforce, not to challenge the structure of power. At the heart of George's approach to understanding media and culture was the importance of storytelling as the defining human attribute, and he argued that the function of storytelling in any society is to fit reality to the social order (Morgan, 2012). George was fond of quoting these words of the 18th-century Scottish patriot, Andrew Fletcher, "If a man were permitted to make all the ballads he need not care who should make the laws of a nation."

The second key to George's analysis was the recognition that, in the modern world, storytelling has become a commercialized, centralized industrial enterprise. In 1959 he wrote, "The rise of cultural mass production, creating audiences, subjecting tastes, views and desires to the laws of the market, and inherently tending toward the standardized and the safe rather than the diversified or critical, creates new problems in the theory and practice of self-government" (Gerbner, 1959, pp. 276–277). In the subsequent decades he developed and deepened this perspective, focusing primarily on television which, as he liked to say, had become the medium that told most of the stories to most of the people most of the time. Thus the study of television became a prime "cultural indicator" for understanding the messages that shape our conceptions of reality.

Having been drawn to communication because of my interest in the role of the arts in society it was not difficult to see that the mass media had subsumed many of the functions previously performed by the arts as the conveyors of core cultural assumptions, beliefs, and values. All human societies have created, shared, and consumed with pleasure the symbolic products we can collectively call "culture" or "the arts." The very processes through which all human societies create and maintain themselves—that distinguish us from our animal ancestors—are those of storytelling in words, pictures, music, and dance. For most of human history the stories, songs, and images people knew were crafted by members of their own communities, with whom they shared the basic conditions of life. In stark contrast to pre-industrial societies, in which the culture communities consumed was almost entirely dependent on what they could produce, we now are faced with endless competing choices, twenty-four hours a day, produced by industrial corporations with which we have no social contact whatever.

Remember: this dizzying array of media options is not there because anyone actually asked for all these images, songs, or stories. Rather, it exists because someone, somewhere, has a commercial interest in selling us a product—or more typically, in attracting our attention so that it can be "sold" to advertisers who wish to sell us something. While major corporations compete to spend millions of dollars to place a thirty-second ad during the Super Bowl halftime, there are usually small businesses eager to spend much lower sums to place their ads during late-night programs or on less popular cable channels. Larger or smaller audiences, prime or less desirable demographics, the media are selling audience attention all the time, on all channels. The general rule is: if you're consuming media and not paying for it, you are the product.

The businesses that manufacture and distribute media fare are increasingly inter-connected, and this helps them coordinate their efforts in packaging and selling their products. The corporations that create media fare also control how particular social groups and issues are represented. Indeed, representation in the media is in itself a kind of power, and their invisibility helps maintain the powerlessness of groups at the bottom of the social heap. Not all interests or viewpoints are treated equally, and judgments are routinely made—by producers and writers, editors and reporters—about what to include or exclude.

In one of our first comprehensive accounts of the cultivation approach, the 1976 article, "Living with Television," we noted that "Representation in the fictional world signifies social existence; absence means symbolic annihilation" (Gerbner & Gross, 1976, p. 182). Media representation as a form of social power was always at the center of George's analysis of the media, and there was always an implicit critique of the social inequities that the media helped perpetuate.

My discussions with George, as we embarked on our collaboration, focused on the challenge of assessing the impact of television's seductively realistic depictions of the real world. In particular, we were interested in those aspects of television drama that illustrated the way important social institutions, such as those entrusted with law enforcement or medical treatment, function: Who are the folks who make decisions, who wield power, and who ultimately achieve their goals; and who are the folks who are at the receiving end of these decisions, who suffer the consequences of others' power, and who end badly?

George's previous empirical investigations had been pretty much limited to content analysis, which was the basis for what he called "message system analysis"—one of the three elements of the "cultural indicators" approach to the understanding of media and culture. My contribution was to be on the second front, measuring the role of these messages in cultivating beliefs and images about the real world (the third component, "institutional process analysis," was the least explored in our work, although it was important to the overall analytic model). Having been trained in social psychology, a field that pioneered the systematic analysis and measurement of attitudes and beliefs, George assumed that I would be equipped for the challenge.

And it was a challenge, as previous research on the effects of the media was mostly focused on assessing the impact of particular messages or campaigns on narrowly defined behavioral outcomes. In most instances the question was whether exposure to a message or campaign made viewers more likely to favor the object of the message: buy a product, vote for a candidate, etc. The core definition of a media effect was the difference between expressed attitudes after exposure to a message compared to the attitude expressed before exposure. But we were interested in assessing the impact of entire "message systems," not merely single messages or even campaigns, and we were focusing on the cumulative impact of exposure many hours per day, over months or years. And, equally critical, the effect we were postulating was not a change in audiences' attitudes or behavior but rather the reinforcement and strengthening of the world views cultivated by the media.

One of our first methodological decisions was also one of the most important. Because we wanted to assess the impact of immersion in the symbolic environment embodied in television's dramatic world, we decided early on that we would ask folks questions about the real world, not about television. We were not ourselves administering exposure as an independent variable in an experiment but rather entering the scene long after our respondents had been exposed to television. The independent variable of media exposure had already been administered through much of our respondents' lives. Our supposition was that those who spent more of their time watching television—and then, as now, most Americans spent more time watching television than almost anything else besides work and sleep—would likely come to project television's patterns onto the real world. Thus, if we asked questions about the real world—such as how likely the average person was to encounter violence, or the proportion of the workforce employed in law enforcement, to chose examples relevant to the then-current preoccupation with television and violence—we could see whether those more exposed to television were more likely to chose answers closer to the television version of reality. The simple technique we employed, adapted from a semi-projective technique called "error choice," was one I brought with me as part of my social psychology training (see Hammond, 1948).

We tested our assumptions initially through a fairly simple quota sample survey—designed to obtain groups divided by amounts of television exposure but otherwise comparable in age, gender, education—on which we asked a series of questions drawn from our analyses of television content. At the time, given our funding and the current target of public interest, these questions focused heavily on violence, victimization, and law enforcement; but there were questions about other aspects of life, in particular relating to the differential life chances of men and women. Our basic analytic focus was the proportion of those more exposed to television—what we called the heavy viewers—who chose the answer more reflective of television's version of the world, in contrast with those less exposed, the light viewers. The difference between these two figures—heavy viewers minus light viewers—we called the *cultivation differential* to signal the difference that viewing made to the beliefs and attitudes held by audiences.

As we expected, those reporting much heavier television viewing were more likely to answer questions about the real world in ways that accorded with television's images, what we called the "television answer." On issue after issue those who watched more television were more likely—whatever their background—to project television's versions of reality on to their conceptions about the world, its people, and how they function.

We later isolated a pattern that we termed *mainstreaming*. The mainstream can be thought of as a commonality of viewpoints and values that television tends to cultivate in its viewers. While light viewers in any particular demographic group may exhibit relatively divergent positions on a given topic, heavy viewers are more likely to agree with the viewpoint proffered by television. In other words, differences explained by the viewers' divergent backgrounds and life situations—differences that are readily apparent in the answers given by light viewers—tend to diminish or even disappear when heavy viewers in the same groups are compared. Heavy television use is thus associated with a convergence of outlooks, a mainstreaming of opinion.

But that was then, and the assumptions we made and the methods we adopted were grounded in a set of circumstances that now seem both quaint and distant. Important among them:

- Starting in the late 1940s, television had come to dominate U.S. society, infiltrating the nation's living rooms and forcing all other media and social institutions to come to terms with its power. By the late 1960s, politics, news, entertainment, including sports, commerce, and just plain social life could not be adequately understood without taking television into account.
- U.S. television was dominated by three (soon to be four) networks that together accumulated a mass audience numbering in the scores of millions. Television brought together audiences that would previously have lived in separate worlds. Never before had all social classes, groups, and ages shared so much of the same cultural fare, while having so little to do with its creation.
- While aiming at the assembling of the largest possible mass audience, television's commercial imperatives dictated that they cater to the interests of those segments of most interest to commercial sponsors: White, middle class, suburban.
- Television, like other mass media, was one-directional, allowing audiences the opportunity to participate only by watching; hopefully (in the minds of media executives and sponsors) by buying advertised products; and, in the astronomically unlikely event of being picked by Nielsen, by having their viewing preferences reflected in audience ratings.
- Television news, the most cited news source for most citizens, was the province of three networks, whose anchors became familiar "opinion leaders" supposedly able to shift public sentiment with the raise of an eyebrow.
- U.S. media offered their audiences a U.S.-centered world-view that was rarely challenged, reflecting as well as reinforcing American ethnocentrism.

Fast forward and we find ourselves in a vastly different media and communications environment, and all of the assumptions and methods that were grounded in the conditions of the "television age" are up for reassessment:

- Just as television infiltrated and ultimately transformed all of U.S. society, the Internet, in its manifold manifestations, is now doing just that. By now, once more, we cannot understand politics, news, entertainment, including sports, commerce, and just plain social life without taking the Internet into account.

- As recently as 1980, when fewer than 5% of U.S. households had VCRs and less than a quarter had cable, the networks could count on dividing a mass audience amounting to 90% of all viewers. By 1997 that number had shrunk to 49%, and the Internet was just getting started. By now, as we know, the networks are struggling to come to terms with the new cable/web world. In today's brave new media/communications world, companies that didn't exist one year ago are being bought for billions by companies that didn't exist five years ago.
- Armed with the information derived from Internet-based data mining, audience segmentation and niche marketing have redefined the terms of commercial media, abandoning the search for the largest audiences in favor of targeted appeals to those most likely to respond.
- Web-based media have made multi-directional, audience-generated communication a reality, giving citizens the opportunity to join the party as producers rather than merely consumers. Even with Pareto's power law dictating that a minuscule fraction of "prosumers" ever reach an audience larger than their immediate circle, the top-down tyranny of the media has been effectively challenged.
- Nowhere has the "consumer generated content" revolution been more powerful than in public life, as the reversible panopticon of the new technologies has deprived politicians of the luxury of speaking "just among ourselves," just as it has exposed the authorities to the lenses of countless smartphone cameras that can turn visual evidence of their behavior into viral hits.

These changes are both a challenge and a blessing, as they open new horizons for media research. While all of the received knowledge from the theories and research developed in the age of television's domination needs to be re-examined in light of new realities, this may be especially true of cultivation analysis. Theories such as the agenda-setting role of the media, or the spiral of silence, to choose two prominent examples from the last third of the 20th century, are not necessarily limited by the particularities of the media system they might be asked to explain. But the fundamental assumptions underlying cultivation analysis presume the existence of an ideologically coherent and consistent world view that is cultivated by the various arms of an industrialized, commercial media system. Given the changes noted above, the existence of such a coherent system cannot be taken for granted; this becomes a matter for thoughtful analysis and for sustained empirical investigation. And, fortunately, this volume represents precisely the sort of theory and research that is called for, both for the further development and testing of cultivation as an approach to understanding the role of media, and for subjecting this approach to the challenge of confronting the changed realities of our time.

It may be that the new realities of the Internet, the World Wide Web, social media, and whatever will come along next, will not reveal the familiar contours of cultivation in the world views, attitudes, and beliefs held by citizens of the future. But decades of working with George Gerbner instilled in me a strong skepticism on this front, and an enduring hunch that the power embedded in media systems will not easily be dislodged by new technologies.

When George retired as dean he turned his boundless energies from understanding and critiquing the role of media to trying to change what he liked to call the cultural environment, which, he insisted, is every bit as precious and vulnerable as the physical environment. As he put it, we need a cultural environmental movement to "mobilize Americans to act as citizens as effectively as commercials mobilize us to act as consumers." Here, it must be said, George finally met a foe he could not defeat, but his efforts to define the terms of the struggle, identify the enemy, and tirelessly raise the standard of humanity in the face of corporate greed and political cowardice will long be an inspiration to those who knew him as teacher, colleague, and friend.

## References

Gerbner, G. (1959). Education and the challenge of mass culture. *AV Communication Review, 7*, 264–278.

Gerbner, G., & Gross, L. (1976). Living with television: The violence profile. *Journal of Communication, 26*(2), 173–199.

Hammond, K. (1948). Measuring attitudes by error-choice: An indirect method. *Journal of Abnormal and Social Psychology, 43*(1), 38–48.

Morgan, M. (2012). *George Gerbner: A critical introduction to media and communication theory.* New York: Peter Lang Publishing.

# *Introduction*

# 1. The Stories We Tell

## Cultivation Theory and Research

*Michael Morgan, James Shanahan, & Nancy Signorielli*

In the context of communication theory and research, what is "cultivation analysis"? Briefly, it's a research approach that examines how the stories we watch on television contribute to our beliefs and attitudes about the "real" world. Hundreds of studies conducted over the past four decades have (mostly) found that there *are* relationships between television exposure and peoples' worldviews. But important questions remain: Just how strong are these relationships, are they real, are some people more vulnerable to them than others, do they vary across different topics, and will we continue to find them in new media environments? The chapters in this book survey important recent developments in this evolving body of work and point us toward new directions and fresh challenges for cultivation theory and research in the future.

## Background

Most readers are probably familiar with the fact that television's social impact is a "perennial and vexing object of passionate debate" (Shanahan & Morgan, 1999, p. 1), particularly for those who want to trace society's ills to easily identifiable sources. But we have more experience with television now, and perhaps we look on it with a somewhat more jaundiced and less hysterical eye. Sixty years have passed since it became the most prominent mass medium (and arguably one of the defining experiences of life) in the 20th century. The decades-old fears about TV violence, gender and ethnic stereotyping, and assorted harmful effects on children and adolescents may seem less urgent, particularly as other technologies (the Internet, social media, video games, cell phones, etc.) draw our attention to these old concerns (and others) in new ways. Cultivation theory and research were hatched in the days when television was younger and the issues seemed more pressing (and cultivation was actually an alternative response to many of those concerns). Still, while television has obviously changed as an institution, as a technology, and in terms of its programming, the fact that "new media" seem to get more attention may mask a situation in which television still garners most of the viewers and the bulk of the advertising dollars.

This book is the latest step in a long process of exploring the relevance of television in the formation and maintenance of people's attitudes, beliefs, and behaviors. For George Gerbner (the author of cultivation theory and the larger Cultural Indicators project of which it is a key part; see Morgan, 2002, 2012), it began as an attempt to say something about television during a time when many believed television was a major cause of social violence. While most investigators (virtually all of those researching the question under the auspices of the Surgeon General (Surgeon General's Scientific Advisory Committee on Television and Social Behavior, 1972) were focused on determining whether audiences imitate television violence immediately after viewing it, Gerbner was more interested in the lessons and impacts of exposure to television over the longer term.

Gerbner argued that television content—or any message—is a socially and historically determined expression of concrete physical and social relationships. Messages imply propositions, assumptions, and points of view that are understandable only in terms of the social relationships and contexts in which they are produced. Yet they also reconstitute those relationships and contexts. They thus function recursively, sustaining and giving meaning to the structures and practices that produce them.

Communication to Gerbner is "interaction through messages," a distinctly human (and humanizing) process that both creates and is driven by the symbolic environment that constitutes culture. The symbolic environment reveals social and institutional dynamics, and because it expresses social patterns it also cultivates them. This, then, is how Gerbner originally conceived of "cultivation": the process within which interaction through messages shapes and sustains the terms on which the messages are premised.

Connecting these views on communication to the more specific problem of television, Gerbner was interested in the social functions that stemmed from its role as the dominant cultural storyteller of the age. "People learn best not what their teachers think they teach or what their preachers think they preach, but what their cultures in fact cultivate," he wrote early on (1963, p. 42). The new features that were most critical to Gerbner were the extensive industrialization and commercialization of storytelling that mass media introduced. This was a profound transformation in the cultural process of storytelling, and television took it to new extremes.

Gerbner was especially fond of quoting Scottish patriot Andrew Fletcher (1655–1716), who wrote: "If a man were permitted to make all the ballads, he need not care who should make the laws of a nation." Such a romantic notion is not easily testable by empirical methods, but that makes it no less compelling. Storytelling occupies a crucial role in human existence, and it is being increasingly monopolized by a small and shrinking group of global conglomerates whose attention does not extend beyond the bottom line and quarterly reports to stockholders. Therefore, the world we are inhabiting and (re)creating is one designed according to the specifications of marketing strategies.

To assess television's importance as a storyteller, Gerbner devised a three-pronged research strategy for a research project called Cultural Indicators (Gerbner, 1973). This research project would have three main components (or "prongs"). The first component, known as *institutional process analysis*, investigates how the flow of media messages is produced and managed, how decisions are made, and how media organizations function.

The second, *message system analysis*, has been used since 1967 to track the most stable, pervasive, and recurrent images in media content, in terms of the portrayal of violence, race and ethnicity, gender-roles, occupations, and many other topics and aspects of life. In formulating this aspect of the Cultural Indicators research program, Gerbner took care to document the parameters and boundaries of the emerging "system" of messages seen on television. Gerbner (see, e.g., 1969) felt that simple (though detailed and comprehensive) measurements of television's world would tell us a lot. He found, not surprisingly, that the world of TV was very violent (Gerbner, 1970). Above and beyond that, though, there were other persistent features, such as the fact that men outnumbered women on TV by a ratio of about three to one and that minorities, older people, and the working class were significantly under-represented. And while there had been similar content analyses before, Gerbner's project was the only one that looked at violence as a social scenario examining whether men, women, Whites, and Blacks (among various other categories of people) were more or less likely to commit violence, and more or less likely to be shown as victims. While earlier studies provided valuable snapshots, Gerbner wanted to measure trends in the cultural environment over time.

The third prong, *cultivation analysis*, is the study of how exposure to the world of television contributes to viewers' conceptions about the real world.

Gerbner was loath to look at the issue from the then-standard "stimulus-response" perspective; as an alternative, he and Larry Gross crafted a strategy that examined the relationship between amount of exposure to television and the worldviews of viewers. In their classic article, "Living with Television" (Gerbner & Gross, 1976; see also Larry Gross's Foreword to this volume), they introduced the "cultivation differential" (CD), which is simply the percentage point difference between light and heavy viewers on any given issue being examined. If, for instance, 40 percent of light viewers but 50 percent of heavy viewers believed that they would likely become victims of violence, the "CD" was +10 points. Since this modest original formulation, the theoretical framework and methodological techniques of cultivation analysis have evolved in many ways over the years. The focus of this book is on current advances in cultivation theory and research. More than 40 years later, we are still trying to figure out how exposure to television contributes to our conceptions of social reality—and, more than ever, what it means to be living with television now.

So, why "cultivation"? Very simply, Gerbner did not care about any "changes" in outlook that were due to viewing in the short-term. Those were questions for persuasion and marketing research. Rather, he saw outlooks as being nurtured, maintained, and reinforced by television's messages over long periods of time. All communication, he argued, cultivates the assumptions, points of view, and relationships on which it is premised. With *mass* communication, what is cultivated is standardized and widely shared to an historically unprecedented degree. The common symbolic environment in which we grow up and live gives shape and meaning to all that we do; the more we "live" in that synthetic but coherent world, the more it cultivates our conceptions of social reality.

To some, this was a common-sense idea. However, it raised the hackles of many social scientists who saw within it a too-simplistic criticism of television or even a misuse of social science research methods; it provided an opportunity for innumerable colloquies, critiques, revisions, and reappraisals. We've contributed a few of these ourselves (there is an extensive review of the various criticisms and responses to them in Shanahan & Morgan, 1999). But despite, or perhaps because of, the enormous amount of criticism that has been leveled at cultivation, it has been one of the most frequently cited theories of mass communication or media effects since the 1970s. Various studies of the media effects literature regularly place cultivation as one of the three most cited theories (along with agenda-setting and uses and gratifications; Bryant & Miron, 2004). Moreover, an analysis of 962 articles on media effects in 16 journals published between 1993 and 2005 found that cultivation was *the* most cited theory (Potter & Riddle, 2007). Indeed, Cultural Indicators research has been prolific. More than 550 relevant studies have been published (two-thirds of which are extensions, replications, reviews, and critiques conducted by independent researchers not associated with Gerbner and the original research team).[1] Cultivation studies have been carried out in Argentina, Australia, Belgium, Brazil, China, England, Germany, Hungary, Israel, Japan, Mexico, Russia, South Korea, Sweden, Thailand, and elsewhere. Clearly, such a large body of work—and all the complex issues and implications it raises—cannot be exhaustively treated here, so this chapter attempts to provide only a general introduction to this area of research. (For a more extensive examination of the cultivation literature, see Morgan, Shanahan, & Signorielli, 2009; Shanahan & Morgan, 1999.)

## Cultivation Analysis Methods

In this section we offer a brief account of how cultivation analysis is usually conducted. Not everyone does it this way, and the chapters of this book will show that there is a good deal of discussion about the best ways to do cultivation analysis. In general, though, cultivation analysis begins by identifying the most common and stable patterns in television content, emphasizing the consistent images, portrayals, and values that cut across program genres. This is accomplished either by conducting a message system analysis or by examining existing content studies.

Once those patterns are identified, the goal is to ascertain if those who spend more time watching television are more likely to perceive the real world in ways that reflect those particular messages and lessons. That is, cultivation analysts develop hypotheses about what heavy viewers would be expected to think about some topic or issue, if they think about it in terms of the way it is presented on television.

To test these hypotheses, survey procedures are typically used to examine relationships between amount of television viewing and conceptions of social reality. The questions used are of several types. Some juxtapose answers reflecting the statistical "facts" of the television world with those more in line with reality. For example, compared to light viewers, heavy viewers would be more likely to think that there are more law enforcement professionals in the workforce (Gerbner & Gross, 1976). These are often referred to as "first-order" measures of cultivation. Other questions examine symbolic transformations and more general implications of the message system data; many call these "second-order" cultivation measures. Some of these questions are "semi-projective" (e.g., asking respondents to estimate some aspect of reality relative to their own situation). Questions about peoples' perceived likelihood of victimization and the extent to which they think others can be trusted fall into this category.

Finally, some simply ask about beliefs, opinions, attitudes, or behaviors. For instance, heavy viewers have been shown to harbor more traditional beliefs about gender roles in many studies (Morgan, 1982; Signorielli, 1993).

Using different types of samples (national probability, regional, convenience) of children, adolescents, or adults, amount of viewing is usually assessed by asking how much time the respondent spends watching on an "average day." These data may be used in their original form (a ratio scale) or may be grouped by level of exposure ("light," "medium," and "heavy" viewing). The determination of what constitutes "light," "medium," and "heavy" is made on a sample-by-sample basis, using as close to an even three-way split of hours of self-reported daily television viewing as possible.

People who regularly consume a great deal of television differ from light viewers in many ways besides simply how much time they spend watching. To deal with this, differences across the responses of light, medium, and heavy viewers are examined within specific demographic subgroups, and the effects of other variables are statistically controlled. Differences associated with amount of viewing are sometimes independent of, but usually interact with, the many social, cultural, and personal factors that differentiate light and heavy viewers. In other words, the strength, shape, and even direction of cultivation relationships may all vary considerably for different types of people and groups. (These variations often suggest a process called "mainstreaming," described below.) In addition, the analysis typically examines associations between amount of viewing and attitudes while applying simultaneous controls, as in partial correlation and multiple regression, although this was not always done in the early days of the research.

## Cultivation: Development and Critique

Early cultivation results were largely focused on violence; Gerbner and Gross (1976) reported that heavy viewers were more likely than light viewers to give "television answers" to questions about law enforcement, crime, danger, and mistrust. Message system analysis had shown that television greatly exaggerates the amount of violence in society and over-represents the number of police, detectives, criminal lawyers, and so on, in the workforce. As discussed above, respondents were asked if they thought the number of people working in law enforcement and crime detection was 1% (closer to the real world figure) or 5% (referred to as the "TV answer," since it is closer to the ways things are in the world of television). The data showed that 50% of the light viewers, compared to 59% of the heavy viewers, said 5%—that is, heavy viewers were more likely to give the "TV answer" (with a cultivation differential of +9).

In the attitudinal realm, when asked if "most people can be trusted," 48% of light viewers but 65% of heavy viewers responded that "You can't be too careful." From these patterns, the notion of the "Mean World Syndrome" emerged, suggesting that television viewing cultivates a complex set of outlooks that includes an exaggerated sense of victimization, apprehension, insecurity, anxiety, and mistrust.

These early findings were elaborated in a series of annual Violence Profiles (e.g., Gerbner, Gross, Jackson-Beeck, Jeffries-Fox, & Signorielli, 1978; Gerbner, Gross, Signorielli, & Jackson-Beeck, 1979), which generally argued that symbolic violence is a demonstration of power and a mechanism of social control. In showing who can get away with what against whom, television violence perpetuates a social hierarchy of power, vulnerability, and control (Morgan, 1983). Cultivating a sense of insecurity and risk can intensify dependence on authority and promote a willingness to accept repressive measures that promise greater security.

From that start, studies expanded to examine the cultivation of sex-role stereotypes, political orientations and behavior, images of aging, health-related beliefs and behaviors, opinions about science, attitudes toward marriage, the family, and work, beliefs about the environment, religion, and many other issues, along with an increasing emphasis on international extensions and cross-cultural comparisons (see Shanahan & Morgan, 1999; Signorielli & Morgan, 1990).

### *Critiques and Refinements*

Few theories of media effects (and perhaps few areas of social research in general) have been critiqued as heavily and fiercely as cultivation. (For some examples, see Doob & Macdonald, 1979; Hirsch, 1980; Hughes, 1980; Potter, 1993, 1994; Wober, 1980; see also Shanahan & Morgan, 1999.) These critiques have focused on many diverse issues, including cultivation's emphasis on overall amount of television exposure (as opposed to specific types of programs), the way television viewing is measured and divided into relative levels of exposure, justifications for interpreting television world answers, the linearity of cultivation associations, and much more. Some of the most heated issues of contention have revolved around questions of spuriousness and the proper use of statistical controls.

One of the main critiques focuses on the fact that powerful predictors of social beliefs and attitudes, such as race, education, income, gender, and so on, are also typically closely associated with amount of television viewing. For instance, higher income respondents and those with more education tend to watch less TV. Therefore, comparisons of light and heavy viewers are always carried out under controls—that is, within important demographic subgroups.

Cultivation differentials are compared for, say, those with and without a college education, males vs. females, and those under or over 30 years old. From the start, it was clear that cultivation patterns were not uniform across demographic subgroups. Associations were stronger in some groups and weaker or non-existent in others.

Yet, early on, cultivation researchers had typically applied a single control variable at a time. In contrast, various critics—reanalyzing the same data—argued that when multiple controls were applied *at the same time*, the relationships between television viewing and attitudes mostly disappeared. This led them to conclude that there was essentially no meaningful evidence to support the cultivation hypothesis.

Gerbner and his colleagues countered that even if a relationship disappears under multiple controls, significant patterns may still exist *within* specific subgroups, often reflecting a pattern they called "mainstreaming" (Gerbner, Gross, Morgan, & Signorielli, 1980). Among light viewers, people who differ in terms of background factors such as age, education, social class, political orientations, and region of residence tend to have sharply different conceptions of social reality regarding violence, interpersonal mistrust, gender-role stereotypes, and a broad range of political and social outlooks. Yet, among heavy viewers across those same groups, those differences tend to be much smaller or even to disappear entirely.

For example, Gerbner et al. (1980) found that low-income respondents were more likely than those with higher incomes to say that "fear of crime is a very serious personal problem." Among low-income respondents, amount of television viewing was not related at all to perceptions of crime. In contrast, although higher-income respondents as a group were less likely to think of crime as a serious personal problem, the heavy viewers with higher incomes were much more likely than the light viewers to be especially worried about crime. In other words, heavy viewers with higher incomes had the same perception as those with lower incomes; among heavy viewers, the difference stemming from income was sharply diminished. Similarly, among lighter viewers, those with more education have been found to express more "progressive" attitudes about gender roles, but this difference disappears among heavy viewers; more educated heavy viewers express the same "traditional" beliefs as do those with less education. In addition, the concept of "resonance" was also developed as a way to explain how cultivation relates to those whose day-to-day lives connect with and exacerbate television's images.

These patterns, and many similar ones discovered in analyses of political ideology and attitudes (Gerbner et al., 1982), suggest that cultivation is like a gravitational process, in which the angle and direction of the "pull" depend on where groups of viewers and their styles of life are with reference to the center of gravity, the mainstream of the world of television. Mainstreaming thus means that heavy television viewing contributes to an erosion of differences in people's perspectives that stem from other factors and influences (Morgan, 1986). People who otherwise have little in common besides television are brought into the same dominant mainstream by cumulative heavy viewing. Cultivation researchers contend that television contributes to a blurring of cultural, political, social, regional, and class-based distinctions, the blending of attitudes into the television mainstream, and the bending of the direction of that mainstream to serve the political and economic tasks of the medium and the institutions that subsidize it.

There were other critiques as well. Critiques were aimed at the content data used in cultivation, suggesting that the definitions of violence were too idiosyncratic to be sustainable. Also, some critics thought that cultivation analysis generalized too much about viewers; they would have preferred a more humanistic critique that allowed for different viewer reactions to violence (Newcomb, 1978).

## Summary

Much of the back-and-forth dialogue took place in the early to middle 1980s, and from it emerged a few important theoretical outcomes. Overall, cultivation theory and its basic research approaches prospered, even as the critiques also gained some level of acceptance among researchers. This climate of theoretical formulation resulted in several ways in which cultivation research grew and expanded. First, the overall focus of cultivation was broadened from its beginnings in violence to, as noted above, issues related to sex roles, aging, politics, health, and many other topics. Second, theoretical specifications, such as mainstreaming and resonance, were incorporated into the approach. Finally, the study of cultivation was taken up by many individual researchers who had not worked or trained with the original Cultural Indicators research team; it became an international research phenomenon. This also led to important extensions and new strands of research, such as those focusing on the cognitive processes underlying cultivation.

At its outset, cultivation was an easy target because it blended critical theory about mass media with empirical research techniques, cutting across the typical division between critical and empirical research that was so common at that time. Also, as a critical theory it made claims against vested interests, so it was not surprising that the early reaction from television networks was particularly strong. Nevertheless, the amount of research continued to grow. By the end of the 1990s, dozens of studies had been conducted, many in other countries and many by independent researchers. Shanahan and Morgan (1999) reviewed over 20 years' worth of studies in a meta-analysis. This analysis found that the body of research exhibited a small but persistent relationship between television exposure and beliefs about the world. But of course, that analysis did not finally settle the question, and cultivation theory and research have continued to evolve, with over 125 new studies published since 2000.

Today, there are many and various views about how cultivation should be studied, and there are many matters of ongoing debate. This book gathers together a variety of these new developments and perspectives, and is the first major book-length review of cultivation since 1999 (Shanahan & Morgan, 1999). Most of the studies and reviews reported here are supportive of the basic idea of cultivation, though many propose extensions and modifications to the methods originally suggested by Gerbner, and there has been continued growth in the ways researchers conceptualize the activity of watching television and its consequences.

## Overview of the Book

This book is organized into three sections. The first section, "Updates and Extensions," deals with advances in research in areas focusing on the "classic" dependent variables in cultivation research (images of crime, sex roles, marginalized minorities, etc.). The next section, "Understanding Cognitive Mechanisms," deals with cultivation "processes" with chapters that look specifically at cognitive processes and their implications. Finally, the last section, "New Theoretical and Methodological Dimensions," deals with new explorations in the intersections of cultivation with other major theories as well as recent methodological advances.

In the first section, Chapter 2 (Oliver, Bae, Ash, and Chung) offers an update and status report on the voluminous research on television viewing and fear of crime. As the archetypical issue that sparked cultivation research, there is much that is new to report about violence and crime. Much of this research ventures out into areas such as genre cultivation, and even the fear of events such as the 9/11 attacks. Chapter 3 (Mastro and Tukachinsky) explores another issue that has received quite bit of attention through the history of cultivation—attitudes about marginalized minorities. Perceptions and views about minorities have changed greatly across the 40+ years of cultivation research, and so have the studies documenting media effects. In Chapter 4, which looks at the relationship of TV viewing with views on homosexuality, Nisbet and Myers bring an innovative multi-level methodology to bear on showing how social change, television depictions, and opinions can be analyzed over time. Similarly, views on gender have changed. In the 1960s, women on television were far outnumbered by men. While the imbalance has eased somewhat, residual forms of sexism persist. The studies in this area are presented and discussed by Scharrer in Chapter 5. Hardy, in chapter 6, explores the area of politics, where not as much has changed; he finds that television viewing still tends to cultivate middle-of-the-road self-perceptions. Hardy brings a cultivation perspective to bear on political communication, a focus that is not frequently explored in political communication research. Finally, in this section, Brossard and Dudo (Chapter 7) update the research on the cultivation of attitudes about science and scientists.

The second section presents a variety of views on the enormous number of advances in understanding the cognitive mechanisms that explain cultivation. Shrum and Lee (Chapter 8) give a very comprehensive summary of Shrum's extensive work on explaining how people make first-order judgments (estimates of frequency and set size in the real world) and second-order judgments (attitudes, opinions, and feelings). This chapter provides an introduction and primer for those who want to learn about cognitive mechanisms relevant to cultivation. Chapter 9 (Busselle and Bilandzic) explores the related issue of (perceived) realism. For many years perceived realism was put forth as one of the important concepts that might yield a better understanding of the cognitive mechanisms of cultivation. Given recent advances on heuristic processing and narrative persuasion, Busselle and Bilandzic are able to put the issue of realism itself in a new light. Ewoldsen and Rhodes (Chapter 10) introduce something new to cultivation: the use of cultural models. These models show how individuals develop shared understandings of situations in the world; the authors relate these theoretically to television use and provide an empirical example dealing with perceptions of romance. Bradley and Matthews (Chapter 11) introduce another novel technique to cultivation: the analysis of neural networks. These networks depict how simulated connections between neurons create memories, and eventually how these memories are then retrieved in judgments that might be related to television viewing. The authors' empirical work shows that hypothetical networks, when given conditions that resemble how we process messages from television, show results consistent with cultivation.

Our final section looks at how cultivation intersects with other theoretical approaches as well as some new methodological developments. Van den Bulck (Chapter 12) examines international cultivation analysis. He offers a systematic view of studies conducted outside the U.S., as well as of studies on immigrants, sojourners, and others exposed to television that is produced outside of their native culture. Bilandzic and Busselle (Chapter 13) explore the implications of genre for cultivation research. While "classic" cultivation research typically rejected such an approach, these authors argue that genre's status as an important component of narrative means that it is useful to look at cultivation within genres (such as crime programs). Their chapter offers a justification for the variety of genre cultivation studies that have already appeared, as well as a future research agenda. A different but complementary view comes from Riddle (Chapter 14), who develops a measure that assesses viewing across a person's lifetime. It addresses the need for a measure in a theory that proposes that systematic, long-term exposure to television is what matters, more so than individuals' current viewing habits. As in Chapter 4 (Nisbet and Myers), the historical over-time dimension also emerges for Riddle as very important (although in a rather different way).

The final four chapters explore new theoretical intersections. Hetsroni and Lowenstein (Chapter 15) suggest a model for linking cultivation and agenda-setting research. They look at both theories in terms of first- and second-order media effects, hypothesizing a single process that might unite the two. In Chapter 16, Diefenbach and West look at the intersection of cultivation with the Third-Person Effect. Because cultivation is an example of a media effect that people can think about (thus generating possible expectations about how others might be affected), looking at the two together makes considerable sense. Shanahan and Scheufele (Chapter 17), in turn, look at cultivation and the spiral of silence, finding some interesting historical similarities between the two theories. They test a model linking the two approaches in relation to the issue of smoking. Finally, Ruddock (Chapter 18) takes an unusual turn for cultivation, examining it through the lens of a critical cultural theorist. His chapter links cultivation with ritual theory, and takes on the issues of digital sports media and fandom from that new perspective. He also shows how the idea of cultivation may become even more relevant as new media emerge.

Cultivation continues to be a theory that is frequently tested, cited, and scrutinized, and it continues to evolve. Our conclusion, in Chapter 19, considers the book's collective chapters in relation to the outline of future research directions provided, over twenty years ago, by Signorielli and Morgan (1990). As we discuss in this concluding chapter, although many of the ideas set forth back then have come to fruition (and many seem to be not so important anymore), as with any workable and viable theory, there are still important insights to be gained as to where cultivation research can go in the future. We believe that cultivation's stature as one of the most well known and used theoretical approaches in communication is well justified, and we hope that this volume provides a useful view of where the research stands at this juncture. We look forward to seeing where research on cultivation will lead us in the next twenty years.

# Note

1. A complete bibliography of Cultural Indicators work is located at: *http://people.umass.edu/mmorgan/CulturalIndicatorsBibliography.pdf.*

# References

Bryant, J., & Miron, D. (2004). Theory and research in mass communication. *Journal of Communication, 54*, 662–704.

Doob, A., & Macdonald, G. (1979). Television viewing and fear of victimization: Is the relationship causal? *Journal of Personality and Social Psychology, 37*(2), 170–179.

Gerbner, G. (1963). A theory of communication and its implications for teaching. In *The nature of teaching* (pp. 33–47). Milwaukee, WI: University of Wisconsin–Milwaukee, School of Education.

Gerbner, G. (1969). Toward cultural indicators: The analysis of mass mediated message systems. *AV Communication Review, 13*, 85–108.

Gerbner, G. (1970). Cultural indicators: The case of violence in television drama. *The Annals of the American Academy of Political and Social Science, 388*, 69–81.

Gerbner, G. (1973.). Cultural Indicators: The third voice. In G. Gerbner, L. Gross, & W. Melody (Eds.), *Communications technology and social policy* (pp. 555–573). New York: John Wiley & Sons.

Gerbner, G., & Gross, L. (1976). Living with television: The violence profile. *Journal of Communication, 26*(2), 173–199.

Gerbner, G., Gross, L., Jackson-Beeck, M., Jeffries-Fox, S., & Signorielli, N. (1978). Cultural indicators: Violence profile no. 9. *Journal of Communication, 28*(3), 176–207.

Gerbner, G., Gross, L., Morgan, M., & Signorielli, N. (1980). The "mainstreaming" of America: Violence profile No. 11. *Journal of Communication, 30*(3), 10–29.

Gerbner, G., Gross, L., Morgan, M., & Signorielli, M. (1982). Charting the mainstream: Television's contributions to political orientations. *Journal of Communication, 32*(2), 100–127.

Gerbner, G., Gross, L., Signorielli, N., Morgan, M., & Jackson-Beeck, M. (1979). The demonstration of power: Violence profile no. 10. *Journal of Communication, 29*(3), 177–196.

Hirsch, P. (1980). The "Scary World" of the nonviewer and other anomalies: A reanalysis of Gerbner et al.'s findings of cultivation analysis, Part I. *Communication Research, 7*(4), 403–456.

Hughes, M. (1980). The fruits of cultivation analysis: A re-examination of the effects of television watching on fear of victimization, alienation, and the approval of violence. *Public Opinion Quarterly, 44*(3), 287–302.

Morgan, M. (1982). Television and adolescent's sex-role stereotypes: A longitudinal study. *Journal of Personality and Social Psychology, 43*(5), 947–955.

Morgan, M. (1983). Symbolic victimization and real-world fear. *Human Communication Research, 9*(2), 146–157.

Morgan, M. (1986). Television and the erosion of regional diversity. *Journal of Broadcasting & Electronic Media, 30*(2), 123–139.

Morgan, M. (Ed.). (2002). *Against the mainstream: The selected works of George Gerbner.* New York: Peter Lang Publishing.

Morgan, M. (2012). *George Gerbner: A critical introduction to media and communication theory.* New York: Peter Lang Publishing.

Morgan, M., Shanahan, J., & Signorielli, N. (2009). Growing up with television: Cultivation processes. In J. Bryant & M. Oliver (Eds.), *Media effects: Advances in theory and research* (3rd ed., pp. 34–49). Mahwah, NJ: Erlbaum.

Newcomb, H. (1978). Assessing the violence profile of Gerbner and Gross: A humanistic critique and suggestion. *Communication Research, 5*(3), 264–282.

Potter, W. J. (1993). Cultivation theory and research: A conceptual critique. *Human Communication Research, 19,* 564–601.

Potter, W. J. (1994). Cultivation theory and research: A methodological critique. *Journalism Monographs, 147,* 1–35.

Potter, W. J., & Riddle, K. (2007). A content analysis of the media effects literature. *Journalism & Mass Communication Quarterly, 84*(1), 90–104.

Shanahan, J., & Morgan, M. (1999). *Television and its viewers: Cultivation theory and research.* Cambridge: Cambridge University Press.

Signorielli, N. (1993). Sex roles and stereotyping on television. *Adolescent Medicine: State of the Art Reviews, 4*(3), 551–561.

Signorielli, N., & Morgan, M. (Eds.). (1990). *Cultivation analysis: New directions in media effects research.* Newbury Park, CA: Sage.

Surgeon General's Scientific Advisory Committee on Television and Social Behavior. (1972). *Television and Growing Up: The Impact of Televised Violence. Report to the Surgeon General, United States Public Health Service.* Washington, DC: National Institute of Mental Health.

Wober, J. (1990). Does television cultivate the British? Late 80s evidence. In N. Signorielli & M. Morgan (Eds.), *Cultivation analysis: New directions in media effects research* (pp. 207–224). Newbury Park, CA: Sage.

# *Updates and Extensions*

# 2. New Developments in Analyses of Crime and Fear

*Mary Beth Oliver, Keunmin Bae, Erin Ash, & Mun-Young Chung*

The diversity of ways that media consumption may cultivate individuals' perceptions of social reality has been documented by scholars examining topics ranging from gender (Signorielli, 1989) to occupations (Signorielli & Kahlenberg, 2001) and even to nutrition (Signorielli & Staples, 1997). However, the effects of violent content on viewers' perceptions of and fears about crime have arguably received the greatest share of attention, presumably because violence is a staple of most television diets and difficult to avoid. Perhaps more than any other single type of portrayal, violence is a theme that runs through different genres of programming such as comedy (Potter & Warren, 1998), sports (Tamborini et al., 2005), and drama (Vorderer & Knobloch, 2000); that is featured in both fictional and realistic portrayals (Potter et al., 1995); that is targeted to both children and adults (Wilson et al., 2002); and that is generally stable over time (Smith, Nathanson, & Wilson, 2002). As a result of the ubiquity of violence in the media landscape, it follows that concerns about TV violence have persisted for more than half a century, with early congressional hearings focused on violent content and its effects on viewers. Therefore, it stands to reason that cultivation scholars have likewise been particularly interested in how this recurrent theme affects not only individuals' social-reality judgments concerning the prevalence of crime and violence but also the affective and attitudinal outcomes of such perceptions, including fear of crime and general feelings of distrust or unease as well as support for more punitive policies that promise to increase individual safety (Morgan

& Shanahan, 2010). Indeed, Gerbner's work broadened the scope of inquiry on media violence beyond that of imitation to also consider the cultivation of public sentiments and cultural values that reflect the dominant storyteller of television.

Given the prevalence of violence and aggression in media content across decades, it may seem somewhat odd to suggest that an "update" to literature in this area will reveal any new findings or suggest novel ways that this important issue can be examined. Yet, media landscapes are rapidly changing with evolving new technologies. Further, national and global events such as school shootings and terrorist attacks focus the public and media agenda on qualitatively different issues that warrant further consideration. Additionally, the development of new means of assessing individuals' affective and cognitive experiences related to their media exposure allows for innovative and perhaps more nuanced means of examining the cultivation of fear. As a consequence, there is a considerable amount of material to consider in an updated overview of research pertaining to media consumption and fear of crime from a cultivation perspective.

Before we begin our overview, we believe it is important to note that we take a broad conceptual and operational view of what is meant by "fear of crime." At its most basic, we understand fear of crime to be manifest in both individuals' self-reported concern for issues of personal safety and in their social-reality judgments concerning the prevalence of violence and aggression in society. However, in our chapter we also include additional manifestations of fearful and alienated perceptions, such as general distrust and cynicism, and also greater support for punitive or authoritarian policies that may be thought to protect one from the dangers of society. Finally, in our chapter we consider not only how media may cultivate fear of crime or perceptions of danger but also how those cultivated fears may lead to a greater consumption of fear-inducing content.

## Television Viewing and Fear of Crime

Because so much scholarship has pointed to media violence as a stable and recurrent theme, the most general hypothesis of cultivation research as it pertains to violence is that heavy viewers, more so than light viewers, are inclined to see the world in ways that are consistent with these violent themes (Gerbner, Gross, Morgan, & Signorielli, 1980). As a result, the hypothesized "Mean World Syndrome" reflects the idea that heavy viewers perceive the world to be more violent than is the case and are therefore more likely to harbor feelings of distrust, concern, and ultimately support for policy that will serve to protect their safety, even if it entails the loss of basic civil liberties.

### Television Programming Overall

Recent research on media content and viewers' concerns or fears about crime generally finds evidence for the idea that the world of television continues to be a place that is overly dangerous and aggressive and that heavy exposure to it therefore may serve to cultivate mean-world views. In terms of violent content, perhaps one of the wider-scale analyses of media violence is the three-year National Television Violence Study examining programs shown between 1994 and 1997 (Federman, 1998; Smith et al., 2002). In the third year of the analysis of over 2700 different programs, 61% of the programs contained at least one act of aggression, with violent interactions occurring 6.63 times per hour on average, and almost a third of the programs (32%) contained more than 8 instances of violence. Importantly, too, these authors found evidence for the prevalence of the very kind of depictions that scholars have argued are most associated with heightened fear among viewers (although they did not themselves also study viewers). Specifically, these authors found that the majority of violent interactions (59%) involved lethal violence, that 25% of the violent scenes featured blood and gore, that over a third of the interactions involved the use of a gun, and that the majority of programs featuring violence (68%) were in realistic settings.

Given the violent world depicted by television, it is perhaps not surprising that studies generally continue to reveal support for the predicted positive correlation between overall television exposure and fear of crime (Morgan & Shanahan, 1997). For example, Van den Bulck's (2004) research compared three different models to explain the relationship between media exposure and fear of crime: that television heightens fear; that fear leads to greater television viewing for purposes of coping; or that the relationship is spurious and reflects the tendency for frightened individuals to stay indoors (thereby watching more television). Van den Bulck concluded that the strongest model supported cultivation's prediction: Television was not only a predictor of fear of crime but was also a better predictor than actual crime victimization. Most recently, Riddle's (2010) research also found support for the relationship between television exposure and heightened estimates of crime prevalence. Importantly, Riddle's work provided evidence for cultivation's argument that television's influence reflects cumulative, long-term exposure to recurrent themes and that the best media predictor of crime perceptions was the respondents' exposure to television over their lifetimes rather than current viewing habits (see also Riddle, Chapter 14, this volume).

### Fictional Crime Dramas

Because cultivation research conceptualizes the influence of media (and especially television) in macro-level terms, many scholars from this tradition have historically argued against measuring the idiosyncratic media diets of individual viewers rather than the overall *amount* of media consumption. At the same time, however, additional scholarship suggests that it may be fruitful to examine certain types of content that are noteworthy for their portrayals of violence or crime, even if such examinations stray from the broad conceptualization of television as a "cultural storyteller" (see Morgan & Shanahan, 2010). In terms of fictional entertainment, this reasoning has led a number of scholars to examine the effects of crime portrayals in particular (see Bilandzic & Busselle, Chapter 13, this volume).

As their name implies, crime dramas obviously feature a host of criminal activities, often interspersed with a variety of violent or aggressive acts. For example, in Smith et al.'s (2002) content analysis of television programming (using data from the National TV Violence Study), certain genres were more likely than others to contain heightened levels of aggression. Specifically, dramas and movies (more so than comedies) were particularly likely to be "saturated" with violence, as were programs appearing on premium cable channels. Likewise, Soulliere's (2003) analysis of *Law & Order*, *The Practice*, and *NYPD Blue* found that the most frequent (and overrepresented) type of criminal act depicted in these programs was murder, accounting for more than 60% of the instances of crime in each of the three programs.

Given that heavy viewers of crime dramas are, by definition, exposed to a particularly high dosage of crime and violence, it follows that heavy viewing should be associated with greater levels of fear and other indicators of fearful perceptions. Consistent with this reasoning, Eschholz, Chiricos, and Gertz (2003) found that greater viewing of television crime dramas was associated with higher levels of fear of crime. Likewise, Holbert, Shah, and Kwak (2004) found that crime-drama viewing was associated with greater support for the death penalty, and Holbrook and Hill (2005) found that greater viewing of (and even mere exposure to a single episode of) crime shows, such as *NYPD Blue*, was associated with the heightened belief that crime is the most important problem facing the country.

### *News*

Despite general support for the idea that crime dramas may be particularly likely to affect viewers' perceptions of and fears of crime, other scholars have suggested that more realistic content may be particularly likely to be influential (e.g., Chiricos, Padgett, & Gertz, 2000). From this perspective, it makes sense that a great deal of research has focused on news content, as news coverage presumably represents the most typical and relied-upon source of information concerning actual crime occurring in viewers' environments.

Insofar as news reports may provide viewers with information relevant to their likelihood of crime victimization, it follows that a number of studies have suggested that *local* news may be particularly consequential. For example, Weitzer and Kubrin (2004) examined a diversity of media types that may be associated with individuals' fear of crime, finding that reliance on and frequency of viewing local news was the only significant media predictor. Likewise, Romer, Jamieson, and Aday's (2003) analysis employing both national and regional (Philadelphia) samples found that local-news viewing predicted fear of crime, whereas exposure to other media (e.g., newspapers, radio) did not. Finally, the idea that more proximate or local crime news is particularly important has also been demonstrated among child viewers. For example, Smith and Wilson (2000) reported that among the children in their sample aged 10 to 11, viewing of stories about a violent crime resulted in stronger fear when the crime was located in a local versus non-local city. Although this study employed experimental methodologies and therefore did not assess the cumulative impact of media as examined in cultivation research, it does speak to the idea that media portrayals may play consequential roles in affecting viewers' perceptions of the safety of their immediate surroundings.

The emphasis on local rather than national news may reflect a number of important variables, including the idea that crime news is more frequently covered by local than national news outlets. However, this focus should not be understood as suggesting that national news plays *no* role in affecting viewers' perceptions. For example, Lowry, Nio, and Leitner (2003) analyzed Gallup poll data, media coverage of crime, and statistics of actual crime rates in the U.S. as reported in the FBI's *Uniform Crime Reports* from the years 1978 through 1998. These authors found that media coverage of crime was a substantially better predictor than actual crime rates of the percentage of individuals naming crime as the most important problem facing the country. Of course, the perception of crime as a problem is distinct from fear of crime. However, like fear, such perceptions seem consistent with the idea the media contribute to beliefs that the world is a violent and dangerous place.

### *Reality Programming*

Whereas news programming is arguably the most "realistic" type of content on television, reality-based police programming such as *Cops* and *America's Most Wanted* has also attracted the attention of numerous researchers, presumably because (at least in part) such programs may be particularly potent in influencing viewers' social-reality beliefs. Consistent with this idea, this body of scholarship tends to show much stronger cultivation effects from reality-based than fictional programming (for further discussion, see Grabe & Drew, 2007). For example, although Holbrook and Hill (2005) found some evidence for the effects of fictional-crime viewing, they found abundant evidence for reality-crime viewing on not only increased support for the death penalty but also on heightened fear of crime, support for police authority, endorsement of gun ownership, and likelihood of owning a gun.

Although reality shows focused on policing were one of the earliest types of reality programming, this genre has obviously expanded tremendously over the last decade, with a large variety of sub-genres enjoying wide-scale popularity (Nabi, Biely, Morgan, & Stitt, 2003). Programs such as *The Real World*, *Big Brother*, and *Survivor* are widely viewed and enjoyed. Research exploring these more contemporary programs generally suggests that many of them contain key themes that imply a mean or hostile society. For example, Reiss and Wiltz (2004) found that life-values and desires pertaining to vengeance were particularly strong predictors of enjoyment of these types of programs. Subsequent research applying cultivation theory to the reality genre echoes this idea. Barton (2007) found that heavy viewers of competition-based reality television were more likely to perceive the world as less trustworthy and to perceive that lying is prevalent in society. Another sub-genre of reality television is the reality dating show. Cultivation studies of this genre have shown effects on increasing hostile attitudes toward dating and members of the opposite sex. Specifically, heavy viewing appears to be associated with adversarial sexual beliefs (i.e., a lot of women seem to get pleasure out of putting men down; men are out for only one thing), and perceptions of dating as a game, of men as sex driven, and of women as sex objects (Ferris, Smith, Greenberg, & Smith, 2007; Zurbriggen & Morgan, 2006).

### *Summary*

Media portrayals of violence run throughout television content and form a common "story" that contributes to mean-world perceptions. At the same time, though, it's evident that the story of crime, danger, and hostility gets heightened play in some types of content over others, including in crime dramas, news, and in newer entertainment forms such as reality programming. Given that violence represents such a prominent and seemingly permanent part of the entertainment landscape, it is crucial that cultivation scholars be vigilant for how these stories continue to be "told" as entertainment and how they continue to expand into newer and therefore under-studied venues (e.g., user-generated media).

## The Importance of Race in Fear of Crime

Although many cultivation studies concerning fear of crime have assessed fears in unspecified or generic contexts (e.g., fear of walking alone, overall concern about crime, etc.), scholars have noted that the ways that crime is portrayed in the media are far from "generic." Specifically, media depictions of crime and aggression continue to reflect stereotypical patterns of portrayals of race and ethnicity, motivating cultivation scholars to suggest that media may cultivate fears of specific groups of individuals such as African Americans (for reviews, see Mastro, 2009; Oliver, Ramasubramanian, & Kim, 2007). In general, research from this perspective has been motivated by a concern that media portrayals may represent one source of Whites' stereotyping of and prejudicial attitudes toward persons of color.

The idea that White individuals may be particularly fearful of certain races or ethnicities is consistent with the stereotypical identification of African Americans and Latinos as criminal, dangerous, and violent. Importantly, content analyses of media portrayals of crime imply that the media may serve as one source of these stereotypes. Although content analyses of prime-time entertainment programming generally show no differences between White and minority involvement in crime as perpetrators or victims (e.g., Signorielli, 2003), content analyses of news coverage paint a very different picture. Namely, analyses of news reports of crime have found that African Americans are over-represented as criminal suspects and under-represented as crime victims (Bjornstrom, Kaufman, Peterson, & Slater, 2010; Dixon & Linz, 2000), and that coverage of potentially prejudicial pre-trial information in the news is more likely for both Black and Latino criminal suspects than for White criminal suspects (Dixon & Linz, 2002).

Research on the effects of biased representations of race and crime generally finds evidence consistent with cultivation influences. For example, Dixon (2008) reported that greater attention to local crime news was associated not only with greater fear of crime per se, but also with greater perceptions of the culpability of Black and race-unidentified criminal suspects, but not of White criminal suspects (see also Mastro, Behm-Morawitz, & Ortiz, 2007). Likewise, earlier work on reality-based police programs found that although viewing these types of shows was related to greater estimates of both Black and White involvement in crime, the associations were more pronounced for estimates of Black than White involvement (Oliver & Armstrong, 1998).

In addition to providing evidence for the cultivation of stereotypes in general, research has also identified important moderators of cultivation effects pertaining to race. In this regard, the proximity of viewers to the stereotyped group has arguably generated the greatest amount of scholarship. However, research in this area has revealed conflicting findings. For example, Eschholz et al. (2003) reported a positive association between television viewing and fear of crime, but particularly among individuals who perceived that their neighborhood had a higher percentage of African Americans. In contrast, Gilliam, Valentino, and Beckmann (2002) found support for the idea that exposure to stereotypical portrayals of African Americans in crime news would have a stronger effect on increasing stereotype endorsement among Whites who live in neighborhoods with low numbers of African Americans. These authors interpreted their research as suggesting that everyday encounters with stereotyped out-group members in non-crime contexts act to "buffer" any harmful effects that media depictions may have. Although there are numerous potential explanations for these seemingly contradictory findings, perhaps it may be useful for scholars to move beyond merely assessing racial composition. For example, Gilliam et al. pointed out that most of their participants were from relatively low-crime areas, implying that Black-White encounters were likely unrelated to perceptions of danger or threat. If this reasoning is correct, then examining the *extent of and nature of* actual interactions among people from different racial backgrounds may prove useful in helping scholars to determine the populations that may be most vulnerable to media depictions of stereotypes (Mastro et al., 2007; for a general discussion of the cultivation of perceptions of minority groups, see Mastro & Tukachinsky, Chapter 3, this volume).

To summarize, although research on the effects of media portrayals of crime suggests heightened fear across the board, the focus of media portrayals of African Americans and Latinos is particularly troublesome, as such portrayals have the potential to reinforce already existing stereotypes. Of course, the focus on the effects of media portrayals on White viewers is understandable, as the majority of research in this area has arguably been motivated by concerns regarding prejudice and discrimination. However, future research may consider the utility of also examining the effects of media portrayals on minority viewers' social-reality perceptions concerning race and crime. Likewise, African Americans and Latinos are not the only racial group stereotypically associated with aggression and crime. Importantly, most recently, fears of terrorism and other global threats have targeted Arabs and Muslims as particularly dangerous or threatening. Our next section on more recent global and national events in the U.S. addresses this issue, as well as additional sources of fear in a national context.

## Global and National Events as the Context of Newer Fears

Research on fear of crime from a cultivation perspective has generally tended to examine more gradual trends in crimes that are routinely catalogued in documents, such as the FBI's *Uniform Crime Report*. As a result, horrifying but nevertheless frequent crimes such as assault, murder, or armed robbery have often been the focus of cultivation-like research, as these crimes unfortunately occur in many communities, and are also frequently featured not only in the news but also in entertainment. In contrast, less frequent (or proximate) events that may be much more severe (e.g., war) have received less coverage in cultivation research, perhaps because single traumatic events may be unlikely to play consequential roles in the cumulative cultivation of attitudes, or because such events are often geographically remote from the viewer, thereby making it less likely that such events may heighten fears for personal safety. Unfortunately, since the earlier days of cultivation research, a number of wide-scale international and national events have unalterably changed the nature and scope of individuals' fears. In this section, we consider both the issue of terrorism and the issue of school-related violence such as Columbine.

### *Terrorism*

Since September 11, fears of crime in the U.S. have arguably expanded from more common, local crimes to now include global and more unpredictable crimes of terrorism, with the focus of the fear largely targeting members of Arab and Muslim communities (Baker, 2010). Analyses of media coverage have revealed primarily negative depictions of these groups in non-fictional Western media (Baker, 2010). For example, Richter and Hafez's (2009) analysis of magazines, talk shows, documentaries, and reports in German public networks found that words such as "Islam," "Islamic," and "Muslim" were primarily connected with violence and conflict-driven issues.

Despite generally negative media portrayals, research is only beginning to emerge concerning the effect of media consumption on viewers' fears. Not surprisingly, early research tends to suggests that fear responses reflect a host of non-media variables, including political views (Scheufele, Nisbet, & Ostman, 2005), gender (Nellis, 2009), and religious affiliation (Slone, 2000; Wicks, 2006). However, this research also points to the importance of media exposure in intensifying viewers' concerns. For example, Scheufele et al. (2005) analyzed phone-survey data collected during the months following the September 11 attacks. This research reported that TV-news viewing and television viewing per se were positively associated with support for restrictive policies presumably designed to protect people from terrorist activities (i.e., police powers and limits on privacy and freedom of information). Interestingly, newspaper reading was negatively associated with public support for these restrictive policies. The fact that both television news and overall viewing were associated with heightened indicators of fear suggests that the demonization of Muslims is not only present in news but also runs throughout media entertainment, including fictionalized content. Although it is unclear why print media failed to reveal similar findings, Scheufele et al. speculated that the vivid, salient, and sometimes sensationalistic coverage on television may have served to exacerbate media influences.

Obviously, as terrorism becomes an increasingly common global concern, the role of media in affecting individuals' fears becomes an even more important issue to examine. Not only may such fears result in stereotyping and prejudicial responses to individuals presumably associated with terrorist activities, but such fears may also be effectively exploited by politicians and policy makers making claims to protect their citizens. Lastly, the implications of fears on issues such as civil liberties are just beginning to emerge, suggesting that the cultivation of fear of terrorism is a particularly fruitful (though potentially distressing) line of future research.

### *School-Related Violence*

In addition to ushering in new fears associated with terrorism, the last several decades have witnessed tragedies such as the 1999 Columbine massacre, which have also introduced new fears related to school safety. Unfortunately, school shootings such as that of Columbine are a growing type of tragedy not only visible in the U.S. but also in other nations (Muschert, 2007). Although research on the effects of media coverage of these types of events is severely lacking at this point (but see Kaminski, Koons-Witt, Thompson, & Weiss, 2010), cultivation research would clearly suggest that media coverage of these events may result in overly heightened concern for personal safety regarding school violence, even among individuals who may be distant from the danger. Muschert (2009) implied this argument in his content analysis of news coverage of Columbine, noting that media coverage of the event evolved from initial descriptions of the specific incident from a local perspective to discussions of safety in schools all across the nation.

The few systematic studies that have been conducted on the effects of school shootings suggest that media coverage can serve to exacerbate fears. For example, Kaminski et al. (2010) conducted a series of surveys among students in South Carolina before and after the shootings at Virginia Tech and Northern Illinois. Whereas these surveys indicated an increase in fear of campus crime after both shootings, the results were stronger after the Virginia Tech than the Northern Illinois event. These researchers speculated that these findings may reflect the fact that the Virginia shooting received more media coverage.

To summarize, over the last several decades of research, cultivation has continued to grapple with issues of crimes such as murder and assault. At the same time, however, different types of crimes such as terrorism and school violence have taken center stage, receiving an abundance of media coverage. Though scholars are only beginning to study the effects of media coverage of these events, their vividness and salience make them obvious topics to explore from a cultivation perspective.

## Enjoyment of Media Crime and Violence

If media portrayals of crime and violence cultivate unrealistic estimates of violence and unnecessarily heightened concerns for personal safety, it is unclear why violence continues to be a staple of media diets. On the one hand, of course, people may *not* enjoy viewing media violence at all (Weaver & Wilson, 2009), but the media industry features it prominently nevertheless. Consistent with this argument, Gerbner (1999) suggested that the prevalence of media violence fails to reflect audience preferences but rather reflects the media-industry's need for cheap, easy-to-produce, and easily exported media content.

In this chapter, we do not want to suggest that media users seek out violence because they get particular pleasures out of witnessing others' suffering or because they desire brutality. At the same time, however, we note that some conceptualizations of the enjoyment of violence appear consistent with cultivation's general arguments. In this section, we consider the argument that fear may lead to the viewing of violence (in addition to the reverse causal direction).

The idea that fear of crime may lead to increased consumption of media violence may seem counter-intuitive, but early research in an actual crime-related circumstance supported the general notion that fearful individuals may be particularly drawn to violent and crime-ridden entertainment (Boyanows, Newtson, & Walster, 1974). Subsequent research argued and found support for the position that fearful viewers may enjoy media violence and portrayals of crime because such portrayals typically are stories about the restoration of justice (Wakshlag, Vial, & Tamborini, 1983; Zillmann & Wakshlag, 1985). As such, the seemingly odd media preferences of fearful viewers may actually reflect the idea that many forms of media violence that feature comforting portrayals in which the "bad guys" are locked up or punished may actually be reassuring.

More recent research on the selection and enjoyment of media violence (and particularly crime dramas) has expanded our theoretical understanding of the variables that may be at work in explaining viewer preference. For example, Raney and Bryant's (2002) application of disposition theory to the enjoyment of this genre identified audience inputs as important predictors of their perceptions and evaluations of the characters and events in a justice sequence (see also Raney, 2005). For example, attitudes about crime, punishment, and even stereotyping can affect viewers' perceptions of the morality of the perpetrator and, hence, the appropriate severity of punishment in the justice sequence. Applied to the issue at hand, this model of crime-drama enjoyment suggests that fearful viewers may be particularly likely to judge crime (and criminals) as dangerous and therefore deserving of punishment, and may consequently experience the greatest level of gratification from viewing dramas where the criminals are unambiguously "put away" and punished for their wrong-doings.

In other research pertaining to the enjoyment of crime drama, Appel (2008) reasoned not only that media violence may cultivate perceptions of fear as predicted by cultivation, but also that media narratives focused on crime resolutions may also cultivate perceptions of fairness and justice. Consistent with this reasoning, Appel found that overall television viewing was positively correlated with mean-world beliefs, and that viewing of fictional crime drama was positively associated with endorsement of "just world beliefs" (e.g., most people get what they deserve).

Finally, scholars have now begun to turn their attention to a relatively newer form of television crime drama—the forensic program. The enormous popularity of these programs is evidenced in a variety of ways, including the diversity of programs that focus on forensic and criminal science (e.g., *Crime Scene Investigation*, *Cold Case*, *Criminal Minds*), as well as the large increase in the number of students interested in studying forensic medicine in college.

Research in a variety of fields, including law, criminology, and criminal justice, in addition to communication, has begun to investigate what is referred to as the "CSI effect" (Bilandzic, Busselle, & Spitzner, 2009; Gever, 2005; Nolan, 2007; Podlas, 2006; Tyler, 2006). One argument made is that the prevalence of these programs on television leads viewers to believe that with the appropriate scientific tools, all crimes can eventually, and arguably quite easily, be solved (Bilandzic et al., 2009; Gever, 2005). As Bilandzic et al. (2009) explain, "Criminals are not safe in the *CSI* world. They cannot commit a crime without leaving a trace that later can be used against them; they also cannot anticipate every possible way in which their bodies leave cues for the investigators" (p. 7).

Given that these newer types of crime dramas typically feature the success of criminal investigations in solving crime, some scholars have suggested that these programs may be psychologically reassuring, with heavy viewing leading to a heightened desire to see real-world crimes solved and real-world perpetrators punished more efficiently and potentially less deliberatively (Bilandzic et al., 2009; Tyler, 2006). Bilandzic et al. (2009), in an empirical test of the cultivation effect of such programs, found that this need for closure was not a motive for watching *CSI*. However, crime drama viewing in general predicted attitudes toward forensic science, including perceptions of the prevalence of such science in solving crimes, its relevance to police work, the infallibility of forensic evidence, and the usefulness of forensic science for solving crimes.

## Directions for Future Research

We hope that it is evident that recent research on media and fear of crime demonstrates the continued significance of cultivation in our contemporary media landscape. Though a number of scholars have rightly suggested the importance of examining the ways in which technologies may challenge some of the assumptions of cultivation theory (Chaffee & Metzger, 2001; Metzger, 2009), in this final section we opt to consider how newer technologies present *opportunities* to examine the implications of new media on fear of crime, as well as possibilities for assessing fear of crime in ways that may be more nuanced than have been possible thus far.

### *Implications of Newer Media on Fear of Crime*

Cultivation is a theory that was born in the age of television. Although television undoubtedly continues to function as the primary storyteller in the lives of most people, it is evident that people are also spending more and more time with additional technologies. We focus here on two such media: the Internet and video games.

**Internet.** Scholars are beginning to examine the applicability of cultivation theory to the Internet. On the one hand, the Internet may not (at least at present) represent a strong departure from the conceptualization of television as the dominant "storyteller" in our culture. Specifically, Morgan and Shanahan (2010) pointed out that due to streaming sites such as Hulu and YouTube, television programs and television-like content remain the most prevalent type of content consumed on the Internet. Further, that content is not restricted to a broadcasting schedule, thereby allowing individuals to watch at their convenience. As a result, these authors suggest that the Internet has led some audiences to watch television programming more frequently than when it was available on television alone (Morgan & Shanahan, 2010). In this regard, rather than challenging the assumptions of cultivation research, the growth of the Internet may actually serve to exacerbate cultivation effects. However, the Internet obviously introduces new considerations that must be addressed by cultivation scholars. For example, in comparison to television audiences, Internet audiences play more active roles when selecting what they wish to view, making it arguably difficult to assess the Internet's cultivation effect when Internet consumption per se is employed as an independent variable.

At the same time that the Internet introduces new challenges, it also presents opportunities to explore novel types of cultivation effects, as the medium itself introduces new types of crimes and fears that are not just *portrayed* by the media, but that are the *result of* these newer technologies. For example, issues such as identity theft and cyber-bullying are now fears that may be related not only to media exposure, but also to media use itself. Currently, identity theft is one of the most rapidly increasing crimes (O'Brien, 2000). In a survey conducted by the Cyber Security Industry Alliance, 48% of the participants responded that they feared the possibility that their financial information could be stolen while making purchases on the Internet (President's Identity Theft Task Force, 2007). Likewise, cyber-bullying has become a phenomenon of rapidly increasing concern. According to a national survey conducted in 2004, 9% of adolescents aged 10–17 who use the Internet had been the target of Internet harassment at least once during that year (Ybarra, Mitchell, Finkelhor, & Wolak, 2007). Although these new types of crimes and concerns have yet to receive systematic attention from cultivation scholars, they represent new venues for the exploration of novel means by which media may serve to exacerbate the fear of crime.

**Video games.** Another newer medium whose popularity has grown exponentially over the last decade is video games. As cultivation theory in its original conception was concerned with television violence, its applicability to video games is a logical direction, as research has shown that more than two-thirds (68%) of games contain some type of violence (Smith, Lachlan, & Tamborini, 2003). More recently, Thompson, Tepichin, and Haninger's (2006) analysis of Mature-rated games showed that 83.3% contained violence, with an analysis of 42 hours of game play featuring the deaths of over 6000 characters.

Most of the research concerning the effects of gaming has focused on short-term effects, such as whether playing a violent game leads to increased levels of aggressive affect, cognition, or behavior immediately following game play. However, theorizing concerning long-term effects of violent game play appears to have important implications for cultivation scholars. For example, the General Aggression Model developed by Anderson and Bushman (2001; Bushman & Anderson, 2002) proposes long-term effects resulting from the formation of knowledge structures after repeated exposure to violence and describes a variety of aggression-related knowledge structures shaped by violent game content. Two of these structures may be related to perceptions of a "mean world"—aggressive perceptual schemata and aggressive expectation schemata. For example, research has shown that after playing a violent video game, individuals are more likely to expect an aggressive response from a character involved in a potential conflict compared to those who played a non-violent game (Bushman & Anderson, 2002; Eastin & Griffiths, 2009).

In addition to focusing on aggressive outcomes, a number of studies employing a variety of methodologies have sought to apply cultivation theory to video games (Robinson, Wilde, Navracruz, Haydel, & Varady, 2001; Van Mierlo & Van den Bulck, 2004; Williams, 2006). For example, a study of elementary-age children participating in an intervention curriculum to reduce their television and video game use showed reduced perceptions of a "mean and scary" world compared to a control group, though the difference did not reach statistical significance (Robinson et al., 2001). Another study of Flemish secondary school students examined the relationship between video game play and perceptions of a mean world (Van Mierlo & Van den Bulck, 2004). Whereas cultivation effects were found for television, no effects for estimates of death by murder, accident, or heart attack were found for video game use. However, violent game play was associated with higher estimates of violent crime and the number of police officers in the workforce. Finally, Williams (2006) examined judgments of the prevalence of game-relevant and game-irrelevant real-world crimes among participants who played a violent role-playing, online PC game for one month. Cultivation effects were observed but only for judgments of crimes related to game content.

Several explanations have been offered for the difficulty in applying cultivation to video games. Perhaps most noteworthy is the issue of the wide diversity of video game experiences. Whereas cultivation theory has traditionally relied on the assumption of a common set of television images consumed by viewers (Gerbner, Gross, Morgan, Signorielli, & Shanahan, 2002), not only does the video game industry produce thousands of titles, but each individual player also controls the experience, including the level of violence portrayed. Thus, some scholars have suggested game and/or genre selectivity may be a useful variable in this line of research (Van Mierlo & Van den Bulck, 2004; Williams, 2006). Regardless of how the issue of selectivity is addressed, however, it is evident that the popularity of gaming points to the idea that future research on perceptions cultivated by video game play is both necessary and warranted.

### *Assessment of Fear*

Just as new media and new types of content provide avenues for future exploration of cultivation effects, advances in technologies and software also make possible additional means for assessing fear that may prove particularly fruitful. Specifically, researchers may find it useful to consider expanding beyond the self-report measures that are typically employed to make greater use of measures that may be more subtle and therefore, able to tap into attitudes and beliefs that may be otherwise difficult to observe. For example, the use of physiological measures could be employed as a means of assessing anxiety about crime that participants may be unwilling or unable to articulate. Likewise, scholars may consider employing less reactive measures to study the influence of media consumption on the stereotypical association of crime/threat with specific racial groups. In this regard, the Implicit Association Test or similar means of assessing unconscious stereotypes may be particularly well suited to measure affective or cognitive associations that may be cultivated for heavy viewers but that are not easily assessed via self-report measures that notoriously suffer from social-desirability problems (Devine & Monteith, 1999; Greenwald, McGhee, & Schwartz, 1998).

Finally, behavioral manifestations of implicit attitudes may also provide further insights into the role of media in cultivating attitudes that have the potential to result in devastating social outcomes. For example, Correll and his colleagues' research showed that their non-Black participants' decisions to shoot or not shoot at Black and White targets in a computer task tend to demonstrate race-biased judgments (Correll, Park, Judd, Wittenbrink, et al., 2007; see also Unkelbach, Forgas, & Denson, 2008). Specifically, participants were quicker and more accurate in decisions that are consistent with prevailing stereotypes—shooting at African American targets shown *with* weapons, and *not* shooting at White targets *without* weapons. Importantly in terms of media influence, Correll, Park, Judd, and Wittenbrink (2007) demonstrated that assignment to an experimental condition involving exposure to news reports featuring African American criminals resulted in even more pronounced race-biased decisions. Consequently, cultivation researchers interested in the ramifications of media exposure on race-related perceptions may find it fruitful to pursue this intriguing (albeit disturbing) means of assessing behavioral outcomes.

## Concluding Comments

Of all of the types of cultivation effects examined in the literature, perhaps the most notable and studied effect is that of the "Mean World Syndrome." In this chapter, we acknowledge not only the stability of portrayals of violence in the media across decades, but we also point to the robustness of research demonstrating media's contribution to heightened fears of crime. At the same time, we hope our overview encourages readers to consider broadening the scope of research in this area, as changes brought on by the evolving media landscape provide unparalleled opportunities to not only extend the boundaries of the types of fears examined in cultivation scholarship but to also become more creative and nuanced in our measures in ways that hold promise of being theoretically productive.

## References

Anderson, C. A., & Bushman, B. J. (2001). Effects of violent video games on aggressive behavior, aggressive cognition, aggressive affect, physiological arousal, and prosocial behavior: A meta-analytic review of the scientific literature. *Psychological Science*, *12*, 353–359.

Appel, M. (2008). Fictional narratives cultivate just-world beliefs. *Journal of Communication, 58*, 62–83.

Baker, P. (2010). Representations of Islam in British broadsheet and tabloid newspapers 1999–2005. *Journal of Language & Politics, 9*, 310–338.

Barton, K. M. (2007). *The mean world effects of reality television: Perceptions of antisocial behaviors resulting from exposure to competition-based reality programming.* Unpublished Dissertation, Florida State University.

Bilandzic, H., Busselle, R., & Spitzner, F. (2009, May). *The CSI cultivation effect: The influences of need for closure and narrative engageability.* Paper presented at the annual convention of the International Communication Association, Chicago, IL.

Bjornstrom, E. E. S., Kaufman, R. L., Peterson, R. D., & Slater, M. D. (2010). Race and ethnic representations of lawbreakers and victims in crime news: A national study of television coverage. *Social Problems, 57*, 269–293.

Boyanows, E. O., Newtson, D., & Walster, E. (1974). Film preferences following a murder. *Communication Research, 1*, 32–43.

Bushman, B. J., & Anderson, C. A. (2002). Violent video games and hostile expectations: A test of the General Aggression Model. *Personality and Social Psychology Bulletin, 28*, 1679–1686.

Chaffee, S. H., & Metzger, M. J. (2001). The end of mass communication? *Mass Communication & Society, 4*, 365–379.

Chiricos, T., Padgett, K., & Gertz, M. (2000). Fear, TV news, and the reality of crime. *Criminology, 38*, 755–785.

Correll, J., Park, B., Judd, C. M., & Wittenbrink, B. (2007). The influence of stereotypes on decisions to shoot. *European Journal of Social Psychology, 37*, 1102–1117.

Correll, J., Park, B., Judd, C. M., Wittenbrink, B., Sadler, M. S., & Keesee, T. (2007). Across the thin blue line: Police officers and racial bias in the decision to shoot. *Journal of Personality and Social Psychology, 92*, 1006–1023.

Devine, P. G., & Monteith, M. J. (1999). Automaticity and control in stereotyping. In S. Chaiken & Y. Trope (Eds.), *Dual-process theories in social psychology* (pp. 339–360). New York: Guilford Press.

Dixon, T. L. (2008). Crime news and racialized beliefs: Understanding the relationship between local news viewing and perceptions of African Americans and crime. *Journal of Communication, 58*, 106–129.

Dixon, T. L., & Linz, D. (2000). Overrepresentation and underrepresentation of African Americans and Latinos as lawbreakers on television news. *Journal of Communication, 50*, 131–154.

Dixon, T. L., & Linz, D. (2002). Television news, prejudicial pretrial publicity, and the depiction of race. *Journal of Broadcasting & Electronic Media, 46*, 112–136.

Eastin, M. S., & Griffiths, R. P. (2009). Unreal: Hostile expectations from social gameplay. *New Media & Society, 11*, 509–531.

Eschholz, S., Chiricos, T., & Gertz, M. (2003). Television and fear of crime: Program types, audience traits, and the mediating effect of perceived neighborhood racial composition. *Social Problems, 50*, 395–415.

Federman, J. (Ed.). (1998). *Executive summary: National Television Violence Study* (Vol. 3). Santa Barbara, CA: Center for Communication and Social Policy, University of California, Santa Barbara.

Ferris, A. L., Smith, S. W., Greenberg, B. S., & Smith, S. L. (2007). The content of reality dating shows and viewer perceptions of dating. *Journal of Communication, 57*, 490–510.

Gerbner, G. (1999). The stories we tell. *Peace Review, 11*(1), 9–15.

Gerbner, G., Gross, L., Morgan, M., & Signorielli, N. (1980). The "mainstreaming" of America: Violence profile no. 11. *Journal of Communication, 30*(3), 10–29.

Gerbner, G., Gross, L., Morgan, M., Signorielli, N., & Shanahan, J. (2002). Growing up with television: Cultivation processes. In J. Bryant & D. Zillmann (Eds.), *Media effects: Advances in theory and research* (2nd ed., pp. 43–67). Mahwah, NJ: Erlbaum.

Gever, M. (2005). The spectacle of crime, digitized: *CSI: Crime Scene Investigation* and social anatomy. *European Journal of Cultural Studies, 8*, 445–463.

Gilliam, F. D., Valentino, N. A., & Beckmann, M. N. (2002). Where you live and what you watch: The impact of racial proximity and local television news on attitudes about race and crime. *Political Research Quarterly, 55*, 755–780.

Grabe, M. E., & Drew, D. G. (2007). Crime cultivation: Comparisons across media genres and channels. *Journal of Broadcasting & Electronic Media, 51*, 147–171.

Greenwald, A. G., McGhee, D. E., & Schwartz, J. L. K. (1998). Measuring individual differences in implicit cognition: The implicit association test. *Journal of Personality and Social Psychology, 74*, 1464–1480.

Holbert, R. L., Shah, D. V., & Kwak, N. (2004). Fear, authority, and justice: Crime-related TV viewing and endorsements of capital punishment and gun ownership. *Journalism & Mass Communication Quarterly, 81*, 343–363.

Holbrook, R. A., & Hill, T. G. (2005). Agenda-setting and priming in prime time television: Crime dramas as political cues. *Political Communication, 22*, 277–295.

Kaminski, R. J., Koons-Witt, B. A., Thompson, N. S., & Weiss, D. (2010). The impacts of the Virginia Tech and Northern Illinois University shootings on fear of crime on campus. *Journal of Criminal Justice, 38*, 88–98.

Lowry, D. T., Nio, T. C. J., & Leitner, D. W. (2003). Setting the public fear agenda: A longitudinal analysis of network TV crime reporting, public perceptions of crime, and FBI crime statistics. *Journal of Communication, 53*, 61–73.

Mastro, D. E. (2009). Racial/ethnic stereotyping and the media. In R. L. Nabi & M. B. Oliver (Eds.), *The Sage handbook of media processes and effects* (pp. 377–392). Newbury Park, CA: Sage.

Mastro, D. E., Behm-Morawitz, E., & Ortiz, M. (2007). The cultivation of social perceptions of Latinos: A mental models approach. *Media Psychology, 9*, 347–365.

Metzger, M. J. (2009). The study of media effects in the era of Internet communication. In R. L. Nabi & M. B. Oliver (Eds.), *The Sage handbook of media processes and effects* (pp. 567–576). Newbury Park, CA: Sage.

Morgan, M., & Shanahan, J. (1997). Two decades of cultivation research: An appraisal and meta-analysis. In B. R. Burleson (Ed.), *Communication Yearbook* (Vol. 20, pp. 1–45). Thousand Oaks, CA: Sage.

Morgan, M., & Shanahan, J. (2010). The state of cultivation. *Journal of Broadcasting & Electronic Media, 54*, 337–355.

Muschert, G. W. (2007). Research in school shootings. *Sociology Compass, 1*(1), 60–80.

Muschert, G. W. (2009). Frame-changing in the media coverage of a school shooting: The rise of Columbine as a national concern. *Social Science Journal, 46*, 164–170.

Nabi, R. L., Biely, E. N., Morgan, S. J., & Stitt, C. R. (2003). Reality-based television programming and the psychology of its appeal. *Media Psychology, 5*, 303–330.

Nellis, A. M. (2009). Gender differences in fear of terrorism. *Journal of Contemporary Criminal Justice, 25*, 322–340.

Nolan, T. W. (2007). Depiction of the "CSI effect" in popular culture: Portrait in domination and effective affectation. *New England Law Review, 41*, 575–589.

O'Brien, T. L. (2000, April 3). Officials worried over a sharp rise in identity theft. *New York Times.*

Oliver, M. B., & Armstrong, G. B. (1998). The color of crime: Perceptions of Caucasians' and African Americans' involvement in crime. In M. Fishman & G. Cavender (Eds.), *Entertaining crime: Television reality programs* (pp. 19–35). New York: Aldine de Gruyter.

Oliver, M. B., Ramasubramanian, S., & Kim, J. (2007). Racism and the media. In D. Roskos-Ewoldsen & J. Monahan (Eds.), *Communication and social cognition* (2nd ed., pp. 273–291). Mahwah, NJ: Erlbaum.

Podlas, K. (2006). The CSI Effect: Exposing the media myth. *Media and Entertainment Law Journal, 16*, 429–465.

Potter, W. J., Vaughan, M. W., Warren, R., Howley, K., Land, A., & Hagemeyer, J. C. (1995). How real is the portrayal of aggression in television entertainment programming? *Journal of Broadcasting & Electronic Media, 39*, 496–516.

Potter, W. J., & Warren, R. (1998). Humor as camouflage of televised violence. *Journal of Communication, 48*(2), 40–57.

President's Identity Theft Task Force. (2007). *Combating identity theft: A strategic plan.* Retrieved from http://purl.access.gpo.gov/GPO/LPS82893.

Raney, A. A. (2005). Punishing media criminals and moral judgment: The impact on enjoyment. *Media Psychology, 7*, 145–163.

Raney, A. A., & Bryant, J. (2002). Moral judgment and crime drama: An integrated theory of enjoyment. *Journal of Communication, 52*, 402–415.

Reiss, S., & Wiltz, J. (2004). Why people watch reality TV. *Media Psychology, 6*, 363–378.

Richter, C., & Hafez, K. (2009). The image of Islam in German public service television programmes. *Journal of Arab & Muslim Media Research, 2*(3), 169–181.

Riddle, K. (2010). Remembering past media use: Toward the development of a lifetime television exposure scale. *Communication Methods and Measures, 4*, 241–255.

Robinson, T. N., Wilde, M. L., Navracruz, L. C., Haydel, K. F., & Varady, A. (2001). Effects of reducing children's television and video game use on aggressive behavior: A randomized controlled trial. *Archives of Pediatrics & Adolescent Medicine, 155*, 17–23.

Romer, D., Jamieson, K. H., & Aday, S. (2003). Television news and the cultivation of fear of crime. *Journal of Communication, 53*, 88–104.

Scheufele, D. A., Nisbet, M. C., & Ostman, R. E. (2005). September 11 news coverage, public opinion and support for civil liberties. *Mass Communication & Society, 8*, 197–218.

Signorielli, N. (1989). Television and conceptions about sex roles: Maintaining conventionality and the status quo. *Sex Roles, 21*, 341–360.

Signorielli, N. (2003). Prime-time violence 1993–2001: Has the picture really changed? *Journal of Broadcasting & Electronic Media, 47*, 36–57.

Signorielli, N., & Kahlenberg, S. (2001). Television's world of work in the nineties.

*Journal of Broadcasting & Electronic Media, 45*, 4–22.

Signorielli, N., & Staples, J. (1997). Television and children's conceptions of nutrition. *Health Communication, 9*, 289–301.

Slone, M. (2000). Responses to media coverage of terrorism. *Journal of Conflict Resolution, 44*, 508–522.

Smith, S. L., Lachlan, K., & Tamborini, R. (2003). Popular video games: Quantifying the presentation of violence and its context. *Journal of Broadcasting & Electronic Media, 47*, 58–76.

Smith, S. L., Nathanson, A. I., & Wilson, B. J. (2002). Prime-time television: Assessing violence during the most popular viewing hours. *Journal of Communication, 52*, 84–111.

Smith, S. L., & Wilson, B. J. (2000). Children's reactions to a television news story: The impact of video footage and proximity of the crime. *Communication Research, 34*, 212–230.

Soulliere, D. (2003). Prime-time murder: Presentations of murder on popular television justice programs. *Journal of Criminal Justice and Popular Culture, 10*, 12–38.

Tamborini, R., Skalski, P., Lachlan, K., Westerman, D., Davis, J., & Smith, S. (2005). The raw nature of televised professional wrestling: Is the violence a cause for concern? *Journal of Broadcasting & Electronic Media, 49*, 202–220.

Thompson, K. M., Tepichin, K., & Haninger, K. (2006). Content and ratings of mature-rated video games. *Archives of Pediatrics & Adolescent Medicine, 160*, 402–410.

Tyler, T. R. (2006). Viewing *CSI* and the threshold of guilt: Managing truth and justice in reality and fiction. *The Yale Law Journal, 115*, 1050–1085.

Unkelbach, C., Forgas, J. P., & Denson, T. F. (2008). The turban effect: The influence of Muslim headgear and induced affect on aggressive responses in the shooter bias paradigm. *Journal of Experimental Social Psychology, 44*, 1409–1413.

Van den Bulck, J. (2004). The relationship between television fiction and fear of crime: An empirical comparison of three causal explanations. *European Journal of Communication, 19*, 239–248.

Van Mierlo, J., & Van den Bulck, J. (2004). Benchmarking the cultivation approach to video game effects: A comparison of the correlates of TV viewing and game play. *Journal of Adolescence, 27*, 97–111.

Vorderer, P., & Knobloch, S. (2000). Conflict and suspense in drama. In D. Zillmann & P. Vorderer (Eds.), *Media entertainment: The psychology of its appeal* (pp. 59–72). Mahwah, NJ: Erlbaum.

Wakshlag, J., Vial, V., & Tamborini, R. (1983). Selecting crime drama and apprehension about crime. *Human Communication Research, 10*, 227–242.

Weaver, A., & Wilson, B. (2009). The role of graphic and sanitized violence in the enjoyment of television dramas. *Human Communication Research, 35*, 442–463.

Weitzer, R., & Kubrin, C. E. (2004). Breaking news: how local TV news and real-world conditions affect fear of crime. *Justice Quarterly, 21*, 497–520.

Wicks, R. H. (2006). Emotional response to collective action media frames about Islam and terrorism. *Journal of Media & Religion, 5*, 245–263.

Williams, D. (2006). Virtual cultivation: Online worlds, offline perceptions. *Journal of Communication, 56*, 69–87.

Wilson, B., Smith, S., Potter, W. J., Kunkel, D., Linz, D., Colvin, C., & Donerstein, E.

(2002). Violence in children's television programming: Assessing the risks. *Journal of Communication, 52*, 5–35.

Ybarra, M. L., Mitchell, K. J., Finkelhor, D., & Wolak, J. (2007). Internet prevention messages: Targeting the right online behaviors. *Archives of Pediatrics & Adolescent Medicine, 161*, 138–145.

Zillmann, D., & Wakshlag, J. (1985). Fear of victimization and the appeal of crime drama. In D. Zillmann & J. Bryant (Eds.), *Selective exposure to communication* (pp. 141–156). Hillsdale, NJ: Erlbaum.

Zurbriggen, E. L., & Morgan, E. M. (2006). Who wants to marry a millionaire? Reality dating television programs, attitudes toward sex, and sexual behaviors. *Sex Roles, 54*, 1–17.

# 3. Cultivation of Perceptions of Marginalized Groups

*Dana Mastro & Riva Tukachinsky*

As cultivation theorists have long articulated, media constitute an important socializing agent, providing audiences with information (whether accurate or not) about societal features, values, and norms that shape audiences' perceptions of the world—including views about marginalized racial and ethnic groups (Gerbner, Gross, Morgan, Signorielli, & Shanahan, 2002; Morgan & Shanahan, 2010). In more specific terms, contemporary cultivation theorizing asserts that heavy consumers of media are more likely than light users to conceptualize reality in a manner consistent with the mediated world (vs. the social world), though no one is entirely immune to its influence. Although the impact of exposure to thematic messages in media content as a whole is given primacy within the cultivation framework, current research also includes genre-specific effects of media consumption and suggests that perceptions are cultivated in the direction of the attributes featured in the content to which consumers are exposed (see Morgan & Shanahan, 2010 for discussion; also see Bilandzic & Busselle, Chapter 13, this volume). In either case (overall or genre-specific), the system of media messages is paramount. Thus, given that cultivation depends, in large part, on the properties of media representations themselves, it is critical to first identify patterns in media content (via content analysis) and determine the extent to which these offerings deviate from real-life data.

Such assessments are particularly important when it comes to understanding the influence of media exposure on perceptions of race/ethnicity, as many factors other than media use are known to contribute to views of different groups. In other words, although cultivation effects are generally understood to be stable and consistent (Morgan, Shanahan, & Signorielli, 2009), individual differences such as real world experiences create contingencies to this relationship (Potter, 1991a, 1991b). As such, cultivation effects can be most clearly illustrated (as distinct from other societal forces) in contexts where media messages and people's direct experiences diverge. Accordingly, when considered in conjunction with viewers' personal experiences, both the number and quality of media portrayals of racial/ethnic minorities can be used to make predictions about the effects of exposure. To this end, the present chapter addresses the conceptual and methodological steps involved in testing the cultivation of racial/ethnic perceptions, starting with evidence of media *mis*representations of various groups (demonstrated by both a meta-analytic examination of existing content analyses as well as a narrative review of this literature) and continuing with an overview of findings from current media effects studies. Recent psychological developments in cultivation research are additionally highlighted, including work isolating the cognitive mechanisms underlying perceptual changes in audience members (in general and with regard to marginalized groups).

## Cultural Indicators: Media Representations of Racial/Ethnic Minorities

Message system analysis constitutes a central feature of cultivation research. It involves a systemic examination of the symbolic environment created by the dominant medium in a given society (Gerbner, 1969). Specifically, television has been recognized as the predominant cultural storyteller that cultivates shared public perceptions in contemporary American society. Thus, periodic quantitative content analyses of television programs are used to reveal the direction in which media trends may socialize viewers. Such content analyses address both the quantity (i.e., numerical prevalence) and the quality (e.g., stereotypicality) of racial/ethnic representations in the media.

### *Quantity of Media Representations*

Over the past fifty years, ample quantitative content analyses have been conducted which document portrayals of racial/ethnic minorities in the media. Given that prime-time network television has historically constituted the lion's share of consumers' media diet, this content has been the focus of the majority of these studies. In order to provide a rigorous summary of the findings stemming from this body of work, we conducted a longitudinal meta-analysis of these content analyses (as Hetsroni, 2007, did with studies of sexual content). Similar to meta-analysis of effect sizes, meta-analysis of content analyses helps overcome the inevitable shortcomings of any individual study. As such, the findings from a meta-analytical review of this nature are less susceptible to biases from sampling, coding procedures, and other idiosyncrasies introduced within individual studies. Thus, content-based meta-analyses such as the one presented here offer a more systematic and precise synthesis of past empirical findings (compared with the more subjective practice of providing summary reviews).

Two procedures were used to identify studies for inclusion in the present content analytic, longitudinal meta-analysis. First, the "Communication and Mass Media Complete" database was searched for articles that included the following search terms in the title or abstract: "television" + ("prime time" OR "primetime" OR "prime-time") + ("rac*" OR "minor*" OR "ethnic*" OR "Black*" OR "African American*" OR "Latin*" OR "Hispanic*" OR "Asian*" OR "Oriental*" OR "Indian*" OR "Native American*"). Second, the reference sections from each of the studies located in this database search were reviewed to identify any additional content analyses that were not previously found. To be included in the current meta-analysis, a study had to report quantitative data about the relative share of at least one racial/ethnic group from among all of the characters in the sample of prime-time television programs.

Studies on commercials, non-primetime shows, and studies examining *only* programs that included racial/ethnic minority characters were eliminated from the current analysis. Three studies also were omitted due to the use of units of analyses that were incompatible with measures used in other studies (Stroman, Merritt, & Matabane, 1989; Weigel, Kim, & Frost, 1995; Wu, 1996). Finally, one study (Lichter, Lichter, Rothman, & Amundson, 1987) was excluded from the analysis because it reported the overall prevalence of characters of different races/ethnicities over several decades (between 1955 and 1986)—an extensive timeframe during which portrayals of race/ethnicity were likely to shift.

These two search strategies coupled with the exclusion criteria yielded a total of 23 journal articles and research reports that provide information about the racial composition of characters in primetime television programming between 1966 and 2008 (these works are noted in the references with an asterisk). For consistency and comparability, only data from network programming were included. Together, these studies examine 90,392 characters appearing in primetime network programs airing in 37 different television seasons. The findings from each study were weighted by the total number of characters coded in the study.[1] Weighted percentages of characters from different ethnic/racial groups were computed for each decade.[2] The weighted averages of television characters in each decade were then compared with census data from the corresponding decade (Census Bureau, 2001, 2010).

The rationale for using decades as the time unit for the analysis was grounded in the fact that most studies included in the meta-analysis reported aggregated data from television programming across multiple years. Thus, for the current study to include as many data points as possible, it was necessary to combine data within each decade. Notably, some studies do report data from individual years, showing some variation in representations of minorities even within a given decade. For instance, Signorielli's (2009a) comparison between individual seasons in the 2000s revealed that the over-representation of African Americans that was prevalent in the early 2000s was followed by a decrease in the presence of Black characters in the 2005–2008 television seasons. Furthermore, some individual studies provide information about the specific nature of changes in racial/ethnic characterizations (e.g., examining differences in gender portrayals across and within racial/ethnic groups). Although these individual studies make a crucial contribution (documenting the year-to-year fluctuations in media content and illuminating the characteristics of these changes), the objective of the current meta-analysis is to present a bird's-eye view of the broad trends in media representations of different groups across time. This goal can be achieved best by synthesizing data from multiple studies across a number of television seasons, therefore overcoming the limitations of sampling and reliability inherent in each individual study.

Results from the meta-analysis can be found in Figure 1, which presents changes (across decades) in the demographic composition of both the U.S. population and the population of primetime television characters. Additionally, Table 1 provides the ratio between the share of each racial/ethnic group in the media and in the U.S. population. Values of less than one indicate under-representation of a given group (such that the prevalence of the group on television is smaller than its proportion in the U.S. Census), whereas values above one indicate over-representation of the racial/ethnic group.

As can be seen in the figure, variability exists (on an absolute and comparative basis) in the extent to which different racial/ethnic groups are depicted on television. Although the number of Whites from the 1970s to the 2000s largely corresponds to their actual proportion of the population, racial/ethnic minorities tend to be under-represented (with one exception, that of African American portrayals). The rate of African American representation on television has gradually increased from *under*-representation in 1970s (compared with U.S. census figures) to *over*-representation in the 1990s and 2000s. The opposite trend characterizes depictions of the most rapidly growing racial/ethnic minorities in the United States—Asian Americans and Latino

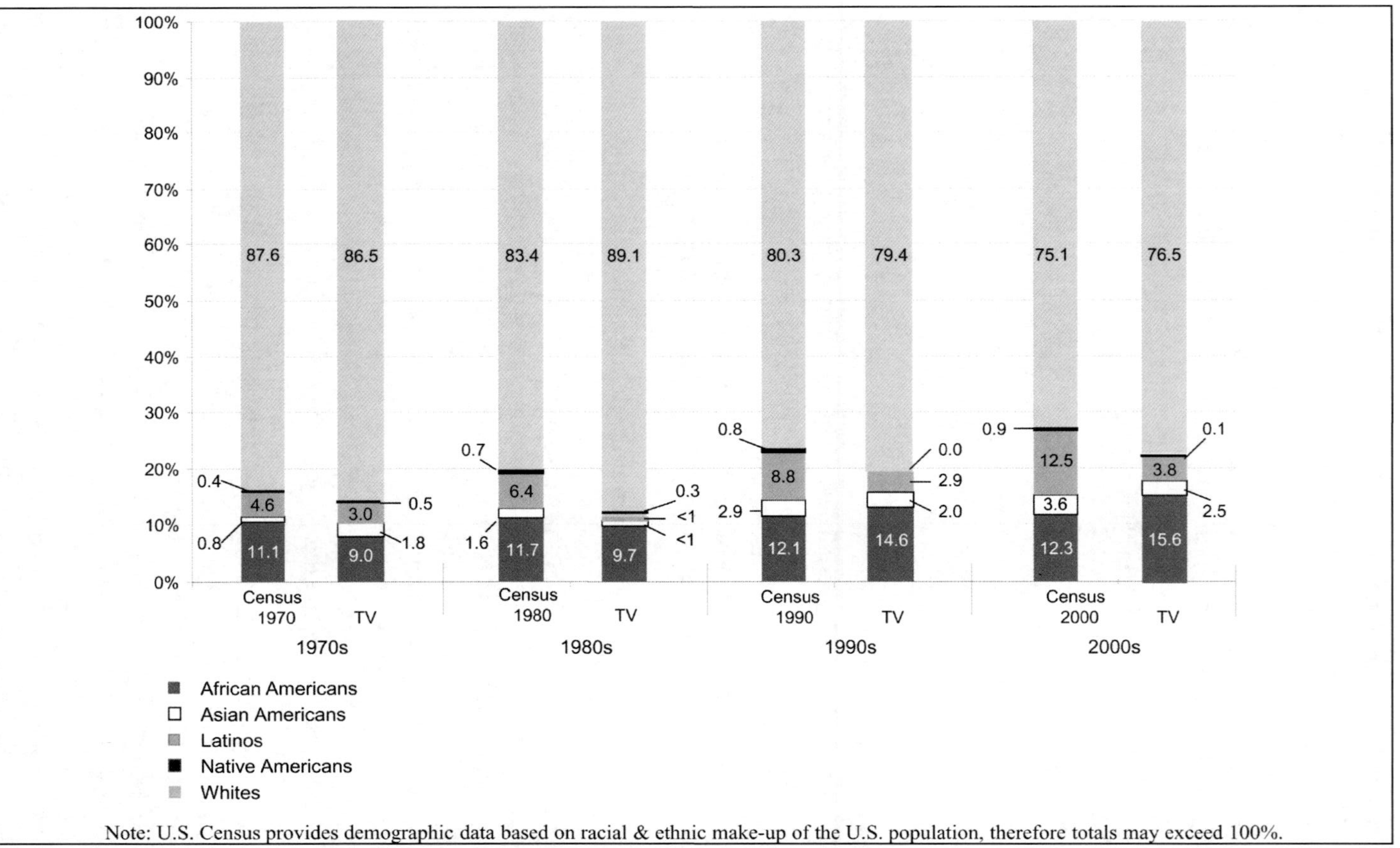


Note: U.S. Census provides demographic data based on racial & ethnic make-up of the U.S. population, therefore totals may exceed 100%.

Figure 1. Racial/ethnic composition of primetime characters and the U.S. population

Americans. Indeed, it appears that these groups proportionately lost ground from the 1970s to the present. From the 1970s to the 1980s both groups saw a drop in their overall rate of representation on primetime, while their share of the U.S. population increased. Modest improvements for both groups were revealed in the 1990s; however, for Latinos this rate of representation still fell below that of the 1970s. By the 2000s, minor increases were again identified, but representations remained strikingly discrepant with real-world census reports. For Latinos, this is most pronounced. Although Latino Americans made up 12.5% of the U.S. population according to the 2000 census, they comprised a mere 3.8% of the characters seen on primetime television—more than three times below their proportion of U.S. society (see Table 1). Although they remained under-represented, at 3.6% of the U.S. population and 2.5% of the TV population, Asian Americans fared better than their Latino counterparts during the decade spanning 2000–2010.

Table 1. Over and under-representations of racial/ethnic groups across decades

| | 1970s | 1980s | 1990s | 2000s |
|---|---|---|---|---|
| African Americans | 0.81 | 0.83 | 1.21 | 1.27 |
| Asian Americans | 2.25 | 0.83 | 0.69 | 0.69 |
| Latinos | 0.65 | 0.16 | 0.33 | 0.30 |
| Native Americans | 1.25 | 0.43 | 0.00 | 0.11 |
| Whites | 0.99 | 1.07 | 0.99 | 1.02 |

Note: The numbers in the table represent the percent of characters (for each group) divided by their real-world proportion of the population according to U.S. Census data.

Native Americans suffer from a distinct form of neglect on primetime. Given the scarcity of Native American characters, many early content analyses (from the 1970s and 1980s) failed to report whether any Native American characters were even identified. However, five studies from the 1990s explicitly noted that within their samples of television programming, not even a single Native American character was found. By the 2000s, American Indians constituted approximately one percent of the U.S. population, while their share of prime time television characters remained meager, at about one tenth of a percent (with four out of seven studies reporting no Native American characters in their samples).

The results from this meta-analysis paint a fairly dire picture when it comes to the equitable distribution of racial/ethnic minority characters on television. With the exception of African Americans, it appears that racial/ethnic minorities have been and continue to be under-represented on primetime (compared with their proportion of the population). From a cultivation perspective, the implications are clear: Audience members, particularly (though not exclusively) heavy consumers, are likely to grossly misconstrue the composition and structure of U.S. society. However, alongside the importance of the sheer quantity of representations, cultivation theory additionally recognizes that the quality of these portrayals is of tremendous consequence. From the standpoint of cultivation theory, the social and cultural status and significance of ethnic minorities on television, rather than their sheer quantitative presence alone, has implications for viewers' perceptions of these groups. Thus, the question remains: When racial/ethnic minority characters are presented on television, *how* are they depicted?

### Quality of Media Representations

Over the decades, content analyses documenting depictions of race/ethnicity have focused on a variety of attributes, applying a diversity of coding schemes and categories. As a result, it is not possible to average findings across studies in a meta-analytic fashion. However, clear patterns emerge from this body of research. Throughout the 1960s and 1970s it was typical to see African Americans cast in comic and minor roles, where they were depicted as less educated and lower in social status positions than their on-air counterparts (Northcott, Seggar, & Hinton, 1975; Stroman et al., 1989; U.S. Commission on Civil Rights, 1979). Beginning in the 1980s and into the 1990s, African Americans were increasingly likely to be seen in major roles playing more diverse kinds of characters (Harwood & Anderson, 2002; Mastro & Greenberg, 2000). By the 2000s, over a quarter (26%) of African Americans on television held prestigious occupations such as physicians or attorneys, with the next largest characterization as law enforcers (21%) and only 10% depicted as law breakers (Children Now, 2004). Despite this overall positive trend, some stereotypical representations persisted. For instance, African Americans in the 2000s were often provocatively dressed and were depicted as less professional (Mastro & Greenberg, 2000) and more criminal than their White, on-air counterparts (Children Now, 2004). Further, compared with television shows with diverse casts and all-White cast programs, television shows with a predominantly ethnic-minority casts were more likely to present characters without occupations or with unclear occupational statuses (Signorielli, 2009b).

According to Gerbner (see Shanahan & Morgan, 1999), media present a bifurcated image of Blacks. In comedies, Blacks are depicted as having high social status. However, in programming designed to represent reality (e.g., news), they are portrayed as criminals posing a threat to the social order. In support of this assertion, recent content analyses of local television news reveal that although the share of African American law-defenders (e.g., police officers) was proportional to their prevalence in society (Dixon & Linz, 2000b), Blacks were overrepresented among lawbreakers (Dixon & Linz, 2000a). Historically, this misrepresentation has been particularly pronounced for crimes perpetrated against White victims (Romer, Jaimeson, & de Coteau, 1998). Moreover, examinations of the narrative frames used in news reporting on crime and race indicate that news coverage has tended to dehumanize African American (vs. White) crime perpetrators/suspects and depict them as a greater threat to society (Entman, 1992). Additionally, it appears that news stories portray African American political leaders as more aggressive than their White peers, engaging in angry rhetoric and striving to promote racial issues at the expense of the public interest (Entman, 1990).

Latinos also have been found to populate unflattering roles on television (Williams & Condry, 1989), most often serving a negative function in the narrative (Harwood & Anderson, 2002). A composite of the typical Latino character on television tends to have a heavy accent and to occupy roles in stereotypical contexts such as crime, violence, and the family milieu—as opposed to professional settings (Mastro & Greenberg, 2000). When compared with other racial/ethnic groups on primetime television, Latinos are also four times more likely to be presented as domestic workers (Children Now, 2004). Further, Latinos (and Latinas in particular) are characterized as the laziest, least motivated, least articulate, most ridiculed figures on television (Mastro & Behm-Morawitz, 2005).

Given the scarcity of other racial/ethnic minority groups on television, relatively little is known about the manner in which they are represented. What can be gleaned from existing work suggests that Asian Americans, although confined to minor and non-recurring parts, tend to be depicted in roles of high occupational status (Children Now, 2004). Representations of Native Americans are limited to two main themes: social delinquency (e.g., criminality) and historical/spiritual festivals (Heider, 2000). Finally, when Arab/Middle Eastern characters are depicted (at a rate of less than 1% of the primetime population), nearly half (46%) are criminals, "...compared to 15% of Asian/Pacific Islander and Latino characters, 10% of African American characters and 5% of White characters" (Children Now, 2004, p. 6).

### *Overarching Implications from a Cultivation Perspective*

Comparisons between census data and the results from content analyses indicate that marginalized racial/ethnic groups other than African Americans are, indeed, underrepresented in mass media offerings (primetime television in particular). Beyond the issue of numeric parity, when these groups appear on television, they are commonly portrayed in a stereotype-consistent, oftentimes negative, manner. At the most basic level, applying cultivation-based assumptions would indicate that long-term, heavy exposure to such characterizations (both quantitative and qualitative) has the potential to shape perceptions of these groups. Thus, given the images documented here, exposure is likely to promote unfavorable racial/ethnic stereotypes among media consumers as well as misperceptions about the demographic features of these groups. Research testing such cultivation hypotheses supports this assertion.

## Cultivation Indicators: Media Effects on Perceptions of Racial/Ethnic Minority Groups

Hawkins and Pingree (1981) distinguish between two types of cultivation outcomes—effects on viewers' perceptions regarding the concrete features of society (demographic measures, often called "first-order" cultivation) and effects on viewers' value systems and worldviews (often called "second-order" cultivation). In the domain of race/ethnicity, evidence of both first- and second-order cultivation effects has been revealed.

### *First-order Cultivation*

As demonstrated above in the meta-analysis, different racial/ethnic groups are depicted on television at varying rates (and for minority communities, largely inconsistently with census figures). It is logical to hypothesize, when considering these data, that exposure to such content will encourage underestimations of Asian Americans and Latinos and overestimations of African Americans in the U.S. population. Although not included in the meta-analysis, it is also plausible that genre-specific consumption patterns will influence such perceptions. If so, given content analytic evidence of the over-representation of African Americans in news reporting on crime (Dixon & Linz, 2000a), it would be expected that news consumers would exaggerate the amount of crime and violence committed by this group.

In fact, multiple sources indicate that Americans hold distorted perceptions about U.S. demographics (e.g., Sigelman & Niemi, 2001). At the broadest level, the 2000 General Social Survey (GSS) reveals that, on average, White Americans believe that they (i.e., Whites) constitute 59 percent of the U.S. population (compared with 75 percent according to the 2000 Census). At the same time, Whites considerably over-estimate the share of racial/ethnic minorities in the population (Wong, 2007), maintaining that the U.S. population consists of 30 percent Blacks (12 percent in the Census), 23 percent Hispanics (13 percent in the Census) and 16 percent Asians (4 percent in the Census). Although the GSS data do not show a link between media use (i.e., television and newspaper) and demographic estimations (Wong, 2007), it is quite possible that this relationship exists but is masked by a study design that was not constructed to specifically examine media effects. Accordingly, it is reasonable to suggest that television exposure may well be one factor in the public's perceptions of the demographics of the American population.

To further illuminate the process by which individuals construct their perceptions regarding the racial/ethnic composition of the U.S., Gallagher (2003) conducted a series of semi-structured interviews and focus groups. The participants in this study exhibited the same demographic innumeracy phenomenon documented in national surveys such as the GSS. When asked to explain how they produced their estimates, many indicated that they relied on television news. For example, a White American, middle-aged woman from Mountain County, Georgia (population: 95.54% White), who rarely traveled outside her community, believed that Blacks comprised 40 percent of the U.S. population, stating: "from watching the news, you see, it [the U.S.] consists of Blacks" (p. 387). Similarly, a 19-year-old Mountain County man estimated that Blacks constitute 60 percent of the U.S. population because "you see them [Blacks] on TV" (p. 387). Curiously, whereas over-estimations of Blacks in the U.S. population appear to be linked with exposure to television news coverage among these participants, over-estimations of Asian Americans in the population seem to be based on interpersonal contact. Given the exploratory nature of these findings, future empirical studies are necessary to more definitively flesh out this relationship.

In addition to examining the estimated prevalence of different racial/ethnic groups, several studies addressing first-order cultivation effects also have investigated the relationship between media exposure and perceptions of African Americans' social and economic standing. Armstrong, Neuendorf, and Brentar (1992) conducted two surveys (1980–81 and 1985–86) in which White university students were asked to estimate the status-based outcomes (average yearly income, social class, educational achievement) and the social contributions (the value of goods/services produced) of Whites and African Americans. Exposure to entertainment television programming (both in 1980 and in 1985) was associated with more positive perceptions of African Americans' status. Alternatively, news exposure (1980 only) was predictive of unfavorable estimations of the contributions of African Americans, once again supporting Gerbner's notion of the "bifurcated image" of African Americans.

Further, in Busselle and Crandall's (2002) research, White college students' exposure to situation comedies (but not dramas) was associated with more favorable perceptions of Blacks' education and income levels. For news consumption, exposure was related to perceptions that African Americans had fewer job opportunities available to them. It is important to note, however, that as news viewing rose, so too did the belief that socioeconomic failings stemmed from a lack of motivation (rather than opportunity). Notably, in this study, news exposure was not predictive of perceived income. Conversely, more recent survey research of a multiracial sample of Los Angeles County residents found that network news exposure (but not exposure to local news) was related to lower estimates of African Americans' income (Dixon, 2008a, 2008b). It is possible that such differences stem from the varying approaches used in assessing both media use (e.g., daily estimates, diaries, etc.) as well as the dependent variables of interest. For example, Jeffres, Atkin, and Neuendorf (2001) found no effect of media exposure (of any kind) on beliefs about African Americans' educational opportunities and discrimination, among respondents in their phone survey of Midwestern metropolitan residents. However, when responses were analyzed for mainstreaming (i.e., the extent to which respondents converged with the modal response), newspaper consumption was found to be associated with holding more extreme views about African Americans' educational opportunities and workplace discrimination.

Finally, research fairly consistently links media use with perceptions of racial/ethnic minorities' involvement in crime and violence. For example, Oliver and Armstrong (1998) found that White viewers' exposure to reality-based crime programs (e.g., *Cops*), but not exposure to fictional crime shows, was associated with elevated perceptions regarding African American crime rates. Similarly, work by Dixon (2008b) revealed exposure to news channels that over-represent Blacks as criminals to be associated with the belief (among a diverse sample of viewers) that Blacks are more violent (Dixon, 2008b).

Taken together, these findings are consistent with the notion that first-order beliefs about racial/ethnic minorities (especially African Americans) are related to the ways in which these groups are depicted in different genres. While entertainment genres (specifically, sitcoms) portray African Americans in diverse roles (Children Now, 2004), news predominantly features them in the context of crime and poverty (Dixon & Linz, 2000b; Entman & Rojecki, 2001). Thus, exposure to news is largely related to more unfavorable views of Blacks' socioeconomic success and criminality. On the other hand, exposure to entertainment media (and comedies in particular) is related to more constructive views of African Americans.

### *Second-order Cultivation*

Second-order cultivation is concerned with the influence of media use on consumers' values and worldviews. In the context of perceptions of race/ethnicity, this can include outcomes such as stereotyping and prejudice (among other things). Consistent with this contention, Mastro, Behm-Morawitz, and Ortiz (2007) found that Whites with higher rates of television consumption (varying based on perceptions of content) were more likely to endorse negative stereotypes about the criminality, intelligence, and work ethic of Latinos. Results from Dong and Murrillo (2007) yielded comparable outcomes, with Whites who reported learning about race/ethnicity from television more likely to endorse negative stereotypes about Latinos (controlling for valence of interpersonal contact). Similarly, a survey of Los Angeles county residents (utilizing a multi-racial sample and controlling for a number of social and demographic features) found that exposure to network news (but not exposure to newspapers and local television news) was related to respondents' endorsement of racial stereotypes and greater prejudice towards African Americans (Dixon, 2008a). Furthermore, television exposure (among a predominantly White sample of college students) was associated with the attribution of more negative personality traits to Asians, Native Americans, and Blacks, and of more positive traits to Whites (Lee, Bichard, Irey, Walt, & Carlson, 2009). For example, watching informational programs corresponded with lower perceptions about the neuroticism of Whites, whereas exposure to entertainment programs was related to perceptions of African Americans as less agreeable, Asians as less conscientious, and Native Americans as less open to new experiences and learning. These perceptions are not necessarily aligned with specific racial stereotypes but rather represent a more general trend of positive ingroup and negative outgroup views. This study did not document any consistent media effects on perceptions of Latinos.

Alongside the implications for stereotyping, media use also has been linked with more tangible, discriminatory responses. To illustrate, news consumption among a diverse sample of adults was found to be related to viewers' perceptions of Black (but not White) criminal suspects' culpability, when controlling for a number of social and demographic features (Dixon, 2008b). Further, reliance on television is associated with greater reports of fear from a diverse sample of residents from multi-racial/ethnic neighborhoods (i.e., with high presence of Blacks, Latinos, etc.), irrespective of actual crime rates (Matei, Ball-Rokeach, & Qiu, 2001).

Altogether, studies support the notion of second-order cultivation effects when it comes to perceptions of racial/ethnic groups. In particular, media consumption (especially but not exclusively among Whites) appears to: (a) cultivate negative views about racial/ethnic minority groups, (b) enhance prejudice, and (c) induce fear of racial/ethnic minorities. However, as in the case of research on first-order cultivation, the bulk of the work in this area focuses on perceptions of African Americans. Although this research is of both theoretical and practical importance, devoting attention to the media's influence on perceptions regarding a wider range of racial/ethnic groups is critical to understanding the breadth of potential cultivation effects. For example, it is possible that variations in both the quality and quantity of representations of different racial/ethnic groups moderate the impact of media on consumers. To illustrate, although Tan, Fujioka, and Lucht (1997) did not find a relationship between television exposure and endorsements of stereotypes of Native Americans, this result may actually reflect the conspicuous under-representation of this group on television (and in other media).

## Moderating Factors

Although many studies have demonstrated overarching race-related cultivation effects, the media's impact can vary across consumers. One important moderating factor is audience members' direct experiences with racial/ethnic groups other than their own. Two opposing hypotheses are posed about the possible implications of such experiences on cultivation effects: the resonance hypothesis and the substitution hypothesis.

According to the resonance hypothesis, media-congruent first-hand experiences reaffirm the lessons learned from the media. In other words, if viewers' direct experiences resonate with television's depictions of reality, the media's effect is enhanced. For instance, personal experiences mirroring the overly violent and dangerous television-version of reality promote fear of victimization among viewers (Chiricos, Padgett, & Gertz, 2000).

Notably, although this effect was initially found to be greater among individuals with low (compared with high) income-levels, residing in urban neighborhoods (Gerbner, Gross, Morgan, & Signorielli, 1980), this relationship has been fine-tuned in more recent research. Specifically, Eschholz, Chiricos, and Gertz's (2003) research links neighborhood racial/ethnic composition and exposure to television (specifically local news and crime drama) with traditional mean world syndrome outcomes. Similarly, White individuals who report having poor interpersonal experiences with Latinos and who watch more criminal-related portrayals on television hold more negative views of Latino criminality (Mastro, Behm-Morawitz, & Ortiz, 2007). No such effect was found for light viewers, for viewers with positive intergroup experiences, or for beliefs about other stereotypes associated with Latinos. Nonetheless, this finding provides support for the resonance hypothesis, indicating that first-hand experiences that parallel thematic media messages about race/ethnicity enhance the media's influence on social perceptions.

Taking a somewhat different tack, the substitution hypothesis asserts that the media's influence will be greater given an absence of personal experiences in a given domain (Gunter, 1987). According to this view, media representations serve as a substitute for direct experiences—with individuals who lack alternative sources of information more dependent on the media and thus more susceptible to media's influence (media dependency; Ball-Rokeach & DeFleur, 1976). Perceptions of marginalized groups are, therefore, hypothesized to be more aligned with media portrayals among those who lack direct contact with these groups. In line with this hypothesis, Armstrong et al. (1992) found that media exposure more consistently predicted perceptions of African Americans in a sample of participants who had little interpersonal contact with Blacks, compared with highly integrated individuals. The substitution hypothesis also can explain why Gallagher's (2003) interviewees (addressed previously) relied heavily on television portrayals in forming their (distorted) perceptions regarding U.S. demographics.

The substitution hypothesis may also partially reconcile results offered in Fujioka's (1999) examination of the effects of media exposure on perceptions of African Americans among White college students and international Japanese students. For White respondents, exposure to negative depictions of Blacks was associated with negative stereotypes of Blacks whereas exposure to positive representations of Blacks was not related to perceptions of this group. The opposite was true of Japanese international students: Exposure to positive portrayals was associated with favorable perceptions of African Americans, whereas exposure to negative portrayals was unrelated to negative stereotypes. It is conceivable that the differences between the media's impact on the two groups stemmed from the viewers' prior experiences (or lack thereof). Perhaps White Americans related media depictions to their own experiences (supporting a resonance effect), whereas Japanese students relied exclusively on media in forming their perceptions of African Americans (given a lack of real-world experience). Of course this line of reasoning does not explain why Japanese students substituted only positive information in their impression formation. Moreover, this result is inconsistent with findings from Tan, Zhang, Zhang, and Dalisay (2009), which link exposure to American movies and television with negative stereotypes of African Americans among Chinese high school students (who had no direct experiences with African Americans). Despite these inconsistencies, studies on both resonance and substitution suggest that the moderating influence of direct real-world experiences (on cultivation outcomes) cannot be ignored. Instead, these results underscore the need for greater explication of these concepts, including identification of the conditions under which these hypotheses will hold. To a degree, recent theoretical advances aimed at accounting for the cognitive-psychological processes underlying cultivation effects address this issue.

## Cognitive Mechanisms Underlying Cultivation of Perceptions of Marginalized Groups

### *Cultivation as Accessibility Heuristic*

Currently, the dominant cognitive explanation of cultivation (Morgan & Shanahan, 2010) is Shrum's heuristic model (Shrum, 1996, 2004; Shrum & O'Guinn, 1993), rooted in Tversky and Kahneman's (1980) research on heuristic decision making (see Shrum & Lee, Chapter 8, this volume). According to this approach, television provides viewers with recurring, vivid instances termed exemplars. With repeated media exposure, these exemplars become particularly easy to retrieve. Hence, when forming social judgments, the more individuals consume media, the more likely they are to rely on media-generated exemplars.

Media, of course, are not the sole source of exemplars. Mental libraries of exemplars include personal experiences, imagination, and interpersonal sources (Busselle & Shrum, 2003). However, some domains might be dominated by media-based exemplars. Thus, in line with the substitution hypothesis, the cultivation effect has been hypothesized to be particularly prevalent when it comes to issues that are frequently portrayed in the media but with which individuals have little first-hand experience (e.g., murders and trials, as opposed to dating or highway accidents; Busselle & Shrum, 2003).

In line with the heuristic model, priming studies have shown that exposure to media-based exemplars of racial/ethnic minorities shapes viewers' overall perceptions of the groups' attributes as well as beliefs about discrimination in society (Bodenhausen, Schwarz, Bless, & Wanke, 1995; Mastro & Tukachinsky, in press). Although these studies have experimentally manipulated media-based exemplar activation, it is also possible for individuals to spontaneously retrieve media-based racial/ethnic exemplars. For example, Busselle (2001) found that when asked to think of a Black physician, most consumers brought to mind fictional media characters. Moreover, the perceived realism of relevant television programs predicted the ease (i.e., speed) in generating an example of a Black doctor. Accordingly, it is reasonable to hypothesize that media exemplars that are perceived to be true representations of the world would be used more commonly as a basis for real world judgments (e.g., Potter, 1986).

The theoretical advances offered by the heuristic model of cultivation allow for refined predictions to be made about the relationships among media use, content, and effects as they pertain to issues of race/ethnicity. First, to increase accessibility, media-based exemplars should be vivid and frequent (Shrum, 1996; Shrum & O'Guinn, 1993). In other words, a critical number of racial/ethnic minority characters has to be present in the media for cultivation to occur. Thus, it should not come as a surprise that media exposure was found to have little or no effect on viewers' perceptions of Native Americans—a group that is largely ignored on television (Fujioka, 1999; Tan et al., 1997).

Second, since exemplars perceived as realistic are more likely to be applied when making real-world judgments (Busselle, 2001), some media exemplars may be more impactful than others. In the context of mediated intergroup encounters, prototypicality appears to be an important dimension along which outgroup members are evaluated (e.g., Mastro, Tamborini, & Hullett, 2005). When a media exemplar is perceived to be atypical of the group, the exemplar is deemed irrelevant/unrepresentative. Once discounted, such exemplars do not contribute to the formation of viewers' judgments about the group (e.g., Bodenhausen et al., 1995).

### *Cultivation as Construction of Mental Models*

The heuristic model focuses on media effects resulting from the activation of accessible constructs stored in memory (rather than from a dynamic process of mental construction of reality). Although second-order beliefs about social groups can be, at least in part, explained by the activation of individual exemplars (e.g., Mastro & Tukachinsky, in press; Power, Murphy & Coover, 1996), the heuristic model does not account for global inferences that viewers generate on the basis of multiple, repeated media exposures. Such effects do not occur due to heuristic judgments but result from online cognitive construction and integration of media representations (Shrum, 2004). This process involves developing mental representations from media messages, updating these mental constructions as additional media-based information becomes available, and integrating these models with data previously stored in memory (Roskos-Ewoldsen, Roskos-Ewoldsen, Yang, & Lee, 2007; Zwaan & Radvansky, 1998; Zwaan, Langston, & Graesser, 1995). Accordingly, media-based and real-world knowledge intermingle in this process. In fact, mental models of the real world assist individuals in comprehending media content (Busselle & Bilandzic, 2008). At the same time, media-based knowledge is also merged into generalized mental constructs of the world (Roskos-Ewoldsen, Davies, & Roskos-Ewoldsen, 2004; see also Ewoldsen & Rhodes, Chapter 10, this volume). To illustrate, Mastro et al. (2007) found that repeated media exposure integrates perceptions of televised Latinos and perceptions of Latinos in reality into a single mental model of Latinos (used in making real-world judgments). Specifically, perceptions of television representations of ethnic minorities and the amount of television exposure interact in predicting White college students' real-world perceptions/stereotypes of Latinos.

## Conclusions and Directions for Future Research

If media are the predominant storytellers in modern society (Gerbner et al., 2002), then the tale they tell about racial/ethnic minorities in the U.S. is an unflattering one. Although some groups' representations have improved over time (in numerical terms), overall, racial/ethnic minorities continue to be underrepresented and depicted in stereotypical, mostly negative contexts. Exposure to these images, in turn, has detrimental effects on majority group viewers' real-world perceptions of minority groups. Although there may be some inconsistencies across studies, research in this area consistently demonstrates that media consumption influences perceptions about the demographic features of society as well as attitudes and perceptions about racial/ethnic groups. Cognitive-psychological developments in cultivation theory (Shrum, 1996; Roskos-Ewoldsen et al., 2004; also see Shrum & Lee, Chapter 8, this volume) further illuminate the processes driving these effects, explicating the importance of both individual exemplars and generalized models (Mastro & Tukachinsky, in press).

Despite the insights offered by this research, many key issues remain which call for further investigation. First, due to obvious methodological and logistic constraints many cultivation studies are based on cross-sectional surveys in which both television viewing and perceptions of social groups are assessed on one occasion. The cultivation hypothesis, however, is concerned with long-term, cumulative effects of repeated media consumption. As in any area of cultivation research, longitudinal studies of race-related issues would be instrumental in: (a) establishing a stronger casual association between exposure and various relevant beliefs and (b) drawing a wider range of conclusions about a broader variety of effects. From a mental models perspective, such studies might examine the degree of flexibility of mental models and the processes by which they are updated based on mediated or direct intergroup experiences. For example, it is possible to identify points in human development in which race-related mental models begin to form and thus are, perhaps, most susceptible to media effects.

Second, although studies have demonstrated that real-life experiences moderate the effects of media exposure (e.g., Mastro et al., 2007), additional theorizing and empirical studies are necessary to more confidently establish this relationship. For instance, while perceived realism is likely to enhance the media's impact (e.g., Busselle, 2001), it is also possible that individuals who already hold negative views of minorities find stereotypical media representations to be more realistic. Future studies can and should explore the ways in which viewers' preexisting mental models guide perception, organization, and integration of media information and how these processes ultimately lead to media effects.

Finally, most media effects studies in the domain of perceptions of minority groups focus on the ways in which media contribute to Whites' perceptions of racial/ethnic minorities. Relatively little research has examined the media's impact on ethnic minorities' self-perceptions, and even less attention has been devoted to the question of ethnic minorities' perceptions of the majority group. The scarcity of research addressing the socialization of marginalized groups calls for further investigation of these questions.

## Notes

1. In four studies the authors did not explicitly indicate the exact number of characters coded in each season. In these instances, an estimate of the number of characters was made based on either (a) the total number of characters coded across all seasons reported in the study, or based on (b) the number of hours and programs coded in the study.
2. Two studies reported an overall percentage of characters across several seasons from different decades, such that it was impossible to differentiate between the contributions of different decades to the study's findings. Since these content analyses focused on a particular decade (contrary to the Lichter et al., 1987, study that was excluded from the analysis) the results of these studies were analyzed as representing the decade from which the majority of the seasons in the sample were coded. For example, Signorielli (1983) reported data based on ten fall seasons from 1969 until 1979, and three winter seasons from 1975, 1976 and 1981. Although this sample extends from 1969 to 1981, the results were treated as if they represent "the 1970s," since the vast majority of the coded characters appeared on television during this decade.

## References

* *Publications included in the content meta-analysis*

Armstrong, G., Neuendorf, K., & Brentar, J. (1992). TV entertainment, news, and racial perceptions of college students. *Journal of Communication, 42,* 153–176.

Ball-Rokeach, S. J., & DeFleur, M. L. (1976). A dependency model of mass-media effects. *Communication Research, 1,* 3–21.

Bodenhausen, G., Schwarz, N., Bless, H., & Wanke, M. (1995). Effects of atypical exemplars on racial beliefs: Enlightened racism or generalized appraisals? *Journal of Experimental Social Psychology, 31,* 48–63.

Busselle, R. W. (2001). Television exposure, perceived realism, exemplar accessibility in the social judgment process. *Media Psychology, 3,* 43–67.

Busselle, R., & Bilandzic, H. (2008). Fictionality and perceived realism in experiencing stories: A model of narrative comprehension and engagement. *Communication Theory, 18,* 255–280.

Busselle, R., & Crandall, H. (2002). Television viewing and perceptions about race differences in socioeconomic success. *Journal of Broadcasting & Electronic Media, 46*, 256–282.

Busselle, R. W., & Shrum, L. J. (2003). Media exposure and exemplar accessibility. *Media Psychology, 5*(3), 255–282.

Census Bureau (2001). Overview of race and Hispanic origin. Retrieved from: http://www.census.gov/prod/2001pubs/cenbr01-1.pdf

Census Bureau (2010). United States—Race and Hispanic origin: 1790 to 1990. Retrieved from: http://www.census.gov/population/www/documentation/twps0056/tab01.pdf

*Children Now (2000). *Fall colors, 1999–2000: Prime time diversity report.* Oakland, CA: Children Now.

*Children Now (2001). *Fall colors, 2000–2001: Prime time diversity report.* Oakland, CA: Children Now.

*Children Now (2002). *Fall colors, 2001–2002: Prime time diversity report.* Oakland, CA: Children Now.

*Children Now (2004). *Fall colors, 2003–2004*: Prime time diversity report. Oakland, CA: Children Now.

Chiricos, T., Padgett, K., & Gertz, M. (2000). Fear, TV news, and the reality of crime. *Criminology, 38*, 755–85.

Dixon, T. L. (2008a). Crime news and racialized beliefs: Understanding the relationship between local news viewing and perceptions of African Americans and crime. *Journal of Communication, 58*, 106–125.

Dixon, T.L. (2008b). Network news and racial beliefs: Exploring the connection between national television news exposure and stereotypical perceptions of African Americans. *Journal of Communication, 58*, 321–337.

Dixon, T. L., & Linz, D. (2000a). Overrepresentation and underrepresentation of African Americans and Latinos as lawbreakers on television news. *Journal of Communication, 50*(2), 131–154.

Dixon, T. & Linz, D. (2000b). Race and the misrepresentation of victimization on local television news. *Communication Research, 27*(5), 547-573.

Dong, Q., & Murrillo, A. (2007). The impact of television viewing on young adults' stereotypes towards Hispanic Americans. *Human Communication, 10*, 33–44.

Entman, R. (1990). Modern racism and the images of Blacks in local television news. Critical *Studies in Mass Communication, 7*(4), 332–345.

Entman, R. (1992) Blacks in the news: Television, modern racism, and cultural change. *Journalism Quarterly, 69*, 341–361.

Entman, R. M., & Rojecki, A. (2001). *The Black image in the White mind: Media and race in America.* Chicago, IL: University of Chicago Press.

Eschholz, S., Chiricos, T., & Gertz, M. (2003). Television and fear of crime: Program types, audience traits and the mediating effect of perceived neighborhood racial composition. *Social Problems, 50*, 395–415.

Fujioka, Y. (1999). Television portrayals and African-American stereotypes: Examination of television effects when direct contact is lacking. *Journalism & Mass Communication Quarterly, 76*, 52–75.

Gallagher, C. A. (2003). Miscounting race: Exploring Whites' misperceptions of racial group size. *Sociological Perspectives, 46,* 81–96.

Gerbner, G. (1969). Toward "cultural indicators": The analysis of mass mediated public message systems. *Communication Review, 17*(2), 137–148.

*Gerbner, G. (1993). Women and minorities on television: A study in casting and fate. Report to the Screen Actors Guild and the American Federation of Radio and Television Artists.

Gerbner, G., Gross, L., Morgan, M., & Signorielli, N. (1980). The "mainstreaming" of America: Violence profile no. 11. *Journal of Communication, 30*, 10–29.

Gerbner, G., Gross, L., Morgan, M., Signorielli, N., & Shanahan, J. (2002). Growing up with television: Cultivation processes. In J. Bryant & D. Zillmann (Eds.), *Media effects: Advances in theory and research* (2nd ed., pp. 43–68). Mahwah, NJ: Erlbaum.

*Gerbner, G., & Signorielli, N. (1979). *Women and Minorities in Television Drama, 1969–1978.* Annenberg School of Communications, University of Pennsylvania.

Gilliam, F., Nicholas, D., Valentino, A., & Beckmann, M. N. (2002). Where you live and what you watch: The impact of racial proximity and local television news on attitudes about race and crime. *Political Research Quarterly, 55,* 755–80.

*Glascock, J. (2001). Gender roles on primetime network television: Demographics and behaviors. *Journal of Broadcasting & Electronic Media, 45,* 656–669.

*Glascock, J. (2003). Gender, race, and aggression in newer TV networks prime time programming. *Communication Quarterly, 51,* 90–100.

*Glascock, J. (2008). Direct and indirect aggression on primetime network television. *Journal of Broadcasting & Electronic Media, 52*(2), 268–281.

*Greenberg, B. S., & Collette, L. (1997). The changing faces on TV: A demographic analysis of network television's new seasons, 1966–1992. *Journal of Broadcasting & Electronic Media, 41*(1), 1–13.

*Greenberg, B. S. Simmons, K., Hogan, L., & Atkin, C. (1980). Three seasons of television characters: A demographic analysis. *Journal of Broadcasting, 24,* 49–60.

Gunter, B. (1987). *Television and the fear of crime.* London: John Libbey and Co.

*Harwood, J., & Anderson, K. (2002). The presence and portrayal of social groups on primetime television. *Communication Reports, 15,* 81–98.

Hawkins, R. P., & Pingree, S. (1981). Uniform content and habitual viewing: Unnecessary assumptions in social reality effects. *Human Communication Research, 7,* 291–301.

Heider, D. (2000). *White news: Why local news programs don't cover people of color.* Mahwah, NJ: Erlbaum.

Hetsroni, A. (2007) Three decades of sexual content on prime-time network programming: a longitudinal meta-analytic review. *Journal of Communication, 57,* 318–348.

*Hunt, D. (2003). *Prime time in black and white: Not much is new for 2002.* Bunche Research Report, 1(1). Los Angeles: CAAS Publications.

Jeffres, L. W., Atkin, D. J., & Neuendorf, K. A. (2001). Expanding the range of dependent measures in mainstreaming and cultivation analysis. *Communication Research Reports, 18*(4), 408–417.

Lee, M., Bichard, S., Irey, M., Walt, H., & Carlson, A. (2009). Television viewing and ethnic stereotypes: Do college students form stereotypical perceptions of ethnic groups as a result of heavy television consumption? *Howard Journal of Communications, 20*(1), 95–110.

Lichter, S. R., Lichter, L., Rothman, S., & Amundson, D. (1987, July/August). Primetime prejudice: TV's images of Blacks and Hispanics. *Public Opinion*, 13–16.

*Mastro, D., & Behm-Morawitz, E. (2005). Latino representation on primetime television: A content analysis. *Journalism & Mass Communication Quarterly, 82*, 110–130.

*Mastro, D., & Greenberg, B.S. (2000). The portrayal of racial minorities on prime time television. *Journal of Broadcasting & Electronic Media, 44,* 690–703.

Mastro, D., Behm-Morawitz, E., & Ortiz, M. (2007). The cultivation of social perceptions of Latinos: A mental models approach. *Media Psychology, 9,* 1–19.

Mastro, D., Tamborini, R., & Hullett, C. (2005). Linking media to prototype activation and subsequent celebrity attraction: An application of self-categorization theory. *Communication Research, 32,* 323–348.

Mastro, D., & Tukachinsky, R. (in press). Exemplar versus prototype-based processing of media content and the influence on racial/ethnic evaluations. *Journal of Communication.*

Matei, S., Ball-Rokeach, S. J., & Qiu, J. L. (2001). Fear and misperception of Los Angeles urban space: A spatial-statistical study of communication-shaped mental maps. *Communication Research, 28*, 429–463.

Morgan, M., & Shanahan, J. (2010). The state of cultivation. *Journal of Broadcasting & Electronic Media, 54*(2), 337–355.

Morgan, M., Shanahan, J., & Signorielli, N. (2009). Growing up with television: Cultivation processes. In J. Bryant & M. B. Oliver (Eds.), *Media effects: Advances in theory and research.* (3rd ed., pp. 34–49). New York, NY: Routledge.

Northcott, H., Seggar, J., & Hinton, J. (1975). Trends in TV portrayals of Blacks and women. *Journalism Quarterly, 52*(4), 741–744.

*O'Kelly, C., & Bloomquist, L. (1976). Women and Blacks on TV. *Journal of Communication, 26*(4), 179–184.

Oliver, M. B., & Armstrong, G. B. (1998). The color of crime: Perceptions of Caucasians' and African Americans' involvement in crime. In M. Fishman & G. Cavender (Eds.), *Entertaining crime: Television reality programs* (pp. 19–35). New York: Aldine de Gruyter.

Potter, W. J. (1986). Perceived reality and the cultivation hypothesis. *Journal of Broadcasting & Electronic Media, 30*(2), 159–174.

Potter, W. J. (1991a). Examining cultivation from a psychological perspective. *Communication Research, 18*, 77–102.

Potter, W. J. (1991b). The relationship between first- and second- order measures of cultivation. *Human Communication Research, 18*, 92–113.

Power, J., Murphy, S., & Coover, G. (1996). Priming prejudice: How stereotypes and counter-stereotypes influence attribution of responsibility and credibility among ingroups and outgroups. *Human Communication Research, 23*, 36–58.

Romer, D., Jaimeson, K., & de Coteau, N. (1998). The treatment of persons of color in local television: Ethnic blame discourse or realistic group conflict? *Communication Research, 25*(3), 286–305.

Roskos-Ewoldsen, B., Davies, J., & Roskos-Ewoldsen, D. R. (2004). Implications of the mental models approach for cultivation theory. *Communications, 29*, 345–363.

Roskos-Ewoldsen, B., Roskos-Ewoldsen, D. R., Yang, M., & Lee, M. (2007). Comprehension of the media. In D. R. Roskos-Ewoldsen & J. Monahan (Eds.), *Communication and social cognition: Theories and methods* (pp. 319–348). Mahwah, NJ: Erlbaum.

*Seggar, J. F. (1977). Television's portrayal of minorities and women 1971–1975. *Journal of Broadcasting, 21*, 201–214.

*Seggar, J. F., Hafen, J. K., & Hannonen-Gladden, H. (1981). Television's portrayals of minorities and women in drama and comedy drama, 1971–80. *Journal of Broadcasting & Electronic Media, 25*(3), 277–288.

Shanahan, J., & Morgan, M. (1999). *Television and its viewers: Cultivation theory and research.* Cambridge: Cambridge University Press.

Shrum, L. J. (1996). Psychological processes underlying cultivation effects: Further tests of construct accessibility. *Human Communication Research, 22*(4), 482–509.

Shrum, L. J. (2004). The cognitive processes underlying cultivation effects are a function of whether the judgments are on-line or memory-based. *Communications, 29*, 327–344.

Shrum, L. J., & O'Guinn, T. C. (1993). Processes and effects in the construction of social reality: Construct accessibility as an explanatory variable. *Communication Research, 20*, 436–471.

*Signorielli, N. (1983). *The demography of the television world.* In O. H. Gandy, P. Espinosa, & J. A. Ordover (Eds.), *Proceedings from the Tenth Annual Telecommunications Policy Research Conference* (pp. 53–74). Norwood, NJ: Ablex.

Signorielli, N. (2009a). Minority representation in prime time: 2000 to 2008. *Communication Research Reports, 26*(4), 323–336.

*Signorielli, N. (2009b). Race and sex in prime time: A look at occupations and occupational prestige. *Mass Communication & Society, 12*(3), 335–352.

Sigelman, L., & Niemi, R. (2001). Innumeracy about minority populations: African Americans and Whites compared. *Public Opinion Quarterly, 65*, 86–94.

Stroman, C. Merritt, B., & Matabane, P. (1989). Twenty years after Kerner: The portrayal of African Americans on prime time television. *Howard Journal of Communication, 2*(1), 44–57.

Tan, A., Fujioka, Y., & Lucht, N. (1997). Native American stereotypes, TV portrayals, and personal contact. *Journalism & Mass Communication Quarterly, 74*, 265–284.

Tan, A., Zhang, Y., Zhang, L., & Dalisay, F. (2009). Stereotypes of African-Americans in China and media use. *Howard Journal of Communications, 20*, 260–275.

Tversky, A., & Kahneman, D. (1980). Rational choice and the framing of decisions. In K. Cook & M. Levi (Eds.), *The limits of rationality* (pp. 60–89). Chicago: University of Chicago Press.

*U.S. Commission on Civil Rights (1977). *Window Dressing on the Set: Women and minorities in television*. Washington, DC.

Weigel, R. H., Kim, E. L., & Frost, J. L. (1995). Race relations on prime time television reconsidered: Patterns of continuity and change. *Journal of Applied Social Psychology, 25*, 223–236.

Williams, M. E., & Condry, J. C. (1989, April). *Living color: Minority portrayals and cross-racial interactions on television.* Paper presented at the biennial meeting of the Society for Research in Child Development, Kansas City, MO.

Wong, C. J. (2007). Little and big pictures in our heads: Race, local context, and innumeracy about racial groups in the United States. *Public Opinion Quarterly, 71,* 391–412.

Wu, H. D. (1996). An enduring schema: The image of the Chinese in American prime time television dramas. *Gazette, 58,* 69–86.

Zwaan, R. A., & Radvansky, G. A. (1998). Situation models in language comprehension and memory. *Psychological Bulletin, 123,* 162–185.

Zwaan, R. A., Langston, M. C., & Graesser, A. C. (1995). The construction of situation models in narrative comprehension: An event-indexing model. *Psychological Science, 6*(5), 292–297.

# 4. Cultivating Tolerance of Homosexuals

*Erik C. Nisbet & Teresa A. Myers*

The original cultivation hypothesis developed by George Gerbner and his colleagues in the 1970s posited that, compared to lighter viewers, those who watch more television would be more likely to express a worldview that mirrors the dominant values, lessons, and messages found in entertainment television (Gerbner, 1970, 1973; Gerbner, Gross, Morgan, & Signorielli, 1980; Morgan & Shanahan, 2010; Shanahan & Morgan, 1999). Since that time, research examining and testing the cultivation hypothesis has become one of the dominant areas of research within the field of mass communication (Bryant & Miron, 2004; Morgan & Shanahan, 2010). However, though the original cultivation hypothesis has evolved conceptually and has been empirically tested across a range of contexts, as Morgan and Shanahan (2010) note, cultivation has not been without its critics (see Shanahan & Morgan, 1999, and Rossman & Brosius, 2004, for reviews). One reason many criticisms have endured is the reliance of most cultivation research on cross-sectional survey data collected at a singular time and place to examine the relationship between television exposure and individual beliefs and/or attitudes (Rossman & Brosius, 2004). Similarly, several scholars have argued that the cultivation hypothesis is one of the theoretical areas of mass communication research that would most benefit from a multilevel, dynamic approach (Lang & Ewoldsen, 2010; McLeod, Kosicki, & McLeod, 2009; Pan & McLeod, 1991).

Taking advantage of advances in methodology and data availability, this chapter expands the conceptual and methodological approaches to evaluating the original cultivation hypothesis as proposed by Gerbner. We move away from reliance on one-shot, cross-sectional survey data and instead attempt to model the *multilevel, dynamic relationships* among media content, individual television exposure, and worldviews of audiences that evolve *across time* by pairing multiple cross-sectional general population surveys conducted over a forty-year period with annual quantitative indicators of television content collected over the same time span. We focus on an important dimension of the cultural life-world: "tolerance" of homosexuality. The issue of homosexuality is apt for this exploration, as it has undergone extensive cultural, social, economic, and political evolution since the early 1970s (see for example Gross, 2001; Tropiano, 2002; Walters, 2001; Yang, 1997) and allows us to examine the *dynamic* relationship between cultural and social change over time, which is at the heart of Gerbner's original cultivation perspective.

## Revisiting the Cultivation Hypothesis

The original cultivation hypothesis, that heavy exposure to entertainment television content is related to audience attitudes and perceptions reflecting the dominant message system found in television content, has been well documented and explored across a variety of contexts. However, the hypothesis evolved out of a larger set of interrelated questions posited by Gerbner about (a) how we can quantitatively evaluate and track cultural shifts and continuities over time and (b) the institutional role of television within modern society (Gerbner, 1973; Shanahan, 2004; Morgan & Shanahan, 2010).

To answer the former question, Gerbner proposed a project to develop indicators for measuring culturally important trends in society that could complement established social and economic indicators. Gerbner (1973) believed that the traditional way of "taking stock" of society using only economic and social indicators could be improved with the addition of cultural indicators, resulting in more informed policy decisions. According to Gerbner (1973), "the social and cultural transformations of our society have made economic and labor statistics and census information less than adequate to meeting our national needs with knowledge and reason" (p. 177). Gerbner believed that a cultural product such as television presented a repository of images, narratives, conceptions, and presentations that could be used as a cultural indicator. Cultural Indicators research was thus meant to broadly monitor TV's message system and to track the broader production of culture over time.

However, in Gerbner's view, and to address the latter question posed above, television was more than simply a repository of culture; it was also an important producer and disseminator of culture within society. Gerbner and his colleagues argued that television had become the dominant "storyteller" in modern society, displacing the power of other social institutions like the family or religion to communicate lessons and values about everyday life that shape audiences' worldviews and perceptions (Gerbner, 1999; Gerbner, Gross, Morgan, & Signorielli, 1982; Shanahan & Morgan, 1999). Gerbner argued that television's "centralized system of storytelling" through "drama, commercials, news, and other programs [brings] a relatively coherent world of common images and messages into every viewing home"(Gerbner et al., 1982, p. 102). Of critical concern to Gerbner were the institutional arrangements that generated television's coherent message system and what interests, values, ideologies, and so on, were being reflected and privileged in television content (Shanahan & Morgan, 1999; Morgan & Shanahan, 2010). Gerbner believed the power structures and decision-making processes inherent in television as an institution resulted in a narrow range of homogeneous cultural values and symbols being diffused—cultural values that reflected the economic, social, and political interests of a small number of cultural producers (Gerbner, 1973, 1999; Shanahan & Morgan, 1999). Daily, cumulative immersion in this coherent, homogeneous message system, through which television was the primary conduit, Gerbner and his colleagues argued, would cultivate perceptions of reality in line with the dominant and prevalent messages within television's cultural "repository"—this is the basis for the cultivation hypothesis regarding the consequences of heavy TV exposure (Gerbner, 1973; Shanahan & Morgan, 1999). In this sense, ***television exposure is a communication process that links two levels of society:*** the individual at the micro-level and the cultural environment (represented by television content) at the macro-level.

However, as Morgan and Shanahan (2010) note, Gerbner's concept of cultivation analysis was much broader than simply understanding the immediate "effect" of media content on individual attitudes and behaviors. Cultivation analysis rejects the "simple, linear 'stimulus-response' model of the relationships between media content and audiences" (Morgan & Signorelli, 1990, p. 18). From a cultivation perspective, television is an institution that encourages social continuity, integrity, and cohesion through socialization into society's dominant norms, values, and identities (Nisbet, 2008; Nisbet & Myers, 2010; Shanahan & Jones, 1999; Shanahan & Morgan, 1999; Viswanath & Demers, 1999). However, being an agent of social *control* does not preclude television from also promoting social *change*, though in a limited capacity (Viswanath & Demers, 1999). As television's content reflects the dominant power relations and norms of society, television is limited in its ability to independently enact social change outside of changes already taking place within society. In other words, television *reinforces social change* already taking place within the social system in its capacity as an agent of social control; as the dominant cultural norms and relations within the social system, and consequently media messages, evolve, so does the nature of the relationship between heavy TV viewing and audience perceptions.

## Cultivation: A Multilevel, Dynamic Theory

Integrating the twin goals of developing indicators of cultural trends over time and understanding the role and power of television in society resulted in the Cultural Indicators project (Gerbner, 1969, 1973; Shanahan, 2004). At the macro-level of analysis, the project endeavored to understand the institutional arrangements and power structure of cultural institutions like television (*institutional process analysis*) and to quantitatively evaluate the dominant cultural symbols, meanings, and values found within media messages in the aggregate (*message system analysis*). At the micro-level of analysis the goal was to understand the influence of these dominant cultural meanings and symbols on individual perceptions and attitudes, which in turn have implications for society as a whole (*cultivation analysis;* Shanahan & Morgan, 1999; Morgan & Shanahan, 2010).

However, even with the formation and undisputed notoriety of the research program that came to be known as "Cultural Indicators," other research questions that were raised by Gerbner, his colleagues, critics, and imitators eventually received much greater attention in the communication research sphere. Gerbner's own research efforts on cultural indicators and focus on the social problem of violence led to a misperception among some scholars that cultivation was about violence indicators specifically rather than a broader, more inclusive program of cultural indicators research (e.g., on family, gender, labor, poverty, etc.).[1] Furthermore, the individualistic and effects-centered biases within the dominant paradigm of mass communication research over the last forty years (see Gitlin, 1978; Lang & Ewoldsen, 2010; McLeod et al., 2009, for discussions) led to a greater focus on explicating the individual cognitive processes underlying the proposed "cultivation effect" of television (e.g., Bradley, 2007; Shrum, 1995, 1996) and less attention to explicating either macro- or multi-level communication processes within Gerbner's original cultural indicators framework.

Some years ago, Pan and McLeod (1991) noted the failure of mass communication research to both theoretically and methodologically integrate communication theories and processes across levels of analysis, specifically citing cultivation as an example. Proposing a "meta-theoretical" framework of macro- and micro- levels of analysis and cross-level relationships connected through social interactions and organizational processes, Pan and McLeod argued that communication theories such as cultivation need to be investigated with more of a society-centered focus, accounting for dynamic relationships and changes over time. Sadly, their call for such research largely has gone unheeded, partly due to the methodological and ontological challenges of linking macro- and micro-levels of analysis combined with the aforementioned micro-focus of the dominant paradigm within mass communication research (McLeod et al., 2009).

As a consequence, many of the empirical cultivation studies that have attempted to explicitly link macro- and micro-levels of analyses have been limited in their conceptualization and methodological approach. As Rossman and Brosius (2004) describe, cultivation researchers typically employ a somewhat disjointed two-stage methodological approach by pairing a quantitative content analysis of TV's message system with a cross-sectional, representative population survey to explicate how closely heavy TV viewers' perceptions match the messages found in television content at a discrete point in time and space (for examples, see Gerbner & Gross, 1976 or Gerbner et al., 1980).

As several scholars explicitly point out (Lang & Ewoldsen, 2010; Pan & McLeod, 1991; Rossman & Brosius, 2004), this approach poorly models the temporal, dynamic, and multilevel properties of Gerbner's original cultivation perspective. The cross-sectional nature of the design also provides fodder for critics questioning the validity of the cultivation hypothesis (Rossman & Brosius, 2004). In addition, by conducting a patchwork of individual cultivation studies at discrete points of time, or by pooling large multi-year survey datasets such the General Social Survey to examine the relationship between TV exposure and audience perceptions (for example, see Shanahan & Morgan, 1999), cultivation researchers may inadvertently overemphasize the social control (static) aspect of Gerbner's cultivation argument and not adequately identify incremental changes in the cultural environment and audience perceptions that are reflective of how television may institutionally reinforce social change.

More recently, several scholars (McLeod et al., 2009; Slater, Snyder, & Hayes, 2006) have reiterated Pan and McLeod's argument for more multilevel research and note that new methodological techniques such as multilevel modeling (sometimes called "hierarchal linear modeling," see also Raudenbush & Bryk, 2002; Snijders & Bosker, 1999) now allow for quantitative empirical research that more closely integrates macro- and micro-levels of analyses. Multilevel modeling does not constrain researchers to a single level of analysis and permits the exploration of cross-level relationships and communication processes over time (Slater et al., 2006). However, to the best of our knowledge, to date no studies have yet employed multilevel modeling to examine cultivation processes across levels of analysis and to link cultural indicators, television exposure, and audience perceptions in an integrated model.

Employing Pan and McLeod's (1991) multilevel framework to cultivation theory, in this chapter we conceptualize the cultural environment, represented by the dominant system of meanings and symbols embedded in television programming, at a macro-level of analysis. In turn, we conceptualize individual cultural systems of meaning and symbols (i.e., attitudes, perceptions, beliefs) at the micro-level of analysis. Television use is a mass communication process that links the cultural environment with the individual (i.e., the macro to the micro). The stronger the link between the two levels, the more likely individuals will employ symbols and meanings in their everyday lives that are representative of dominant cultural environment (i.e., the cultivation hypothesis). Moreover, the macro-level cultural environment and its system of meaning *are not necessarily static* but may evolve over time in response to social, economic, or political change. As a consequence, across time, individuals with the strongest connection (i.e., heavy TV exposure) to this macro-level cultural repository (i.e., TV content) should be more likely to reflect changes in the macro-level cultural environment in their own personal systems of meaning than individuals with weaker macro-micro links (i.e., light TV exposure).

Thus, employing multilevel modeling as both our theoretical and methodological approach, we explicate a multilevel model of cultivation analysis that (a) empirically tests our multilevel conceptualization of the cultivation hypothesis described above, (b) bridges the macro and micro levels of analysis in a more sophisticated manner than previous cultivation research, (c) takes into account the temporal (and dynamic) nature of cultural indicators, and (d) broadens the focus of inquiry beyond the typical focus on TV violence to a socio-cultural issue that has undergone a great deal of cultural evolution over the last forty years: tolerance of homosexuality.

### *The Case of Homosexuality*

Employing homosexuality as the substantive context in which to examine our theoretical and methodological approach affirms Gerbner's original vision of cultural indicators spanning a range of social and cultural issues beyond violence. The issue of homosexuality within the United States has gone through a transformation over the last forty years, especially in terms of public visibility (Gross, 2001; Walters, 2001), and thus it provides a useful case study for examining the multilevel relationship among the cultural environment, television viewing, and audience perceptions over time. Social attitudes have evolved, with the number of Americans who believe gay and lesbian relations are morally acceptable rising from 34% in 1982 to 52% in 2010 (Gallup, 2010a). Likewise, the percentage of Americans who believe same-sex marriage should be legalized increased from 27% in 1996 to 44% in 2010 (Gallup, 2010b). As of 2010, a majority of the American public (67%) had come to support allowing gays and lesbians to openly serve in the U.S. military (Gallup, 2010c).

Correspondingly, gays and lesbians have increasingly gained political equality over time, moving from a "hidden" vote to a voting segment that political candidates actively pursue (Walters, 2001). This increased political tolerance combined with political empowerment has resulted in substantial gains in civil liberties for homosexuals since 2000, with inclusion in federal hate crime legislation, legal protections against discrimination based on sexual orientation in twenty states, the repeal of the military's "Don't Ask, Don't Tell" policy, the striking of sodomy laws from the books, and legalized gay marriage in a growing number of states (and the District of Columbia). As the cultural representations of sexual minorities in media often "reflect the biases and interests of those elites who define the public agenda" (Gross, 1991, p. 190), these evolving social and political trends raise the question of how television has portrayed homosexuals/homosexuality over time and the corresponding effects of television exposure on attitudes and opinions about homosexuality.

Historically, there is an inverse relationship between media visibility and tolerance toward minorities in American society, with many minority groups "symbolically annihilated" from media content until social and cultural changes lead to gradual visibility (Gross, 1984, 1991, 2001). For example, analysis by Gross (1984) of the 1977 and 1980 General Social Surveys, at a time when homosexuality was all but invisible on America's TV airwaves, found that heavy television exposure was associated with greater intolerance of homosexuality. Twenty-five years later, after the visibility of homosexuality in television content has substantially increased (Calzo & Ward, 2009; Fisher, Hill, Grube, & Gruber, 2007; Hetsroni, 2007), recent research has shown that television exposure is associated with more tolerant attitudes toward homosexuality, though the relationship varies considerably across TV genres and demographic groups (Calzo & Ward, 2009).

We assert that the increased *visibility of homosexuality* in television content is both an indicator of, and contributor to, the increased *tolerance of homosexuality* in American society. Furthermore, we conceptually differentiate individuals' *tolerance of homosexuals* from their attitudes toward homosexuality such as liking, agreement, favorability, or moral acceptance of homosexual sexual practices. Tolerance is about acknowledging and accepting gay men and women as members of mainstream society, even if one disapproves of homosexual relations or has unfavorable opinions or perceptions of gays and lesbians. Thus, although negative depictions and stereotypes of homosexuals are still quite prevalent in television content (e.g., Fisher et al., 2007; Fouts & Inch, 2005;Gross, 2001; Herman, 2005), the increased visibility of homosexuality in TV content should be associated with increased (political) tolerance of, if not necessarily favorability towards, gays and lesbians.

Based on this theoretical framework, we explore two ideas. First, we examine whether the meanings and symbols of the macro cultural environment (i.e., television content) will be generally reflected in individual systems of meaning (i.e., attitudes) over time, specifically. That is, we determine whether increased visibility of homosexuality in prime-time television content over time is associated with greater individual tolerance toward homosexuality.

In addition, we argue that the stronger connection (i.e., television exposure) an individual has to the macro-cultural environment the more likely he or she is to possess personal systems of meaning that reflect that cultural environment. Furthermore, these macro-micro systems of meaning are *dynamic* and co-evolve: As dominant meanings of the cultural environment change, these changes will be most reflected in individual systems of meaning for those who have the strongest connection to the cultural environment. Thus, we propose a "cross-level interaction" between our (a) cultural indicators of homosexuality (i.e., the macro cultural environment) and (b) strength of connection to that environment (i.e., individual television exposure) that (c) influences the individual-level meanings and symbols associated with homosexuality (i.e., attitudes about tolerance) over time. In this sense, we argue that *television institutionally reinforces dynamic processes of social change among heavy TV users.* Summarized briefly, as the visibility of homosexuality on television increases over time, heavy TV users will express greater tolerance of gay men and women than light or moderate TV users.

### *Visibility of Homosexuality and Attitudes across Time*

In order to assess our hypotheses about how the cultural visibility of homosexuality has evolved over time and its relationship with public opinion, we developed a set of quantitative cultural indicators based on television content. Our key indicator was the number of male and female homosexual characters that had leading, supporting, or recurring roles (appearing in a minimum of three episodes) within American prime-time television series on major broadcast networks (ABC, CBS, NBC, FOX, UPN, WB, CW) between 1972 and 2008. We selected 1972 as the starting point for our examination based on the availability of indicator data, the fact that homosexuality first appeared on television around that time (the first regular homosexual TV character was in 1972), and the fact that gay men and women first began to emerge as a socially visible minority in American society in the wake of the 1969 Stonewall Riots (Gross 1984, 2001; Walters, 2001). We limited our scope to broadcast networks and excluded basic or subscriber cable channels, as well as rebroadcast network shows in syndication in order (1) to have a comparable set of channels that represent the widest mainstream viewership for comparisons over time and (2) to avoid over-representing the visibility of homosexual characterizations, as many basic and pay cable channels have very small, niche audiences.The list of homosexual characters was developed using a variety of online and print resources (Capsuto, 2000; GLAAD, 2003–2009; Tropiano, 2002; Wyatt, 2001). Furthermore, the collected data were checked and cross-referenced with television series credits found in the Internet Movie Database at www.imdb.com. The results indicate that a total of 557 different homosexual characters appeared on prime-time broadcast television between the years of 1972 and 2008, with an average of 15.1 characters appearing each year, though the number of characters appearing each year during the selected time span varies greatly (from 1 to 43).

Figure 1 charts the visibility of homosexuality on American prime-time broadcast TV from 1972 to 2008. In addition, the aggregated mean tolerance of homosexuals from available years of the General Social Surveys[2] is also plotted for same time period. Both indices are standardized and *z*-scored in order to compare the relationship between the two sets of cultural (number of TV characters) and social (aggregated mean tolerance) indicators over time. As Figure 1 illustrates, the two sets of indicators are highly correlated ($r$ =.88), with both the visibility and the tolerance of homosexuality relatively low in the 1970s and 1980s, then rising substantially in the early 1990s, and beginning to plateau in the late 2000s. Though this macro to macro relationship is suggestive of highly correlated cultural and social change over time, any conclusion we may draw about a direct relationship between TV's message system at the macro-level and individual tolerance of homosexuality at the micro-level is limited, as doing so would be committing an ecological fallacy (Robinson, 1950).

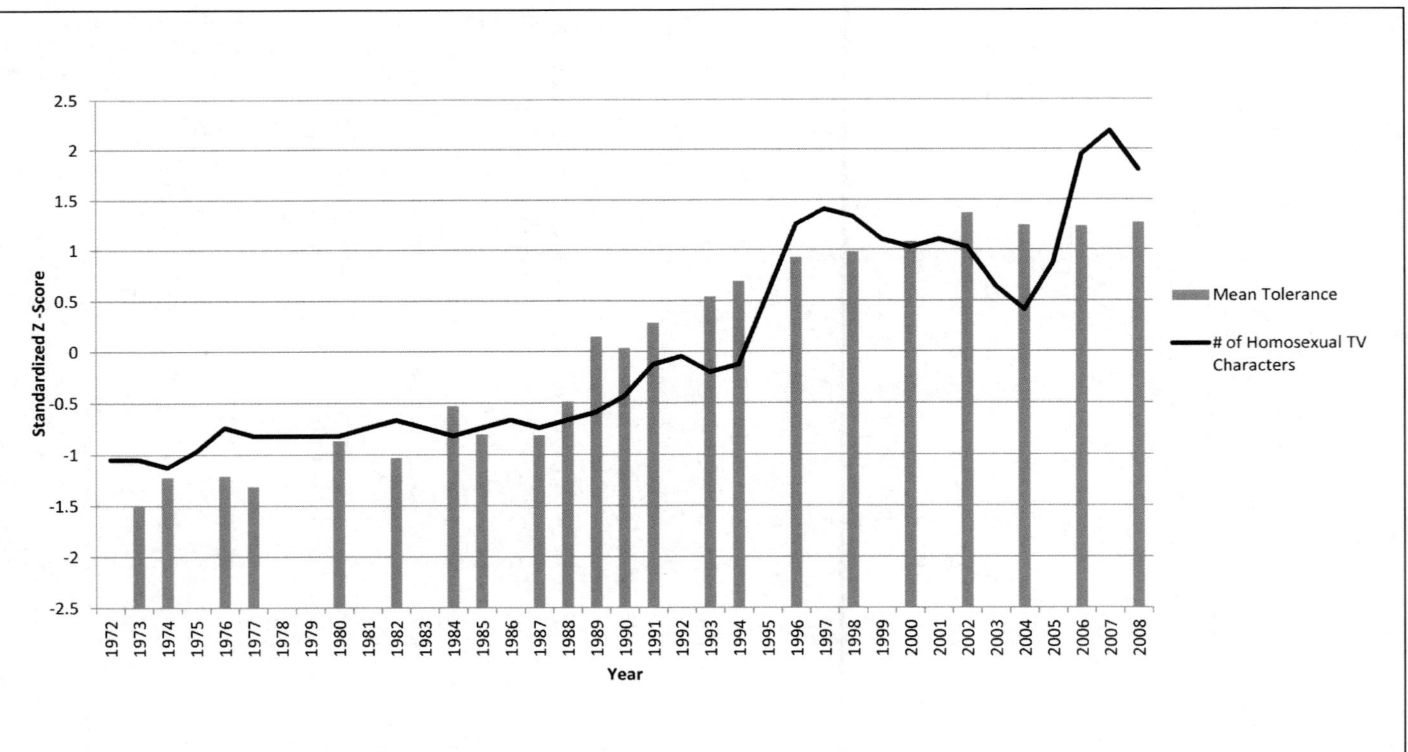


Figure 1. Visibility of homosexuality on prime-time broadcast TV and mean tolerance of homosexuals 1972–2008

## Developing a Multilevel Cultivation Model of Tolerance for Homosexuals

To properly assess our multi-level hypotheses, we employed multi-level modeling, sometimes called hierarchical linear modeling, to examine the relationships between our macro- and micro-level indicators (for a discussion of HLM in the field of communication, see Slater, Snyder, & Hayes, 2006). At the micro-level of analysis we employed 16 different cross-sectional GSS surveys conducted between 1972 and 2008 that included measures of attitudes about homosexuality and television exposure, as well as other important controls.

At the individual-level of analysis, four sets of variables were included: (a) socio-demographic controls, (b) ideological and religious orientations, (c) media exposure, and (d) tolerance of homosexuals. Socio-demographic controls included measures of *educational attainment* ($M = 13$, $SD = 3.1$) measured in years of formal schooling, *race* with being White coded into a dichotomous variable (80%), *gender* with male coded high (54%), and *age* measured as a continuous variable ($M = 45.9$, $SD = 17.3$).

*Political ideology* was measured on a seven-point scale ranging from very liberal to very conservative (M=4.1, $SD$=1.38). *Religious orientations* were assessed by coding whether the respondent was a self-identified Christian evangelical (30.4%) or not and how often respondents *attended church* services on a nine-point scale ranging from "never" to "more than once a week" ($M = 3.8$, $SD = 2.7$).

Two measures of media use were included in the analysis, one that assessed the amount of daily *television exposure* by asking respondents how many hours of television they watch each day ($M = 2.9$, $SD = 2.0$). The other assessed how often the respondent *reads the daily newspaper* on a five-point scale ranging from "never" to "every day" ($M = 3.9$, $SD = 1.3$). The dependent variable in our model, *tolerance toward homosexuals*, was constructed from three items, with higher scores indicating more willingness to allow homosexual individuals to participate in various community endeavors (see Endnote 2 for more details).

At the macro-level of analysis, we included the measure of *homosexual visibility on prime-time broadcast television* also described above. This annual index of homosexual TV characters was paired with the corresponding annual GSS survey data, with each year of available survey data in the GSS matched with a two-year moving average of homosexual characters on TV that included the mean number of characters that appeared during both the corresponding and preceding year to the GSS.[3]

Table 1. Hierarchical linear model predicting tolerance of homosexuality.

| | Model 1 | Model 2[a] | Model 3[b] | Model 4[b] |
|---|---|---|---|---|
| Intercept | 7.305*** | 7.362*** | 7.354*** | 7.354*** |
| *# of TV Characters*[c] | | | .186*** | .193*** |
| Age | | -.020*** | -.019*** | -.020*** |
| Education | | .188*** | .188*** | .188*** |
| Sex | | .242*** | .241*** | .244*** |
| Ideology | | -.144*** | -.144*** | -.144*** |
| White | | .011 | .023 | .029 |
| Church Attendance | | -.120*** | -.119*** | -.119*** |
| Evangelical | | -.673*** | -.668*** | -.668*** |
| Newspaper Exposure | | .075*** | .079*** | .080*** |
| TV Exposure | | -.014 | -.013 | -.012 |
| Interaction: Exposure X *# of TV Characters*[c] | | | | .014* |
| $\tau_{00}$ | .200*** | .112*** | .073*** | .071*** |
| $\sigma^2$ | 4.806 | 3.935 | 3.936 | 3.935 |

* $p < .05$, **$p < .01$, ***$p < .001$

Note: Italicized coefficients are level-2 predictors

[a] Individual-level predictors are grand-mean centered

[b] Individual-level predictors are centered within context

[c] In units of ten characters

## *Results*

A hierarchical linear model (Raudenbush & Bryk, 2002; Snijders & Bosker, 1999) employing HLM 6.08 and restricted maximum likelihood was estimated to assess our hypotheses. First, as is customary in multilevel regression, an empty, intercept-only model predicting tolerance toward homosexuals was estimated, testing whether there was evidence of variation across time. Results are shown in Table 1, Model 1. Evidence of variation in tolerance toward homosexuality across years existed, with approximately 4 percent of the variance in tolerance toward homosexuality attributable to year.[4]

In a second, conditional model, all individual-level predictors were added (grand-mean centered). The model tested whether there was evidence that the effect of these individual-level predictors varied according to year (testing whether the random effect should be fixed). The random effects of age, education, gender, and being an evangelical Christian on tolerance were all significant, indicating that the effect of these predictors differed by year. Thus, in subsequent analyses, the effect for these four individual level predictors was allowed to vary across years; the random component for all other individual-level predictors was fixed at zero. Results indicated that individuals who were younger, more educated, male, less politically conservative, read the newspaper more frequently, attended church relatively less often, and not evangelical Christians, were relatively more tolerant toward homosexuals (see Table 1, Model 2). Next, the number of homosexual television characters in a given year was included as a contextual-level variable, grand-mean centered (reported in units of ten characters for ease of interpretation; Table 1, Model 3). Results showed that the number of homosexual television characters was positively related to an individual's tolerance of homosexuality, $\gamma = .186, p < .001$ (tolerance increased by .186 for an increase of every ten homosexual TV characters). Including the number of homosexual television characters as a predictor explained 34 percent of the *between-year variance* in tolerance toward homosexuality (in other words, the number of homosexual television characters explained 34% of the level-two variance—the variance in tolerance toward homosexuals that remained between years after including level-one predictors).

A final model interacted the number of homosexual television characters with an individual's average daily television exposure, showing that as an individual's television exposure increased, the *effect* of the number of television characters on tolerance toward homosexuality increased, $\gamma$interaction = .014, $p < .01$. At all levels of television exposure, an increase in the number of homosexual television characters depicted was associated with an increase in tolerance toward homosexuality; but as illustrated in Figure 2, this effect was amplified among those who were exposed to more television. Therefore, among those individuals who watched less than the average amount of television (one standard deviation below the mean), every increase of ten additional homosexual television characters was associated with an increase of .16 units in tolerance toward homosexuality (on a nine-point scale). Among those who watched relatively more television (one standard deviation above the mean), this effect was amplified, so that an increase of ten homosexual television characters was associated with an increase of .22 units in tolerance toward homosexuality.

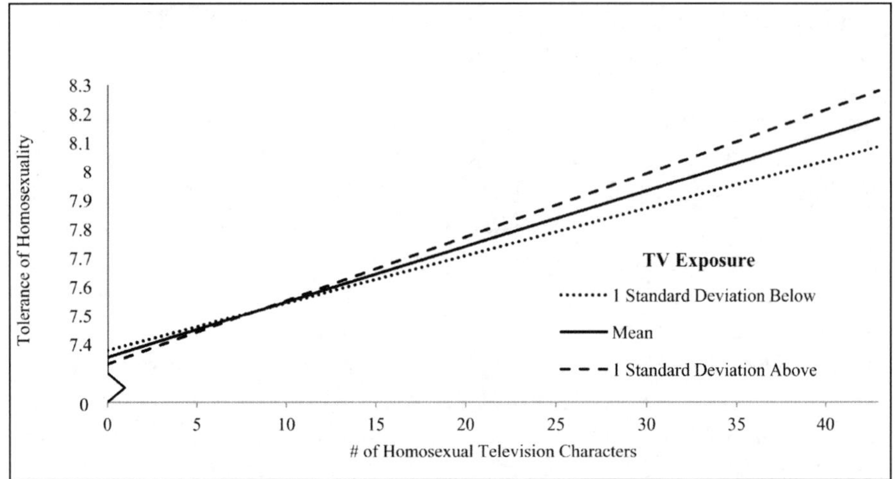


Figure 2. Effect of the number of homosexual television characters on tolerance of homosexuality, by levels of individual television exposure

# Discussion

## *Cultivation: A Multilevel, Dynamic Theory of Mass Communication*

Unlike many other academic disciplines such as psychology or sociology, communication is a *variable* field that focuses on dynamic social and psychological processes across levels of analysis (Paisley, 1984). Gerbner's original vision of a program of mass communication research exploring the dynamic, evolving relationships between society and culture and how institutions, messages, and individuals are linked through communication processes embodies this definition. However, as discussed, individualistic and behavioral biases within the field of communication, the methodological challenges of multi-level research, and Gerbner's own decisions about research focus led to important dimensions of cultivation theory remaining relatively underdeveloped over the last forty years.

In this context, this study is an initial step toward moving cultivation research forward from both a methodological and theoretical perspective. Methodologically, we have demonstrated how researchers may combine empirical, quantitative macro indicators of the cultural environment with individual-level survey data into an integrated model. This form of conceptual/statistical modeling allows cultivation researchers to better explore the dynamic relationship between cultural indicators and individual attitudes over time, as well as to directly evaluate how the relationship between communication processes like television viewing and attitude formation is contingent upon the available meanings and symbols in the cultural environment. The same methodological approach may also be employed to explore how cultural environments defined by spatial (i.e., TV markets, regions, countries, etc.) units of analysis, rather than temporal ones (i.e., years, TV seasons, etc.) may be associated with individual attitudes, beliefs, and behaviors.

From a theoretical perspective, this chapter heeds the recent call of communication scholars to envision mass communication as a *multi-level* (McLeod et al., 2009), *dynamic* (Lang & Ewoldsen, 2010) process, rather than simply a static individual-level "effect." In this way, it enriches cultivation theory and research by opening new avenues of inquiry while simultaneously contributing to the validity of Gerbner's original cultivation hypothesis. Our results show not only a general co-evolution between cultural indicators of homosexuality and individual attitudes about homosexuality over time (controlling for any year-to-year variance in individual-level characteristics), but also that the alignment between the changing visibility of homosexuality in the cultural environment and individual attitudes was strongest for those who were most connected to society's primary storyteller: *heavy TV users.*

These findings demonstrate television's role in managing (moderating) social change envisioned by Gerbner and others (e.g., Shanahan & Morgan, 1999; Viswanath & Demers, 1999). In this view, television is often described as a regulating institution; the boundaries and limits of social roles and representations are established within the medium. However, as our findings demonstrate, social or cultural shifts can eventually enter the mainstream of television content, in this case, as public acceptability of homosexuality increases. In turn, shifts in television content toward more representations of gays and lesbians are reflected in the views of heavy television users that reinforce the newly established cultural order. Furthermore, television's tendency to hypostatize and stereotype everything and the politics of political correctness may push television toward ever more positive portrayals of newly emerging minority groups such as homosexuals, a path previously followed by African Americans (Gross, 1984), and may explain the rapid explosion in the visibility of homosexual characters in recent years (see Figure 1).

## Challenges and Opportunities

Though this study has some challenges, it also identifies some new opportunities for cultivation research. First, in terms of challenges, our measurements at both the macro- and micro-levels of analysis were limited in some regards. Our cultural indicators of homosexuality only tapped one dimension of "meaning," visibility, and did not capture how gay characters were portrayed in terms of tone, valence, roles, and so on. At the individual level of analysis, GSS survey data were only available for 16 time periods (see Table 1) with intermittent gaps. Furthermore, additional measures of media use (i.e., genre, entertainment vs. news, medium) and a more robust measure of individual tolerance (beyond political visibility) would have been useful. However, at the same time, we did employ a wider-range of individual control variables (i.e., church attendance, Evangelical Christian, newspaper use) than is typical of many cultivation studies in order to help guard against spurious relationships.

Though our study does not fully address the concerns about cultivation and causality expressed by some critics as it is not a longitudinal panel or time-series design (Rossman & Brosius, 2004), we believe the dynamic relationships over time explicated in our multilevel analysis strengthen the causal arguments of the cultivation hypothesis. The alternative causal explanation to our findings based on the concept of selective exposure, that individuals who were less tolerant of homosexuals watched more TV in the 1970s and 1980s than those who were more tolerant, and in turn beginning in the 1990s and 2000s began to watch less TV compared to viewers who were more tolerant, seems much less plausible.

However, it may be argued that our findings about the effect of the number of homosexual television characters on tolerance of homosexuality may simply be a spurious relationship due to some other set of variables that increase with time, as we are not controlling for the passage of time at the contextual (macro) level. There is a high correlation between the number of homosexual television characters and the passage of time ($r = .92$, $p < .001$), and this high degree of multi-collinearity prevents the inclusion of both predictors in the model. Therefore, we were unable to statistically disentangle the unique effect of the visibility of homosexual television characters from the simple passage of time. However, the finding that this effect is amplified among high television viewers lends credence to the claim that something unique about television content is associated with changes in opinion. If it was simply the passage of time that was driving the effect on tolerance, and not the number of visible characters, then it would be expected that this effect would operate independently of how much an individual chose to watch television. As the relationship between the number of characters shown and tolerance varied by an individual's television use, however, there is increased confidence that television content is uniquely associated with changes in tolerance of gay men and women.

While some challenges remain, we also wish to highlight several opportunities for cultivation scholarship moving forward. This study contributes to Gerbner's original goal of developing cultural indicators for a range of cultural spheres (i.e., family, race, gender, health, class, etc.). Furthermore, we believe that cultivation theory and research needs to be further expanded at both the macro- and micro-levels of analysis. At the macro level of analysis, with the acceleration of media concentration (ownership) and convergence (technology) in the last decade, developing cultural indicators across range of cultural products (e.g., books, magazines, plays, movies, advertising, video games) is necessary in order to fully explicate the dominant meanings and stories in the cultural environment.

Similarly, at the micro-level of analysis we need to re-examine how we conceptualize the manner in which audiences are "connected" (e.g., television, magazines, Internet, video games, mobile devices) to the cultural environment in terms of cultivation effects, and how these communication channels and processes may be mutually reinforcing. Integrating expanded measurement and conceptualization of macro cultural indicators and micro communication processes/outcomes with new methodological approaches will allow a more sophisticated, multilevel, and dynamic model of cultivation to emerge—a model that moves us further toward fulfilling Gerbner's original goal of understanding the role of mass communication in long-term social and cultural change.

## Notes

1. For a fuller discussion of the history of Cultural Indicators (CI) and its research program see Shanahan (2004) and Shanahan & Morgan (1999).
2. Tolerance toward homosexuals was measured by combining three items on the General Social Survey (GSS) asking respondents how tolerant they were of homosexuals in three different contexts: allow a homosexual to make a speech in their community, allow a homosexual to teach in a college or university, and remove a book about homosexuality written by a homosexual from their local library. These three measures were coded into a three-point scale (disagree, unsure, agree) and combined into one additive index of mean tolerance toward homosexuals ($M = 7.3$, $SD = 2.2$, $\alpha = .81$). More information about the GSS methodology and data collection procedures may be found at www.gss.norc.org.
3. Since the GSS did not include measures of tolerance and television exposure each year and was not conducted annually beginning in the 1990s, there were gaps in the GSS time series ranging from 2 to 5 years. In addition, since cultivation effects are conceptualized as cumulative and long-term, we believed that pairing each available GSS survey year with a moving average of homosexual visibility most accurately modeled the cultural TV environment for GSS respondents.
4. Intraclass Correlation Coefficient [ICC] = .04; $\tau_{00} = .200$, $\chi^2(15) = 950.961$, $p < .001$.

## References

Bradley, S. D. (2007). Neural network simulations support heuristic processing model of cultivation effects. *Media Psychology, 10*(3), 449-469.

Bryant, J., & Miron, D. (2004). Theory and research in mass communication. *Journal of Communication*, *54*(4), 662–704.

Calzo, J., & Ward, L. (2009). Media exposure and viewers' attitudes toward homosexuality: Evidence for mainstreaming or resonance? *Journal of Broadcasting & Electronic Media, 53*(2), 280–299.

Capsuto, S. (2000). *Alternate channels: The uncensored story of gay and lesbian images on radio and television.* New York: Ballantine Books.

Fisher, D., Hill, D., Grube, J., & Gruber, E. (2007). Gay, lesbian, and bisexual content on television: A quantitative analysis across two seasons. *Journal of Homosexuality, 52*(3/4), 167–188.

Fouts, G., & Inch, R. (2005). Homosexuality in TV situation comedies: Characters and verbal comments. *Journal of Homosexuality, 49*(1), 35–45.

Gallup (2010a, May 25). Americans' Acceptance of Gay Relations Crosses 50% Threshold. Washington, DC: Gallup Organization. Retrieved from http://www.gallup.com/

Gallup (2010b, May 24). Americans' Opposition to Gay Marriage Eases Slightly. Washington, DC: Gallup Organization. Retrieved from http://www.gallup.com/

Gallup (2010c, December 9). In U.S., 67% Support Repealing 'Don't Ask, Don't Tell.' Washington, DC: Gallup Organization. Retrieved from http://www.gallup.com/

Gerbner, G. (1969). Toward "cultural indicators": The analysis of mass mediated message systems. *AV Communication Review, 17*(2), 137–148.

Gerbner, G. (1970). Cultural indicators: The case of violence in television drama.*The Annals of the American Academy of Political and Social Science, 388,* 69–81.

Gerbner G. (1973). Cultural indicators: The third voice. In G. Gerbner, L. P. Gross, & W. H. Melody (Eds.), *Communications technology and socialpolicy* (pp. 555–573). New York: John Wiley & Sons.

Gerbner, G.(1999). The stories we tell. *Peace Review, 11*(1), 9–15.

Gerbner, G., & Gross, L. (1976). Living with television: The violence profile. *Journal of Communication, 26*(2), 173–199.

Gerbner, G., Gross, L., Morgan, M., & Signorielli, N. (1980). The "mainstreaming" of America: Violence profile no. 11. *Journal of Communication, 30*(3), 10–29.

Gerbner, G., Gross, L., Morgan, M., & Signorielli, N. (1982). Charting the mainstream: Television's contributions to political orientations. *Journal of Communication,32*(2), 100–127.

Gitlin, T. (1978). Media sociology: The dominant paradigm. *Theory and Society, 6*(2), 205–253.

GLAAD (2003). *Where are we on TV Report 2002–2003.* New York: Gay & Lesbian Alliance Against Defamation. Retrieved from http://www.glaad.org

GLAAD (2004). *Where are we on TV Report 2003–2004.* New York: Gay & Lesbian Alliance Against Defamation. Retrieved from http://www.glaad.org

GLAAD (2005). *Where are we on TV Report 2004–2005.* New York: Gay & Lesbian Alliance Against Defamation. Retrieved from http://www.glaad.org

GLAAD (2006). *Where are we on TV Report 2005–2006.* New York: Gay & Lesbian Alliance Against Defamation. Retrieved from http://www.glaad.org

GLAAD (2007). *Where are we on TV Report 2006–2007.* New York: Gay & Lesbian Alliance Against Defamation. Retrieved from http://www.glaad.org

GLAAD (2008). *Where are we on TV Report 2007–2008.* New York: Gay & Lesbian Alliance Against Defamation. Retrieved from http://www.glaad.org

GLAAD (2009). *Where are we on TV Report 2008–2009.* New York: Gay & Lesbian Alliance Against Defamation. Retrieved from http://www.glaad.org

Gross, L. (1984). The cultivation of intolerance: Television, blacks and gays. In G. Melischek, K. E. Rosengren, & J. Stappers (Eds.), *Cultural indicators: An international symposium* (pp. 345–363). Vienna, Austria: Osterreichischen Akademie der Wissenschaften.

Gross, L. (1991). Out of the mainstream: Sexual minorities and the mass media. In M. Wolf & A. Kielwasser (Eds.), *Gay people, sex, and the media* (pp. 19–46). New York: Haworth.

Gross, L. (2001). *Up from invisibility: Lesbians, gay men, and the media in America.* New York: Columbia University Press.

Herman, D. (2005). "I'm gay": Declarations, desire, and coming out on prime-time television. *Sexualities, 8*(1), 7–29.

Hetsroni, A. (2007). Three decades of sexual content on prime-time network programming: A longitudinal meta-analytic review. *Journal of Communication, 57*, 318–348

Lang, A., & Ewoldsen, D. (2010). Beyond effects: Conceptualizing communication as dynamic, complex, nonlinear, and fundamental. In S. Allan (Ed.), *Rethinking communication: Keywords in communication research.* (pp. 111–122). New York: Hampton Press.

McLeod, J. M., Kosicki, G. M., & McLeod, D. M. (2009). Levels of analysis and communication science. In C. R. Berger, M. Roloff, & D. Roskos-Ewoldson (Eds.), *Handbook of communication science* (2nd ed., pp. 183–200). Los Angeles: Sage Publications.

Morgan, M., & Shanahan, J. (2010). The state of cultivation. *Journal of Broadcasting & Electronic Media. 54*(2), 337–355.

Morgan, M., & Signorielli, N. (1990). Cultivation analysis: Conceptualization and methodology. In N. Signorielli & M. Morgan (Eds.), *Cultivation analysis: New directions in media effects research* (pp. 13–34). Newbury Park: Sage Publications.

Nisbet, E. C. (2008). Media use, democratic citizenship, and communicating gaps in a developing democracy. *International Journal of Public Opinion Research, 20*, 454–482.

Nisbet, E. C., & Myers, T. (2010). Challenging the state: Transnational TV and political identity in the Middle East. *Political Communication, 27*(4), 1–20.

Paisley, W. J. (1984). Communication in the communication sciences. In B. Dervin & M. J. Voigt (Eds.), *Progress in communication sciences* (Vol. 5, pp. 1–43). Norwood, NJ: Ablex.

Pan, Z., & McLeod, J. M. (1991). Multi-level analysis in mass communication research. *Communication Research, 18*, 138–171.

Raudenbush, S. W., & Bryk, A. S. (2002). *Hierarchical linear models*(2nd ed.). Newbury Park, CA: Sage Publications.

Robinson, W.S. (1950). Ecological correlations and the behavior of individuals. *American Sociological Review, 15*(3), 351–357.

Rossman, C., & Brosius, H. (2004). The problem of causality in cultivation research. *Communications, 29*, 379–397.

Russo, V. (1981). *The celluloid closet: Homosexuality in the movies.* New York: Harper & Row.

Shanahan, J. (2004). A return to cultural indicators.*Communications, 29*, 277–294.

Shanahan, J., & Jones, V. (1999). Cultivation and social control. In D. Demers & K.

Viswanath (Eds.), *Mass media, social control, and social change: A macrosocial perspective* (pp. 31–50). Ames, IA: Iowa State University Press.

Shanahan, J., & Morgan, M. (1999) *Television and its viewers: Cultivation theory and research.* Cambridge: Cambridge University Press.

Shrum, L. J. (1995). Assessing the social-influence of television: A social cognition perspective on cultivation effects. *Communication Research, 22*, 402–429.

Shrum, L. J. (1996). Psychological processes underlying cultivation effects: Further tests of construct accessibility. *Human Communication Research, 22*, 482–509.

Slater, M., Snyder, L., & Hayes, A. (2006). Thinking and modeling at multiple levels: The potential contribution of multilevel modeling to communication theory and research. *Human Communication Research, 32*(4), 375–384.

Snijders, T., & R. J. Bosker. (2003). *Multi-level analysis.* London: Sage Publications.

Tropiano, S. (1999). *Prime time closet.* New York: Applause Theatre & Cinema Books.

Viswanath, K., & Demers, D. (1999).Mass media from a macrosocial perspective. In D. Demers & K. Viswanath (Eds.), *Mass media, social control, & social change* (pp. 3–28). Ames, Iowa: Iowa State University Press.

Walters, S. D. (2001). *All the rage: The story of gay visibility in America.* Chicago: University of Chicago Press.

Wyatt, D. (2001). *Gay/Lesbian/Bisexual television characters.* Located at http://home.cc.umanitoba.ca/~wyatt/tv-characters.html

Yang, A. S. (1997). The polls: attitudes toward homosexuality. *Public Opinion Quarterly, 61*, 477–507.

Zarnowitz, V. (1987) Indicators. In J. Eatwell, M. Milgate, & P. Newman (Eds.),*The new Palgrave dictionary of economics* (Vol. 2, pp. 783–786). London: Macmillan Press.

# 5. Television and Gender Roles

## Cultivating Conceptions of Self and Others

*Erica Scharrer*

Television is one of the most influential socializing agents of the modern era, informing its viewers through stories told in programming and advertising of cultural norms, beliefs, and expectations. Although television has many stories to tell, one of its most vocal messages is about gender. Viewing the men and women and boys and girls who appear on television—what they say, what they do, what they look like, and how they interact—shapes audience members' views of gender roles and their conceptions of themselves and others. Television has the potential to enculturate individuals young and old into a set of gendered roles and to form their ideas about femininity and masculinity. This chapter examines the latest cultivation-related research on the consequences of attending to television's stories about gender for the ideas, beliefs, and behavior of audiences. In doing so, it will briefly reference the most recent content analyses documenting patterns in representations of gender and gender roles and then examine enduring as well as newer directions in cultivation and media effects research. From messages about romance and dating received from reality programming to depictions of mothers and fathers on domestic sitcoms, and from views of "ideal" bodies to perceptions of sexual stereotypes, the chapter will provide important insights into the ways in which social norms about gender are reflected and shaped through the lens of television.

As the research evidence will show, viewers do, indeed, learn from cumulative exposure to consistent configurations in depictions on the screen, picking up on television's lessons about what is valued and what is devalued in society. Implicit messages are sent to viewers when particular people are privileged with extensive, positive, and complex portrayals on screen, as they are when particular people are rarely seen and/or are restricted to negative or narrow portrayals. Thus, viewers learn about both what is normative and what disrupts social norms, and their conceptions of themselves and others shift in response.

Although it is difficult to isolate gender from other aspects of identity, its investigation is of the utmost importance. From a very young age, individuals develop a sense of themselves and of others based in no small part on biological sex and socially constructed gender. The implications of such concepts extend to critical areas including, but not limited to, romantic and sexual interactions, satisfaction or lack thereof with their own appearance, the division of household chores and domestic responsibilities, the setting of occupational goals, and opportunities and barriers in society at large. In other words, the depiction of gender and gender roles on television has the ability to define and to delimit one's concept of the self and of others, of one's potential and of one's restrictions. Such defining and delimiting also shape social interactions in inter- and intra-gendered dynamics and contributes to larger enculturation processes.

The existing research on television's cultivation of gender roles includes meta-analyses and other large-scale research projects that examine gender stereotypes broadly as well as individual studies that center around the subtopics of beauty and body, romance and sexuality, housework and domestic roles, and occupations and professional roles. Therefore, this chapter is organized accordingly. However, it is important to make an overall observation about television's representation of characters by gender, more generally, before launching into these more specific analyses. Early content analysis showed that males outnumbered females on television by 3 to 1 (Head, 1954). The distribution of males and females had improved to a 60/40 split in favor of males by the mid-1990s (Signorielli & Bacue, 1999), and that pattern has remained largely in place since (Signorielli, in press). Therefore, as we consider the ways in which males and females are depicted on television and the ways in which audience members' views may correspond, it is important to recall that such depictions occur within the context of continued underrepresentation of female characters on television.

## Overall Effects on Gender-Role Conceptualizations

Perhaps the most important and lasting contribution of cultivation analysis is its most simple and most central hypothesis: that repeated exposure to the consistent themes and patterns in the stories told on television shapes viewers' conceptions of social reality. In other words, heavy television viewers perceive the "real world" as more closely approximating the television world compared to lighter viewers, as cumulative exposure blurs the boundaries between fact and fiction and blends ideas and assumptions about the "real world" with the television world.

Of course, the prominence of the medium in most individuals' lives means that even lighter viewers view a substantial amount of television, and these kinds of images are by no means exclusive to television. Because of the dominance of television in the contemporary world and its command of even lighter viewers' time, all viewers are often exposed to the sorts of gender depictions and stereotypes described here. Thus, the "cultivation differential"—the gap between the perceptions of heavy and light viewers—is likely to be small, although by no means inconsequential (Morgan, Shanahan, & Signorielli, 2009). And in some cultural contexts, television's depictions of gender may be more progressive than the messages received from other socializing agents. In these cases, therefore, we see television cultivating an acceptance of wider and less restrictive gender roles rather than a rejection.

Meta-analysis is one useful way to examine the role of television in shaping gender role attitudes and behaviors. A number of such meta-analyses exist, spanning decades of research and multiple methodologies. Each points to the same conclusion: television exerts a small but important influence on the development and expression of gender roles. In one of the earlier such meta-analyses, Herrett-Skjellum and Allen (1996) amassed 30 studies and found an average effect size of .10 between television and gender role stereotypes. The relationship held regardless of age of the research participant, and among the strongest associations was that between television exposure and views of occupational roles. An average effect size of .10 was also found by Morgan and Shanahan (1997) whose meta-analysis comprised 14 studies of television and gender roles from the cultivation analysis literature. Oppliger's (2007) meta-analysis included 31 studies (narrowed from an original 52 studies on the topic after eliminating those that failed to include means and standard deviations for each variable, those in which the dependent variable involved the research participants' ratings of or responses to particular characters, those that did not measure amount of viewing, and those that were conducted in non-English speaking contexts). Once again, the statistical relationship between television exposure and gender role outcomes among experimental ($r = .24$) and—most importantly for cultivation effects—non-experimental ($r = .12$) studies was positive, pointing to television's role in contributing to stereotypes and more traditional outlooks.

Examination of multiple public opinion polls conducted over time also provides a "big picture" interpretation of the topic. Signorielli (1989) examined the link between amount of television viewing and gender-stereotypical attitudes among responses to the General Social Survey (GSS) used by NORC from 1975 to 1986. Although she found that fewer people agreed with more rigid gender-typed views in the 1980s compared to the 1970s, there remained a statistical association between television viewing and holding more traditional views of the role of women in society. In the meta-analyses and in this study of opinions over time, therefore, overall amount of television use is consistently associated with traditional views of gender.

Other studies examine particular subgroups of the population and/or particular genres of television programming. For example, Ward, Hansbrough, and Walker (2005) found that African American high school students who watched more music videos and more sports programming had more gender-role stereotyped attitudes than those who watched less of those genres. Yet, exposure to other genres such as situation comedies, dramas, and movies was not related to gender-related views. Rivadeneyra and Ward (2005) surveyed a sample of Latino high school students in the Los Angeles area, measuring their exposure to English- and Spanish-language primetime programming, soap operas, and talk shows. Items used to measure gender-related attitudes included "the husband should make all the important decisions in the marriage" and "a wife should do whatever her husband wants" (p. 462). The authors found that girls who watched more television, especially talk shows and situation comedies, were more likely to support restricted roles for women. Across gender of respondent, exposure to Spanish-language programs also contributed to traditional gender-role attitudes. Importantly, the association between television use and these attitudes was heightened when participants had higher levels of perceived realism and viewer involvement.

Television's contribution to generalized gender role attitudes has also been supported in research outside the United States. Morgan (1990), for instance, found evidence of television cultivating gender-role stereotypes among adolescent samples from the United States, Argentina, China, and South Korea. Later, Saito (2007) analyzed survey responses from 417 adults in Japan and determined that amount of television viewing was significantly associated with more gender-stereotyped responses to selected items from the Scale of Egalitarian Sex Role Attitudes, and the association remained marginally significant ($\beta = -.094$, $p = .07$) when controlling for age, education, occupational status, and political orientation in hierarchical regression analysis. Follow-up analyses revealed stronger or weaker results depending on subgroup. Heavier-viewing females, for instance, but not males, revealed more stereotypical ideologies in their responses to the scale. Interestingly, politically conservative respondents who were heavy television viewers had less stereotyped responses to the scale than heavier viewing liberal counterparts. These analyses support the concept of mainstreaming, the ability of television viewing to reduce differences in conceptions often found based on demographics (Morgan et al., 2009).

In fact, the ability of television to cultivate progressive, non-traditional gender role attitudes in other cultural contexts has been further supported. In Kuwait, for instance, Abdulrahim, Al-Kandari and Hasanen (2009) found that amount of viewing of American television programming was associated with more liberal, non-traditional views of gender roles, measured using such items as "Women should have the same rights as men in every way" and "Men and women should get equal pay when they are in the same jobs" (p. 64). Exposure to U.S. television remained a significant predictor of less stereotypical views of gender even when accounting for demographic variables and additional variables pertaining to perceptions of that programming (including, for instance, its capacity to provide trans-cultural knowledge). The role of television can change, therefore, depending on its comparative emphasis alongside other social and cultural forces. If television is more progressive in its treatment of gender roles than other messages from the culture, it can contribute to the opening up of individuals' conceptualizations of gender. If it is more conservative in its treatment of gender than other messages from the culture, it can play a part in constraining conceptualizations of gender. The phenomenon is not likely to be confined to one particular area of the world (such as Kuwait), as a prior study had found the same pattern among college students in Korea (Kang & Morgan, 1988).

## Beauty and Body

Television presents a narrow definition of attractiveness, emphasizing thinness as an essential component, particularly for females. Fouts and Burggraf (2002) found, for instance, that sitcoms underrepresent above-average weight individuals compared to population statistics, and in particular overrepresent under-weight females. Females were coded as more attractive than males in a study of Spanish-language primetime programming, as well, and their appearance was emphasized to a greater degree in the narrative (Glascock & Ruggiero, 2004). In an analysis of the newer television networks' programming, that on Fox, the WB, and UPN (the latter two now merged together but then separate networks), Glascock (2003) also determined that female characters were dressed more provocatively than male characters, again calling attention to their attractiveness and sexuality.

In commercial content, males outnumber females for all product types except health- and beauty-related and household products (Bartsch, Burnett,

Diller, & Rankin-Williams, 2000; Ganahl, Prinsen, & Netzley, 2003), thereby illustrating the associations of female gender roles with beauty and all things domestic. Female characters are typically younger than male characters and older women are the least visible group appearing in advertising (Ganahl et al., 2003). Stern and Mastro (2004) found, further, that young adult females were the most attractive as well as the thinnest group of characters appearing in television advertising, while older females were coded as less attractive and heavier.

Television has been found to cultivate viewers' ideals and standards of beauty, with especially deleterious outcomes when viewers feel that they do not measure up well against such standards. Harrison and Cantor (1997) and Tiggemann (2003) each found significant links between overall amount of television exposure and body dissatisfaction, thereby supporting the notion that television's failure to veer from a thin ideal in its depictions can have a negative consequence for the level of contentment individual viewers have with their own bodies. Zhang and Lien (2010) found within a sample of 301 Taiwanese adolescent girls that among those with low self esteem and heavier body weight, television viewing was associated with body dissatisfaction. Among heavy viewers but not among light, low self esteem was correlated with body dissatisfaction.

An even larger set of studies has found evidence for viewing specific genres and types of programming (such as programs that are particularly "thinness depicting") to be associated with body image disturbances (Bissell & Zhou, 2004; Harrison, 2003; Park, 2005; Stice, Schupak-Neuberg, Shaw, & Stein, 2004; Tiggemann, 2003, 2005). Although the literature is marked by the occasional study that fails to show a link between negative body image and either overall amount of television exposure (Botta, 1999; Tiggemann, 2005) or viewing of specific genres (Botta, 1999; Stice, Spangler, & Agras, 2001), one can conclude from the majority of the evidence that television is likely to exert an influence on body image, but the effect is small or moderate in size and, like all media effects, not universal.

A newer subtopic is emerging within the realm of media and body image, as well. Two recent studies have investigated the effects of exposure to television programs that focus on appearance-related makeovers in which participants, usually women, are transformed via new clothing, hairstyles, and even cosmetic surgery into versions of themselves that ostensibly more closely meet societal standards for beauty. Kubic and Chory (2007) found that amount of viewing of such makeover programs is negatively related to self esteem and positively associated with dissatisfaction with one's body and a drive toward "perfectionism." Nabi (2009) surveyed 170 undergraduates, who reported both their overall amount of television viewing and their exposure to a long list of reality-based programs, including three focusing specifically on cosmetic surgery makeovers, *The Swan, Extreme Makeover*, and *I Want a Famous Face.* Significant partial correlations (controlling for age, gender, race, and Body Mass Index) emerged between overall television viewing and level of body consciousness and between exposure to the three cosmetic surgery makeover programs and self-reported likelihood to engage in "appearance-enhancing procedures" if cost were no object, including those minimally as well as more invasive. Television appears to underscore a drive toward thinness and an idealized definition of beauty, therefore, both overall in its programming across genres and titles and, in particular, within the relatively new yet popular programs with an emphasis on makeovers.

## Romance and Sexuality

An analysis of 124 programs aired on the broadcast networks during the 2005–2006 television season found female characters more often depicted in roles and scenarios having to do with interpersonal relationships—including familial, between friends, and with romantic partners—than male characters (Lauzen, Dozier, & Horan, 2008). The overwhelming majority of romantic and sexual relationships depicted on television are heterosexual, although more gay and lesbian characters are appearing than in the past. Fisher and colleagues (Fisher, Hill, Grube, & Gruber, 2007) found that from 2001 to 2003, 15% of all television shows contained some same-sex sexual content, and such content was more prevalent on cable, in variety and comedy genres, and in feature films broadcast on TV. A later analysis of 98 episodes of prime-time programs on broadcast and cable television estimated that 7.5% of all characters appearing in such programs are gay (Netzley, 2010).

Research has also explored television's effects on views and attitudes regarding romantic and sexual relationships. The messages sent implicitly and explicitly about marriage from television, for example, tend to be rather complex and sometimes even contradictory. Signorielli (1991) found among a sample of high school students that overall amount of television viewing was significantly associated with negative views of marriage, such as thinking of marriage as too restrictive, preferring cohabitation, and calling into question whether marriage is necessary. Yet, she also found a positive link between television viewing and respondents' stated intentions to get married and stay married later in life. In a single study, therefore, we see that television viewing is associated with incongruous views.

That ambivalence is further reflected in a second study on the topic. Segrin and Nabi (2002) surveyed 285 undergraduate students, measuring their generalized marriage expectations (asked via an open-ended question of what they think marriage would be like), "fantasy ruminations" about marriage (e.g., "I have put a lot of thought into what kind of wedding I might have"), idealistic expectations for intimacy (e.g., "You should know each other's innermost feelings"), "eros love style," which taps attitudes about romance and passion in relationships (e.g., "My partner and I would be attracted to each other immediately after we first met"), and marriage intentions (e.g., when and under what conditions respondents expected marriage to occur; p. 252). They measured both overall exposure to television and exposure to romantic comedies, soap operas, daytime talk shows, and reality programs with a particular focus on romantic relationships. Regression results showed genre-specific television viewing was a positive predictor of responses to the eros love style scale, fantasy ruminations about marriage, the number of fantasy-oriented themes respondents listed in the open-ended item, and the marriage intentions scale. Overall television exposure was a negative predictor of expectations for intimacy, but genre-specific exposure was a positive predictor of such expectations. From this study, therefore, we can conclude that the overall picture painted on television is rather challenging to the institution of marriage but through romance-based television genres, positive and even idealistic views of marriage are also nurtured.

Additional analyses have studied perceptions of dating and intimate relationships rather than marriage, and have generally supported the hypothesis that specific forms of television viewing promote gender-related stereotypes. Ward (2002) found in a sample of 259 undergraduate students that amount of exposure to prime-time comedies, prime-time dramas, soap operas, and music videos was each associated with seeing women as sexual objects and men as both driven by sex and unable to maintain a monogamous relationship. Ferris, Smith, Greenberg, and Smith (2007) discovered similar gender-based dating and sex stereotypes, but in this case they were expressed by males and appeared to stem from the single genre that was the focus of their analysis: reality-based dating programs. Male heavy viewers of these dating programs were more likely to endorse the same sorts of stereotypes that surfaced in the Ward (2002) study (women as sex objects, men as sex driven) compared to their lighter viewer counterparts.

The daytime talk show has been identified as one genre in which depictions of dating and of sex are particularly prevalent and often portrayed as problematic (Greenberg, Sherry, Busselle, Hnilo, & Smith, 1997). Researchers, therefore, have studied whether exposure to such portrayals cultivates beliefs and attitudes regarding interpersonal relationships. Davis and Mares (1998) found that high school students who were heavier viewers of daytime talk shows were more likely than lighter viewing respondents to perceive greater prevalence of teenage pregnancy, teenage sex, and other such scenarios in society. Yet, they were no more likely to trivialize these issues than their lighter viewing counterparts, suggesting that the often negative depiction of intimate relationships on talk shows communicates a degree of caution among young viewers. Woo and Dominick (2001) conducted a similar study, yet added an international element, positing that international students would experience a stronger cultivation effect from daytime talk shows than domestic students. Within a sample of 320 college students, they found American students' amount of exposure to daytime talk shows predicted all 13 of their dependent variables (which included estimates of infidelity and of premarital sex and views of married couples and couples in romantic relationships on a series of semantic differentials including honest-dishonest, aggressive-peaceful), whereas their overall amount of television viewing predicted just two. Among the international students, exposure to talk shows predicted 8 of the 13 dependent variables, talk show exposure dominance (the ratio between exposure to talk shows and overall amount of exposure) predicted 10, and overall television viewing again predicted just two. For both groups, therefore, exposure to the specific genre was more likely to cultivate beliefs consonant with the genre's portrayals, whereas for international students the proportion of talk show exposure within total television time was a critical variable as well, likely because the American students watched more television, overall.

Calzo and Ward (2009) tested whether television cultivates perceptions of gay men and lesbians, using a large sample of over 1,700 fairly diverse undergraduates for their research. They measured both overall television use and exposure to particular genres (as well as exposure to other media forms). Within the entire sample, overall television viewing was not associated with accepting attitudes toward homosexuality (AATH) under multiple controls, but music video viewing and primetime television viewing were significantly correlated with AATH. They found further that the influence of television appears to bring views of homosexuality among less and more religious individuals together toward a "mainstream" outlook. For those from whom we would expect greater acceptance of homosexuality based on less strongly held religious beliefs, television appears to exert an influence toward a less accepting outlook. For those from whom we would expect less acceptance of homosexuality based on more strongly held religious beliefs, television appears to exert an influence toward a more accepting outlook (see also Nisbet & Myers, Chapter 4, this volume).

## Housework and Domestic Roles

Content analysis has found that female characters' marital status is more likely to be readily identified compared to male characters on television (Signorielli & Kahlenberg, 2001), thereby communicating to the audience the relative importance of marriage to and for women. Female characters in *telenovelas* and serial dramas on Spanish-language television were shown to be responsible for childcare more than were male characters (Glascock & Ruggiero, 2004). Indeed, within televised families, studies have found some key differences in how mothers and fathers are represented. The general trend for women and mothers has been toward roles progressively reflecting more independence and fewer domestic duties (Reep & Dambrot, 1994). Yet, father figures in domestic sitcoms from the 1950s through the 1990s have been increasingly negatively depicted, struggling with authority and competence in parenting, often to humorous ends (Scharrer, 2001).

Perhaps in no other television genre are gender stereotypes regarding the domestic sphere more vivid than in advertising on television, both within the United States (Browne, 1998; Coltrane & Messineo, 2000; Scharrer, Kim, Lin, & Liu, 2006) and in such countries as Spain (Royo-Vela, Aldas-Manzano, Kuster, & Vila, 2008), the United Kingdom (Lewin-Jones & Mitra, 2009), and Australia (Milmer & Higgs, 2004). Household responsibilities tend to be distributed stereotypically, according to these analyses, with women, for instance, doing the majority of the cleaning and cooking and men doing the majority of the outdoor chores and household repairs in commercials. Moreover, in the few instances in which males do take on chores that run counter to gender expectations, their efforts are often presented as humorously inept (Kaufman, 1999; Scharrer et al., 2006).

Effects research examines television's influence on gender-related responsibilities in and around the home. Here the research evidence has found an interesting dichotomy. Television use seems to be related to traditional attitudes about who should be or is ideally suited for particular roles and responsibilities, such as females doing the cooking and cleaning and males taking care of repairs and taking out the trash. Yet, the influence of television does not appear to extend to who actually does these tasks within the household. Rather, the distribution of actual housework and chores (although often quite gendered) is carried out without drawing directly on television's messages.

For example, Morgan (1987) used longitudinal data from a sample of 287 adolescents and determined that television viewing contributed to changes in adolescents' gender-role attitudes over time but was not related to their performance of specific household responsibilities. Signorielli and Lears (1992) examined similar relationships in a younger sample of fourth and fifth graders, also finding significant associations between television consumption and gender-typed attitudes toward housework but no such connection between viewing and actually doing gender-stereotyped chores around the house. In this case, the role of television in attitude development is direct whereas the role of television in behavior appears to be more limited.

Finally, a single study has examined the role of television in cultivating expectations of motherhood. Ex, Janssens, and Korzilius (2002) examined responses among 166 female adolescents and young women (aged 15 to 22) in the Netherlands and found that exposure to sitcoms and soap operas that feature more conventional gender-role depictions, but not overall television viewing, predicted the anticipation of a more traditional approach to motherhood, one in which the family and children were the focus more so than work. In addition to conceptions about marriage, therefore, specific television programs can also shape the visions that girls and young women hold regarding potential future roles for themselves as mothers.

## Occupations and Professional Roles

Male characters are more likely to be explicitly presented on television as having a job outside the home than female characters. Signorielli and Kahlenberg (2001) found that approximately 60% of female characters were identified as having an occupation compared to about three quarters of male characters. That disparity lingers in later analyses of prime-time television programs as well (Signorielli, in press). Additional analyses have determined the sorts of occupations that are taken on by male and female characters on television, defining "traditionally male" occupations such as doctors, lawyers, and politicians and "traditionally female" occupations such as teachers and those in the service sector, as well as "gender neutral" occupations. Here we see some progress as well as remaining obstacles standing in the way of wider roles. In terms of progress, women are just as likely as men on television to be found in white-collar or professional occupations (Signorielli, in press; Signorielli & Kahlenberg, 2001). Furthermore, only about 20% of female characters are currently in "traditionally female" occupations, with an estimated one third crossing traditional gender boundaries by occupying "traditionally male" jobs (Signorielli, in press). Limiting circumstances persist for male characters, however, in that an estimated one half has "traditionally male" jobs and careers, and just 5% are depicted in "traditionally female" occupational roles (Signorielli, in press).

One of the first studies finding effects in this area was conducted by Jeffries-Fox and Jeffries-Fox (1981), who studied 200 7th through 9th graders and found that television exposure made a small but significant contribution to their conceptions of gender roles regarding occupations and work-related skills and capacities. Zemach and Cohen (1986) discovered in a sample of over 1,200 Israeli adults that heavy television viewing was associated with a smaller gap between perceptions of the ways in which television depicts gender and occupations and actual population statistics regarding gender and occupations. In a study conducted by Wroblewski and Huston (1987), fifth and sixth grade girls who were frequent viewers of television programs with traditional gender depictions and infrequent viewers of programs with counter-stereotypical gender depictions expressed stronger aspirations toward more traditionally feminine occupations such as those featured on the screen. Both boys and girls in the study had negative attitudes about male characters participating in traditionally female-associated occupations on television.

Yet, with the changing nature of television depictions toward more working women and a greater range of occupations for female characters, the size of the television effect and its direction are not always clear. As early as the mid-1980s, for instance, Wroblewski and Huston (1987) found that early adolescents critiqued television occupations as more gender stereotyped than real-life occupations. Television had been shown to foster a desire for a relatively easy yet high-paying job among both boys and girls in past research (Signorielli, 1993). Yet, a more recent analysis showed no such association between amount of viewing and particular work values, although the respondents' own aspirations and values were related to their favorite characters' occupations (Hoffner, Levine, & Touhey, 2008).

## Conclusions and New Directions in Effects Research

An overarching conclusion from this review is that although one can point to some progress in wider and more encompassing gender roles on television, stereotypical portrayals persist. Due in large part to the commercial constraints of television (Morgan, Shanahan, & Harris, 1990), television's treatment of gender remains rather restrictive, and earns considerable criticism from scholars and activists regarding both the quantity and the quality of roles. The reliance on advertising income (most certainly within the United States and increasingly beyond), the high cost of program production, and the generally risk-averse nature of the industry means many conventional or even stereotypical depictions linger.

The effects research points decidedly to a single conclusion: Television's depiction of gender matters for members of the audience. Heavy viewers can learn gender stereotypes from television, for instance, including those pertaining to specific arenas such as physical appearance, romantic and sexual relationships, and roles taken up in both domestic and professional realms. Yet, we have also seen that television can be a counter-stereotypical force as well if its messages are among the more "gender-progressive" in a culture.

A trend in gender-related cultivation research as clearly indicated in the literature reviewed in this chapter is the growing tendency to explore the role of exposure to particular genres and program types in predicting outcomes in addition to or even instead of overall amount of viewing. This trend defies the original cultivation premise, which calls specifically for the analysis of the influence of overall amount of television use and which, in turn, approximates viewers' exposure to themes that cut across content categories in producing the cultivation effect (Morgan et al., 2009). Yet, as Morgan and Shanahan (2010) have written, cultivation researchers faithful to the original premise have certainly never suggested that other effects tied more closely to specific programs or genres would not occur. On the contrary, genre- and program-specific effects have been reviewed concurrently with overall television effects in recent reviews of cultivation research, although whether the former can accurately be called "cultivation" has been questioned (Morgan et al., 2009; Morgan & Shanahan, 2010). As is evident from many of the studies identified in this chapter, some gender-related effects do stem more readily from viewers' exposure to particular program types—such as those that are more "thinness depicting," those that feature cosmetic makeovers, and the like—whereas other effects continue to be attributed to overall exposure to the medium. Future research, therefore, would do well to accrue more empirical evidence and extend theory regarding the conditions under which an overall television versus a specific type of cultivation effect might be expected. (For an extended discussion of this issue, see Bilandzic & Busselle, Chapter 13, this volume.)

Another fruitful new trend in effects research regarding television's influence on gender role conceptualizations is combining and integrating cultivation theory with other theoretical perspectives. Morgan and Shanahan (2010) have noted this trend across a variety of topics, but since the present chapter is focused exclusively on gender roles, a single example is best and is provided by a recent study. Nabi (2009) examined exposure to cosmetic surgery-based reality television programming and a number of outcome variables through the lenses of cultivation theory, social cognitive theory (Bandura, 1986, 2002), and social comparison theory (Festinger, 1954). Nabi reasoned that cultivation theory would predict effects manifested in views of society (estimated prevalence of cosmetic surgery procedures) and one's own desire to undergo such a procedure, whereas social comparison theory would predict effects through body dissatisfaction (when the self is compared to characters on the programs), and social cognitive theory would predict effects primarily through identification with characters. Using responses from a survey of 271 undergraduate women, she found support for many of these predictions. Although there was no association between exposure to cosmetic makeover programs and estimates of the prevalence of cosmetic surgery in society, exposure to the programs was associated with respondents' desire to undergo appearance-enhancing procedures of all levels of invasiveness. Furthermore, overall television viewing was associated with both lower body satisfaction in general as well as lower body area satisfaction (in which respondents expressed concern about how specific parts of their body looked). These data support a cultivation theory explanation.

Yet, data were also found to support social comparison processes (e.g., "I judge how attractive I am by comparing myself with the people on the program") in predicting body dissatisfaction and desiring cosmetic procedures of all sorts and identification processes (e.g., "I feel I am watching people like myself") in explaining desire to undergo invasive procedures, in particular. Therefore, Nabi integrated measures from each of the three explanations to arrive upon a combined theoretical interpretation. She explains the results of her path analysis:

> The model suggests that cosmetic surgery makeover program viewing associates directly with desire for invasive procedures as well as indirectly through its effects on social comparison and perception of positive outcomes. Social comparison, identification, and perceived positive outcomes also maintained direct relationships with desire for invasive procedures as well as indirect relationships via their associations with one another and through the perceived positive outcome-identification interaction. (p. 20)

Thus, we can see that for this phenomenon specific to gender—feeling discontent with what one looks like and desiring to alter one's body size and shape through surgical procedures—the media effects processes hypothesized by cultivation theory retain their explanatory power, but they do so in concert with other processes posited through additional theoretical perspectives. A new direction in cultivation-related effects research, then, involves reaching across multiple theoretical traditions to draw from and combine multiple concepts and build integrative theories that allow greater flexibility to explain complex phenomena.

Finally, a third trend in research regarding the cultivation of gender roles is another extension beyond the original assumptions and focus of cultivation analysis, in that scholarly inquiries have reached beyond television toward other media forms with increasing frequency over the years (Morgan &

Shanahan, 2010). Researchers have found that amount of exposure to fashion and women's magazines, in addition to television, for example, also relates to negative body image perceptions (see Murnen, Levine, Groesz, & Smith, 2007 for a meta-analytic review). Moreover, because video games have been shown to feature profoundly stereotypical gender-role depictions (Scharrer, 2004; Williams, Martins, Consalvo, & Ivory, 2009), it is likely that future research will investigate overall amount of video game playing and gender-related outcomes as well. Indeed, one recent study found heavy video game players made more frequent social comparisons between female video game characters and real women in terms of beauty and body shape compared to light video game players (Rask, 2007). The research record to date suggests that future studies examining the contribution of overall amount of time spent with media other than television will be conceived and conducted under the aegis of cultivation analysis.

### *Future Research*

There is no indication that research regarding television and gender is slowing or stagnating. To the contrary, this review has shown important new updates to the content analysis literature, innovative directions in studying effects, and durable evidence that underscores the importance of this topic for society at large. Yet, this review has identified perennially important areas in which the available research evidence is aging as well as gaps in the literature in which potentially important variables have yet to be explored at all. The body of knowledge on television and the cultivation of gender roles, as we have seen, is extensive and robust. But key unanswered questions remain.

New content analyses, new subtopics in effects studies pertaining to gender (dating, marriage, etc.), and new independent variables (talk shows, makeover shows, video games, etc.) have provided critical updates and extensions to this topic area. Yet, the more "basic" analyses of the relationship between overall television viewing and gender-related perceptions and attitudes are beginning to show their age. The most recent studies in these areas were conducted as far back as the 1980s or in the early to mid-1990s. Perhaps researchers have been heartened or otherwise convinced by content analysis work in this area, work that (as we have seen) has pointed to some signs of progress in terms of the opening up of gender roles on television, particularly those for women, both within and outside the home. Yet, a careful review of the content patterns suggests there still exists reason for concern in this area, with some gendered depictions proving more stubborn to overturn, including roles for men, the overt connection of marital status to women and occupational status to men, and, perhaps most decidedly, the continued strict assignment of individuals to specific housework, parenting, and domestic care roles, particularly in advertising. Moreover, little is known about the prevalence and persistence of more subtle stereotypes, for example those portraying females as "emotional" and "dependent." It is essential to update the research regarding how these messages and lessons are impacting audiences, and whether amount of television viewing overall or amount of exposure to particular program types that hold on to these stereotypes helps frame gender-related expectations and roles.

It is also quite evident from this review that men's roles and the depiction of masculinity have received much less attention than women's roles and the depiction of femininity, in both content analysis and effects/reception-related research (Scharrer, 2012). The relative failure to explore the cultivation of images of masculinity is a considerable gap in the literature that should be addressed in future research. Like Whiteness, masculinity is often assumed to be a "default" category, so dominant in the culture as to defy inquiry. Yet, increasingly, scholars from sociology, psychology, cultural studies and other fields are recognizing that the study of masculinity is a worthwhile enterprise, providing a means for examining social and cultural norms, dominance and power in society, and the resulting implications for everyday interactions between and within people of varying genders. With some evidence that men's roles, too, are often restricted and constrained in television depictions (once again, as we have seen in this chapter), it is likely that television viewing would cultivate conceptualizations of male roles accordingly. New research in this area would make an important contribution to the body of knowledge regarding gender and media.

Finally, the advances in a cognitive/processing explanation for the cultivation influence that have been tested with other topics (see Shrum & Lee, Chapter 8, this volume, for a review) should be applied to the important topic of the formation of gender-role conceptualizations as well. Is the cultivation of gender-related beliefs best explained by heuristics or cognitive accessibility? How do recency, frequency of activation, and other key concepts shape individuals' responses to gender-related survey questions? Much of the cognitive accessibility-related cultivation research has centered on the issue of violence and crime (Shrum, 2009), a topic that may seem rather hypothetical and remote to many individuals who are fortunate enough to lack first-hand experiences in this area. The topic of gender roles, in contrast, is likely to be proximate to most if not all individuals, a distinction which may call for new inquiries in the processing explanation for cultivation. These vital questions regarding how cultivation occurs merit further consideration within the area of media and gender in the future as well.

# References

Abdulrahim, M. A., Al-Kandari, A. A. J., & Hasenen, M. (2009). The influence of American television programs on university students in Kuwait. *European Journal of American Culture, 28*(1), 57–74.

Bandura, A. (1986). *Social foundations of thought and action: A social cognitive theory.* Englewood Cliffs, NJ: Prentice-Hall.

Bandura, A. (2002). Social cognitive theory of mass communication. In J. Bryant & D. Zillmann (Eds.), *Media effects: Advances in theory and research* (2nd ed., pp. 121–153). Mahwah, NJ: Erlbaum.

Bartsch, R. A., Burnett, T., Diller, T. R., & Rankin-Williams, E. (2000). Gender representation in television commercials: Updating an update. *Sex Roles, 43*(9/10), 735–743.

Bissell, K. L., & Zhou, P. (2004). Must-see-TV or ESPN: Entertainment and sports media exposure and body-image distortion in college women. *Journal of Communication, 54,* 5–21.

Botta, R. (1999). Televised images and adolescent girls' body image disturbance. *Journal of Communication, 49*(2), 22–41.

Browne, B. A. (1998). Gender stereotypes in advertising on children's television in the 1990s: A cross-national analysis. *Journal of Advertising, 27*(1), 83–96.

Calzo, J., & Ward, L. M. (2009). Media exposure and viewers' attitudes toward homosexuality: Evidence for mainstreaming or resonance? *Journal of Broadcasting & Electronic Media, 53*(2), 280–300.

Coltrane, S., & Messineo, M. (2000). The perpetuation of subtle prejudice: Race and gender imagery in 1990s television advertising. *Sex Roles, 42* (5/6), 363–389.

Davis, S., & Mares, M. (1998). Effects of talk show viewing on adolescents. *Journal of Communication, 48*(3), 69–86.

Ex, C. T. G. M., Janssens, J. M. A. M., & Korzilius, H. P. L. M. (2002). Young females' images of motherhood in relation to television viewing. *Journal of Communication, 52*(4), 955–971.

Ferris, A. L., Smith, S., Greenberg, B. S., & Smith, S. L. (2007). The content of reality dating shows and viewer perceptions of dating. *Journal of Communication, 57*(3), 490–510.

Festinger, L. (1954). A theory of social comparison processes. *Human Relations, 7,* 117–140.

Fisher, D. A., Hill, D. L., Grube, J. W., & Gruber, E. L. (2007). Gay, lesbian, and bisexual content on television: A quantitative analysis across two seasons. *Journal of Homosexuality, 52*(3/4), 167–188.

Fouts, G., & Burggraf, K. (2002). Television situation comedies: Female body images and verbal reinforcements. *Women and Language, 25*(2), 473–481.

Ganahl, D. J., Prinsen, T. J., & Netzley, S. B. (2003). A content analysis of prime time commercials: A contextual framework of gender representation. *Sex Roles, 49*(9/10), 546–551.

Glascock, J. (2003). Gender, race, and aggression in newer TV network's primetime programming. *Communication Quarterly, 51*(1), 90–100.

Glascock, J., & Ruggiero, T. E. (2004). Representations of class and gender on primetime Spanish language television in the United States. *Communication Quarterly, 52*(4), 390–402.

Greenberg, B., Sherry, J. L., Busselle, R. W., Hnilo, L. R., & Smith, S. (1997). Daytime television talk shows. *Journal of Broadcasting & Electronic Media, 41*(3), 412–426.

Harrison, K. (2003). Television viewers' ideal body proportions: The case of the curvaceously thin woman. *Sex Roles, 48*, 255–264.

Harrison, K., & Cantor, J. (1997). The relationship between media consumption and eating disorders. *Journal of Communication, 47*(1), 40–66.

Head, S. (1954). Content analysis of television drama programs. *Quarterly Journal of Film, Radio, and Television, 9*, 175–194.

Herrett-Skjellum, J., & Allen, M. (1996). Television programming and sex stereotyping: A meta-analysis. In B. R. Burleson (Ed.), *Communication Yearbook 19* (pp. 157–185). Thousand Oaks, CA: Sage Publications.

Hoffner, C. A., Levine, K. J., & Touhey, R. A. (2008). Socialization to work in late adolescence: The role of television and family. *Journal of Broadcasting & Electronic Media, 52*(2), 282–302.

Jeffries-Fox, S., & Jeffries-Fox, B. (1981). Gender differences in socialization through television to occupational roles: An exploratory approach. *The Journal of Early Adolescence, 1*(3), 293–302.

Kang, J. G. & Morgan, M. (1988). Culture clash: US television programs in Korea. *Journalism Quarterly*, 65(2), 431–438.

Kaufman, G. (1999). The portrayal of men's family roles in television commercials. *Sex Roles: A Journal of Research, 41*, 439–458.

Kubic, K. N., & Chory, R. M. (2007). Exposure to television makeover programs and perceptions of self. *Communication Research Reports, 24*(4), 283–291.

Lauzen, M. M., Dozier, D. M., & Horan, N. (2008). Constructing gender stereotypes through social roles in primetime television. *Journal of Broadcasting & Electronic Media, 52*(2), 200–214.

Lewin-Jones, J., & Mitra, B. (2009). Gender roles in television commercials and primary school children in the UK. *Journal of Children and Media, 3*(1), 35–50.

Livingstone, S. M. (1987). The representation of personal relationships in television drama: Realism, convention, and morality. In R. Burnett, P. McGhee, & D. Clark (Eds.), *Accounting for personal relationships: Explanation, representation, and knowledge* (pp. 248–268). London: Methuen.

Milmer, L. M., & Higgs, B. (2004). Gender sex-role portrayals in international television advertising over time: The Australian experience. *Journal of Current Issues and Research in Advertising, 26*(2), 81–95.

Morgan, M. (1987). Television, sex-role attitudes, and sex-role behavior. *The Journal of Early Adolescence*, 7(3), 269–282.

Morgan, M. (1990). International cultivation analysis. In N. Signorielli & M. Morgan (Eds.), *Cultivation analysis: New directions in media effects research* (pp. 225–248). Newbury Park: Sage Publications.

Morgan, M., & Shanahan, J. (1997). Two decades of cultivation research: An appraisal and meta analysis. In B. R. Burleson (ed.), *Communication Yearbook 20* (pp. 1–46). Thousand Oaks, CA: Sage Publications.

Morgan, M., & Shanahan, J. (2010). The state of cultivation. *Journal of Broadcasting & Electronic Media, 54*(2), 337–355.

Morgan, M., Shanahan, J., & Harris, C. (1990). VCRs and the effects of television: New diversity or more of the same? In J. R. Dobrow (Ed.), *Social and cultural aspects of VCR use* (pp. 107–123). Hillsdale, NJ: Erlbaum.

Morgan, M., Shanahan, J., & Signorielli, N. (2009). Growing up with television: Cultivation processes. In J. Bryant & M. Oliver (Eds.), *Media effects: Advances in theory and research* (3rd ed., pp. 34–49). New York: Routledge.

Murnen, S. K., Levine, M. P., Groesz, L., & Smith, J. (2007, August). *Do fashion magazines promote body dissatisfaction in girls and women? A meta-analytic review.* Paper presented at the 115th meeting of the American Psychology Association, San Francisco, CA.

Nabi, R. (2009). Cosmetic surgery makeover programs and intentions to undergo cosmetic enhancements: A consideration of three models of media effects. *Human Communication Research, 35*(1), 1–27.

Netzley, S. B. (2010). Visibility that demystifies: Gays, gender, and sex on television. *Journal of Homosexuality, 57*(8), 968–986.

Oppliger, P. A. (2007). Effects of gender stereotyping on socialization. In R. W. Press, B. M. Gayle, N. Burrell, M. Allen, & J. Bryant (Eds.), *Mass media effects research: Advances through meta-analysis* (pp. 199–214). Mahwah, NJ: Erlbaum.

Park, S. (2005). The influence of presumed media influence on women's desire to be thin. *Communication Research, 32*, 594–614.

Rask, A. (2007, May). *Video game vixens: Shaping men's perceptions of beauty?* Paper presented at the annual meeting of the International Communication Association. San Francisco, CA.

Reep, D. C. & Dambrot, F. H. (1994). TV parents: Fathers (and now mothers) know best. *Journal of Popular Culture, 28*(2), 13–23.

Rivadeneyra, R. & Ward, L. M. (2005). From *Ally McBeal* to *Sábado Gigante*: Contributions of television viewing to the gender role attitudes of Latino adolescents. *Journal of Adolescent Research,* 20, 453–475.

Royo-Vela, M., Aldas-Manzano, J., Kuster, I., & Vila, N. (2008). Adaptation of marketing activities to cultural and social context: Gender role portrayals and sexism in Spanish commercials. *Sex Roles, 58* (5/6), 379–390.

Saito, S. (2007). Television and the cultivation of gender-role attitudes in Japan: Does television contribute to the maintenance of the status quo? *Journal of Communication, 57*(3), 511–531.

Scharrer, E. (2001). From wise to foolish: The portrayal of the sitcom father, 1950s to 1990s. *Journal of Broadcasting & Electronic Media, 45*(1), 23–41.

Scharrer, E. (2004). Virtual violence: Gender and aggression in video game advertisements. *Mass Communication & Society, 7*(4), 393–412.

Scharrer, E. (2012). More than 'just the facts'? Portrayals of masculinity in police and detective programs over time. *Howard Journal of Communications, 23*, 1-21.

Scharrer, E., Kim, D. D., Lin, K., & Liu, Z. (2006). Working hard or hardly working? Gender, humor, and the performance of domestic chores in television commercials. *Mass Communication & Society, 9*(2), 215–238.

Segrin, C. & Nabi, R. L. (2002). Does television viewing cultivate unrealistic expectations about marriage? *Journal of Communication, 52*(2), 247–264.

Shrum, L. J. (2009). Media consumption and perceptions of social reality: Effects and underlying processes. In J. Bryant & M. B. Oliver (Eds.), *Media effects: Advances in theory and research* (pp. 50–73, 3rd ed.). New York: Routledge.

Signorielli, N. (1989). Television and conceptions about sex-roles: Maintaining conventionality and the status quo. *Sex Roles, 21*(5/6), 341–360.

Signorielli, N. (1991). Adolescents and ambivalence toward marriage: A cultivation analysis. *Youth and Society, 23*, 121–149.

Signorielli, N. (1993). Television and adolescents' perceptions about work. *Youth & Society, 24*, 314–341.

Signorielli, N. (in press). Gender role socialization in the 21st century. In E. Scharrer (Ed.), *Media effects/media psychology*. Boston, MA: Wiley Blackwell.

Signorielli, N., & Bacue, A. (1999). Recognition and respect: A content analysis of prime-time television characters across three decades. *Sex Roles, 40*(7/8), 527–544.

Signorielli, N., & Kahlenberg, S. (2001). Television's world of work in the nineties. *Journal of Broadcasting & Electronic Media, 45*(1), 1–19.

Signorielli, N., & Lears, M. (1992). Children, television and conceptions about chores: Attitudes and behaviors. *Sex Roles, 27*, 157–170.

Stern, S. R., & Mastro, D. E. (2004). Gender portrayals across the life span: A content analytic look at broadcast commercials. *Mass Communication & Society, 7*(2), 215–236.

Stice, E., Schupak-Neuberg, E., Shaw, H. E., & Stein, R. I. (1994). Relation of media exposure to eating disorder symptomatology: An examination of mediating mechanisms. *Journal of Abnormal Psychology, 103*, 836–840.

Stice, E., Spangler, D. L., & Agras, W. S. (2001). Exposure to media-portrayed thin-ideal images adversely effects vulnerable girls: A longitudinal experiment. *Journal of Social and Clinical Psychology, 20*, 271–289.

Tiggemann, M. (2003). Media exposure, body dissatisfaction, and disordered eating: Television and magazines are not the same! *European Eating Disorders Review, 11*, 418–430.

Tiggemann, M. (2005). Television and adolescent body image: The role of program content and viewing motivation. *Journal of Social & Clinical Psychology, 24*, 361–381.

Ward, L. M. (2002). Does television exposure affect emerging adults' attitudes and assumptions about sexual relationships? Correlational and experimental confirmation. *Journal of Youth and Adolescence, 31*(1), 1–15.

Ward, L. M., Hansbrough, E., & Walker, E. (2005). Contributions of music video exposure to Black adolescents' gender and sexual schemas. *Journal of Adolescent Research, 20*(2), 143–166.

Williams, D., Martins, N., Consalvo, M., & Ivory, J. (2009). The virtual census: Representations of gender, race, and age in video games. *New Media & Society, 11*(5), 815–834.

Woo, H. J., & Dominick, J. R. (2001). Daytime television talk shows and the cultivation effect among U.S. and international students. *Journal of Broadcasting & Electronic Media, 45*(4), 598–615.

Wroblewski, R., & Huston, A. (1987). Televised occupational stereotypes and their effects on early adolescents: Are they changing? *The Journal of Early Adolescence, 7*(3), 283–297.

Zemach, T., & Cohen, A. A. (1986). Perception of gender equality on TV and in social reality. *Journal of Broadcasting & Electronic Media, 30*(4), 427–444.

Zhang, Y. B., Lien, S. C. (2010). Television viewing and Taiwanese adolescent girls' perceptions of body image. *China Media Report Overseas, 6*(4), 15–24.

# 6. Cultivation of Political Attitudes in the New Media Environment

*Bruce W. Hardy*

Political communication studies have all but abandoned cultivation as a theoretical force driving hypotheses and research designs. While much of the published political communication research focuses on short-term persuasion and learning effects, there is a substantial amount of work dedicated to understanding long-term cumulative media effects on political attitudes. Yet cultivation is rarely applied in studies examining the effects of consistent and dominant frames in politically oriented media on audiences. In this chapter, I confirm that there is still empirical support in the political sphere for cultivation—specifically the "mainstreaming hypothesis"—by presenting new analyses from the 2008 National Annenberg Election Survey. I also present analyses from the 2004 National Annenberg Election Survey and a 2005 survey sponsored by the Annenberg Democracy Project[1] that suggest that campaign coverage and political information found on 24-hour cable channels and the Internet cultivate a sense of mistrust of political candidates and government. I conclude by discussing a few areas of political communication where cultivation could be used to extend theory and research. Framing, political socialization, and selective exposure hypotheses are used as illustrations to show how cultivation theory can be applied in future political communication research.

## The Cultivation of Political Orientations and Attitudes: Revisiting the Mainstream

Although the work of George Gerbner may be most closely identified with the study of television violence that began with his 1967–1968 study for the National Commission of the Causes and Prevention of Violence and continued under the sponsorship of multiple federal agencies, Gerbner and his team were also very interested in the cultivation of political orientations and attitudes. During the early and mid-1980s, the Cultural Indicators team published works such as "Charting the Mainstream: Television's Contributions to Political Orientations" (Gerbner, Gross, Morgan, & Signorielli, 1982) and "Political Correlates of Television Viewing" (Gerbner, Gross, Morgan, & Signorielli, 1984). The team found consistent support for their "mainstreaming" hypothesis, reporting a "convergence and homogenization of heavy [television] viewers across political groups" (Gerbner et al., 1982, p. 116). Compared to light television viewers, those who spent a considerable amount of time with television were significantly more likely to self-identify as holding moderate political views. While the Cultural Indicators team found a centering effect on self-identification, in terms of ideology they reported that heavy viewers often take a more conservative position on many social issues. This was especially true for self-identified liberals. These researchers theorized that the economic pressures to reach the buying public from advertising clients resulted in the cultivation of consumer values and gratifications. Gerbner and his colleagues (1982) concluded:

> The cultural—and evidently political—television mainstream tends to absorb the divergent tendencies that traditionally shaped the political process and to contain its own cross-currents. Heavy television viewers tend more than comparable light viewers to call themselves 'moderate' but take positions that are unmistakably conservative, except on economic issues.
>
> Our analysis shows that although television viewing brings conservatives, moderates, and liberals closer together, it is the liberal position that is weakest among heavy viewers. Viewing blurs traditional differences, blends them into a more homogenous mainstream, and bends the mainstream toward a 'hard line' position on issues dealing with minorities and personal rights. Hard-nosed commercial populism, with its mix of restrictive conservatism and pork-chop liberalism, is the paradoxical—and potentially volatile—contribution of television to political orientations. (p. 126)

Other studies have produced similar results, finding for example that heavy television viewers are significantly more likely to discriminate on gender (Signorielli, 1989), or in terms of race and sexual identification (Gross, 1984).

In the 1984 article, "Political Correlates of Television Viewing," the team extended support for the mainstreaming hypothesis. Testing to see if this effect was truly television-specific rather than a general media phenomenon, they found that newspaper readers were more likely to hold a conservative self-identification, and radio listeners said they were liberals, while heavy television viewers were more likely to report holding moderate views. Interestingly, this relationship held across 24 sub-groups, suggesting that the mainstreaming effect is not specific to a certain type of individual, just heavy television viewers.

In their book, *Television and Its Viewers: Cultivation Theory and Research*, Shanahan and Morgan (1999) analyzed data from the General Social Survey (GSS) from 1972–1994 and, like many past studies, found support for the mainstreaming hypotheses. Heavy television viewers were more likely to identify as moderate yet at the same time hold conservative views on minority or personal rights issues. An interesting finding was that "effects generally are larger in regions where the 'natural' opinion base is more liberal" (p. 154). The stronger evidence for cultivation in geographic areas with a high liberal bias further demonstrates the phenomenon of mainstreaming.

In testing television's cultivation of political attitudes among adolescents in Argentina, Morgan and Shanahan (1991) found results similar to what the Cultural Indicators team found in the U.S. They concluded:

> As we expected, television in Argentina serves the same overall formal function as in the United States—preservation of a political status quo—although the salient political issues are different. Cultivation analysis has shown that in the United States amount of television viewing is consistently, if moderately, related to a variety of political attitudes, beliefs, and behaviors. For the most part, these associations suggest that television is a conservative force that generally does not encourage a supportive atmosphere for overall systemic change. Commercial television must serve (and follow) the political and social mainstream to fulfill its mandate of sustaining and increasing consumption (p. 101).

In the years since these studies, only a few publications have applied cultivation with an explicitly political focus. Analyzing European Social Survey data from ten countries, Besley (2006) found entertainment television use to be negatively associated with levels of political participation. He found that the association between TV viewing and participation is strongest for those with progressive values such as "openness to change" and "self-transcendence." Following the theoretical argument of past research on materialism (Burroughs, Shrum, & Rindfleisch, 2002; Shrum, Wyer, & O'Guinn, 1998), Besley concluded that his results may be in part due to television's emphasis on private individual consumption and not on public and civic life.

While not straightforwardly political in nature, many other studies have looked at various issues that have strong political implications such as family, health, the environment, attitudes towards homosexuality, mental illness, etc. (e.g., Diefenbach & West, 2007; Glynn, Huge, Reineke, Hardy, & Shanahan, 2007; Shanahan & McComas, 1999). For example, Glynn and her colleagues found exposure to daytime talk shows was positively related to support for government involvement in social issues and redistribution programs. The effect of daytime talk shows, like *The Oprah Winfrey Show*, was most pronounced for conservatives. As these researchers noted, conservatives have "further to go" than non-conservatives concerning support for government involvement in family issues, meaning that "their opinions have to change *more* than those of liberals to get to that mainstream" (Glynn et al., 2007, p. 241).

## Televised Campaign Information and Mainstreaming During the 2008 Presidential Elections

Data from the 2008 National Annenberg Election Survey (NAES) produced some interesting results that support the mainstreaming hypothesis.[2] The first model (Table 1) presents a logistic regression predicting respondents' self report of holding "moderate" political views.[3] In the presence of socio-demographic controls, party identification, and how closely respondents are following the election, the more one viewed campaign information on television,[4] the more likely one was to report holding moderate views. It is important to understand that this is not a measure of general, overall television viewing, or even of general news viewing, but that it specifically deals with exposure to information about the 2008 campaign, which is a clear departure from measures used by the Cultural Indicators team in the studies previously outlined.

There are a couple of things to note concerning the results reported in Table 1: First, this is not a large effect, especially given the very large sample size. However, the relationship (significant at the $p < .001$ level) holds in the face of party identification and how closely respondents are following the election. The television variable in the model is measured in days in the past week, meaning that the coefficients in the statistical model represent the difference of individual responses on a zero- to seven-point scale. The translation of the coefficient into a quantifiable effect size requires us to talk in terms of "one-day increases" in our television variable. However, it is important to note this does not mean changes within individuals across time. It represents the differences between individuals in a fixed period of time. Additionally, because the logistic regression model is based on probabilities of being a self-identified moderate or not, it's important to take into consideration that television cannot have an effect on those respondents who already have a 100 percent probability of being a moderate. The same is true for respondents who already hold a zero percent chance. Therefore, by definition the less chance one has of already being or not being a moderate, the greater impact television can have. In the model reported here a one-day increase in TV between respondents has an impact of 0.9 percent on someone with a 50 percent baseline probability to self-identify as a moderate.

Table 1. Logistic regression predicting self-identified moderates

| | B | S.E. | Odds Ratios |
|---|---|---|---|
| Female (1=yes, 0=no) | 0.024 | 0.019 | 1.025 |
| Age (in years) | 0.002 | 0.001 | 1.002*** |
| Black (1=yes, 0=no) | 0.138 | 0.034 | 1.148*** |
| Education (in years) | 0.004 | 0.004 | 1.004 |
| Hispanic (1=yes, 0=no) | -0.026 | 0.039 | 0.974 |
| Republican (1=yes, 0=no) | -0.738 | 0.024 | 0.478*** |
| Democrat (1=yes, 0=no) | -0.188 | 0.022 | 0.828*** |
| Closely Following the Election (1= not closely at all, 4 = very closely) | -0.134 | 0.012 | 0.875*** |
| Days saw campaign information on television in past week | 0.035 | 0.004 | 1.036*** |
| *Cox & Snell $R^2$ = .022* | | | |
| *Nagelkerke $R^2$ = .031* | | | |
| *N = 55,054* | | | |

*** $p < .001$, ** $p < .01$, * $p < .05$

Source: 2008 National Annenberg Election Survey.

While this measurement of television use is quite specific and the data were collected during an election period with a great deal of information available, the statically significant relationship reported here supports a main assumption of the mainstreaming hypothesis, even though it is a departure from the studies Gerber and his team conducted in the 1980s. While this television measure is specific in content, it is also broad in terms of where the campaign information could be seen in that the question does not specify certain channels such as CNN or FOX News. What this means is that this measure taps both the active news junkie and the more nonchalant viewer who may be accidentally exposed to campaign advertisements and information via non-hard news outlets like late night talk shows, *Saturday Night Live, The View, The Daily Show,* and the like. Although we have seen a rise in partisan media (see Jamieson & Cappella, 2008), mainstream news for the most part is not ideologically bent. The campaigns themselves refrain from offering extreme ideological communication in order to sway the undecided moderate voters. Most of the non-news shows where candidates make guest appearance focus on character (e.g., Bill Clinton playing the saxophone on *The Arsenio Hall Show* in 1992) and not on ideologically rooted rhetoric.

The communication surrounding presidential campaigns focuses on valence issues and leadership credentials framed in reference to times of war or the economy. Position issues that are contested on ideological grounds such as gay marriage, abortion, and stem cell research receive relatively less mainstream discussion and the rhetoric surrounding these issues is delivered to small groups of susceptible voters through microtargeting capabilities of radio (Kenski, Hardy, & Jamieson, 2010). Past research on news coverage of campaigns has found more of a focus on the "horserace" and candidate personality than on substantive issues (Cappella & Jamieson 1996, 1997; Patterson, 1993). Research has also shown that post-presidential-debate news coverage devotes most of its time to discussion of candidate traits, leaving little room for coverage of the content of the policy debate (Sears & Chaffee, 1979). In an experiment that exposed participants to the 1988 presidential debates, Pfau and Kang (1991) found that voters focused on candidates' communication that was considered friendly, sincere, and honest and not on their policy stands. Overall, campaign information on television is centered more on candidates' character and less on political parties and ideology (Wattenberg, 1991), leading to the ideological mainstreaming effect reported here.

## Campaign Coverage and the Cultivation of Mistrust

As a rhetoric of contest frames campaign coverage and two-party politics more generally, some have argued that the press is not fulfilling its democratic functions (e.g., Bennett, 2001; Bennett & Serrin, 2005; Patterson, 1980, 1993). When politicians succeed in deceiving the public, the press fails to act as a "custodian of fact" (Jamieson & Hardy, 2007). Past research has noted that news about campaigns is dominated by tactical and strategic coverage (Cappella & Jamieson 1996, 1997; Patterson, 1993) and that there is an over-reliance on "he-said-she-said reporting" (Jamieson & Hardy, 2007). Patterson (1993) wrote that "election news, rather than serving to bring candidates and voters together, drives a wedge between them" because of the focus on the horserace and politicking of the campaign. Cappella and Jamieson (1997) reported that strategic news coverage that focused on the political moves and electoral game rather than on relevant issues depressed learning and activated cynicism toward politics and political actors. By "reporting about politicians and their policies repeatedly framed as self-interest and seldom in terms of the common good—whether such characterizations are correct or incorrect," they noted, "the public's experience of their leaders is biased toward attributions that induce mistrust" (Cappella & Jamieson, 1997, p. 142). The press is an "actor in today's political drama, conveying a steady stream of unambiguously negative cues about government and politics" (Neustadt, 1997, p. 97). Lost in strategic news coverage is the press' focus on adjudicating fact.

The reliance on horserace coverage and "he-said-she-said" reporting in campaign coverage as the standard narrative of campaigns lends itself to thinking about this type of news content in a cultivation framework. Because there is a steady and consistent narrative surrounding political campaigns, repeated exposure to such narratives may help shape the worldview of those exposed to it. Morgan and Shanahan (1992) found that heavy television viewers were politically apathetic and proposed that television may have a narcotizing effect (also see Lazarsfeld & Merton, 1948) and promote cynicism among the electorate. Therefore, exposure to campaign coverage and its focus on strategic framing may cultivate a sense of mistrust among the electorate. At the same time, politicians in fictional entertainment programs are frequently represented as corrupt and incompetent. While many viewers actively seek out campaign coverage, non-selective everyday viewing will also provide audiences with negative images of politicians.

For evidence, I turn to the 2004 presidential election. This election was particularly noted for horserace coverage and deceptive campaign techniques (see Jackson & Jamieson, 2007). This contest between incumbent president George W. Bush and Democratic Senator John Kerry focused primarily on leadership credentials and levels of trustworthiness. Senator Kerry was framed as a "flip-flopper." President Bush was attacked on his military service during the Vietnam War for allegedly receiving preferential treatment. Senator John Kerry campaigned on his war hero-status only to be undercut by the 527 group Swift Boat Veterans for Truth which explicitly attacked Kerry's leadership ability and his honesty.

For the analyses below I rely on the 2004 Annenberg Post Election Deception Survey of 3,400 voting age Americans conducted as part of the 2004 National Annenberg Election Survey. Political cynicism, for these first analyses, was not measured as a general lack of confidence in institutions as is usually done in political communication research. Instead, a more focused set of questions was used to tap respondents' beliefs that the presidential candidates were deceitful about each other's record. A measure of respondents' belief that candidates lie about each other was combined from two rotated and reverse-coded questions on the survey: "How often do you think John Kerry told the truth about George W. Bush's record?" and "How often do you think George W. Bush told the truth about John Kerry's record?—1) none of the time, 2) some of the time, and 3) all of the time." This combined variable was then dichotomized, where respondents who reported a belief that at least one of the candidates never told the truth received a score of one (30.1 per cent—16.0 percent believed that Kerry never told the truth and 18.9 percent believe that Bush never told the truth) and respondents who believed that both candidates always or sometimes told the truth received a score of zero (see Hardy, Jamieson, & Winneg, 2008 for additional analyses using this measure and dataset).

Table 2 reports a logistic regression model predicting the belief that candidates never tell the truth about the record of their competitors. Interestingly, exposure to 24-hour cable news and the Internet—the homes of partisan journalism—produced positive and significant relationships. Getting campaign news from either broadcast television or newspaper reading, however, was not significantly related to the dependent variable. Given the content differences between these media it makes sense as cable news and the Internet are often highlighted by partisan bickering. A study by Mutz and Reeves (2005) found that while mediated incivility in public discourse increased viewers' interest it also negatively affected levels of political trust. Another study by Mutz (2007) found that "in-your-face" televised discourse—found mostly on 24-hour cable news channels—tended to delegitimize political opposition and debate. Concerning the Internet, Sweetser and Kaid (2008) found that even though Internet users are more politically active than non-users "they remain cynical about elected officials" (p. 83).

A similar pattern appears when we look at the broader measure of political trust, using the 2008 NAES question: "Thinking about the federal government in Washington, how much of the time do you think you can trust the federal government to do what is right? 1) always, 2) most of the time, 3) some of the time, 4) or never." As reported in Table 3, those who saw campaign information on television and the Internet are more likely to distrust the federal government. On the other hand, newspaper readership produced the opposite pattern.

To further the point and triangulate results, an OLS regression model on data from a 2005 survey sponsored by the Annenberg Institutions of American Democracy Project (Table 4) produced similar findings regarding media use and levels of trust in the federal government. In this model, 24-hour cable news

Table 2. Logistic regression predicting the belief that presidential candidates always lie

| | B | S.E. | Odds Ratios |
|---|---|---|---|
| Female (1=yes, 0=no) | 0.019 | 0.081 | 1.019 |
| Age (in years) | 0.013 | 0.003 | 1.013*** |
| Black (1=yes, 0=no) | 0.303 | 0.142 | 1.354* |
| Education (in years) | -0.024 | 0.017 | 0.977 |
| Hispanic (1=yes, 0=no) | 0.028 | 0.160 | 1.028 |
| Republican (1=yes, 0=no) | 0.296 | 0.103 | 1.344** |
| Democrat (1=yes, 0=no) | 0.361 | 0.100 | 1.435*** |
| Ideology (1=very liberal, 5= very conservative) | -0.056 | 0.045 | 0.946 |
| Days got news from broadcast TV in past week | -0.032 | 0.016 | 0.969 |
| Days got news from 24 hour cable news channel in past week | 0.036 | 0.014 | 1.037** |
| Days got news from newspaper in past week | 0.018 | 0.015 | 1.018 |
| Days got news from Internet in past week | 0.065 | 0.020 | 1.067*** |

*Cox & Snell* $R^2$ *= .023*

*Nagelkerke* $R^2$ *= .033*

*N = 3,137*

*** $p < .001$, ** $p < .01$, * $p < .05$

Source: 2004 Annenberg Post Election Deception Survey

is broken out from general television news viewing and is significantly related to lower levels of trust.

A more specific measure of cynicism found on the 2008 NAES is a battery of questions designed to tap beliefs that Black public officials are more likely to support policies that favor Black communities and constituents: "Do you think Black elected officials are more likely to 1) Favor Blacks for government jobs over White applicants? 2) Support government spending that favors Blacks? 3) Give special favors to the Black community?" These items were measured on a four-point scale where 1 equals "strongly disagree" and 4 equals "strongly agree" and combined into a "favoritism scale" ($\alpha$ = .88).

Past research has shown that among other social reinforcing agents, television cultivates stereotypes of racial and ethnic minorities and dominantly portrays

Table 3. OLS regression predicting trust in federal government

| | B | S.E. | Standardized Beta |
|---|---|---|---|
| Female (1=yes, 0=no) | 0.002 | 0.011 | 0.002 |
| Age (in years) | 0.001 | 0.000 | 0.025** |
| Black (1=yes, 0=no) | 0.041 | 0.020 | 0.020* |
| Education (in years) | -0.006 | 0.002 | -0.026** |
| Hispanic (1=yes, 0=no) | -0.165 | 0.023 | -0.068*** |
| Republican (1=yes, 0=no) | -0.120 | 0.013 | -0.096*** |
| Democrat (1=yes, 0=no) | -0.100 | 0.013 | -0.084*** |
| Closely Following the Election (1= not closely at all, 4 = very closely) | -0.011 | 0.007 | -0.016 |
| Days saw campaign information on television in past week | 0.005 | 0.002 | 0.020* |
| Days saw campaign information on newspaper in past week | -0.005 | 0.002 | -0.027** |
| Days saw campaign information on the Internet in the past week | 0.005 | 0.002 | 0.025* |

$R^2 = .015$

$N = 11,271$

*** p < .001, ** p < .01, * p < .05

Source: 2008 National Annenberg Election Survey

Whiteness as the norm (Cummings, 1988; Mastro & Greenberg, 2000; Mastro & Robinson, 2000). Ramasubramanian (2010) wrote:

> Ingroup favoritism, the systematic tendency to privilege ingroup norms over outgroup ones, is aided by pervasive portrayals of Whiteness on television as law-abiding role models, in contrast to dehumanizing depictions of non-Whiteness as criminal and unmotivated. The simultaneous juxtaposing of Whiteness as normative along with non-Whiteness as inferior helps maintain the status quo by justifying discriminatory policies against subordinated racial groups and privileging benefits for dominant racial groups (p. 105).

Content analyses of news have found that African Americans are over-represented as criminals and Whites are mostly law-enforcers or victims (Mastro & Robinson, 2000; Ramasubramanian, 2010).

This ingroup/outgroup narrative was very salient during the 2008 presidential election. One of the more memorable moments during the 2008 primaries was

Table 4. OLS regression predicting trust in federal government

| | B | S.E. | Standardized Beta |
|---|---|---|---|
| Female (1=yes, 0=no) | -0.074 | 0.044 | -0.044 |
| Age (in years) | 0.001 | 0.001 | 0.013 |
| Black (1=yes, 0=no) | 0.115 | 0.071 | 0.045 |
| Education (in years) | 0.023 | 0.011 | 0.056* |
| Republican (1=yes, 0=no) | -0.385 | 0.057 | -0.220*** |
| Democrat (1=yes, 0=no) | -0.044 | 0.056 | -0.025 |
| Ideology (1=very liberal to 5=very conservative) | -0.057 | 0.023 | -0.071* |
| Political interest | -0.034 | 0.008 | -0.119*** |
| Days got news from broadcast TV in past week | -0.011 | 0.009 | -0.034 |
| Days got news from newspaper in past week | -0.010 | 0.008 | -0.034 |
| Days got news from 24 hour cable news channel in past week | 0.018 | 0.008 | 0.061* |
| Days got news from Internet in past week | 0.001 | 0.009 | 0.004 |

$R^2 = .078$

*N* = *1,338*

*** p < .001, ** p < .01, * p < .05

Source: Annenberg Democracy Project: Media Survey.

the emergence of incendiary recorded statements made by Obama's Chicago mentor and pastor, Reverend Wright. While the videos were replayed on news and went viral over the Internet during the primaries, the controversy lost traction after Obama's successful Philadelphia speech addressing Wright and race relations in the U.S. However, during the general election when Republican Vice Presidential nominee Sarah Palin was fond of saying that "Obama palled around with terrorists," the 527 group Our Country Deserves Better ran an ad that tried to activate the stereotype of the angry, resentment-filled Black man ("Too radical. Too risky.") and by implication one who is un-American and against the status quo. Although he had explicitly repudiated Wright's views, the spot implied that Obama shared them. "For 20 years, Barack Obama followed a preacher of hate," it began, as "hate, hate" appeared on a pictured film strip, followed by a picture of Wright preaching. Then a repetition of "hate."

Obama "said nothing as Wright raged against our country," asserted the spot. After Wright shouts "Not God bless America. God damn America," Obama is shown stating, "I don't think my church is particularly controversial." The ad then intercuts a clip of the pastor shouting, "U.S. of KKK-A." The spot closed with the claim, "Wright was his mentor, adviser, and close friend. For 20 years, Obama never complained until he ran for president." The same set of associations was the subject of ads by the Republican Federal Committee of Pennsylvania and the Judicial Confirmation Network.

Appearing in the last week before the election, a National Rifle Association Victory Fund spot showed a terrified woman in a bathrobe clutching a handgun in her darkened living room as the announcer ominously stated, "Imagine your child screaming in the middle of the night when a convicted felon breaks into your home. Worse, he comes back a second time. You use a firearm. Unbelievably, Barack Obama voted to make you the criminal." The clearest racial cue concluded the ad with a photo of Obama dressed in a suit and tie superimposed on prison bars, a juxtaposition that suggests that he is a white-collar criminal protecting the unseen villain whom race-based fears would cast as Black. "It's a true story and it gets worse," added the announcer. "Obama voted four times to deny citizens the right of self-protection even in their homes."

Other assertions during the 2008 election tried to define Obama's identity as an outsider, un-American criminal. Alleged connections to Franklin Raines, the embattled former head of the Federal National Mortgage Association, convicted former Detroit mayor Kwame Kilpatrick, and former Weatherman William Ayers pervaded the campaign. Additionally, rumblings over Obama's lack of an American flag lapel pin, a picture of him not putting his hand over his heart during the pledge of allegiance, and accusations that he was not born in the U.S. but in Kenya added to the narrative that Obama was an outsider.

As past research has shown, entertainment and news television foster an ingroup/outgroup status quo between Whiteness and non-Whiteness. As some campaign messages painted Obama as a member of the outgroup, the favoritism scale was included on the NAES to tap respondents' beliefs that Black elected officials are likely to promote policies that favor Black communities and constituents. Exposure to campaign information on television advanced this view (Table 5).

Cultivation is based on the premise of a shared mediated narrative and its influence on the "very process of humanization, the process that makes human beings out of *Homo sapiens*" (Gerbner, 1983–1984, p. 14). Therefore, to stay somewhat true to theoretical core of cultivation, these analyses should have been conducted with measures of overall exposure regardless of content. On the other hand, an important part of the process of theory refinement is the examination of genre-and content-specific media effects (see Morgan & Shanahan, 2010),

Table 5: OLS regression predicting the "favoritism scale"

| | B | S.E. | Standardized Beta |
|---|---|---|---|
| Female (1=yes, 0=no) | -0.411 | 0.030 | -0.073*** |
| Age (in years) | 0.016 | 0.001 | 0.092*** |
| Black (1=yes, 0=no) | -0.934 | 0.056 | -0.092*** |
| Education (in years) | -0.088 | 0.006 | -0.077*** |
| Hispanic (1=yes, 0=no) | 0.075 | 0.063 | 0.006 |
| Republican (1=yes, 0=no) | 0.654 | 0.037 | 0.106*** |
| Democrat (1=yes, 0=no) | -0.454 | 0.036 | -0.078*** |
| Closely Following the Election (1= not closely at all, 4 = very closely) | -0.117 | 0.020 | -0.033*** |
| Days saw campaign information on television in past week | 0.018 | 0.006 | 0.016** |

$R^2 = .064$

*N* = 33,597

*** p < .001, ** p < .01, * p < .05

Source: 2008 National Annenberg Election Survey

which adds to our understanding of how campaign information may cultivate political attitudes. Additionally, 24-hour cable news channels and the Internet as we know them today did not exist in any meaningful way when Gerbner and his team conducted their work on political attitudes.

It should be noted that the $R^2$ statistic for each model reported suggests that not much of the variance in the dependent variables is being explained by the independent variables combined, let alone by the media variables. Consequently, the influence of the media variables in predicting the dependent variables is actually quite small. However, the measures that are used in the analyses are bounded temporally. Moreover, the data employed are cross-sectional in nature and do not lend themselves to providing insight into the kind of long term cumulative media effects upon which the cultivation hypothesis is built. Therefore, in the quick snapshots of public opinion presented in this chapter the effect size may seem miniscule, but an aggregate inference of these small effects to one of a complete lifetime of exposure may actually suggest larger, more consequential media effects. Shanahan and Morgan (1999) surmised:

> Cultivation theory certainly accepts, and common sense predicts, that TV viewing will play a smaller statistical role than major demographic variables, so it is no surprise that the average cultivation relationship is less than .20. Also, television

> viewing tends to co-vary in significant ways with important demographic variables, so that tends to restrict the variance we can detect as well. Judged within those parameters and by the parameters of social science more generally, then, a significant and consistent relationship of .10 is something important, even though it is not a 'large' effect size. Particularly when one considers that TV viewing's effects are cumulative and repetitive, a relationship of .10 is something that can make a difference over time. Slow but consistent effects can also have noticeable and important influences. (p. 121)

Additionally, these analyses look at overall, sample-wide patterns only, with stringent multiple simultaneous controls and some of these associations may be substantially stronger within certain population segments.

## Other Areas of Political Communication Where Cultivation May Be Applied

Perhaps one of the most researched areas within the political communication sub-field is framing. Cultivation analysis definitely has a place in this area when we think of the idea of certain persistent frames presented in mediated content. One well-known contribution of Shanto Iyengar to the framing literature is his dichotomy between "episodic" versus "thematic" frames:

> The episodic news frame takes the form of a case study or event-oriented report and depicts public issues in terms of concrete instances (for example, the plight of a homeless person or a teenager drug user, the bombing of an airliner, or an attempted murder). The thematic frame, by contrast, places public issues in some more general or abstract context and takes the form of a 'takeout,' or a 'backgrounder,' report directed at general outcomes or conditions. (Iyengar, 1991, p. 14)

Iyengar (1991) also finds that episodic framing is much more abundant and consistent than thematic framing and that exposure to episodic framing leads viewers to an individualistic causal attribution of responsibilities compared to holding more systematic and structural forces accountable. Iyengar concludes that the dominance of episodic framing has systematically protected government and society from responsibility. Moreover, as empirically shown, Americans attribute deep-seated chronic problems such as poverty and crime to individuals and do not attribute responsibility to more structural forces such as economic or social conditions. Consistent with the assumptions underlying cultivation, Iyengar paints a picture of the news media as promoters of the status quo explained by a hegemonic model of communication. He argues that television news "operates in a systematic fashion to shape viewers' attributions of responsibility for political affairs in a way that tends to undermine the democratic norm of electoral accountability" (p. 141). In short, episodic framing allows political actors to ignore deep-seated social problems and issues. This type of broad cultural theorizing of persistent news frames is in line with the work of George Gerbner, both because of the focus on a broad media influence on shared experiences and because of its shaping of the cultural understanding of the political world. Moreover, both conclude that the lessons of media messages can be found in an end result that protects dominant commercial and political interests.

Another area of research where cultivation should be applied is the political socialization of youth. Gerbner et al. (1984) point this out and cite Conway, Wyckoff, Feldbaum, and Ahern's (1981) seminal work on the news media's impact on children's political socialization. Morgan and Shanahan's (1991) study of adolescents in Argentina also illustrates how cultivation theory can be applied to the political socialization of youth. Today's children spend more time than ever with media. According to the Kaiser Family Foundation, the amount of time young people spend with entertainment media has risen dramatically in recent years, and 8–18-year-olds spend an average of 7 hours and 38 minutes a day with entertainment media. This report also stated that because children multi-task they may actually spend up to 11 hours a day with media (Rideout, Foehr, & Roberts, 2010). In today's media environment, where political information is spread across social networks sites and blogs, and where politically charged comments posted in reference to seemingly apolitical content combine with adolescents' increased media use, the political narratives youths are exposed to will likely shape their long-term political identities and beliefs. Understanding these narratives and how they are affecting children is a daunting task that political communication scholars need to tackle but is true to the vision of the Cultural Indicators project.

Connected to socialization is the notion of selective exposure to partisan news content (see Stroud, 2008; Sunstein, 2007). In a world where conservatives turn to Fox News, Rush Limbaugh, and Redstate.com and liberals to MSNBC, NPR, and DailyKos, the political narrative is polarized. While selectivity may initially drive someone to one source or another, there is likely a reinforcement effect from consistent exposure to a central narrative that is either pro-right or pro-left. Using cultivation as a research framework may help explain this reiterative relationship. What does the fragmented media universe of today mean for the kind of political mainstreaming found in the studies from the 1980s noted above? By the data presented here, even the measure of attending to campaign news on TV still seems to go with choosing a "moderate" self-designation. But these effects are small. Television may be losing its mainstreaming effect because of niche media. Future research could also see if the convergence of liberals, moderates, and conservatives (and the erosion of the liberal position) still holds despite the fragmentation of audiences and channels.

As cable-news, talk radio, and the Internet foster selective exposure and ideological enclaves, today's political information environment is also marked by aggressive discourse and deception (Mutz, 2007; Jackson & Jamieson, 2007). The "in-your-face" combative nature of politics, which has always been present in the Senate Chamber and House Floor but mostly hidden from the public when there were only three networks, is now front and center and encouraged in the public sphere because of the cable talk news shows, talk radio, blogs, YouTube, and other public forums on the Internet. While ideological enclaves may be taking different sides on issues, a common narrative is not what they say but how they are saying it and a sense of political incivility may be cultivated in the electorate. Instead of thoughtful deliberation, uncivil name calling is becoming the political norm, which could have detrimental effects on decision and policy making.

One final point is one of methodology. Currently there are multiple research firms that collect Internet panel data from millions of respondents (e.g., Knowledge Networks, Polimetrix, etc.). This presents an opportunity for communication researchers to track respondents across long periods of time, allowing for analyses of cumulative media effects. While the analyses reported in this chapter are cross sectional in nature, a better design would be a within-subject analysis across many years and many data points in order to untangle how the complex processes of cultivation, reinforcement, and selectivity operate, and perhaps interact, over time.

## Notes

1. All three of the datasets analyzed for this chapter are available to the academic community at http://www.annenbergpublicpolicycenter.org/ResearchDataSets.aspx
2. Throughout this chapter, I rely on the NAES sample of 57,967 voting age adults living in the continental United States surveyed from December 17, 2007 to November 3, 2008 on a daily rolling cross-sectional design (see Romer et al., 2004). Because the survey is specifically designed to track shifts in public opinion across time, many questions were added and deleted throughout the survey's time in the field. In the analyses below I present multiple models with different sample sizes and different dates of collection due to the dynamic nature of the NAES codebook.
3. Exact question wording: "Generally speaking, would you describe your political views as: 1) Very conservative, 2) Somewhat conservative, 3) Moderate, 4) Somewhat liberal, or 5) Very liberal?" Moderates were coded as 1 and all other responses were coded as zero.
4. Exact question wording: "Thinking now about the past week, how many days did you see information on broadcast or cable television about the 2008 presidential campaign? This includes seeing programs on television, on the internet, your cellphone, iPod, or PDA."

## References

Bennett, W. L. (2001). *News: The politics of illusion* (4th ed.). New York: Longman.

Bennett, W. L., & Serrin, W. (2005). The watchdog role. In G. Overholser & K. H. Jamieson (Eds.), *Institutions of American democracy: The press* (pp. 169–188). Oxford: Oxford University Press.

Besley, J. C. (2006). The role of entertainment television and its interactions with individual values in explaining political participation. *Harvard International Journal of Press/Politics, 11*(2), 41–62.

Burroughs, J. E., Shrum, L. J., & Rindfleisch, A. (2002). Does television viewing promote materialism? Cultivating American perception of the good life. *Advances in Consumer Research, 29*, 442–443.

Cappella, J. N., & Jamieson, K. H. (1996). News frames, political cynicism, and media cynicism. *The Annals of the American Academy of Political and Social Science, 546*, 71–85.

Cappella, J. N., & Jamieson, K. H. (1997). *Spiral of cynicism: The press and the public good.* Oxford: Oxford University Press.

Conway, M. M., Wyckoff, M. L., Feldbaum, E., & Ahern, D. (1981). The news media in children's political socialization. *Public Opinion Quarterly, 45*, 164–178.

Cummings, M. (1988). The changing image of the Black family on television. *Journal of Popular Culture, 22*, 75–85.

Diefenbach, D. L., & West, M. D. (2007). Television and attitudes toward mental health issues: Cultivation analysis and the third-person effect. *Journal of Community Psychology, 35*(2), 181–195.

Gerbner, G. (1983–1984). Liberal education in the information age. *Current Issues in Higher Education, 39*(1), 14–18.

Gerbner, G., Gross, L., Morgan, M., & Signorielli, N. (1982). Charting the mainstream: Television's contributions to political orientations. *Journal of Communication, 32*(2), 100–127.

Gerbner, G., Gross, L., Morgan, M., & Signorielli, N. (1984). Political correlates of television viewing. *Public Opinion Quarterly, 48*(1), 283–300.

Glynn, C. J., Huge, M., Reineke, J. B., Hardy, B. W., & Shanahan, J. (2007). When Oprah intervenes: Political correlates of daytime talk show viewing. *Journal of Broadcasting & Electronic Media, 51*(2), 228–244.

Gross, L. (1984). The cultivation of intolerance: Television, Blacks, and gays. In G. Melischek, K. E. Rosengren, & J. Stappers (Eds.), *Cultural indicators: An international symposium* (pp. 345–363). Vienna, Austria: Verlag der Osterreichischen Akademie der Wissenschaften.

Hardy, B. W., Jamieson, K. H., & Winneg, K. (2008). Wired to facts: The utility of the internet in identifying deception during the 2004 US presidential campaign. In A. Chadwick & P. Howard (Eds.), *Handbook of internet politics.* (pp.131–143). New York and London: Routledge.

Iyengar, S. (1991). *Is anyone responsible?* Chicago: The University of Chicago Press.

Jackson, B., & Jamieson, K. H. (2007). *Un-spun: Finding fact in a world of disinformation.* New York: Random House.

Jamieson, K. H., & Cappella, J. N. (2008). *Echo chamber: Rush Limbaugh and the conservative media establishment.* New York: Oxford University Press.

Jamieson, K. H., & Hardy, B. W. (2007). Unmasking deception: The capacity, disposition, and challenges facing the press. In D. Graber, D. McQuail, & P. Norris (Eds.), *The politics of news: The news of politics* (2nd ed., pp. 117–138). Washington, DC: CQ Press.

Kenski, K., Hardy, B. W., & Jamieson, K. H. (2010). *The Obama victory: How media, money, and messages shaped the 2008 election.* New York: Oxford University Press

Lazarsfeld, P. F., & Merton, R. K. (1948). Mass communication, popular taste, and organized social action. In L. Bryson (ed.), *The communication of ideas* (pp. 95–118). New York: Harper.

Mastro, D. E., & Greenberg, B. S. (2000). The portrayal of racial minorities on prime time television. *Journal of Broadcasting & Electronic Media, 44,* 690–703.

Mastro, D. E., & Robinson, A. L. (2000). Cops and crooks: Images of minorities on prime-time television. *Journal of Criminal Justice, 28,* 385–396.

Morgan, M., & Shanahan, J. (1991). Television and the cultivation of political attitudes in Argentina. *Journal of Communication, 41*(1), 88–103.

Morgan, M., & Shanahan, J. (1992). Television viewing and voting 1972–1989. *Electoral Studies, 11*(1), 3–20.

Morgan, M., & Shanahan, J. (2010). The state of cultivation. *Journal of Broadcasting & Electronic Media, 54,* 337–355.

Mutz, D. C. (2007). Effects of "in-your-face" television discourse on perceptions of a legitimate opposition. *American Political Science Review, 101*(4), 621–635.

Mutz. D. C. & Reeves, B. (2005). The new videomalaise: Effects of televised incivility on political trust. *American Political Science Review, 99*(1), 1–15.

Neustadt, R. E. (1997). The politics of mistrust. In J. N. Nye, Jr., P. D. Zelikow, & D. C. King (Eds.), *Why people don't trust government* (pp. 197–202). Cambridge, MA: Harvard University Press.

Patterson, T. E. (1980). *The mass media election.* New York: Praeger.

Patterson, T. E. (1993). *Out of order: How the decline of political parties and the growing power of the news media undermine the American way of life.* New York: Knopf.

Pfau, M., & Kang, J. G. (1991). The impact of relational messages on candidate influence in televised political debates. *Communication Studies, 42,* 114–128.

Ramasubramanian, S. (2010). Television viewing, racial attitudes, and policy preferences: Exploring the role of social identity and intergroup emotions in influencing support for affirmative action. *Communication Monographs, 77*(1), 102–120.

Rideout, V. J., Foehr, U. G., & Roberts, D. F. (2010). *Generation $M^2$: Media in the lives of 8- to 18-Year-Olds.* A Kaiser Family Foundation Study: Henry J. Kaiser Foundation, Menlo Park, CA.

Romer, D., Kenski, K., Waldman, P., Adasiewicz, C., & Jamieson, K. H. (Eds.). (2004). *Capturing campaign dynamics: The National Annenberg Election Survey.* Oxford: Oxford University Press.

Sears, D. O., & Chaffee, S. H. (1979). Uses and effects of the 1976 debates: An overview of empirical studies. In S. Kraus (Ed.), *The great debates: Carter vs. Ford, 1976* (pp. 223–261). Bloomington, IN: Indiana University Press.

Shanahan, J., & McComas, K. A. (1999). *Nature stories: Depictions of the environment and their effects.* Cresskill, NJ: Hampton Press.

Shanahan, J., & Morgan, M. (1999). *Television and Its Viewers: Cultivation Theory and Research.* London: Cambridge University Press.

Shrum, L. J., Wyer, R. S., & O'Guinn, T. (1998). The effects of television consumption on social perceptions: The use of priming procedures to investigate psychological processes. *Journal of Consumer Research, 24*(4), 447–58.

Signorielli, N. (1989). Television and conceptions about sex-roles: Maintaining conventionality and the status quo. *Sex Roles, 21*(5/6), 341–360.

Stroud, N. J. (2008). Media use and political predispositions: Revisiting the concept of selective exposure. *Political Behavior, 30*(3), 341–366.

Sunstein, C. R. (2007). *Republic.com 2.0.* Princeton: Princeton University Press.

Sweetser, K. D., & Kaid, L. L. (2008). Stealth soapboxes: political information efficacy, cynicism and uses of celebrity weblogs among readers. *New Media & Society, 10*(1), 67–91.

Wattenberg, M. P. (1991). *The rise of candidate-center politics: Presidential elections of the 1980s.* Cambridge, MA: Harvard University Press.

# 7. Cultivation of Attitudes Toward Science

*Dominique Brossard & Anthony Dudo*

Science is largely an unobtrusive issue. Most citizens have little or no direct experience with scientific research, have never set foot in a lab, seldom visit a science center and have limited understanding of even basic scientific principles (U.S. Department of Education, 2006).

So, apart from our schooling, how do we learn about science? And how do our dispositions toward science sustain and change throughout our lives given our experiential distance from this topic? One primary source of the public's scientific information is the media (Allan, 2002; Gregory & Miller, 1998; Nelkin, 1995; National Science Board [NSB], 2010). As with other unobtrusive issues, the public, whether consciously or not, relies largely on the media for their understanding of, and attitudes toward, science. Brossard and Nisbet (2007) note: "When formal education in science ends, media become the most available and sometimes the only source for the public to gain information about scientific discoveries, controversies, events, and the work of scientists" (p. 9). With this scenario in mind, over the last few decades a growing body of research has examined how informational and entertainment media contribute to public understanding and opinion formation about science, and of specific scientific and environmental issues.

In this chapter, we provide an overview of the research that has explored links between the use of entertainment media and science-related outcomes for its viewers. More specifically, we focus on the studies grounded in cultivation analysis. Cultivation researchers study how exposure to the world of television contributes to viewers' conceptions about the real world (Signorielli & Morgan, 2009).

Cultivation analysis does not (as persuasion-based theoretical frameworks would imply) study direct effects from messages sent and received in the short term. Instead, it is interested in "broad patterns of relationships between the social consumption of media messages and stable, aggregate belief structures among large groups of people" (Shanahan & Morgan, 1999, p. 6). In short, cultivation analysis rests on the thesis that television's "socially constructed version of reality bombards all classes, groups, and ages with the same perspective at the same time," contributing to the cultivation of "shared conceptions of reality among otherwise diverse publics" (Signorielli & Morgan, 2009, p. 108)

Our chapter is divided into five sections. In the first, we provide a brief synopsis of the relationship between science and the public, covering general trends about public awareness, knowledge, and attitudes related to science. Our second section provides a review of research examining the cultivation of science attitudes. This review traces the history of science cultivation research from Gerbner and colleagues' earliest work in the early 1980s through work on the cultivation of science attitudes conducted during the 1990s. In the third section, we discuss the cultivation of science attitudes in the 21st century, highlighting changes in the media environment relevant to the context of science cultivation (e.g., the increased complexity of media content, the growing use of the Internet as an information source) and recent research on the cultivation of techno-scientific issues. The remaining two sections of our chapter focus on new directions in science-related cultivation research. Using an analysis of national survey data, the fourth section provides results from an analysis examining how the use of specific genres of TV programming contributes to individuals' general attitudes toward science. And the final section, in part based on our analysis, outlines numerous directions for future research on the cultivation of science attitudes.

## Science and the Public

The National Science Foundation has conducted, since 1979, a series of biannual surveys that have tracked, among numerous other variables, knowledge levels, understanding, and attitudes toward science among the American public. Known as the "Science and Engineering Indicators," results of these surveys show that levels of knowledge of basic scientific facts among the American public have traditionally been quite low. In 1988, out of 10 basic true/false knowledge-related questions, individuals were on average able to answer correctly 6.5 (NSB, 1989). Between 1992 and 2008, the dates for which comparable data were collected, the percentage of adults able to answer correctly all the questions included in the "factual knowledge scale" questions was still relatively low, although it increased from 59% to 64% (NSB, 2010).

Despite these relatively low knowledge levels, Americans have consistently been mostly positive about science. In 2008, a majority of Americans thought the benefits of science outweighed the risks, support for public spending on science was strong, and most of the public was confident in scientific leaders. These results are very similar to those obtained since 1992 (NSB, 2010).

Where do Americans hear about science? Until the late 1990s, Americans received most of their exposure to science content through television (as we will discuss in a later session, this has been changing in the last two decades). Indeed, television has been the primary source of information about science for most people since the late 1970s. From 1979 to 1999, the Science and Engineering Indicators consistently reported that Americans viewed a self-reported average of around 2.8 hours of television per day, and relied mainly on television for information about science (NSB, 2002). It therefore made sense to hypothesize a potential cultivation effect of entertainment television content on public attitudes toward science.

## Cultivation of Science Attitudes: A Review of the Early Research

The first formal cultivation study of science attitudes dates back to the mid-1980s, when George Gerbner and colleagues examined television's impact on perceptions of science. (Prior to receiving the grant funding this research, the team had conducted some pilot studies on the portrayal of science on television as well as some preliminary cultivation analyses focusing on science; see Gerbner, Gross, Morgan, & Signorielli, 1981.) Following the typical practice in the Cultural Indicators research program, the researchers first evaluated how science and scientists were depicted on television through a message system analysis. They showed that scientists appeared rarely on television, were mainly portrayed as "good" ("bad" scientists were, however, more numerous than "bad" doctors or law enforcers), and were more likely to be shown as "strange" characters ending up confronting death or failure. In line with the cultivation perspective, survey results showed that television's heavy viewers had attitudes consistent with the entertainment content identified through the message analysis and were less likely than individuals who watched less television to have positive attitudes toward science. And as "mainstreaming" would predict, relationships between television viewing and holding negative views about science were stronger for the individuals otherwise more predisposed to view science positively: the well-educated, more affluent, and younger (Gerbner, Gross, Morgan & Signorielli, 1985; Gerbner, 1987).

The 1990s and early 2000s saw little research specifically devoted to the study of public science attitudes from a cultivation perspective. However, scholarly examinations of the cultivation of environmental attitudes were increasingly appearing in the research literature. These studies (e.g., Holbert, Kwak, & Shah, 2003; McComas & Shanahan, 1999; Shanahan & McComas, 1999; Shanahan, Morgan, & Stenbjerre, 1997) showed that the world of television drama was one with few environmental problems. Consistent with the cultivation perspective, and since the environment was portrayed in relatively positive (or innocuous) terms on television, television exposure was negatively correlated to environmental concerns but not related to perceptions of specific threats to the environment.

## Moving Forward: Studying the Cultivation of Science Attitudes in the 21st Century

According to the 2000 Science and Engineering report, television and print were still seen as the most important sources of information about science in the late 1990s. However, large increases in Internet and computer use were also documented, as well as increasing concerns about an emerging "digital divide." By 2004, although television still led in terms of overall time spent with media, the Internet was clearly displacing traditional print sources for information about science and had become the primary venue for those actively seeking information. Science-related content on cable channels was significantly increasing, suggesting that potential exposure to science content was clearly much more diversified than in the prior two decades (the 2006, 2008, and 2010 reports later confirmed these trends; NSB, 2004, 2006, 2008, 2010). But although an increasing reliance on the Internet for science-related information is clear, some demographic differences are worthwhile noting. Although those who pay attention to science primarily on the Internet are diverse as far as age is concerned (with one-fourth between 18 and 34 years old), they tend to be more knowledgeable about science, highly educated, male, and slightly more diverse racially than those who rely on other media (Anderson, Brossard,& Scheufele, 2010). (The question of whether or not the Internet is contributing to gaps in science knowledge and to differences in science attitudes among diverse audiences is one worth asking, and we will discuss it later on.)

These changes in the media environment have important implications for cultivation research. First, the media landscape is far more complex than it was 10 years ago, and particularly more complex than when cultivation theory was formulated (see, for example, Jenkins, 2006). For instance, the existence of science-specific cable networks might mean that even casual heavy viewers of television will see more science-related images and messages than such audiences would have two decades ago. Second, and potentially due to the proliferation of television channels, television content is clearly far more multifaceted than it was in the mid-1980s. A review of the content analysis literature performed in 2002 suggests that images of scientists are not as uniform as Gerbner had originally concluded and that scientists are portrayed as unusual in both positive and negative ways (Nisbet et al., 2002). Specific entertainment television programming could therefore have multilevel direct and indirect effects on people's attitudes about science and the environment. And third, cultivation processes may be taking place through Internet platforms as well as through traditional television use.

Consistent with these developments, the first decade of the 2000s saw the birth of studies proposing more refined approaches to the potential cultivation effects of entertainment television on attitudes toward science. Acknowledging the complexity of modern science, researchers began exploring potential cultivation effects for specific scientific developments while taking into account potential other influences. For instance, after controlling systematically for social background factors including education and political ideology, Besley and Shanahan (2005) found that entertainment and news viewing were associated with differing perceptions of agricultural biotechnology. More importantly, heavier entertainment television viewers were more likely to support agricultural biotechnology, a finding that was contrary to previous cultivation research suggesting that entertainment TV's effect on science attitudes is negative. Besley and Shanahan concluded that TV use may encourage people to process information heuristically, to rely on mental shortcuts and peripheral information rather than engaging in close examination of a topic. In this case, audiences' strong general belief in the promise of science (shared by most Americans) may likely serve as a natural shortcut in forming opinions about agricultural biotechnology.

Noting that little research has examined media depictions of science across different types of media and their effects on perceptions of science, Nisbet et al. (2002) proposed a media effects model centered on the interrelationships between different types of media use (including science TV and general TV), two types of science knowledge (factual and procedural), and belief in either the promise of science or reservations about its impact on society. Although heavy television viewers were more likely to hold reservations about science, they also expressed stronger beliefs in its promise. This showed how "the dual nature of depictions of science and technology appears to play out" (p. 600). Nisbet et al.'s innovation in terms of cultivation research was to look at science knowledge as a mediating variable. Television viewing was negatively correlated with both "procedural" science knowledge (about science as a mode of inquiry, what it means to study something scientifically) and "factual" science knowledge (about terms, concepts, and some basic scientific facts). Greater factual and procedural knowledge were both associated with having fewer reservations about science. The association between amount of television viewing and holding reservations about science was mediated by knowledge. That is, the data suggested that heavier television viewing goes with less knowledge about science, and that lower levels of knowledge in turn tend to heighten reservations about science.

Dudo et al. (2011) provide the most recent report on the depictions of scientists in prime-time television programming, with an analysis of entertainment television aired between 2000 and 2008. The study identifies several key trends. First, scientists rarely appear in prime-time programming: Only 1% of prime-time characters with occupations are portrayed as scientists. Second, when scientists are portrayed, they are most often White. Third, scientists are considerably more likely to be categorized as "good" (81%) than as bad (3%), although science is sometimes portrayed as one of the more violent professions (in terms of violence and victimization, 3.2% of scientists kill others, compared to 2.2% of medical personnel and 2.5% of lawyers). The authors contextualize these findings, noting that the results extend what Gerbner et al. found in the mid-1980s but that their empirical findings are at odds with the common claim that entertainment television consistently depicts scientists in a negative light. Also, in contrast to earlier studies, overall time spent viewing television was not found to be significantly related to negative attitudes toward science as early studies had suggested. Television use, however, does appear to displace the use of other media that would lead to higher levels of science knowledge and that would contribute both directly and indirectly to more positive attitudes toward science. And more importantly, the relationship between television use and attitudes toward science is different among audience groups. Among people without college science experience, heavy television use is associated with more positive views about science. Conversely, among people with college science experience, heavy television use is associated with more negative views about science. This finding holds after controlling for other demographic variables as well as science knowledge (Dudo et al., 2011).

Research in the last decade also illustrates that exposure to specific types of entertainment television programming can be related to specific attitudes about science and the environment. For instance, viewing televised nature documentaries predicts individuals' propensity to exhibit behaviors that are favorable to the environment (Holbert et al., 2003). As noted above, exposure to dramas and situation comedies is related to support for agricultural biotechnology (Besley & Shanahan, 2005), while exposure to science documentaries is related to support for embryonic stem cell research (Nisbet & Goidel, 2007) and greater belief in both scientific promise and scientific reservations (Nisbet et al., 2002). Recent findings also suggest that exposure to science fiction and religious programs may influence attitudes toward science. Specifically, viewing science fiction shows (e.g., *The X-Files*) predicts support for therapeutic cloning, while watching religious programming (e.g., *The 700 Club*) predicts more negative beliefs about embryonic stem cell research (Nisbet & Goidel, 2007).

Following up on these findings and acknowledging the potential conflicting views of science and the environment depicted on different television channels, Dahlstrom and Scheufele (2010) stressed the importance of "exposure diversity." They concluded that beyond the amount of television viewed, and after controlling for several individual differences, the diversity of television channels accessed is a factor that explains the cultivation of concern about environmental risks. Exposure diversity should therefore be taken into account when examining the cultivation of science and environmental attitudes (Dahlstrom & Scheufele, 2010), as well as in other areas of cultivation research.

In sum, recent research supports the idea that exposure to entertainment television contributes to public attitudes about science but also suggests that these effects occur in complex ways that often cut against conventional assumptions and earlier findings. Although the fragmentation of the media landscape and the importance of the online environment are often acknowledged, most of this research has, with a few exceptions exploring attitudes toward specific scientific innovations, measured exposure and/or attention to undifferentiated media television content. While this approach is consistent with the traditional operationalization of "television exposure" used in cultivation research, it also limits our understanding of how a wider array of media content might influence the public's perceptions of science. It also does not allow for an exploration of the potential mediating role specific entertainment content might play in the cultivation of science-related values, orientations, and science attitudes.

## A Pilot Study: Exploring the Cultivating Effects of Three Types of Entertainment Programs

In an effort to broaden our understanding of the relationship between entertainment media use and attitudes toward science while taking into account the reality of today's entertainment televisual landscape, we conducted a pilot study to explore how specific types of television entertainment programs might influence science attitudes, either through direct or indirect links. Notably, we were interested in media's potential mediating role between various value predispositions and attitudes toward science.

### *Rationale for the Study*

Different genres of entertainment programming depict the epistemological potency of science differently and could therefore cultivate a variety of different attitudes toward science. We were particularly interested in three specific genres of entertainment television—religious, science fiction, and pro-science dramas—each of which has a large and loyal audience. "Pro-science dramas" are fictional programs whose overall content tends to depict science as well suited to solving most of the problems encountered in daily life. In these shows, science is the means through which questions are commonly answered, problems solved, and/or catastrophes averted. An example of this type of programming is *ER*, which shares with viewers the practice of science by showing its tests, procedures, vocabulary, and rhetoric (Gregory & Miller, 1998), and how the scientific practice of medicine can solve complex health issues. In fact, one experimental study found that viewers of an *ER* episode gained substantial short-term awareness of important health issues (Kaiser Family Foundation, 1997). Another example is *CSI* (*Crime Scene Investigation*), which depicts the practice of science in a forensic context and routinely illustrates how science is used to solve crimes and help justice prevail. In both shows, science is depicted as a positive force in the world.

On the opposite end of the spectrum, "religious programming" portrays religion, not science, as the key to solving questions and alleviating problems. Whereas *CSI* and *ER* often depict science as a purveyor of truth and an efficient cure for life's uncertainties, a program such as *Touched by an Angel* portrays religion and spirituality as fulfilling these same roles and depicts religion as omniscient. In sum, pro-science dramas and religious programs, in general, seem to exhibit divergent viewpoints on the epistemological potency of science.

The third type of programming, "science-fiction programming," offers a range of images regarding science, from negative to positive. Science fiction programs often depict science negatively (Basalla, 1976; Turney, 1998). For example, some critics (including scientists, such as Richard Dawkins) argue that science fiction programming (e.g., *The X-Files*) depicts "mystical speculation" as more capable of explaining extraordinary events than science (Nisbet et al., 2002, p. 585). At the same time, science fiction programs often portray science in a positive light. For example, Banks and Tankel (1990) argue that science fiction programs designed for prime-time television (e.g., *Star Trek*) depict scientific technology as socially beneficial and as a means to secure a positive, stable future. Other scholars contend that shows like *The X-Files* promote important characteristics of science and suggest that teachers use these shows to spur interest in scientific concepts among their students (Dhingra, 2003; Simon, 1999). In sum, it seems that the omniscience of science is depicted inconsistently in science fiction programs.

Clearly, these three types of television entertainment programs seem to provide varying depictions of scientific omniscience. The extent to which they cultivate different attitudes toward science among their viewers is an empirical question. And as discussed earlier, potential cultivation effects do not take place in a vacuum. A useful framework to think of other potential influences on cultivating effects is the O-S-O-R model (Markus & Zajonc, 1985).

The O-S-O-R model takes into account that individuals' values, orientations, cognitions, and so on, interact with their media experiences en route to their social responses (McLeod, Kosicki, & McLeod, 2002). It acknowledges that individuals are more active in their media consumption and provides a means through which to link media consumption and media effects (McQuail, 2005). It assumes that—beyond basic demographic and socioeconomic variables—audiences bring two types of orientations to the table. The first set of orientations (the first "O") are the long-term, stable predispositional values that provide the context in which people use and process media content (the communication stimulus "S"). The second-order intervening orientations (the second "O") potentially mediate or moderate the links between media and the final outcome variable or response (the "R"), in this case attitudes toward science.

Beyond the three specific types of entertainment programs presented above, the model tested in our pilot study includes one pair of first-order orientations (religiosity and ideology) and one pair of second-order orientations (science knowledge and trust in science).

**First-order orientations: Religiosity and ideology**. Individuals often use heuristics such as value predispositions (e.g., religion, ideology, etc.) when forming attitudes toward many issues (Fiske & Taylor, 1991) and particularly scientific issues. In other words, individuals will likely use their ideological predispositions as cues when interpreting media content and defining their attitudes toward science. With science and religion providing different paradigms for understanding the nature of the world, the interplay between religious beliefs and attitudes toward science has always been complex. More specifically, research has shown that citizens can use their religious beliefs to make sense of what they see in mass media regarding scientific issues. In particular, individuals can use their religious values as perceptual filters through which to accept arguments that are consistent with their religious values and dismiss those that are not (Brossard, Scheufele, Kim, & Lewenstein, 2009; Scheufele, 2006a, 2006b). Ideology also has been shown to play an important role in shaping science-related attitudes (Brossard & Nisbet, 2007; Ho, Brossard, & Scheufele, 2008; Nisbet, 2005).

**Second-order orientations: Science knowledge and trust in science.** As discussed earlier, the role science knowledge may play in cultivation is likely to be complex. Heavier television viewing goes with less knowledge about science, and lower levels of knowledge in turn means heightened reservations about science (Nisbet et al., 2002). Television use does also appear to displace the use of other media that would lead to higher levels of science knowledge and that would contribute both directly and indirectly to more positive attitudes toward science (Dudo et al., 2011). It seems therefore important to include levels of knowledge in a model exploring potential cultivation effects of specific television genres on attitudes toward science.

Finally, levels of trust in science may have an important role to play. Research has shown that trust strongly influences how the public regards science (Gregory & Miller, 1998; Wynne, 1995). Especially in the absence of scientific knowledge, trust is a heuristic shortcut that enables individuals to make sense of the complex world of science as depicted in entertainment media. For instance, trust in particular scientific institutions is a more significant factor than general knowledge in explaining support for agricultural biotechnology applications (Brossard & Nisbet, 2007).

With this in mind, our pilot study examined the extent to which exposure to pro-science dramas, religious programming, and science fiction programming interacted with value predispositions (religion and ideology), science knowledge, and trust in science, in the cultivation of science attitudes. In order to test the potential links between television entertainment programming and attitudes toward science in an externally valid fashion, it was necessary to test these links relative to informational science news use. Television science news use was therefore controlled in our comprehensive model in order to provide a real-world test of the interplay between these three types of entertainment programming and the other variables in the model. Specifically, our model tests whether exposure to religious entertainment television programs is related to negative science attitudes, and whether exposure to pro-science dramas and televised science news is related to positive attitudes about science.

In addition, our model explores the question: In what ways are the three specific types of television programming—religious, science fiction, and pro-science dramas—related to value predispositions, televised science news use, science knowledge, and trust in science, to explain attitudes toward science?

### *Sources of Evidence*

To get a sense of how religious entertainment, pro-science drama, science fiction, and news programming on television affect scientific attitudes, along with other orientation variables, we relied on a three-wave national panel survey conducted in February 2002, November 2004, and June/July 2005.[1] The waves asked the same questions in all years, with some additional questions added to Waves 2 and 3. A benefit of this multi-wave panel design is that it enables analyses in which the explanatory variables are not measured within the same social context as the outcome variables of interest (Bartels, 1999). For example, our exogenous and endogenous variables (i.e., ideology, religiosity, television entertainment media, television science news, science knowledge, and trust in science) were measured in the first two survey waves, and our criterion variable (attitude toward science) was measured in the third wave. While this design does not enable causal claims about the relationships among the variables, it does help control for the potential reverse causation commonly associated with cross-sectional surveys since it measures variables at different points in time, and it controls for potential intervening and spurious factors (Kendall & Lazarsfeld, 1950). In addition, we controlled for four standard demographic variables: age, sex, education, and income.[2]

Wave 1 of the survey included two first-order orientations (i.e., value predispositions) and entertainment media exposure. The value predispositions included were ideology (political affiliation) and religiosity (whether religion is an important part of life). The three entertainment exposure variables were *exposure to pro-science television dramas*, which included *ER* and *CSI*, *religious television programs*, which included *Touched by an Angel* and a question measuring "other religious programs," and *science fiction television programs*, or *The X-Files* and *Star Trek: Enterprise*.

Nielsen Media Research Ratings for February 2002 reveal that these genre-specific shows were among the most popular in their categories at the time of data collection. While the pro-science drama programs (*ER* and *CSI*) had higher program ratings than the religious and sci-fi programs used in this study, these programs still had high ratings when compared to competing shows in the same genres. Although we may not have included an extensive catalogue of television shows, the shows included in our analysis reached a large number of viewers. More importantly, our study also has unique advantages over other comparable data sets (e.g., the General Social Survey, National Science and Engineering Indicators, etc.) that do not include measures of entertainment media use. And it is reasonable to assume that, if anything, more reliable multi-item television entertainment programming measures would produce stronger overall effects than the ones observed with the measure we used.

Wave 2 included a science television news media exposure variable and two second-order orientation variables: trust in science and level of scientific knowledge. Exposure to *televised news stories about science* was assessed using two measures, one asking respondents to indicate how many days in the last week they watched news stories related to science, technology, and medicine and the other asking respondents how much attention they paid to stories related to science, technology, and medicine. *Trust in scientists* was measured by asking respondents how much they agree or disagree with the statement: "Scientists know best what is good for the public." *Scientific knowledge* was measured using five items: (1) "Light travels faster than sound," (2) "Antibiotics kill viruses as well as bacteria," (3) "Adult stem cells are used to develop treatment for disease," (4) "Electrons are smaller than atoms," and (5) "Stem cells can only be developed from human embryos."

Wave 3 of the survey measured *attitude toward science* by asking participants how much they agree with the statements: "Overall science does more harm than good" and "We depend too much on science and not enough on faith."

## *Relationships Between Science Television Programming and Orientations with Attitudes Toward Science*

Of the three different types of entertainment programming, only religious programming had a main effect on attitudes toward science (see Table 1 for the details of the hierarchical OLS regression analysis). People who had watched more religious programs tended to have less positive attitudes toward science, which we expected. However, neither pro-science dramas nor science fiction programming were significantly related to the criterion variable as we had anticipated. Use of televised science news had a main effect on attitudes toward science: People who watched more science news had more positive attitudes toward science.

Regarding the second-level orientation variables, people who had more trust in scientists also had more favorable attitudes toward science. Science knowledge, however, had no significant main effect on attitudes toward science.

Table 1. Hierarchical multiple regression predicting positive attitudes toward science

| | Total effects | Model 1 | Model 2 | Model 3 | Model 4 | Model 5 |
|---|---|---|---|---|---|---|
| Block 1: Demographics | | | | | | |
| Age | -.06* | -.03 | .03 | .04 | .04 | .04 |
| Sex (female=1) | -.07* | -.06 | .00 | .00 | .01 | .01 |
| Education | .25*** | .18*** | .17*** | .16*** | .14*** | .14*** |
| Income | .26*** | .18*** | .16*** | .14*** | .13*** | .13*** |
| Incremental $R^2$ (%) | | 9.8*** | | | | |
| Block 2: Value Predispositions | | | | | | |
| Ideology (liberal high) | .20*** | | .15*** | .14*** | .13*** | .13*** |
| Religiosity | -.32*** | | -.30*** | -.25*** | -.25*** | -.24*** |
| Incremental $R^2$ (%) | | | 11.6*** | | | |
| Block 3: Television Entertainment Programming use | | | | | | |
| Pro-science entertainment programming | .03 | | | .04 | .03 | .03 |
| Religious entertainment programming | -.15*** | | | -.15*** | -.15*** | -.15*** |
| Science fiction entertainment programming | .01 | | | .01 | .00 | .00 |
| Incremental $R^2$ (%) | | | | 2.0*** | | |

| | Total effects | Model 1 | Model 2 | Model 3 | Model 4 | Model 5 |
|---|---|---|---|---|---|---|
| Block 4: Science television News use | | | | | | |
| Exposure and attention paid to science television news | .13*** | | | | .13*** | .12*** |
| Incremental $R^2$ (%) | | | | | 1.4*** | |
| Block 5: Knowledge and Trust | | | | | | |
| Trust in science | .07* | | | | | .07* |
| Science knowledge | .01 | | | | | .00 |
| Incremental $R^2$ (%) | | | | | | .06* |
| Total $R^2$ (%) | | | | | | 25.04* |

NOTE: $N$ = 1,073. Cell entries for the total effects column are before-entry betas and are equivalent to zero-order correlations. The remaining cell entries are standardized regression coefficients.
*$p$<.05, **$p$<.01, $p$<.001***

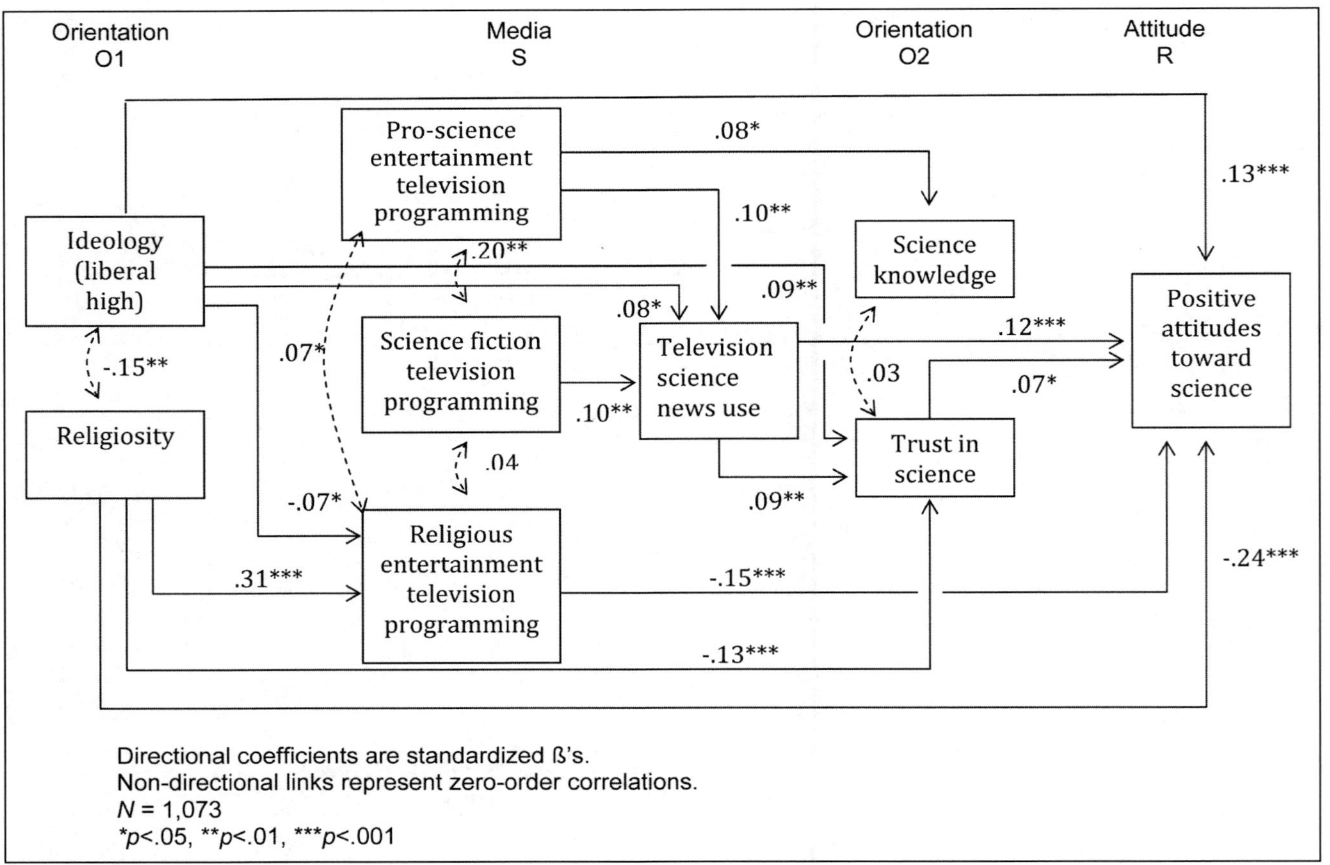


Figure 1. Path analysis exploring mediating links

As a second step and in order to explore more in depth the processes linking the variables in our model we also tested a regression path model against our data (see Figure 1). More particularly, this approach allowed us to explore our research question in greater detail.[3] Demographic variables were included in the path analysis as controls but are not presented in Figure 1.

As the figure shows, the relationship between religiosity and attitudes toward science worked in part through exposure to religious programming. Thus, watching religious programming contributes to religious individuals' negative perceptions of science, beyond other potential influences. Exposure to science fiction and pro-science programming was not directly linked to attitudes toward science. Although exposure to pro-science dramas was linked to higher levels of scientific knowledge, consistent with the original regression model, there was no relationship between science knowledge and attitudes toward science.

Interestingly, indirect links that were not apparent in the initial regression analysis were significant in the path analysis. In particular, exposure to televised science news linked a number of endogenous variables to the criterion variable. People who watched pro-science dramas were more likely to watch science news and, in turn, were more likely to have positive attitudes toward science. Individuals who watched science fiction programs were also more likely to watch science news, and, consequently, they too were more likely to have positive attitudes toward science.

While there was no relationship between science news use and science knowledge, the relationship between ideology and attitudes toward science worked in part through science news use. Liberals who viewed science news were more likely to have positive attitudes toward science.

The relationship between religiosity and attitudes toward science also worked in part through trust in scientists. Religiosity had both a direct effect on attitudes toward science and an indirect effect on attitudes toward science through trust in scientists. This result suggests that (mis)trust of scientists contributes to religious individuals' negative perceptions of science.

In sum, the findings of our pilot study suggest that exposure to different types of entertainment programming can cultivate different attitudes toward science through complex mechanisms that involve reliance on value predispositions, and potential indirect effects involving sciences news exposure, knowledge, and trust in science. Building on these findings, our final section offers some suggestions for research directions in the cultivation of science attitudes.

## Suggested Future Research Directions

### *Do More Empirical Content Analysis*

As our review suggests, it is important to note that there is a paucity of recent content analytic studies examining entertainment media's messages about scientists and science (Dhingra, 2003; Lewenstein, 2001). And although Dudo et al. (2011) examined television portrayals of scientists, they did not analyze portrayals of science itself. How scientists themselves are portrayed (as done in other studies) is a useful starting point but is obviously only part of the picture. As discussed in the previous section, different types of programming are likely to present science in very different light. Although future research should empirically test the validity of the types of television programs we examined in our pilot study, we believe that the categories we used depict scientific omniscience in varying and distinguishable ways and see them as a first step in a research program that should explore dimensions of entertainment television use in a more granular fashion.

It is also worth reflecting on the wider implications of some of the content studies reviewed in this chapter. It has been assumed for decades that entertainment media overwhelmingly portrayed science and scientists negatively and therefore contributed to a potential lack of public support for science (this view has been publicized in popular books such as Mooney & Kirshenbaum, 2009, or Perkowitz, 2007). This type of assumption has led to the creation by the National Academy of Sciences of The Science and Entertainment Exchange, a program aiming to improve depictions of science and scientists in television and film. While it is true that early cultivation studies suggested a negative contribution of television's portrayals of scientists to public attitudes (e.g., Gerbner et al., 1985; Gerbner, 1987), studies such as Dudo et al. (2011) would argue differently. Televised portrayals of scientists, though still rare, are nowadays mostly positive on network television. Moreover, Dudo et al. (2011) not only did not find support for a negative relationship between television use and attitudes toward science, they also showed that heavy television use can in some cases enhance attitudes toward science for people who share certain common experiences, such as few science classes in college. And this leads to our second, and important, suggestion.

### *Cultivation Should Be Tested in Complex Models*

As illustrated by some of the studies discussed in our chapter and exemplified by our pilot study, the cultivation of science attitudes is likely to take place through complex processes that should be analyzed with appropriate statistical techniques. Notably, it seems clear that future research needs to consider television viewing as at least a double-edged sword: television, it seems, has the potential to influence views of science through direct symbolic annihilation (as shown in previous cultivation research), and/or through displacement. We believe that these mechanisms should be explored in more detail.

### *The Role of Science Knowledge as a Mediator*

Although our pilot study did not find evidence that science knowledge is a mediator between entertainment media exposure and attitudes toward science, other studies have suggested that it is. Finding support for the displacement hypothesis (as did Nisbet et al., 2002) suggests that the potential mediating role of knowledge should be an important part of cultivation research dealing with attitudes toward science. Heavier television viewing can mean less knowledge about science, and lower levels of knowledge in turn tend to heighten reservations about science (Nisbet et al., 2002). Television use does also appear to displace the use of other media that would lead to higher levels of science knowledge and that would contribute both directly and indirectly to more positive attitudes toward science (Dudo et al., 2011). On the other hand, the results of our pilot study complement a growing body of research that shows people often form their science-related attitudes regardless of their level of scientific knowledge (Brossard et al., 2009). As such, these results further substantiate a "cognitive miser" model of information processing, which suggests that people often use cognitive shortcuts (e.g., value predispositions) when formulating their perspectives on science-related issues (Brossard et al., 2009; Ho et al., 2008).

### *Controlling for Demographics and Value Predispositions (Ideology, Religiosity, Deference to Scientific Authority)*

Our pilot study makes a number of initial contributions to our understanding of how values provide the context for media effects on science attitudes, and how the links between television use and attitudes are potentially mediated by trust and levels of knowledge. First, religiosity and ideology played significant roles in shaping attitudes toward science. Conservatives and religious individuals had more negative attitudes toward science. Together, these two value variables explained the largest amount of variance in science attitudes (nearly 12%). These findings corroborate a growing body of science communication research that has found these same relationships. From the second-order orientations, trust in science also had a significant main effect on science attitudes. Individuals who had more trust in science had more positive attitudes toward science. This result is consistent with past research that showed that trust in science institutions was a significant predictor of support for agricultural biotechnology (Brossard & Nisbet, 2007; Priest, 2001). It should be noted that Dudo et al. (2011) partially controlled for the potential influence of value predispositions when attempting to identify the potential cultivation effects of television on attitudes toward science.

### *Expand Cultivation Analysis to Incorporate Exposure to Differentiated Media Content*

With the diversification of today's televisual content, it will be extremely important to integrate exposure to specific content (either online or on traditional television) in cultivation research. We discussed earlier how heavier genre-specific television viewing can influence perceptions of science and specific scientific issues. The traditional cultivation approach focusing on overall exposure to the system of televised messages may be outdated. Instead, as our pilot study suggests, more micro-level approaches that explore how different genres of television programming (while controlling for potential confounding influences of traditional science news use on television) can influence perceptions of science in different ways for different people may be more appropriate in the case of science. Our pilot study shows that television entertainment programs with different portrayals of scientific omniscience had significant links to general attitudes toward science. In particular, even after controlling for religious and ideological predispositions and informational science television use, heavier viewers of religious programs had significantly more negative attitudes toward science. Moreover, watching these religious programs went with lower levels of trust, which may further undermine respondents' attitudes toward science. This finding substantiates the *a priori* assumption that religious entertainment television shows might not depict science as beneficially omniscient, and, moreover, that this depiction likely reinforces any negative science-related attitudes its viewers might have. Our results also speak to media consumption and effects; people for whom religion provided more guidance were more inclined to watch these religious programs—most likely because the content was consistent with their beliefs—and this consumption pattern was connected with science attitudes that are consonant with these beliefs. This is not to say that religious programming is inherently anti-science, or that science and religion are inherently incompatible. Rather, our findings suggest that preferred communication channels and personal predispositions have a combined effect for viewers and produce some of the outcomes observed in our analyses.

Conversely, science fiction programs and pro-science dramas had no main effect on attitudes toward science. However, they were both connected to science attitudes through science news use. Our path analysis revealed that these two types of entertainment media were indirectly linked to positive attitudes toward science through use of televised science news (measured in a later wave). This shows that televised science news is not the only televised media format that has the potential to cultivate positive attitudes toward science. Use of pro-science dramas and science fiction programs, in conjunction with use of science news, also can predict positive attitudes toward science.

Overall, these media-related findings legitimize the notion that both the use of specific television entertainment programs and science news use should be considered in future research that has a goal of assessing the cultivation of science attitudes, more particularly in light of the viewing patterns of the American population. Television continues to be the primary source of science news and information for the American public (NSB, 2010). Television entertainment programs (e.g., *CSI*) have considerably more viewers than informational science programming and have the inherent potential to bring science to widespread, heterogeneous audiences (NSB, 2008). But the potential cultivation effects of online sources should not be underestimated. This leads to our last suggestion.

### *Analyze Science Exposure Through Internet Channels and Develop More Sophisticated Measures*

Last but not least, it should be stressed that although television is still a dominant media source for the vast majority of Americans (who spend a great deal of time watching television every day), time spent viewing online videos on websites such as YouTube and Hulu is growing exponentially (Global Information Industry Center, 2009). Individuals are therefore likely to be choosing their viewing content more actively than a decade ago by turning to the Internet to watch their favorite shows, independently of when they were aired in the first place. Teenagers spend countless hours on YouTube watching short movies likely to depict science in a specific way. And numerous searches performed on the Internet expose users to a variety of portrayals of science through processes that were unthinkable two decades ago and are just starting to be unveiled (Anderson et al., 2010; Ladwig et al., 2010).

The cultivation of science attitudes through Internet use may therefore be different than for straightforward television exposure. Indeed, in the recent study by Dudo and colleagues, Internet use was a significant predictor of positive science attitudes, directly and through an increase of scientific knowledge (Dudo et al., 2011). This result, along with the aforementioned shifts in media consumption, indicate that cultivation research will have to take the Internet into account in the future, and rely on sophisticated exposure measures for this medium.

# Notes

1. The data collection was carried out by Synovate on behalf of DDB-Chicago, a subsidiary of the OmnicomMediaGroup, Inc. A stratified quota sampling method was used to generate the initial sample of 5,000 respondents for the 2002 "Life Style Study" (hereafter known as "Wave 1"). A total of 3,580 responses was returned in Wave 1 thereby yielding a response rate of 71.6%. These same individuals was re-contacted in November 2004 (hereafter known as "Wave 2") with another custom questionnaire. As a result of panel erosion since Wave 1 was mailed, 2,450 questionnaires were mailed. A total of 1,484 responses was returned, yielding a response rate of 60.1% and a panel retention rate of 41.4%. Individuals who completed the 2004 survey were contacted again in June/July 2005 (hereafter known as "Wave 3"). A total of 1,446 questionnaires was mailed as a result of panel erosion since Wave 2
2. Respondents' *age* was measured as a continuous variable ($M$ = 54.3, $SD$ = 14.9). Respondents' *sex* was a dichotomous variable with male coded 0 and female coded 1 (60.9%). The *education level* of respondents was a seven-point ordinal measure ranging from "attended elementary school" (coded 1) to "attended 5–8 year graduate school" (coded 7) ($M$ = 5.0, $SD$ = 1.2). Last, respondents' *annual household income* was assessed using an eight-point ordinal measure ranging from "under $20,000" (coded 1) to "$100,000 or more" (coded 8) ($M$ = 4.1, $SD$ = 2.3). The data representing these variables came from Wave 1 of the survey.
3. In an effort to provide the most rigorous investigation of our research questions, we used the MPLUS software program (Muthen & Muthen, 2007) to test a structural equation model against our data. The results of the structural model corroborated the results of the regression path model and provided us with model fit statistics. The Root Mean Square Error of Approximation, a measure of approximate fit proposed by Browne and Cudeck (1993) and considered to be a more realistic test of model fit than other indicators (see Kaplan, 2000), showed the model had fair approximate fit ($RMSEA$ = 0.05, $CI$: 0.049—0.066, $SRMR$ = 0.045).

# References

Allan, S. (2002). *Media, risk and society*. Philadelphia, PA: Open University Press.

Anderson, A. A., Brossard, D., & Scheufele, D. A. (2010). The changing information environment for nanotechnology: Online audiences and content. *Journal of Nanoparticle Research, 12*(4), 1083–1094.

Banks, J., & Tankel, J. D. (1990). Science as fiction: Technology in prime time telelvision. *Critical Studies in Mass Communication, 7*, 24–36.

Bartels, L. M. (1999). Panel effects in the American National Election Studies. *Political Analysis, 8*(1), 1–20.

Basalla, G. (1976). Pop science: The depiction of science in popular culture. In G. Holton & W. Blanpied (Eds.), *Science and its public* (pp. 261–178). Boston: Beacon.

Besley, J. & Shanahan, J. (2005). Media attention and exposure in relation to support for agricultural biotechnology. *Science Communication, 26*(4), 347–367.

Brossard, D., Scheufele, D. A., Kim, E., & Lewenstein, B.V. (2009). Religiosity as a perceptual filter: Examining processes of opinion formation about nanotechnology. *Public Understanding of Science, 18*(5), 546–568.

Brossard, D., & Nisbet, M. C. (2007). Deference to scientific authority among a low information public: Understanding U.S. opinion on agricultural biotechnology. *International Journal of Public Opinion Research, 19*(1), 24–52.

Brossard, D., & Shanahan, J. (2003). Do citizens want to have their say? Media, agricultural biotechnology, and authoritarian views of democratic processes in science. *Mass Communication & Society, 3*, 291–312.

Browne, M. W., & Cudeck, R. (1993). Alternative ways of testing model fit. In K. A. Bollen & J. S. Long (Eds.), *Testing structural equation models* (pp. 136–162). Newbury Park, CA: Sage Publications.

Dahlstrom, M. F., & Scheufele, D. A. (2010). Diversity of television exposure and its association with the cultivation of concern for environmental risks. *Environmental Communication: A Journal of Nature and Culture, 4*(1), 54–65.

Dhingra, K. (2003). Thinking about television science: How students understand the nature of science from different program genres. *Journal of Research in Science Teaching, 40*(2), 234–256.

Dudo, A., Brossard, D., Shanahan, J., Scheufele, D. A., Morgan, M., & Signorielli, N. (2011). Science on television in the 21st century: Recent trends in portrayals and their contributions to public attitudes toward science. *Communication Research, 38*(6), 754–777.

Fiske, S. T. & Taylor, S. E. (1991). *Social cognitions* (2nd ed.). New York: McGraw-Hill.

Gaskell, G., Ten Eyck, T., Jackson, J., & Veltri, G. (2004). Public attitudes to nanotechnology in Europe and the United States. *Nature Materials, 3*(8), 496.

Gerbner, G. (1987). Science on television: How it affects public conceptions. *Issues in Science and Technology, 3*(3), 109–115.

Gerbner, G., Gross, L. Morgan, M.,& Signorielli, N. (1981). Scientists on the tv screen. *Society, 42*, 41–44.

Gerbner, G., Gross, L. Morgan, M., & Signorielli, N. (1985). *Science and television.* A Research Report by the Annenberg School of Communications.

Gregory, J., & Miller, S. (1998). *Science in public: Communication, culture, and credibility.* New York: Plenum Press.

Ho, S., Brossard, D., & Scheufele, D. (2008). Effects of value predispositions, mass media use, and knowledge on public attitudes toward embryonic stem cell research. *International Journal of Public Opinion Research, 20*(2), 171–192.

Holbert, R. L., Kwak, N., & Shah, D. (2003). Environmental concern, patterns of television viewing, and pro-environmental behaviors: Integrating models of media consumption and effects. *Journal of Broadcasting & Electronic Media, 47*(2), 177–196.

Jenkins, H. (2006). *Convergence culture: Where old and new media collide.* New York: New York University Press.

Kaiser Family Foundation. (1997). *Documenting the power of entertainment television:The impact of a brief health message in one of TV's most popular dramas.* Menlo Park, CA: Kaiser Family Foundation.

Kaplan, D. (2000). *Structural equation modeling: Foundations and extensions.* Thousand Oaks, CA: Sage Publications, Inc.

Kendall, P. L., & Lazarsfeld, P. F. (1950). Problems of survey analysis. In R. K. Merton &

P. F. Lazarsfeld (Eds.), *Continuities in social research: Studies in the scope and method of 'The American Soldier'* (pp. 148–154). Glencoe, IL: Free Press.

Ladwig, P., Anderson, A. A., Brossard, D., Scheufele, D. A., & Shaw, B. (2010). Narrowing the nano discourse? *Materials Today, 13*(5), 52–54.

Lee, C., & Scheufele, D. A. (2006).The influence of knowledge and deference toward scientific authority: A media effects model for public attitudes toward nanotechnology. *Journalism & Mass Communication Quarterly, 83*(4), 819–834.

Lewenstein, B. (2001). Science and the media. In S. Jasanoff, G. E. Markle, J. C. Peterson, & T. Pinch (Eds.), *Handbook of science and technology studies* (pp. 343–360). Thousand Oaks, CA: Sage.

Markus, H., & Zajonc, R. B. (1985). The cognitive perspective in social psychology. In G. Lindzey & E. Aronson (Eds.), *The handbook of social psychology* (3rd ed., Vol. 1, pp. 137–229). New York: Random House.

McComas, K., & Shanahan, J. (1999). Telling stories about global climate change: Measuring the impact of narratives on issue cycles. *Communication Research, 26*(1), 30–57.

McLeod, D. M., Kosicki, G. M., & McLeod, J. M. (2002). Resurveying the boundaries of political communications effects. In J. Bryant & D. Zillman (Eds.), *Media effects: Advances in theory and research* (2nd ed., pp. 215–268). Mahwah, NJ: Erlbaum.

McQuail, D. (2005). *Mass communication theory* (5th ed.). London: Sage.

Mooney, C., & Kirshenbaum, S. (2009). *Unscientific America: How scientific illiteracy threatens our future.* New York: Basic Books.

Muthen, L. K., & Muthen, B. O. (2007). MPLUS (Version 4.2). Los Angeles: Muthen & Muthen.

National Science Board. (1989). *Science and Engineering Indicators 1989.* (NSB 89–01). Washington, DC: U.S. Government Printing Office.

National Science Board. (1996). *Science and Engineering Indicators 1996.* Arlington, VA (NSB 96–21). Washington, DC: U.S. Government Printing Office.

National Science Board. (2002). *Science and Engineering Indicators 2002.* Arlington, VA (NSB-02-1). Washington, DC: U.S. Government Printing Office.

National Science Board. (2004). *Science and Engineering Indicators 2004.* Arlington, VA (NSB 04–01). Washington, DC: U.S. Government Printing Office.

National Science Board. (2006). *Science and Engineering Indicators 2006.* Arlington, VA (NSB 06–02). Washington, DC: U.S. Government Printing Office.

National Science Board. (2008). Science and technology: Public attitudes and understanding. In *Science and engineering indicators* (pp. 7.1–7.44). Washington, DC: U.S. Government Printing Office.

National Science Board. (2010). Science and technology: Public attitudes and understanding. In *Science and engineering indicators.* Washington, DC: U.S. Government Printing Office.

Nelkin, D. (1995). *Selling science: How the press covers science and technology.* New York: Freeman.

Nisbet, M. C. (2005). The competition for worldviews: Values, information, and public support for stem cell research. *International Journal of Public Opinion Research, 17*(1), 90–112.

Nisbet, M. C., & Goidel, R. K. (2007). Understanding citizen perceptions of science controversy: Bridging the ethnographic-survey research divide. *Public Understanding of Science, 16*, 421–440.

Nisbet, M. C., Scheufele, D. A., Shanahan, J., Moy, P., Brossard, D., & Lewenstein, B. V. (2002). Knowledge, reservations, or promise? A media effects model for public perceptions of science and technology. *Communication Research, 19*(5), 584–608.

Perkowitz, S. (2007). *Hollywood science: Movies, science, and the end of the world.* New York: Columbia University Press.

Priest, S. H. (2001). Misplaced faith: Communication variables as predictors of encouragement for biotechnology development. *Science Communication, 23*(2), 97–110.

Scheufele, D. A. (2006a). Five lessons in nano outreach. *Materials Today, 9*(5), 64.

Scheufele, D. A. (2006b). Messages and heuristics: How audiences form attitudes about emerging technologies. In J. Turney (Ed.), *Engaging science: Thoughts, deeds, analysis and action* (pp. 20–25). London: The Wellcome Trust.

Scheufele, D., & Lewenstein, B. (2005). The public and nanotechnology: How citizens make sense of emerging technologies. *Journal of Nanotechnology Research, 7,* 659–667.

Shanahan, J., & McComas, K. (1999). *Nature Stories: Depictions of the environment and their effects.* Cresskill, NJ: Hampton Press.

Shanahan, J., & Morgan, M. (1999). *Television and its viewers: Cultivation theory and research.* Cambridge: Cambridge University Press.

Shanahan, J., Morgan, M., & Stenbjerre, M. (1997). Green or brown? Television and the cultivation of environmental concern. *Journal of Broadcasting & Electronic Media, 41*(3), 305–323.

Signorielli, N., & Morgan, M. (2009). Cultivation analysis: Research and practice. In M. Salwen & D. Stacks (Eds.), *An integrated approach to communication theory and research* (2nd ed., pp. 106–121). Hillsdale, NJ: Erlbaum.

Simon, A. (1999). *The real science behind the X Files.* New York: Simon & Schuster.

Turney, J. (1998). *Frankenstein's footsteps: Science, genetics, and popular culture.* New Haven, CT: Yale University Press.

U.S. Department of Education. (2006). *The nation's report card: Science 2005.* National Assessment of Educational Progress. Retrieved from http://nces.ed.gov/NAEP/pdf/main2005/2006466.pdf

Wynne, B. (1995). Public understanding of science. In S. Jasanoff, G. E. Markle, J. C. Petersen, & T. Pinch (Eds.), *Handbook of science and technology studies* (pp. 361–368). Thousand Oaks, CA: Sage.

# *Understanding Cognitive Mechanisms*

# 8. Multiple Processes Underlying Cultivation Effects

## How Cultivation Works Depends on the Types of Beliefs Being Cultivated

*L. J. Shrum & Jaehoon Lee*

With research on cultivation effects now going on 40 years, cultivation has clearly established itself as a theory with staying power. As Morgan and Shanahan have noted, and this volume attests, following the usual fits and starts that mark the arrival of any new theory, cultivation research has moved into a period of increasing both its breadth and depth (Morgan & Shanahan, 2010). This includes investigations that range from the many different types of attitudes and beliefs that can be cultivated, to investigations of how these effects occur in viewers' heads. In this chapter, we focus on the latter. As we detail presently, like cultivation research, research on the psychological mechanisms underlying the effect also began in fits and starts. However, as more and more process research has accumulated, a clearer picture has begun to develop about how cultivation proceeds from viewing to doing.

In this chapter, we present two models of the psychological processes underlying cultivation effects and discuss research that has tested these models. The two models pertain to separate psychological processes. We argue that there are different types of cultivation effects, and these differences aren't just the usual function of the different messages that are portrayed on television (crime, affluence, mistrust), but also are a function of the different types of beliefs that are produced (attitudes, values, normative perceptions). In combination, these models can address some inconsistencies and peculiarities in prior process research. We conclude by discussing the utility of understanding the processes underlying cultivation effects and their implications for mitigating the effects.

## A Social Cognition Perspective on Cultivation: First- versus Second-Order Cultivation Effects

In order to tap into different aspects of cultivation, Gerbner and colleagues used a number of operationalizations of their dependent variables (for a review, see Shanahan and Morgan, 1999). In some cases, they measured respondents' perceptions of how often various things occur or appear in the real world (e.g., the proportion of men employed in law enforcement, the percentage of people involved in violence each week), or asked respondents to assess their own levels of risk (e.g., "What are your chances of being involved in a violent crime in the next year?"). In other cases, the researchers asked respondents to make more general assessments about their views of the world, particularly with respect to crime and violence. Respondents were asked to indicate their level of agreement with beliefs such as "one can't be too careful," "people can't be trusted," or "the world is a mean and violent place."

Gerbner and colleagues understandably treated these various measures as indicators of the same general concept. That is, perceiving high levels of societal crime and personal likelihood of victimization, and holding strong beliefs that the world is a mean and violent place and that people can't be trusted, were viewed as convergent measures of a single underlying construct. However, Hawkins and Pingree (1982, 1990) observed that, from a psychological process perspective, these items actually represent different types of measures. They noted that first-order judgments (which they termed "demographic" measures) were usually measures of frequency or probability of occurrence. As such, they represent concrete, factual measures that can be objectively determined for both the real world and the television world (e.g., base rates in the U.S. for the probability of being involved in a violent crime vs. the probability of a television character being involved in violence). Thus, the extent of cultivation in terms of differences between television and real world estimates could be directly assessed (hence, *first* order). In contrast, second-order judgments (which they termed "value-systems" measures) represent more subjective measures of values, attitudes, and beliefs. Thus, they have no direct counterpart in the television world, but can only be inferred from analysis of television content (hence, *second* order).

Along with the differences in the forms of the measures, Hawkins and Pingree (1982, 1990) also made two other important observations. The first was that, based on their review of cultivation research to date, first-order cultivation effects appeared to be more robust and reliable than second-order effects. This was particularly true when multiple statistical controls were applied simultaneously. The second important observation was that the processes by which television influences the two judgments may be different.

This observation was motivated by their early process research that showed that first-order judgments did not predict second-order judgments, as they had initially speculated. Instead, the two measures were relatively independent. This led them to the speculation that both types of judgments may not be explained by the same process. Although the first assertion that second-order effects were not robust did not hold up over time (see Morgan & Shanahan, 1997 for a meta-analysis), the second assertion regarding different psychological processes turned out to be on the money.

In the following sections, we present two separate models for the processes that underlie first- and second-order cultivation effects. We argue that the types of judgments underlying first- and second-order cultivation effects (first- and second-order judgments) are fundamentally different and are constructed in very different ways. Moreover, we argue that because the processes of judgment construction are so fundamentally different, so too are the ways in which television viewing influences those judgments.

## Memory-Based versus Online Processing Models

The most fundamental way in which first-order and second-order cultivation judgments differ is that first-order judgments are, for the most part, memory-based judgments, whereas second-order judgments are, for the most part, constructed through an online (real-time) process. Memory-based judgments are just as the label implies: They are constructed through the recall of information stored in long-term memory (Hastie & Park, 1986). For example, suppose you are asked to provide an estimate of the length of the Mississippi River. The answer to this question is one that most people do not have easy access to in memory (accessibility), if they have it stored in memory at all (availability). Consequently, they will attempt to answer the question by recalling information that may have bearing on the answer (they know it runs from the Great Lakes to the Gulf of Mexico, that it runs the lengths of several states, that the length of one of these states (Illinois) is about 400 miles long, etc.). In a similar manner, most people do not know the answer to a person's likelihood of being a victim of sexual assault or being a doctor. Thus, people will attempt to bring to mind information stored in memory that may help construct those particular judgments.

In contrast, imagine you're asked to indicate your attitude about the death penalty or whether it is safe to walk alone at night in your neighborhood. In both cases, it is likely that you have already constructed your attitude or belief. In this case, you would just recall your attitude and report it. But how did that attitude get constructed in the first place? In all likelihood, it is based on information you have read, heard, or experienced over time. There may have been a particularly poignant story on the news, an editorial in the newspaper, or a personal experience with violent crime. In all of these cases, the judgment is based on information as it is encountered. This is known as online processing (Hastie & Park, 1986). In such cases, the information that is encountered in real time is used to form a judgment rather than relying on information that is stored in memory.

Given that the types of judgments that are fundamental to cultivation research are constructed through different processes, it seems plausible that the processes by which television information influences these judgments are correspondingly different. If so, it also implies that the mediators and moderators of the cultivation effect for each type of judgment may differ. In the next sections, we explicate independent models for each type of cultivation judgment and show that not only do particular mediators or moderators produce different effects as a function of type of cultivation judgment, but in some instances they have almost opposite effects.

## The Accessibility Model for First-Order Cultivation Effects

The accessibility model rests on two general assumptions. The first is that television viewing increases the accessibility in memory of information relevant to a typical cultivation judgment (crime, wealth, occupations). Accessibility refers to the ease with which something can be recalled (accessed) from memory. The second assumption is that first-order cultivation judgments are memory-based ones that are generally constructed through heuristic processing. Heuristic processing refers to the tendency to take cognitive shortcuts when trying to answer difficult questions. That is, rather than making an exhaustive search of memory for information bearing on a particular judgment, people may take a cognitive shortcut and use only a subset of relevant information. More specifically, people will rely on the general ease with which the information is recalled, rather than the implications of the information itself, to form their judgments. This metacognitive tendency to base judgments on perceived ease of recall is referred to as the availability heuristic (Schwarz, 2004; Tversky & Kahneman, 1973), and it is a nonconscious, automatic process.

Based on these two general propositions, more specific propositions pertaining to cultivation processes and effects can be generated. Five particular propositions comprise the model: 1) television viewing influences accessibility; 2) accessibility mediates the cultivation effect; 3) television exemplars are not source-discounted; 4) motivation to process information moderates the cultivation effect; and 5) ability to process information moderates the cultivation effect. In the following sections, we elaborate on these propositions and discuss supporting research.

### *Proposition 1: Viewing Increases Accessibility*

The first proposition is that television viewing increases the accessibility of constructs frequently portrayed on television. For example, as Gerbner and colleagues clearly document in their Violence Profiles (for a review, see Shanahan & Morgan, 1999), violence is a common theme running through many different types of television programming, and thus is very frequently portrayed. In addition, because of their centrality and attention-getting features, these portrayals are often quite vivid. These two aspects of constructs (frequency and vividness) have been shown to increase construct accessibility (Higgins, 1996; Shrum, 1995; Wyer & Srull, 1989). Thus, viewing television should increase construct accessibility of those things relevant to cultivation research (crime, violence, marital discord, occupational prevalence, affluence), and should do so in proportion to viewing frequency.

Proposition 1 was first tested by Shrum and O'Guinn (1993). We tested the hypothesis that amount of television viewing would be positively correlated with the accessibility of information portrayed on television. Participants were asked to provide a variety of first-order cultivation judgments (e.g., percent likelihood of being a victim of a violent crime, percentage of Americans with a drinking problem), and the speed with which they provided the judgments was measured. The assumption was that the more accessible the information pertaining to the judgments, the faster the judgments would be constructed. Consistent with our reasoning, heavier viewers not only provided higher estimates for the judgments than did lighter viewers, they made them faster as well. These results held when a variety of individual difference variables were statistically controlled. These general findings have been replicated using multiple operationalizations of television viewing frequency, dependent measures, and control variables (O'Guinn & Shrum, 1997; Shrum, 1996; Shrum, O'Guinn, Semenik, & Faber, 1991). Other studies that have directly assessed ease of recall of television exemplars as a function of amount of television viewing also found support for the accessibility proposition (e.g., Busselle & Shrum, 2003).

### *Proposition 2: Accessibility Mediates the Cultivation Effect*

The second proposition is based on the application of the availability heuristic (Tversky & Kahneman, 1973). The availability heuristic is the tendency to infer frequency of occurrence from ease of recall (accessibility of relevant exemplars). Because things that occur frequently are generally easy to recall, people may also infer that if things are easy to recall, then they probably occur frequently. If so, and if television makes certain exemplars easy to recall (as Proposition 1 states), then the accessibility effect should lead to increased estimates of frequency or probability.

Support for this mediation process was also provided by Shrum and O'Guinn (1993). When the speed of response to the judgments (accessibility) was controlled, the cultivation effect was reduced to nonsignificance. More direct support, however, was provided by Shrum (1996). Path analyses were used to establish that a) television viewing influenced both speed of response (accessibility effect) and magnitude of estimates (cultivation effect) in the expected ways, b) that speed of response also was inversely related to magnitude of estimates (i.e., faster responses were associated with higher estimates), and c) that controlling for speed of response significantly reduced the cultivation effect. Meeting these three conditions demonstrates mediation (Baron & Kenny, 1986). This mediation effect held across two of the three different dependent measures (crime and occupational prevalence but not marital discord). A summary representation of the pattern of effects can be seen in Figure 1 (numbers represent averages for crime and occupational prevalence). All paths in Figure 1 are significant, including the path between television viewing and judgments. This latter path indicates that although accessibility (response latencies) mediated the cultivation effect, the mediation was only partial.

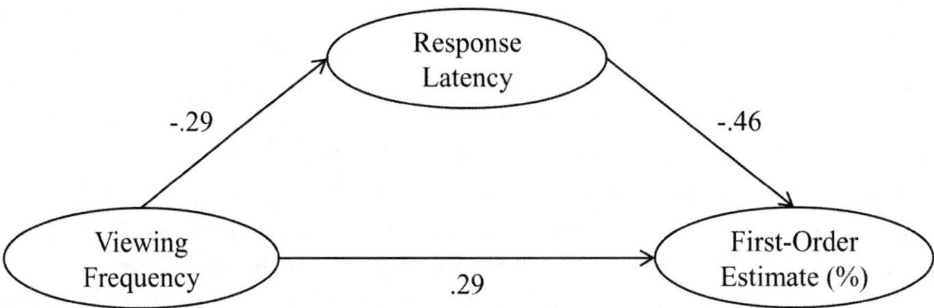


Figure 1. Path model showing mediating role of accessibility in the cultivation effect. Represents pattern of results across dependent variables (see Shrum, 1996).

Other research that has directly manipulated accessibility has also provided support for the second proposition. Busselle (2001) had some participants provide cultivation judgments in the usual manner, but asked other participants to first recall an example of the construct being estimated (e.g., the percentage of people who have extramarital affairs). The latter was expected to eliminate an accessibility advantage for heavier viewers by making exemplars equally accessible for all participants, and in doing so, eliminate the cultivation effect. Consistent with predictions, a cultivation effect was observed in the first condition but not in the second.

### *Proposition 3: Television Exemplars Are Not Source-Discounted*

The third proposition is that television exemplars are not source-discounted when constructing judgments. That is, when people attempt to construct a first-order judgment by recalling a relevant exemplar, they do not ignore exemplars from television, including fictional representations. This is an important proposition because it addresses the counterintuitive notion that people would base their judgments of real-world prevalence on the ease with which a television example could be recalled. On the one hand, we know that viewers do not believe that television information is particularly reflective of the real world (Shrum, 2007a), and thus would be unlikely to consider television information applicable to a real-world judgment. On the other hand, we also know that accessibility influences judgment only when the accessible information is considered applicable to the judgment (Higgins, 1996). Thus, for all of these conditions to hold simultaneously, it must be that people do not generally attend to the source of the information they retrieve. This would be consistent with a heuristic process model in which people base their judgments on the ease of exemplar retrieval without attending to the individuating details (including the source) of each exemplar.

Support for this proposition was provided in two experiments (Shrum, Wyer, & O'Guinn, 1998). To test the hypotheses that people generally do not source discount when constructing cultivation judgments, we created conditions in which we induced people to source discount, and then compared these conditions to the usual (control) conditions. To do so, for some participants, we manipulated the salience of television information prior to them making their judgments. We reasoned that if people normally do not usually attend to source characteristics, then we should observe the usual cultivation effect when source characteristics are not made salient (control condition). However, calling attention to their television viewing habits should make source characteristics salient, and they should thus discount the television information under these circumstances.

The results were consistent with our predictions, and the general pattern of results can be seen in Figure 2. When we simply asked respondents to make the standard cultivation judgments, and then asked them to estimate their television viewing frequency (no priming), we observed a sizeable cultivation effect. However, when we made their television viewing habits salient by asking them to report their frequency of viewing before they reported their cultivation judgments (source priming), or reminded them that television information might influence their judgments (relation priming), the cultivation effect was eliminated. An additional point about the results is worth noting. As the figure shows, source discounting occurred only among the heavy television viewers; the difference across conditions for light viewers was not significant. This is consistent with our theoretical reasoning. Light viewers should have relatively few television-based exemplars stored in memory in the first place. Consequently, they should be relatively unaffected by conditions that encouraged them to discount television-based information.

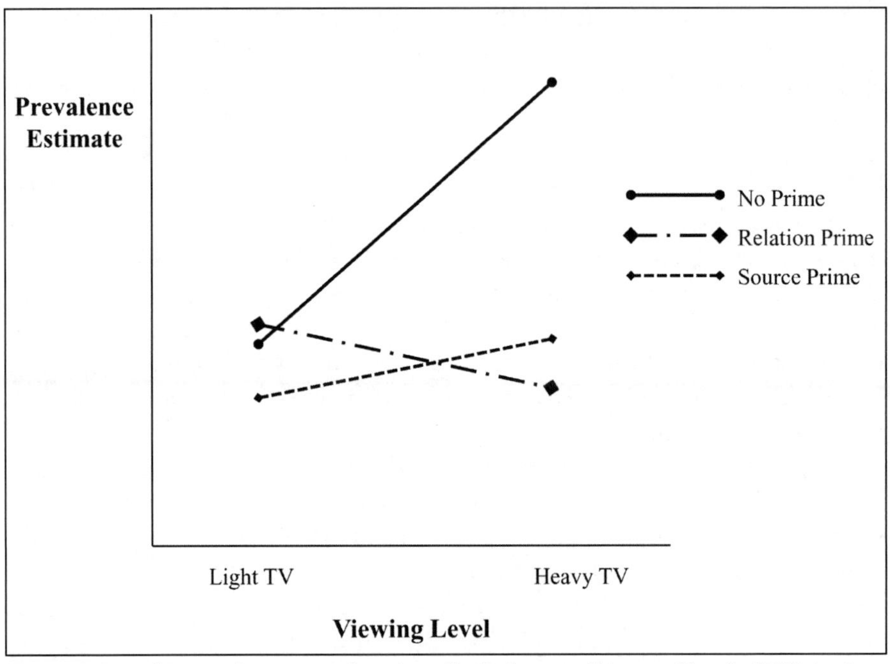


Figure 2. Prevalence estimates as a function of priming condition and level of TV viewing. Rep-resents pattern of results across dependent variables (see Shrum et al., 1998).

Thus far, propositions 1–3 have focused on testing characteristics of the heuristic process itself and whether it plays a role in the cultivation effect. Propositions 4 and 5 focus on situations in which heuristic processing is more or less likely to be used in the judgment construction process. As mentioned earlier, heuristics are considered to be effort-reduction processes for constructing difficult judgments, and they are employed without conscious awareness (Kahneman & Frederick, 2002). Consequently, heuristics are more likely to be employed when motivation to form a difficult judgment is low. An example is a situation in which respondents do not care a great deal if their judgments are accurate. Heuristic processing is also more likely to be employed when the ability to form a difficult judgment is low. An example is a situation in which processing conditions are hurried or distracting. Propositions 4 and 5 propose that motivation and ability moderate the cultivation effect in just these ways.

### *Proposition 4: Motivation to Process as Moderator*

Proposition 4 is based on research that indicates that there are certain conditions under which the tendency toward heuristic processing is attenuated (Sherman & Corty, 1984). One condition is motivation to process information. As noted earlier, the tendency to use heuristics is a cognitive shortcut to reduce processing effort. However, if people are sufficiently motivated, they will expend effort to more systematically process information, and thus avoid cognitive heuristics. More pertinent to our case, if sufficiently motivated, respondents will attempt to retrieve relevant information from memory and avoid relying simply on the ease with which an example can be brought to mind. In such cases, the accessibility of television information should play less of a role.

To test Proposition 4, motivation to process information was induced by manipulating participants' motivation to be accurate in their judgments (Shrum, 2001). A third of the participants provided their judgments in the standard manner (control group). We expected that these participants would process heuristically and demonstrate a cultivation effect. Another third of the participants were asked to provide their answers by giving the first figure that came to mind, "off the top of their heads" (heuristic group). We expected this group to also demonstrate a cultivation effect and one similar in magnitude to the control group. That is, if people spontaneously process heuristically when making typical cultivation judgments, then asking them to do what they normally do anyway should have little effect. In contrast, for the third group, we increased their motivation to be accurate by telling them their answers would be compared to the average student, that the experimenter would discuss their answers with them after the experiment, and that they would be expected to justify their answers (systematic group). We expected that participants in this condition would be motivated to think more carefully and consider information other than that which was most accessible (i.e., not process heuristically), which should reduce the cultivation effect.

The results were consistent with expectations and are summarized in Figure 3. The control and heuristic groups exhibited sizeable cultivation effects that did not differ from each other in magnitude. However, the cultivation effect was eliminated in the systematic condition. Also, just as in Figure 2, it is worth noting that the systematic manipulation only affected heavy viewers. The differences across conditions for light viewers were not significant, and in fact the pattern of the interaction between the control and priming conditions in Figure 2 is almost identical to the pattern of the interaction between the control and systematic conditions in Figure 3. These results are again consistent with the model: Light viewers were not influenced by television information in control conditions (because they don't have much of it stored in memory), so inducing them to think harder should have little effect on the use of accessible television information when they form their judgments.

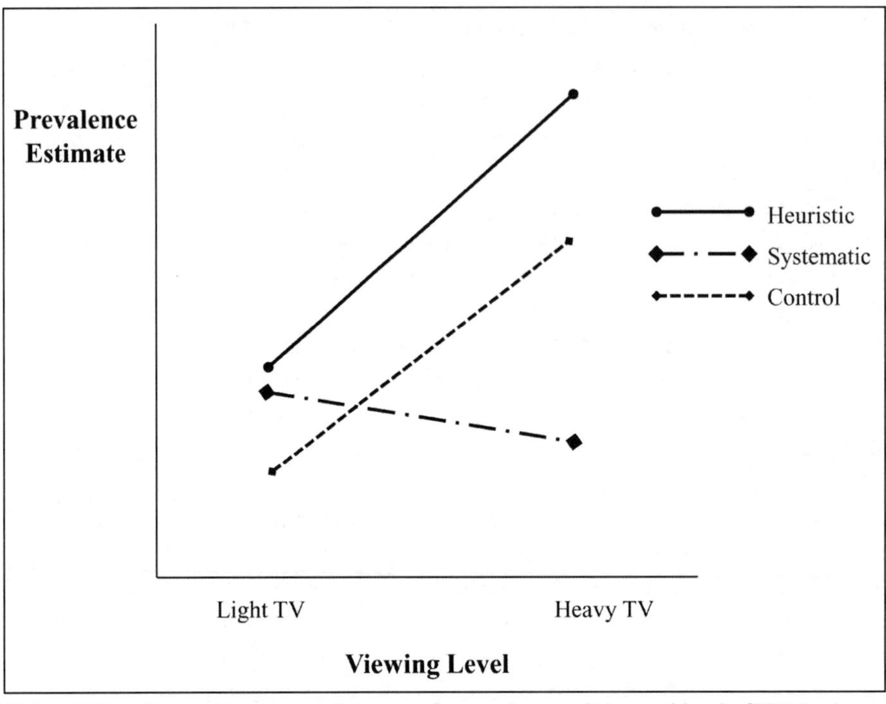


Figure 3. Prevalence estimates as a function of processing condition and level of TV viewing. Represents pattern of results across dependent variables (see Shrum, 2001).

### *Proposition 5: Ability to Process as Moderator*

Proposition 5 follows from the same research on which Proposition 4 was based. In this case, however, we were interested in conditions that may increase (rather than decrease) the propensity to process heuristically. Because heuristics are task simplification procedures, it follows that making a judgment task more difficult should facilitate heuristic processing. One such condition that facilitates heuristic processing is making the judgment task difficult by reducing the ability to process information. Shrum (2007b) accomplished this via a field experiment that manipulated type of survey method: whether data were collected via mail or telephone surveys. Pretests had shown that both survey methods elicited the same level of involvement, but participants in telephone survey conditions reported greater levels of time pressure than did participants in mail survey conditions. We therefore reasoned that respondents would be more likely to process heuristically in telephone survey conditions because time pressure would make the judgments more difficult for telephone survey respondents than for mail survey respondents.

These predictions were confirmed. Across six different dependent variables, cultivation effects were larger in telephone conditions (average $\beta = .26$) than in mail conditions (average $\beta = .10$) for five of the six dependent variables. The average effect size for the mail condition is in line with most general population mail surveys (Morgan & Shanahan, 1997), but increases by a factor of six in telephone survey conditions. Thus, the greater sense of time pressure generated by a telephone survey seems to increase the extent of heuristic processing, which in turn augments the observed cultivation effects.

### *Model Integration and Summary*

The five propositions test different aspects of the accessibility model. An integration of all five propositions into one overarching framework is shown in Figure 4. The model is presented as a flow chart that specifies a series of links which ultimately connect television viewing with judgments, and the particular route taken determines whether a cultivation effect is observed.

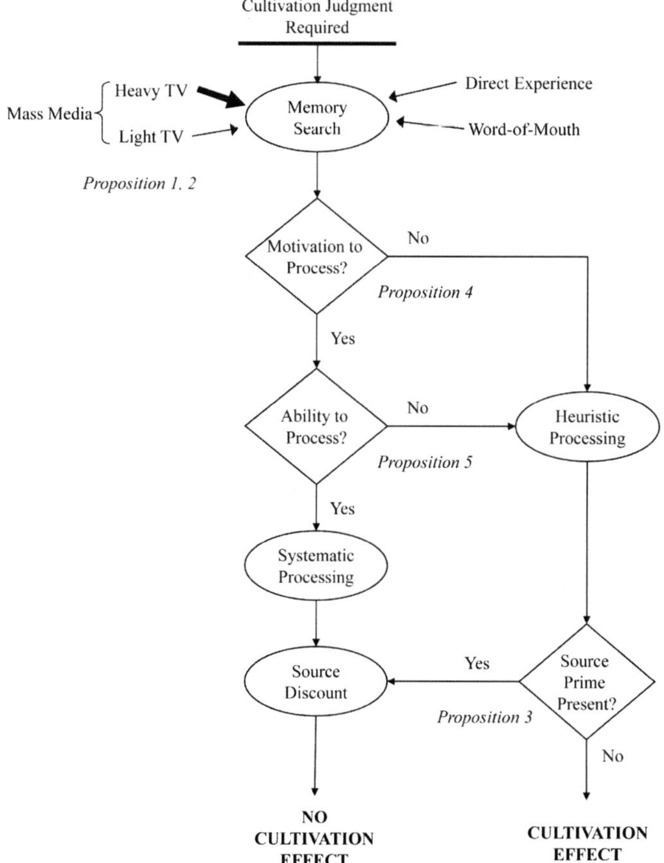


Figure 4. Flow diagram of the heuristic processing model of television effects. Circles represent mental processes. The thicker arrow from Heavy TV to Memory Search indicates a greater contribution to the search process.

The accessibility model addresses the processes underlying cultivation effects for first-order judgments. First-order judgments are memory based and particularly influenced by the accessibility of relevant information (exemplars) in memory. Television viewing increases the accessibility of this information, which, in turn, increases the magnitude of estimates, and this process occurs automatically with little attention to the details of the information, including its source. However, conditions can occur in which people do not rely as much on heuristics such as accessibility. Thus, when people are sufficiently motivated to make accurate judgments, and have the ability to do so, they will rely less on simple heuristics and make the effort to seek out more valid information on which to base their judgments.

The accessibility model helps explain why television influences first-order judgments. However, aspects of the model beyond the five propositions also are important in understanding previous cultivation findings. One in particular is the implication of the memory-based nature of first-order judgments. This process implies that judgments are constructed through recall of information, and that this occurs at the time the judgment is elicited, not during the viewing process. In other words, the cultivation effect manifests itself (in the form of higher estimates for heavier viewers) when people are required to make a judgment, usually for some external reason (asked by an experimenter, teacher, relative). Consequently, variables that measure aspects of processing during viewing, such as viewer involvement, may have relatively little effect. In fact, the results of prior research show just that: Involvement has little impact on the cultivation effect (Carveth & Alexander, 1985; Rouner, 1984; Shrum, 1996, 2001). That is not to say that viewing variables necessarily have no effect at all. Viewing process variables such as attention, involvement, and transportation may affect the accessibility of information in memory, which may in turn affect first-order judgments. However, thus far researchers have not been able to detect such effects consistently.

Although understanding the processes that underlie first-order cultivation judgments is important, it does little to illuminate the processes underlying second-order cultivation judgments. This is unfortunate for two reasons. First, whether and how television exerts its influence on the formation of attitudes and beliefs, and becomes integrated into general value systems, are arguably more important than whether and how it influences general societal perceptions. Moreover, second-order judgments also seem to better capture the original notion of cultivation and its pernicious nature (Gerbner & Gross, 1976). Second, it is important to move beyond first-order measures because they are actually quite rare, are infrequently made, and are difficult to produce, even in the lab (Hastie & Park, 1986). Thus, second-order judgments, arguably the most important and most ubiquitous types of cultivation judgments, have received relatively little attention with respect to underlying processes. In the next section, we describe new developments in our efforts to construct and test a process model for these types of judgments.

## The Online Process Model for Second-Order Cultivation Effects

In contrast to memory-based judgments, in everyday life online judgments are frequently made, occur spontaneously, and require little effort. Examples of online judgments include attitudes, values, and beliefs. Online judgments occur as information is received and processed. Common examples include impression formation and stereotyping ("what do I think about this person or group of people?"), assessment of a situation ("is it safe?"), and attitudes toward objects or lifestyles (valuing being rich or famous). In terms of television viewing, these types of judgments would be influenced by television portrayals during the viewing process and made spontaneously. This type of process generally describes a model in which television portrayals function as a persuasive communication that may potentially affect the values, attitudes, and beliefs of viewers.

If the persuasion model analogy is accurate, it has implications for the processes that underlie second-order cultivation effects. For one, it suggests that frequent viewing of consistent and repetitive messages would lead to attitude shifts toward the dominant messages and themes of television. However, it also goes beyond the simple prediction of a cultivation effect. Theories of attitude formation and change, such as the Elaboration Likelihood Model (Petty & Cacioppo, 1986), provide specific predictions about how different processing factors may affect persuasion. For example, the Elaboration Likelihood Model states that increased motivation to process information can enhance persuasion (at least when the persuasive arguments are strong). When motivation is high, people will follow the central route to persuasion and think more carefully about arguments and process them more deeply. Applied to the cultivation effect, greater motivation to process information should result in a larger cultivation effect. Similarly, the ability to process information also enhances persuasion. For example, when people are able to pay close attention to a message and are not distracted from it, persuasion is enhanced. Applied to the cultivation effect, higher ability to process information should result in a larger cultivation effect. *It is worth noting that these two predictions are exactly opposite of the effects of motivation and ability that were predicted and observed in the case of first-order cultivation effects, as just reviewed* (cf. Shrum, 2001, 2007b).

### *Model Tests*

**Motivation and ability**. The first studies to address the online processing model tested the proposition that both motivation and ability to process information during viewing would moderate second-order cultivation effects (Shrum, Burroughs, & Rindfleisch, 2005). Specifically, the studies examined the effect of television viewing on material values (Richins & Dawson, 1992). Although a number of studies have investigated the relation between television viewing and perceptions of societal affluence (a first-order judgment), cultivation research on materialism itself has been scarce. Because television portrays clear messages that possessions increase happiness and signal success (O'Guinn & Shrum, 1997), we expected that television viewing frequency would be positively correlated with levels of materialism.

However, we also expected that motivation and ability would moderate this effect. Higher levels of motivation and ability to process information were each expected to increase cultivation effects. Motivation to process was operationalized as need for cognition (Cacioppo & Petty, 1982), which is an individual difference measure of the extent to which people enjoy processing information, being cognitively active, and solving puzzles. Ability to process was operationalized as chronic attention to programming while viewing (Rubin, Perse, & Taylor, 1988). The results supported the model and the general pattern can be seen in Figure 5. Cultivation effects (positive correlations between television viewing and materialism) were stronger for those higher in need for cognition and those who generally pay more attention during viewing. However, as the figure shows, cultivation effects were obtained for everyone: They were just stronger for the high need for cognition and high attention groups. A follow-up experiment confirmed that viewers with a high need for cognition tend to elaborate more during viewing than viewers with a low need for cognition; the former also produce more positive elaborations and generally are more immersed in the programs.

**Narrative transportation**. Although the Shrum et al. (2005) studies provided support for the model, the studies were hampered by several limitations. For one, the primary study (Study 1) that tested the moderating roles of motivation and ability to process information was correlational, and thus makes assertions of causality problematic. Second, and relatedly, the survey nature of the study precluded any determination of what actually goes on during viewing, but instead relied on self reports of general dispositions while viewing.

To remedy these shortcomings, Shrum, Lee, Burroughs, and Rindfleisch (2011) conducted an experiment that manipulated levels of materialistic content. As part of a study to ostensibly investigate the relations between ads and television content, some participants viewed a 20-minute excerpt from *Wall*

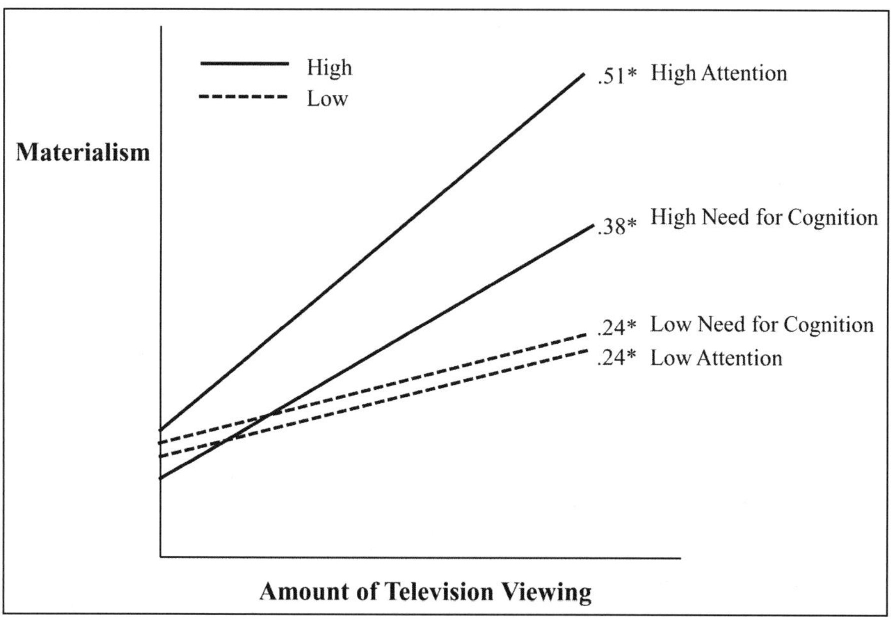


Figure 5. Materialism as a function of need for cognition and television viewing and as a function of attention and television viewing. Represents general pattern of effects (see Shrum et al., 2005).

*Street* (high materialism), and other participants viewed a 20-minute excerpt from *Gorillas in the Mist* (low materialism). In addition, participants indicated the extent to which they were "transported" into the narrative (Busselle & Bilandzic, 2008; Green & Brock, 2000). Narrative transportation is an individual difference variable that measures the extent to which audience members (readers, listeners, viewers) are absorbed into the world of the narrative. Transported viewers become engrossed in the story, are highly involved and cognitively engaged, think vivid thoughts, and react emotionally to the narrative (Green & Brock, 2000). To achieve and maintain this state of transportation, viewers may suspend disbelief and actively avoid counterarguing, thereby ignoring facts that may contradict the narrative's message (Green, Garst, & Brock, 2004). Research shows that transportation is associated with more positive feelings toward sympathetic characters in the narrative, more narrative-consistent beliefs, and fewer negative thoughts.

Based on these findings, we expected that viewing the more materialistic narrative (*Wall Street*) would increase levels of materialism relative to those who viewed the less materialistic narrative (*Gorillas in the Mist*), but that this effect would be moderated by narrative transportation. Those who were more transported into the narrative were expected to be more influenced by the narrative theme. The

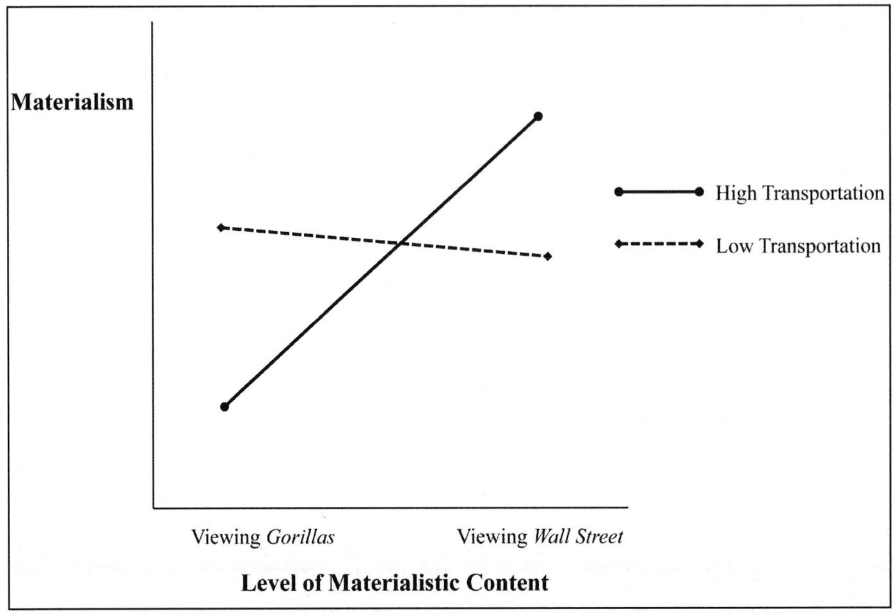


Figure 6. Materialism as a function of narrative transportation and media exposure. Represents general pattern of effects (see Shrum et al., 2011).

results were in line with expectations, and the general pattern of results can be seen in Figure 6. As the figure shows, only those who reported being transported into the narrative were influenced by the manipulation of materialistic content.

### *Summary*

Taken together, the studies just described that tested various aspects of the online processing model provide good support for the general theoretical framework. For online, second-order cultivation judgments such as values, attitudes, and beliefs, the influence of television on judgment occurs during viewing, as information is processed. These judgments are internally and spontaneously generated, and are affected by the extent to which people are involved in the program, pay attention to it, and are transported into the narrative. Contrast this with memory-based, first-order cultivation judgments such as frequency and probability estimates. These judgments are usually externally generated through some elicitation, and thus television influences judgments at the time of that elicitation through recall of relevant information in memory, some of which comes from television programs. The judgments are affected by the extent to which people have the motivation and ability to search through memory for information pertaining to the required judgment. Clearly, first- and second-order judgments are influenced by television viewing through quite different processes.

## Implications and Future Directions

Having spent considerable time explicating the processes underlying first- and second-order cultivation effects and describing their explanatory models, it seems fair to ask why these issues are important in the first place. There are at least three reasons we would like to propose for why process issues matter. First, process models provide important steps toward strengthening the validity of the cultivation effect (Hawkins & Pingree, 1990). If process models can be developed that specify and demonstrate clear links between television viewing, mediating factors, and cultivation judgments, then threats to internal validity such as reverse causality and spuriousness are greatly reduced.

A second contribution of process models, particularly the notion that separate models are needed for first- and second-order cultivation judgments, is that they may explain a number of inconsistencies and seemingly counterintuitive findings. For example, it seems intuitive that viewer involvement should enhance the cultivation effect, yet few studies have found this to be the case (e.g., Carveth & Alexander, 1985; Rouner, 1984; Shrum, 1996, 2001). However, taken together, the online and accessibility models suggest that viewer involvement should affect only second-order judgments. Because much of the early cultivation research found robust cultivation effects only for first-order measures (Hawkins & Pingree, 1982), the potential effect of viewer involvement on second-order measures may have been overlooked because of small and often nonsignificant effects.

A third reason process models are important is their potential for inhibiting or facilitating cultivation effects. Process models establish conditions under which the effect should or should not hold. Once these boundary conditions are established, intervention methods can be employed to reduce or eliminate the effect under naturally occurring conditions. For example, process models could inform media literacy programs that teach viewers how to reduce unwanted effects of television viewing. However, cultivation effects are not solely negative, and thus television programs might be used for prosocial purposes, such as reducing drinking, smoking, and other vices, promoting racial equality, or increasing pro-environmental behavior, by inducing cultivation-type effects. Process models suggest conditions that would facilitate the effect (e.g., via narratives rather than rhetoric, increasing narrative engagement).

Thus, understanding that different types of cultivation-related judgments have different underlying processes becomes particularly important. For example, for memory-based (first-order) judgments, individuals need to understand that these types of judgments are influenced by the accessibility of information when they attempt to construct their judgments, and this accessibility may have an unwanted influence from television viewing. If so, then individuals need to consider information other than the most immediately accessible when constructing judgments. In contrast, for online (second-order) judgments, which are influenced by program content during viewing, people may need to either reassess their attitudes and beliefs after viewing and attempt to adjust for unwanted influence at that point, or actively counterargue and resist particular messages that they may be unconsciously adopting during viewing but are antithetical to their personal values and beliefs (e.g., the attractiveness of torture or revenge in the pursuit of a just end). Of course, the latter may likely produce an unsatisfying viewing experience! Nevertheless, process models suggest particular avenues for managing the influence of television messages on social judgments.

In terms of future research, there is clearly more to be done in understanding the different processes that underlie second-order cultivation effects. It is readily apparent when comparing the research on first- and second-order cultivation processes that the latter is still in its infancy. The research on second-order processes represents only a first step in the process of better understanding how the cultivation of second-order judgments works. If, as our model suggests, factors that influence the processing of information during viewing moderate the cultivation effect for second-order judgments, then there are likely quite a number of factors that could be examined. Further investigations into these process variables should contribute to a much richer and more advanced process model for second-order judgments.

Another possible route to studying cultivation effects and their underlying processes is the use of more implicit measures of values, attitudes, and beliefs. For example, the Implicit Association Test (IAT; Greenwald, McGhee, & Schwartz, 1998) is designed to measure attitudes that may be subject to a socially desirable response bias (e.g., reporting racial attitudes) or are attitudes which people are truly unaware that they hold (Erdelyi & Zizak, 2004). Employing such methods may allow cultivation researchers to uncover effects that had previously gone undetected.

Because of premature reports of the death of television, people may think that cultivation research is also on its last legs. However, as Morgan and Shanahan (2010) point out, this is far from the case. Although new media have changed the communication and entertainment landscape, television viewing levels have remained relatively unchanged over the last decade, and if anything, absolute hours of viewing have increased (Nielsen Wire, 2009). One challenge for cultivation researchers in the next decade is to determine whether there are any interesting interactions between the new media and the old, whether the new media enhance traditional cultivation effects, and whether new media may create some of their own. A related challenge is to better understand the cognitive processes involved in consumption of new media. Clearly, the ways in which new and old media are processed may be quite different, whether they are functions of the media themselves (e.g., computer vs. television) or the situations in which they are traditionally processed (e.g., multi-tasking). As with cultivation research, establishing both the existence of the effect and its underlying processes should be dual goals.

## References

Baron, R. M., & Kenny, D. A. (1986). The moderator-mediator variable distinction in social psychological research: Conceptual, strategic and statistical considerations. *Journal of Personality and Social Psychology, 51*, 1173–1182.

Busselle, R. W. (2001). The role of exemplar accessibility in social reality judgments. *Media Psychology, 3*, 43–67.

Busselle, R., & Bilandzic, H. (2008). Fictionality and perceived realism in experiencing stories: A model of narrative comprehension and engagement. *Communication Theory, 18*, 255–280.

Busselle, R. W., & Shrum, L. J. (2003). Media exposure and the accessibility of social information. *Media Psychology, 5*, 255–282.

Cacioppo, J. T., & Petty, R. E. (1982). The need for cognition. *Journal of Personality and Social Psychology, 42*, 116–131.

Carveth, R., & Alexander, A. (1985). Soap opera viewing motivations and the cultivation process. *Journal of Broadcasting & Electronic Media, 29*, 259–273.

Erdelyi, M. H., & Zizak, D. M. (2004). Beyond gizmo subliminality. In L. J. Shrum (Ed.), *The psychology of entertainment media: Blurring the lines between entertainment and persuasion* (pp. 13–44). Mahwah, NJ: Erlbaum.

Gerbner, G., & Gross, L. (1976). Living with television: The violence profile. *Journal of Communication, 26*(2), 172–194.

Green, M. C., & Brock, T. C. (2000). The role of transportation in the persuasiveness of public narratives. *Journal of Personality and Social Psychology, 79*, 701–721.

Green, M. C., Garst, J., & Brock, T. C. (2004). The power of fiction: Determinants and boundaries. In L. J. Shrum (Ed.), *The psychology of entertainment media: Blurring the lines between entertainment and persuasion* (pp. 161–176). Mahwah, NJ: Erlbaum.

Greenwald, A. G., McGhee, D. E., & Schwartz, J. K. L. (1998). Measuring individual differences in implicit cognition: The Implicit Association Test. *Journal of Personality and Social Psychology, 74*, 1464–1480.

Hastie, R., & Park, B. (1986). The relationship between memory and judgment depends on whether the judgment task is memory-based or online. *Psychological Review, 93*, 258–268.

Hawkins, R. P., & Pingree, S. (1982). Television's influence on constructions of social reality. In D. Pearl, L. Bouthilet, & J. Lazar (Eds.), *Television and behavior: Ten years of scientific progress and implications for the eighties* (Vol. 2, pp. 224–247). Washington, DC: Government Printing Office.

Hawkins, R. P., & Pingree, S. (1990). Divergent psychological processes in constructing social reality from mass media content. In N. Signorielli & M. Morgan (Eds.), *Cultivation analysis: New directions in media effects research* (pp. 33–50). Newbury Park, CA: Sage.

Higgins, E. T. (1996). Knowledge activation: Accessibility, applicability, and salience. In E. T. Higgins & A. W. Kruglanski (Eds.), *Social psychology: Handbook of basic principles* (pp. 133–168). New York: Guilford Press.

Kahneman, D., & Frederick, S. (2002). Representativeness revisited: Attribute substitution in intuitive judgment. In T. Gilovich, D. Griffin, & D. Kahneman (Eds.), *Heuristics and biases: The psychology of intuitive judgment* (pp. 49–81). Cambridge: Cambridge University Press.

Morgan, M., & Shanahan, J. (1997). Two decades of cultivation research: An appraisal and meta-analysis. In B. R. Burleson (Ed.), *Communication Yearbook 20* (pp. 1–45). Newbury Park, CA: Sage.

Morgan, M., & Shanahan, J. (2010). The state of cultivation. *Journal of Broadcasting & Electronic Media, 54,* 337–355.

Nielsen Wire. (2009, Nov. 10). Average TV viewing for 2008–09 TV season at all-time high. Retrieved from http://blog.nielsen.com/nielsenwire/media_entertainment/average-tv-viewing-for-2008–09-tv-season-at-all-time-high/

O'Guinn, T. C., & Shrum, L. J. (1997). The role of television in the construction of consumer reality. *Journal of Consumer Research, 23,* 278–294.

Petty, R. E., & Cacioppo, J. T. (1986). *Communication and persuasion: Central and peripheral routes to attitude change.* New York: Springer-Verlag.

Richins, M. L., & Dawson, S. (1992). A consumer values orientation for materialism and its measurement: Scale development and validation: *Journal of Consumer Research, 19,* 303–316.

Rouner, D. (1984). Active television viewing and the cultivation hypothesis. *Journalism Quarterly, 61,* 168–174.

Rubin, A. J., Perse, E. M., & Taylor, D. S. (1988). A methodological examination of cultivation. *Communication Research, 15,* 107–134.

Schwarz, N. (2004). Meta-cognitive experiences in consumer judgment and decision making. *Journal of Consumer Psychology, 32,* 332–348.

Shanahan, J., & Morgan, M. (1999). *Television and its viewers: Cultivation theory and research.* Cambridge: Cambridge University Press.

Sherman, S. J., & Corty, E. (1984). Cognitive heuristics. In R. S. Wyer & T. K. Srull (Eds.), *Handbook of social cognition* (Vol. 1, pp. 189–286). Hillsdale, NJ: Erlbaum.

Shrum, L. J. (1995). Assessing the social influence of television: A social cognition perspective on cultivation effects. *Communication Research, 22,* 402–429.

Shrum, L. J. (1996). Psychological processes underlying cultivation effects: Further tests of construct accessibility. *Human Communication Research, 22,* 482–509.

Shrum, L. J. (2001). Processing strategy moderates the cultivation effect. *Human Communication Research, 27,* 94–120.

Shrum, L. J. (2007a). Cultivation and social cognition. In D. R. Roskos-Ewoldsen & J. L. Monahan (Eds.), *Communication and social cognition: Theories and methods* (pp. 245–272). Mahwah, NJ: Erlbaum.

Shrum, L. J. (2007b). The implications of survey method for measuring cultivation effects. *Human Communication Research, 33,* 64–80.

Shrum, L. J., Burroughs, J. E., & Rindfleisch, A. (2005). Television's cultivation of material values. *Journal of Consumer Research, 32*, 473–479.

Shrum, L. J., Lee, J., Burroughs, J. E., & Rindfleisch, A. (2011). An online process model of second-order cultivation effects: How television cultivates materialism and its consequences for life satisfaction. *Human Communication Research, 37*, 34–57.

Shrum, L. J., & O'Guinn, T. C. (1993). Processes and effects in the construction of social reality: Construct accessibility as an explanatory variable. *Communication Research, 20*, 436–471.

Shrum, L. J., O'Guinn, T. C., Semenik, R. J., & Faber, R. J. (1991). Processes and effects in the construction of normative consumer beliefs: The role of television. In R. H. Holman & M. R. Solomon (Eds.), *Advances in consumer research* (Vol. 18, pp. 755–763). Provo, UT: Association for Consumer Research.

Shrum, L. J., Wyer, R. S., & O'Guinn, T. C. (1998). The effects of television consumption on social perceptions: The use of priming procedures to investigate psychological processes. *Journal of Consumer Research, 24*, 447–458.

Tversky, A., & Kahneman, D. (1973). Availability: A heuristic for judging frequency and probability. *Cognitive Psychology, 5*, 207–232.

Wyer, R. S., & Srull, T. K. (1989). *Memory and cognition in its social context.* Hillsdale, NJ: Erlbaum.

# 9. Cultivation and the Perceived Realism of Stories

*Rick Busselle & Helena Bilandzic*

> The poet does not require us to be awake and believe; he solicits us only to yield ourselves to a dream and this too with our eyes open, and with our judgment *perdue* behind a curtain, ready to awaken us at the first motion of our will: and meantime, only, not to *dis*believe. (Coleridge, 1817/1907, p. 189)

Theory and research suggest that relationships between media exposure and media effects are influenced by the extent to which audience members judge media content to be realistic. One is tempted to conclude that as perceived realism increases so does media's influence. However, conceptual and methodological complications challenge too simplistic a conclusion (see Hall, 2009a). These complications fall into three interrelated categories: (1) conceptualizations of perceived realism, (2) how realism varies across different content categories (fiction, non-fiction, or reality-based) and from one genre to another within categories (e.g., reality dating or fly-on-the-wall reality), and (3) the extent to which we are by nature either disbelieving or credulous in our consumption of media content.

Cultivation theory describes how mediated stories construct reality for audience members and societies (Gerbner, 1998, 1999; Gerbner & Gross, 1976; Morgan, Shanahan, & Signorielli, 2009; Gerbner, Gross, Morgan, Signorielli, & Shanahan, 2002). In this chapter we are not directly concerned with the social construction of reality as cultivation theory articulates it. Instead we focus on perceived realism as the comparisons audience members make between the constructed realities they interpret as the actual world and the representations of those realities they observe in media. We might think of perceived realism as the extent to which viewers judge that the people and events they encounter in media are portrayed as would be expected, given the socially constructed understandings of the actual world that a given viewer brings to the media experience. There are two important elements to this definition. First, it recognizes that the actual world audience members take as "reality" is a social construction based on their immediate and mediated experiences as well as their own traits and tendencies. Second, it defines perceived realism as based on an expectation audiences have of content that originates in that socially constructed reality.

An array of conceptual and operational definitions of perceived realism exists in the literature (for reviews, see Busselle & Greenberg, 2000; Potter, 1988), and scholars continue both to redefine the concept (e.g., Shapiro, Barriga, & Beren, 2010) and to question its efficacy (Pouliot & Cowen, 2007). Such a lack of consensus might suggest that scholars have yet to identify the best definition of perceived realism. We argue that this is not the case. Instead, we suggest that what constitutes realism or authenticity, and therefore perceived realism, varies depending on what one is watching. In essence, audience members use different criteria to judge realism in different media contexts. Thus, the appropriate conceptualization of perceived realism depends on the nature of realism in a given genre or content category. Further, it is not clear from the research whether viewers, listeners, or readers actively and routinely evaluate realism or only object to its absence (Busselle & Bilandzic, 2008). One approach suggests that individuals are incredulous by nature but suspend disbelief to a greater or lesser extent while consuming fictional stories (for an overview, see Worth, 2004). An alternative is that audiences are accepting by nature, assuming authenticity until challenged otherwise (e.g., Gerrig & Rapp, 2004). Thus, the task for media scholars with respect to realism is to understand what "realism" means in different contexts and when and under what conditions audience members make judgments about it.

Cultivation theory, with its focus on storytelling (Gerbner & Gross, 1976), is an especially useful domain for considering realism. This is because a considerable amount of research has focused on perceived realism as a moderator or mediator of cultivation effects (e.g., Busselle, 2001; Potter, 1986; Quick, 2009). It is also because cultivation theory relies on stories as the primary communicative unit of influence (Busselle, Ryabovolova, & Wilson, 2004; Gerbner, 1999). Pinpointing the story as a starting point for investigating realism helps to focus theoretical considerations related to both processes and outcomes and allows us to narrow and frame our discussion in useful ways.

In this chapter we explore the concept of perceived realism from the perspectives of cultivation theory and narrative processing. We begin with issues of definition.

## Conceptualizing Realism

Scholars have generated a range of items and scales to assess audiences' interpretations of the accuracy, authenticity, or verisimilitude of media content. In doing so, they have struggled with several issues. One is a difficulty in knowing what criteria audiences use to judge realism. A second is that the criteria for judging realism may change from one genre to another. A third complication relates to the specificity of realism judgments. Judgments about specific content, such as a program or segment shown in an experimental setting, may be very different from more abstract judgments about an entire genre, such as responses to perceived realism questions asked in a survey.

These complications have contributed to a proliferation of realism items and scales that vary in at least three ways (Busselle & Greenberg, 2000). First, realism instruments purport to assess different conceptual dimensions, such as whether television reflects the reality of social interactions and situations (e.g., Dorr, Kovaric, & Doubleday, 1990; Wright, Huston, Reitz, & Piemayat, 1994), the extent to which events typically happen in real life as they are portrayed in media (Shapiro & Chock, 2003), or whether representations are plausible in the real world (Elliott, Rudd, & Good, 1983; Elliott & Slater, 1980). Second, they ask about different objects within media content, such as people, events, and behaviors (e.g., Greenberg & Reeves, 1976). Third, they ask about realism at different levels of specificity, ranging from a specific story or episode (e.g., Bahk, 2001; Slater, Rouner, & Long, 2006; Ward & Rivadeneyra, 1999) to genres or categories (e.g., Rubin, Perse, & Powell, 1985; Perse, 1990) to television in general (e.g., Busselle, 2003; Potter, 1986).

In some experimental settings realism has been manipulated rather than measured. Typically participants are shown stimulus content that is fictional or nonfictional, or they are told that the same stimulus is real or not real. In some cases the participants respond differently depending on the manipulation (e.g., Atkin, 1983; Berkowitz & Alioto, 1973; Konijn, Walma van der Molen, & van Nes, 2009), although not in all cases (e.g., Feshbach, 1976), suggesting that perceived realism is open to the interpretation of the viewer as much as the definition of the researcher (Potter, 1988).

With respect to conceptual dimensions, nearly a dozen separate terms can be found in the literature describing realism (for reviews, see Busselle & Greenberg, 2000; Potter, 1988). Early research focused on the notion of similarity when comparing portrayals to their real world counterpart, such as police officers or teachers (e.g., Greenberg & Reeves, 1976; Wright et al., 1994) and actions or events, such as crimes or emergencies (e.g., Busselle, 2001; Reeves, 1978). This may have been under the assumption that television images which do not look or feel like the real world have no influence on perceptions of real life. In this context a portrayal was thought to be realistic if people or events were represented as they were assumed to appear in the actual world. A second element of these comparisons recognized that fictional representations may vary with respect to the likelihood or probability of people existing or events occurring (e.g., Hall, 2003; Wright et al., 1994), whether similar people or events could plausibly occur (e.g., Elliott et al., 1983), or the nature of how events would typically occur if they were to occur (Shapiro & Chock, 2003; Shapiro & Fox, 2002).

In fantasy genres there may be no apparent relation between a portrayal and the real world. Events and creatures may not exist or be possible in the real world. But, at the same time, these portrayals may seem authentic, or not inauthentic, in meaningful ways. Potter (1988) recognized a distinction between the extent to which people and objects look like modern day, real life—*syntactic* realism—and the realism of human interactions and relations, regardless of surface appearances—*semantic* realism (for a slightly different conceptualization of this distinction, see Pouliot & Cowen, 2007). For example, *Harry Potter's* Dumbledore is a 150-year-old wizard. At one level he is absurdly unrealistic and could not exist in the actual world. Yet, his grandfatherly relationship with the protagonist, Harry Potter, may seem realistic to the extent that Dumbledore's death was devastating for both Harry Potter and the audience, evoking emotions in both that are quite real.[1]

Busselle and Bilandzic (2008) outlined a number of ways in which portrayals might be seen as *un*realistic based on the potential for audiences to observe inconsistencies. They argue that a portrayal may seem unrealistic if it is inconsistent with an audience member's expectations based on previous real life experience, previous mediated experience, or previous experience with a genre or media category. Further, portrayals may seem unrealistic if the story is internally inconsistent (Hall, 2003) or incoherent (Graesser, Olde, & Klettke, 2002; Rapp & Gerrig, 2002). Here realism may depend on the extent to which people and events are logical or appropriate given earlier events and character development. Recently, Shapiro et al. (2010) demonstrated a relation between perceived realism and causal attributions made in a text about characters' behaviors, suggesting that logical inferences play a role in realism perceptions.

It is important to recognize that some studies have allowed respondents to define realism for themselves by simply asking, "how realistic" is a given program, genre, or medium. For example, Quick (2009) asked viewers of the medical drama, *Grey's Anatomy*, to rate the series on three continua—realistic-unrealistic, believable-unbelievable, and credible-not credible—which were combined into a single scale. The study found that the scale positively mediated the relation between viewing level and favorable perceptions of doctors. One limitation of using an open definition such as this is uncertainty about what viewers mean when they report that content is realistic, believable, or credible. At the same time, there is an advantage in reducing the likelihood that a respondent does not share the researcher's definition. That is, while we may be uncertain about what realism means for viewers in a given context (e.g., to *Grey's Anatomy* viewers), the empirical evidence that realism plays a role in the relation between exposure and perception is important.

In summary, conceptualizations of perceived realism originated as judgments about the similarity of portrayed characters and events to their real world counterparts. This may have followed the assumption that content with no obvious connection to the actual world would have no influence. The concept was expanded to include assessments of the plausibility or likelihood of fictional events occurring in the actual world. Then, the concept was expanded further to recognize that even stories of fantastical people and events are "realistic" to the extent that they make sense according to an internal logic. Finally, there is some evidence that part of perceived realism is related to causal attributions suggested in a portrayal. We now turn to the nature of realism in different genres and content categories.

## A Moving Target

Research on cultivation theory most frequently tests the central hypothesis that exposure to media (typically television) is related to perceptions of the actual world. Usually exposure is operationalized as hours of television viewed on an average day (Morgan, Shanahan, & Signorielli, 2009) or in terms of the viewing of specific genres (Bilandzic & Busselle, 2008; Bilandzic & Rössler, 2004), such as soap operas (Shrum, 1996), crime-dramas (Busselle & Shrum, 2003) or action-adventure programs (Potter & Chang, 1990). Stories told in different genres vary in both topic and structure (e.g., Pyrhönen, 2007). For example romantic comedies deal with topics related to relationships and tend to follow an explication-complication-resolution structure (Lyden, 2003). Mysteries typically begin with the commission of a crime and are resolved with the revelation of the culprit and his or her method (Mittell, 2004). Our present concern is less with different genres per se than with the role of realism across the broader content categories of fiction, nonfiction, and the hybrid, reality-based genres.

With the exception of abstract media art, all media content is *representation*, usually of people (or creatures), places, and events. Representations are not reality, but "stake a claim on reality" through an implied relationship with the actual world (Grossberg, Wartella, Whitney, & Wise, 2006, p. 196). The nature of that relationship depends on the content in question and determines what judgments are available about the realism of that content.

Nonfiction has a direct relationship to specific, real people and events. Therefore, judgments related to realism are limited to the realm of accuracy and representativeness. Available criticisms focus on bias, sensationalism, or the veracity of facts (Maier, 2002; Newhagen & Nass, 1989). At a more abstract level, questions about the realism of nonfiction may focus on the representativeness of the events and facts linked to an inferred category, such as whether news reports in general represent news events as they are in life (Rubin, Perse, & Powell, 1985; Perse, 1990) or if topics, such as crime, are exaggerated or underrepresented in news programs (Chiricos, Padgett, & Gertz, 2000). Realism judgments about both specific events and content categories assume that the people and events represented do or did exist in the actual world. Thus, realism is limited to the accuracy with which those events are reported or documented.

Conversely, fictional representations typically make no claim about specific real individuals or events. Instead, representations are linked to categories of the real world through fictional characters and events. In fiction, the realm of story elements to which accuracy can be applied is determined by the story world. Story world includes time and place as well as the logic and rules of the story. For example, modern day London is governed by the logic of the actual world, unless Jack The Ripper has time-travelled to the present from the past, in which case the story world includes the ability to time travel as well as all of the logical implications of that possibility. In a work of fiction that takes place in an actual world setting (e.g., a crime-drama), perceptions of accuracy in the form of similarity to the perceived real world likely play a larger part in realism judgments. This may be because we use the actual world as the default reality unless a representation constructs an alternative reality (Segal, 1995). For example, participants listing thoughts after viewing an episode of *Law & Order*, a modern crime-drama, were quick to notice when police officers "busted" into an apartment without a search warrant or failed to read suspects their Miranda Rights (Quintero Johnson & Busselle, 2005). As story worlds depart from the actual world, the requirement for accuracy applies to fewer elements of the representation. For example, some audience members object when a cowboy appears to have an unlimited supply of bullets in his "six-shooter," but not when a Storm Trooper's "blaster" can fire ad infinitum.

Here we can draw two conclusions. First, as the story world departs from the actual world there is a diminishing of the realm of the story to which realism vis-à-vis perceived similarity to the actual world applies. At the same time there is a limit to how much a story can deviate from the actual world because realism always applies at the level of basic human behavior and basic logic. For example, the generally accepted conventions of human behavior prohibit a character from intentionally causing his or her own death except as a result of mental illness or altruism, assuming non-altruistic suicide is always caused by some form of mental illness. Similarly, the laws of logic preclude the reversal of temporal order in causally related events; while time travel is possible in many stories, a character can never go forward in time to change the past.

The second conclusion is that as one moves from nonfiction to fiction, realism as representativeness and accuracy gives way to realism as plausibility. Shapiro and colleagues (Shapiro et al., 2010; Shapiro & Chock, 2003) have pointed out that audience members may imagine how fictional events would occur if they were to occur. In this case audiences assess realism by considering the relation between the portrayal and their image of what could or probably would happen or how people could or probably would behave under a given set of circumstances.

Existing between fiction and non-fiction are hybrid, reality-based genres (Hill, 2005; Nabi et al., 2006; Ouellette & Hay, 2008). As Nabi, Biely, Morgan, & Stitt (2003) point out, categorizing reality-based programs is difficult because there are so many variations, and new iterations are introduced with each new television season. Reality-based programs' claim on the real world differs from both fiction and nonfiction. This relationship appears to manifest in two forms. In one case ostensibly naturally occurring, real events are captured on video and replayed for the audience (e.g., *Cops, America's Funniest Home Videos*). Here, realism may depend largely on the viewer's sense that the video is not staged (Antony, 2010), which probably matters to the extent that viewers' expectations of actuality are met or violated. That is, if one expected to see actual police procedures or actual accidents, the sense that an event was staged would not meet expectations.

In another type of reality-based program events are real in the sense that they are not the product of special effects or computer-generated imagery. So when a man eats a handful of live worms, he is actually eating live worms. In this sense, the relation between the representation and the event may be more direct than is the case in traditional nonfiction. For example, news reports often do not have video of a news event itself, but only images of the aftermath and possibly eye-witness testimonies. In reality-based programming the representation is real and linked to an actual person in the real world. At the same time, the real event is staged (Hill, 2005) or manipulated

(Hall, 2009b). The staged nature of events in many reality-based genres challenges the logic of traditional realism judgments. For example, staged events are both unlikely to occur in the real world but do occur when program producers create artificial situations; these situations are both implausible in reality and do occur under artificial conditions; and events would both not happen as portrayed and apparently did happen as witnessed. In reality-based genres assessments of realism may be based on the extent to which characters or participants behave as one would expect them to, given the unrealistic or contrived situation in which they find themselves. Of course, the staged nature of reality-based programming varies. But even in so-called "fly-on-the-wall" programs, in which participants ostensibly go about their normal lives while being recorded, audience members appear to be aware that behavior may be influenced by the presence of cameras and recording devices. In interviews with reality-TV viewers, Hill (2005) found that audience members appear to adjust their expectations to account for the artificial nature of the situation presented in the program.

Nabi et al. (2007) provides an interesting illustration of how perceived realism might work in reality-based content. She asked respondents to rate 33 reality programs representing a broad range of sub-groups of the genre (e.g., crime, make-over, talent contests) on 12 dimensions, including realism. Despite the fact that all the programs were reality-based and covered a wide range of potential perceived realism—from very unrealistic to very realistic—the perception of realism was not a strong determinant of how the programs clustered in the minds of respondents. This suggests that rather than categorizing reality programming along a realism continuum, individuals adjust their interpretations of what realism means in different programs or categories.

The important point is that the variety of relationships between representations and the real world across the media landscape makes perceived realism different from other constructs of interest to communication scholars (e.g., information seeking, probability estimates, behavioral intention) because the nature of "realism" itself changes from one content category to the next. The types of judgments people may make about realism also change from one genre to the next. People "see" different genres as more or less realistic (Busselle, 2003). But more importantly, when considering different categories, people make fundamentally different kinds of realism judgments, applying different criteria and maybe using different judgment processes.

This has important implications for the issue of genre-specific cultivation effects (Bilandzic & Busselle, 2008; Bilandzic & Rössler, 2004; Morgan & Shanahan, 2010). Audiences likely have different realism expectations about portrayals in different genres or content categories. A premise or situation may be noticeably unrealistic in one genre or context (e.g., a medical drama) but may seem perfectly normal in another (e.g., fantasy, reality-contests). The challenge for scholars is to match conceptualization and measurement with content, context, and research focus (Konijn et al., 2009).

## Real as the Default

When reflecting on his own writing of *Lyrical Ballads,* Samuel Coleridge said that he sought "…a semblance of truth sufficient to procure for these shadows of imagination that *willing suspension of disbelief* for the moment, which constitutes poetic faith" (Coleridge, 1817/1907, p. 6, emphasis added).[2] The concept has come to represent a set of implicit assumptions about audiences' negotiations of the transition between reality and fiction. Coleridge described a willingness to believe, a withholding of rational judgment, and a willingness to reactivate judgment or "bring judgment back into play" (Bormann, 1972, p. 58). We consider these three processes in turn.

The notion of a willingness to believe, which facilitates a suspension of disbelief, requires the assumption that media consumers are incredulous by default. This assumption is questionable. Certainly, individuals may approach content skeptically, for example, when faced with content one perceives as persuasive or with news content from a distrusted source. However, even to reject media content, audiences must comprehend information before disbelieving it. Then, subsequent to comprehension, we may evaluate the veracity of that information and conclude that it is in some way flawed. However, such subsequent evaluation requires both cognitive resources and motivation (Gilbert, 1991; Gilbert & Gill, 2000; Gilbert, Tafarodi, & Malone, 1993). This reasoning prompted Prentice and Gerrig (1999) to conclude that disbelief is *constructed* rather than *suspended*. When applied to the notion of media realism, this suggests that individuals may evaluate information and conclude that it is unrealistic, but without such evaluation, story relevant information is simply accepted (Bradley & Shapiro, 2004; Busselle & Bilandzic, 2008; Shapiro et al., 2010). Indeed, Coleridge (1817/1907) foreshadowed this when referring to "…that negative faith, which simply permits the images presented to work by their own force, without either denial or affirmation of their real existence…" (p. 107).

The point is that one does not anticipate the possibility of unrealistic content, any more than one assumes that a barista cannot make a good cappuccino or that a friend's offer to buy a cappuccino is insincere. Both are possibilities, but not possibilities we necessarily consider. Moreover, if we are unaware of the possibilities, we also must be unaware of their absence or that the possibilities did not materialize. Simply stated, we cannot dismiss a possibility that we have not previously considered.

The second process suggested by Coleridge—a withholding of rational judgment—has two components. First, fictional spaces open up a possible alternative world; this, however, is not the same as falseness, against which audiences need to argue. If fictional content does not make a claim of truth, then audiences do not have to withhold judgment about falseness. Thus, we argue that audiences are not bothered by fictionality. Instead, as with any other judgment, audiences evaluate when necessary. Individuals make judgments and draw conclusions about the people and events they witness in stories, regardless of whether those stories are fictional, nonfictional, or some hybrid of the two, just as they make judgments about all types of information; we are disappointed in the woman who succumbs to an unworthy suitor, and concerned for the child who becomes separated from his mother. This is true regardless of whether it occurs in a sci-fi film, in a documentary, or in our own neighborhood as told to us by a friend.

The third process suggested by Coleridge focuses on activating rational judgment. We have argued that rational judgment is not suspended. But we have also argued that judgment about truth status is activated only when prompted or required. In order to address this we need to consider narrative processing in more detail.

## Narrative Processing and Realism Judgments

Consumers of narratives are active in constructing mental models of the story world, the characters who populate that world, and the events that impact them (Bordwell, 1985; Ohler, 1994; Oatley, 2002; Zwaan, Magliano, & Graesser, 1995). Readers and viewers combine information from a text (novel, film, television program) with previously existing, story-relevant knowledge, to construct these mental representations (Prentice, Gerrig, & Bailis, 1997; Rapp, Gerrig, & Prentice, 2001). The primary activity of the reader or audience member is to progressively construct a mental representation that is coherent both with respect to earlier points in the story and with what the individual brings to the story in the form of previous knowledge and experience (Busselle & Bilandzic, 2008; Graesser et al., 2002). The event-indexing model (Zwaan, Langston, & Graesser, 1995) suggests that during the process of comprehending a story, readers monitor changes in five dimensions (time, space, protagonists' identity, causality, and intentionality).[3] To the extent that these changes can be incorporated into existing mental representations, the narrative is coherent and comprehension progresses relatively smoothly. Conversely, if new information is inconsistent with existing representations then construction should be interrupted and comprehension should suffer (Albrecht & O'Brien, 1993; Zwaan, Magliano, & Graesser,

1995). Worth (2004) suggested that the consumer of narrative *creates* belief rather than suspends disbelief, and that one cannot construct a narrative world and at the same time believe that world is false.

Bordwell (1985) pointed to the hypothesis-testing nature of narrative comprehension. As new information becomes available audience members anticipate its implications for characters and events. Based on characters' traits and motivations some behaviors can be reasonably expected from a character, but others cannot (Rapp et al., 2001). In fact, some reactions would seem absurd. Consider a scenario in which a man meets two muggers on the street at night. The man is threatened at knife point and ordered to hand over his wallet. First, in the mind of the audience, the man and the muggers are neither real nor unreal. They simply are a potential victim and two muggers. Second, depending on previous character development, the audience suspects a range of possible responses from the potential victim. The victim as a sensible man may remain calm and hand over the wallet, hoping the muggers will be satisfied. The victim as a cowardly man may sob and beg for his life while forfeiting his wallet. The victim as an action hero may employ his martial arts skills to teach a lesson in retaliatory justice. Each of these responses would be coherent relative to the way the character has been developed, or the mental model of the character (Rapp et al., 2001). Comprehension of the narrative and construction of the story will progress to the extent that the man's response is consistent with the audience's expectations, given their knowledge of the character and his situation. Of course, the man's responses are not so strictly proscribed. The coward may remain calm; the sensible man may cower, and the action hero may not use violence. But the response must be consistent with the character. The coward cannot inexplicably become a martial artist and the hero cannot cower, unless the inconsistent behavior is somehow justified in the story. Moreover, unless fantastical story-world rules have been introduced, none of the men can shape-shift or become invisible.

From this one can conclude, generally, that information that is inconsistent with the characters, situations, or the story world should activate some type of realism evaluation in the audience. But without such observed inconsistency, the audience has no reason to consider the authenticity, verisimilitude, or realism of the information presented. This suggests we should fundamentally change the way we think about perceived realism. It seems unlikely that audience members assess realism in the narratives they consume, at least while consuming them. Conversely, they *should* notice if the narrative is unrealistic. This is because not being realistic manifests as inconsistency between observations and expectations. These expectations are based on what is known about characters, situations, and story worlds as well as assumptions based on real world experience. These inconsistencies should interrupt the smooth construction of mental representations of the story, which, in turn, should lower engagement and enjoyment.

This has implications for audiences seeking programs as well as genres. For example, Papacharissi and Mendelson (2007) adapted realism items to measure "how true to life viewers understand reality [-TV] depictions to be" (p. 363). They found that the perceived realism of reality programming was positively related to hours of viewing and watching for entertainment and relaxation motivations. Thus, perceiving a lack of realism in a reality-based program, within the constraints of realism expectations about that program, may deter future viewing of similar content.

## Implications for Perceived Realism and Cultivation Research

Research into the perceived realism of media and its role in media effects has focused on the extent to which audiences find what they consume to be realistic. Gerbner and Gross (1976) argued that "viewers assume [television stories] take place against the backdrop of reality" and wondered "how often and to what degree viewers suspend their disbelief in the reality of the symbolic world" (p. 178). Potter (1986) concluded that "viewers who believe that televised content is real are more likely to be influenced by it than viewers who believe the content to be fictional or stylized" (p. 161). This assumption of active realism monitoring also is apparent in the most recent research (e.g., Barriga, Shapiro, & Jhaveri, 2009; Konijn et al., 2009; Quick, 2009; Shapiro et al., 2010) and prevails across research into different content areas including non-fiction (e.g., Chiricos et al., 2000), fiction (e.g., Quick, 2009), reality-based content (Nabi et al., 2006), and even public service announcements (e.g., Pinkleton, Austin, & Van de Vord, 2010).

Conventional wisdom suggests that mediated stories are taken as fundamentally different from real world events. Then the two somehow become confused, or one is recognized as a reflection of the other, resulting in the mediated world contaminating understandings of the actual world. However, our arguments suggest that mediated and actual worlds are not perceived as fundamentally different, at least as they are being experienced. For example, as we have argued elsewhere, while watching a mystery, viewers do not think of a detective as a fictional detective or a realistic detective. They think of him or her only as a detective trying to solve a crime (Busselle & Bilandzic, 2008). Given this, it may be more productive to ask how often, under what conditions, and to what effect viewers find content to be *un*realistic. There are a number of reasons to consider changing our focus from realism to unrealism.

First, when we measure other communication-related constructs, such as an attitude, we assume that the construct is salient or will become salient in the future, perhaps in a purchase or voting decision. However, perceived realism may be an example of what we have referred to as an "asymmetrical" construct, one that individuals become aware of only when it is in a negative state (Busselle & Bilandzic, 2009). This may be true of attention and understanding as well as realism; we typically are not consciously aware that we are paying attention, that we understand, or that something is realistic. Instead, we become aware only when our attention wanes, when we have difficulty understanding, or when a portrayal seems unrealistic. If this is the case, common realism measures do not directly measure the construct of interest—observed unrealism. Instead, at best, they indirectly measure its absence. The implication here is that cultivation surveys that measure realism may capture very little of the unrealism respondents observe while viewing. The unrealism observed in data may be more a reaction to generalizations about genres or social desirability related to negative opinions about the medium than instances of actually observing in stories some lack of authenticity. One suggestion to address this is the development of measures that more directly assess *un*realism. One might ask respondents, for example, if they recall thinking that anything about a medical drama seemed implausible or hard to believe. This may take the form of a counter-arguing measure (e.g., Jacks & Cameron, 2003; Wellins & McGinnies, 1977) through a prompted thought listing procedure. Such a measure may be useful because perceived unrealism judgments could be thought of as a manifestation of counter-arguing in narrative context. A similar alternative may be to ask respondents how often they find themselves thinking that a story or portrayal is inaccurate or inauthentic. We might find that people who report "often" or "very often" are less susceptible to cultivation-type effects than those who say "never" or "rarely."

Second, if viewers do not evaluate the realism of content and do not conceive of it as a continuum ranging from less to more realistic then realism cannot moderate cultivation in the sense we typically think of. Shrum (2001) demonstrated that television exposure has little influence on social judgments when viewers are made aware that their judgments may be based on television sources or examples. It appears that respondents dismiss these sources, upon reflection, as somehow unreliable or irrelevant. A similar but reverse process may be at work with perceived realism. When participants are asked about content realism, an evaluation process is activated that otherwise may remain dormant. If the default state is acceptance when realism judgments are dormant, then merely asking the question may activate a process that can only move the judgment toward the negative. That is, if the default is acceptance, then the accurate response on a scale would be the most positive option. But when realism judgments are prompted respondents may search for evidence that content is unrealistic—evidence that may be unrelated or tangentially related to the process of cultivation and may indicate response values that suggest moderate levels of perceived realism, which inaccurately reflect the acceptance that typically occurs during viewing. Thus, asking about the perceived realism of content may activate a process and introduce variance that is not present under real world conditions.

Third, the proposition that people are susceptible to media effects such as cultivation *unless* they perceive content to be unrealistic (and that perceiving content as unrealistic may be more the exception than the rule) is consistent with research in narrative persuasion. That research has shown that higher levels of transportation or absorption in stories positively relate to changes in beliefs and attitudes (Appel & Richter, 2010; Escalas, 2007; Green & Brock, 2000, Vaughn, Hesse, Petkova, & Trudeau, 2009). From this we might suspect that stories which are more engaging play a stronger role in the cultivation process. There are two reasons for this. First, if noticing instances of unrealism is distracting and interferes with engagement and enjoyment, it also should interfere with a story's influence on attitudes and beliefs about the real world. Moreover, to the extent that viewers choose content that is rewarding and avoid content that is not, viewers should avoid content they perceive as unrealistic for the very reason that it is less engaging and enjoyable. Thus, over time, individuals' overall viewing patterns should tend to move away from content they perceive to be unrealistic (given their own expectations for that content) and toward that which does not promote evaluations or judgments related to realism. Put simply, we should expect people to gravitate toward content that does not fail to meet their implicit expectations of authenticity. If this is the case, realism may not mediate cultivation in a traditional, statistical sense, but in a way that is more consistent with cultivation theory itself. Specifically, the effect of perceived *un*realism should be to guide individuals' media choices toward content they find more engaging, more enjoyable, more consistent with their extant perceptions of reality, and ultimately to content that is more likely to contribute to and reinforce the social construction of the perceived "real" world.

## Notes

1. For discussions of emotions in fictional contexts, see Gendler and Kovakovich (2005) and Tan (1996).
2. Coleridge was referring to *Lyrical Ballads*, a collection of poems by Samuel Coleridge and William Wordsworth, published in 1798.
3. There are a number of different theoretical models that fall under this constructionist paradigm (Graesser et al., 2002). While they differ in the specific mechanisms they describe, each proposes some type of construction or integration process in which the individual must make sense of incoming information in light of existing knowledge.

# References


Albrecht, J., & O'Brien, E. (1993). Updating a mental model: Maintaining both local and global coherence. *Journal of Experimental Psychology: Learning, Memory, and Cognition, 19,* 1061–1070.

Antony, M. G. (2010). *When it's not fake: Empathic distress and affective responses to real media violence.* Doctoral Dissertation, Washington State University.

Appel, M., & Richter, T. (2010). Transportation and need for affect in narrative persuasion: A mediated moderation model. *Media Psychology, 13,* 101–135.

Atkin, C. (1983). Effects of realistic TV violence vs. fictional violence on aggression. *Journalism Quarterly, 60,* 615–621.

Bahk, C. M. (2001). Perceived realism and role attractiveness in movie portrayals of alcohol drinking. *American Journal of Health Behavior, 25,* 433–446.

Barriga, C. A., Shapiro, M. A., & Jhaveri, R. (2009). Media context, female body size and perceived realism. *Sex Roles, 60,* 128–141.

Berkowitz, L., & Alioto, J. (1973). The meaning of an observed event as a determinant of its aggressive consequences. *Journal of Personality and Social Psychology, 28,* 206–217.

Bilandzic, H., & Busselle, R. (2008). Transportation and transportability in the cultivation of genre-consistent attitudes and estimates. *Journal of Communication, 53,* 508–529.

Bilandzic, H., & Rössler, P. (2004). Life according to television. Implications of genre-specific cultivation effects: The gratification/cultivation model. *Communications: The European Journal of Communication Research, 29,* 295–326.

Bordwell, D. (1985). *Narration in the fiction film.* Madison, WI: University of Wisconsin Press.

Bormann, D. R. (1972). The willing suspension of disbelief: Kames as a forerunner of Coleridge. *Central States Speech Journal, 23,* 56–60.

Bradley, S., & Shapiro, M. A. (2005). Parsing reality: The interactive effects of complex syntax and time pressure on cognitive processing of television scenarios. *Media Psychology, 6,* 307–333.

Brehm, S. S., & Brehm, J. W. (1981). *Psychological reactance: A theory of freedom and control.* San Diego, CA: Academic Press.

Busselle, R. W. (2001). The role of exemplar accessibility in social reality judgments. *Media Psychology, 3,* 43–67.

Busselle, R. W. (2003). Television realism measures: The influence of program salience on global judgments. *Communication Research Reports, 20(4),* 367–375.

Busselle, R., & Bilandzic, H. (2008). Fictionality and perceived realism in experiencing stories: A model of narrative comprehension and engagement. *Communication Theory, 18,* 255–280.

Busselle, R. W., & Greenberg, B. S. (2000). The nature of television realism judgments: A reevaluation of their conceptualization and measurement. *Mass Communication & Society, 3,* 249–258.

Busselle, R. W., Ryabovolova, A., & Wilson, B. (2004). Ruining a good story: Cultivation, perceived realism and narrative. *Communications: The European Journal of Communication Research, 29,* 365–378.

Busselle, R. W., & Shrum, L. J. (2003). Media exposure and exemplar accessibility. *Media Psychology, 5*(3), 255–282.

Chiricos, T., Padgett, K., & Gertz, M. (2000). Fear, TV news, and the reality of crime. *Criminology, 38,* 755–785.

Coleridge, S. T. (1907). *Biographia Literaria*, Vol. 2, Clarendon Press: Oxford.

Dorr, A., Kovaric, P., & Doubleday, C. (1990). Age and content influences on children's perceptions of the realism of television families. *Journal of Broadcasting & Electronic Media, 34,* 377–397.

Elliott, W. R., Rudd, R. L., & Good, L. (1983). *Measuring perceived reality of television: Perceived plausibility, perceived superficiality, and degree of personal utility.* Paper presented at the Association for Education in Journalism and Mass Communication, Corvallis, OR.

Elliott, W. R., & Slater, D. (1980). Exposure, experience and perceived TV reality for adolescents. *Journalism Quarterly, 57,* 409–414, 431.

Escalas, J. (2007). Self-referencing and persuasion: Narrative transportation versus analytical elaboration. *Journal of Consumer Research, 33,* 421–429.

Feshbach, S. (1976). The role of fantasy in response to television. *Journal of Social Issues. 32*(4), 71–85.

Gendler, T. S., & Kovakovich, K. (2005). Genuine rational fictional emotions. In M. Kieran (Ed.), *Contemporary Debates in Aesthetics and the Philosophy of Art* (pp. 241–253). Oxford: Blackwell.

Gerbner, G. (1998). Cultivation analysis: An overview. *Mass Communication & Society, 1*(3/4), 175–194.

Gerbner, G. (1999). Foreword: What do we know? In J. Shanahan & M. Morgan, *Television and its viewers: Cultivation theory and research* (pp. ix-xiii). Cambridge: Cambridge University Press.

Gerbner, G., & Gross, L. (1976). Living with television: The violence profile. *Journal of Communication, 26*(2), 172–199.

Gerbner, G., Gross, L., Morgan, M., Signorielli, N., & Shanahan, J. (2002). Growing up with television: Cultivation processes. In J. Bryant & D. Zillmann (Eds.), *Media effects: Advances in theory and research* (2nd ed., pp. 43–67). Mahwah, NJ: Erlbaum.

Gerrig, R. J., & Rapp, D. N. (2004). Psychological processes underlying literary impact. *Poetics Today, 25,* 266–281.

Gilbert, D. T. (1991). How mental systems believe. *American Psychologist, 46,* 107–119.

Gilbert, D. T., & Gill, M. J. (2000). The momentary realist. *Psychological Science, 11,* 394–398.

Gilbert, D. T., Tafarodi, R. W., & Malone, P. S. (1993). You can't not believe everything you read. *Journal of Personality and Social Psychology, 65,* 221–233.

Graesser, A. C., Olde, B., & Klettke, B. (2002). How does the mind construct and represent stories? In M. C. Green, J. J. Strange, & T. C. Brock (Eds.), *Narrative impact: Social and cognitive foundations* (pp. 229–262). Mahwah, NJ: Erlbaum.

Green, M. C., & Brock, T. C. (2000). The role of transportation in the persuasiveness of public narratives. *Journal of Personality and Social Psychology, 79,* 701–721.

Greenberg, B. S., & Reeves, B. (1976). Children and the perceived reality of television. *Journal of Social Issues, 32,* 86–97.

Grossberg, L., Wartella, E., Whitney, D. C., & Wise, J. M. (2006). *Media making: Mass media in popular culture.* Thousand Oaks, CA: Sage.

Hall, A. E. (2003). Reading realism: Audiences' evaluations of the reality of media texts. *Journal of Communication, 53,* 624–641.

Hall, A. E. (2009a). Perceptions of media realism and reality TV. In R. L. Nabi & M. B. Oliver (Eds.), *The Sage handbook of media processes and effects* (pp. 423–438). Thousand Oaks, CA: Sage.

Hall, A. E. (2009b). Perceptions of the authenticity of reality programs and their relationships to audience involvement, enjoyment, and perceived learning. *Journal of Broadcasting & Electronic Media, 53,* 515–531.

Hill, A. (2005). *Reality TV: Audiences and popular factual television.* New York: Routledge.

Jacks, Z. J., & Cameron, K. A. (2003). Strategies for resisting persuasion. *Basic and Applied Social Psychology, 25*(2), 145–161.

Konijn, E. A., Walma van der Molen, J. H., & van Nes, S. (2009). Emotions bias perceptions of realism in audiovisual media: Why we may take fiction for real. *Discourse Processes, 46,* 309–340.

Lyden, J. C. (2003). *Film as religion. Myths, morals, and rituals.* New York: New York University Press.

Maier, S. R. (2002). Getting it right? Not in 59 percent of stories, *Newspaper Research Journal, 23,* 10–24.

Mittell, J. (2004). *Genre and television. From cop shows to cartoons in American culture.* New York: Routledge.

Morgan, M., Shanahan, J., & Signorielli, N. (2009). Growing up with television: Cultivation processes. In J. Bryant & M. B. Oliver (Eds.), *Media effects* (pp. 34–49). New York: Routledge.

Moyer-Gusé, E., & Nabi, R. (2010). Explaining the effects of narrative in an entertainment television program: Overcoming resistance to persuasion. *Human Communication Research, 36,* 26–52.

Nabi, R. L., Biely, E. N., Morgan, S. J., & Stitt, C. R. (2003) Reality-based television programming and the psychology of its appeal. *Media Psychology, 5,* 303–330.

Nabi, R., Stitt, C., Halford, J., & Finnerty, K. (2006). Emotional and cognitive predictors of the enjoyment of reality-based and fictional television programming: An elaboration of the uses and gratifications perspective. *Media Psychology, 8,* 421–447.

Newhagen, J., & Nass, C. (1989). Differential criteria for evaluating credibility of newspapers and TV news. *Journalism Quarterly, 66,* 277–284.

Oatley, K. (2002). Emotions and the story worlds of fiction. In M. C. Green, J. J. Strange, & T. C. Brock (Eds.), *Narrative impact: Social and cognitive foundations* (pp. 39–69). Mahwah, NJ: Erlbaum.

Ohler, P. (1994). *Kognitive Filmpsychologie. Verarbeitung und mentale Repräsentation narrativer Filme [Cognitive psychology of film. Processing and mental representation of narrative films].* Münster: MAkS Publikationen.

Ouellette, L., & Hay, J. (2008). *Better living through reality TV.* Oxford: Blackwell.

Papacharissi, Z., & Mendelson, A. (2007). An exploratory study of reality appeal: Uses and gratifications of reality TV shows. *Journal of Broadcasting & Electronic Media, 51*(2), 355–370.

Perse, E. M. (1990). Predicting attention to local television news: Need for cognition and motives for viewing. *Communication Reports, 5,* 40–49.

Petty, R. E., Tormala, Z. L., & Rucker, D. D. (2004). Resisting persuasion by counterarguing: An attitude strength perspective. In J. Jost, M. Banaji, R. Mahzarin, & D. Prentice (Eds.), *Perspectivism in social psychology: The yin and yang of scientific progress. APA Science Series. APA Decade of Behavior Series.* (pp. 37–51). Washington, DC: American Psychological Association.

Pinkleton, B. E., Austin, E. W., & Van de Vord, R. (2010). The role of realism, similarity, and expectancies in adolescents' interpretation of abuse-prevention messages. *Health Communication, 25,* 258–265.

Potter, W. J. (1986). Perceived reality and the cultivation hypothesis. *Journal of Broadcasting & Electronic Media, 30,* 159–174.

Potter, W. J. (1988). Perceived reality in television effects research. *Journal of Broadcasting & Electronic Media, 32,* 23–41.

Potter, W. J., & Chang, I. C. (1990). Television exposure measures and the cultivation hypothesis. *Journal of Broadcasting & Electronic Media, 34,* 313–333.

Pouliot, L., & Cowen, P. (2007). Does perceived realism really matter in media effects? *Media Psychology, 9,* 241–259.

Prentice, D. A., & Gerrig, R. J. (1999). Exploring the boundary between fiction and reality. In S. Chaiken & Y. Trope (Eds.), *Dual-process-theories in social psychology* (pp. 529–546). New York: Guilford Press.

Prentice, D. A., Gerrig, R. J., & Bailis, D. S. (1997). What readers bring to the processing of fictional texts. *Psychonomic Bulletin & Review, 4,* 416–420.

Pyrhönen, H. (2007). Genre. In D. Herman (Ed.), *The Cambridge companion to narrative* (pp. 109–123). Cambridge: Cambridge University Press.

Quick, B. L. (2009). The effects of viewing *Grey's Anatomy* on perceptions of doctors and patient satisfaction. *Journal of Broadcasting & Electronic Media, 53,* 38–55.

Quick, B. L., & Stephenson, M. T. (2007). Further evidence that psychological reactance can be modeled as a combination of anger and negative cognitions. *Communication Research, 34,* 255–276.

Quintero Johnson, J., & Busselle, R. (2005). *Processing narrative: The relationships among perceived realism, experiential involvement, and critical, cognitive, and emotional thoughts.* Paper presented to the Mass Communication division of the National Communication Association, Annual Convention, Boston, November.

Rapp, D. N., & Gerrig, R. J. (2002). Readers' reality-driven and plot-driven analyses in narrative comprehension. *Memory & Cognition, 30,* 779–788.

Rapp, D. N., Gerrig, R. J., & Prentice, D. A. (2001). Readers' trait-based models of characters in narrative comprehension. *Journal of Memory and Language, 45,* 737–750.

Reeves, B. (1978). Perceived TV reality as a predictor of children's social behavior. *Journalism Quarterly, 55,* 682–689, 695.

Rubin, A. M., Perse, E. M., & Powell, R. (1985). Loneliness, parasocial interaction, and local television news viewing. *Human Communication Research, 12,* 155–180.

Segal, E. M. (1995). A cognitive-phenomenological theory of fictional narrative. In J. F. Duchan, G. A. Bruder, & L. E. Hewitt (Eds.), *Deixis in narrative: A cognitive science perspective* (pp. 61–78). Hillsdale, NJ: Erlbaum.

Shapiro, M. A., Barriga, C. A., & Beren, J. (2010). Causal attributions and perceived realism of stories. *Media Psychology, 13,* 273–300.

Shapiro, M. A., & Chock, T. M. (2003). Psychological processes in perceiving reality. *Media Psychology, 5,* 163–198.

Shapiro, M. A., & Fox, F. R. (2002). The role of typical and atypical events in story memory. *Human Communication Research, 28,* 109–135.

Shrum, L. J. (1996). Psychological processes underlying cultivation effects: Further tests of construct accessibility. *Human Communication Research, 22,* 482–509.

Shrum, L. J. (2001). Processing strategy moderates the cultivation effect. *Human Communication Research, 27*(1), 94–120.

Slater, M. D., Rouner, D., & Long, M. (2006). Television dramas and support for controversial public policies: Effects and mechanisms. *Journal of Communication, 56*, 235–252.

Tan, E. S. (1996). *Emotion and the structure of narrative film: Film as an emotion machine.* Mahwah, NJ: Erlbaum.

Vaughn, L., Hesse, A., Petkova, Z., & Trudeau, L. (2009). "This story is right on": The impact of regulatory fit on narrative engagement and persuasion. *European Journal of Social Psychology, 39*, 447–456.

Ward, L. M., & Rivadeneyra, R. (1999). Contributions of entertainment television to adolescents' sexual attitudes and expectations: The role of viewing amount versus viewer involvement. *Journal of Sex Research, 36*, 237–249.

Wellins, R., & McGinnies, E. (1977). Counterarguing and selective exposure to persuasion. *Journal of Social Psychology, 103*, 115–127.

Worth, S. (2004). Fictional spaces. *Philosophical Forum, 35*, 439–455.

Wright, J. C., Huston, A. C., Reitz, A. L., & Piemayat, S. (1994). Young children's perceptions of television reality: Determinants and developmental differences. *Developmental Psychology, 30*, 229–239.

Zwaan, R. A., Langston, M. C., & Graesser, A. C. (1995). The construction of situation models in narrative comprehension: An event-indexing model. *Psychological Science, 6*, 292–297.

Zwaan, R. A., Magliano, J. P., & Graesser, A. C. (1995). Dimensions of situation model construction in narrative comprehension. *Journal of Experimental Psychology: Learning, Memory, and Cognition, 21*, 386–397.

# 10. Cultural Models and the Media

## Exploring the Interplay between Culture and the Individual

*David R. Ewoldsen & Nancy Rhodes*

Cultivation theory has spawned an amazing number of empirical studies testing its various predictions (Gerbner, 1998). In a content analysis of three major communication journals, Bryant and Miron (2004) identified cultivation theory—along with agenda-setting and uses and gratifications—as among the dominant three theories in the discipline. However, there are differing views as to the importance of cultivation theory. The overwhelming amount of evidence supporting cultivation theory elevates it to a class of grand theories. On the other hand, cultivation theory has been heavily criticized because most of the effects associated with cultivation research are very small. For example, a meta-analysis limited to the survey research testing cultivation theory included over 75 published studies that tested various predictions made by the theory (Morgan & Shanahan, 1997). That meta-analysis found an overall effect size of .09. This suggests, at least to some scholars, that support for cultivation theory is weak, and to the extent research does support the theory, it suggests it is not a particularly important phenomenon (Nabi & Oliver, 2010).

However, we argue that much of the research on cultivation—while important and certainly informing our understanding of media effects—misses a central point of the theory (Lang & Ewoldsen, 2010). The original formulation of the theory focused on the dynamic interplay between television and culture. Unfortunately, the cultural focus of cultivation theory has been lost (Lang & Ewoldsen, 2010; Roskos-Ewoldsen et al., 2004). In this chapter, we propose to revive the focus on the dynamic interplay between culture and television by drawing on theoretical and methodological developments in cognitive anthropology, focusing on cultural models and their relationship to media use (D'Andrade, 1995; Dressler, 2006; Shore, 1996; Strauss & Quinn, 1997). In addition, we will discuss the methodological issues involved in studying cultural models and summarize recent research on cultural models of romance.

## Contemporary Approaches to the Study of Cultivation Theory

Starting in the early 1980s, a major strand of cultivation research emerged that had a decidedly psychological orientation (Morgan, Shanahan, & Signorielli, 2009). Much of the research within this psychological tradition has focused on the classic and important distinction between first-order and second-order effects (Hawkins & Pingree, 1982; Shrum, Lee, Burroughs, & Rindfleisch, 2011). First-order effects deal with perceptions of the relative frequency of events such as the amount of violence in the world, how often people are divorced, the prevalence of law enforcement personnel in the United States and so forth. In other words, first-order effects deal with perceived "states of the world."

In contrast, second-order cultivation effects involve how perceptions about the state of the world influence judgments such as "the world is a mean place" or "marriages in the United States are unstable." In other words, second-order effects deal with how people evaluate the state of the world (Shrum et al., 2011). The prevalence of so much crime or so many law enforcement professionals certainly means that the world must be a dangerous place. Both first- and second-order cultivation effects deal with people's perceptions of the world. Whereas first-order effects deal with how frequently certain things occur, second-order effects are more concerned with the implications of these occurrences for their perceptions of the world.

One of the mechanisms through which cultivation may work is by increasing the accessibility of constructs depicted on TV in the memory of viewers (Shrum et al., 2011; Shrum & Lee, Chapter 8, this volume). This focus on the accessibility of constructs and attitudes is, in our view, some of the most important recent work in cultivation theory. Numerous studies have demonstrated that heavy viewing of particular television genres increases the accessibility of related constructs from memory (Busselle & Shrum, 2003; Shrum, 1996). Constructs that are more accessible from memory bias our judgments about and perceptions of our social environment (Anderson, Moskowitz,

Blair, & Nosek, 2007; Fazio, Roskos-Ewoldsen, & Powell, 1994). In particular, the accessibility of these constructs to some extent mediates the influence of television on perceptions of social reality (Shrum et al., 2011). Thus, the cultivation effect of the media appears to operate, at least in part, by increasing the accessibility of constructs that are related to what heavy viewers are watching. For example, if a person watches a lot of crime dramas, then crime and related constructs (e.g., guns, police, etc.) would be more accessible from memory for that person than for someone who sees few crime dramas. In turn, when that person walks around his or her neighborhood, that person would be more likely to interpret various elements of the social environment as involving violence (e.g., two boys wrestling will be interpreted as a fight; someone carrying a small pipe might be interpreted as carrying a gun).

Based on this research, Shrum et al. (2011) developed the heuristic processing model of cultivation effects. To explain the model, we will use the example of someone who watches a lot of crime dramas. According to this model, when this person is asked to make a judgment (e.g., "What percentage of the population engages in violent crime?") and she does not already have a judgment stored in memory, she will search memory for relevant information in order to make her judgment (e.g., "How many people can I think of who have engaged in a violent crime?"). This is referred to as a memory-based judgment because memory is searched for information to aid in making the decision (Hastie & Park, 1986). If the person is not highly motivated to make this judgment, then she will use heuristic processes, and information that is highly accessible from memory will exert a stronger influence on her judgments. Consequently, if this is a domain where the person watches a lot of television, the information that television has made highly accessible from memory (e.g., muggings, assaults, armed robbery, murders, etc.) will be more likely to influence her judgments. To the extent that television viewing has made relevant information more accessible in memory, then television viewing has influenced her judgment. According to Shrum et al. (2011), this is how first-order cultivation effects occur. However, if she is highly motivated to make a correct judgment, our viewer will engage in a more exhaustive search of memory, and the more easily accessible information will be less likely to influence her judgments (Fazio, 1990).

To explain second-order cultivation effects, Shrum et al. (2011) draw on an online process model. People typically make judgments of information as they encounter that information in what are called online judgments (Hastie & Park, 1986). To continue our example, our TV viewer also watches the local news after her favorite crime drama. If the local news has several stories about violent assaults and murders in the section of the town where she lives, she will probably make the judgment immediately that this is a dangerous place to drive. If someone later asks her about renting an apartment in that part of town, rather than recalling the different news stories about crime in that part of town, she will immediately recall the judgment that she has already made that this is a dangerous place. Television has influenced her judgment about this part of town (second-order cultivation effect) by influencing her judgments while watching television. To the extent that this judgment is made repeatedly, her judgment will be more accessible from memory and more likely to influence how she responds to queries about that topic and how she perceives relevant information and acts in relevant situations (Arpan, Rhodes, & Roskos-Ewoldsen, 2007).

Understanding how the media influence first- and second-order cultivation effects is important. However, we believe that as originally proposed, cultivation theory was more concerned with how television interacts with how people understand the world. To extend this example, instead of asking how frequently violent crimes occur, or whether a certain neighborhood is dangerous, we are concerned with the question of whether people who watch a lot of violent television *understand* what constitutes a violent action differently than a person who does not watch a lot of violent television.

## Cultivation and Culture

The research described above has clearly explicated how heavy viewing of the media can influence both judgments of states of the world and people's evaluations of these states. However, to us, cultivation theory implies that the media influence how people *understand* their world as opposed to simply how they perceive it. We believe this is a subtle but important distinction. Our reading of cultivation theory is that TV operates as a primary socializing agent in today's world (Gerbner, 1969, 1998; Gerbner & Gross, 1976; Gerbner, Gross, Morgan, Signorielli, & Shanahan, 2002). In other words, the culture that people learn is influenced heavily by the culture portrayed on TV. This is especially so for heavy viewers of TV. Although focusing on construct accessibility provides an explanation for individual level cultivation effects, it does not adequately account for the dynamic relationship between TV and culture. One of the dangers of a purely psychological explanation of cultivation theory is that its original focus on the dynamic relationship between television and culture may be lost. Nevertheless, it provides a valuable starting point for understanding cultivation effects.

At a basic level, cultivation theory maintains that the media cultivate our conceptions of social reality: What we watch influences how we understand the world. Cultivation theory has been, and continues to be, useful in a metaphoric understanding of the influence of the media. The very name of the theory—cultivation—is a metaphor drawing upon agriculture to help highlight the basic idea of the theory—that the media help to create a structured reality instead of a disorganized random weed patch reality. There are other metaphors used to understand media's influence. For example, gravity has been used to highlight the nonlinear nature of the theory: Heavy users of TV are drawn to the "TV reality" as if TV had a gravitational force. Metaphors are used to make certain characteristics of something more salient and often, more can be learned about the object of a metaphor by exploring the metaphor in more detail (Collins & Gentner, 1987). The cultivation metaphor is useful because it highlights the influence of culture within cultivation theory. Culture operates as the "glue" that binds people together so that they can work together—even when they are in conflict—by following basic rules of behavior.

Although cultivation is a good metaphor and has had enormous heuristic value in terms of generating research, from our perspective, a critical question remains about the theory. If television has been cultivating culture since its introduction over sixty years ago, how has it managed to do so *at a cultural level?* Research has done an excellent job of explicating the psychological mechanisms that account for individual-level cultivation effects, but our understanding of the societal-level mechanisms underlying this phenomenon is embarrassingly inadequate. Specifically, very little is known about the reciprocal influences of television viewing and culture. We draw upon a growing body of literature in cognitive anthropology to provide a new approach to understanding the mechanism underlying cultivation theory; namely, a cultural models approach.

One explanation for the lack of research attention devoted to the cultural component of cultivation theory is the difficulty in defining exactly what is meant by "culture." Indeed, there have been moves in anthropology—the discipline most closely aligned with the study of culture—to abandon the study of culture because of the elusiveness of the concept (Dressler, 2006; Strauss & Quinn, 1997). If it is difficult even for the experts in culture to define what is meant by culture, how are we supposed to study the relationship between media use and culture?

Historically, the problem with the definition of culture is several fold. First, the term is often defined so broadly that it becomes everything and hence captures only the most general themes of a culture and misses the details that comprise the richness of that culture (Dressler, 2006). For example, Hofstede's (2001) work to identify five dimensions along which cultures differ has been fruitful (his dimensions are individualism, masculinity, power distance, uncertainty avoidance, and long-term orientation). Indeed, extensive research by media scholars has utilized the dimensional approach (for example, Kwak, Zinkhan, & Dominick, 2002). But Hofstede's dimensional approach certainly captures few of the details and none of the nuances of culture. Consequently, research in this tradition often ignores very large differences in the cultures that exist within a given country or between countries that exist at similar points along Hofstede's dimensions. Second, culture is often talked about as if it is a "thing" that different groups of people possess (Strauss & Quinn, 1997), and while this focus on the concreteness of culture may make it easier to operationalize, culture is not a "thing" but rather a process. Third, there has been difficulty reconciling the apparent paradox that culture is something that exists across groups of people yet operates at the level of the individual (Dressler, 2005; Shore, 1996). However, the cultural models approach within cognitive anthropology addresses these shortcomings in the study of culture.

## Cultural Models: Making the Cognitive Social

Within cognitive anthropology, culture is often defined as the knowledge that one must possess to function adequately as a member of that society (Dressler, 2006). The knowledge that is necessary to function effectively resides in *cultural models*, which are intersubjectively shared mental models (D'Andrade, 1995; Dressler, 2005; Holland & Quinn, 1987; Romney & Moore, 1998; Shore, 1996). Cultural models are mental models of different culturally important elements of the world that are broadly shared by the people within that culture. These models allow people to make sense of their social world and how to act within that world (D'Andrade, 1995; Holland & Quinn, 1987; Romney & Moore, 1998). One way to think about cultural models is that they are highly shared mental models (D'Andrade, 1995; Roskos-Ewoldsen et al., 2004; Quinn, 1987).

Typically, research on cognition focuses on the individual, but work on cultural models focuses on the *shared* aspects of cognitive representations (D'Andrade, 1995; Romney & Moore, 1998; Shore, 1996; Strauss & Quinn, 1997). Within this perspective, culture is found at both the aggregate and individual levels. Cultural models focus on the aggregate because they involve the knowledge that is necessary for people to function in a coordinated and cooperative way—this is knowledge that must be distributed across individuals. But cultural models also operate at the individual level because these models are located within the individual's cognitive system.

Research in cognitive anthropology has demonstrated that cultural models are shared widely within cultural groups (Atran, Medin, & Ross, 2005;

Dressler, Borges, Balieiro, & dos Santos, 2005; Handwerker, 2002; Minoura, 1992; Quinn, 1987). For example, Quinn (1987) found a high degree of consensus concerning the cultural model of marriage in the United States. Specifically, in the cultural model of marriage in the U.S. there are eight elements: Marriages are enduring, mutually beneficial, unknown at the outset, difficult, effortful, a joint endeavor, may succeed or fail, and risky. Metaphors used to talk about marriage almost invariably include at least some of these elements. For example, a common metaphor for marriage is that it is a manufactured product (e.g., "we worked hard at making this marriage work"). This metaphor reflects the effortful and joint endeavor components of the marriage model. Not only are these cultural models shared, they also serve as the foundation on which people reason about marriage (Quinn, 1987). In other words, cultural models can shape how we view a cultural phenomenon such as marriage.

But where do these cultural models come from? How does shared knowledge arise within a person's idiosyncratic cognitive system? Certainly, our day-to-day experiences reflect a constant repetition of common themes and experiences ranging from greeting rituals to work and leisure-time activities to the behaviors long-term partners engage in and so on. Importantly, these patterns are fairly consistent and are repeated over and over again. This repetition and consistency create the ideal situation for a mental representation to form within the individual (D'Andrade, 1995; Shore, 1996; Strauss & Quinn, 1997), but because these patterns are widespread, similar mental representations should form across individuals, resulting in shared mental representations. For a more extensive discussion of these processes, Strauss and Quinn (1997) provide a general theory for the different ways in which these shared representations are created, passed across generations, and also change. But the basic point is that these cognitive structures emerge through our patterns of interaction with each other as well as those interactions we observe in both our social environment and by way of the media.

This is not to say that all of the cognitive representations found within a person's cognitive system are cultural models. There are a wide variety of cognitive representations which reflect a wide variety of influences. People clearly have their own idiosyncratic experiences that also are reflected in their cognitive representations as autobiographical memories as well as mental models and schemas (Roskos-Ewoldsen et al., 2004). Likewise, there are idiosyncrasies in people's cultural models that reflect their own unique experiences. Equally importantly, not all consensually shared knowledge reflects cultural knowledge. Some consensually shared knowledge reflects universals that arise because we are a biological species (Strauss & Quinn, 1997). The shared understanding that rain is wet reflects our experiences as a biological species. The shared understanding of kissing leads to the interpretation that the two people you see kissing in the United States are in a close relationship. However, in other parts of the world kissing is a greeting ritual that says very little about the relationship between the two people. This difference in the interpretation of kissing is cultural knowledge. The knowledge of rain and kissing are probably highly shared across people, but they arise out of different processes. As humans living in this world, we learn that rain is wet by idiosyncratically experiencing getting wet in the rain. Conversely, most people probably learn the meaning of a kiss between two people by observing this behavior countless times enacted in our cultural environment.

Clearly, some of these patterns—such as greeting rituals or patterns of behaviors in romantic relationships—reflect the larger culture within which we live. Because these behaviors reflect the culture, they are patterns that people are repeatedly exposed to in their day-to-day lives both in their day-to-day interactions and through the media. This repetition creates the ideal conditions for the formation of mental representations of these patterns. A dynamic relationship exists between these patterns of behavior and the resulting mental representations. The representations drive the behaviors but the behavior reinforces the representation within the individual and other individuals operating in the cultural environment (Strauss & Quinn, 1997). Culture reproduces itself through the cultural models which influence behavior. The enacted behavior in turn influences the cultural models.

Of course, this same process should operate with television. To the extent that television presents programming that reflects that larger culture within which it operates, it provides a rich resource for the repetitive presentation of culturally enacted behaviors. The extant research on cultivation theory suggests that this is the case and that television and the media should play an important role in the development and reinforcement of cultural models. Likewise, cultural models should influence what programming people watch as well as how they interpret that programming (Eno & Ewoldsen, 2010; Roskos-Ewoldsen et al., 2004). However, while the general expectation is that television will reinforce people's cultural models, there may be situations where television (and other media) undermines people's cultural models. Television typically presents fairly idealized representations of the world, and certain subgenres of programming are particularly prone to present idealized representations of a domain that may be at odds with the cultural model. For example, in certain subgenres of romantic programming, the events always seem to work out for the main characters to find each other at the end of the story. We hypothesize that heavy viewers of certain subgenres of programming such as idealized romantic programming may develop models of a domain that are at odds with the cultural model.

When discussing culture, there are a wide variety of potential models. Shore (1996) proposed three broad categories of cultural models. One broad domain of cultural models is *task models*. Task models involve how things get done such as what people do in a restaurant (Schank & Abelson, 1977), what grocery shopping entails, or the procedures involved in placing someone under arrest. The second category is *conceptual models*, which involve how people understand their social world. Conceptual models might include such things as what is marriage, what constitutes the game of soccer, or what is a bedtime story. The third category involves *orientation models*, which deal with relationships between things within the physical and social environment. Orientation models can include spatial layouts such as how to set a table or the appropriate use of interpersonal space as well as models of kin relationships and even medical diagnosis (e.g., the relationship between symptoms and a disease).

This process, discussed earlier, of the mutual reinforcement between television viewing and culture should be ongoing for all three of the different types of cultural models. Certainly, people learn what various culturally relevant concepts mean such as marriage (Signorielli, 1991) or materialism (Kwak et al., 2002; Shrum et al., 2011) from television (conceptual models). In addition, television presents numerous depictions of how various activities or goals are accomplished within a culture such as going grocery shopping, eating at a restaurant, or remodeling a house (e.g., task models). Finally, television contains many portrayals that should play a role in transmitting knowledge of how things go together such as families but also influence people's understanding of spatial and temporal relationships (orientation models). However, it is difficult to identify research that has explicitly tested these different types of models from a cultivation perspective. Indeed, one of the strengths of the cultural models approach in our view is that it highlights different domains of knowledge that have rarely been studied from a cultivation perspective. What is the role of television in transmitting cultural knowledge of how people accomplish different types of tasks or learn about relationships within their social and physical world? More research is needed on these types of topics in order to develop a fuller understanding of the relationship between television use and culture.

## *Romantic Media and Cultural Models*

We believe that work on cultural models in cognitive anthropology provides a way to combine psychological and cultural approaches to understanding cultivation effects (Roskos-Ewoldsen et al., 2004). From the perspective of cultivation theory, the media should be able to shape an intersubjectively shared mental model at a cultural level. Research suggests that this may be true. Segrin and Nabi (2002) found that heavy viewing of the romance genre of TV (e.g., romantic comedies, daytime talk shows, and reality-based shows about relationships) is related to holding idealized expectations about romance. Although the research did not specifically test cultural models of romance, their results suggest a relation between heavy viewing of romantic programming and a distorted cultural model of romance. We believe that the model of romance cultivated by the romance genre of TV would be distorted because the depictions of romance found in the romance genre of TV are idealistic (Bachen & Illouz, 1996). To the extent that these representations can be characterized as idealistic, it suggests that they do not represent what is perceived as typical or the norm. In contrast, the cultural model should be more related to what are perceived as normative romantic relationships because the model should serve as the standard for making these judgments (Shore, 1996).

Based on Segrin and Nabi's (2002) findings, we decided that our first foray into studying cultivation from a cultural models perspective would involve romance. Romance is a critical part of people's everyday life. Because a cultural model allows us to understand the world around us (Holland & Quinn, 1987), and given the importance of romance in our culture, we hypothesized that there would be a cultural model of romance. That is to say, we should be able to identify a model of how romance is cognitively represented. Furthermore, to establish that this model is a cultural model, we would have to establish that the structure of this model is shared across individuals. In the next section of this chapter, we will describe how to identify the model of a domain and establish whether it is a cultural model or not.

From a cultivation perspective, we were also interested in whether there is a relationship between TV viewing and the structure of people's model of romance. While not directly related to romance, a content analysis of television programming found that the representation of marriage was ambivalent with many married couples presented on TV, but divorced individuals also frequently portrayed (Signorielli, 1991). As predicted by cultivation theory, this study found that heavy viewing of television was related to perceptions of marriage. Adolescents who watched more television were more likely to indicate they planned on getting married, but they were also more likely to agree that "One sees so few good or happy marriages that one questions it as a way of life" (p. 127), suggesting that heavy-viewing adolescents were influenced by the ambivalent representations of marriage presented on TV. Indeed, Signorielli's (1991) results suggest that the heavy-viewing adolescents had a model of marriage that closely matched the cultural model of marriage identified by Quinn's (1987) research.

The representation of romance found in certain genres of movies (e.g., romantic comedies), television programming (reality romance programming such as *The Bachelorette*), magazines (e.g., beauty and teen magazines), books (e.g., romance novels), and Internet sites (e.g., dating sites) tends to be more idealistic than found in real life (Bachen & Illouz, 1996). In romantic television programming, the themes, for example, that everyone has a "soul mate" and that soul mates fall in love at first sight are common (Hefner, 2008). This portrayal of romance in the media may cultivate idealistic expectations about romance (Bachen & Illouz, 1996; Chernin & Fishbein, 2007) and, indeed, that is what Segrin and Nabi (2002) found.

Although cultural models are shared, clearly there are differences in the representation of any given cultural model across people based on any number of factors including their immediate social environment, their life experiences, and, we would hypothesize, their media consumption. In terms of testing the relationship between media use and a cultural model of romance, the critical issue is whether heavy viewers of romantic media have a model of romance that diverges from the identified cultural model. In other words, although there may be consensus regarding the structure of a cultural model, not all people may share the model. We hypothesized that viewers of highly romanticized media would have representations of romance that diverged from the cultural model of romance because of the idealized portrayals of romance represented in this genre of programming.

## How to Study Cultural Models

Given the relative newness of measuring cultural models within anthropology—the practice only really started in the 1980s—we assume that most communication scholars are probably not familiar with this methodological technique. Furthermore, identification of a cultural model requires several steps (Atran et al., 2005; Dressler, Borges, Balieiro, & dos Santos, 2005; Handwerker, 2002; Romney & Moore, 1998; Ross & Medin, 2005; Weller & Romney, 1988). In this section, we outline the steps that are involved in establishing the existence of a cultural model.

The first major objective is to establish that there is a cultural model. This involves four steps. First, the attributes or characteristics of the domain must be identified. Second, the structure or dimensions of the model must be determined, typically by applying multidimensional scaling (MDS) to the identified attributes of the domain (Roskos-Ewoldsen & Roskos-Ewoldsen, 2008). Third, how the cultural model is interpreted is established by identifying the interpretation of the dimensions identified through MDS. The fourth and final task is to determine whether there is consensus regarding the meaning of the different characteristics of the model. Each of these steps is discussed in greater detail below.

Our example comes from our ongoing study of cultural models of romance (Ewoldsen, Rhodes, Nevin, & Dressler, n.d.). This research illustrates at least one way to approach each of the steps involved in identifying a model and determining whether it is a cultural model.

After the cultural model is identified we can begin to focus on whether heavy use of the media is related to these models and explore the nature of the relationship between media exposure and cultural models. Numerous hypotheses can be explored from a cultural models perspective. For example, in the romantic media use research, we hypothesized that the unrealistic representations of romantic relationships prevalent in the media result in heavy users of romantic media having models of romance that are at odds with the cultural model.

### *The Nature of the Domain*

First, the attributes or characteristics of the domain must be identified. A cultural model involves a domain of knowledge which is composed of various attributes. The game of checkers has a number of attributes including a board with a certain configuration of spaces on the board, types of spaces on the board, a certain number of pieces of a certain type, types of moves and conditions for when certain types of moves are allowed, and so forth. The goal of cultural modeling is to identify whether there is agreement as to what the various attributes of a domain are and what they mean.

Initially, the boundaries of the domain of study must be clearly articulated so that the objects may be properly chosen for inclusion or exclusion from the set of attributes of the domain. Researchers must clearly delineate the focus of the study and include only those objects that are within this boundary. It is important to exclude those attributes that are not part of the domain but, at the same time, be sure to include the attributes that represent the entirety of the domain in question. In our study on romance, initial discussions involved whether the focus of the study would be romance, marriage, or both. Almost immediately, the decision was made to limit it to either romance or marriage (we chose romance) because earlier work on cultural models of marriage had clearly demonstrated that they are two separate cultural domains (Quinn, 1987). Furthermore, we wanted to be clear that we were interested in the attributes of everyday romances and not idealized romances.

Once the boundaries of the domain have been identified (e.g., everyday romance and not marriage), the second issue is to identify those objects or attributes that represent that domain. This stage is critical because if the domain of objects is incomplete, the ultimate solutions that are identified will be incomplete and only a partial representation of the cultural model will be identified (Weller & Romney, 1988). Likewise, if attributes from outside the domain are included, there will be distortions in the identified cultural model that may reflect a blending of two or more models. There are at least two sources for finding relevant objects or attributes within a domain. The first is existing scholarship. One should conduct an extensive literature review of the research within the domain (Roskos-Ewoldsen, 1997).

A second source is to ask members of the culture to describe the objects of attributes of that domain. This often takes the form of interviews or focus groups with members of the population of interest. In the romance study, we initially interviewed 45 college students one at a time concerning their concept of romance. Specifically, the participants were instructed to list all the important characteristics they perceived to be part of a romantic relationship. To avoid participants only listing characteristics of idealized romances, participants were instructed to think of a number of different romantic relationships that ranged from very good to very poor. While thinking of these relationships, the participants were asked to identify those attributes or characteristics that made these relationships romantic.

Once the list of romantic attributes was obtained, we validated them through additional interviews. Specifically, the set of identified attributes was presented to new respondents with three goals in mind: (1) determine if any of the listed attributes are not really attributes of that domain (e.g., romance), (2) identify any groups of attributes that could be combined because they are redundant, and (3) identify any attributes of the domain that are missing from the list and should be added. Using this procedure we compiled a set of 59 unique attributes. For more information on how to identify the attributes of a domain, see Weller and Romney's (1988) volume.

### *The Structure of the Domain*

Once the attributes of a domain are identified, the next step involves identifying the structure or number of dimensions in the model. This is accomplished using multidimensional scaling. Multidimensional scaling requires proximity or similarity data between all of the attributes of the domain. Proximity data are collected by having participants rate the items on similarity scales or by having participants sort the attributes into groups (for a more detailed discussion of the issues involved in multidimensional scaling, see Roskos-Ewoldsen & Roskos-Ewoldsen, 2008, or Kruskal & Wish, 1978).

**Similarity ratings.** One way to determine the similarity between two objects is to use a direct rating of their similarity using a standard 7- or 11-point scale. All possible pairs of the attributes must be rated. Consequently, a disadvantage of using similarity ratings to collect proximity data is the number of judgments required to obtain the necessary data. For our study of romance there were 59 attributes of romantic relationships, which would have required 1,711 similarity judgments, so we did not use this technique. Clearly, the number of judgments required by this technique can be prohibitive. Further details of this procedure can be found in Roskos-Ewoldsen and Roskos-Ewoldsen (2007).

**Card sorting.** A card-sorting task is probably the most utilized method for measuring similarity with larger sets of objects and is the technique we used in the romance study. In a sorting task, each attribute is placed on a card (though some computer programs exist that allow a sorting task to be done on a computer), and participants are instructed to place similar attributes into piles with other similar attributes so that the items in the pile are more similar to each other than they are to the attributes in other piles. For useful discussions of several different variants of the card-sorting task see Weller and Romney (1988), Rosenberg and Kim (1975) and Wish (1967). After completing the sorting task, dissimilarity scores can be obtained through procedures described in Roskos-Ewoldsen and Roskos-Ewoldsen (2008), and the MDS analysis can be conducted.

From the perspective of cultural modeling, the reason for using MDS is to identify the number of dimensions represented by the attributes of the domain. There are no set rules for determining the appropriate number of dimensions for a set of objects. Issues to consider when determining the appropriate number of dimensions in an MDS analysis include stress, which is a goodness of fit index that provides a measure of how well the dissimilarity data match the distances in the MDS configuration and the interpretability of the dimensions (Kruskal & Wish, 1978; Roskos-Ewoldsen & Roskos-Ewoldsen, 2008). For the romance data, stress and ease of interpretability both pointed to a two-dimensional solution.

### *Interpreting the Structure of the Domain*

Once the number of dimensions in the model has been determined, the third step involves the interpretation of those dimensions. Although most statistical software packages will produce a visual representation of the multidimensional space including dimensions that run through the space, it is important to recognize that these spaces are determined arbitrarily (Roskos-Ewoldsen & Roskos-Ewoldsen, 2008).

The first step in interpreting an MDS space is to identify possible dimensions that run through the space. Potential dimensions can be identified in a number of ways including examining the literature for clues, asking participants to describe how they sorted the attributes into piles, or by considering clearly distinct attributes and identifying dimensions they may differ along. Once possible dimensions have been identified, participants provide ratings of each of the attributes along each of the prospective dimensions identified by the researchers. For example, in our research on romance, one possible dimension was the level of emotion involved in each attribute. A second dimension involved whether the attribute concerned the physical aspects of romance or was more nonphysical. A third possible dimension was whether the attribute involved long-term or short-term features of the relationship. All told, we tested five potential dimensions by having participants rate each of the 59 attributes along each of the five dimensions. To determine how well the possible dimensions capture the actual dimensions in the data, a multiple regression is conducted for each of the possible dimensions using procedures outlined by Roskos-Ewoldsen (1997; see also Kruskal & Wish, 1978; Roskos-Ewoldsen & Roskos-Ewoldsen, 2008). In the romance study, it turned out that two dimensions defined the MDS space: whether the attributes were physical or nonphysical and whether they involved long-term or short-term components of romance.

Once the dimensions of a model are identified, a model for the domain of study has been identified. But this does not establish that it is a *cultural* model. As discussed earlier, a cultural model requires a high degree of consensus regarding the meaning of the various attributes within the model (Atran et al., 2005; Dressler et al., 2005; Handwerker, 2002). The final task, then, is to determine whether there is consensus regarding the meaning of the different characteristics of the model. The basic assumption of cultural modeling is that if there is consensus regarding the meaning of the attributes of the model, then there should be consensus among people as to where the attributes fall along the dimensions of the model (Romney & Moore, 1996). To the extent that people perceive each attribute as falling at the same point along the dimensions of the identified model, then there is consensus as to the structure of that model and a cultural model can be said to exist.

Statistically, whether there is consensus on the identified model is established using principal components factor analysis (Atran et al., 2005; Dressler et al., 2005; Handwerker, 2002; Ross & Medin, 2005). Similar to the logic of a factor analysis in psychological measurement, in which questions in a questionnaire are analyzed to examine subsets that tend to be answered similarly, in this procedure participants are analyzed to discern whether their ratings of the attributes are in agreement along one of the dimensions of the cultural model. To the extent that all of the participants rate the attributes similarly, the participants should load on a single factor. If participants are rating the attributes in different ways either multiple factors will emerge (this would suggest that there are different subgroups of participants who are rating the characteristics similarly to each other in that subgroup but differently from the other subgroups), or no clear solution will emerge (Atran et al., 2005; Dressler et al., 2005; Ross & Medin, 2005). There was a high degree of consensus for both the short-term/long-term and the physical/nonphysical dimensions, indicating that there is a cultural model of romance for college-aged participants at the university where this research was conducted. One of the important considerations for cultural modeling is that cultural models can exist for fairly small groups of people, so we would not want to say that this is the cultural model of romance for older adults or for the college-age population in general or in a different region of the country (Atran et al., 2005).

### *Media Use and Cultural Models*

Bringing this back to cultivation theory, the critical issue is whether media use is related to the cultural model. In other words, do heavy or light viewers of television have a cultural model of the domain that diverges from the identified cultural model? While there may be consensus regarding the structure of a cultural model, not all people will share this model (Shore, 1996; Strauss & Quinn, 1997). Anthropologists have developed the idea of *consonance* as a measure of the degree to which a person's knowledge is consistent with or in agreement with the cultural model (Atran et al., 2005; Dressler, 2005; Handwerker, 2002). People whose representation of the domain closely matches the cultural model have a high level of consonance with the model, and people whose knowledge diverges from the cultural model have a low level of consonance with the cultural model.

Consonance is measured using the results of the principal components factor analysis that establishes whether there is a cultural model. If a single factor emerges from the factor analysis—which indicates there is consensual interpretation along the dimensions of the model—then participants' factor loadings on that first factor serve as an empirical measure of their consonance with the model. Participants whose ratings of the characteristics of the cultural model more closely resemble the consensus rating of the attributes across the dimension will have higher factor loadings than participants whose ratings of the characteristics of the cultural model do not match the consensus rating of the attributes (Dressler, 2005).

The influence of the media on the cultural model can then be determined by using a measure of media use to predict consonance with the cultural model. A cultural models approach to cultivation theory would predict that media use should be related to consonance with the cultural model. For example, in the romance data, we found that use of romantic media (including TV, movies, books, the Internet, and magazines) is related to consonance with one of the two dimensions (the physical dimension) of the cultural model such that heavy users of romantic media had lower consonance with the model along that dimension. But media use was not related to the other dimension of the cultural model (the short-term/long-term dimension). Our interpretation of this finding is that heavy use of romantic media, which tends to focus more on identifying one's soul mate than on the physical components of romance (Bachen & Illouz, 1996; Chernin & Fishbein, 2007; Hefner, 2008), results in less emphasis on the physical/nonphysical dimension to evaluate relationships. This diverges from the cultural model, which recognizes that there is a physical dimension of relationships, but this is not the sole dimension on which relationships can be evaluated.

## Conclusions

We believe that the cultural models approach provides a useful perspective for studying cultivation theory. This perspective nicely meshes with our view that culture and media should have a dynamic relationship. Theoretically, the idea that heavy media use might either reinforce or modify an individual's cultural model is important because it captures the influence of the media at both the cultural and the individual level. By focusing on knowledge on which there is a broad consensus, a cultural models approach captures that important component of cultivation theory involving the influence of the media on shared frames of reference—the cultivation of order out of the weed patch of reality. But the cultural models approach also retains that focus on the individual that has received so much attention in cultivation research during the past 25 years.

Indeed, the cultural models approach is consistent with the research focusing on the individual cognitive processes underlying cultivation theory. The accessibility component of Shrum's model (Shrum et al., 2011; Shrum & Lee, Chapter 8, this volume) reflects a dynamic interplay between media, individual constructs, and consonance with a cultural model. Cultural models should influence what information people attend to in their environment (Strauss & Quinn, 1997), including what information they focus on while using the media. Consequently, heavy viewers should have more accessible constructs that represent the intersection of their cultural model and the content of the media they are using. Consistent with research by Shrum and others, we hypothesize that this interaction between the cultural model and media use should result in more accessible constructs in the memory system. If the information found in the media is consistent with the meaning of the information within the cultural model (which is what we would anticipate is happening the majority of the time), then media use could result in heightened consonance with the cultural model. This prediction is perfectly consistent with Gerbner's (1969, 1998; Gerbner & Gross, 1976) ideas that the media reinforce culture. Conversely, if the information found in the media is inconsistent with the meaning of the cultural model, then media use could increase the accessibility of information that is related to the cultural model but inconsistent with the prevailing view within the culture. In this instance, consonance with the cultural model would decrease. Clearly, this is a hypothesis that needs to be tested longitudinally. However, these ideas reflect the dynamic relationship among media use, cultural models, and construct accessibility (Lang & Ewoldsen, 2010), and our cross-sectional data on romantic media use are consistent with this view.

Before ending this chapter, we highlight several issues to keep in mind when doing this type of research. One issue that faces cultivation scholars is whether to measure general media use or genre-specific media use (see Bilandzic & Busselle, Chapter 13, this volume). Previously, research has focused on overall viewing of TV rather than watching particular types of shows. However, many scholars maintain that heavy viewing of particular genres of TV has stronger and more specific effects than overall TV viewing (Hawkins & Pingree, 1981; Segrin & Nabi, 2002). For example, Segrin and Nabi (2002) found a weak negative relationship between general TV viewing and idealistic expectations about romance. However, they found a strong positive relationship between watching romantic media and unrealistic expectations about romance. Similarly, we found no relationship between overall media use and consonance with cultural models of romance, but we did find a negative relationship between genre-specific media use and consonance with one dimension of the cultural model.

Second, research on cultural models is likely to have the most impact if it examines long-term media use. Research on cultivation theory typically measures people's current viewing patterns (e.g., how much TV do you watch in a typical week?). However, research on the development of cultural models suggests that the development of such models occurs over an extended time frame. For example, Minoura (1992) found that Japanese students who had moved to the United States with their parents took between 3 and 4 years to learn the United States' cultural model of peer interpersonal behavior. Cultivation researchers would probably find stronger effects of heavy TV viewing if they measured viewing patterns across years instead of weeks. A college sophomore who has watched romance programming all of her life is bound to have stronger cultivation effects than a college sophomore who began heavy viewing of romance programming when she moved into her sorority. Scales for long-term media use have been developed such as Riddle's (2010) *Lifetime Television Exposure Scale* (see also Riddle, Chapter 14, this volume). Although the scale was first designed to measure general television viewing, it was later modified to measure genre-specific viewing as well.

Finally, a knee-jerk hypothesis is that heavy viewers should have more consonance with the cultural model than light viewers. While this is probably true the majority of the time, there is no reason why that necessarily needs to be the case. If the model represented in the media overlaps with the cultural model, then heavy viewers should show higher levels of consonance than light viewers. For example, it has been argued that part of the popularity of soap operas is that viewers can identify with the characters in the show and the show's storyline (Radway, 1984). If the TV program mirrors people's lived reality, then heavy viewers may well have higher levels of consonance with the cultural model than light viewers. However, in those instances where the media depart from the cultural model, then heavy users of that genre of media may have low consonance with the cultural model of that domain.

In conclusion, we hope that this introduction to the cultural models approach to the study of cultivation theory will pique the interest of other scholars interested in these processes. Although the work as described here may sound labor intensive, it is fascinating and enlightening work to conduct. We believe the potential to better understand the role of the media in the culture we live in is great, and we believe these tools can shed unique light on this process.

## References

Anderson, S. M., Moskowitz, G. B., Blair, I. V., & Nosek, B. A. (2007). Automatic thought. In A. W. Kruglanski & E. T. Higgins (Eds.), *Social psychology: Handbook of basic principles* (2nd ed., pp. 138–175). New York: Guilford Press.

Arpan, L., Rhodes, N., & Roskos-Ewoldsen, D. R. (2007). Accessibility, persuasion, and behavior. In D. R. Roskos-Ewoldsen & J. Monahan (Eds.), *Communication and social cognition: Theories and methods* (pp. 351–375). Mahwah, NJ: Erlbaum.

Atran, S., Medin, D. L., & Ross, N. O. (2005). The cultural mind: Environmental decision making and cultural modeling within and across populations. *Psychological Review, 112*, 744–776.

Bachen, C. M. & Illouz, E. (1996). Imagining romance: Young people's cultural models of romance and love. *Critical Studies in Mass Communication, 13*, 279–308.

Bryant, J., & Miron, D. (2004). Theory and research in mass communication. *Journal of Communication, 54*, 662–704.

Busselle, R. W. & Shrum, L. J. (2003). Media exposure and the accessibility of social information. *Media Psychology, 5*, 255–282.

Chernin, A., & Fishbein, M. (2007, May). *The association between adolescents' exposure to romantic-themed media and the endorsement of unrealistic beliefs about romantic relationships.* Paper presented to the International Communication Association, San Francisco, CA.

Collins, A., & Gentner, D. (1987). How people construct mental models. In D. Holland & N. Quinn (Eds.), *Cultural models in language & thought* (pp. 243–265). Cambridge: Cambridge University Press.

D'Andrade, R. (1995). *The development of cognitive anthropology.* Cambridge: Cambridge University Press.

Dressler, W. W. (2005) What's *cultural* about bio*cultural* research? *Ethos, 33,* 20–45.

Dressler, W. W. (2006). Taking culture seriously in health research. *International Journal of Epidemiology, 35,* 258–259.

Dressler, W. W., Borges, C. D., Balieiro, M. C., & Dos Santos, J. E. (2005). Measuring cultural consonance: Examples with special reference to measurement theory in anthropology. *Field Methods, 17,* 331–355.

Dressler, W. W., Dos Santos, J. E., & Balieiro, M. C. (1996). Studying diversity and sharing in culture: An example of lifestyle in Brazil. *Journal of Anthropological Research, 52,* 331–353

Eddison, A. (2006). *The cultivation of perceptions and behavioral expectations of romantic relationships through the media* (Unpublished master's thesis). University of Alabama, Tuscaloosa.

Eno, C. A. & Ewoldsen, D. R. (2010). The influence of explicitly and implicitly measured prejudice on interpretations of and reactions to black film. *Media Psychology, 13,* 1–30.

Ewoldsen, D. R., Rhodes, N., Nevin, K., & Dressler, W. (n.d.). *Cultivation theory and cultural models of romance.* Manuscript under review.

Fazio, R. (1990). Multiple processes by which attitudes guide behavior: The MODE model as an integrative framework. In M. P. Zanna (Ed.), *Advances in experimental social psychology* (pp. 75–109). New York: Academic Press.

Fazio, R. H., Roskos-Ewoldsen, D. R., & Powell, M. C. (1994). Attitudes, perception, and attention. In P. M. Niedenthal & S. Kitayama (Eds.), *The heart's eye: Emotional influences in perception and attention* (pp. 197–216). San Diego, CA: Academic Press.

Gerbner, G. (1969). Toward "cultural indicators": The analysis of mass mediated message systems. *AV Communication Review, 6,* 137–148.

Gerbner, G. (1998). Cultivation analysis: An overview. *Mass Communication & Society, 1,* 175–194.

Gerbner, G., & Gross. L. (1976). Living with television: The violence profile. *Journal of Communication, 26*(2), 173–199.

Gerbner, G., Gross, L., Morgan, M., Signorielli, N., & Shanahan, J. (2002). Growing up with television: Cultivation processes. In J. Bryant & D. Zillmann (Eds.), *Media effects: Advances in theory and research* (2nd ed., pp. 43–68). Mahwah, NJ: Erlbaum.

Handwerker, W. P. (2002). The construct validity of cultures: Cultural diversity, culture theory, and a method for ethnography. *American Anthropologist, 104,* 106–122.

Hastie, R., & Park, B. (1986). The relationship between memory and judgment depends on whether the judgment task is memory-based or on-line. *Psychological Review, 93,* 258–268.

Hawkins, R. P., & Pingree, S. (1981). Uniform messages and habitual viewing: Unnecessary assumptions in social reality effects. *Human Communication Research, 7,* 291–301.

Hawkins, R. P., & Pingree, S. (1982). Television's influence on social reality. In D. Pearl, L. Bouthilet, & J. Lazer (Eds.), *Television and behavior: Ten years of scientific progress and implications for the eighties* (pp. 224–247). Washington, DC: Government Printing Office.

Hefner, V. (2008, November). *Romantic relationship ideal in mass media: An explication of a construct.* Paper presented to the National Communication Association, San Diego, CA.

Hofstede, G. (2001). *Culture's consequences: Comparing values, behaviors, institutions and organizations across nations.* Thousand Oaks, CA: Sage Publications.

Holland, D., & Quinn, N. (1987). *Cultural models in language and thought.* Cambridge: Cambridge University Press.

Kruskal, J. P., & Wish, M. (1978). *Multidimensional scaling.* Thousand Oaks, CA: Sage.

Kwak, H., Zinkhan, G. M., & Dominick, J. R. (2002). The moderating role of gender and compulsive buying tendencies in the cultivation effects of TV shows and TV advertising: A cross cultural study between the United States and South Korea. *Media Psychology, 4,* 77–111.

Lang, A., & Ewoldsen, D. (2010). Beyond effects: Conceptualizing communication as dynamic, complex, nonlinear, and fundamental. In S. Allan (Ed.), *Rethinking communication* (pp. 109–120). Cresskill, NJ: Hampton Press.

Minoura, Y. (1992). A sensitive period for the incorporation of a cultural meaning system: A study of Japanese children growing up in the United States. *Ethos, 20,* 304–339.

Morgan, M., & Shanahan, J. (1997). Two decades of cultivation analysis: An appraisal and meta-analysis. In B. Burleson (Ed.), *Communication Yearbook 20* (pp. 1–45). Thousand Oaks, CA: Sage.

Morgan, M., Shanahan, J., & Signorielli, N. (2009). Growing up with television: Cultivation processes. In J. Bryant & M. B. Oliver (Eds.), *Media effects: Advances in theory and research* (3rd ed., pp. 34–49). New York: Routledge.

Nabi, R. L., & Oliver, M. B. (2010). Mass media effects. In C. R. Berger, M. E. Roloff, & D. R. Roskos-Ewoldsen (Eds.), *Handbook of communication science* (2nd ed., pp. 255–272). Los Angeles: Sage.

Quinn, N. (1987). Convergent evidence for a cultural model of American marriage. In D. Holland & N. Quinn (Eds.), *Cultural Models in Language and Thought* (pp. 173–192). Cambridge: Cambridge University Press.

Radway, J. A. (1984). *Reading the romance: Women, patriarchy, and popular literature.* Chapel Hill, NC: University of North Carolina Press.

Riddle, K. (2010). Remembering past media use: Toward the development of a lifetime television exposure scale. *Communication Methods & Measures, 4,* 241–255.

Romney, A. K., & Moore, C. (1998). Toward a theory of culture as shared cognitive structures. *Ethos, 26,* 314–337.

Romney, A. K., Weller, S. C., & Batchelder, W. H. (1986). Culture as consensus: A theory of culture and informant accuracy. *American Anthropologist, 88,* 313–338

Rosenberg, S., & Kim, M. P. (1975). The method of sorting as a data-gathering procedure in multivariate research. *Multivariate Behavioral Research, 10,* 489–502.

Roskos-Ewoldsen, B., Davies, J., & Roskos-Ewoldson, D. (2004). Implications of the mental models approach for cultivation theory. *Communications, 29,* 345–363.

Roskos-Ewoldsen, D. R. (1997). Implicit theories of persuasion. *Human Communication Research, 24,* 31–63.

Roskos-Ewoldsen, D. R., & Roskos-Ewoldsen, B. (2008). Multidimensional scaling and cluster analysis. In A. F. Hayes, M. D. Slater, & L. Snyder (Eds.), *The Sage sourcebook of advanced data analysis methods for communication research* (pp. 275–310). Thousand Oaks, CA: Sage.

Ross, N., & Medin, D. L. (2005). Ethnography and experiments: Cultural models and expertise effects elicited with experimental research techniques. *Field Methods, 17*, 131–149.

Schank, R. C., & Abelson, R. P. (1977). *Scripts, plans, goals and understanding: An inquiry into human knowledge structures.* Mahwah, NJ: Erlbaum.

Segrin, C. & Nabi, R. L. (2002). Does television viewing cultivate unrealistic expectations of marriage? *Journal of Communication, 52*, 247–263.

Shore, B. (1996). *Culture in mind.* New York: Oxford University Press.

Shrum, L. J. (1996). Psychological processes underlying cultivation effects: Further tests of construct accessibility. *Human Communication Research, 22*, 482–509.

Shrum, L. J., Lee, J., Burroughs, J. E., & Rindfleisch, A. (2011). An online process model of second-order cultivation effects. *Human Communication Research, 37*, 34–57.

Signorielli, N. (1991). Adolescents and ambivalence toward marriage: A cultivation analysis. *Youth & Society, 23*, 121–149.

Strauss, C. & Quinn, N. (1997). *A cognitive theory of cultural meaning.* Cambridge: Cambridge University Press.

Weller, S. C., & Romney, A. K. (1988). *Systematic data collection.* Thousand Oaks, CA: Sage.

Wish, M. (1976). Comparisons among multidimensional structures of interpersonal relations. *Multivariate Behavioral Research, 11*, 297–324.

# 11. Temporal and Narrative Bases of Cultivation

## Insight from Neural Networks

*Samuel D. Bradley & Curtis B. Matthews*

Cultivation is, broadly speaking, a society-level occurrence that relies upon societal phenomena, including the shared symbols and messages of television splashed across the collective psyche. In more than a hundred million American homes, the mesmerizing pixels of television saturate the background of existence for almost one-third of the hours in a given day. This omnipresence necessitates a societal-level investigation. However, cultivation must have an accompanying psychological-level explanation. Despite the consistent image of a violent, affluent society nearly universally portrayed on television, any distortion of reality happens in the mind of one single viewer at a time. Thus, any complete explanation of cultivation must be multilevel, incorporating a psychological component as well as a societal and institutional analysis. However, the ubiquity of television's messages makes it almost impossible to control all potential mediating and moderating variables.

Incorporating the use of artificial neural networks, relevant hypotheses regarding cultivation can be tested within an entirely controlled environment. These neural networks instantiate an associative model of memory that represents the world as distributed patterns of activation across artificial neurons. Due to this distributed representation, similar situations are more confusable than dissimilar situations. As more memories come from mediated sources, these models are more likely to generalize those types of situations to novel scenarios. This closely resembles the observed cultivation differential between heavy and light television viewers. At the most basic level, these simulations merely show that a given hypothesis is possible. That is, the models are able to demonstrate that changes in a given independent variable lead to predicted outcomes among dependent variables. However, these models take an important additional step unavailable to traditional analyses. Due to the fact that the researcher governs the entire architecture of the model, these models provide the opportunity to demonstrate whether a given effect occurs in the manner predicted by theory. This simulated environment allows us to examine not only whether an effect will occur but also exactly how it will occur.

## The Primacy of Time

Consider, for a moment, the Grand Canyon—a tourist magnet located in Northern Arizona that draws millions of visitors annually. Over millions of years the rolling water of the Colorado River carved a gash more than a mile deep into the Colorado Plateau (Polyak, Hill, & Asmerom, 2008). Rather than a single cataclysmic event, the story of the Grand Canyon is a story about time. Water clearly starred as the lead protagonist in this drama. But the Grand Canyon is not a story about water. It's a story about time. Time alone provides a framework within which to understand this geological marvel.

Time affects the very basis of cognition and how humans perceive causality. In a series of elegant experiments, Michotte (1963) employed small shapes to assess inferences about causation. In the base experiment, participants saw two 5 mm squares, one red and one black, that were 40 mm apart. At a given moment, the red square moved toward the black square at 30 cm per second. When the two touched, the red square stopped, and the black square continued on the red square's trajectory at the same rate, which Michotte dubbed the "launching effect." At the time, several hundred participants had completed the experiment, and only two failed to describe the scene as the red square *causing* the black one's movement. However, if a delay as short as 200 ms intervened when the objects first touch and when the black square began moving, the attributions of causality disappear. This dissociation cannot be understood by pondering the movement of the squares as two separate events. Instead, Michotte writes,

> . . . it is possible, theoretically, to distinguish two successive events, the movement and the contact. But actually there are not *two events*; there is only one event which develops progressively.…the impact is not really limited to the coming into contact of the two objects; it constitutes a whole *process*, of which the movement and the contact are both constitutive parts. The process evolves. (Michotte, 1963, p. 24, emphasis in original)

Between the delay and no-delay conditions, the constitutive parts are identical. However, when a temporal delay of just one-fifth of a second intervenes, perception of causation goes from nearly universally present to nearly universally absent. Only by linking these objects to the fabric of time can this be understood.

The story of cultivation is, at its most basic, a story about time. Whether cultivating a farmer's fields or cultivating a worldview among mass media audiences, the process unfolds over time. In many ways, the traditional three-prong approach of the Cultural Indicators project prominently also incorporates time. Institutional process analysis tracks changes within and among industries over time, and message analysis chronicles the development of messages across decades. Yet the cultivation differential itself proves more elusive to investigate over time. Measures of time spent viewing obviously include a temporal component because television must be viewed over time. That is, 20 hours of viewing consumes 20 hours. Yet the cultivation differential is not a story of hours. It is a story of years and decades.

Furthermore, cultivation is especially slippery to drag into the experimental laboratory, the likely home for those who want to study its cognitive underpinnings. If one subscribes to the most basic conceptual definitions of cultivation analysis, then the relationships of worldview to television use are seen among communities over long time spans. This cannot be replicated in the lab. "If nearly everyone 'lives' to some extent in the world of television, clearly we cannot find unexposed groups who would be identical in all important respects to the viewers" (Gerbner & Gross, 1976, p. 182). Even classic work, such as Zillmann's investigation of pornography effects (work that likely would not be permitted under the institutional review board scrutiny applied today), shows the limits of approximating long-term exposure in an experimental setting. In a series of studies fundamental to the study of media effects, Zillmann and colleagues randomly assigned participants to one of three conditions of pornography exposure: none, intermediate, and massive (Zillmann & Bryant, 1984). In the massive condition—the closest analog to anything resembling cultivation—participants viewed about 48 minutes of pornography per week for a series of six weeks. In an era prior to ubiquitous VHS, DVD, and eventually online pornography, this "massive" exposure of fewer than six hours spread across six weeks affected a host of measures ranging from increased aggression and enjoyment to decreases in repulsion or recommended sentences for hypothetical convicted rapists.

Despite the impressiveness of the breadth of effects, changes resulting from fewer than six hours of exposure more closely resemble habituation and desensitization rather than cultivation. To illustrate this, compare this amount of exposure to the lifetime television exposure the average undergraduate brings to the lab (see also Riddle, Chapter 14, this volume). A quarter of a century ago, Gerbner and Gross (1976) reported that nearly half of the 12-year-olds they studied watched at least 6 hours of television per day. A 2010 Kaiser Family Foundation report showed that 11- to 14-year-olds watched, on average, 5.03 hours of television content per day, a figure that had increased since 2004 (Rideout, Foehr, & Roberts, 2010). Although perhaps an hour less than three decades before, data show that myriad new media choices have increased total media exposure. Clearly this social force's ubiquitousness persists. Using these estimates combined with previous work (Rideout, Vandewater, & Wartella, 2003) and our own data for college students, the *average* 20-year-old college student has logged more than 23,500 hours in front of television content when she walks in the door of the lab. Given that the expertise literature suggests that about 10,000 hours of learning is needed in order to become an "expert" (e.g., Ericsson, Prietula, & Cokelyo, 2007), these students are experts twice over on the world of television.

## Human Learning

The human brain represents the most effective general-purpose learning device in the known universe. More than any other creature in the planet's history, humans have spread and thrived in every environment. This is not to dismiss global health disparities or problems of poverty, but humans exist and thrive from the Alaskan bush north of the Arctic Circle, to the shores of the piranha-laden Amazon River, to the trust-fund-encrusted confines of the Upper East Side. In order to accomplish this, a newborn human must be able to observe and master the rules, symbols, and conventions of the society into which it is born.

The world represents an intricate linkage of statistical regularities, and the human mind has evolved to best make use of those regularities. Despite the seeming agony of many students when they formally study statistics, strong evidence exists that even newborns engage in statistical learning (Kirkham, Slemmer, & Johnson, 2002), perhaps even deciphering statistical regularities of their native language *in utero* (Baron, 2000). However, this statistical analysis of the natural world is not invariant, and it is finely tuned to helping the human make optimal decisions at each passing moment. Consider the static viewed on an old analog television tuned between channels. This static, or "snow," is a matrix of random black and white pixels upon the screen. Given the random nature, any two screenshots of this snow should show almost perfect noncorrelation. That is, knowing that a particular pixel is white in a given screenshot tells one nothing about the likelihood of the same pixel being white in a subsequent screenshot. Thus, any two images are as different as any two images could be, statistically speaking. To a computer, distinguishing among these screenshots is exceedingly easy. For a human, though, the task is nearly impossible. Changing the task slightly, consider two screenshots of a courtroom television drama. The first image was captured during a wide shot of the judge, witness stand, and courtroom stenographer from the perspective of an attorney's table. The second image was captured from the same vantage point; however, it represents a close-up of the judge. For the computer, distinguishing between these images becomes a much more difficult task. Although the images *seem* entirely different to the human viewer, they contain considerable regularity. First, the second shot is essentially contained inside the first. The wood paneling in the courtroom remains constant, so there is a good chance that a brown pixel in one shot also is brown in the next. Although far from a perfect correlation, statistical analysis reveals strong correlations between shots such as these (Bradley, 2004). That is, knowing something about a pixel in one shot tells you something about a pixel in the next shot.

How does distinguishing between two screenshots become *more* difficult for a computer while simultaneously becoming *easier* for the human? The answer lies in the design of the computer as a general-purpose information processor and the evolved design of the human as a carbon-based lifeform that achieves maximum success when it survives, reproduces, and ensures that its offspring reach reproductive age. In order to accomplish these tasks, the brain must make the most efficient use of limited-capacity resources. This entails exploiting useful statistical regularities and storing information in an associative network. Rather than anything resembling a file cabinet, the brain stores information by slowly varying strengths of connections among neurons. These trillion-plus connections (i.e., synapses) among billions of neurons constitute human memory. The basis of human information storage rests upon similarities among stimuli.

Although physicists ponder the very existence of time, it is a universal constant for the human realm. Despite the wishes of countless fiction writers, time (at least as experienced by humans on Earth) marches steadily forward. This constant temporal progression allows humans to make judgments about cause and effect and to make learned predictions about the future. The more often an event is repeated, the more one should expect it to occur. Indeed the very notion of conditioned reflexes suggests the ability to abstract such generalizations. It is a mistake to view Pavlov's (1927) dogs as merely pairing two unrelated stimuli. Instead, these reflexes tell the tale of canines learning a repeated story over time. The ringing of a bell at one time indicates the presence of food at a subsequent (and always later) time. By repeatedly experiencing these events in a specific time order, the dogs learn the causal sequence of the narrative, and they use that information to predict subsequent events. Their eventual salivation at the sound of the bell signifies such a prediction: At the most primal levels of their physiology the body predicts the next event in the story and makes appropriate preparations by salivating digestive enzymes. Time matters fundamentally. For instance, the presence of food never signals the coming of a bell.

## Optimal Perception

Thankfully for most television viewers, little time is invested in securing the lowest levels of needs in Maslow's hierarchy, those associated with basic physiological survival. Yet despite the relative comfort of modern humans, they inhabit bodies governed by brains that evolved in far leaner times. As is still the case for almost every species of animal today, our ancestors lived in a world of scarce opportunity and plentiful threat. The human brain is a metabolic glutton, consuming 20% of the body's blood supply. Natural selection clearly favored brains that made the best survival-related decisions with the fewest resources. Surviving and thriving requires maximal allocation of limited cognitive capacity toward opportunity seeking, while still responding instantly to potential threats. This produces a system tuned to optimally perceive the world at each passing moment, and that is what we see in humans (Bradley, 2006). Despite this elegant capacity allocation (for a discussion of capacity constraints, see Kahneman, 1973), most resource allocation occurs well below conscious awareness. Thus, humans must make sense of an ever-changing world while learning the symbols that reliably predict opportunity (as with Pavlov's bell) and yet never missing a threat. For all but the most recent humans in evolution, a missed threat meant the end of your genetic lineage.

Perception is about the "now," and memory is about the past. Or so it seems. Memory researchers increasingly report that memory is about the future and not the past (Schacter & Addis, 2007). The idea may seem farcical at first, but only acting as a servant of the future provides a rational explanation for memory. Nostalgia can be pleasing, but natural selection would never divert 20% of the body's blood flow to this end. Instead, it appears, that memory exists to allow optimal prediction of the future. Once again, time is paramount. The present is merely a fixed point in space. There is no trajectory in "now." However, when mixed with "where I've been," the now can be used to predict where I'm going. Memory predicts the future. At least, it predicts the immediate future.

To illustrate this concept, imagine how a young child learns about gravity. Surely the child has fallen and dropped many things, but neither of these implies that the child will have learned a general principle of gravity. If, however, the child were given a model of an irregular surface (such as the one in the left panel of Figure 1) and a handful of marbles, the child would have the tools to begin to develop such a theory. Whenever the child places a marble on the surface and lets go, the marble rolls. This happens over time, and the child can learn where the marbles end up. Albeit imperfect, there is a regularity and a systematicity to this world, and repeated paths of the marble reveal this pattern. Figure 1 shows the modeled trajectories of 2,000 marbles placed at random points on this surface. In the panel at left, the dashed lines show the trajectories of individual marbles. Thicker lines indicate paths taken by more marbles. In the right panel, a two-dimensional representation of the same space is shown. In this right panel, the placement of a marble is marked with an ×, and the ending points are marked with circles. There are hundreds of ×'s but only a handful of circles. There is great regularity in this world. No matter where they begin, the marbles end up in one of a few spots: at the bottom of the two valleys or pinned against the edge of the space in the flatlands. In getting to these ending spots, marbles take reliable paths. Our argument is that this hypothetical 3-dimensional space is a close metaphor for human memory. Experiences etch pathways in mental space. Often-repeated experiences etch deeper pathways. When faced with the future, we expect the world to take one of our learned trajectories, and we are surprised when it does not. From this view, cultivation results from thousands of hours of television content carving deep grooves in memory space.

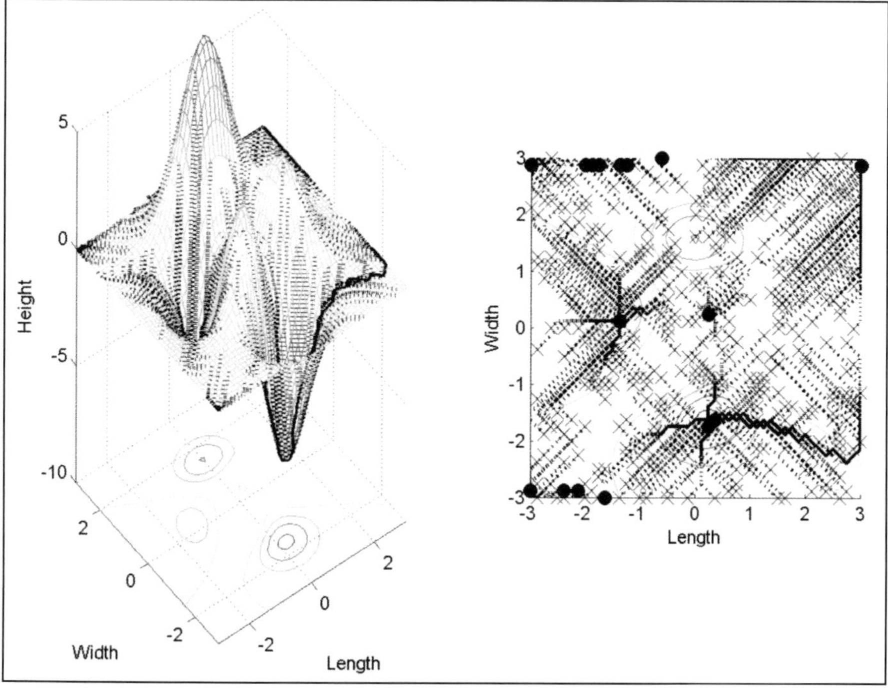


Figure 1. Hypothetical 3-dimensional space (left panel) showing the trajectory of randomly placed marbles. More frequent pathways are shown as darker lines. The right panel shows a 2-dimensional view of the same space with starting points marked as x's and endpoints marked as circles.

## Telling Stories

Viewed from this perspective, memory sounds much like narrative. At its most basic, narrative is "a series of temporally related events involving oneself or other persons, along with the states of affairs that either cause or result from these events" (Wyer, Adaval, & Colcombe, 2002, p. 131). We argue that narrative is more than a structural feature or trait of a message. We argue that narrative is the very basis of cognition and how we understand the world. In this sense, time is the backbone and narrative is the structure that guides cognition. For the human brain, the world is a story. To Gerbner as well, the world *was* one of stories, a point he repeatedly emphasized:

> Popular culture is the stories we share every day. Call it news, fiction, education, mythology, or just media, that great and uniquely human process governs much of what we do.
>
> Who is the most prolific and tireless storyteller in your home? It used to be the parent, grandparent, or older sibling. Today in most homes it is television. Television has achieved what all emperors and popes could only dream about: a pulpit in every living room, with a charismatic messenger providing the common ritual of entertainment and information with a central underlying sales message for all (Gerbner, 1978, p. Va. 11).

Gerbner's emphasis on storytelling was well placed. Human culture largely centers on the stories that we tell. The epic poems of Homer define our knowledge of the Trojan War, and Shakespeare's iambic pentameter remains on stages large and small around the world. Today's stories are predominantly mediated, and the industries that create these stories are profit-driven. Media content production revolves around ratings and box office takes, leaving little if any room for deeper themes. One seeming constant from the great works of literature past to present-day television content is a reliance on sex and violence. Given the unique cultural history of America, mediated violence is more prevalent than sex. From this perspective, it is not surprising that television cultivates a "mean" worldview.

One cannot deny that the mediated world presents a very distorted mirror of the actual world. In terms of themes portrayed, dozens of content analyses reveal great systematicity in these distortions. Media portrayals do not reflect a random or haphazard view of nonmediated life. Instead these misrepresentations provide a constant supply of programming that elicits physiological arousal—and concomitantly eyes on screen—by magnifying the intensity and frequency of violence. Yet to focus merely on the content is to overlook something fundamental both to understanding human cognition and the cultivation process. Is it not merely the stories that differ but also the ways in which they are told.

Many consider *The Great Train Robbery* (1903) to be a landmark in the development of mediated communication. It is acknowledged as the first film to include armed criminals (Cook, 1990), thus laying the foundation for much of the entertainment that would lead to cultivation research. What director Edwin S. Porter uncovered was not just the foundation of modern narrative storytelling, but the way in which these stories were told. Since the very beginning of film, directors have selected not only the most arousing topics, but also tell stories by focusing on the most arousing parts. Deadweight transitions that define so much of day-to-day life scarcely exist in mediated stories. Authors write stories to rivet the viewer. Consider this advice from a leading book used in screenwriting classes: "*Nothing moves forward in a story except through conflict*" (McKee, 1997, p. 210, emphasis in original). Good stories are not merely about conflict, they *are* conflict, would-be writers are taught. Although to some extent this characterizes daily life, it is easy to see how the mediated world is that much louder, brighter, and more interesting.

A voluminous amount of literature outlines the power of narrative, only a subset of which will be outlined here (for a review, see Bradley, 2010). Before the mass-market introduction of television, Heider and Simmel (1944) showed participants a film that portrayed three geometric shapes moving around a two-dimensional plane at varying speeds and directions. At the center of the plane was the outline of a rectangle, part of which was hinged and opened and closed much like a door. After viewing the film, participants were asked to describe the action. The consistency of the narrative and "character" descriptions offered by the participants is stunning. For instance, the larger of two triangles is described by 97% of participants as being bad-tempered or a bully. Not only do people see story where one doesn't really exist, but they see the same story. Journalists tell stories every day, and due to a host of professional conventions, they put the most interesting part of the story first, a style known as the inverted pyramid. Although this makes news more interesting, it also makes it less memorable (Lang, 1989). Furthermore, recall of television messages with even an extremely low degree of narrative structure shows that viewers remember them embedded in a story framework (Lang, Sias, Chantrill, & Burek, 1995).

Given the overwhelming power of narrative structure, Gerbner seems well justified in focusing on stories, and any true model of the cultivation process must not only incorporate narrative, it must be based in it. Gerbner and Gross (1976) argued that to understand cultivation requires a new toolset. They were right. Nonviewers represent extreme outliers. The reliable but modest cultivation differential reported by Shanahan and Morgan (1999) may owe its modesty more to light viewers being merely "less heavy" viewers than to the effect itself. Given the difficulties of truly studying cultivation in the experimental laboratory and the difficulties in studying psychological processes in a broader setting, we propose that neural network simulations and the epistemological framework of cognitive modeling provide an excellent environment to study and further our understanding of cultivation.

## Insight from Modeling

As computing power has increased, researchers interested in the human mind have increasingly turned to the computer to simulate the billions of neurons and trillions of connections in the average human brain. The brain is a massively parallel information processor. Information is not transmitted down long pathways of single (or few) neurons but across the distributed pattern of activation of thousands or millions of neurons over short distances. This processing method contrasts starkly with modern computers, which, unencumbered by moisture, allow information to flow at nearly the speed of light with massively serial processes. Simulation work increased in the 1980s, culminating with the two-volume set, *Parallel Distributed Processing* (Rumelhart & McClelland, 1986a, 1986b). At the heart of this work is the idea of the simple feed-forward artificial neural network, such as the one shown in Figure 2 (left side).

At its most basic, this type of network involves a set of processing units, a pattern of connectivity among these units, and some rule governing how one unit activates another. Drawing an analogy to the human brain, the units represent neurons, the connections represent synapses, and the activation rule represents the threshold at which one neuron fires in response to input from other neurons. These processing units are arrayed in layers, typically beginning with input—some perception of the state of the world. There need be only two layers, and the second necessary layer is output, or the network's response to the input. Most often, however, there is at least one additional "hidden" layer. Such layers are hidden in the sense that they do not receive input from or produce output to the outside world. The greatest power of the networks lies within these hidden units, which allow the network to re-represent the problem in a manner that allows it to be solved. Consider human vision, which begins with photons hitting photoreceptors in the retina. Eventually these photons become the pictures in the head, which in no way resemble photons. Along the way, the presence or absence of a photon hitting a given cone or rod is re-represented several times. Without such transformations, vision would not be possible. Artificial neural networks learn by adjusting the weights between processing units, just as neurons adjust the strength of their connections based upon neural activity (Hebb, 1949). This makes these neural networks powerful general-purpose learning devices that solve many problems very much like humans solve them. Importantly, this often means that these net-

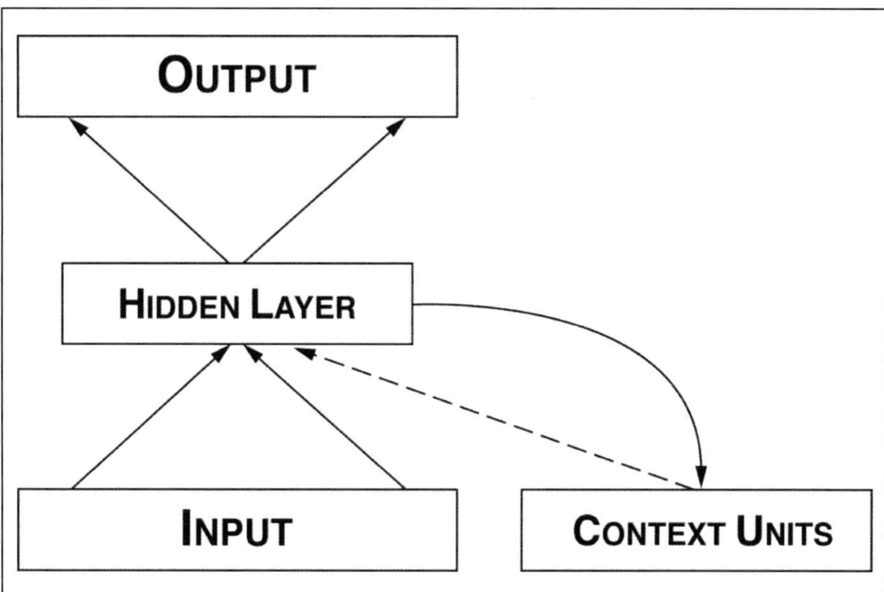


Figure 2. Illustration of a simple feed-forward neural network (solid arrows) and a recurrent Elman (1990) network (dashed arrows). The recurrent layer gives the model access to its own internal representations from the previous timestep.

works not only get correct what humans do, but also that they make very similar errors to actual humans. During the past two decades of research, parallel distributed processing has taken on a number of monikers, but it is perhaps most commonly called "connectionism," owing to the vast array of connections among processing units.

For most fields of inquiry, modeling represents the rule rather than the exception. Sir Isaac Newton has been dead for almost 300 years, yet when he offered a Law of Universal Gravitation in the late 17th century, he presented it as a mathematical model rather than as a series of statements, which is the more common form theory takes within the field of communication. Unpacking the equation, Newton predicted that the gravitational attraction between two objects was directly proportional to the masses of the two objects and inversely proportional to the square root of the distance between the two objects. All of this was multiplied by a gravitational constant, which was derived from observation. This seemingly simple straightforward model makes the extremely counterintuitive but testable (and subsequently verified) prediction that a feather and an apple will fall toward the earth at the same rate (in the absence of wind resistance). When Newton's ideas were substantially updated in the 20th century, they were again updated with a testable model, this time with perhaps the most famous equation in science, Albert Einstein's $E = MC^2$, which defined energy as mass times the speed of light squared. Equations always can be unpacked into prose, but the converse is less often true.

Although both Newton's law and Einstein's special theory of relativity clearly permit field experiments (e.g., dropping apples or nuclear fission, respectively), they also allow investigation of the predictions of the models themselves detached from actual observation. The question for the modeler is not merely whether the model represents or fails to represent the data; rather, the model can be dissected to investigate the specific ways in which it appears to have succeeded or failed.

In modeling human cognition, one aspiration is to explain as many phenomena as possible without appending extra components to account for specific behaviors. All theory building strives for parsimony, but cognitive modeling especially attempts to account for as much behavior as possible with the simplest model possible. A model's explanatory power increases greatly when its performance mimics human performance without special contrivances to force the parallel. That is to say, a model is more impressive when its behavior takes shape as an emergent property of basic modeling rather than purpose-built architecture. Applying this to cultivation research, the goal of the current model is to explore the basic hypothesis of whether an abstract, general-purpose learning device produces similar performance to actual human viewers of television. Viewed this way, we gain knowledge of whether cultivation can emerge from the basic cognitive structure that we shared with preliterate, media-free humans.

## The Current Model

Computational modeling provides an ideal environment in which to test theoretical propositions involving the mechanisms that produce cultivation because these models afford the opportunity to precisely specify the paths of causation. The first neural network simulation of Shrum's (2001) heuristic processing model of cultivation effects demonstrated that both cultivation and the effects of systematic and heuristic processing can occur *in the way that this model predicts* (Bradley, 2007b). This is important, because these simulations showed that a general-purpose learner fits existing data and theory. However, that model was limited in that it could not capture the dimension of time or narrative. To truly represent psychological processes thought to underlie cultivation, a model must represent a dynamic system, or one that unfolds over time (e.g., Bradley, 2007a). Human cognitive capacity is finite, and a host of evolved processes attempt to optimally allocate attentional resources at each moment. As events—both mediated and live—unfold, what is attended to and stored changes. Any account that neglects time, by definition, misses these changes altogether. Imagine trying to understand language with no verb tense: Are you going to the store, already there, or putting away groceries? Time matters.

Any neural network simulation begins with a representation of the world. That is, stimuli must be converted from abstract ideas into representations amenable to computing, which most often means numerical values. Without question, this process involves a great number of assumptions, and these assumptions affect both the model's ability to function and its credibility as an explainer of phenomena. If the simulated task is represented specifically to achieve the desired result, then the model is nothing more than tautology.

In a simple feed-forward model such as the one in Figure 2 (left side), the neural network attempts to learn an association between input and output. However, no temporal dimension exists. Given an input, the model produces an output. Although the model learns along the way, it has no conception that the *next* input follows the preceding one. Its memory is only long-term, and it knows nothing of the immediate past or the immediate future. Such networks exist in a time vacuum, and as such can make no inferences about how the world unfolds over time. This is a crippling limitation for a theorist who believes that narrative (i.e., the temporal linkage of actors, objects, and agents) plays a key role in the phenomenon under study.

Neural networks have incorporated time in various ways (e.g., Jordan, 1986); however, one of the most robust models that does so is commonly known as an Elman Net after its creator (Elman, 1990). Known as a "recurrent" network because it incorporates feedback, an elegant change to the simple feed-forward neural network produces profound changes. At any given "timestep" (neural network parlance for a moment in time), an Elman Net has access to its own hidden layer activation from the previous time step (see Figure 2, curved arrow). This means in the "now," the model not only has access to the current state of the world, but it also has access to its own internal representation of the immediate past. For situations lacking a temporal component, these connections add nothing, and the models quickly learn to ignore them. For problems with a temporal component, however, these recurrent units prove invaluable. At first glance, it appears on Figure 2 that the model has access only to its *immediate* past, and in the strictest sense, this is true. However, as an Elman net learns, it builds the ability to have something akin to a short-term memory that extends well beyond one timestep.

To illustrate this, consider the very beginning of a model simulation. At Time 0 ($T_0$), there is no temporal component. The model has access to the state of the world at $T_0$, but the recurrent units are blank because there was no previous timestep. This is roughly analogous to entering a room for the first time. Since there was no past, there were no internal representations to copy. At the next timestep, $T_1$, the model has access to the state of the world at $T_1$ *and* its own internal representations at $T_0$—representing just the immediate past. However the next timestep, $T_2$, gives the model access to the state of the world at $T_2$ and its own internal representation at $T_1$. The elegance and power of this model derive from the fact that the $T_1$ internal representations were a product of *both* the input representations at $T_1$ but also the model's own hidden layer activation at $T_0$. This means that at $T_2$ the model has indirect access to $T_0$ even though that is not explicitly visible in Figure 2. This regress continues through time. At $T_3$, the model "sees" the world at $T_3$ and has its internal representations from $T_2$, which were a product of the state of the world at $T_2$ and its own internal representation at $T_1$, itself influenced by $T_1$ and $T_0$. One layer of recurrent connection provides access to much more than the immediate past. Importantly, as these models learn, and the problems with which they are presented grow more complex (see Elman, 1993), this indirect short-term memory reaches back farther and farther in time. Consider an analogy to motion. A snapshot of an airborne baseball at a given moment tells one nothing. However, the more one knows about the previous trajectory of the baseball, the more accurate the predictions about where the baseball is headed. The same is true of an Elman Net: The more it learns how the world unfolds over time, the better it is at predicting what will happen next.

A well-trained Elman Net is a powerful story prediction device. If you teach an Elman Net a series of stories and then begin a new story, it will begin to predict what will happen in the story. If many of the learned stories contain a certain element (e.g., violent attacks by strangers), then the network will begin to expect stories containing strangers to contain violence. Much like the amalgamation of neurons in the actual human brain, these "expectations" do not clearly "live" anywhere in the model. Instead, the weights of connections among units have systematically varied over time in order for the model (and the brain) to learn the "world" in which it lives. But the predictions do not live in the weights, either. Instead, model predictions arise from the dynamic interaction of connection weights, present input, and the recent past. Artificial neural networks are powerful statistical learners, and these models will learn whether the world is "mean" by the proportion of input-output pairs that reflect this reality. Previous work showed that simple feed-forward models *do* learn the world in this manner and that alerting the model to attend to source cues eliminates the cultivation differential (Bradley, 2007b), as suggested by real-world data (Shapiro, 1991). However, most first-order cultivation estimates involve some *prediction* about what would happen given a novel scenario.

Consider the following question that requires participants to respond with a percentage estimate: "What do you think the chances are that if you were to walk home alone at night on residential streets in New York City each night for a month, that you would be the victim of a violent crime?" This question has been included in a variety of cultivation-related studies for more than two decades, and participants seamlessly respond to the question (our data show that participants answer these questions in 6–14 seconds including reading time and the time required to type the response), yet the temporal nature of the question could not be clearer. In order to answer this question, participants must imagine not just a single instance but multiple instances that might make up a given month. In order to answer the question, then, participants must use memory to make repeated predictions of the future. To describe this phenomenon, a model must incorporate both narrative and time.

### *Model Architecture*

Unlike the first attempt to model the cultivation process (Bradley, 2007b), time (as expressed through narrative) is the key element in the new model, *trajectories across learned experiences*, or TALE. During a stage simulating lifetime learning, the model is presented with the co-occurrences of objects, agents, and actions over time in a variety of contexts and owing to a variety of sources. As with the actual world, there is both systematic and random variance among these occurrences. Certain actions, for example, are more strongly associated with certain agents, objects, and contexts. Take, for instance, snow skiing. Skiing should be linked with skis, boots, and gloves. Similarly, some people are skiers, and some are not. And skiing typically occurs in a relatively narrow range of contexts, such as mountainous terrain and winter. This does not mean that anomalies (e.g., scorching hot Dubai's indoor skiing) are incomprehensible, but such anomalies are atypical and are less likely to be brought to mind as an exemplar.

Thus, each simulated model's lifetime learning consists of a mixture of "personally" experienced events, information learned from other people, and mediated events that unfold over time. In each case, the model's sole purpose is to attempt to predict the immediate future based upon patterns over time. In a sense, the model searches for central tendencies in the world. Along the way, it does learn about tangential information, such as sources, but this is not the focus of learning. The model does not have to be instructed or taught to make the most relevant predictions for novel events. Instead it is an inherent property of the system.

The model is an implementation of a recurrent Elman (1990) network. The basis of this network is much like the simple feed-forward network outlined by Bradley (2007b), just larger and more complex. However, unlike the previous instantiation, TALE has recurrent connections on its hidden layer activation, providing access to its own internal representations from the previous timestep. The model's long-term memory is stored in the connections among weights, but the recurrent connections provide the model a short-term, or working, memory. When predicting the future, Elman Nets use the present (current input), the recent past (recurrent connections), and the long-term past (connection weights).

At the heart of TALE is a group of 100 context units, approximately 20% of which are active at any given timestep. The context units serve as the backdrop to the world, much like soft jazz playing at a coffeeshop. The information is there to be perceived if you so choose, but chances are that you cannot remember what was playing during your last latte. Conversely, you surely would remember if soft jazz were played during a football halftime—that context doesn't "go with" that event. Likewise, imagine seeing your dentist at a salad bar. You know the face but cannot place it. The context is wrong. These context units attempt to capture that phenomenon (see Figure 3). For each simulated participant, the degree to which that participant is associated with a given contextual unit ranges from very strong ($p$[occurrence] = .9999) to very weak ($p$[occurrence] = .0001), but averages 20%. This is akin to actual life, where some elements are often encountered (e.g., one's house) and others most likely have never been encountered (e.g., the inside of a nuclear missile silo). The model is strictly probabilistic rather than deterministic. That is, some things are far more likely to be encountered by the simulated participant, but nothing is prohibited. Within the world, there are a range of agents (i.e., other people), actions, objects, and information sources. For each of these, each simulated participant is strongly associated with only a small subset, again along a continuum. Even the most Renaissance among us doesn't know everyone, hasn't done everything, and hasn't experienced every object in the world. Just as a subset is associated with the individual, another subset is associated with the media, and these two subsets, on average, overlap very little. Finally, in addition to the continuum of sources, there are specific source bits, just as in Bradley (2007b), that always identify the general source category. Thus, personal experiences, interpersonal stories, and media sources are always uniquely identified. However, this does not guarantee that source information is learned or memorized. Models make use of only relevant information, and the presence of randomness in the model and requiring the model to re-represent the world in fewer hidden units assure that nothing is perfectly learned. This function is largely useful only in post-learning testing.

The "lifetime" of a simulated participant is a series of stories from a variety of sources. Each story begins with random activation of approximately 20% of the context units, which then activate the most closely associated agents,

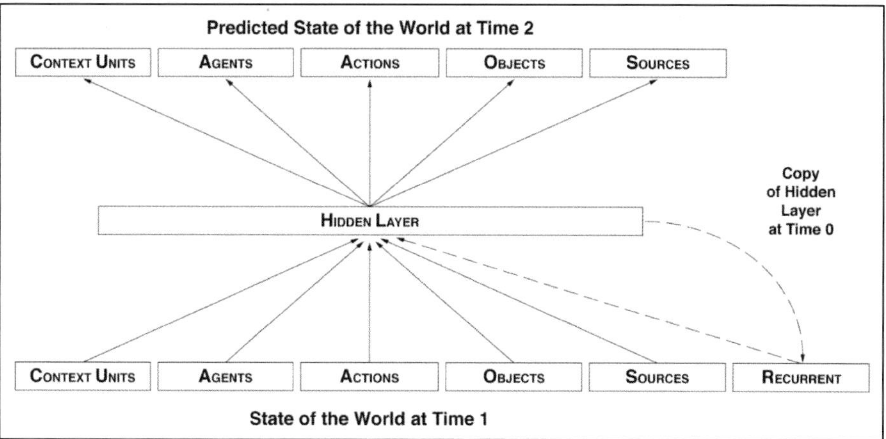


Figure 3. Schematic representation of the model *trajectories across learned experiences*. This model perceives the state of the world at a given time and uses that information combined with its internal representations from the immediate past (shown by dashed arrows) to make predictions about the immediate future.

actions, objects, and sources. Once again, this is probabilistic, such that the most closely associated action is more likely to become active but is not guaranteed to be (e.g., your favorite barista at the local coffee shop sometimes calls in sick for work). After this initial randomness, an additional degree of randomness is added to ensure stochastic variation, such that typical units are switched off and atypical ones are switched on (this was set to 0.5%). In keeping with both the literature and common sense, episodes of personal experience last far longer than either mediated or interpersonal stories. The exact story length was varied randomly for every story so that the model could not learn exactly when a story should end. Furthermore, media and interpersonal stories are more likely to cut to the chase, whereas personally experienced events ramp up slowly. This was implemented by constraining the number of active elements at the beginning and end of interpersonal stories.

Overall, stories were constrained such that about 20% of context units and 10% of other units were active at any given timestep. This constraint was added so that a story could be about neither nothing nor everything. After the first timestep, every element in the story constrained the development of events probabilistically with each active unit vying to add its most closely associated items. Returning to the example above, making the action "skiing" active would put pressure on activation of the object "ski lift" but not deterministically. Stories unfolded over time by copying the immediately previous timestep and making both random and probabilistic changes. Thus, each preceding moment closely resembled the previous, but the possibility of two successive timesteps being identical was virtually zero. Once again to resemble the actual world, all three types of sources allowed for the possibility of rapid changes of subjects, similar to "cuts" in television. This was most probable for media stories and least likely for personally experienced events. This—combined with varying story length—ensured that the future was predictable but never obvious. At any given moment, an interpersonal source might function like a conversation partner saying, "Hey, that reminds me . . ." and launching off on a new topic.

Although the objects, actions, agents, and sources portrayed on television did not overlap greatly with personal experience, an even smaller subset was constrained to overlap especially little. For the purposes of this chapter, these are denoted as "crime-related." However, given that TALE has no true semantics, these can be generalized to anything overrepresented on television. For each simulated participant, somewhere between 5,100 and 5,500 timesteps constituted a lifetime. The size of the model and its parts were constrained by hardware limitations (i.e., computer RAM). The simulations were as large as possible. Each participant was simulated using MATLAB (MathWorks Inc., Natick, MA) Neural Network Toolbox for 700 epochs (i.e., lifetime learning involved 700 trials of each timestep), at which time learning showed a clear asymptote. Five simulated participants were generated for both the high and low TV exposure conditions. Although this is admittedly a small *N*, computer-processing time placed the limit here; however, small-scale tests repeatedly demonstrated that additional participants strengthened rather than weakened results. Once trained, the models could be simulated. That is, once each model learned the narrative that was its unique life, it could start to tell new stories. By activating a very small subset of the units, it is possible to see where the model "went" over time. Two overall simulations are presented here: One attempts to capture the cultivation differential by presenting the model with a task similar to a social reality estimate, and the second examines the model's more generic view of the world.

### *Simulation Results*

For readers unfamiliar with modeling, this dissection of the world into context, agents, actions, objects, and sources might seem highly artificial. However, consider the task presented to the prototypical participant in a cultivation study. Sitting at a table, the participant stares at a white piece of paper with black type (much like this page). On that page are a series of questions regarding social reality estimates. Care has been taken by the researchers not to mention media habits in any way before these estimates are made. Then the question is posed: "What proportion of crimes are committed by strangers?" What cues does the participant have here? Very few. There is no context, and if the questionnaire is being completed in a dedicated research space, the context is highly unlike anything previous in the participant's lifetime. So context is unhelpful. Both the action "crime" and the agent "stranger" are generic. No objects are mentioned. And care has been taken not to prime sources. Thus, it is argued here that a participant makes this estimation by attempting to activate the concept of a relatively unknown set of agents and relatively ill-specified crime actions. In our lab, these types of dependent measures reliably reproduce the cultivation differential.

For these simulations, the models received some abstract initial "seed" to begin their stories. Providing the model absolutely nothing would be equivalent to placing a human subject in a sensory deprivation chamber. For the second timestep and every subsequent timestep, the model was fed back its own prediction from the previous timestep with the only caveat being that the seeds remained "on" where indicated below. Thus, other than the seeds, the model's predictions received no interference from the world. For each simulated participant for each trial, the results were recorded. Data were averaged for each timestep for actions and objects associated with crime and those not associated with crime.

### *The Cultivation Differential*

In order to model abstract judgment, groups of simulated participants representing both Heavy and Light TV viewers had two randomly chosen agent units activated (i.e., individuals highly likely to be strangers). It seemed tautological to directly activate crime units, so each simulated participant also had two arbitrary source bits activated. These sources, which we dubbed arbitrary, had no strong connections to the simulated participant, its friends, or the media. No context, action, or object information was activated. Each simulated participant (both heavy and light media) then attempted to predict where this story would go for 40 total timesteps, which was the median length of interpersonal stories. After this point, the models would begin to strongly expect the story to end. This process was repeated 25 times for each simulated participant, with each trial randomly selecting two agents and two arbitrary sources. Keep in mind that through more than 5,000 timesteps of lifetime learning, the models had never seen an input as sparse as this. Thus, these simulations required the models to heavily generalize from the abstract. In keeping with this notion, the random seeds could not be eliminated after the first time step. Given that the models had never seen anything like this input pattern, they would quickly deactivate the units and search for a well-known story.

Thus, for each trial, the four seeds were held constant for the first 5 timesteps, which can be seen in Figure 5. After the 5th timestep, each model generated its own predictions. Here we scored the average activation (ranging

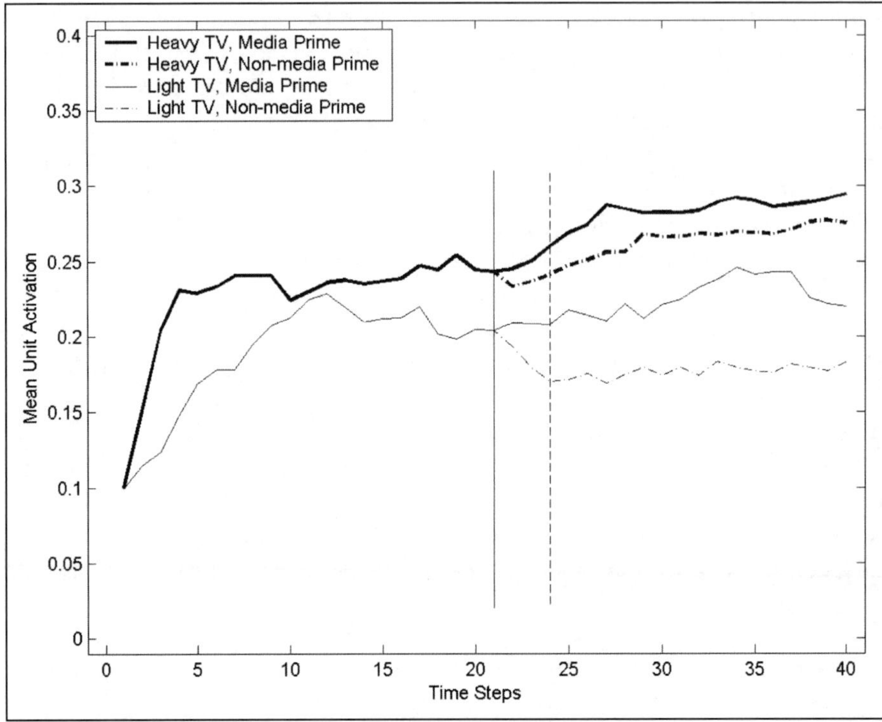


Figure 4. Over time crime-related predictions of neural networks simulations as either Heavy TV or Light TV viewers. Between the vertical lines, models were either seeded with media primes or with non-media primes.

from 0.1 to 0.9) for every crime-related action, object, and agent it knows. As can be seen, the heavier TV simulated participants show greater activation of crime-related units, and this difference is immediate. When thinking of strangers, these neural nets predict a greater prevalence of crime. Interestingly, the steep initial activation slope is an artifact of training. The Heavy TV models saw more TV stories, which get to the point more quickly, than real-world events. This small adjustment in the ratio of these stories makes these models expect the world to happen faster. This was not initially predicted, but it is an idea worth exploring.

Beginning at the 21st timestep (shown as the solid vertical line in Figure 4), these models had the source category units activated, either media or a combination of personal and interpersonal. Although these media primes were held constant for 4 timesteps (i.e., to ensure the models did not instantly dismiss them), the divergence of performance is immediate. It should be noted here that predictions *before* the 21st timestep are perfectly parallel for Heavy TV and Light TV viewers. This is due to the fact that learning can be turned off in these models, so within-subjects type comparisons can be made between-subjects. These models have no testing effects, so the same models can be simulated multiple ways. Given that each simulated subject required approximately 12 straight hours of CPU time, this is preferable. This means simply that the models do not show the kind of error variance expected among typical human subjects. Thus performance before the source primes is identical. As soon as the primes begin and long after they are removed, these models tell a different story. When primed with a media source, crime activation jumps for both Heavy TV and Light TV simulated participants. When primed with non-media sources, the prediction of crime immediately drops, although this effect is more pronounced for Light TV simulated participants. The data in Figure 4 replicate and extend Bradley (2007b). As was the case before, neural networks that see more TV expect more crime. However, in this case, the simulations suggest that this effect persists over time and occurs even when the model was allowed to predict its own story from the onset. As with Bradley (2007b), priming a model with non-mediated sources causes crime expectations to lower.

Interestingly, the so-called Light TV simulated participants show an increasing activation of crime-related elements until the seeds are removed, at which point activation levels off for the duration of the story. Heavy TV units also level off, but this happens before the seeds are removed. The data show a strong cultivation differential between the models designated Heavy TV viewers and Light TV viewers. From the beginning of the story, the presence of these disconnected units activates agents and objects associated with crime. Consistent with cultivation expectations, however, the activation of crime is both greater and more immediate for simulated participants with greater media exposure. Furthermore, once the seeds are removed, the activation persists across the duration of the story. Although the model has never experienced a situation such as this, it has a strong prediction that the narrative will end with a crime. This is especially impressive given that we attempted to make this task more difficult by not activating *any* crime units. Cultivation measures typically mention crimes; we merely mentioned strangers.

### *Self-generated Stories*

One of the benefits of these models is that once trained, many queries can be made, and questions can be "asked" of the models that are less easily asked of human participants. In order to show that these models were not merely elaborate demonstrations of a cultivation machine, an additional set of simulations were run. Clearly even the heaviest viewers do not merely sit and cower in fear of crime at every moment. So how do these models perform in a more routine environment? In this second batch of simulations, we presented each model only with 5 randomly chosen context units (out of 100). Throughout their lifetimes, these models had an average of 20 context units active, so 5 units are merely a suggestion. These simulations basically entail asking the model, "Tell me a story. The first thing that comes to mind." Nothing about this demands a media story. The random seeds were held constant for the first 5 trials, after which each simulated participant proceeded with no guidance. Once again, each line in Figure 5 represents the average of 25 trials for each of the 5 simulated participants in each condition.

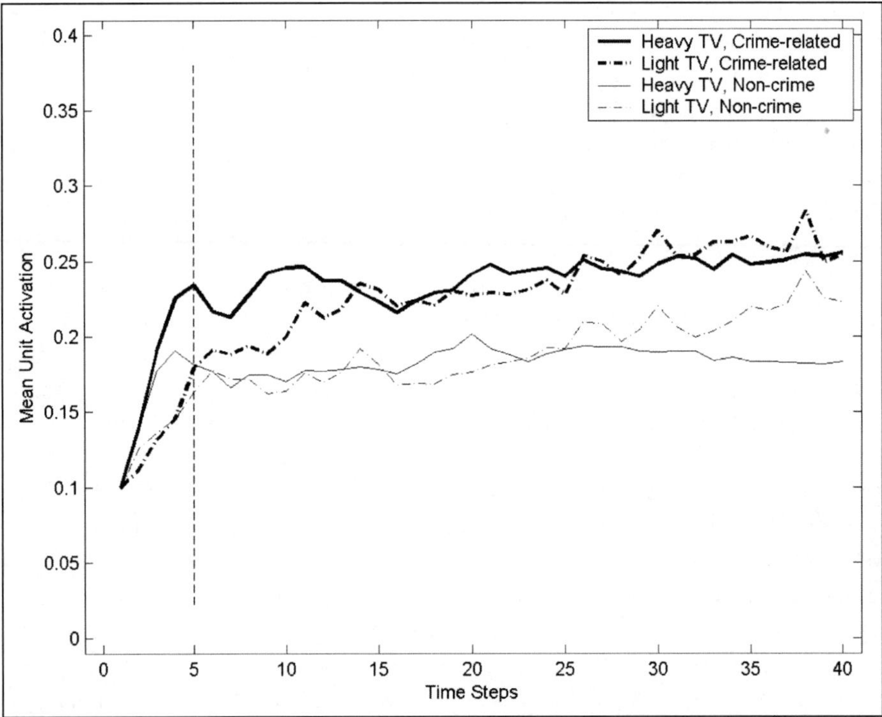


Figure 5. Over time predictions of crime-related and non-crime related of neural networks simulations as either Heavy TV or Light TV viewers. Before the vertical line, all models were seeded with random context.

A very different picture emerges here. Once again, the Heavy TV models expect stories to begin more quickly. They activate more units—both crime-related and not—more quickly than the light TV units. However, most interestingly, the difference in crime between Light and Heavy TV is negligible. These models simply do not live in a crime-filled world. Recall that after the seeds are removed (shown by the vertical line in Figure 5), these models get no feedback from the world. They simply predict how a story would unfold given no feedback. Due to the initial quicker crime activation of Heavy TV units, if *any* feedback were given suggestive of crime, these activations would have quickly risen. But when nothing in the world suggests crime, these models show very little difference, and this lack of difference persists over time. We believe this underscores the importance of interpreting cultivation as a phenomenon of both time and narrative. On average, model predictions are steady over time, although any given trial waxes and wanes typical of narrative.

## Discussion

Returning to television, we see the remarkable constancy of narrative first posited by Gerbner. This is a commercial enterprise that survives only when millions of eyes voluntarily and habitually attend to the screen. First with the development of motion pictures and then television, producers, directors, and screenwriters have crafted the art of telling compelling stories. With great regularity, these stories make use of the elements most relevant to survival: sex and violence. In the study of television institutions and effects, it is taken as axiomatic that the intensity of the televised world scarcely resembles actual life. That is, if television were no more exciting than real life, why would people watch? At the same time, much of television's reality must be similar to the actual world, or the content becomes implausible or even unintelligible. A series of studies shows that viewers can make snap-second accurate judgments about the plausibility or typicality of a given mediated event (Bradley & Shapiro, 2004). Furthermore, source information is encoded as part of the story. However, this source information appears unheeded for at least two reasons. First, when compared with the relative invariance presented in prominent themes on television, source information and context vary widely. Thus source and context information are more poorly stored and are relatively less accessible. When necessary—and through the work of excessive elaboration—this information can be recalled and used to discount media-learned information (Shapiro, 1991; Shrum, 2001).

The simulations offered here approach this topic from a unique perspective: Is cultivation an emergent property of an evolved brain tuned to optimally perceive the world at each passing moment? The data suggest that a general-purpose learner does a strong job of exhibiting a cultivation pattern while at the same time not perpetually cowering in the corner expecting crime and violence at every turn. When thinking of strangers, crime seems more likely, and this is especially true for Heavy TV viewers. When focusing on television (not source discounting), this expectation of crime increases for both Heavy and

Light viewers. When focusing on personal and interpersonal experience, this decreases, especially for Light viewers.

Life happens over time, and these simulations make a compelling argument to study the cultivation process over time. Gerbner and Gross (1976) said, "Plots weave a thread of causality into the fabric of dramatic ritual, as stock characters act out familiar parts and confirm preferred notions of what's what, who's who, and who counts for what" (p. 182). Repeated, heavy exposure, however, weaves more than causality into drama. Recent work in neuroscience, human memory, cognitive science, and communication all point to the primacy of time and narrative. We use time to make sense of the world, weaving narratives to establish causal relations of actions, objects, and agents. Without this fabric, the world simply does not make sense. And we argue that neural network simulations advance the study of cultivation. Although the robustness of the effect is without question, these and past data (Bradley, 2007b) illustrate that the kind of general-purpose learning device already shown to underlie so many human cognitive functions also predicts and demonstrates the cultivation process. Viewing the world and predicting the future means drawing upon a lifetime of learned experiences. These past experiences are combined with the now to make a trajectory that we use to predict the future. When those past experiences are dominated by television, the TV stories color our trajectories through time. Importantly, however, we are neither blinded nor completely overwhelmed by the discolorations. Perhaps the greatest power of television is just that: It colors predictions ever so slightly such that we don't notice the bending effects of our predictions. We cross the street when a stranger approaches, never thinking that our 20,000 hours of viewing compelled us to act.

## References

Baron, N. S. (2000). *Growing up with language: How children learn to talk.* New York: Da Capo Press.

Bradley, S. D. (2004). Visual expectancy and orienting behavior in an artificial neural network [Abstract]. *Psychophysiology, 41*(Suppl. 1), S62.

Bradley, S. D. (2006). Exploring the validity and reliability of the acoustic startle probe as a measure of attention and motivation to television programming (Doctoral dissertation, Indiana University, 2005). *Dissertation Abstracts International, 66*(08), 4527B.

Bradley, S. D. (2007a). Dynamic, embodied, limited-capacity attention and memory: Modeling cognitive processing of mediated stimuli. *Media Psychology, 9*, 211–239.

Bradley, S. D. (2007b). Neural network simulations support heuristic processing model of cultivation effects. *Media Psychology, 10*, 449–469.

Bradley, S. D. (2010). Narrative theory. In C. Baehr & B. Schaller (Eds.), *Writing for the Internet: A guide to real communication in virtual space* (pp. 81–93). Santa Barbara, CA: Greenwood.

Bradley, S. D., & Shapiro, M. A. (2004). Parsing reality: The interactive effects of complex syntax and time pressure on cognitive processing of television scenarios. *Media Psychology, 6*, 307–333.

Cook, D. A. (1990). *A history of narrative film* (2nd ed.). New York: W. W. Norton.

Elman, J. L. (1990). Finding structure in time. *Cognitive Science, 14*, 179–211.

Elman, J. L. (1993). Learning and development in neural networks: The importance of starting small. *Cognition, 48*, 71–99.

Ericsson, K. A., Prietula, M. J., & Cokelyo, E. T. (2007). The making of an expert. *Harvard Business Review, 85*(7/8), 114–121.

Gerbner, G. (1978, Feb. 9). Television and state: The public's own money is used to sell public audiences to the highest bidders. *The Washington Post*, p. Va. 11.

Gerbner, G., & Gross, L. (1976). Living with television: The violence profile. *Journal of Communication, 26*(2), 173–199.

Hebb, D. (1949). *The organization of behavior*. New Work: Wiley.

Heider, F., & Simmel, M. (1944). An experimental study of apparent behavior. *The American Journal of Psychology, 57*, 243–259.

Jordan, M. (1986). *Serial order: A parallel distributed processing approach* (No. ICS Report 8604, Institute for Cognitive Science). La Jolla, CA: University of California at San Diego.

Kahneman, D. (1973). *Attention and effort*. New York: Prentice-Hall.

Kirkham, N. Z., Slemmer, J. A., & Johnson, S. P. (2002). Visual statistical learning in infancy: evidence for a domain general learning mechanism. *Cognition, 83*, B35–B42.

Lang, A. (1989). The effects of chronological presentation of information on processing and memory for broadcast news. *Journal of Broadcasting & Electronic Media, 33*, 441–452.

Lang, A., Sias, P. M., Chantrill, P., & Burek, J. A. (1995). Tell me a story: Narrative elaboration and memory for television. *Communication Reports, 8*, 102–110.

McKee, R. (1997). *Story: Substance, structure, style, and the principles of screenwriting*. New York: Harper Collins.

Michotte, A. (1963). *The perception of causality*. New York: Basic Books.

Pavlov, I.P. (1927). *Conditioned reflexes: An investigation of the physiological activity of the cerebral cortex*. Cambridge: Oxford University Press.

Polyak, V., Hill, C., & Asmerom, Y. (2008). Age and evolution of the Grand Canyon revealed by U-Pb dating of water table-type speleothems. *Science, 319*, 1377–1380.

Rideout, V. J., Foehr, U. G., & Roberts, D. F. (2010). *Generation $M^2$: Media in the lives of 8- to 18-year-olds*. Menlo Park, CA: Kaiser Family Foundation.

Rideout, V. J., Vandewater, E. A., & Wartella, E. A. (2003). *Zero to six: Electronic media in the lives of infants, toddlers and preschoolers*. Menlo Park, CA: Kaiser Family Foundation.

Rumelhart, D. E., & McClelland, J. L. (Eds.). (1986a). *Parallel distributed processing: Explorations in the microstructure of cognition, Volume 1: Foundations*. Cambridge, MA: MIT Press.

Rumelhart, D. E., & McClelland, J. L. (Eds.). (1986b). *Parallel distributed processing: Explorations in the microstructure of cognition, Volume 2: Psychological and biological models*. Cambridge, MA: MIT Press.

Schacter, D. L., & Addis, D. R. (2007). The cognitive neuroscience of constructive memory: Remembering the past and imagining the future. *Philosophical Transactions of the Royal Society B: Biological Sciences, 362*, 773–786.

Shanahan, J., & Morgan, M. (1999). *Television and its viewers: Cultivation theory and research.* Cambridge: Cambridge University Press.

Shapiro, M. A. (1991). Memory and decision processes in the construction of social reality. *Communication Research, 18*, 3–24.

Shrum, L. J. (2001). Processing strategy moderates the cultivation effect. *Human Communication Research, 27*(1), 94–120.

Wyer, R. S., Adaval, R., & Colcombe, S. J. (2002). Narrative-based representations of social knowledge: Their construction and use in comprehension, memory and judgment. In M. P. Zanna (Ed.), *Advances in experimental social psychology* (Vol. 34, pp. 131–197). San Diego: Academic Press.

Zillmann, D., & Bryant, J. (1984). Effects of massive exposure to pornography. In M. Malamuth & E. Donnerstein (Eds.), *Pornography and sexual aggression* (pp. 115–138). Orlando, FL: Academic Press.

# *New Theoretical and Methodological Dimensions*

# 12. International Cultivation

*Jan Van den Bulck*

The cultivation hypothesis was conceived and developed in the U.S., where most of the early research was conducted. Soon, however, researchers from other countries started to examine this theory. In 1978 Wober published his "View from Great Britain," a replication of cultivation research which failed to reproduce any evidence of a cultivation effect in the U.K. Even though this very brief report was extremely limited, both in its definition of the exposure variable and the dependent variables, the study and the way in which it was used by others introduced an important modification of the cultivation hypothesis. Morgan and Shanahan (1997) argued that differences in viewing levels and a "more diversified and balanced flow of media messages that [are] not driven entirely by commercial interests" meant that one might not actually expect to find a cultivation effect in that particular context (p. 11). Other authors also argued that the content of television was more homogenous and violent in the U.S. than in other countries (Blumler, Brynin, & Nossiter, 1986; von Feilitzen, Strand, Nowak, & Andrén, 1989). In other words, Wober's (1978) study and his subsequent book (Wober & Gunter, 1988) introduced a strong suggestion that cultivation might be essentially an American phenomenon. Kolbeins (2004) repeated virtually all these arguments to explain why an Icelandic study found no significant relationships between watching television and typical cultivation measures such as trust in other people and fear of walking alone at night.

This chapter must therefore start by answering the question: "Is cultivation exclusively an American phenomenon?" In other words, does it make sense to look for cultivation effects outside of the U.S. or among non-U.S. audiences? The question is further complicated by the presence in the U.S. of large groups of immigrants not born in the U.S. Tamborini and Choi (1990) therefore made a distinction between three types of people among whom cultivation effects might be researched: a) foreigners living in the U.S. and exposed to U.S. television; b) people living in other countries, but exposed to U.S. TV in those countries; and c) people living in other countries exposed to television programs produced in that country. Generally speaking, cultivation research with an international perspective can therefore be divided into two broad types. First, there are studies that examine American television specifically, and deal with three types of questions:

a) What is the impact of American television on the perceptions that non-American viewers not living in the U.S. have of the U.S.?
b) What is the impact of American television on the perceptions of non-American viewers living in the U.S.? (In other words, does American TV play a role in the acculturation of immigrants?)
c) What is the impact of American television on general perceptions of viewers not living in the United States? (In other words, does American TV influence fear of crime, attitudes, etc., in other countries?)

Second, there are studies conducted in other countries that treat the cultivation hypothesis as if it were a *general* theory of the effects of television fiction, regardless of the country in which it is conducted or where the programming is produced. Such studies often imply that the fact that they were conducted in Belgium, Germany, Israel, or some other country is irrelevant for the theoretical assumptions or the empirical findings of the study.

This chapter cannot do justice to all the authors who have written in and about this field. In addition, this text is limited to references published in English and focuses mainly on studies published since 2000. There will, therefore, undoubtedly be important omissions. There are countless studies of cultivation in many different countries, published in many different languages. Some of these studies will certainly contain new ideas for the cultivation research community and a wider dissemination of these studies would further our knowledge of cultivation processes. This chapter aims to address key conceptual issues and challenges rather than to provide a comprehensive and exhaustive review of all international cultivation studies. As there has been no overview or synthesis of this aspect of cultivation research for some years, it ends with a typology that aims to organize this body of literature in a way that can help lead to new developments and identifies areas of research that need more attention in the years to come.

## American Television Outside of the U.S.

Even if the cultivation hypothesis only applied to audiovisual fiction produced in the U.S., it would still be legitimate to wonder about its impact outside of the U.S. Virtually all countries around the world broadcast a lot of American fiction on TV. Data from 2009 showed that 54% of all TV fiction series and 59% of all feature films shown on TV in European countries were produced in the U.S. (European Audiovisual Observatory, 2010). Earlier studies have shown that it was safe to conclude that U.S.-made fiction is widely distributed, even during prime time (De Bens & de Smaele, 2001). Consequently, many of the programs Gerbner and his colleagues studied in the U.S. have been shown around the world. As recently as 2010, Fu and Sim wrote of the "growing prominence of the U.S. media exports over the past decades" (2010, p. 137).

The fact that American programs are a steady part of the TV diet in many countries, and have been for decades, is not enough to conclude that effects attributed to American television in the U.S. are likely to be found in those other countries. First, American television programs may be interpreted differently in different cultures. The fact that American programs can be seen around the world has sometimes been referred to as the "Dallasification" of television (De Bens & de Smaele, 2001), referring to the success of the prime-time soap opera popular in the late 1970s through the 1990s. *Dallas* led, however, to the birth of reception theory, based on the findings of Ien Ang (1985) and Liebes and Katz (1990) who showed that people from different cultures may attach meanings to television programs that are very different from those attached to the same program by viewers in the country where it was first produced. As such, it is possible that a program associated with feelings of fear in the U.S. might have a very different effect—or no effect—in another culture. An extreme example can be found in the work of Granzberg (1982), who studied the effects of the introduction of television in a community of Algonkian Indians in Central Canada. The Algonkians had no previous experience with television and had a culture in which storytelling had such a central and particular role that they were inclined to take American television fiction as literal truth. This difference in attributing meaning to stories strongly influenced the way in which these people were affected by television.

Second, even if there were no differences in interpretation, the same stimulus might have a different effect on members of another culture. A number of researchers have, in fact, suggested that American television might even be *more* powerful *outside* of the U.S. The *impersonal impact hypothesis*, for instance, argues that a distinction has to be made between perceptions that refer to a person's personal situation and perceptions at the societal level. It has been argued that direct experience is probably the most important source of knowledge regarding personal situations and that the media are more likely to be influential regarding matters with which a person has no personal experience (see Shrum, 2001). Another school of thought believes that effects only occur in areas that do not really concern the viewer. Adoni, Cohen, and Mane (1984) referred to Berger and Luckmann's sociology of knowledge to distinguish "fields of relevance." Some areas in life are very relevant because they refer to "immediate pragmatic interests" (Berger & Luckmann, 1976), which Adoni et al. defined as "close." Other areas in life refer to "my general situation in society"; these were called "remote." Adoni et al. (1984) believed that what is close will be learned through direct experience, while what is remote may be learned through mediated experience. Both approaches to media effects suggest that American television, which refers to American society, may be very successful in affecting people's perceptions of the United States in other countries, regardless of whether it plays any role in their views of their own societies.

## Cultivation and non-U.S. TV

Cultivation theory was not conceived as a theory exclusively about the effects of U.S. TV on U.S. audiences. Even though the original authors did not mention nationality in this sense it is clear that they wanted to present a general theory on the effects of television or, more precisely, storytelling. In their review of two decades of cultivation theory, Morgan and Shanahan, for instance, described the empirical strategy of cultivation research as aiming to chart "the degree to which heavy viewers are more likely to give responses that are demonstrably emphasized in the television world" (1997, p. 11). The essence of cultivation theory is the hypothesis that "television viewing cultivates assumptions about the facts of life that reflect the medium's most recurrent portrayals" (p. 8). In another definition, Gerbner, Gross, Morgan, Signorielli, and Shanahan (2002) delineated cultivation effects as "the independent contributions television viewing makes to viewer conceptions of social reality" (p. 47). None of this involves the assumption that cultivation is, in essence, a specifically American effect or an effect limited to American TV.

Another misconception, implicit in much of the criticism of Gerbner's work, is that cultivation theory is only about crime and violence. The absence of relationships between TV viewing and perceptions or beliefs about crime and violence is, therefore, not enough to conclude that TV does not cultivate worldviews in a particular culture. Violence was an important concept in the early works of Gerbner and his co-workers because

> TV violence is a dramatic demonstration of power which communicates much about social norms and relationships, about goals and means, about winners and losers, about the risks of life and the price for transgressions of society's rules. Violence-laden drama shows who gets away with what, when, why, how and against whom. (Gerbner & Gross, 1976, p. 176)

Nevertheless, the theory only saw violence as a vehicle for socialization. It suffices to replace the references to violence in the quote from Gerbner and Gross by references to "emergency medicine" to have a passable definition of how the many stories about emergency medicine on the street and in hospitals might cultivate perceptions in a similar way. The developers of cultivation theory did not limit themselves to studies of the effects of violence. They also looked at gender-roles, health, politics, and so forth (for early reviews see Signorielli, Gross, & Morgan, 1982; Signorielli & Morgan, 1990). There is no suggestion in cultivation that effects are only expected to occur if and when enough (and the right kind of) violence is present in a particular television culture. The idea that other cultures may have other meta-narratives, another view of society presented through storytelling, may only mean that other types of cultivation effects are to be expected. Thus, at best all that Wober (1978) demonstrated was that the operationalizations he utilized and the statistical methodology he employed failed to reproduce the findings of Gerbner and associates in the U.K.

One limitation to this broad view of the applicability of cultivation is, however, that cultivation is not a theory about television effects, but about the effects of storytelling. Elaborating on Gerbner and Gross's (1976) argument that "representational realism" is the "dominant convention" in the way stories are told in Western cultures, Shanahan and Morgan summarized it as "the form of storytelling in which the hearer or viewer is convinced that, if certain assumptions are taken for granted, the events taking place could happen 'in reality'" (1999, p. 21). This characteristic of television may not apply to every television culture. As well, the question of what constitutes representational realism itself may be culture-specific. Western audiences may feel that the special effects that allow fighters to leap to physically impossible heights in Asian martial arts movies are "unrealistic," thus spoiling the temporary suspension of disbelief, but may have little trouble being transported into a movie in which a robot is sent back through time to prevent a certain baby from being born.

## Impact of American Television on Perceptions of the U.S.

Tan, Li, and Simpson have argued: "To many foreign audiences, American television is the only or main source of information about American culture and people" (1986, p. 809). Tan et al. based their hypothesis on the observation that U.S. TV is omnipresent and on the assumption that the influence of television "will be greatest when dependence on the medium is high, and when direct experience with the response to be learned is limited" (Tan et al., 1986, p. 809). Framing their study as a test of both cultivation theory and contemporary psychological research on stereotypes, Tan et al. (1986) administered surveys in Taiwan and Mexico. They found that the top five characteristics of Americans, as perceived by 788 adult Chinese respondents in Taiwan, were *individualistic*, *conceited*, *practical*, *athletic*, and *ambitious*. In a separate study, 150 Mexican college students felt that Americans were *materialistic*, *ambitious*, *artistic*, *practical*, and *industrious*. Many of these perceived characteristics, such as lack of marital faithfulness, high divorce rates, a penchant for pleasure, and so on, seemed to resemble the meta-narratives of TV shows such as *Dallas* and *Dynasty*, which the authors mentioned as sources of such stereotypes. Exposure to *Dallas* correlated significantly with perceptions of Americans as dishonest and materialistic in the Chinese sample and exposure to *Dynasty* correlated significantly with perceptions of Americans as individualistic and pleasure loving in the Mexican sample. Similar conclusions were reached in a study of high school students in the Philippines (Tan, Tan, & Tan, 1987) and a study of undergraduates in Thailand (Tan & Suarchavarat, 1988).

Tan added an interesting new idea to his original studies about 30 years later. He realized that the stereotypical images of Americans and the stereotypical beliefs they appeared to engender mainly referred to White Americans. Tan, Zhang, Zhang, and Dalisay (2009) found a relationship between exposure to American TV programs and negative stereotypes of African Americans among Chinese high school students. Interestingly, these perceptions were less negative than the image they had of White Americans, but exposure to Chinese media correlated with much more positive stereotypes. In addition, a study of South Korean high school students showed a similar relationship between exposure to American TV and negative stereotypes of African Americans (Tan, Dalisay, Zhang, Han, & Merchant, 2010).

Other researchers have conducted similar studies to ascertain whether exposure to American TV is related to perceptions of what the U.S. is like. Hetsroni, Elphariach, Kapuza, & Tsfoni (2007), for instance, found that among 655 Israeli students, viewing American TV shows was related to giving the so-called TV answer to forced-choice questions regarding the prevalence of certain professions in the U.S. workforce.

## Television and the Acculturation of American Immigrants

When immigrants arrive in a new country they come equipped with a fully fledged culture. The new host country will have its own culture. To thrive in the host country immigrants have to acquire knowledge of the new culture. The processes whereby immigrants learn the new culture are generally referred to as *acculturation* (wherein different groups adjust to the presence of each other's culture) and *adaptation* (the effect of acculturation on an individual; Berry, 2001). Even though acculturation theorists such as Berry have stressed that both the host and the immigrant cultures will have to adjust to each other's presence, research tends to focus on the extent to which immigrants adjust to the host culture. It is commonly assumed that the mass media of the host country will play an important part in the acculturation process (Tamborini & Choi, 1990). Raman and Harwood (2008) therefore argued that "cultivation theory is a sensible framework within which to examine acculturation" (p. 297). In many ways this is an understatement. Because new arrivals in a host culture usually have little or no previous exposure to the new culture and often have limited contacts within the new culture (Moon & Park, 2007), the mass media may be one of their most important sources of knowledge (a process which may have started long before they arrived in the new culture). As such, acculturation is a true field-experiment in cultivation. This is best expressed by Moon and Park (2007), who argued that mass media reflect the cultural values of a society and are therefore perfect vehicles for the transmission of knowledge and values. They found two processes that interact: Korean immigrants in Los Angeles who watched a lot of American TV were more likely to accept American cultural values, but they were also more likely to display less affinity for Korean culture. This suggests that television might have two different effects on acculturation: it encourages knowledge of and thus acceptance of the host culture, and it diminishes the attractiveness of the immigrant's original culture. As such, storytelling might considerably speed up the acculturation process. Moon and Park concluded that exposure to American media led to cultural homogenization of immigrants and not to biculturalism.

In acculturation research some have studied what are referred to as *sojourners* instead of *immigrants*. Sojourners are defined as "individuals who travel abroad to attain a particular goal within a specified period of time" (Bochner, 2006, p. 181). While an example might be an expatriate worker who stays in another country with a temporary work permit, the concept is most commonly used to refer to foreign undergraduate or high school students. While the convenient access researchers have to this group probably explains their presence in so much research, using them makes particular sense in the case of acculturation research. Even though foreign students are unlikely to be a representative sample of the culture to which they belong, comparing foreign undergraduates with native undergraduates assures that both groups are fairly homogeneous as far as such control variables as age, level of education, and certain interests are concerned (see also Tamborini & Choi, 1990). One of Tan's earliest studies compared 187 American students and 114 Chinese studying in the U.S. (Tan, 1982). Among the Chinese students, perceptions of Americans as pleasure-loving and materialistic were significantly related to TV use (the correlations ranged between .20 and .42). A study of 83 Japanese students and 166 White students at a university in the Northwest suggested that in both groups television viewing was related to stereotypical perceptions of African Americans (Fujioka, 1999). Unlike these earlier studies, a survey of 114 students from India by Raman and Harwood (2008) failed to find any evidence of a relationship between exposure to American (or other) TV and acculturation. While the study explicitly referred to cultivation theory, the dependent variables did not include perceptions of American reality or beliefs about the real world; instead, the researchers used an Asian Self-Identity Acculturation Scale that measured identity aspects such as language preferences, food preferences, and cultural and socio-religious participation. Self-identity may not be a measure commonly used by cultivation researchers, but it does appear to be a logical end-result of socialization processes. As such it would be interesting for cultivation researchers to pay more attention to it in future research.

There have been other studies in the area of acculturation that add to cultivation theory by introducing new research questions. Woo and Dominick (2001, 2003), for instance, looked at the relationship between exposure to daytime television talk shows and perceptions of and attitudes towards Americans among international students. They found that exposure to these shows was related to higher estimates of the frequency of what they referred to as "inappropriate or undesirable behaviors" (2001, p. 604) that are common themes on those shows, such as infidelity, premarital sex, and running away from home. Exposure to this type of TV fare was also related to more negative perceptions of human relationships in the U.S.

Chaffee, Nass, and Yang (1990), while writing about the acculturation effects of television news, offered an interesting hypothesis for all students of the effects of the media on immigrants and sojourners. They remarked that the processes leading to the acculturation of an immigrant operate differently in adults and in adolescents. To illustrate this they introduced two metaphors. Adults, they argued, undergo a *bridging* process. They arrive in a new culture fully socialized and have to be resocialized to "move laterally" (p. 269) from the old culture to the next (hence the bridge metaphor). Adolescents, on the other hand, "climb the ladder to adulthood" (p. 269) and become socialized in a number of steps (hence a *stair step* metaphor). The same media message may therefore play a different role in the acculturation of an adult or an adolescent; and the messages may affect adolescents on differing steps of the ladder in different ways.

## The Impact of Television on General Perceptions and Beliefs

It is not difficult to see how images of another culture, even if the storylines are fictional, may affect viewers' perceptions of that culture. A different matter is the question of whether "foreign" cultural products might affect a viewer's perception of his or her own lifeworld and environment. For instance, might an Australian viewer who watches a lot of U.S. crime fiction be more concerned with his or her own safety in Australia?

In his study of the introduction of television among Algonkian Indians in Central Canada, Granzberg (1982) found "observational evidence of increased fears and aggression" that was "most readily apparent in children's play" (p. 45). One of the more remarkable observations the author made was that "the number of eyes lost in fights increased greatly" (p. 45) after the children started acting out things they had seen on TV. The Algonkian people he studied had, however, no previous exposure to this powerful medium and, as noted above, their own culture had an attitude towards storytelling that made them very susceptible to treating fictional stories as if they were real. This response may therefore have been very culture-specific and also dependent upon the level of experience the culture previously had with the modern mass media. The study by Tan et al. (1987) of 225 high school students in the Philippines found that heavy viewers of U.S. TV were more likely than infrequent viewers to feel that some of the values U.S. TV appeared to promote were important to them, too. The authors concluded that "There is some evidence, then, that frequent viewing of American television is related to *some* erosion of traditional Filipino values in our samples" (p. 144). Pingree and Hawkins (1981) studied 1280 children from the 2nd to the 11th grades in Australia and found that watching U.S. television correlated significantly with perceptions of Australia as a mean and dangerous place. Such relationships were not found between watching Australian drama and these same beliefs or between watching U.S. drama and the belief that the U.S. was a mean and dangerous place.

Not all studies have found a relationship between exposure to U.S. television and fear in (or perceptions of) one's own environment. Kolbeins (2004), for instance, found no cultivation relationships at all in an Icelandic study. The fact that a British study found a relationship between the viewing of U.S. television and fear but not between the viewing of British television and fear (Wober, 1990) was seen by Kolbeins as evidence that something was wrong with the cultivation hypothesis. A theoretical explanation for this apparent contradiction can be found in Yang, Ramasubramanian, and Oliver (2008), who studied the relationship between TV viewing and feelings of relative deprivation in India and South Korea. The authors found that exposure to U.S. television was associated with the perception of Americans as very affluent. This perception in turn was associated with feelings of relative deprivation. In other words, the authors described a kind of two-step model of intercultural cultivation. They used the distinction between first- and second-order cultivation effects (cf. Hawkins & Pingree, 1981, 1990) to describe what they believe happened: Watching U.S. television might influence perceptions of affluence in the U.S. (a "first-order" perception), and these perceptions might then affect feelings of relative deprivation (a "second-order" judgment). Research on social comparison theory, often quoted by communication scholars in other contexts (Yang & Oliver, 2010), may therefore be particularly relevant for researchers in the field of international cultivation.

While the theory of Yang et al. (2008) offers a hypothesis that explains how certain real-world judgments of non-residents of the U.S. might be affected by exposure to U.S. television, it cannot explain why some have found that viewing U.S. programs is associated with perceptions of risk and feelings of fear pertaining to the viewer's own country and environment. In a qualitative cultivation study, Van den Bulck and Vandebosch (2003) found that first-time prisoners held clear expectations of what life in a Belgian prison would be like. They explicitly referred to U.S. television and movie images of prison as a source of their "knowledge." The prisoners literally could not imagine any reality except the one they had become so familiar with through their TV exposure. This example suggests an explanation for the effect of U.S. television on people's perceptions of their own (non-U.S.) environments. As Busselle and Greenberg (2000) have argued, viewers exposed to TV fiction make constant reality judgments. What they view is perceived as realistic if they judge it as being both possible and plausible. Combined with Shrum's theorizing on the availability heuristic (2007), this leads to the hypothesis that when people see something on television that refers to a reality of which they have no direct experience they wonder whether what they see is possible and plausible. When they have to make a real world judgment at a later date (for instance, when they wonder what prison life might be like), the "probable" TV images may be the only input available. If they cannot imagine anything else, then the U.S. TV image becomes the most likely exemplar from which to draw inferences. If they have no other knowledge, then the TV image goes from a picture of how things are probably done in the U.S. to the most likely example of how things are done in general.

## Cultivation Without Borders

Many authors outside of the U.S. have treated cultivation as a theory that has no particular bearing on the United States. They have conducted studies in Belgium, Germany, or Israel, to name just a few, with respondents recruited in those countries, assuming that the presence or absence of relationships between TV viewing and particular outcome variables teaches us something about cultivation theory *in general*. All these studies have focused on advancing our understanding of cultivation theory and of the processes underlying the cultivation effect assuming (usually implicitly) that the fact that the study was conducted outside of the U.S. neither increased nor reduced the validity of the findings.

Even though there is a lot of variety among the studies conducted outside the U.S., a number of subjects have received particular attention. The first is the methodology of cultivation research. In Belgium, Van den Bulck (2003) examined the validity of Hirsch's (1981a, 1981b) accusation that the mainstreaming effect of cultivation was a statistical artifact known as *regression to the mean*. Regression to the mean occurs when subgroups with the lowest and highest scores on some variable are selected to be remeasured on that variable after some "treatment." Because some will end up in the extreme highest or lowest scoring group as a result of random or measurement error, they will often appear to show a score closer to the overall mean (and their "true" score) on the subsequent measure. In mainstreaming research, however, an entirely different approach is used. Typically, it examines the mean scores of the light viewers of two groups (e.g., men and women) on some variable (e.g., crime estimates) and compares them to the mean scores of the heavy viewers on the same variable. Random effects are comparable for those groups and cannot account for any reduction in differences between heavy viewers versus light viewers. Van den Bulck thus concluded that Hirsch was wrong and that mainstreaming could not be explained by regression to the mean.

Gerbner and his co-authors remarked that cultivation theory was not a stimulus-response theory (Morgan & Signorielli, 1990, p. 18). "Thus, television neither simply 'creates' nor 'reflects' images, opinions and beliefs. Rather, it is an integral aspect of a dynamic process" (Gerbner et al., 1994, p. 23). The original theory was not framed in terms of causality. A number of studies conducted since 2000 have, however, looked at causality issues that arise as a result of the fact that most cultivation research is based on cross-sectional survey data. Van den Bulck (2004) used structural equation modeling and found that a cultivation model, in which television viewing predicted fear of crime, fit the data of a survey of 909 adults from Belgium better than a *mood management* model, in which fear predicted television exposure, a *withdrawal* model, in which the relationship between fear and viewing was spurious, and a *null* model in which there was no relationship. In Germany, Rossman and Brosius (2004) discussed the causality problem in detail and offered a number of solutions. They compared various alternatives to survey research, including laboratory experiments, experiments in a natural setting, and longitudinal studies. They concluded that progress in cultivation research cannot depend on one "ideal" method but needs to come from using different approaches that complement one another. One example is Rössler and Brosius's (2001) study in which both an unusual methodology (a prolonged exposure experiment) and an unusual type of TV exposure (talk shows) were used. Others have tried to chart cultivation processes by doing experiments with written stories (Appel & Richter, 2007). These studies assume that cultivation processes are not limited to television fiction but can also occur when exposed to written fiction or to other types of television entertainment. Similarly, Van Mierlo and Van den Bulck (2004) examined whether the relationship between video game play and traditional cultivation measures was comparable to the relationships found between those dependent variables and TV exposure.

A second type of international cultivation study (conducted in various countries outside the U.S.) has tried to enrich the theory by introducing new concepts. Hetsroni (2008), for instance, proposed that viewers in Israel may give correct estimates of the TV world or may over- or underestimate TV reality, which in itself may or may not depict the real world accurately. Both over- and underestimations of real world phenomena may thus be cultivation effects. Hetsroni and Tukachinsky (2006) believed that heavier viewers (again in Israel) were more likely to be in a group they called "overcultivated," meaning that viewers felt the real world looked like the TV world but overestimated what was shown in the TV world. Appel and Richter (2007) used a German sample to remind cultivation researchers of the old concepts of *absolute* and *relative sleeper effects* to argue that narrative fiction can have persistent persuasive effects that can even grow stronger over time. Custers and Van den Bulck (2011a, b) argued from Belgian data that cultivation research on the relationship between viewing and fear of crime had been inconsistent and inaccurate in its use of the concept of fear. They argued that perceived risk (a cognition) and fear (an emotion) were too often used as if they were synonyms. They also remarked that fear could be a state (which they referred to as *situational fear*), but could also be a trait (called *dispositional fear*), as some people have a higher propensity for becoming afraid than others (Custers & Van den Bulck, 2011b). The authors concluded that progress in cultivation research on fear of crime should start by paying closer attention to the definition of core variables.

Studies have examined the processes explaining or moderating the cultivation effect. Particular attention has been given to the potential role of *transportation* in the cultivation process by authors such as Bilandzic and Busselle, who used German or American samples or combinations of both for their research (Bilandzic & Busselle, 2008; Busselle & Bilandzic, 2009). The concept of transportation refers to the experience of becoming immersed in a narrative, of being transported into the story, defined as "a flow-like state accompanied by a loss of awareness of self and the actual world" (Busselle & Bilandzic , 2008, p. 256). Whether a trait called *transportability* might exist and how it might be measured has also been explored (Bilandzic & Busselle, 2008) along with whether transportation in turn is predicted by a trait called *need for affect* (Appel & Richter, 2010).

Hetsroni's (2008) study also looked at beliefs about the real world that were over- or underrepresented on television and found that television viewing was related to these beliefs, regardless of whether they were concerned with over- or underrepresented elements. These findings challenge the idea that the frequency with which certain elements are shown on TV creates the cultivation effect. Van den Bulck & Vandebosch (2003) have suggested that the consistency of the portrayal might be more important than the frequency. Even if something is shown only rarely on television heavy viewers will still end up being exposed to it regularly. If the picture presented by these rare occurrences is consistent, this may be enough to affect reality judgments over time. These are just some of the findings and issues that have emerged from studies of cultivation undertaken outside of the U.S.

## Towards a Typology of International Cultivation

What makes a cultivation study "international"? Is it any cultivation study not conducted in the United States? To an extent, that is probably what most would assume. Such studies have to start by providing a response to the Wober assumption, which can be paraphrased as: Cultivation is a quintessentially American process, and there is no reason to assume it can occur outside of the U.S. This approach would limit the cultivation hypothesis to processes occurring among people native to the U.S. and living there. The studies discussed above show that the cultivation hypothesis has been used in many other contexts as well. Table 1 gives an overview of the types of cultivation studies that can be discerned. In the table, *primary cultivation* refers to the processes occurring when American viewers are exposed to American TV messages. When an immigrant or sojourner arrives in the United States two types of cultivation effects might occur. When this person learns about the United States and is influenced by perceptions created and values or attitudes supported by American TV, acculturation occurs. This is the learning of a second culture and might therefore also be labeled *secondary cultivation*. As cultivation generally refers to unintended media effects, secondary cultivation would, by definition, need to be distinguished from intentional acculturation efforts. The end product of acculturation is adaptation to the new culture or even assimilation if the ties to the culture of origin weaken considerably. When the immigrant or sojourner is still exposed to media messages produced in the country of origin another type of cultivation effect can occur. This could be labeled *culture maintenance* (cf. Moon & Park, 2007) as it would keep the cultural values, practices, and perceptions from the country of origin alive.

However, all cultivation can act as a form of culture maintenance. Gerbner and his colleagues have remarked that all too often people have assumed that "no change means no effects" (Gerbner et al., 1994, p. 25), but maintenance of the status quo might be a typical cultivation effect. American TV may therefore also act as a kind of culture maintenance for Americans. *Heritage maintenance* (cf. Ruggierro, Taylor, & Lambert, 1996) might be a better concept, because it emphasizes the link with the culture of origin. When people in other countries are exposed to TV programs produced in the U.S. for a U.S. audience, *transcultural cultivation* occurs as these viewers are influenced by a culture which is not their own. Finally, viewers in and from another country might be cultivated by the programs produced in their home country. If one accepts that cultivation can occur in non-Americans and can be produced by non-American TV, then this is a form of *primary cultivation* as well.

Accepting this last proposition would simplify the model considerably (see Table 2). *Primary cultivation* can then be defined by paraphrasing Gerbner et al. (2002) as *the independent contributions viewing television programs produced in a particular country make to the conceptions of social reality held by viewers from that country residing in that country*. This is the process of learning from depictions of one's own culture and can therefore be seen as an *enculturation* process. *Acculturation through cultivation* would be: *the independent contributions viewing television programs produced in country A make to the conceptions of social reality held by viewers from country B, residing in country A*. The definition of *transcultural cultivation* then becomes: *the independent contributions*

Table 1: A typology of international cultivation

| | | Viewer is | | |
|---|---|---|---|---|
| | | American in America | Non-American | |
| | | | In America | In native country |
| TV produced in | U.S. | Primary cultivation | Acculturation | Transcultural cultivation |
| | Outside of U.S.* | Transcultural cultivation | Culture maintenance | Primary cultivation |

* Outside of U.S.: refers to the native country if the subject is non-American.

Table 2: A simplified typology of international cultivation

| | | Viewer is in | |
|---|---|---|---|
| | | Native culture | Non-native culture |
| TV produced in | Native culture | Primary cultivation (Enculturation) | Heritage maintenance |
| | Non-native culture | Transcultural cultivation<br>Secondary acculturation<br>Integration | Secondary cultivation (Acculturation) |

*viewing television programs produced in country A make to the conceptions of social reality held by viewers from country B, residing in country B.* Transcultural cultivation can take two forms. Viewers not from the U.S. and not living there may either learn about the U.S. or be influenced in their own worldview. The former is an example of *secondary acculturation*, and the latter (as in Pingree & Hawkins, 1981) is an example of what Berry (2005) called *integration*, which occurs when the confrontation of two cultures leads to a synthesis. Finally, *heritage maintenance through cultivation* becomes: *the independent contributions viewing television programs produced in country A make to the conceptions of social reality held by viewers from country A residing in country B.*

One type of potential source of cultivation is not indexed explicitly in this typology. A Korean migrating to the U.S. might develop a picture of England as a result of exposure to British movies or TV programs viewed in the U.S. This, however, is another example of secondary acculturation.

It has to be noted that this typology describes processes. This implies dynamic models in which individuals (and even groups) change over time. Acculturation may result in assimilation, which occurs when an individual becomes more and more detached from his or her culture of origin and takes on the host culture, but anthropologists have remarked that three other evolutions are possible as well. Migrants may end up rejecting the new culture (separation), may develop a mixture of their original culture and of the host culture (integration), or may become marginalized when they become alienated from both their original and their host culture (Berry, 2001). Cultivation processes might change with the evolution in the individual. As the immigrant loses touch with the home culture, the heritage maintenance effect of the home media may turn into secondary acculturation. If the immigrant never or hardly ever visits the culture of origin, the image he or she has of that country may start to shift from an enculturated image (what was learned as a member of the culture of origin) to an acculturated image (whereby knowledge of the culture depends upon exposure to home media). Such dynamic changes in the cultivating potential of home and host media appear not to have been studied in depth so far. There are obvious links to media dependency theory (Ball-Rokeach, 1985) to look at in this context.

An obvious gap in research on the processes described in this chapter is a dearth of studies on secondary acculturation among U.S. viewers. What do American viewers learn about other cultures from exposure to non-American media (however rare this type of exposure may be)?

## The Limitations of International Cultivation and an Agenda for Research

Studies of cultivation in an international setting as discussed in the typology presented above are particularly relevant to the development of cultivation theory and research in general. They offer a return to the origins of the study of socialization processes. Van den Bulck and Van den Bergh (2005) remarked that the study of socialization began with the study of adult immigrants (Thomas & Znaniecki, 1927). The influence of an emerging developmental psychology led to a shift towards the study of socialization processes in children, to the extent that present-day researchers seem to have a hard time realizing that socialization can also occur in adults or can even be a bi-directional process (with children socializing parents, another common process in immigrant acculturation).

The existing research on international cultivation suffers from a number of limitations. First, not much attention appears to have been paid to the issue of causality. While a significant relationship may exist between an immigrant's exposure to the host-country's media and the extent to which the immigrant has assimilated the norms and values of the host culture, there is little or no reflection about the direction of the relationship. Exposure to the host media may reinforce assimilation, but increasing assimilation may be what explains why the immigrant exposed him- or herself to the host media in the first place. To further our knowledge in this field, experimental and longitudinal designs would be needed.

Second, more attention to processes explaining cultivation should be paid by the studies focusing on acculturation. While it is customary to list cultivation among the "explanations" of acculturation, most studies fail to explain how exposure to host country fiction might lead to acculturation and, more specifically, assimilation. While the transfer of knowledge about the host culture may be similar to learning from fiction taking place among natives, the same may not be true of the assimilation of norms and values. Immigrants may learn from the American media that Americans have certain norms and values, but the step from knowing these facts to internalizing these norms and values as one's own still needs to be explored.

Third, among researchers studying primary cultivation outside the U.S., there is a marked lack of attention to the Wober assumption. They study primary cultivation as if the fact that it is being studied outside the U.S. is irrelevant. There are, however, several important issues to be considered. The presence or absence of relationships has to be interpreted carefully. Does the absence of a relationship mean that a certain meta-narrative was absent in the media diet of the culture in which the relationship was studied—or does it mean that members enculturated in this culture are inured against TV's cultivation appeal?

An example of the dangers involved can be found in the limited number of studies that have looked at the potential impact of the way in which cardio-respiratory resuscitation (CPR) has been portrayed in medical TV fiction. A study conducted in the U.S. (Diem et al., 1996) found that in shows such as *Chicago Hope* and *ER*, CPR was predominantly successful. On average, 67% of the patients suffering cardiac arrest were saved by the application of CPR, in stark contrast with real-world rates that are closer to 18%. A second study conducted in the U.S. found that there appeared to be a significant relationship between exposure to these shows and overestimation of the success rate of CPR (Jones et al., 2000). A study among Flemish Belgians found a similar relationship between exposure to television and overestimation of the success rate of CPR (Van den Bulck, 2002). The Belgian study assumed that the picture of CPR to which the Flemish Belgian viewers had been exposed had been the same. One argument in favor of this conclusion was the observation that the television shows analyzed in the first study were broadcast in Belgium as well. Later, a content analysis of Belgian hospital fiction showed that the CPR success rate to which Flemish viewers watching during prime time were exposed was actually 18% (Van den Bulck & Damiaans, 2004). The American shows, broadcast late at night on channels with limited audiences, had very low numbers of viewers and could therefore not explain the over-estimation found by Van den Bulck (2002). This example illustrates, first, the dangers of assuming too readily that what has been found in and about the U.S. can be applied elsewhere and, second, that more attention to these intercultural differences may lead to new hypotheses regarding (or new challenges to) the nature of the cultivation effect. Van den Bulck and Damiaans (2004) hypothesized that the proportion of successful CPR attempts probably was not as important as the suggestion created by a limited number of dramatic successes. Lay viewers believing that life ends when the heart stops beating may be affected strongly by convincing depictions of successful CPR, regardless of the success rate of the televised procedure.

Fourth, international researchers studying *integration*—that is the effect of, for instance, American fiction on perceptions or attitudes of non-Americans regarding their own environment—should develop models explaining this phenomenon. Are these memory errors, when elements derived from another culture's fiction are accidentally stored as if they pertained to the native environment? Or is integration the result of a more fundamental process? Perhaps television's meta-narratives operate at a much higher level of abstraction. Perhaps foreign fiction does not teach us only about the other culture where the program was produced, but perhaps, and particularly when it is perceived as being highly realistic, it suggests that it offers the only imaginable way in which the world may operate. Van den Bulck and Vandebosch's (2003) study of Belgian first-time prison inmates suggests the Belgian inmates expected prison to be as it was in American movies. They knew they had gotten their ideas from foreign fiction, but they literally could not imagine reality being anything else.

Fifth, there is some discussion about the use of genre as an exposure variable in cultivation research (Morgan & Shanahan, 2010; see also Bilandzic & Busselle, Chapter 13, this volume). International cultivation processes further complicate this issue. The discussion about genre deals with the question of whether the meta-narratives of television are stable across different content types. Do the messages of crime fiction differ from those of romantic comedies or of situation comedies? Traditional views of cultivation maintain that cultivation deals with the overall effect of a television culture or television system, while those looking at genres assume that exposure to crime fiction is more likely to affect crime-related judgments than exposure to genres with less or no attention to crime would. In the context of international cultivation an extra level is added to the discussion. Even if the meta-narrative of television is stable across program types *within* a culture, it may be different *between* cultures. Local programming may even have created message systems which oppose the meta-narratives of American television, as both Tamborini and Choi (1990) and Morgan (1990) have suggested. Researchers studying genre exposure should therefore pay careful attention to whether they are studying genres or cultures. If situation comedies in a particular country are mainly produced locally while crime drama is imported, correlations between "genres" and cultivation measures may not tap into genre differences, but into cultural differences. Conversely, the correlates of U.S.-made crime shows may not be the same as those of home-grown shows or those from third countries.

Finally, all acculturation research emphasizes the fact that acculturation is a bi-directional process. A classic definition, for instance, reads: "acculturation comprehends those phenomena which result when groups of individuals having different cultures come into continuous first-hand contact, with subsequent changes in the original culture patterns of either or both groups" (Redfield, Linton, & Kerskovits, 1936, p. 149). In media research the bi-directional issue of acculturation and similar processes has not been studied. Yet, even media cultures and meta-narratives can change over time. As immigrants become more visible in cultures, they may find their way into the demography of television fiction as well. The meta-narrative of television would then change accordingly.

## Concluding Remarks

International cultivation is an under-valued aspect of cultivation research. It has been limited to correlates of media use by immigrants by some and ignored by others who assumed that their studies of cultivation do not even need to acknowledge that they were not conducted in the U.S. One might argue, however, that international cultivation is the ideal experimental lab for cutting edge cultivation research, because it deals with the issues of socialization, enculturation, or even de-culturation (Somani, 2010) by the media. Studying how Americans learn about their own culture from realistic and believable depictions of that culture is difficult enough. Studying how people absorb the norms and values, the knowledge, and the social order of another culture in opposition to their own culture may be an even bigger challenge. Taking up this gauntlet should, however, teach us a lot about cultivation.

# References

Adoni, H., Cohen, A. A., & Mane, S. (1984). Social reality and television news: Perceptual dimensions of social conflicts in selected life areas. *Journal of Broadcasting, 28*, 33–49.

Ang, I. (1985). *Watching* Dallas: *Soap opera and the melodramatic imagination*. London: Methuen.

Appel, M., & Richter, T. (2007). Persuasive effects of fictional narratives increase over time. *Media Psychology, 10*, 113–134.

Appel, M., & Richter, T. (2010). Transportation and need for affect in narrative persuasion: A mediated moderation model. *Media Psychology, 13*, 101–135.

Ball-Rokeach, S. J. (1985). The origins of individual media-system dependency: A sociological framework. *Communication Research, 12*, 485.

Berger, P., & Luckmann, T. (1976). *The social construction of reality: A treatise in the sociology of knowledge*. Harmondsworth: Penguin.

Berry, J. W. (2001). A psychology of immigration. *Journal of Social Issues, 57*, 615–631.

Berry, J. W. (2005). Acculturation: Living successfully in two cultures. *International Journal of Intercultural Relations, 29*, 697–712.

Bilandzic, H., & Busselle, R. W. (2008). Transportation and transportability in the cultivation of genre-consistent attitudes and estimates. *Journal of Communication, 58*, 508–529.

Bilandzic, H., & Kinnebrock, S. (2009). Narrative experiences and effects of media stories: An introduction to the special issue. *Communications: The European Journal of Communication Research, 34*, 355–360.

Blumler, J. G., Brynin, M., & Nossiter, T. J. (1986). Broadcasting, finance and programme quality: An international review. *European Journal of Communication, 1*, 343–364.

Bochner, S. (2006). Sojourners. In D .L. Sam & J. W. Berry (Eds.), *The Cambridge handbook of acculturation psychology* (pp. 181–197). Cambridge: Cambridge University Press.

Busselle, R. W., & Bilandzic, H. (2008). Fictionality and perceived realism in experiencing stories: A model of narrative comprehension and engagement. *Communication Theory, 18*, 255–280.

Busselle, R. & Bilandzic, H. (2009). Measuring narrative engagement. *Media Psychology, 12*, 321–347.

Busselle, R. W., & Greenberg, B. S. (2000). The nature of television realism judgments: A reevaluation of their conceptualization and measurement. *Mass Communication & Society, 3*, 249–268.

Chaffee, S. H., Nass, C. I., & Yang, S.-M. (1990). The bridging role of television in immigrant political socialization. *Human Communication Research, 17*, 266–288.

Custers, K. & Van den Bulck, J. (2011a). Mediators of the association between television viewing and fear of crime: Perceived personal risk and perceived ability to cope. *Poetics,* 39, 107–124

Custers, K. & Van den Bulck, J. (2011b). The relationship of dispositional and situational fear of crime with television viewing and direct experience with crime. *Mass Communication & Society*, 14, 600–619.

De Bens, E., & de Smaele, H. (2001). The inflow of American television fiction on European broadcasting channels revisited. *European Journal of Communication, 16*, 51.

Diem, S. J., Lantos, J. D., & Tulsky, J. A. (1996). Cardiopulmonary resuscitation on television: Miracles and misinformation. *New England Journal of Medicine, 334*, 1578–1582.

European Audiovisual Observatory (2010). *Trends in European Television Yearbook, Vol. 2.* Strasbourg: European Audiovisual Observatory.

Fu, W. W., & Sim, C. (2010). Examining international country-to-country flow of theatrical films. *Journal of Communication, 60*, 120–143.

Fujioka, Y. (1999). Television portrayals and African-American stereotypes: Examination of television effects when direct contact is lacking. *Journalism & Mass Communication Quarterly, 76*, 52–75.

Gerbner, G., & Gross, L. (1976). Living with television: The violence profile. *Journal of Communication, 26*(2), 173–199.

Gerbner, G., Gross, L., Morgan, M., & Signorielli, N. (1994). Growing up with television: The cultivation perspective. In J. Bryant & D. Zillmann (Eds.), *Media effects: Advances in theory and research* (pp. 17–41). Hillsdale, NJ: Erlbaum.

Gerbner, G., Gross, L., Morgan, M., Signorielli, N., & Shanahan, J. (2002). Growing up with television: Cultivation processes. In J. Bryant & D. Zillmann (Eds.), *Media effects: Advances in theory and research* (2nd ed., pp. 43–67). Mahwah, NJ: Erlbaum.

Granzberg, G. (1982). Television as storyteller: The Algonkian Indians of central Canada. *Journal of Communication, 32*(1), 43–52.

Hawkins, R. P., & Pingree, S. (1981). Uniform messages and habitual viewing: Unneccesary assumptions in social-reality effects. *Human Communication Research, 7*, 291–301.

Hawkins, R. P., & Pingree, S. (1990). Divergent psychological processes in constructing social reality from mass media content. In N. Signorielli & M. Morgan (Eds.), *Cultivation analysis: New directions in media effects research* (pp. 35–50). Newbury Park, CA: Sage.

Hetsroni, A. (2008). Overrepresented topics, underrepresented topics, and the cultivation effect. *Communication Research Reports, 25*, 200–210.

Hetsroni, A., Elphariach, H., Kapuza, R., & Tsfoni, B. (2007). Geographical proximity, cultural imperialism, and the cultivation effect. *Communication Monographs, 74*, 181–199.

Hetsroni, A., & Tukachinsky, R. H. (2006). Television-world estimates, real-world estimates, and television viewing: A new scheme for cultivation. *Journal of Communication, 56*, 133–156.

Hirsch, P. M. (1981a). Distinguishing good speculation from bad theory: Rejoinder to Gerbner et al. *Communication Research, 8*, 73–95.

Hirsch, P. M. (1981b). On not learning from one's own mistakes: A reanalysis of Gerbner et al.'s findings on cultivation analysis, Part 2. *Communication Research, 8*, 3–37.

Jones, G. K., Brewer, K. L., & Garrison, H. G. (2000). Public expectations of survival following cardiopulmonary resuscitation. *Academic Emergency Medicine, 7*, 48–53.

Kolbeins, G. H. (2004). The non-finding of the cultivation effect in Iceland. *NORDICOM Review, 25*, 309–314.

Liebes, T., & Katz, E. (1990). *The export of meaning: Cross-cultural readings of* Dallas. Oxford: Oxford University Press.

Moon, S.-J., & Park, C. Y. (2007). Media effects on acculturation and biculturalism: A case study of Korean immigrants in Los Angeles' Koreatown. *Mass Communication & Society, 10*, 319–343.

Morgan, M. (1990). International cultivation analysis. In N. Signorielli & M. Morgan (Eds.), *Cultivation analysis: New directions in media effects research* (pp. 225–247). Newbury Park, CA: Sage.

Morgan, M., & Shanahan, J. (1997). Two decades of cultivation research: An appraisal and a meta-analysis. In B. R. Burleson (Ed.), *Communication Yearbook 20* (pp. 1–45). Thousand Oaks, CA: Sage.

Morgan, M., & Shanahan, J. (2010). The state of cultivation. *Journal of Broadcasting & Electronic Media, 54*, 337–355.

Morgan, M., & Signorielli, N. (1990). Cultivation analysis: Conceptualization and methodology. In N. Signorielli & M. Morgan (Eds.), *Cultivation analysis: New directions in media effects research* (pp. 13–34). Newbury Park, CA: Sage.

Pingree, S., & Hawkins, R. (1981). U.S. programs on Australian television: The cultivation effect. *Journal of Communication, 31*(1), 97–105.

Raman, P., & Harwood, J. (2008). Acculturation of Asian Indian sojourners in America: Application of the cultivation framework. *Southern Communication Journal, 73*, 295–311.

Redfield, R., Linton, R., & Kerskovits, M. J. (1936). Memorandum for the study of acculturation. *American Anthropologist, 38*, 149–152.

Rössler, P., & Brosius, H.-B. (2001). Do talk shows cultivate adolescents' views of the world? A prolonged-exposure experiment. *Journal of Communication, 51*, 143.

Rossmann, C., & Brosius, H.-B. (2004). The problem of causality in cultivation research. *Communications: The European Journal of Communication Research, 29*, 379–397.

Ruggiero, K. M., Taylor, D. M., & Lambert, W. E. (1996). A model of heritage culture maintenance: The role of discrimination. *International Journal of Intercultural Relations, 20*, 47–67.

Shanahan, J., & Morgan, M. (1999). *Television and its viewers: Cultivation theory and research.* Cambridge: Cambridge University Press.

Shrum, L. J. (2001). Mainstreaming, resonance, and impersonal impact: Testing moderators of the cultivation effect for estimates of crime risk. *Human Communication Research, 27*, 187–215.

Shrum, L. J. (2007). Cultivation and social cognition. In D. R. Roskos-Ewoldsen & J. L. Monahan (Eds.), *Communication and social cognition: Theories and methods* (pp. 245–272). Mahwah, NJ: Erlbaum.

Signorielli, N., Gross, L., & Morgan, M. (1982). Violence in television programs: Ten years later. In D. Pearl, L. Bouthilet, & J. Lazar (Eds.), *Television and behavior: Ten years of scientific progress and implications for the eighties, volume 2, Technical reviews* (pp. 158–175). Rockville, MD: National Institute of Mental Health.

Signorielli, N., & Morgan, M. (1990). *Cultivation analysis: New directions in media effects research.* Newbury Park, CA: Sage.

Somani, I. S. (2010). Becoming American. *Journal of International & Intercultural Communication, 3*, 59–81.

Tamborini, R., & Choi, J. (1990). The role of cultural diversity in cultivation research. In

N. Signorielli & M. Morgan (Eds.), *Cultivation analysis: New directions in media effects research* (pp. 157–180). Newbury Park, CA: Sage.

Tan, A. (1982). Television use and social stereotypes. *Journalism Quarterly, 59*, 119–122.

Tan, A., Dalisay, F., Zhang, Y., Han, E.-J., & Merchant, M. M. (2010). A cognitive processing model of information source use and stereotyping: African-American stereotypes in South Korea. *Journal of Broadcasting & Electronic Media, 54*, 569–587.

Tan, A., Li, S., & Simpson, C. (1986). American TV and social stereotypes of Americans in Taiwan and Mexico. *Journalism Quarterly, 63*, 809–814.

Tan, A., & Suarchavarat, K. (1988). American TV and social stereotypes of Americans in Thailand. *Journalism Quarterly, 65*, 648–654.

Tan, A., Tan, G. K., & Tan, A. S. (1987). American TV in the Philippines: A test of cultural impact. *Journalism Quarterly, 64*, 65–144.

Tan, A., Zhang, Y., Zhang, L., & Dalisay, F. (2009). Stereotypes of African Americans and media use among Chinese high school students. *Howard Journal of Communications, 20*, 260–275.

Thomas, W. I. & Znaniecki, F. (1927). *The Polish peasant in Europe and America*. Boston: Gorham.

Van den Bulck, J. (2002). The impact of television fiction on public expectations of survival following inhospital resuscitation by medical professionals. *European Journal of Emergency Medicine, 9*, 325–329.

Van den Bulck, J. (2003). Is the mainstreaming effect of cultivation an artifact of regression to the mean? *Journal of Broadcasting & Electronic Media, 47*, 289–295.

Van den Bulck, J. (2004). The relationship between television fiction and fear of crime: An empirical comparison of three causal explanations. *European Journal of Communication, 19*, 239–248.

Van den Bulck, J., & Damiaans, K. (2004). Cardiopulmonary resuscitation on Flemish television: Challenges to the television effects hypothesis. *Emergency Medicine Journal, 21*, 565–567.

Van den Bulck, J., & Van den Bergh, B. (2005). The child effect in media and communication research: A call to arms and an agenda for research. *Communication Yearbook 29*, 35–47.

Van den Bulck, J., & Vandebosch, H. (2003). When the viewer goes to prison: Learning fact from watching fiction. A qualitative cultivation study. *Poetics, 31*, 103–116.

Van Mierlo, J., & Van den Bulck, J. (2004). Benchmarking the cultivation approach to video game effects: A comparison of the correlates of TV viewing and game play. *Journal of Adolescence, 27*, 97–111.

von Feilitzen, C., Strand, H., Nowak, K., & Andrén, G. (1989). To be or not to be in the TV world: Ontological and methodological aspects of content analysis. *European Journal of Communication, 4*, 11–32.

Wober, J. M. (1978). Televised violence and paranoid perception: The view from Great Britain. *Public Opinion Quarterly, 42*, 315.

Wober, J. M. (1990). Does television cultivate the British? Late 80s evidence. In N. Signorielli & M. Morgan (Eds.), *Cultivation analysis: New directions in media effects research* (pp. 207–224). Newbury Park: Sage.

Wober, J. M., & Gunter, B. (1988). *Television and social control.* Avesbury: Aldershot.

Woo, H.-J., & Dominick, J. R. (2001). Daytime television talk shows and the cultivation effect among U.S. and international students. *Journal of Broadcasting & Electronic Media, 45*, 598–614.

Woo, H.-J., & Dominick, J. R. (2003). Acculturation, cultivation, and daytime TV talk shows. *Journalism & Mass Communication Quarterly, 80*, 109–127.

Yang, H., & Oliver, M. B. (2010). Exploring the effects of television viewing on perceived life quality: A combined perspective of material value and upward social comparison. *Mass Communication & Society, 13*, 118–138.

Yang, H., Ramasubramanian, S., & Oliver, M. B. (2008). Cultivation effects on quality of life indicators: Exploring the effects of American television consumption on feelings of relative deprivation in South Korea and India. *Journal of Broadcasting & Electronic Media, 52*, 247–267.

# 13. A Narrative Perspective on Genre-Specific Cultivation

*Helena Bilandzic & Rick Busselle*

Genre-specific cultivation deals with the long-term contribution of viewing types of television programs (crime shows or sitcoms, for instance) to viewers' perceptions of social reality. Exposure to specific genres may influence the formation of norms and values as well as overarching world views and ideologies (e.g., Morgan & Shanahan, 2010; Morgan, Shanahan, & Signorielli, 2009). Genres carry specific and typical patterns of cultural indicators, expressed in characteristic plots, character constellations, and story morals. The basic logic of genre-specific cultivation is that viewers internalize messages from the genres they watch. At its origin, cultivation was seen as a force coming from television in general, not individual genres or shows—a force coming from the *system of messages* rather than *specific content* (Morgan & Shanahan, 2010). George Gerbner (2001) argued that television composes a coherent cultural environment, a "seamless web" (p. 5) of meaning that serves as unquestioned background for the lives of a mass audience. Television presents "organically related fact and fiction" (Gerbner & Gross, 1976, p. 175) where basic rules and structures of society are replicated across a variety of different programs and form the consistent ideology of the television world. From the beginning, cultivation scholars have stressed the importance of looking at television as a system and an organic unit: "Despite obvious surface-level differences across genres and programs, deeper analysis often shows that surprisingly similar and complementary images of society, consistent ideologies, and stable accounts of the 'facts' of life cut across many different types of programs" (Morgan et al., 2009, p. 36).

Some changes in the television environment challenge these early assumptions. Available television channels have multiplied and serve more and more fragmented audiences that are more selective today than in the early years of television (Hawkins & Pingree, 1981; Potter, 1993). One way to capture this specialization on both the content and the audience side is to address genre content and genre use as a cultivation issue. Research on genre-specific cultivation rests on the assumption that, within the realm of television, we can find provinces of meaning defined by genre that create idiosyncratic views of how the social world functions. Often, it is reasonable to assume that cultural indicators are not equally spread over all genres but accumulate in some and are lacking in others. For example, murder is indispensable for most crime dramas but virtually absent in sitcoms. Cosmetic enhancement does not usually appear in crime drama, but is the main theme of cosmetic surgery makeover programs. Some genres do have potential "influence monopolies" over some topics.

This chapter argues that genre is useful as a unit of analysis for cultivation, provided that we have a conceptual grip on "genre." The quality of genre-specific cultivation research depends on our ability to conceptualize and articulate the content of a genre. To advance this goal, our chapter takes a different approach from existing literature on genre-specific cultivation. Rather than summarizing research along content dimensions (e.g., crime, relationships, gender roles, etc.), we will first look at conceptualizations of genre from narrative theory and, based on that, develop a taxonomy of cultivation dimensions emerging from the literature on genre. Along these dimensions, we will then synthesize cultivation research where it exists and point out gaps where it does not. Such a narrative view on genre-specific cultivation should strengthen our theoretical foundation for empirical research—and continue to develop Gerbner's original idea that cultivation originates from the consistent social narrative that society's main storyteller, television, provides.

## Genres as Content Units

Genres group content together that shares a "'repertoire of elements' which mainly consists of characters, setting, iconography, narrative and style of a text" (Lacey, 2000, p. 133). A crime series, for example, usually features a crime, victims, witnesses, policemen, and is set in a contemporary story world. A subset of crime series, forensic programs like *CSI*, is additionally characterized by specific iconography (e.g., forensic technology), and specific stylistic elements (e.g., computer-animations and flash-backs to crime scenes).

How genres emerge in social practice and how they can be defined for scholarly purposes has long been debated in film studies. Textual definitions (see Staiger, 2003) use specifics of the text to find similarities and commonalities that define genre. Todorov (1990) argues against text-driven analytic definitions: "it is always possible to discover a property common to two texts, and thus to put them together in a class. Is there any virtue in calling the result of such a combination a 'genre'?" (p. 17). Todorov proposes a historical approach, by which he does not necessarily mean going back in time but rather looking at how the label of a genre has been used in social practice. Simply put: If people use a genre label, the genre exists. This is reflected by other scholars, for example, in what Staiger (2003) identifies as the social convention definition or Tudor's conviction that genre "is what we collectively believe it to be" (Tudor, 1979, p. 122). Once a genre is identified socially, researchers may go back into texts labeled with a genre and analyze their common properties (Todorov, 1990).

Understanding genre as discursive practice goes beyond identifying categories and texts belonging to them: It also implies looking at meanings constructed in genres. Mittell (2004) specifies genre as a construction process, in which authors, critics, audiences, and industries are involved: "anyone who uses generic terms is participating [in] the constitution of genre categories" (p. 13). Lacey (2000) describes a triangle of spheres that need and use genre categories: artists, audiences, and institutions (p. 134). Artists use genre to guide their artistic production; well-known generic conventions can be assumed to be known by audiences and used to generate audience expectations as part of the intended experience. Audiences classify texts with the help of genre labels. Institutions use genres to label and market their products.

Neale (2003) assigns primacy to institutional definitions of genre, arguing that while idiosyncratic definitions may exist, they "play little part, if any, in the public formation and circulation of genres and generic images. In the public sphere, the institutional discourses are of central importance. Testimony to the existence of genres and evidence of their properties is to be found primarily here" (p. 167). One might add that genres created by the industry only come into actual existence when they become somewhat popular. A genre would not form without resonance in the viewership. Success ensures that genre categories are actually known and accepted: "Genre texts, because of their commerciality, are very useful for this [making links to society] because if a particular generic variant does not find an audience, it is usually unlikely that many similar texts will be made" (Lacey, 2000, p. 142).

The argument that institutional categories are most instrumental in finding the communicative common ground between audiences and programs serves to legitimize their use in cultivation research. If genre categories denote territories of meaning within the realm of narrative texts, and authors/industries produce for genre use, and audiences select and read according to genre conventions, then it makes sense to use genre as a meaningful unit in cultivation. This is in line with Casetti's (2001) notion of genre as a communicative contract between author and audience. The basic idea is that authors produce texts labeled as a specific genre in full awareness that audiences will understand the text as a generic instance and that a specific set of expectations will be evoked as a result of a particular reading. In this sense, authors and audiences negotiate meaning about a text with the help of genre labels. This negotiation may be regarded as a contract: Authors using a genre may expect audiences to understand genre clues. Audiences, reading texts as genre texts, may expect the authors to follow conventions of the genre. Here, the relationship between program and viewer seems especially important. Genre is an instrument for mutual negotiation about the meaning of the narrated plot; for example, the fact that a conflict is presented generates the expectation that the conflict will be solved. This type of agreement is preparatory in that expectations from both sides exist before the actual viewing experience; expectations are generated in repeated exposures and represent, in a sense, hypotheses that are confirmed across different viewing occasions. Jauss (1982) called this the "horizon of expectations"—the set of rules associated with a specific genre. Also, through repeated exposure to genre texts, viewers gain a "generic competence, that is an ability (1) to recognize and interpret the codes typical of a given genre, and (2) to perceive departures from it" (Pyrhönen, 2007, p. 112).

For cultivation, the agreement about the genre label is extended beyond the usual players in the genre game—audiences, authors, and institutions—to the researchers. Thus, researchers should only use genre labels that are established by many instances in the television environment (e.g., commercial descriptions, film criticism, program announcements) and are commonly used as descriptors across several "metadiscursive discourses" (Todorov, 1976, p. 162). It is important to recognize that genre should not be a category forced upon respondents by researchers, but that researchers participate in a discourse that has already been established by those "naturally" involved in production and reception.

On the side of the audience, genre knowledge can be thought of as a generic concept in memory, as schema, representing typical aspects of genres such as objects, situations, and plots (e.g., Ohler, 1994). Incoming information about the story at hand is interpreted with the help of schemas, which guide viewers in making sense of the text more quickly and biases interpretation according to genre schema. A different approach is worth considering for cultivation purposes: Schweinitz (1994) argues that genres are too open, dynamic, and fuzzy to be understood as having a set of describable properties, as schema theory suggests. Genres are more likely to be defined through prototypes, paradigmatic texts that dominate perceptions and expectations of a genre based on the most representative member of a category. All other members are grouped and linked to this prototype to form a cluster around it. The advantage is that membership in a category is not exclusive but gradual; media texts need not belong to a category according to a definition but may be linked to the prototype through several other media texts.

Whether a text is considered to belong to a category is not determined by general rules but by judging it as a variation of the prototype. This has repercussions for cultivation research. A survey may list one or two films or series that are considered to be at the center of a genre. Respondents need not have a definition of the genre to recognize their media behavior but simply need to evaluate whether what they watch is similar to the prototype.

## Relevance for Cultivation

Cultivation is a long-term-process in which it is difficult to trace causal effects (e.g., Morgan & Shanahan, 2010). In fact, the overwhelming majority of cultivation research is correlational and cannot distinguish between romantic comedy viewing leading to positive attitudes about romantic love and positive attitudes about romantic love leading to heavier romantic comedy viewing. As a long-term process, it is likely that both causal directions are involved in cultivation processes. Moreover, genres are linked to both content selection and cultivation effects (Bilandzic & Busselle, 2008).

Genres not only share specific common characteristics in plots and characters but may also predict the type of experience that viewers can expect. Over time, viewers develop preferences for genres with which they have had pleasurable individual experiences. Gehrau (2006) argues that the "basic" genres of comedy, drama, and thriller signify different emotional experiences that viewers come to expect when they choose content: to be happy, sad, or afraid.

Here it is important to recognize the role of narrative processing and engagement in linking genres with cultivation effects. Narrative engagement (or "transportation") is a complex experience of immersion into a narrative, characterized by an intense cognitive focus on the plot as well as intense emotions for the characters (Busselle & Bilandzic, 2008; Green & Brock, 2000). It is the experiential product of the smooth construction of mental models of meaning that represent a narrative text (Busselle & Bilandzic, 2008). Such immersion experiences have been related to enjoyment and repeated genre use (Bilandzic & Busselle, 2008). Engagement is enjoyable for several reasons: People enjoy experiencing deep emotions which are usually rare in actual life;

for a given time, they are relieved from their own identities and lives—very effectively indeed, because cognitive capacity is consumed in processing the narrative rather than ruminating about one's own problems (Bilandzic & Busselle, 2011). Narrative engagement and enjoyment of a story are highly related (Bilandzic & Busselle, 2011; Busselle & Bilandzic, 2009; Green, Brock, & Kaufman, 2004); as a result, to the extent that viewers associate specific genres with opportunities to experience higher levels of narrative engagement, and thus higher levels of enjoyment, they are motivated to seek out those genres (Bilandzic & Busselle, 2008).

At the same time, narrative engagement is important for effects: If a perceiver's mental systems are occupied with constructing mental models of the story's characters, events, locations, and its progression in time, little cognitive energy is left for critical examination of or counterarguing with the story's assertions (Green & Brock, 2002). In turn, reduced counterarguing generally increases the likelihood of persuasion (Green & Brock, 2002; Petty, Tormala, & Rucker, 2004). At the same time, watching stories in an intensive narrative engagement mode facilitates encoding the message as well as inferences and elaboration, increasing the likelihood of adopting story-consistent beliefs. In cultivation processes, with each exposure, genre-consistent beliefs should be adjusted a little towards the general lines of the genre. Over time, knowledge and attitudes should shift towards genre-consistent levels. We need to emphasize that cultivation through high-level engagement exposures is not the only way for cultivation effects to emerge. Repeated exposures in low-involvement modes should also result in cultivation effects. Single low-involvement exposures should result in smaller effects than high-involvement exposures. It seems reasonable to assume that low-involvement exposures cumulate over time but have a smaller impact than cumulated high-involvement exposures (Bilandzic & Busselle, 2008). Nonetheless, low-involvement exposures may be the more common case in television viewing and be responsible for most of the cultivation effects we know today.

In addition to learning genre-consistent messages, viewers acquire more and more competence in understanding a genre. They extract rules about typical plots of the genre, typical themes as well as typical characters. With refined genre conventions, viewers can process new genre texts more easily, decode significant symbols and generate expectations as well as extract meaning from an individual story. Knowing the rules of a genre not only facilitates the interpretation of a new text in that genre but also helps to instantiate a story-world model with a genre-adequate story-world logic. For example, in science fiction, it is normal to see advanced technology which does not exist (yet) in the actual world. For a regular viewer of science fiction, this is normal. In contrast, a novice may spend some time thinking about how unrealistic the story is, which may disrupt narrative engagement and initiate counterarguing. Thus, being familiar with genre conventions helps viewers focus on the actual plots without having to think about the prerequisites of the genre; ultimately, this will (1) increase effects, and (2) encourage more exposure to the genre, because processing is easy (Bilandzic & Busselle, 2008).

This model of cultivation deviates from the traditional approach by considering processes leading to effects and motivations for selective exposure over time. Specifically, regarding selective exposure as a part of the cultivation process runs counter to the claim that television viewing is relatively non-selective (e.g., Gerbner, Gross, Morgan, Signorielli, & Jackson-Beeck, 1979). Clearly, viewing is less likely to be non-selective in the modern television age, with countless programs available (e.g., Potter, 1993). We carry this argument further: While Gerbner et al. downplayed the role of selectivity, the model presented here explicitly uses selective exposure to explain how cultivation works as a process over time.

## Insights Derived from a Genre-Theoretic View: A Taxonomy of Dimensions in Genre-Specific Cultivation

Cultivation scholars need to have a clear picture of the content in order to determine how much viewers share the definition of social reality presented in television. This is why, in Gerbner's original research paradigm, a content analysis ("message system analysis") was integral, feeding into the cultivation survey and being contrasted with actual-world data (e.g., Gerbner & Gross, 1976). The cultural indicators collected in these content analyses were mostly simple facts of the television world—simple, but revealing of power relations, social roles, and demographic structure—for example, violence, occupational roles, gender roles, or the justice system. While the message system analysis serves a good purpose in describing facts and indicating possible influences on the frequency and risk estimates of viewers, no equivalent method exists to anchor cultivation attitudes (or second-order-beliefs; see Shrum & Lee, Chapter 8 this volume, for a fuller discussion) in the television content. Second-order cultivation measures are mostly derivatives of television facts, not found directly in television content. Often, the facts of television allow quite different consequences for attitudes. For example, romantic comedies highlight betrayals and lies as central plot elements. What viewers should learn as "fact" is that betrayals and lies often occur in romantic relationships and may conclude that these behaviors are norm violations and detrimental to relationships (see Ewoldsen & Rhodes, Chapter 10, this volume, for a discussion of the cultivation of beliefs about romance). Alternatively, they may conclude that deception is everyday business in relationships and that one is forgiven as long as one shows remorse. Depending on the interpretation, betrayals and lies may be considered unforgivable norm violations or as a relationship's normal and remediable troubles.

Thus, two aspects merit closer theoretical and methodological attention: First, how do we select which facts to analyze as facts of the television world? While systematic content analyses exist, of course, the theoretical view on the content is often rather unsystematic and leaves open to eclecticism and intuition the question of which aspects of the genre or show should be analyzed in a content analysis. Second, how we select and analyze more abstract conclusions that may manifest as attitudes in regular viewers is unclear. For both questions, genre considerations may help. The following section presents a taxonomy of cultivation dimensions based on elements defined in the genre literature. To some extent, these dimensions have been dealt with in cultivation research already. However, a systematic approach based on conceptual considerations derived from the genre literature has the advantage that new uncharted fields can be discovered and gaps in the research landscape can be identified. For the taxonomy, we distinguish among (1) elements and conventions of a genre, (2) complex plot messages, and (3) cross-genre perspectives.

## Genre Elements and Conventions

Lacey (2000) identifies elements that comprise the basic schema of a genre: characters, setting, iconography, narrative, and style. This schema will serve as a systematic backbone to structure research fields that refer to single elements within a genre.

### *Characters*

In many accounts of narrative meaning construction, characters are the key to understanding (Bordwell, 1989; M. Smith, 1995; Tan, 1996). When assuming the point of view of a character and emoting with and for them, viewers come to understand basic motivations (and hence reasons for actions), the relation between characters in the story, as well as narrative evaluations (Busselle & Bilandzic, 2008). Moreover, emotional reactions to a story always involve characters and reflect the connection between viewer and agents of a story. Thus, viewers have to pay attention to characters in order to understand a story, and their narrative engagement will to some extent be determined by and depend upon their emotional connection with the characters.

Characters in any given genre often follow certain patterns in behavior and traits. Lacey (2000) distinguishes stereotypes, which exist in reality and fiction, from generic types, which are typical of persons appearing in a genre story, but have no referent in the actual world (for example, the good cowboy, the heroine in the domestic context, the villain; p. 137). Lacey's notion of generic types resonates with more general types extracted by Campbell (1949) as the common ground from myths and tales, for example, the hero, the helper, the goddess, the temptress, or the father. Stories make use of both types of characters: Generic types generate expectations in the viewer which can be satisfied or played with; and stereotypes (e.g., about minorities, gender, occupation) drive the process of sense making by the viewer. Not only does the media text contain and play with stereotypes, but viewers also use stereotypes and other knowledge from everyday interactions to construct their model of the characters in a story (Busselle & Bilandzic, 2008; M. Smith, 1995). This interaction between textual cues and viewers' person schemata has several consequences for cultivation. First, recognizing generic types helps viewers process stories with ease—they develop generic competence. Second, repeated exposure to specific person schemata may consolidate and intensify stereotypes of social groups.

A growing body of research on the relationship between television viewing and stereotyping follows a cultivation paradigm and looks at the specific contribution of genre exposure to gender stereotypes (Signorielli, 2001; Smith & Granados, 2009). While the cultivation of gender stereotypes is predominantly attributed to overall television exposure, there are a number of studies that turn to specific genre influences (see also Scharrer, Chapter 5, this volume).

Soap opera viewing, for example, is related to holding stereotypical beliefs about occupational roles (Buerkel-Rothfuss & Mayes, 1981; Carveth & Alexander, 1985). Perceptions of the percentage of women working were higher for those with more exposure to action adventure programs in a study by Potter and Chang (1990); in the same study, attitudes about working women were positively related to some genres (sitcoms, news, movies, talk shows, and game shows), and negatively to others (action adventure, sports). No relationships to any of these indicators were found with overall television exposure. Rivadeneyra and Ward (2005) found relationships between some genres (Spanish-language prime time television, English talk shows) and traditional gender roles among Latina adolescents (for conflicting evidence, see Ward & Rivadeneyra, 1999). Among African American high school students, Ward, Hansbrough, and Walker (2005) found a positive correlation between music video consumption and gender roles. Counter-stereotypical portrayals in specific television shows such as *The Cosby Show* relate to counter-stereotypical gender role attitudes (Rosenwasser, Lingenfelter, & Harrington, 1989). This matters all the more since longitudinal content analyses show that gender role portrayals are less consistent today than they were some decades ago (Signorielli & Bacue, 1999).

Similarly, stereotypes of ethnic minorities have been under intense investigation in a cultivation paradigm (Mastro, 2009; Mastro & Tukachinsky, Chapter 3, this volume), less so, however, with a differentiation among genres. For example, attitudes towards the socio-economic success of Blacks and Whites differentially relate to exposure to television entertainment and news (Armstrong, Neuendorf, & Brentar, 1992) as well as drama and sitcom exposure (Busselle & Crandall, 2002). Local television news exposure (Dixon, 2008) and reality-based crime shows (Oliver & Armstrong, 1995) are related to racial stereotypes. Other social groups have also been the focus of genre-specific investigation, albeit studies are less frequent here. For example, in a study by Calzo and Ward (2009), exposure to daytime talk shows and soap operas was related to more accepting attitudes towards homosexuality, and talk show exposure was related to less restrictive attitudes about lesbian or gay relationships in a study by Rössler and Brosius (2001). Other examples are attitudes towards occupational groups, for example, doctors (Chory-Assad & Tamborini, 2003; Pfau, Mullen, & Garrow, 1995; Quick, 2009) or attorneys (Pfau, Mullen, Deidrich, & Garrow, 1995).

Not only are *perceptions* of social groups shaped in this way; these perceptions also have consequences for everyday social interactions (e.g., expectations towards doctors; Quick, 2009), influence the interpretation of social situations (e.g., attributing race to unidentified perpetrators; Dixon, 2007), and may reflect upon one's own self-concept (e.g., self-esteem; Rivadeneyra, Ward, & Gordon, 2007).

### *Setting*

Setting refers to the time and location of a story (Lacey, 2000). A possible cultivation outcome is that viewers learn certain facts about a time period; for example, regular viewers of Westerns may learn "facts" about the American frontier and life at the end of the 19th century. While no studies exist about setting specifically, Woo and Dominick (2001) found that daily talk show viewing was related to estimates and attitudes about American culture more for international students than for American students.

Setting also comprises what is possible in a certain story world and what is not: the story-world logic (Busselle & Bilandzic, 2008). For example, one might ask how technological progress is perceived as a fact of today's world, even if it is presented in a science-fiction context and not yet existent in the actual world. A similar effect can be observed with forensic series, which suggest that DNA testing is available within minutes, or that finding usable DNA traces is the rule and not the exception (e.g., Podlas, 2006; Schweitzer & Saks, 2007).

### *Iconography*

Iconography refers to symbols, both visual and auditory, that are common in certain genres (Lacey, 2000, p. 138), for example, police cars and crime scene tape in crime shows, or laser guns and space ships in science fiction. In many cases, iconography will be difficult to translate into cultivation outcomes, because many genre-typical signs are also present in everyday life (horses, police cars). However, some of the typical iconography is divergent from the actual world ("false facts") or comes from a context that is usually unavailable to the common citizen. In these rare cases, we may follow the classic cultivation paradigm and observe whether viewers adopt unique iconography. This type of cultivation outcome is different from first-order effects, which refer to frequency, probability, or risk estimation. Being acquainted with iconography has a different quality. It is not likely that regular Western viewers will overestimate the frequencies of horses in the actual world. It is more likely that viewers will associate horses with certain values and attributes. Another possible form of cultivation outcome is that viewers learn about the existence of a fact—a process Van den Bulck (2010) calls "data setting." Van den Bulck exemplifies this with forensic procedures that determine blood stains and other bodily fluids using a special substance which changes color after contact with blood or ultraviolet light. This type of cultivation outcome is not about estimating the frequency with which a procedure is used in forensics (first-order estimate), but about knowing that a blood stain will turn pink when sprayed with the substance or that the light beam is violet. The only question is whether these effects are cumulative and increase with more exposure, or whether a one-time exposure is enough to learn one fact. While this is an empirical question, speed and accuracy of retrieval from memory may increase in regular viewers. A systematic, cultivation-relevant content analysis for iconography may open up a new field in cultivation research.

### *Plot*

The plot is the event structure of a story, events or actions connected with certain causal relations. Depending on the level of abstraction and the focus, the plot offers several options for cultivation outcomes, some of which are very common in cultivation research, and some of which have received little if any attention.

**Single actions and events.** Exposure to single events and actions within the plot gives viewers an impression of their frequency and likelihood, and manifests in first-order estimates used in cultivation research (e.g., Gerbner & Gross, 1976). Not all first-order measures fall into this plot category but only those that refer to single actions and events. For example, while likelihood of theft and bodily harm are plot oriented and refer to single actions and events, the percentage of violent crimes committed by non-Caucasians is a generalization made from television characters (examples from Grabe & Drew, 2007).

The results of genre-specific cultivation in this category are distributed across a large variety of themes, two of which have received a fair amount of attention: crime and marriage.

Regarding crime, in a study by Goidel, Freeman, and Procopio (2006), perceptions of the incidence of juvenile crime and overall crime were related to exposure to television news and reality crime shows, respectively. Romer, Jamieson, and Aday (2003) found that an index of four risks to family and the American public (drugs, violent crime, hand guns, street drugs) was related to viewing local television news but not to national television news. Exposure to crime drama on the other hand did not correlate with single action/event indicators such as the incidence of violent crime or burglary (Bilandzic & Busselle, 2008; Grabe & Drew, 2007; O'Keefe, 1984). Soap opera exposure, as a non-crime genre, was related to crime perceptions such as estimates of rape incidence, using the services of a private detective, being the victim of a gunshot (Shrum, 1996), or overestimating the percentage of men employed in the police force (Cohen & Weimann, 2000).

For marriage, Buerkel-Rothfuss and Mayes (1981) and Potter and Chang (1990) report positive correlations between soap opera exposure and estimates of marriages that end in divorce. Carveth and Alexander (1985) only replicated this result when "years watching soap operas" was used as an indicator of exposure. Conversely, Perse (1986) did not find any influence of soap opera viewing on the estimate of divorce. Interestingly, soap opera viewing became a significant predictor when the question was phrased slightly differently, relating to *people* and not to the *event* of divorce: Heavy viewers of soap operas overestimate the number of males and females whose marriage ends in divorce. This may be an indication that the reference point (humans versus actions/events) matters. Shrum (1996) used an index of four estimates relating to marriage and relationships: extramarital affairs, divorce, women marrying men who they do not love, and executives having affairs with their secretaries. He found a positive correlation of this index with soap opera viewing. In contrast, Davis and Mares (1998) report that talk show viewing does not influence the estimate of the percentage of husbands and wives who cheat.

**Scripts.** According to Schank and Abelson (1977), a script is a generalized sequence of actions that shows how actors typically handle and are expected to handle social situations. Considering that a television genre is characterized by formulaic plots and roles, viewers may, on top of single actions and events, learn genre-specific scripts. An example that may be interpreted as a script (though not called this by the author), is the recent investigation by Van den Bulck (2010) of how Flemish viewers learn the Miranda Rights from American television and acquire knowledge about when Miranda should be read (see Van den Bulck, Chapter 12, this volume, for a fuller discussion of cultivation in international settings). Television viewing increased the likelihood of being able to list at least one part of the Miranda rights.

Apart from such general action scripts, other scripts seem equally worth pursuing. Plantinga (2009) describes a type of script which combines a typical situation with adequate emotional reactions. These scripts are ***paradigm scenarios***—"scenarios that are consistently repeated until they become conventional" (p. 82). Paradigm scenarios may be learned through constant repetition in genre television; they connect particular situations to specific emotions, serve as a basis for interpretation in actual world situations, and guide emotional reactions. Viewers may learn which emotional reactions are appropriate at funerals, in a marital argument, or in court trials. Processes of identification and sympathy with the characters facilitate this type of effect: Viewers are led through the emotional structure of a story and feel emotions in a way similar to actual world situations. Repeated exposures provide occasions to rehearse a particular type of emotional reaction and, over time, display it as an automatic and habituated reaction to specific situations. Winterhoff-Spurk, Unz, and Schwab (2001) expressed the idea that emotions, like cognitions, can be cultivated through repeated exposures to emotional television ("cultivation of emotions").

Related to paradigm scenarios, scripts for norm violations may serve the same purpose and present typical sequences of norm violations and appropriate reactions attached to them. The portrayal of norm violations is connected to a narrative context that informs the viewer about the reason for a norm violation, a justification, reactions of the victim, and consequences for the perpetrator as well as appropriate emotional reactions when the norm violation is uncovered (Bilandzic, 2011). These complex scripts may be learned by viewers over a large number of formulaic genre repetitions.

## *Style*

The formal style of media texts is most often neglected in cultivation research (see Bilandzic & Rössler, 2004; Grabe & Drew, 2007). Formal (or structural) features such as cuts and edits, camera perspective, lighting, colors, music, or special effects do not carry meaning per se but influence sense-making and recall in the viewer (Ohler, 1994).

Moreover, generic conventions are not only content related but also tied to formal conventions which aid in understanding the media text at hand. Formal features themselves also have effects outside of understanding a story. They alter the mode of processing and consequently the effects of the content. For example, some formal techniques elicit stronger emotions: Close-ups of a character's face provide a focus on the character's emotions and invite an intimate bonding of the viewer with the character (Katz, 1991). Other formal features are known to produce arousal in viewers (Lang, 2009). Certain genres or individual shows are always accompanied by arousing style features; either formal features such as rapid pacing and special effects or content-related techniques that create extreme suspense and fear (for example, shows like *24* or *Lost*). If repeated exposures always happen under conditions of high bodily arousal, effects may intensify. A cultivation study that compares "high-" and "low-arousal" programs may illuminate this point.

## Complex Plot Messages

While individual elements of the plot, as outlined above, may yield cultivation outcomes, there are also more complex messages that viewers extract from a story that cannot be traced back to patterns in single actions/events, characters, setting, or style. Complex messages are deduced from the whole plot line: From the initial event that the protagonist lies to his fiancé to the final event where he is forgiven after a lengthy period of apologies; from the initial event of the murderer killing her victim to the final one where she is led to prison. The first sequence may convey that lying is a severe norm violation but may be remedied by sincere remorse; the second sequence presents a world in which justice prevails. We can distinguish between two types of complex plot messages: *grand lessons* invoked by the typical plot of a genre, and homogeneous world views with typical constellations of norms and values, which weave a texture of *ideology* in the genre text.

### *Grand Lessons*

Grand lessons are messages that emerge as a moral from the story taken as a whole, points made by a narrative. They are mirrored on the respondent's side by the concept of second-order effects (e.g., Hawkins & Pingree, 1981). It makes sense to anchor the attitudes in their corresponding textual counterparts and specifically look at grand lessons that emerge from genres as a whole. For example, Bilandzic and Busselle (2008) systematically derive grand lessons from genre literature. They investigate the influence of romantic comedy viewing on favorable attitudes towards romantic love, the influence of science fiction films on critical attitudes towards technology, and the influence of crime thrillers on punitiveness and vigilantism. Results show that genre exposure was only related to critical attitudes towards technology.

Apart from genre lessons, general story schemas can apply to several genres or generalize as a pattern to all fictional programming. Appel (2008) argues that fictional programming is often characterized by an ending where justice is achieved, bad characters are punished, and good ones are rewarded. As a consequence, viewers may conclude that the world is just. Appel found a positive relation between fiction exposure and the belief in a just world.

Extracting grand lessons also works with non-fictional stories. For example, Lee and Niederdeppe (2010) argue that local television news coverage focuses on cancer causes without stressing options for prevention; a possible conclusion is that prevention is of little use. Indeed, they report a correlation between exposure to local news and fatalistic beliefs about cancer prevention.

While the examples given so far relate to adopting grand lessons on a general level, other grand lessons may transfer the grand message to one's own life where viewers arrive at judgments that are not contained in the genre message but represent implications for themselves specifically. For example, several studies found relationships between news exposure and fear of crime (e.g., Chiricos, Padgett, & Gertz, 2000; Romer et al., 2003; Weitzer & Kubrin, 2004). In addition, crime drama exposure correlates with fear of crime (e.g., Carlson, 1985; Kort-Butler & Sittner Hartshorn, 2011). Note that fear of crime, although it is a "cultivated" emotion, is different from paradigm scenarios, where people learn to associate situations and emotions. Other examples of such generalization are body dissatisfaction (Nabi, 2009), quality of life (Shrum, Lee, Burroughs, & Rindfleisch, 2011; Yang & Oliver, 2010), or marriage dissatisfaction (Segrin & Nabi, 2002).

## *Ideology*

Cultivation's emphasis on homogeneous, consistent television content that shows the norms and values of a society as well as its underlying power relations has often involved the term "ideology" (e.g., Morgan et al., 2009). Herman and Vervaeck (2007) define ideology as "a body of norms and values that appear natural as a result of their continuous and mostly tacit promotion by the dominant forces in society" (p. 217). Ideology is implicitly contained in television content but not made explicit; it is taken for granted as the background and interpretational frame for experiencing the world (Herman & Vervaeck, 2007). As socially grounded categories, genres always have (confirming, opposing) connections with the dominant ideology (Pyrhönen, 2007). Indeed, early cultivation research had a critical impetus to uncover power relations and values hidden in the overall pattern of television messages, indicative of a commercial and mass-produced product that needs to be broadly acceptable to the mainstream of society. Ideology was most often indicated by simple facts of the television world. For example, one indicator of power was the demography of victims and perpetrators (e.g., Gerbner & Gross, 1976). Rather than taking an indirect approach to approximate ideology by single actions/events or characters, a small number of studies exists that directly investigate ideological domains. For example, Shrum and colleagues (Shrum, Burroughs, & Rindfleisch, 2005; Shrum et al., 2011) found relationships between materialism and television viewing. Hoffner, Levine, and Toohey (2008) considered work-related values and how identification with favorite characters influences them. Potter (1990) identified values associated with television, for example, "truth wins out in the end," "honesty is the best policy," and "good wins out over evil," and found different relationships with different genres. For example, prime-time soap opera exposure was related to the belief that "Truth wins" and "Luck is important," while sports viewing was related to "Truth wins" and "Hard work yields rewards."

It would be worthwhile to systematically investigate these common ideologies, and find semantic criteria to identify them in television content—for example, by using analyses of ideology from film studies. Wood (2003) identifies thematic fields of ideology common to film, for example, capitalism, the work ethic, marriage, nature as wilderness, or progress/technology/the city, which may serve that purpose.

## View Across Genres

So far, the focus has been on single genres. However, analyses across genres may also provide valuable insights into the nature of cultivation. This can be done in three different ways: First, we can look at how the same theme is presented in different genres and how these differences are expressed in regular viewers. Second, we can look at the diversity versus the homogeneity of genre exposure. Third, we can compare exposure to genre fiction versus non-genre fiction.

### *Same Theme in Different Genres*

The same theme (crime, occupations, gender roles, etc.) may cut across genres and be treated differently in the different genres; these differences should be mirrored in the respective genre viewers' beliefs. For example, lying may be an issue in romantic comedies as well as action movies. In romantic comedies, lying is almost always punished in the end; in action films, lying is functional in achieving goals. These two genres may cultivate different attitudes with respect to how justifiable lying is.

While many studies have investigated differences in how attitudes or estimates are related to exposure to different genres (e.g., Hawkins & Pingree, 1981; Potter, 1990; Potter & Chang, 1990), they most often do not have firm knowledge or assumptions of how content differs from genre to genre. Without that, research across genres will remain descriptive.

One example of research that made assumptions about how content in different genres varies is a study by Armstrong, Neuendorf, and Brentar (1992). The researchers derive from previous research that television news presents a negative view of the socioeconomic success of African Americans, while fictional entertainment and sports on television present a more positive view; they found that perceptions of the socioeconomic success of African Americans were cultivated by the genre viewers watched. Busselle and Crandall (2002) conducted a similar study and found a positive relationship between perceptions of the socioeconomic success of African Americans and exposure to situation comedies. Beullens and Van den Bulck (2008) base their argument on content analyses of risky driving portrayals and accidents in different genres. While news consistently shows consequences of risky driving (i.e., accidents), fictional programs as well as music videos rarely show the deadly consequences of risky driving and often even depict it in a positive light (e.g., connected to masculinity). The researchers found that news exposure indeed was connected to perceiving more risks of drunk driving and speeding, while music video consumption negatively correlated with these two indicators.

### *Diversity vs. Homogeneity of Genre Exposure*

Diversity means that a person's overall television budget is spent with varied genre exposures, while homogeneity means that exposure is concentrated in a few genres or just one. Two hours of watching soap operas should have different relevance and impact if this is one's only contact with television, or whether it is only one third of six hours of viewing. Potter and Chang (1990) found that a measure of the proportion of overall viewing time devoted to one genre was a better predictor of cultivation than overall television viewing and in some instances also better than absolute exposure to a genre.

An interesting variation of looking at the mixture of different content and genre viewed was employed by Dahlstrom and Scheufele (2010), where diversity was operationalized by the number of different television channels watched by a person. They found a weak relationship between channel diversity and environmental concern, although it was stronger than the association with overall viewing. It would be a good extension of their work to explore how genres, combined into a measure of diversity, perform as predictors.

### *Genre versus Non-Genre*

As we stated earlier, genre is not only content. It also is a simple schema that is held and expected to be observed by producers and audiences alike. Similarly, preference for genre is not only a preference for specific content but also preference for the security of the strict conventions of a genre, the predictable plots and character types, and the viewing experiences and emotions which viewers may reliably expect. Watching a given genre provides the viewer with the "happiness of repetition" (Casetti, 2001, p. 172). Prior knowledge facilitates the process of sense-making as viewers may concentrate on deviations from the genre schema rather than building their understanding from scratch. Thus, genre relieves the viewer from effortful processing. The genre categorizes newly encountered media programs and stories and makes repeated exposures possible. Thus, on a meta-level, genre exposure may cultivate the states which are typical for ritualistic actions, for example, a sense of security and protection, and the sense that one can handle a less complex and more predictable world. For this type of cultivation outcome, the actual genre of fiction that people watch should matter less than the fact that they prefer genre fiction over non-genre fiction (e.g., independent films).

## Conclusions

"In sum, although genre-specific studies have not yet outlined a clear rationale for how they are similar to or different from the more global concept of cultivation, [...] it seems clear that they will continue"—this laconic statement is taken from a recent overview by Morgan and Shanahan (2010). Indeed, making a distinction between cultivation and genre-specific cultivation ultimately triggers the need to articulate the advantage of using genre rather than overall television viewing on a theoretical level. On the empirical level, countless studies have explored relationships between genre exposure and world views in a wide range of thematic fields. On the theoretical level, there are still many pieces of the puzzle missing. One piece is finding an angle on the content, and the relationship between content and world view. This chapter is a first step in this direction. We provided a narrative account of how content may be conceptualized beyond thematic categories. Using a scheme from genre theory and narrative literature as a heuristic, we developed a taxonomy of genre-specific cultivation dimensions, which we used to synthesize existing research and identify fields that still need work (see Figure 1).

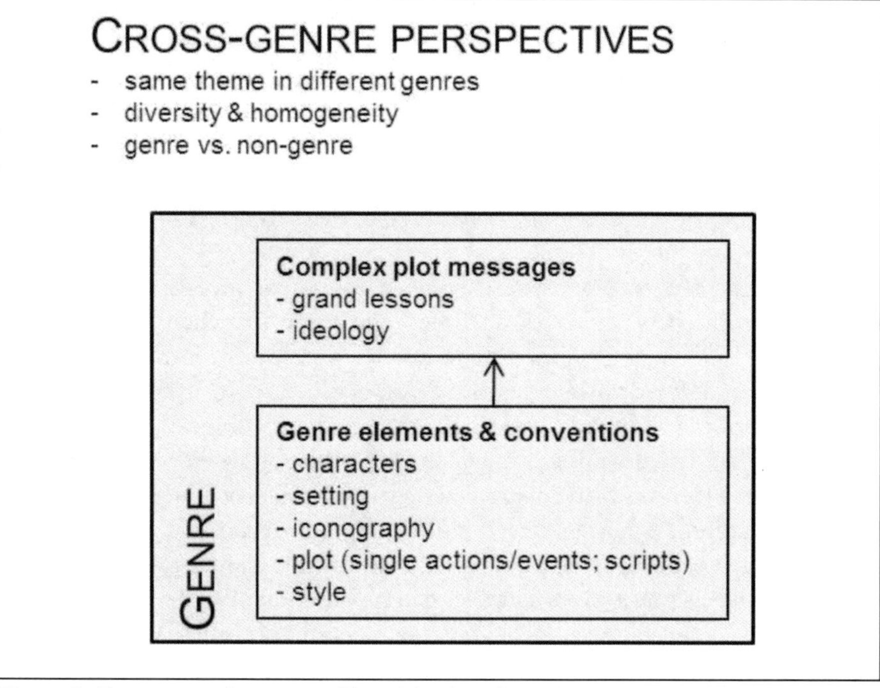


Figure 1: Taxonomy of genre-specific cultivation dimensions

The genre-theoretic approach presents a methodological challenge: Traditional content analyses have limitations with some of the structures we identified in the taxonomy. For example, ideology or grand messages are not easily accessible through content analysis. Mainly, the problem is that content analysis destroys the narrative nature of a story (Hyvärinen, 2008). The challenge is to make use of more open, qualitative methods (possibly from other disciplines such as film studies) or develop hybrids between content analysis and interpretive procedures specifically for this purpose (Bilandzic, Sukalla, & Kinnebrock, 2008).

The upsurge of genre-specific research has fueled the discussion about the definition and range of cultivation. There is a tendency in the cultivation literature to suggest that genre-specific investigations fall outside of the cultivation paradigm, because the initial reliance on the aggregate message system has been replaced with individual exposure situations as well as messages limited to particular genres (e.g., Morgan & Shanahan, 2010, p. 340). We argue that the basic idea of cultivation is *not* altered by including the assumption of genre-specific effects; however, we do agree with the argument that cultivation needs to be defined more clearly.

Regarding the first issue: Why do genre-specific studies not alter the basic cultivation logic? Any theory of genre-specific cultivation must provide a connection between the content and the audience's world views. It is clear that cultivation is not a simple, unidirectional effect, but an interaction among exposure to content, effects, and repeated exposure fueled by effects. Nonetheless, there *is* an effects component. Considering this, genre-specific investigations only make the logic of research more specific; they do not fall outside of cultivation.

Regarding the second issue: Are all studies that investigate effects of media on world views cultivation studies? We argue that they are not. What is the essence of cultivation then? The essence does not lie in the effects part only, and certainly not in the (selective) exposure part. It is the *combination of both effects and voluntary, habitual exposure* that is unique to cultivation. Researchers study cultivation if they consider both parts—viewing habits and general world views. A forced-exposure situation does not implement a cultivation paradigm; it may, however, illuminate micro-processes going on after or before each exposure, which is equally important. Defining the essence of cultivation in this way is more suitable than insisting on overall television viewing. Moreover, this definition is independent of methods; it is not the experiment per se that excludes a study from being cultivation, and it is not the cross-sectional survey that is a necessary and sufficient condition for cultivation. Such a restriction would impoverish the field. Again, it is the inclusion of *effects and voluntary, habitual exposure*, notwithstanding the method and design. This can be realized in a traditional cross-sectional survey correlating viewing habits with world views, a quasi-experimental design following participants over an extended period of time, or with trend data observing the development of the cultivation relationship over time and combining it with content analyses. Defining cultivation may seem peculiar after 40 years of ongoing research. However, it is indeed the first step towards methodological and theoretical innovation within what can be considered cultivation research.

## References

Appel, M. (2008). Fictional narratives cultivate just-world beliefs. *Journal of Communication, 58*, 62–83.

Armstrong, G. B., Neuendorf, K. A., & Brentar, J. (1992). TV entertainment, news, and racial perceptions of college students. *Journal of Communication, 42*(3), 153–176.

Beullens, K., & Van den Bulck, J. (2008). News, music videos and action movie exposure and adolescents' intentions to take risks in traffic. *Accident Analysis & Prevention, 40*, 349–356.

Bilandzic, H. (2011). The complicated relationship between media and morality: A response to Ron Tamborini's model of "Moral Intuition and Media Entertainment" from a narrative perspective. *Journal of Media Psychology, 23,* 46–51.

Bilandzic, H., & Busselle, R. W. (2008). Transportation and transportability in the cultivation of genre-consistent attitudes and estimates. *Journal of Communication, 58,* 508–529.

Bilandzic, H., & Busselle, R. W. (2011). Enjoyment of films as a function of narrative experience, perceived realism and transportability. *Communications: The European Journal of Communication Research, 36,* 29–50.

Bilandzic, H., & Rössler, P. (2004). Life according to television. Implications of genre-specific cultivation effects: The gratification/cultivation model. *Communications: The European Journal of Communication Research, 29,* 295–326.

Bilandzic, H., Sukalla, F., & Kinnebrock, S. (2008). Die Moral von der Geschichte: Methodische Probleme und Methodenentwicklung in der Medienanalyse. [The story morale: Methodological problems and method development in media analysis] In J. v. Gottberg & E. Prommer (Eds.), *Verlorene Werte? Medien und die Entwicklung von Ethik und Moral* [Lost values? Media and the development of ethics and moral] (pp. 245–256). Konstanz: UVK-Verlag.

Bordwell, D. (1989). *Making meaning. Inference and rhetoric in the interpretation of cinema.* Cambridge, MA: Harvard University Press.

Buerkel-Rothfuss, N. L., & Mayes, S. (1981). Soap opera viewing: The cultivation effect. *Journal of Communication, 31*(3), 108–115.

Busselle, R. W., & Bilandzic, H. (2008). Fictionality and perceived realism in experiencing stories: A model of narrative comprehension and engagement. *Communication Theory, 18,* 255–280.

Busselle, R. W., & Bilandzic, H. (2009). Measuring narrative engagement. *Media Psychology, 12,* 321–347.

Busselle, R. W., & Crandall, H. (2002). Television viewing and perceptions about race differences in socioeconomic success. *Journal of Broadcasting & Electronic Media, 46,* 265–282.

Calzo, J. P., & Ward, L. M. (2009). Media exposure and viewers' attitudes toward homosexuality: Evidence for mainstreaming or resonance? *Journal of Broadcasting & Electronic Media, 53,* 280–299.

Campbell, J. (1949). *The hero with a thousand faces.* New York: Pantheon Books.

Carlson, J. M. (1985). *Prime time law enforcement: Crime show viewing and attitudes toward the criminal justice system.* New York: Praeger.

Carveth, R., & Alexander, A. (1985). Soap opera viewing motivations and the cultivation process. *Journal of Broadcasting & Electronic Media, 29,* 259–273.

Casetti, F. (2001). Filmgenres, Verständigungsvergänge und kommunikativer Vertrag [Film genres, negotiation processes and communicative contract]. *Montage/AV, 10,* 155–173.

Chiricos, T., Padgett, K., & Gertz, M. (2000). Fear, TV news, and the reality of crime. *Criminology, 38,* 755–785.

Chory-Assad, R. M., & Tamborini, R. (2003). Television exposure and the public's perceptions of physicians. *Journal of Broadcasting & Electronic Media, 47,* 197–215.

Cohen, J., & Weimann, G. (2000). Cultivation revisited: Some genres have some effects on some viewers. *Communication Reports, 13,* 99–114.

Dahlstrom, M. F., & Scheufele, D. A. (2010). Diversity of television exposure and its association with the cultivation of concern for environmental risks. *Environmental Communication: A Journal of Nature and Culture, 4*, 54–65.

Davis, S., & Mares, M.-L. (1998). Effects of talk show viewing on adolescents. *Journal of Communication, 48*, 69–86.

Dixon, T. L. (2007). Black criminals and white officers: The effects of racially misrepresenting law breakers and law defenders on television news. *Media Psychology, 10*, 270–291.

Dixon, T. L. (2008). Crime news and racialized beliefs: Understanding the relationship between local news viewing and perceptions of African Americans and crime. *Journal of Communication, 58*, 10–125.

Gehrau, V. (2006). Basisgenres und die geschlechtspezifische Rezeption fiktionaler Unterhaltungsgenres [Basic genres and gender-specific perception of fictional entertainment genres]. In H. Schramm, W. Wirth & H. Bilandzic (Eds.), *Empirische Unterhaltungsforschung [Empirical research about entertainment]* (pp. 29–46). München: R. Fischer.

Gerbner, G. (2001). Who is telling all the stories? *InterSections, 1*, 5–8.

Gerbner, G., & Gross, L. (1976). Living with television: The violence profile. *Journal of Communication, 26*(2), 173–199.

Gerbner, G., Gross, L., Morgan, M., Signorielli, N., & Jackson-Beeck, M. (1979). The demonstration of power: Violence profile no. 10. *Journal of Communication, 29*(3), 177–196.

Goidel, R. K., Freeman, C. M., & Procopio, S. T. (2006). The impact of television viewing on perceptions of juvenile crime. *Journal of Broadcasting & Electronic Media, 50*, 119–139.

Grabe, M. E., & Drew, D. G. (2007). Crime cultivation: Comparisons across media genres and channels. *Journal of Broadcasting & Electronic Media, 51*, 147–171.

Green, M. C., & Brock, T. C. (2000). The role of transportation in the persuasiveness of public narratives. *Journal of Personality and Social Psychology, 79*, 701–721.

Green, M. C., & Brock, T. C. (2002). In the mind's eye. Transportation-imagery model of narrative persuasion. In M. C. Green, J. J. Strange, & T. C. Brock (Eds.), *Narrative impact: Social and cognitive foundations* (pp. 315–341). Mahwah, NJ: Erlbaum.

Green, M. C., Brock, T. C., & Kaufman, G. F. (2004). Understanding media enjoyment: The role of transportation into narrative worlds. *Communication Theory, 14*, 311–327.

Hawkins, R., & Pingree, S. (1981). Uniform messages and habitual viewing: Unnecessary assumptions in social reality effects. *Human Communication Research, 7*, 291–301.

Herman, L., & Vervaeck, B. (2007). Ideology. In D. Herman (Ed.), *The Cambridge companion to narrative* (pp. 217–230). Cambridge: Cambridge University Press.

Hoffner, C. A., Levine, K. J., & Toohey, R. A. (2008). Socialization to work in late adolescence: The role of television and family. *Journal of Broadcasting & Electronic Media, 52*, 282–302.

Hyvärinen, M. (2008). Narrative form and narrative content. In I. Järventie & M. Lähde (Eds.), *Methodological challenges in childhood and family research* (pp. 43–63). Tampere: Tampere University Press.

Jauss, H. R. (1982). *Towards an aesthetic of reception*. Brighton: Harvester Press.

Katz, S. D. (1991). *Film directing shot by shot. Visualizing from concept to screen*. Studio City, CA: Michael Wiese.

Kort-Butler, L. A., & Sittner Hartshorn, K. J. (2011). Watching the detectives: Crime programming, fear of crime, and attitudes about the criminal justice system. *The Sociological Quarterly, 52*, 36–55.

Lacey, N. (2000). *Narrative and genre: Key concepts in media studies*. Basingstoke: Palgrave.

Lang, A. (2009). The limited capacity model of motivated mediated message processing. In R. L. Nabi & M. B. Oliver (Eds.), *The Sage handbook of media processes and effects* (pp. 193–204). Los Angeles: Sage.

Lee, C., & Niederdeppe, J. (2010). Genre-specific cultivation effects: Lagged associations between overall TV viewing, local TV news viewing, and fatalistic beliefs about cancer prevention. *Communication Research*. Advance online publication. DOI: 10.1177/0093650210384990

Mastro, D. (2009). Effects of racial and ethnic stereotyping. In J. Bryant & M. B. Oliver (Eds.), *Media effects: Advances in theory and research* (3rd ed., pp. 325–341). New York: Routledge.

Mittell, J. (2004). *Genre and television. From cop shows to cartoons in American culture*. New York, London: Routledge.

Morgan, M., & Shanahan, J. (2010). The state of cultivation. *Journal of Broadcasting & Electronic Media, 54*, 337–355.

Morgan, M., Shanahan, J., & Signorielli, N. (2009). Growing up with television: Cultivation processes. In J. Bryant & M. B. Oliver (Eds.), *Media effects: Advances in theory and research* (3rd ed., pp. 34–49). New York: Routledge.

Nabi, R. L. (2009). Cosmetic surgery makeover programs and intentions to undergo cosmetic enhancements: A consideration of three models of media effects. *Human Communication Research, 35*, 1–27.

Neale, S. (2003). Questions of genre. In B. K. Grant (Ed.), *Film genre reader III* (pp. 160–184). Austin: University of Texas Press.

Ohler, P. (1994). *Kognitive Filmpsychologie. Verarbeitung und mentale Repräsentation narrativer Filme [Cognitive psychology of film. Processing and mental representation of narrative films]*. Münster: MAkS Publikationen.

O'Keefe, G. J. (1984). Public views on crime: Television exposure and media credibility. In R. N. Bostrom & B. H. Westley (Eds.), *Communication Yearbook 8* (pp. 514–535). Beverly Hills: Sage.

Oliver, M. B., & Armstrong, G. B. (1995). Predictors of viewing and enjoyment of reality-based and fictional crime shows. *Journalism & Mass Communication Quarterly, 72*, 559–570.

Perse, E. M. (1986). Soap opera viewing patterns of college students and cultivation. *Journal of Broadcasting & Electronic Media, 30*, 175–193.

Petty, R. E., Tormala, Z. L., & Rucker, D. D. (2004). Resisting persuasion by counterarguing: An attitude strength perspective. In J. Jost, M. Banaji, R. Mahzarin, & D. Prentice (Eds.), *Perspectivism in social psychology: The yin and yang of scientific progress*. (pp. 37–51). Washington, DC: American Psychological Association.

Pfau, M., Mullen, L. J., Deidrich, T., & Garrow, K. (1995). Television viewing and public perceptions of attorneys. *Human Communication Research, 21*, 307–330.

Pfau, M., Mullen, L. J., & Garrow, K. (1995). The influence of television viewing on public perceptions of physicians. *Journal of Broadcasting & Electronic Media, 39*, 441–458.

Plantinga, C. (2009). *Moving viewers. American film and the spectator's experience*. Berkeley: University of California Press.

Podlas, K. (2006). The *CSI* effect: Exposing the media myth. *Media & Entertainment Law Journal, 16*, 429–465.

Potter, J. W. (1990). Adolescents' perceptions of the primary values of television programming. *Journalism Quarterly, 67*, 843–851.

Potter, J. W. (1993). Cultivation theory and research: A conceptual critique. *Human Communication Research*, 19, 564–601.

Potter, J. W., & Chang, I. C. (1990). Television exposure measures and the cultivation hypothesis. *Journal of Broadcasting & Electronic Media, 34*, 313–333.

Pyrhönen, H. (2007). Genre. In D. Herman (Ed.), *The Cambridge companion to narrative* (pp. 109–123). Cambridge: Cambridge University Press.

Quick, B. L. (2009). The effects of viewing *Grey's Anatomy* on perceptions of doctors and patient satisfaction. *Journal of Broadcasting & Electronic Media, 53*(1), 38–55.

Rivadeneyra, R., & Ward, L. M. (2005). From *Ally McBeal* to *Sábado Gigante*: Contributions of television viewing to the gender role attitudes of Latino adolescents. *Journal of Adolescent Research, 20*, 453–475.

Rivadeneyra, R., Ward, L. M., & Gordon, M. (2007). Distorted reflections: Media exposure and Latino adolescents' conceptions of self. *Media Psychology, 9*, 261–290.

Romer, D., Jamieson, K. H., & Aday, S. (2003). Television news and the cultivation of fear of crime. *Journal of Communciation, 53*, 88–104.

Rosenwasser, S. M., Lingenfelter, M., & Harrington, A. F. (1989). Nontraditional gender role portrayals on television and children's gender role perceptions. *Journal of Applied Developmental Psychology, 10*, 97–105.

Rössler, P., & Brosius, H.-B. (2001). Do talk shows cultivate adolescents' views of the world? A prolonged-exposure experiment. *Journal of Communication, 51*, 143–163.

Schank, R. C., & Abelson, R. P. (1977). *Scripts, plans, goals and understanding: An inquiry into human knowledge structures*. Hillsdale, NJ: Erlbaum.

Schweinitz, J. (1994). "Genre" und lebendiges Genrebewusstsein: Geschichte eines Begriffs und Probleme seiner Konzeptualisierung in der Filmwissenschaft ["Genre" and living awareness of genre: History of a concept and problems of its conceptualization in film studies]. *montage /av, 3*, 99–118.

Schweitzer, N. J., & Saks, M. J. (2007). The *CSI* effect: Popular fiction about forensic science affects the public's expectations about real forensic science. *Jurimetrics, 47*, 357–364.

Segrin, C., & Nabi, R. L. (2002). Does television viewing cultivate unrealistic expectations about marriage? *Journal of Communication, 52*, 247–263.

Shrum, L. J. (1996). Psychological processes underlying cultivation effects: Further tests of construct accessibility. *Human Communication Research, 22*, 482–509.

Shrum, L. J., Burroughs, J. E., & Rindfleisch, A. (2005). Television's cultivation of material values. *Journal of Consumer Research, 32*, 473–479.

Shrum, L. J., Lee, J., Burroughs, J. E., & Rindfleisch, A. (2011). An online process model of second-order cultivation effects: How television cultivates materialism and its consequences for life satisfaction. *Human Communication Research, 37*, 34–57.

Signorielli, N. (2001). Television's gender role images and contribution to stereotyping.

In D. G. Singer & J. L. Singer (Eds.), *Handbook of children and the media* (pp. 341–358). Thousand Oaks, CA: Sage.

Signorielli, N., & Bacue, A. (1999). Recognition and respect: A content analysis of prime-time television characters across three decades. *Sex Roles, 40*, 527–544.

Smith, M. (1995). *Engaging characters. Fiction, emotion, and the cinema.* Oxford: Oxford University Press.

Smith, S. L., & Granados, A. D. (2009). Content patterns and effects surrounding sex-role stereotyping on television and film. In J. Bryant & M. B. Oliver (Eds.), *Media effects: Advances in theory and research* (3rd ed., pp. 342–361). New York: Routledge.

Staiger, J. (2003). Hybrid or imbred. The purity hypothesis and Hollywood genre history. In B. K. Grant (Ed.), *Film genre reader III* (pp. 186–199). Austin: University of Texas.

Tan, E. S. (1996). *Emotion and the structure of narrative film. Film as an emotion machine.* Mahwah, NJ: Erlbaum.

Todorov, T. (1976). The origin of genres. *New Literary History, 8*, 159–170.

Todorov, T. (1990). *Genres in discourse.* Cambridge: Cambridge University Press.

Tudor, A. (1979). Genre and critical methodology. In W. Nichols (Ed.), *Movies and methods* (pp. 118–126). Berkeley and Los Angeles: University of California Press.

Van den Bulck, J. (2010). The datasetting effect: Learning facts about the real world from viewing fiction. Paper presented at the annual meeting of the International Communication Association, Singapore.

Ward, L. M., Hansbrough, E., & Walker, E. (2005). Contributions of music video exposure to Black adolescents' gender and sexual schemas. *Journal of Adolescent Research, 20*, 143–166.

Ward, L. M., & Rivadeneyra, R. (1999). Contributions of entertainment television to adolescents' sexual attitudes and expectations: The role of viewing amount versus viewer involvement. *Journal of Sex Research, 36*, 237–249.

Weitzer, R., & Kubrin, C. E. (2004). Breaking news: How local TV news and real-world conditions affect fear of crime. *Justice Quarterly, 21*, 497–520.

Winterhof-Spurk, P., Unz, D., & Schwab, F. (2001). "In the mood"—Zur Kultivierung von Emotionen durch Fernsehen ["In the mood"—About the cultivation of emotions through television]. *magazin forschung (Universität des Saarlandes), 2*, 20–33.

Woo, H.-J., & Dominick, J. R. (2001). Daytime television talk shows and the cultivation effect among U.S. and international students. *Journal of Broadcasting & Electronic Media, 45*, 598–614.

Wood, R. (2003). Ideology, genre, auteur. In B. K. Grant (Ed.), *Film genre reader* (pp. 61–74). Austin: University of Texas Press.

Yang, H., & Oliver, M. B. (2010). Exploring the effects of television viewing on perceived life quality: A combined perspective of material value and upward social comparison. *Mass Communication & Society, 13*, 118–138.

# 14. Developing a Lifetime Television Exposure Scale

## The Importance of Television Viewing Habits During Childhood

*Karyn Riddle*

For decades, media effects scholars have been exploring the myriad ways mediated messages can affect audiences over both the short and long term. Although a number of theoretical approaches to media effects processes have guided this research, cultivation theory (Gerbner, 1969) has emerged as one of the most prominent theories focusing on long-term effects processes. Cultivation scholars have amassed a body of research that suggests the mass media—especially television—exert a small but statistically significant impact on people's views of social reality. Cultivation is among the most frequently cited theories in the field of mass communication (Potter & Riddle, 2007), but it has not suffered from a lack of criticism (e.g., Doob & Macdonald, 1979; Hirsch, 1980, 1981; Newcomb, 1978; Potter, 1993, 1994). Chief among the concerns raised by critics are the methods used to test cultivation, including the operationalization of the theory's key predictor variable, television exposure.

To date, the primary controversy surrounding the measurement of cultivation's predictor variable has centered on the issue of genre specificity. Whereas numerous cultivation scholars argue that cultivation theory addresses the effects of overall television exposure and see television as portraying a system of common messages (e.g., Gerbner, Gross, Jackson-Beeck, Jeffries-Fox, & Signorielli, 1978; Shanahan & Morgan, 1999), other scholars insist that we should focus on individuals' exposure to certain genres or themes, arguing that television today does not convey the common themes it did in the past (e.g., Bilandzic & Rössler, 2004; Hawkins & Pingree, 1981; Potter, 1993). This is indeed an important issue (see Bilandzic & Busselle, Chapter 13, this volume, for a fuller discussion), but in the present chapter I will explore a separate yet equally important concern regarding the measurement of cultivation's predictor variable: the issue of time period. In this chapter, I make the argument that cultivation scholars should explore the possibility that measuring *current* television exposure levels may not be the optimal strategy for operationalizing long-term television viewing levels. To that end, I propose we also consider individuals' *past* television exposure levels, especially during the critical childhood and adolescent time periods.

The primary goal of this chapter, therefore, is to address measurement issues related to cultivation's predictor variable. First, this chapter will review the conceptual definition of this variable. Next, I will provide a brief review of the primary ways the predictor variable has been operationalized in cultivation studies over the past 15 years. I will then critique the field's focus on current television viewing levels and will argue that we should also measure actual long-term viewing levels, especially those during childhood and adolescence. I will introduce a new strategy for measuring childhood and adolescent viewing levels and present data in support of these measures. Finally, recommendations for future research will be provided.

## Cultivation Theory and the Issue of Exposure

Cultivation theory states that the more time people spend "living" in the TV world, the more likely they are to believe social reality is congruent with TV reality. Cultivation theory is based on the assumption that the mass production and distribution of media messages across time, space, and social groupings results in the cultivation of collective consciousness (Gerbner, 1969). Although much cultivation research focuses on the topic of media violence, the theory has also been applied to content areas such as sex role stereotypes (Preston, 1990), images of love and marriage (Segrin & Nabi, 2002), divorce (Carveth & Alexander, 1985), and portrayals of ethnic minorities (Allen & Hatchett, 1986), among other topics.

Cultivation theory very clearly posits that the cultivation effect only occurs after long-term, cumulative exposure to stable patterns of content on television (Shanahan & Morgan, 1999). Gerbner and colleagues (Gerbner,

Gross, Morgan, & Signorielli, 1982), for example, wrote about the importance of "*growing up* in a symbolic environment" shaped by television (p. 66, emphasis added). In their review of cultivation research, Shanahan and Morgan (1999) argue that television creates an impact by exposing people to images "over and over again" (p. 12) and state that the internalization of television messages is "steady and cumulative" (p. 17). In fact, their justification for the use of overall television exposure measures (versus genre-specific measures) is rooted in the assumption that heavy viewing over long periods of time will expose even heavy viewers of non-violent genres to "more of everything" (p. 30).

Due to its emphasis on long-term effects processes, therefore, cultivation research poses significant methodological challenges to researchers. For example, manipulating media exposure that is truly "long-term" is extremely difficult, which is one reason why experimental tests of cultivation are quite rare. In fact, some have argued that experiments are an inappropriate method altogether, due to cultivation's focus on long-term *immersion* in the television world (e.g., Potter, 1994; Shanahan & Morgan, 1999). Nonetheless, some studies have employed either single or prolonged exposure experimental designs to test whether television has a causal effect on cultivation-type outcomes (e.g., Bryant, Carveth, & Brown, 1981; Mares, 1996; Ogles & Hoffner, 1987; Riddle, 2010a; Rössler & Brosius, 2001; Tamborini, Zillmann, & Bryant, 1984).

Because it is so difficult to manipulate viewers' long-term immersion into television, the vast majority of cultivation research employs survey methods in which television exposure is a measured variable. Ideally, the majority of surveys exploring cultivation effects would be longitudinal in design, as they would allow researchers to look at changes over time in terms of exposure and beliefs. Unfortunately, however, there are only a handful of cultivation studies that are longitudinal in nature (e.g., Morgan, 1982; Morgan, 1987; Morgan & Shanahan, 1991; Vergeer, Lubbers, & Scheepers, 2000), in large part because they are often costly and, by definition, time consuming.

The vast majority of cultivation research, therefore, is conducted through the use of cross-sectional surveys. Researchers are thus faced with the challenge of measuring long-term exposure to television. As the following review will demonstrate, however, very few cross-sectional cultivation studies actually do this. Instead, cultivation scholars using cross-sectional surveys tend to measure participants' current television viewing levels and use them as an indicator of lifetime use. In the following section, I will review these measures and will criticize the assumption that current viewing levels are indicative of long-term exposure.

## Measuring Exposure in Cross-Sectional Survey Research

In cross-sectional survey research exploring cultivation, researchers typically measure television (or other media) exposure and compare it to a variety of outcomes. There is no standard measure in the literature, however, for assessing exposure levels, and therefore the methods used vary significantly from study to study. As discussed above, the most controversial area of disagreement in terms of measuring exposure is the conceptual definition of the variable "television exposure," with some cultivation researchers focusing on overall television exposure levels and others focusing on exposure to specific types of content. Researchers disagree on more than just the issue of genre specificity, however. They also differ in terms of the types of measures used (e.g., open-ended vs. Likert scale items) as well as the type of information collected from participants (e.g., number of shows vs. number of hours vs. number of times viewed) and the time frame (e.g., viewing in an average week vs. on an average day).

Take, for example, some of the most common measures used by researchers exploring the effects of overall exposure. One strategy for measuring overall exposure is to present participants with a list of television dayparts and ask them to report the number of hours viewed within each daypart in the average week (e.g., Nabi & Sullivan, 2001). In other studies, researchers present participants with a list of television genres and ask them to list the number of hours per week spent watching each genre (e.g., Busselle, 2001; O'Guinn & Shrum, 1997, Study 1). Other studies use both of these measures and then average the totals together (Shrum, Wyer, & O'Guinn, 1998, Study 1). Some studies ask participants to state the number of hours of television viewed on the day prior to the study, often averaging that amount with participants' estimates of average daily hours of viewing (Mastro, Behm-Morawitz, & Ortiz, 2007; Shrum & Bischak, 2001). Finally, at least one cultivation study employed a Likert-type scale question to measure overall exposure, asking participants to agree or disagree with statements such as "I spend time watching television almost every day," and "I often watch television on weekends" (Shrum, Burroughs, & Rindfleisch, 2004).

Among cultivation studies measuring genre-specific exposure, we also see inconsistencies in measurement strategies. A study focusing on crime and violence, for example, asked participants to indicate their exposure to violence in the news (on television, radio, and newspapers) using a 4-point frequency scale (Romer, Jamieson, & Aday, 2003, Study 1). Bilandzic and Busselle (2008) also used frequency scales, asking participants to rate how often they view specific movie genres on scales ranging from 0 (never) to 7 (very often). The more common strategy for measuring genre-specific viewing, however, appears to be the use of open-ended questions, with great variation in what researchers ask participants to report. Quick (2009) asked participants to state the number of episodes of *Grey's Anatomy* they had viewed in the current and prior season in a study of viewers' perceptions of doctors. Similarly, Chory-Assad and Tamborini (2003) asked participants to state the number of *times* they had viewed primetime doctor shows within a stated time period, which was then converted into the number of hours viewed per week. Some studies ask participants directly to state the number of hours per week they view each of a long list of genres, and then the researchers focus on the genres most relevant to their content area (Busselle, 2003; Busselle & Shrum, 2003). In yet other studies (e.g., O'Guinn & Shrum, 1997, Study 2; Shrum, 1999), researchers ask participants to report only the number of hours they watch one particular genre (e.g., soap operas) within a specified time period.

Certainly, the preceding paragraphs do not represent an exhaustive review of all exposure measures used in cultivation research, but even this brief review reveals a significant lack of consistency in the literature. There is one thing, however, that all of the exposure measures reviewed above have in common: They all assess participants' *current* television viewing habits, either explicitly or implicitly. For example, some studies ask participants to state their media exposure from the day prior (e.g., Jeffres et al., 2001; Mastro et al., 2007). Others ask participants to state their viewing habits over recent time periods, such as, "in the last 8 weeks" (Chory-Assad & Tamborini, 2003) or "last week" (Grabe & Drew, 2007). On the other hand, the focus on current exposure levels is strongly implied in other studies. For example, Bilandzic and Busselle (2008) asked participants, "How often do you watch rented or televised movies from the categories listed below?" Although the researchers did not use the word "currently" in their question, their use of the present tense seems to clearly imply that the researchers want participants to think about their current lifestyle and habits.

The big question, therefore, is whether or not these measures of current television use are accurate indicators of long-term use. On the one hand, research suggests that viewing levels are relatively stable over the course of the lifetime (for a review, see Comstock & Paik, 1991), which does provide some rationale for the use of current exposure measures. However, disruptions in viewing levels can be caused by major life events such as becoming a teen, marriage, childbirth, or job loss. The college years, in particular, are a time period in which exposure levels diminish, and patterns of viewing reflect the periods of availability allowed by college students' schedules (Pingree et al., 2001). Given that college students are often used as research participants in cultivation studies, their "current" television viewing habits may not be representative of long-term viewing habits. In addition, several of the factors that predict television exposure are not permanent and may fluctuate based on a person's stage in their life cycle, such as dissatisfaction with one's life (Rubin, 1985), interest in socializing (Babrow, 1987), loneliness, availability of free time, and emotional difficulties (Kubey & Csikszentmihalyi, 1990). Thus, a person who was a heavy television viewer as a child or young adult may not be a heavy viewer later in life.

Even if measures of current viewing levels are accurate indicators of both current and past television viewing levels, they cannot distinguish between amounts of exposure of people from different age cohorts. As Potter (1993) argued, a heavy television viewer who is 65 years old has been exposed to much more television than a heavy-viewing 18-year-old. More specifically, Kubey (1980) points out that adults raised on television since childhood will have spent an average of over 9 full years watching TV by the time they reach 65. And although the availability of certain genres or programs will certainly change over the course of a person's lifetime, the overall amount of television messages consumed by a heavy-viewing older adult will be higher than that of a younger heavy viewer. Accordingly, any study of long-term media effects comparing individuals from different age groups should employ an exposure measure that operationalizes long-term viewing levels accurately: by measuring *long-term*, lifetime exposure levels in addition to current levels.

## Lifetime Television Exposure

There is theoretical support for the argument that television-viewing levels from the distant past might affect social reality beliefs today. Shrum's research on the heuristic processing model, for example, proposes that construct accessibility is the psychological mechanism underlying the cultivation effect, at least for first-order measures (Shrum, 1996; see also Shrum & Lee, Chapter 8, this volume). His research demonstrates that frequent and recent exposure to vivid media leaves related images easily accessible in memory, and these highly accessible thoughts are used in the formation of social reality beliefs. The heuristic processing model draws from research on chronic accessibility (e.g., Higgins & King, 1981), which suggests that frequent exposure to stimuli results in the habitual, or chronic, accessibility of related constructs. Given that small levels of repetition have been shown to increase chronic accessibility (e.g., Downing, Judd, & Brauer, 1992), there is likely to be a difference in construct accessibility between people who have watched more, versus less, television over the course of an entire lifetime.

There is also reason to suspect that television viewing during one's childhood and adolescence, in particular, might play a critical role in the formation of social reality beliefs in adulthood. After all, childhood and adolescence are particularly important time periods for the formation of cultural models (Roskos-Ewoldsen, Davies, & Roskos-Ewoldsen, 2004) and schema (Huesmann, 1988; Huston, Wright, Fitch, Wroblewski, & Piemyat, 1997). Therefore, television content viewed during childhood and adolescence may impact the formation of schemata and mental models, which may in turn impact social reality beliefs in adulthood. For these reasons, others have already suggested that cultivation research may benefit from focusing on people's television viewing levels during adolescence (Roskos-Ewoldsen et al., 2004).

One of the greatest barriers, however, to measuring long-term, lifetime television exposure levels—especially those during one's childhood—is that it requires people to remember their television viewing habits from the distant past. Research into autobiographical memory, however, suggests that people do tend to remember *patterns* of behavior from their past. Linton (1975), for example, argued that as episodes of a similar kind are experienced over time, a general representation of the event is built up. Although it might be difficult to retrieve any individual past episode, people can remember events from the distant past that occurred routinely by relying on this general representation. Schank (1982) argued that these memories are organized into a structure called a "script," which refers to a collection of specific memories created after a person experiences repeated encounters with a stimulus or event. Others use the term *event clusters,* which exist in a narrative, story-like state and can contain memories that are old and unimportant (Brown & Schopflocher, 1998). Most importantly, these generic representations in memory are in fact based upon actual, experienced events. Although general schemata tend to replace actual memories for repeated experiences (Hudson & Nelson, 1986), these general schemata tend to be based upon actual prior experiences (Baker-Ward, Gordon, Ornstein, Larus, & Clubb, 1993).

The accumulated research strongly suggests, therefore, that people should have a generic representation in memory for daily *routines* they regularly enacted in the past. A grown adult may not be able to remember a specific Tuesday evening during childhood but should have a general schema that represents the types of activities that took place on weeknights during childhood. As a result, the degree to which television was (or was not) a part of one's daily routine in the past should also be embedded into schemata, or scripts, for daily routines. With the proper measurement techniques, therefore, researchers should be able to trigger adults' memories for patterns of television use from the distant past.

To my knowledge, however, only three cultivation studies have attempted to measure past media exposure. First, Carveth and Alexander (1985) conducted a cultivation study focusing on soap operas and asked participants to report their current soap opera viewing habits in addition to the number of years they had been viewing soap operas. They found that current viewing levels exhibited a low correlation with the number of years of past viewing; that is, current exposure was not necessarily indicative of self-reported long-term habits. Furthermore, both variables were positively correlated with numerous cultivation outcomes. Second, Calzo and Ward (2009), in their study of perceptions about homosexuality, argued that the current media landscape is significantly different from that of the past in terms of the portrayals of homosexual characters. In the past (e.g., prior to the year 2000), homosexual characters were almost entirely absent from television programs and, when portrayed, were shown in highly stereotyped manners. Although that stereotyping continues beyond the year 2000, Calzo and Ward noted many advances in terms of the number and diversity of homosexual characters on television. Therefore, in addition to measuring current exposure levels, Calzo and Ward also presented participants with a list of primetime programs, soap operas, and music videos that were popular four years prior to the study. Using 5-point scales, they asked participants to indicate how frequently they *used to view* the programs. Their findings revealed that television use in the past (music videos and primetime TV exposure) was correlated with current attitudes toward homosexuality, whereas current television exposure levels were not.

Third, Riddle (2010b) developed and tested a scale for assessing Lifetime Television Exposure (LTE), which measures participants' current and childhood television viewing levels. The development of the LTE scale relied heavily on the theories of long-term memory storage cited above. In addition, the LTE scale draws from a theoretical approach called the self-memory system (SMS; Conway & Pleydell-Pearce, 2000), which expands upon the research reviewed above and posits that memories are organized based on the major stages in a person's lifetime. The SMS suggests that we possess an autobiographical knowledge base containing memories at three levels of specificity: event-specific knowledge, general event knowledge, and lifetime periods. *Event-specific knowledge* refers to memories for specific, individual events. *General event knowledge* refers to memories for past events that were repeated on a regular basis, such as the scripts and schema reviewed above. Finally, *lifetime periods* represent broad periods of a person's life (e.g., "when I was in college," or "when I lived in Spain"). The SMS says that event-specific knowledge and general event knowledge are embedded within lifetime periods.

Guided by the SMS, the LTE scale triggers participants' memories of prior television use by cueing them think about a particular lifetime period.

Specifically, the LTE focuses on three lifetime periods: elementary school (i.e., early childhood), high school (i.e., adolescence), and the current time period. Rather than measure genre-specific exposure, the original version of the LTE scale (Riddle, 2010b) measured overall television viewing levels during each lifetime period by presenting participants with a chronological list of dayparts on weekdays and weekends. The LTE scale asks participants to think of their daily routine within a particular lifetime period and then asks participants to recall the degree to which television fit into the chronological progression of their daily routine.

In its initial test, the LTE scale predicted cultivation outcomes above and beyond traditional exposure measures focusing on current television viewing levels. These findings lend support to the argument that it is important to measure lifetime, long-term exposure levels—especially exposure during childhood and adolescence—in addition to measuring current exposure. There are several limitations to the LTE scale, however, as well as the study employed to test its validity. First, the LTE scale has thus far only been administered to a sample of college students, for whom childhood and adolescent television exposure is much more recent than it would be for a sample of older adults. Second, the original LTE scale measured overall television exposure levels by daypart, as mentioned above, regardless of genre. It would be useful to determine whether genre-specific exposure from the past is also predictive of cultivation outcomes such as social reality beliefs.

Additional research is therefore needed before we can make firmer conclusions regarding the utility of measuring television exposure levels from the distant past in cultivation research. To that end, data were collected among a nationwide sample of adults to further explore the effects of past television exposure on current cultivation outcomes. The details of this research project are described below.

## New Research on LTE

Building on that first LTE study of the effects of childhood and adolescent television viewing on cultivation outcomes in adulthood (Riddle, 2010b), follow-up research was conducted that expanded it in several respects. For example, the scale was administered to a sample of adults over the age of 18, rather than a sample of college students. The three lifetime periods employed in the scale, however, did not change (e.g., elementary school, high school, and current), due to the formation of mental models and schema during childhood and adolescence. In addition, this study focuses on genre-specific television exposure levels from the past and present rather than overall viewing levels. The primary goal of this research project is to determine whether childhood exposure to violent genres predicts social reality beliefs above and beyond measures of current exposure to violent genres.

Using the online research panel Toluna, an internet-based survey was distributed to a nationwide sample of adults over the age of 18 over a period of one week. Toluna maintains a demographically diverse panel of members who participate in online survey research for rewards.[1] Despite the size and diversity of Toluna's panel, however, it does not generate a representative sample, as members not only have to have internet access but also opt into every study based on their interests.

The final sample collected in the present study ($n$ = 535) ranged in age from 18 to 89 years old ($M$ = 49.3, $SD$ = 16.8), with approximately 20–30% falling into each of the major age subgroups (18–29, 30–49, 50–64, and 65+). A fairly even gender balance was achieved (females = 52%, males = 48%), with a majority of participants self-reporting as Caucasians (78%). Other ethnic groups included African Americans (8%), Asian Americans (5%), Hispanics (4%), and other (5%).

The questionnaire was designed so that participants could state their social reality beliefs before being primed by questions measuring television exposure. The television exposure measures were divided into three sections: elementary school television exposure, high school television exposure, and current television exposure. All participants indicated their television exposure levels in that order, with the "current" section including measures of control variables.

Consistent with prior research (e.g., Gerbner, Gross, Morgan, & Signorielli, 1980; Nabi & Sullivan, 2001; Shrum, 1996; Shrum & Bischak, 2001; Shrum et al., 1998), social reality beliefs were measured using prevalence estimates. Participants were presented with 13 questions asking them to estimate the prevalence of events related to crime and violence. For example, participants were asked questions such as, "What percentage of murders is committed by strangers?" and "When police arrive at the scene of a crime, what percentage of the time must they use force and violence?" All 13 questions asked participants to state their answer in the form of a percentage, and thus answer options ranged from 0—100, with higher numbers reflecting the "television answer" (i.e., more violent). Participants' responses to the 13 questions were averaged together to create one social reality belief scale ($M$ = 25.9, $SD$ = 18.5) that was normally distributed and exhibited strong reliability ($\alpha$ = .94).

Childhood violent television exposure was measured by asking participants to report television exposure levels during the two key lifetime periods mentioned above: elementary school and high school. Participants answered questions pertaining to elementary school viewing first, followed by high school viewing. When participants entered the "Elementary School" section of the survey, they were told to think back to when they were younger children, during elementary school (i.e., ages 5—10). They were told to think about the lifestyle they experienced during this time period, and based on their lifestyle during the ages of 5–10, they were told to answer a series of questions about their exposure to television.

Participants were then presented with a list of 20 television genres (daytime soap operas, sitcoms, sports, cartoons, educational TV, music television, movies on television, variety shows, crime/police dramas, medical dramas, lawyer/courtroom dramas, science fiction, relationship dramas, daytime talk shows, nighttime talk shows, game shows, reality television, celebrity news, local news, and national news). Examples of programs that fall within each genre were not provided, and thus participants were allowed to judge for themselves the types of programs that would fall in each genre in a particular time period. For each genre, participants were asked to indicate how frequently they used to watch during elementary school on a scale ranging from 1—7 (*never, very rarely, somewhat rarely, once in a while, somewhat often, very often, all the time*). This strategy of presenting participants with a list of television genres is consistent with prior cultivation research (e.g., Busselle, 2003; Busselle & Shrum, 2003), although the present study employs a 7-point frequency scale rather than an open-ended measure. The decision to use this kind of scale in the present study was driven by research into long-term memory. Reporting the number of hours of television watched is an appropriate strategy when asking people about their current television viewing patterns but is not likely to be accurate when measuring past viewing levels. Furthermore, recent research reveals moderate to strong correlations between ordinal measures of current media exposure and open-ended measures asking for number of hours a day (Jordan, Trentacoste, Henderson, Manganelo, & Fishbein, 2007).

Consistent with prior research focusing on genre-relevant television programs, the present study averaged together 8 of the 20 genres that have been demonstrated as being violent in prior content analyses. Specifically, prior research has considered local and national news (Gross & Aday, 2003; Romer et al., 2003), music videos and music television (Sherman & Dominick, 1986), movies on television (Busselle, 2003), dramatic programs such as crime/police and lawyer/courtroom shows (Busselle, 2003; Busselle & Shrum, 2003), science fiction (Greenberg, 1974), and cartoons (NTVS, 1997) to be violent. Therefore, participants' elementary school exposure to these eight genres were averaged together to create an *elementary school violent TV exposure* variable ($M$ = 3.26, $SD$ = 1.48, $\alpha$ = .89).

The same procedure was repeated when participants entered the "High School" section of the survey. Specifically, they were told to think back to the high school years (i.e., ages 14—18). They were told to think about the lifestyle they experienced during this time period and base their answers on that lifestyle. Participants were then presented with a list of the same 20 television genres and were asked to indicate how frequently they used to watch them during high school on the same 1–7 scale. Once again, participants' responses to the eight violent genres were averaged together to create a *high school violent TV exposure* variable ($M = 3.56$, $SD = 1.36$, $\alpha = .86$).

The relationship between elementary and high school exposure to violent television was strong ($r = .75$, $p < .001$). To create the final *childhood violent TV exposure* variable, therefore, the two time periods were averaged together. The final variable ranges in value from 1—7 ($M = 3.41$, $SD = 1.32$) and is normally distributed.

When participants entered the "current" section of the survey, they were asked to think about their current lifestyle (i.e., the last few months). Once again, they were presented with the list of 20 television genres and were asked to indicate their exposure on the 7-point frequency scale, and once again, the eight violent genres were averaged together to create a current violent TV exposure scale ($M = 3.78$, $SD = 1.20$, $\alpha = .79$). Current exposure to violent genres is only moderately correlated with childhood exposure to violent genres ($r = .53$, $p < .001$). Its correlation with high school violent genre viewing ($r = .55$, $p < .001$) is slightly higher than its relationship with elementary school violence viewing ($r = .45$, $p < .001$).

Finally, age, gender, ethnicity, and education level were included as control variables, consistent with prior cultivation research (Hetsroni & Tukachinsky, 2006; Potter & Chang, 1990; Shrum, 2001). The data reveal the sample is somewhat educated. For example, 32% of the sample had completed at least some college (without graduating to date), and 18% graduated with a 4-year degree. Only 22% of the sample indicated their highest degree was a high school diploma, and 10% indicated their highest degree was vocational school or junior college. Participants were divided into two groups based on education: one group represents the "higher education" group, and includes individuals with some college or beyond (67%). The second group represents the "lower education" group, and includes those whose highest education level was elementary school, high school, junior college, or trade school (33%).

### *Results of Research Study*

It was expected that measures of childhood violent television exposure would positively predict social reality beliefs above and beyond measures of current violent television exposure. Consistent with prior cultivation research (Shrum,

1999; Shrum et al., 1998), a hierarchical multiple regression was first conducted to determine whether current television exposure levels relate to social reality beliefs after taking demographic control variables measures into account. As such, demographic control variables were entered in Block 1 (age, gender, ethnicity, and education), and current violent television exposure was entered in Block 2. Childhood violent television exposure was entered in Block 3. The dependent variable was social reality beliefs as measured by the 13-item prevalence estimate scale.

The overall regression model was significant, $F(6, 483) = 10.18, p < .001$, and data pertaining to the model are provided in Table 1. Consistent with prior research, the combination of demographic variables in Block 1 contributed a significant amount of explained variance in social reality beliefs ($R^2 = .10, p < .001$). Furthermore, the addition of current violent television exposure in Block 2 contributed a small but statistically significant amount of incremental explained variance in social reality beliefs. Supporting prior cultivation research, current violent television exposure is a positive predictor of social reality beliefs ($\beta = .09, p < .05$). Interestingly, however, once childhood violent television exposure is entered in Block 3, the effect of current violent exposure on social reality beliefs becomes non-significant. Furthermore, the addition of childhood television exposure levels in Block 3 adds a small but statistically significant amount of incremental explained variance in social reality beliefs ($\Delta R^2 = .01, p < .05$). An examination of the standardized beta coefficient reveals childhood violent television exposure to be a positive predictor of social reality beliefs ($\beta = .12, p < .05$).

Table 1. Hierarchical regression analysis predicting prevalence estimates

| | Block 1 | | Block 2 | | Block 3 | |
|---|---|---|---|---|---|---|
| | $\beta$ | $\Delta R^2$ | $\beta$ | $\Delta R^2$ | $\beta$ | $\Delta R^2$ |
| Block 1: Demographics | | .10*** | | | | |
| Age | -.14** | | -.13** | | -.09 | |
| Gender ( 1 = male, 2 = female) | .14** | | .13** | | .14** | |
| Ethnicity ( 1 = Non-white, 2 = White) | -.11* | | -.10* | | -.09* | |
| Education (1 = lower, 2 = higher) | -.19*** | | -.19*** | | -.19*** | |
| Block 2: Current Violent TV Exposure | | | .09* | .01* | .03 | |
| Block 3: Childhood Violent TV Exposure | | | | | .12* | .01* |

*Note.* Beta coefficients reflect standardized values.

* $p < .05$

** $p < .01$

*** $p < .011$

## Future Directions

Media exposure is one of the central variables in mass communication research, yet the field as a whole—cultivation research included—still exhibits great inconsistency in its use of measures for this key concept. The issue of measuring television exposure in particular has been an ongoing hot topic, with scholars publishing literature reviews summarizing and criticizing measurement tactics (Slater, 2004) as well as empirical comparisons of various exposure measures (Jordan et al., 2007; Lee, Hornik, & Hennessy, 2008; Potter & Chang, 1990; Price, 1993). The empirical comparisons have demonstrated that even minute changes in questionnaire wording can significantly alter people's self-reports of media use. For example, Price (1993) found that self-reported television viewing levels are significantly lower when people are asked to state their viewing in the *past* week as opposed to in the *typical* week. With regard to cultivation in particular, varying the television exposure measure can determine the magnitude of a cultivation effect (Potter & Chang, 1990). Thus, the fact that television exposure measures vary so significantly is no small matter and might account for many discrepancies in findings across cultivation studies.

This research strongly suggests, therefore, that media scholars must continuously challenge themselves by questioning the validity and reliability of their media exposure measures in an effort to achieve the optimal self-report measures. In the following sections, I make some specific suggestions that might help cultivation scholars, in particular, achieve these goals.

### *Measuring Past Television Exposure Levels*

Although there are already vast differences in the way cultivation scholars measure their key predictor variable, I nonetheless argue that cultivation research needs to consider one more factor when measuring exposure levels: television viewing levels in the past. The conceptual definition of cultivation's predictor variable clearly emphasizes the importance of long-term exposure, and as such, researchers need to make attempts to match their operationalization of the concept to its actual definition. The new research described here attempts to achieve this goal by measuring television viewing levels from the past in addition to current television viewing levels.

Indeed, the data presented here suggest that television-viewing levels during early childhood and adolescence predict cultivation outcomes above and beyond current viewing levels. This has now been found both in a sample of young adults (Riddle, 2010b) and in the more general sample from an on-line survey. Even more striking in the present study is the finding revealed in Table 1: Current viewing levels no longer predict social reality beliefs once childhood viewing levels are included in the equation. This suggests that childhood exposure to television violence might be an antecedent variable that can help explain the relationship between current viewing and social reality beliefs. Perhaps it is the case that current viewing levels predict social reality beliefs only due to past viewing, with which it exhibited a moderate correlation. As research on mental models suggests, perhaps we generate mental models for real-world violence at a young age, driven in part by the patterns of content viewed on television during childhood.

Although these findings provide some evidence of the validity of these measures, further tests of validity and reliability are needed before researchers can feel fully comfortable using any versions of these LTE scales. In addition, this line of research raises a number of interesting questions about long-term viewing patterns. For example, this chapter has focused on the effects of television exposure during the elementary and high school time periods. Future research should explore whether television viewing levels within other lifetime periods also have an effect on social reality beliefs. Furthermore, what are the effects of variations in viewing across lifetime periods? For example, we might see different cultivation effects in an individual who has maintained heavy viewing throughout his or her life as opposed to someone who was a heavy viewer during childhood but since then decreased. There are also issues related to changes in genres and programming over time to consider. That is, violent television 40 years ago looked very different from violent television today. How might research exploring lifetime viewing levels account for this? Future studies should explore these questions.

### *The Issue of Genre Specificity*

It is beyond the scope of this chapter to resolve the decades-old debate regarding the issue of genre specificity. As the brief review above demonstrates, there are numerous scholars who continue to measure overall television exposure levels, and there are just as many (if not more) measuring exposure to particular genres. Cultivation theorists who advocate for the measurement of overall viewing levels do not deny that genre-specific viewing has effects—they just question whether it constitutes a "cultivation" effect (for a review, see Morgan & Shanahan, 2010). Perhaps the best compromise to this controversy, therefore, is to employ both strategies. To date, there are several cultivation studies that measure both overall and genre-specific exposure and compare each of their effects on outcome variables (e.g., Calzo & Ward, 2009; Segrin & Nabi, 2002). If more scholars adopted this approach, we could provide tests of cultivation theory (i.e., the effects of a system of messages) as well as tests of genre-specific exposure.

### *The Importance of Longitudinal Research*

As stated above, it is unfortunate that there are so few cultivation researchers conducting longitudinal research. Given the nature of cultivation and its emphasis on long-term effects processes, it would appear to be ideally suited for longitudinal research. It is undeniable that there are significant cost and time limitations that make longitudinal research, in general, challenging. Still, cultivation theory would benefit tremendously if future researchers would make attempts to secure the funding that is necessary to conduct quality longitudinal research. In particular, a longitudinal study that starts during childhood or adolescence and continues into adulthood would be extremely valuable.

### *The Difference between Content and Platforms*

A final issue that is worth briefly mentioning is that of media content versus media platforms. In today's media environment, what constitutes "television" exposure is constantly evolving, with fewer individuals watching television content on an actual television set during the program's designated time. For example, individuals can watch television content via DVRs, they can rent or buy their favorite television program on DVD, or they can stream episodes from the Internet. Current media audiences, therefore, might be confused when participating in a cultivation study and asked by a researcher to report their "television" viewing habits.

A report by the Kaiser Family Foundation (Rideout, Foehr, & Roberts, 2010) might provide guidance on this issue. This particular study aimed to document the amount of time spent with media by 8–18-year-olds, and in doing so, provided useful methods for categorizing media. For example, the KFF study was clear to distinguish media content from the platform on which it is delivered when asking children and teens to report their media use. In the case of television, for example, they asked participants to report their exposure to television *content* regardless of the platform. In other words, participants were told to consider television content viewed on live TV, On Demand, via DVR, via VCRs or DVDs, online, on a cell phone, or on an MP3 player.

Cultivation researchers could (and should) adopt this measurement strategy, regardless of the television exposure measure being used. That is, whether measuring current or past television exposure, or overall versus genre specific exposure, any cultivation exposure measure could easily define for participants what constitutes "television" exposure. Furthermore, asking participants to focus on the content, not the platform, can achieve several goals. One, it could alleviate confusion on the part of respondents who might be unclear what researchers mean by "television" exposure in today's environment. Equally important, a focus on television content—rather than platforms—aligns with the original intent of cultivation theory. Cultivation theory was interested in exploring the effects of a system of messages, and therefore the technology used to disseminate the messages should be less important than the messages themselves. Indeed, the original cultivation theorists never predicted certain types of effects for viewers of color television sets compared to viewers of black and white TV. Nor did they alter the predictions of the theory based on the screen size on which a person viewed television content. This is not to say that formal features such as color and size do not matter, but cultivation theory focuses more on the messages. As such, the platforms used in today's contemporary environment should be less of a focus than the content that is being consumed.

## Conclusion

A cultivation scholar would make extraordinary contributions to the field by focusing his or her efforts on the issue of measuring media—especially television—exposure. Several scholars have made progress toward this goal, but clearly more work needs to be done. Given the centrality of this variable within the cultivation literature, it is imperative that we continue to explore the best strategies that will allow individuals to self-report their use of various media.

## Note

1. Participants in Toluna's panel accumulate points for every survey in which they participate. Panelists manage their points and can exchange these points for vouchers and gifts within their reward partner network. Worldwide, Toluna has 4 million participants in their panels.

## References

Allen, R. L., & Hatchett, S. (1986). The media and social reality effects: Self and system orientations of blacks. *Communication Research, 13*, 97–123.

Babrow, A. S. (1987). Student motives for watching soap operas. *Journal of Broadcasting & Electronic Media, 31*(3), 309–321.

Baker-Ward, L., Gordon, B. N., Ornstein, P. A., Larus, D. M., & Clubb, P. A. (1993). Young children's long-term retention of a pediatric examination. *Child Development, 64*, 1519–1533.

Barsalou, L. W. (1988). The content and organization of autobiographical memories. In U. Neisser & E. Winograd (Eds.), *Remembering reconsidered: Ecological and traditional approaches to the study of memory* (pp. 193–243). Cambridge: Cambridge University Press.

Bilandzic, H., & Busselle, R. W. (2008). Transportation and transportability in the cultivation of genre-consistent attitudes and estimates. *Journal of Communication, 58*, 508–529.

Bilandzic, H., & Rössler, P. (2004). Life according to television. Implications of genre-specific cultivation effects: The gratification/cultivation model. *Communications, 29*, 295–326.

Brown, N. R., & Schopflocher, D. (1998). Event clusters: An organization of personal events in autobiographical memory. *Psychological Science, 9*, 470–475.

Bryant, J., Carveth, R. A., & Brown, D. (1981). Television viewing and anxiety: An experimental examination. *Journal of Communication, 31*(1), 106–119.

Busselle, R. W. (2001). Television exposure, perceived realism, and exemplar accessibility in the social judgment process. *Media Psychology, 3*, 43–67.

Busselle, R. W. (2003). Television exposure, parents' precautionary warnings, and young adults' perceptions of crime. *Communication Research, 30*, 530–556.

Busselle, R. W., & Shrum, L. J. (2003). Media exposure and exemplar accessibility. *Media Psychology, 5*, 255–282.

Calzo, J., & Ward, L. (2009). Media exposure and viewers' attitudes toward homosexuality: Evidence for mainstreaming or resonance? *Journal of Broadcasting & Electronic Media, 53*, 280–299.

Carveth, R., & Alexander, A. (1985). Soap opera viewing motivations and the cultivation process. *Journal of Broadcasting & Electronic Media, 29*, 259–273.

Chory-Assad, R. M., & Tamborini, R. (2003). Television exposure and the public's perceptions of physicians. *Journal of Broadcasting & Electronic Media, 47*, 197–215.

Comstock, G., & Paik, H. (1991). *Television and the American child*. San Diego, CA: Academic Press, Inc.

Conway, M. A., & Pleydell-Pearce, C. W. (2000). The construction of autobiographical memories in the self-memory system. *Psychological Review, 107*, 261–288.

Doob, A. N., & Macdonald, G. E. (1979). Television viewing and fear of victimization: Is the relationship causal? *Journal of Personality and Social Psychology, 37*, 170–179.

Downing, J. W., Judd, C. M., & Brauer, M. (1992). Effects of repeated expressions on attitude extremity. *Journal of Personality and Social Psychology, 63*, 17–29.

Gerbner, G. (1969). Toward "cultural indicators": The analysis of mass mediated message systems. *AV Communication Review, 17*, 137–148.

Gerbner, G., Gross, L., Jackson-Beeck, M. Jeffries-Fox, S., & Signorielli, N. (1978). Cultural indicators: Violence profile no. 9. *Journal of Communication, 28*(3), 176–207.

Gerbner, G., Gross, L., Morgan, M., & Signorielli, N. (1980). The "mainstreaming" of America: Violence profile no. 11. *Journal of Communication, 30*(3), 10–29.

Gerbner, G., Gross, L., Morgan, M., & Signorielli, N. (1982). Charting the mainstream: Television's contributions to political orientations. *Journal of Communication, 32*(3), 100–127.

Grabe, M. E., & Drew, D. (2007). Crime cultivation: Comparisons across media genres and channels. *Journal of Broadcasting & Electronic Media, 51*, 147–171.

Greenberg, B. (1974). British children and televised violence. *Public Opinion Quarterly, 38*, 531–547.

Gross, K., & Aday, S. (2003). The scary world in your living room and neighborhood: Using local broadcast news, neighborhood crime rates, and personal experience to test agenda setting and cultivation. *Journal of Communication, 53*, 411–426.

Hawkins, R. P., & Pingree, S. (1981). Using television to construct social reality. *Journal of Broadcasting, 25*, 347–364.

Hetsroni, A., & Tukachinsky, R. (2006). Television-world estimates, real-world estimates, and television viewing: A new scheme for cultivation. *Journal of Communication, 56*, 133–156.

Higgins, E. T., & King, G. (1981). Accessibility of social constructs: Information-processing consequences of individual and contextual variability. In N. Cantor & J. F. Kihlstrom (Eds.), *Personality, cognition and social interaction* (pp. 69–121). Hillsdale, NJ: Erlbaum.

Hirsch, P. M. (1980). The "scary world" of the nonviewer and other anomalies: A reanalysis of Gerbner et al.'s findings on cultivation analysis, Part I. *Communication Research, 7*, 403–456.

Hirsch, P. M. (1981). On not learning from one's own mistakes: A reanalysis of Gerbner et al.'s findings on cultivation analysis, Part II. *Communication Research, 8*, 2–37.

Hudson, J., & Nelson, K. (1986). Repeated encounters of a similar kind: Effects of familiarity on children's autobiographical memory. *Cognitive Development, 1*, 253–271.

Huesmann, L. R. (1988). The role of social information processing and cognitive schema in the acquisition and maintenance of habitual aggressive behavior. In R. G. Geen & E. Donnerstein (Eds.), *Human aggression: Theories, research, and implications for social policy* (pp. 73–109). San Diego, CA: Academic Press.

Huston, A. C., Wright, J. C., Fitch, M., Wroblewski, R., & Piemyat, S. (1997). Effects of documentary and fictional television formats on children's acquisition of schemata for unfamiliar occupations. *Journal of Applied Developmental Psychology, 18*, 563–585.

Jeffres, L. W., Atkin, D. J., & Neuendorf, K. A. (2001). Expanding the range of dependent measures in mainstreaming and cultivation analysis. *Communication Research Reports, 18*, 408-417.

Jordan, A., Trentacoste, N., Henderson, V., Manganelo, J., & Fishbein, M. (2007). Measuring the time teens spend with media: Challenges and opportunities. *Media Psychology, 9*, 19–41.

Kubey, R. W. (1980). Television and aging: Past, present, and future. *The Gerontologist, 20*, 16–35.

Kubey, R., & Csikszentmihalyi, M. (1990). *Television and the quality of life: How viewing shapes everyday experience*. Hillsdale, NJ: Erlbaum.

Lee, C.-J., Hornik, R. & Hennessy, M. (2008). The reliability and stability of general media exposure measures. *Communication Methods and Measures, 2*, 6–22.

Linton, M. (1975). Memory for real-world events. In D. A. Norman & D. E. Rumelhart (Eds.), *Explorations in cognition* (pp. 376–404). San Francisco: Freeman.

Mares, M.-L. (1996). The role of source confusions in television's cultivation of social reality judgments. *Human Communication Research, 23*, 278–297.

Mastro, D., Behm-Morawitz, E., & Ortiz, M. (2007). The cultivation of social perceptions of Latinos: A mental models approach. *Media Psychology, 9*, 347–365.

Morgan, M. (1982). Television and adolescents' sex role stereotypes: A longitudinal study. *Journal of Personality and Social Psychology, 43*, 947–955.

Morgan, M. (1987). Television, sex-role attitudes, and sex-role behavior. *Journal of Early Adolescence, 7*(3), 269–282.

Morgan, M., & Shanahan, J. (1991). Do VCRs change the TV picture? VCRs and the cultivation process. *The American Behavioral Scientist, 35*, 122–135.

Morgan, M., & Shanahan, J. (2010). The state of cultivation. *Journal of Broadcasting & Electronic Media, 54*, 337–355.

Nabi, R. L., & Sullivan, J. L. (2001). Does television viewing relate to engagement in protective action against crime? *Communication Research, 28*, 802–825.

*National television violence study* (Vol. 1). (1997). Thousand Oaks, CA: Sage.

Newcomb, H. (1978). Assessing the violence profile of Gerbner and Gross: A humanistic critique and suggestion. *Communication Research, 5*, 264–282.

Ogles, R. M., & Hoffner, C. (1987). Film violence and perceptions of crime: The cultivation effect. In M. L. McLaughlin (Ed.), *Communication Yearbook 10* (pp. 384–394). Beverly Hills, CA: Sage.

O'Guinn, T. C., & Shrum, L. J. (1997). The role of television in the construction of consumer reality. *Journal of Consumer Research, 23*, 278–294.

Pingree, S., Hawkins, R. P., Bush Hitchon, J. C., Gilligan, E., Radler, B., Kahlor, L.,... Kannaovakum, P. (2001). If college students are appointment television viewers... *Journal of Broadcasting & Electronic Media, 45*, 446–463.

Potter, W. J. (1993). Cultivation theory and research: A conceptual critique. *Human Communication Research, 19*, 564–601.

Potter, W. J. (1994). Cultivation theory and research: A methodological critique. *Journalism Monographs, 147*, 1–34.

Potter, W. J., & Chang, I. C. (1990). Television exposure measures and the cultivation hypothesis. *Journal of Broadcasting & Electronic Media, 34*, 313–333.

Potter, W. J., & Riddle, K. (2007). A content analysis of the media effects literature. *Journalism & Mass Communication Quarterly, 84*, 90–104.

Preston, E. H. (1990). Pornography and the construction of gender. In N. Signorielli & M. Morgan (Eds.), *Cultivation analysis: New directions in media effects research* (pp. 107–122). Newbury Park: Sage.

Price, V. (1993). The impact of varying reference periods in survey questions about media use. *Journalism Quarterly, 70*, 615–627.

Quick, B. (2009). The effects of viewing *Grey's Anatomy* on perceptions of doctors and patient satisfaction. *Journal of Broadcasting & Electronic Media, 53*, 38–55.

Riddle, K. (2010a). Always on my mind: Exploring how frequent, recent, and vivid television portrayals are used in the formation of social reality judgments. *Media Psychology, 13*, 155–179.

Riddle, K. (2010b). Remembering past media use: Toward the development of a Lifetime Television Exposure scale. *Communication Methods and Measures, 4*, 241–255.

Rideout, V. J., Foehr, U. G., & Roberts, D. F. (2010). *Generation $M^2$: Media in the Lives of 8- to 18-year-olds.* Menlo Park, CA: Henry J. Kaiser Family Foundation.

Romer, D., Jamieson, K. H., & Aday, S. (2003). Television news and the cultivation of fear of crime. *Journal of Communication, 53*, 88–104.

Roskos-Ewoldsen, B., Davies, J., & Roskos Ewoldsen, D. R. (2004). Implications of the mental models approach for cultivation theory. *Communications: The European Journal of Communication Research, 29*, 345–363.

Rössler, P., & Brosius, H.-B. (2001). Do talk shows cultivate adolescents' views of the world? A prolonged-exposure experiment. *Journal of Communication, 51*, 143–163.

Rubin, A. M. (1985). Use of daytime television soap operas by college students. *Journal of Broadcasting & Electronic Media, 29*, 241–258.

Schank, R. C. (1982). *Dynamic memory: A theory of learning in computers and people.* New York: Cambridge University Press.

Segrin, C., & Nabi, R. L. (2002). Does television viewing cultivate unrealistic expectations about marriage? *Journal of Communication, 52*, 247–263.

Shanahan, J., & Morgan, M. (1999). *Television and its viewers: Cultivation theory and research.* Cambridge: Cambridge University Press.

Sherman, B. L., & Dominick, J. K. (1986). Violence and sex in music videos: TV and rock 'n' roll. *Journal of Communication, 36*(1), 79–93.

Shrum, L. J. (1996). Psychological processes underlying cultivation effects: Further tests of construct accessibility. *Human Communication Research, 22*, 482–509.

Shrum, L. J. (1999). Television and persuasion: Effects of the programs between the ads. *Psychology and Marketing, 16*, 119–140.

Shrum, L. J. (2001). Processing strategy moderates the cultivation effect. *Human Communication Research, 27*, 94–120.

Shrum, L. J., & Bischak, V. D. (2001). Mainstreaming, resonance, and impersonal impact: Testing moderators of the cultivation effect for estimates of crime risk. *Human Communication Research, 27*, 187–215.

Shrum, L. J., Burroughs, J. E., & Rindfleisch, A. (2004). A process model of consumer cultivation: The role of television is a function of the type of judgment. In L. J. Shrum (Ed.), *The psychology of entertainment media: Blurring the lines between entertainment and persuasion* (pp. 177–191). Mahwah, NJ: Erlbaum.

Shrum, L. J., Wyer, R. S., Jr., & O'Guinn, T. C. (1998). The effects of television consumption on social perceptions: The use of priming procedures to investigate psychological processes. *Journal of Consumer Research, 24*, 447–458.

Slater, M. (2004). Operationalizing and analyzing exposure: The foundation of media effects research. *Journalism & Mass Communication Quarterly, 81*, 168–183.

Tamborini, R., Zillmann, D., & Bryant, J. (1984). Fear and victimization: Exposure to television and perceptions of crime and fear. In R. N. Bostrum (Ed.), *Communication Yearbook 8* (pp. 492–513). Beverly Hills, CA: Sage.

Vergeer, M., Lubbers, M., & Scheepers, P. (2000). Exposure to newspapers and attitudes toward ethnic minorities: A longitudinal analysis. *Howard Journal of Communications, 11*, 127–143.

# 15. Cultivation and Agenda-Setting

## Conceptual and Empirical Intersections

*Amir Hetsroni & Hila Lowenstein*

Cultivation and agenda-setting are media effects theories that came to the fore in the 1970s, cementing the shift from the minimal effects paradigm to a longer-term cumulative effects conception (Perse, 2001). Both theories relate to the impact that popular media have on our worldview. Agenda-setting theory posits that the prevalence of topics in the media instructs us about the most urgent issues on the political agenda and the attributes that we ascribe to these issues. Cultivation theory postulates that over-representation of certain issues in the media brings us to see these issues in a unified manner and as overly frequent. Both agenda-setting and cultivation view the audience as a relatively non-selective and homogeneous whole, consumers of messages produced by organizations that have various purposes, which can be political, economic, or socio-cultural.

The two theories do differ, however, on a number of parameters. This chapter reviews in detail some of the differences and similarities between the theories and suggests a testable model that may connect them. We are not the first to examine the two theories simultaneously (cf. Gross & Aday, 2003), but we are the first to offer a framework that systematically maps resemblances and dissimilarities between the theories and to suggest a model that unifies them into a more comprehensive model of reality construction.

# Overview

Both agenda-setting and cultivation deal with the connection between the world as it is presented in the media and our beliefs about the reality of our surroundings (Weimann, 2000).

### *Cultivation*

The basic tenet of the cultivation hypothesis is that the more time one spends watching television (a very pervasive medium), the more likely one is to perceive the world as an approximate reflection of televised images of the world. Television programming is conceived of as the mass production of popular messages, as a noteworthy communication agent and most importantly as an effective storyteller (Morgan & Shanahan, 2010). Due to this, heavy television viewing implies the adoption of estimates and the internalization of the views that are represented on the screen, often in disproportion to their actual presence in the world (Shanahan & Morgan, 1999). However, cultivation is not an imitation of what takes place on the small screen but is conceived of more as an internalization of norms, beliefs, and evaluations of social reality (Gerbner, Gross, Morgan, Signorielli, & Shanahan, 2002). Furthermore, over the years several studies have succeeded in establishing cultivation-type relationships with media other than traditional television broadcasting (Hetsroni, 2010a; Perse, Ferguson, & McLeod, 1994).

Evidence of cultivation has been found for a wide range of topics. Much of the research pertains to estimates of the likelihood of various occurrences and phenomena such as the rate of crime and violence (Gerbner, Gross, Eleey, Jackson-Beeck, Jeffries-Fox, & Signorielli, 1977; Hetsroni & Tukachinsky, 2006; Ogles & Sparks, 1989; Potter, 1991), the number of women in professional occupations (Carveth & Alexander, 1985), divorce rates (Carveth & Alexander, 1985; Potter, 1991), affluence prevalence (Fox & Philliber, 1978; Potter, 1991) and the number of older people who live in the world (Gerbner, Gross, Signorielli, & Morgan, 1980a; Hetsroni & Tukachinsky, 2006).

Other evidence comes from studies that correlated the level of television viewing with beliefs regarding issues such as personal safety (Gross & Aday, 2003; Shrum & Bischak, 2001), fear of crime (Romer, Jamieson, & Aday, 2003), and immigration intentions (Hetsroni, 2010a). The first type of evidence, which revolves around reality estimates, is known as a *first-order effect*. The interrelatedness between heavier media consumption and beliefs that derive from televised messages, for example supporting severe punishment for crimes that are often depicted on television as causing severe harm, is termed a *second-order effect* (the two "orders" are phrases coined by Gerbner, Gross, Morgan, & Signorielli, 1986, on the basis of an earlier classification by

Hawkins & Pingree, 1982). More recently, Shrum has been able to establish different cognitive processes that explain first- and (to some extent also) second-order effects (see Shrum & Lee, Chapter 8, this volume, for a detailed review).

The *relationship* between first- and second-order cultivation effects remains an unresolved matter: There is evidence that both first- and second-order conceptions are associated with heavier television viewing (and heavier media consumption in general), but studies that have attempted to measure the correlation between the two effects in order to point at a causal chain have yielded contradictory or inconsistent results. The work of Hawkins, Pingree, and Adler (1987) and Potter (1988), which did not come up with unequivocal findings, convinced Gerbner's research group to abandon altogether the distinction they had offered earlier between first- and second-order effects (Shanahan & Morgan, 1999, p. 177). However, Potter (1991) did find evidence of what he termed "generalization," that is, a significant positive correlation between first- and second-order effects that in his opinion indicates that second-order beliefs are construed on the basis of first-order estimates. We do not necessarily agree that there is a conscious attitude formation process at work here (in fact, the existence of such a process would go against the grain of the heuristic processing idea that is the most widely accepted psychological model of first-order cultivation effects; again see Shrum & Lee, Chapter 8), but we do contend that the classification of cultivation effects into first-order estimates and second-order beliefs is valuable because they represent different parts of one's worldview.

## Agenda-setting

Agenda-setting's central hypothesis is encapsulated by the theorem "the media aren't always successful at telling us what to think, but they are stunningly successful at telling us what to think about" (Cohen, 1963, p. 13). The premise is that the media set the public agenda of issues by establishing and altering their salience and share throughout stories, reports, and news items. The more frequently issues are presented in the media, the more pressing these issues are regarded to be by the public (McCombs & Reynolds, 2008). The basis for this relationship is that audiences do not only gain information on certain topics from the media—they also learn about the relative importance of these topics (Weimann, 2000, p. 34). Because heuristic processing of information often connects "frequent" with "important," cultivation and agenda-setting are conceptually related.

Like cultivation, agenda-setting also has its *first-level effects* (a correlation between the salience of issues in the media and the frequency with which they are elicited as the most important issues in the eyes of the public) and *second-*

*level effects* (a correlation between the characteristics attributed to an issue in the media and the characteristics ascribed to this issue by the public; McCombs & Reynolds, 2008). However, while the dependent variable in agenda-setting studies is quite unequivocal (answers given to the question, "*what is the number one problem facing our country?*" or listing issues according to their importance in the respondents' agenda), the independent variable ranges from the media agenda itself (determined by an analysis of relevant media content) to the level of media consumption (Wanta & Ghanem, 2007).

A meta-analysis of 90 first-level agenda-setting studies detected an average significant effect that is much larger in magnitude than the effect of cultivation ($r = .53$ vs. $r = .09$). However, the average effect of agenda-setting studies that used a cultivation-type measure (media exposure) as their independent variable was significantly smaller than the effect of agenda-setting studies that used media content as the independent variable ($r = .49$ vs. $r = .54$). Furthermore, the only agenda-setting study that examined whether the individual agenda of viewers fully reflects the media agenda and not only corresponds to it in some of the major topics found correlations that are quite similar in size to what we witness in cultivation studies (Wanta & Ghanem, 2007).

### *Refinements*

Over the years, parameters have been added to cultivation and agenda-setting. Gerbner, Gross, Morgan and Signorielli (1980b) introduced the terms "resonance" and "mainstreaming" to cultivation. *Resonance* describes the idea that certain populations whose life is more similar to reality as depicted in the media sometimes show a stronger cultivation effect. *Mainstreaming* stands for the narrowing of an attitudinal gap between diverse groups (e.g., liberals and conservatives) in relation to media exposure, or—in other words—the convergence in second-order cultivation measures such as views of appropriate gender roles, legitimacy of homosexuality, and so on, associated with prolonged exposure to the media. Interestingly, a sort of mainstreaming effect has also been detected in agenda-setting. Shaw and Martin (1992) showed that demographically based differences in the magnitude of the agenda-setting effect (i.e., differences between men and women or between Caucasians and ethnic minorities in the magnitude of the correlation between the public agenda and the media agenda) are smaller when the different demographic clusters consist of heavy media consumers.

In addition to this variation on mainstreaming, agenda-setting has also added two concepts to its model: "priming" and "framing." *Priming* is the process in which mental schemas are activated (Domke, Shah, & Wackman, 1998). This term is often presented as a psychological explanation as to how agenda-setting works (Ghanem, 1997), insofar as news items and stories activate mental schemes that may otherwise remain dormant (Price & Tewksbury, 1997). *Framing* is the highlighting of certain aspects of a news story in order to make them more noticeable (Entman, 1993). There is a commonly made distinction between "episodic" framing that depicts public issues in terms of concrete instances or specific events and "thematic" framing that places public issues in a more abstract context (Perse, 2001, p. 95).

All in all, framing is eventually almost synonymous with the attributes of issues on the agenda, which constitute the dependent variables in second-level agenda-setting studies (Takeshita, 1997). However, another opinion is that framing is an example of cultivation because framing is about the way a certain presentation of topics in the media leads heavy media consumers to make certain inferences about these issues (Ghanem, 1997).

This last suggestion highlights a recurrent characteristic (and potentially a problem) that is probably common to both theories: the use of confounded terms which leads to trespassing of theoretical boundaries. For example, Holbrook and Hill (2005) showed that watching crime drama is significantly associated with greater concerns about crime; they contended that their findings were an indication of agenda-setting attributed to entertainment media. However, a cultivation reading of the study would suggest that it was, in fact, an investigation of second-order cultivation.

Hester and Gibson (2003) presented a time series analysis of the relationship between the content of economic news and the public's economic evaluations as an indication of agenda-setting. Yet, Hetsroni (2010b) considered a conceptually similar correlation an example of cultivation, as did Tims, Fan, and Freeman (1989) in examining the relationship between consumer sentiment and exposure to economic news content. Payne (1978) even used the most typical agenda-setting measure ("name the most important issue on the agenda") as part of a multi-item cultivation index in a study that examined the effect of watching foreign TV programs on views about foreign countries. All in all, we agree with Tims et al. (1989, p. 758) that "while research on the agenda-setting function of the press and research on entertainment television's influence in cultivating perceptions of social reality are quite distinct areas of inquiry, they have far more in common than one might expect." In light of that, a conceptual analysis that would mark points of resemblance between cultivation and agenda-setting, highlight dissimilarities between the theories, clarify where one theory starts and where the other ends, and attempt to put them into one comprehensive framework is due. In the next section, we review eight noteworthy parameters: on four of them (historical context, cumulative type of the effect, cross-sectional design, and emphasis on non-obtrusive issues), agenda-setting and cultivation resemble one another; on the other four parameters (effect size, moderating variables, effect source, and critical view of the media), the theories differ in their assumptions, background, and predictions. The final section of the chapter presents a model that combines the two theories into one "reality construction" framework.

## Points of Resemblance between Cultivation and Agenda-setting

### *Historical Context*

Many media effects studies tend to adopt an ostensibly ahistorical and non-ideological approach in an attempt to reach generalizations that cross over cultural and other boundaries and that are (again, ostensibly) not impacted by the researcher's ideology. However, the theories on which media effects studies rely are always drafted against a certain historical backdrop, and the people who conduct the studies come from a certain ideological background, which may have tremendous influence on their premises.

Cultivation and agenda-setting were framed as scientific hypotheses in the late 1960s. It was a time of political turmoil, civil disobedience, and urban unrest in the United States. 1968 was an exceptionally troublesome year, with two political assassinations (presidential candidate Robert Kennedy and Nobel Peace Prize laureate Martin Luther King, Jr.) and numerous demonstrations against the Vietnam War, whose images of violence (e.g., the My Lai Massacre) were brought into the American home on TV every night and via newspapers every day. It was an election year in which the Democratic Party's national convention (where the party was about to nominate Hubert Humphrey as its presidential candidate after Robert Kennedy's assassination) was disrupted by violent protest. This election (won by the GOP's Richard Nixon, who promised to bring back "law and order") set the background for the first agenda-setting research project (McCombs & Shaw, 1972). The campaign offered a good opportunity to test the theory, because the innumerable twists in the media agenda enabled the researchers to examine how the public agenda reacted to changes in the media agenda (Rogers & Dearing, 1988). Since then, the theory has generated many studies that deal with sensitive political issues, for example, changes in public opinion about civil rights (Winter & Eyal, 1981).

The political unrest and violent protest of the 1960s were also part of what drove George Gerbner, the founder of cultivation theory—eventually joined by colleagues at The Annenberg School for Communication at the University of Pennsylvania (first Larry Gross, Nancy Signorielli, and then Michael Morgan)—to study the content and consequences of televised violence. Funded by the National Institute of Mental Health as part of the Surgeon

General's studies on television and social behavior, Gerbner and colleagues conducted a multi-year content analysis that documented trends in the level of violence in TV programming (which has been very stable over the years; see Gerbner et al., 2002) and attempted to gain insight into the relationship between the viewing of TV violence and viewers' conceptions of issues relating to social violence. Cultivation theory was pushing towards a radically new reading of this connection (instead of correlating television viewing with violent behavior, Gerbner and his colleagues were associating routine exposure to TV with attitudes about violence, fear, and even support for measures that could be taken to control violence). Possibly, Gerbner and his associates could not have completed this research without the financial help of Washington, where politicians were motivated to show the public that they were "doing something" to stop the violent escalation in American society (Grimes, Anderson, & Bergen, 2008). Television seemed like an easy target, but no serious attempt was made to decrease the amount of violence on TV throughout the Congressional hearings on the matter that took place throughout the 1970s and 1980s. Partly, this was due to the networks' successful leaning on the First Amendment to prevent external interferences in their programming (Cooper, 1996); partly, this was, in our opinion, because if the TV screen was to be "cleaned up," an essential scapegoat would be lost.

Overall, both agenda-setting and cultivation marked an historical departure from the *law of minimal consequences*—the small effects conception that set the tone in the academic media literature since the 1950s, when the predictions of the *large immediate effects* paradigm, represented by the *hypodermic needle* metaphor, was falsified (Klapper, 1960). They offered a reasonable explanation as to how a more pervasive media system can bring about significant social changes over time (or block such changes from occurring) without having notable behavioral immediate effects on the audience.

## *Cumulative Long-Term Effects*

Agenda-setting and cultivation are theories of cumulative effects (Perse, 2001). This has a couple of meanings and implications. First, it means that the effect—even if small in size as in the case of cultivation—accumulates over the years (Shanahan & Morgan, 1999; see also Riddle, Chapter 14, this volume). Another aspect of cumulative media effects is that they result from prolonged routine contact with the mass media and are not an outcome of a single exposure to a specific text (Perse, 2001). Thus, the effect can (and even should) be measured over a long period of time. Agenda-setting did that in a few studies, such as Winter and Eyal's (1981) overview of changes in the public agenda about civil rights across 25 years and Funkhouser's (1973) ten-year overview of Gallup polls asking about the nation's number one problem and comparing the answers to the coverage of prominent national problems in current affairs magazines. Longitudinal cultivation studies are scarcer, but some attempts have been made. For example, Lett, DiPietro, and Johnson (2004) measured the impact of exposure to TV's live coverage of the September 11th terror attack on estimations made about the prevalence of Islamist terrorism and views concerning Moslems as individuals months after the live broadcast. That study detected a significant second-order effect but presented no indication of a longitudinal first-order effect.

The cumulative effect paradigm is appropriate for both theories because it provides a reasonable account of the media's societal influence in surroundings saturated with a growing number of mass communication channels, and in which the immediate effects paradigm (e.g., the hypodermic needle metaphor) does not seem to work. The cumulative effects paradigm is also consistent with the speed of change in public response to dependent measures. Thus, if we examine GSS surveys, which often serve as a source for cultivation second-order items in American surveys, we notice slow-paced change in public opinion. For example, between 1973 and 2002 the percent of people who advocated removing books whose authors are homosexuals from a public library dropped from 44% to 22% (*American Attitudes*, 2005, p. 103), but on an annual basis the magnitude of change in public opinion was less than three percentage points per year. Thus, cumulative effects theories seem to match well with slow rates of observed aggregate opinion change.

The final implication of the cumulative effect paradigm is that most of the power of the influence lies with the media content. While both agenda-setting and cultivation have acknowledged the impact of moderating variables (particularly audience socio-demographics), these factors play relatively minor roles in both theories (Perse, 2001).

### *Cross-Sectional Design and Sociological Emphasis*

Both cultivation and agenda-setting started as and continue to be theories whose predictions are primarily tested with cross-sectional designs. Such studies sacrifice some internal validity in favor of greater external validity. However, the cross-sectional approach is appropriate when theories conceive of media effects as a macro-sociological phenomenon. Nevertheless, during the last decade, researchers in both traditions have explored experimental designs that radically diverge from the macro-sociological approach and delve into psychological models. For instance, Shrum's studies of cognitive processes in cultivation (Shrum, 2007, 2009; see also Shrum & Lee, Chapter 8, this volume) have contributed to our understanding of the cultivation mechanism by suggesting heuristic processing as a model of first-order effects. Succinctly, Shrum's model posits that television viewing (or media consumption in general) increases the accessibility of exemplars that are relevant to set-size judgments of which reality estimates consist (e.g., assessing the percentage of law enforcement personnel in the workforce). The accessibility of media exemplars is higher among heavy media consumers, and consequently heavy media consumers are more likely to give reality estimates that resemble the world as it is reflected in the media. A recent meta-analysis of 14 cultivation experiments (Dossche, 2010) that were conducted by Shrum and others produced an average effect ($r = .16$) that is only marginally higher than the effect of cross-sectional studies ($r = .09$; Shanahan & Morgan, 1999, p. 134). This pattern of differences in effect magnitude is common in comparisons of experimental designs and surveys (see, for instance, Paik & Comstock, 1994, for a comparison of surveys and experiments measuring the effect of TV violence on viewers).

Some agenda-setting surveys stand on firmer ground than cultivation cross-sectional studies when it comes to the issue of causation because an electoral campaign (the domain of several agenda-setting studies) is a sort of a natural laboratory (McCombs & Reynolds, 2008, p. 3). In some cases, agenda-setting researchers even cooperated with broadcasters and newspaper editors to conduct field experiments, where a random sample of the public was asked about the agenda before and after the airing of an investigative newscast and the publishing of an investigative report (Protess, Leff, Brooks, & Gordon, 1985). Still, some scientists insisted on bringing respondents into the lab itself, where they were exposed to manipulated news clips and were asked about their agenda before and after seeing the clips. The results corroborated agenda-setting effects observed in the field (Iyengar, Peters, & Kinder, 1982; Wang, 2000).

In our opinion, the most troublesome question about agenda-setting and cultivation experiments is whether their operational definitions truly capture the essence of cumulative effects which result from prolonged exposure to the media in a natural environment. Gerbner and his colleagues even raised the claim that the very concept of causation is not fully applicable to the steady flow of images and messages that comprise much of contemporary popular culture (Gerbner, Gross, Jackson-Beeck, Jeffries-Fox, & Signorielli, 1978). Including multiple controls in agenda-setting and cultivation questionnaires helps to rule out spurious relationships (Zhu & Blood, 1997), but the problem of causation may not have a perfect solution because of the prolonged nature of media exposure.

## Non-Obtrusive Issues

Agenda-setting and cultivation define themselves as theories of issues and outlooks rather than accounts of discrete events or specific attitudes (Gerbner et al., 2002; Rogers & Dearing, 1988). This self-definition fits well with the theories' macro-social orientation. However, despite the ambition to portray people's worldviews, both theories actually predict their most consistent effects in relatively peripheral content domains, where non-obtrusive topics predominate. A topic is "obtrusive" if the public has direct experience with it; it is non-obtrusive when the public has less direct contact with it (Zucker, 1978). The domestic economy is often cited as an obtrusive topic, whereas foreign affairs issues are non-obtrusive. Non-obtrusive issues yield stronger agenda-setting effects (Eyal, 1979; Hügel, Degenhardt, & Weiss, 1989), possibly because for these issues the public has to rely mainly on the media as a source of information (Zucker, 1978). Non-obtrusive topics also produce stronger cultivation effects (Hetsroni, Elphariach, Kapuza, & Tsfoni, 2007), because when people respond to cultivation items about topics that are within the focus of their interest they undergo *experiential closeness* and tend to engage in a systematic "recount and count" that is likely to culminate in answers which quite accurately represent real world facts and do not reflect media exemplars (Bilandzic, 2006). In contrast, when the questions pertain to peripheral topics, about which the respondents have less prior knowledge, the condition of *experiential remoteness* activates cognitive shortcuts, which bring about the retrieval of TV exemplars and leads to a stronger cultivation effect. The framing of this idea within a geographic context led Tyler and Cook (1984, pp. 693–694) to suggest that first-order cultivation occurs only when the required assessment is not personal. Although Tyler and Cook underestimated the capability of TV viewing to result in cultivation even on self-related domains, there is evidence that the cultivation effect is significantly lower for personal victimization likelihood than it is for crime prevalence estimates at the country level (Nabi & Sullivan, 2001), the county level (Wåhlberg & Sjöberg, 2000), and even the neighborhood level (Coleman, 1993; Heath & Petraitis, 1987).

## Points of Dissimilarity between Cultivation and Agenda-setting

### *Effect Size*

The variance accounted for by the average agenda-setting effect is approximately 25 times larger than the variance accounted for by the average cultivation effect. One potential theoretical explanation of this gap is that cultivation is a more ambitious theory than agenda-setting in that it aims to explain people's overall assessment of a subject and not solely to predict its relative importance (Gross & Aday, 2003). However, the truth may be more prosaic than that. The gap in correlation size is possibly an artifact of the use of rank-order coefficients (such as Spearman's rho) among a small number of issues in many agenda-setting studies, as opposed to the large-sample individual-level-correlations that are common in cultivation. Relatively high rank-order correlations can be observed even if the actual ranking of issues differs substantially between the media agenda and the audience agenda (Scheufele, 2000). Wanta and Ghanem's meta-analysis of agenda-setting research (2007) found only one study that attempted to verify whether the complete individual-level agenda (that consists of several issues) mirrors the overall media agenda (which consists also of many issues). That study (McLeod, Becker, & Byrnes, 1974) indicated correlations in the range of .05-.16, which are not much different in strength from what is typically witnessed in cultivation studies. The sole simultaneous search for both agenda-setting effects and cultivation effects yielded significant findings only for the former. The authors of that research explained that "cultivation theory posits far more powerful and worrisome effects of watching television than merely making certain issues seem more important than others" (Gross & Aday, 2003, p. 412). However, one may criticize this conclusion by noting that the search for any linkage between personal fear of crime (the measure of second-order cultivation used by Gross and Aday) and the political agenda regarding crime (which they operationalized as a measure of first-level agenda-setting) is too far fetched. In the absence of more research that would simultaneously assess the effects of agenda-setting and cultivation, any conclusion about differences in effect size should be taken with caution.

### *Moderating Variables*

Shanahan and Morgan's meta-analysis shows that the cultivation effect is partly moderated by socio-demographics and by economic indicators. Income, education level, and political orientation significantly reduce the magnitude of cultivation, while there is an insignificant effect reduction for sex, age and race (Shanahan & Morgan, 1999, pp. 133–134). Some of these moderators, particularly political self-designation and education level, *increase* the size of the agenda-setting effect (MacKuen, 1981). What mechanism(s) might explain this difference? In cultivation, the measured impact is mostly an effect of popular entertainment on our worldview. It makes sense that more highly educated persons, who earn higher salaries, are less likely to be avid consumers of such media and be more immune to media effects in general. Indeed, higher education somewhat reduces the cultivation effect (Shanahan & Morgan, 1999, pp. 133–134). In agenda-setting, on the other hand, the measured effect is most often an effect of news media on what we consider to be the most pressing political problems. One's *need for orientation* may play a pivotal role here

(Weaver, 1977). A recent study has shown that a greater need for orientation considerably increases the size of a first-level agenda-setting effect, although its effect on second-level agenda-setting is less consistent (Matthes, 2007). Even more consistent is the tendency of people with high education and a significant amount of savings to be more interested in politics and the economy, to consume more news media, and to be more susceptible to agenda-setting (McCombs & Reynolds, 2008). Even if the distinction between entertainment and news in the current media environment is more blurred than it used to be due to the rise of hybrid formats such as infotainment, the conceptual difference in dependent measures between agenda-setting and cultivation remains, and may partly account for the differential effects of socio-demographic moderators.

### *Effect Source*

We already mentioned that agenda-setting started as a theory of news media effects, while cultivation started as a framework to explore the impact of exposure to entertainment TV programs. Over the years, both theories have generated studies that diverge from this distinction: Holbrook and Hill (2005) examined the agenda-setting effect of TV drama; Romer, Jamieson, and Aday (2003) tested the cultivation potential of local news; and Gross and Aday (2003) attempted to examine concurrently agenda-setting and cultivation on the basis of a single news text. Since the distinction between news and entertainment is becoming less noticeable in the modern media environment, we suggest that the distinction between agenda-setting and cultivation, when it comes to the source of the effect, is less a matter of formal genre (news vs. entertainment) and more a matter of the content of the media (factual or fictional).

### *Critical View of the Media*

Cultivation was read by its opponents as an empirical version of the Frankfurt School, a sort of Marxism with numbers (see Potter, 1993, for a review of the criticisms). While cultivation research has maintained high scientific standards, it is true that the critical view of the media in general and of television in particular as a cultural arena that documents power relations and social control in order to assist in maintaining the political status quo is not alien to cultivation researchers (Shanahan & Morgan, 1999). Gerbner himself rejected the idea that commercial broadcasting only shows what the viewers want to see:

> We are awash in a tide of violent representations the world has never seen. There is no escape from the massive invasion of colorful mayhem into the homes and cultural life of ever larger areas of the world....What you see on TV is not what the people want. (Gerbner, 2002, pp. 477–478)

In a way, then, cultivation is an "anti-media" school of thought, as Grimes et al. (2008, p. 120) put it. This conception, of course, has political implications, but the range of what constitutes "politics" in the eyes of cultivation researchers is very broad—from attitudes toward government to accepting traditional gender role distinctions (Gross & Jeffries-Fox, 1978). Despite this broadness, because higher amounts of television viewing are most often associated with moderate views on political matters and avoidance of extremism (Gerbner et al., 1982), and with refusal to take active part in politics (Gerbner, 1987a), cultivation means an absorption into a homogeneous passive mainstream and support of strong government that would use restrictive measures against deviants (Gerbner et al., 1982). This tendency is noted probably because the typical messages that are embedded in successful TV programs (and in popular culture in general) emphasize fear and mistrust and express a need for security (Shanahan & Morgan, 1999, p. 40). Gerbner used the term "New Populism" in describing the finding that heavy TV viewers demand the adoption of strong measures against crime and social deviance to make them feel more secure, but are unwilling to support fiscal measures such as tax increases that are needed in order to put these measures into action (Gerbner, 1987b).

Agenda-setting has little to say politically beyond determining that the public would consider (positively or negatively) what the media prominently present (Gross & Aday, 2003). This apolitical stance (Zhu & Blood, 1997) may partly explain why agenda-setting did not face the harsh political criticism that cultivation encountered in the 1970s and 1980s. That criticism hinted more than once that anti-capitalist views drive the theory's proponents.

## A Combined Model for Agenda-setting and Cultivation

We propose a model that intertwines cultivation and agenda-setting into one framework, which we term a *reality construction process.* This is a multi-step model that purports to predict four types of effects: first-order cultivation, second-order cultivation, first-level agenda-setting, and second-level agenda-setting, relating them to media consumption habits and to the manner of presentation of the world in the media. The model consists of paths that can (and should) be tested empirically. Figure 1 presents a scheme of the model.

The arrows stand for correlation coefficients that can be measured by a questionnaire addressed to a heterogeneous sample of media consumers. Media content does not appear in Figure 1 because we limit the model to the processes experienced by media consumers and leave the texts that initiate the process out of the scheme. However, it is understood that a certain presentation of reality in the media is mandatory to ignite the reality construction process, and that this presentation, which is termed "agenda building" in the agenda-setting literature and "institutional process analysis" in cultivation scholarship, is motivated by the political and economic aims of media institutes (Cobb & Elder, 1971; Gerbner, 1973). Our scheme also does not include pertinent factors that may moderate the associations (e.g., demographics), but it is taken for granted that any serious examination of the model would have to consider control variables in order to ascertain that the correlations are non-spurious.

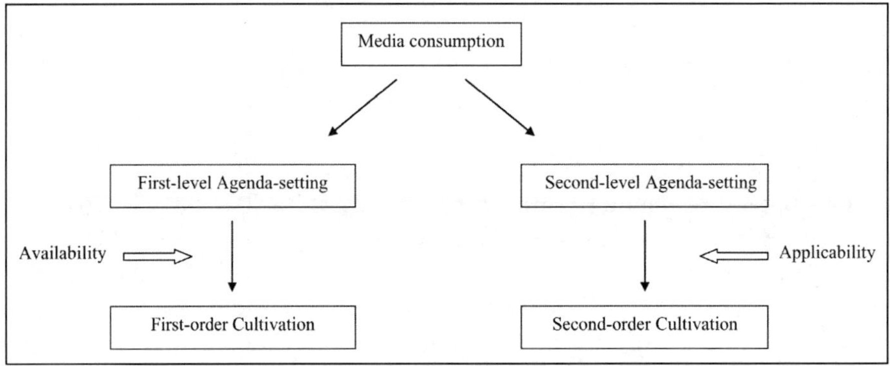


Figure 1. Reality construction model that combines agenda-setting and cultivation

The left path of the model connects media consumption with first-level agenda-setting effects, and first-level agenda-setting with first-order cultivation. The right section of the model connects media consumption with second-level agenda-setting, and second-level agenda-setting with second-order cultivation.

Let us start our discussion with the left path. The dominant heuristic aide in establishing the effects here is *availability*, which prioritizes the processing and retrieval of the most readily available exemplars mainly due to their notable prevalence (Scheufele, 2000). The direct linking of media consumption to the ranking of reality events in the eyes of the audience (public agenda) is an agenda-setting first-level effect. We do not mark a direct path between media consumption and reality estimation (that could represent a first-order cultivation effect) because in our opinion first-order cultivation effects may be contingent and mediated by agenda-setting for a number of reasons. First, as Shrum and his colleagues have demonstrated, set-size judgments, of which first-order cultivation measures are a part, are formed only when a need arises. Heuristic processing of information that occurs when a person is watching TV can start a chain reaction that would lead to a first-order cultivation effect, but the effect itself is established much later (Shrum et al., 2004). Second, from a conceptual standpoint, the ranking of an issue as high on the public agenda (first-level agenda-setting) may explain why people make a mistake in over-assessing this issue's prevalence (first-order cultivation). Likewise, it makes more sense that we over-estimate the frequency of problems that seem important to us (Scheufele, 2000)

The right part of Figure 1 shows how developing attitudes regarding an issue (second-order cultivation) stem from the attributes we ascribe to this issue (second-level agenda-setting).The fact that something is deemed "good" or "bad" (second-level agenda-setting) leads us to favor or reject it (second-order cultivation). The main heuristic aide in this part of the model is applicability, which prioritizes the retrieval of information that seems applicable to the topic (Scheufele, 2000)

Our model is testable for almost any given topic. We have chosen to exemplify it with a topic that is recognized as a hot potato across the western world—the influx of migrant workers. This test of the model relates to the situation in Israel (the authors' country). The current status of migrant workers in Israel is as follows: By the end of 2009, approximately 220,000 residents of foreign countries were residing and working in Israel. Approximately 55% of them had work permits; the rest were working illegally. Altogether, migrant workers constitute 8% of the workforce (Israeli Central Bureau of Statistics, 2010). Two thirds of the migrant workers come from East Asian countries such as Thailand, the Philippines, and China; the rest come from Eastern Europe, particularly Moldova and Russia (Israel Central Bureau of Statistics, 2010). Most of the migrant workers are employed in nursing (60%) and agriculture (25%); the rest work in construction and infrastructure projects or assist in restaurants (Population, Immigration and Borders Authority, 2010).

Migrant workers started to arrive in Israel in significant numbers in the mid-1990s in order to provide cheap labor for an expanding economy and to replace Palestinians who moved to work in the semi-independent Palestinian Authority. The deepening economic recession towards the end of the 2000s brought the migrant workers to the center of the political agenda: On one side of the political fence, right-wing parties call to send them back to their homeland in order to maintain an ethnically homogeneous society and provide work for young inexperienced Israelis; on the other side of the political fence, left-wing activists propose to naturalize the migrant workers on humanitarian grounds (according to present law, migrant workers cannot be naturalized in Israel on the basis of residency tenure).

Our observation and examples from other western countries (see Bauder, 2008) suggest that the issue of migrant workers occupies a salient spot in media reports. Migrant workers appear in news items concerning illegal immigration; their characters also play a considerable role in entertainment fare (e.g., satirical skits, roles in dramatic series, and oriental music troupes that take part in talent competition broadcasts). However, the fact that no content analysis of local media reports on this topic has been published necessitates, as a preliminary step in testing the model, that we conduct a content analysis of relevant Israeli media to assess the actual salience of migrant workers and identify their attributes across the broadcasts. Let us emphasize that the term *relevant media* does not refer solely to *news*. The presentation of migrant workers in *TV drama* or in *reality shows* might be just as relevant. Apart from identifying the share of items concerning migrant workers in the media, the content analysis should also search for statistical facts in the media world whose likelihood would constitute the basis of cultivation first-order measures. Correlating media consumption with first-level agenda-setting indicators (e.g., the relative rank of migrant workers in the list of "most important problems" in the eyes of the public) and then correlating these indicators with first-order cultivation measures (e.g., "What, in your opinion, is the share of migrant workers in the workforce in Israel?") would test the media consumption → first-level agenda-setting → first-order cultivation section of the model (the left path on Figure 1).

The testing of the other part of the model, which describes the relations of media consumption, second-level agenda-setting, and second-order cultivation, would start with the coding of repeating attributes in the description of migrant workers in the media (a potential for a second-level agenda-setting effect and a precursor for attitudes about migrant workers which are evidence of a second-order cultivation effect). The second-level agenda-setting effect would be tested by presenting the respondents with a list of adjectives from which they would have to choose those that best describe, in their opinion, migrant workers (e.g., "industrious," "unreliable," "efficient," "lazy," etc.) and correlating the order in which adjectives are picked up with their relative media prevalence. The measurement of second-order cultivation would use statements that express opinions towards migrant workers, which are related to the above attributes and can be assumed from media texts (e.g., "foreign workers should not be employed because they are unreliable"). The respondents would note their level of agreement or disagreement with the statements. Their level of agreement would be correlated with their level of media consumption. The path between second-level agenda-setting and second-order cultivation would be measured by correlating the tendency to ascribe certain characteristics to migrant workers (e.g., industrious, efficient) with expressing agreement with statements that describe this tendency (e.g., "foreign workers are more diligent than any other workers").

## Suggestions for Further Research

This chapter reviewed points of resemblance and difference between agenda-setting and cultivation and offered a model that combines the two theories into one framework. The actual testing of this model should rely on a large dataset and include a considerable number of potential moderators renowned for their influence on cultivation or agenda-setting (e.g., demographics, attentive exposure to the media) to ascertain the non-spuriousness of the associations. Longitudinal investigations would enable the verification of the direction of the correlations. Specifically, they would teach us whether the perceived importance of topics leads people to see them as overly prevalent (in line with our suggestion that first-level agenda-setting leads to first-order cultivation) or if the perceived frequency of topics leads people to view them as important (which would mean that first-order cultivation leads to first-level agenda-setting). Finally, future studies should also examine the cross-cultural robustness of the model and its applicability to different types of media.

## Acknowledgment

The authors are indebted to the book editors (Michael Morgan, James Shanahan, Nancy Signorielli) for their helpful comments and to Maxwell McCombs for providing insightful suggestions regarding the model, when it was first discussed at a conference on the Development of Agenda-Setting Theory and Research: Between West and East (Wroclaw, Poland, November 2009). Finally, we thank Katarżyna Markiewicz for the careful proofreading

## References

*American attitudes: What Americans think about the issues that shape their lives* (4th ed.). (2005). Ithaca, NY: New Strategist Publications.

Bauder, H. (2008). Foreign farm workers in Ontario (Canada): Exclusionary discourse in the newsprint media. *Journal of Peasant Studies, 35*(1), 100-118.

Bilandzic, H. (2006). The perception of distance in the cultivation process: A theoretical consideration of the relationship between television content, processing experience, and perceived distance. *Communication Theory, 16*(3), 333–355.

Carveth, R., & Alexander, A. (1985). Soap opera viewing motivations and the cultivation process. *Journal of Broadcasting & Electronic Media, 29*, 259–273.

Cobb, R. W., & Elder, C. (1971). The politics of agenda-building: An alternative perspective for modern democratic theory. *Journal of Politics, 33*, 892–915.

Cohen, B. C. (1963). *The press and foreign policy.* Princeton, NJ: Princeton University Press.

Coleman, C. (1993). The influence of mass media and interpersonal communication on societal and personal risk judgments. *Communication Research, 20*(4), 611–628.

Cooper, C. A. (1996). *Violence on television: Congressional inquiry, public criticism, and industry response: A policy analysis.* Lanham, MD: University Press of America.

Domke, D., Shah, D. V., & Wackman, D. (1998). Media priming effects: Accessibility, association and activation. *International Journal of Public Opinion Research, 10*, 51–74.

Dossche, D. (2010, May). *A meta-analysis of cultivation experiments: The priming effect on John and Jane, who are watching prime time television.* Paper presented at the 60th annual meeting of the International Communication Association, Suntec City, Singapore.

Entman, R. M. (1993). Framing: Toward clarification of a fractured paradigm. *Journal of Communication, 43*(4), 51–58.

Eyal, C. H. (1979, May). *The roles of newspapers and television in agenda setting.* Paper presented at the annual meeting of the American Association for Public Opinion Research, Buck Hill Falls, PA.

Fox, W., & Philliber, W. (1978). Television viewing and the perception of affluence. *The Sociological Quarterly, 19*, 103–112.

Funkhouser, G. R. (1973). The issues of the sixties: An exploratory study in the dynamics of public opinion. *Public Opinion Quarterly, 37*(1), 62–75.

Gerbner, G. (1973). Cultural indicators: The third voice. In G. Gerbner, L. Gross, & W. H. Melody (Eds.), *Communications technology and social policy* (pp. 555–573). New York: John Wiley & Sons.

Gerbner, G. (1987a). The electronic church in American culture. *New Catholic World*, May/June, 133–135.

Gerbner, G. (1987b). Television's populist brew: The three Bs. *Et Cetera, 44*(1), 3–7.

Gerbner, G. (2002). TV ratings' deadly choice. In M. Morgan (Ed.), *Against the mainstream: The selected works of George Gerbner* (pp. 474–478). New York: Peter Lang.

Gerbner, G., Gross, L., Eleey, M., Jackson-Beeck, M., Jeffries-Fox, S., & Signorielli, N. (1977). TV violence profile No. 8: The highlights. *Journal of Communication, 27*(2), 171–180.

Gerbner, G., Gross, L., Eleey, M., Jackson-Beeck, M., Jeffries-Fox, S., & Signorielli, N. (1978). Cultural indicators: Violence profile No. 9. *Journal of Communication, 28*(3), 176–207.

Gerbner, G., Gross, L., Signorielli, N., & Morgan, M. (1980a). Aging with television: Images on television drama and conceptions of social reality. *Journal of Communication, 30*(1), 37–47.

Gerbner, G., Gross, L., Morgan, M., & Signorielli, N. (1980b). The "mainstreaming" of America: Violence profile No. 11. *Journal of Communication, 30*(3), 10–29.

Gerbner, G., Gross, L., Morgan, M., & Signorielli, N. (1982). Charting the mainstream: Television's contribution to political orientations. *Journal of Communication, 32*(2), 100–127.

Gerbner, G., Gross, L., Morgan, M., & Signorielli, N. (1986). Living with television: The dynamics of the cultivation process. In J. Bryant & D. Zillmann (Eds.), *Perspectives on media effects* (pp. 17–40). Hillsdale, NJ: Erlbaum.

Gerbner, G., Gross, L., Morgan, M., Signorielli, N., & Shanahan, J. (2002). Growing up with television: Cultivation processes. In J. Bryant & D. Zillmann (Eds.), *Media effects: Advances in theory and research* (2nd ed., pp. 43–67). Mahwah, NJ: Erlbaum.

Ghanem, S. (1997). Filling in the tapestry: The second level of agenda setting. In M. McCombs, D. L. Shaw, & D. Weaver (Eds.), *Communication and democracy: Exploring the intellectual frontiers in agenda-setting theory* (pp. 3–14). Mahwah, NJ: Erlbaum.

Grimes, T., Anderson, J., & Bergen, L. (2008).*Media violence and aggression: Science and ideology.* Thousand Oaks, CA: Sage.

Gross, K., & Aday, S. (2003). The scary world in your living room and neighborhood: Using local broadcast news, neighborhood crime rates, and personal experience to test agenda setting and cultivation. *Journal of Communication, 53*(3), 411–426.

Gross, L., & Jeffries-Fox, S. (1978). What do you want to be when you grow up, little girl? In G. Tuchman, A. K., Daniels, & J. Benet (Eds.), *Hearth and home: Images of women in the mass media* (pp. 240–265). New York: Oxford.

Hawkins, R. P., Pingree, S., & Adler, I. (1987). Searching for cognitive processes in the cultivation effect. *Human Communication Research, 13*(4), 553–577.

Heath, L., & Petraitis, J. (1987). Television viewing and fear of crime: Where is the "Mean World"? *Basic and Applied Social Psychology, 8*, 97–123.

Hester, B., & Gibson, R. (2003). The economy and second-level agenda setting: A time series analysis of economic news and public opinion about the economy. *Journalism & Mass Communication Quarterly, 80*(1), 73–90.

Hetsroni, A. (2010a). When the wind changes direction: The impact of content shift on the cultivation effect. *Communications: The European Journal of Communication Research, 35*(4), 439–460

Hetsroni, A. (2010b, May). *Dangerous liaisons: A cultivation investigation of the relationship between media consumption and economic expectations.* Paper presented at the 60th annual meeting of the International Communication Association, Suntec City, Singapore.

Hetsroni, A., Elphariach, H., Kapuza, R., & Tsfoni, B. (2007). Geographical proximity, cultural imperialism, and the cultivation effect. *Communication Monographs, 74*(2), 181–199.

Hetsroni, A., & Tukachinsky, R. H. (2006). Television-world estimates, real-world estimates, and television viewing: A new scheme for cultivation. *Journal of Communication, 56*(1), 133–152.

Holbrook, R. A., & Hill, T. (2005). Agenda-setting and priming in prime time television: Crime dramas as political cues. *Political Communication, 22*, 277–295.

Hügel, R., Degenhardt, W., & Weiss, H. J. (1989). Structural equation models for the analysis of the agenda-setting process. *European Journal of Communication, 4*, 191–210.

Israeli Central Bureau of Statistics. (2010). *At the end of 2009 in Israel: 118,000 foreign workers who entered with work permits, and 101,000 who entered as tourists.* Retrieved from http://www.cbs.gov.il/reader/newhodaot/ hodaa_template.html?hodaa=201020168

Iyengar, E., Peters, M. D., & Kinder, D. R. (1982). Experimental demonstrations of the "not-so-minimal" consequences of television news programs. *American Political Science Review 76*, 848–858.

Klapper, J. T. (1960). *The effects of mass communication*. Free Press: New York.

Lett, M. D., DiPietro, A. L., & Johnson, D. I. (2004). Examining effects of television news violence on college students through cultivation theory. *Communication Research Reports, 21,* 39–46.

MacKuen, M. B. (1981). Social communication and the mass policy agenda. In M. B. MacKuen & S. L. Combs (Eds.), *More than news: Media power in public affairs* (pp. 19–144). Beverly Hills, CA: Sage.

Matthes, J. (2007). *The need for orientation in agenda-setting theory: Testing its impact in a two-way panel study*. Paper presented at the 57th annual meeting of The International Communication Association, San Francisco, CA.

McCombs, M., & Reynolds, A. (2008). How the news shapes our civic agenda. In J. Bryant & M. B. Oliver (Eds.), *Media effects: Advances in theory and research* (3rd ed., pp. 1–16). London: Routledge.

McCombs, M., & Shaw, D. L. (1972). The agenda setting function of the mass media. *Public Opinion Quarterly, 36*, 176–187.

McLeod, J. M., Becker, L. B., & Byrnes, J. E. (1974). Another look at the agenda-setting function of the press. *Communication Research, 1*, 131–165.

Morgan, M., & Shanahan, J. (2010). The state of cultivation. *Journal of Broadcasting & Electronic Media, 54*(2), 337–355.

Nabi, R. L., & Sullivan, J. (2001). Does television viewing relate to engagement in protective action against crime? A cultivation analysis from a theory of reasoned action perspective.*Communication Research, 28*, 804–825.

Ogles, R. M., & Sparks, G. G. (1989). Television violence and viewers' perceptions of criminal victimization. *Mass Communication Review, 16*(1), 2–11.

Paik, H., & Comstock, G. (1994). The effects of television violence on antisocial behavior: A meta-analysis. *Communication Research, 21*(4), 516–546.

Payne, D. E. (1978). Cross-national diffusion: The effects of Canadian TV on rural Minnesota viewers. *American Sociological Review, 43,* 740–756.

Perse, E. M. (2001). *Media effects and society.* Mahwah, NJ: Erlbaum.

Perse, E. M., Ferguson, D., & McLeod, D. (1994). Cultivation in the newer media environment. *Communication Research, 21*, 79–104.

Population, Immigration and Borders Authority. (2010). *Data of foreign workers in Israel.* Retrieved from http://piba.gov.il/PublicationAndTender/ForeignWorkersStat/Documents/2010Dec.pdf

Potter, W. J. (1988). Three strategies for elaborating the cultivation hypothesis. *Journalism Quarterly, 65*(4), 930–939.

Potter, W. J. (1991) Examining cultivation from a psychological perspective: Component subprocesses. *Communication Research, 18*(1), 77–102.

Potter, W. J. (1993). Cultivation theory and research: A conceptual critique. *Human Communication Research, 19*, 564–601.

Price, V., & Tewksbury, D. (1997). News values and public opinion: A theoretical account of media priming and framing. In F. J. Boster & G. A. Barnett (Eds.), *Progress in the communication sciences,* Vol. 13 (pp. 173–212). New York: Ablex.

Protess, D.L., Leff, D. R., Brooks, S. C., & Gordon, M. T. (1985). Uncovering rape: The watchdog press and the limits of agenda setting. *Public Opinion Quarterly 49*, 19–37.

Rogers, E. M., & Dearing, J. W. (1988). Agenda-setting research: Where has it been, where is it going? *Communication Yearbook 11*, 555–594.

Romer, D., Jamieson, K. H., & Aday, S. (2003). Television news and the cultivation of fear of crime. *Journal of Communication, 53*, 88–104.

Scheufele, D. A. (2000). Agenda-setting, priming, and framing revisited: Another look at cognitive effects of political communication. *Mass Communication & Society, 3*, 297–316.

Shanahan, J., & Morgan, M. (1999). *Television and its viewers: Cultivation theory and research.* Cambridge: Cambridge University Press.

Shaw, D. L., & Martin, S. E. (1992). The function of mass media agenda setting. *Journalism Quarterly, 69*, 902–920.

Shrum, L. J. (2007). Cultivation and social cognition. In D. R. Roskos-Ewoldsen & J. L. Monahan (Eds.), *Communication and social cognition: Theories and methods* (pp. 245–272). Mahwah, NJ: Erlbaum.

Shrum, L. J. (2009). Media consumption and perceptions of social reality: Effects and underlying processes. In J. Bryant & M. B. Oliver (Eds.), *Media effects: Advances in theory and research* (3rd ed., pp. 50–73). London: Routledge.

Shrum, L. J., & Bischak, V. D. (2001). Mainstreaming, resonance, and impersonal impact: Testing moderators of the cultivation effect for estimates of crime risk. *Human Communication Research, 27*, 187–215.

Shrum, L. J., Burroughs, J. E., & Rindfleisch, A. (2004). A process model of consumer cultivation: The role of television is a function of the type of judgment. In L. J. Shrum (Ed.), *The psychology of entertainment media: Blurring the lines between entertainment and persuasion* (pp.177-191). Mahwah, NJ: Erlbaum.

Shrum, L. J., Burroughs, J. E., & Rindfleisch, A. (2005). Television's cultivation of material values. *Journal of Consumer Research, 32*, 473–479.

Takeshita, T. (1997). Exploring the media's roles in defining reality: From issue-agenda setting to attribute-agenda setting. In M. McCombs, D. Shaw, & D. Weaver (Eds.), *Communication and democracy: Exploring the intellectual frontiers in agenda-setting theory* (pp. 15–27). Mahwah, NJ: Erlbaum.

Tims, A. R., Fan, D. P., & Freeman, J. R. (1989). The cultivation of consumer confidence: A longitudinal analysis of news media influence on consumer sentiment. *Advances in Consumer Research, 16*, 758–770.

Tyler, T., & Cook, F. (1984). The mass media and judgments of risk: Distinguishing impact on personal and societal level judgments. *Journal of Personality & Social Psychology, 47*, 693–708.

Wåhlberg, A., & Sjöberg, L. (2000). Risk perception and the media. *Journal of Risk Research, 3*, 31–50.

Wang, T. L. (2000). Agenda-setting online: An experiment testing the effects of hyperlinks in online newspapers. *Southwestern Mass Communication Journal, 15*(2), 59–70.

Wanta, W., & Ghanem, S. (2007). Effects of agenda setting. In R. W. Preiss, B. M. Gayle, N. Burell, M. Allen, & J. Bryant (Eds.), *Mass media effects research: Advances through meta-analysis* (pp. 37–52). Mahwah, NJ: Erlbaum.

Weaver, D. H. (1977). Political issues and voter need for orientation. In D. L. Shaw & M. E. McCombs (Eds.), *The emergence of American public issues: The agenda setting function of the press* (pp. 107–119). St. Paul, MN: West.

Weimann, G. (2000). *Communicating unreality: Mass media and the reconstruction of reality*. Thousand Oaks, CA: Sage.

Winter, J., & Eyal, C. H. (1981). Agenda setting for the civil rights issue. *Public Opinion Quarterly, 45*, 376–383.

Zhu, J. H., & Blood, D. (1997). Media agenda-setting theory: Telling what the public think about. In B. Kovacic (Ed.), *Emerging theories of human communication* (pp. 88–114). Albany, NY: State University of New York Press.

Zucker, H.G. (1978). The variable nature of news media influence. In B. D. Rubin (Ed.), *Communication Yearbook 2* (pp. 225–240). New Brunswick, NJ: Transaction Books.

# 16. Cultivation and the Third-Person Effect

*Donald L. Diefenbach & Mark D. West*

People tend to believe that media messages influence others more than themselves. This is the basic premise of the third-person effect. First articulated by W. Phillips Davison in 1983, the phrase "third-person effect" refers to the idea that the media's "greatest impact will not be on 'me' or 'you,' but on 'them'—the third persons" (p. 3). At first glance the third-person effect seems to be a public opinion measure about the perceived strength and nature of media effects. On the surface this is true. In third-person effects research survey respondents or experimental participants are generally asked how much they believe various types of media messages affect others and how much they believe these same messages affect themselves. The difference between the estimations of influence for "self" and "others" provides an index of a third-person effect. So what does this have to do with cultivation? We posit that the third-person effect can offer additional insights into cultivation as well as interesting avenues for both theory development and research for cultivation scholars as well as for media researchers in general.

## The Third-Person Effect

Although Davison (1983) coined the phrase "third-person effect," he notes in his seminal article that the idea that people tend to believe media messages affect others more than themselves is not new. Davison cites several historical examples of the third-person effect in applied communication practice, including the case of the Japanese dropping propaganda leaflets over the position of an African American unit on Iwo Jima during World War II. The leaflets stated that the Japanese had no quarrel with the African American soldiers and encouraged them to desert the "White man's war." What is interesting to Davison is not the effect that these leaflets had on desertion rates—apparently no one deserted as a result of the leaflets—but rather their effect on the (White) American military commanders who withdrew the unit the next day. Davison observes that it was the *perceived* influence that these leaflets would have on others (the soldiers) that caused the real effect—moving troops.

Davison conducted four small exploratory surveys to systematically test his anecdotal observation of a third-person effect in communication. In all four trials a third-person effect was present. In the decade following Davison's article, thirteen of fourteen published studies demonstrated a third-person effect (Perloff, 1993). Of note to cultivation scholars, two of these early studies centered on entertainment television and both of these reported the presence of a third-person effect (Lasorsa, 1989; Perloff, Neuendorf, Giles, Chang, & Jeffres, 1992).

Paul, Salwen, and Dupagne (2000) conducted a meta-analysis of 32 published and unpublished studies in order to quantify the magnitude of the third-person effect. They converted all measures of self-other disparities to the common *r* metric, to allow easier comparisons across studies, and found the effect to be significant with a mean *r* coefficient of .50. Sun, Pan, and Shen's (2008) more recent and larger-scale meta-analysis of 106 studies concluded that the third-person perception is a robust finding, with difference scores that fall between a "medium" and "large" effect, and equivalent to an overall effect size of .307 when converted to the *r* metric.

Thus, the third-person effect is a reliable phenomenon, but it is important to note that the third-person effect is not a "theory" (Perloff, 1993). Theories seek to explain why effects happen, but the third-person effect starts with the observation of an outcome. Andsager and White (2007) conclude that no one can really say for sure exactly what mechanisms line up to explain third-person effects, and some explanations fit better than others depending on the specific conditions and variables tested, but a number of prominent and plausible explanations have emerged.

Some frequently cited explanations include cognitively based theories such as "biased optimism," which is the idea that people believe that they are less likely than others to encounter negative experiences and negative consequences (e.g., Gunther 1995; Gunther & Mundy, 1993). "Attribution theory" demonstrates that people tend to attribute media influence on the self to the intent of the message or the overall influence of media, but they are more likely to attribute the effects of media on others to their dispositional weaknesses (Gunther, 1991).

Some motivational explanations include a "self-enhancement bias," which predisposes people to project a superior or more positive self-image in making assessments of media influence on self and others (Gunther & Mundy, 1993; Perloff, 2002). Eveland and McLeod (1999) consider third-person effects to be the result of an "ego-defense mechanism," which is of particular value when considering undesirable media content commonly thought to yield negative effects, such as media violence.

In addition to isolating the underlying theories behind the third-person effect, scholars have worked to identify moderating variables that influence the strength of the effect. Some demographic variables are associated with greater third-person effects under some conditions (see Andsager & White, 2007), but these associations are highly variable across studies depending on specific conditions. Perloff (1989) identified involvement as a moderator. People who were more involved in a specific issue were more likely to think that media content would affect others. Increased social distance also yields greater third-person effects (Cohen, Mutz, Price, & Gunther, 1988). On the other hand, Eveland, Nathanson, Detenber, and McLeod (1999) argue that the social distance corollary might be an artifact and found support for perceived "likelihood of exposure" as a predictor of the third-person effect. Sun et al. (2008) determined that message desirability was the most important moderator, with media content perceived as undesirable producing the greatest third-person effects.

Davison (1983) suggested that the third-person phenomenon has a behavioral component—moving troop positions on Iwo Jima, for example. It is this extension to behavioral effects, such as supporting media censorship, which takes the third-person effect out of the realm of a simple curiosity and puts it into a sphere of potentially significant audience effects.

Some studies report the presence of a "reverse third-person effect" (e.g., Cohen & Davis, 1991; Gunther & Thorson, 1992). Specifically, a reverse third-person effect occurs when people believe they personally will be *more* influenced by media messages than others. While negative or antisocial media messages (pornography; media violence) are likely to produce third-person effects, positive or pro-social media messages (health-promoting PSAs, for example) are more likely to result in reverse third-person effects. While third-person effect findings are quite consistent, reverse third-person effects (first-person effects) are less predictable. It seems that respondents are reluctant to admit media influence in many cases even when the content is pro-social.

## Third-Person Effects and Cultivation

The third-person effect was recognized by the 1990s as a tool for developing and integrating established mass communication theories including agenda-setting (Matera & Salwen, 1995) and the spiral of silence (Willnat, 1996). Cultivation has also been explored in conjunction with third-person effects. There are inherent characteristics of the third-person effect that make it a natural for synthesis with cultivation. Media channel is not a significant moderator, so the third-person effect works as well for television as other media (Paul et al., 2000). Also, "The third-person perception occurs for entertainment and news media as often as it does for advertising and other forms of persuasion" (Andsager & White, 2007, p. 11). Most important for integration, however, might be the fact that both the third-person effect and cultivation are, at their core, about the social construction of reality and audience distortions of reality.

Violence on television was central to early cultivation theory and analysis (Gerbner, 1970; Gerbner & Gross, 1976) and is still considered a major component of cultivation today. Similarly, scholars have long utilized media violence as a subject for measuring third-person effects. Innes and Zeitz (1988) were among the first to explore third-person effects questions about media violence. They compared an anti-drunk driving campaign (positive content), a political advertisement (neutral content), and media violence (negative content), and found the greatest third-person effects for media violence. Third-person effects research on the topic of media violence has continued since that time (e.g., Salwen & Dupagne, 2001; Scharrer, 2002) and large violence-related third-person effects have consistently been found (Andsager & White, 2007).

Hoffner et al. (1999) implicitly combined third-person and cultivation research. Respondents were asked the amount of influence they thought television had on shaping their beliefs and the beliefs of others in "viewing the world as a dangerous place (mean-world perceptions)" (p. 732). They also asked about television violence and its effect on aggression on self and others. The third-person effect for aggression predicted support for censorship of television violence, but the third-person effect for mean-world perceptions did not. Hoffner et al. (2001) expanded this line of inquiry in a second study and found a third-person effect for both aggression and mean-world perceptions, and the effects were larger as the social distance between self and others increased.

Recent research has more explicitly linked cultivation and third-person effects. Diefenbach and West (2007) conducted a cultivation analysis that included a message system analysis of network prime-time portrayals of mental health issues. They found TV portrayals to be both false and negative, and that mentally disordered characters were 10 times more likely to be portrayed as violent criminals than other characters. A companion survey found that heavier television viewers were more likely to believe that locating mental health services in residential neighborhoods would endanger the residents and that heavier viewers of television news were less likely to support living next to someone who was mentally ill.

Diefenbach and West also asked respondents to agree or disagree, on a five-point scale, with the following two statements: "Watching television affects my attitudes about mental illness" and "Watching television affects the attitudes of people in general about mental illness." While only 22% agreed that they were personally affected, 58% agreed that television viewing affected others. The cultivation component of the study demonstrates that television affects audience attitudes on mental health issues. The third-person component demonstrates that respondents are correct in identifying that others are affected by television, but what is notable is the general lack of recognition that they themselves are affected. These findings point to the common goals of both cultivation and third-person effects research of examining the construction of social reality, and it is only in this combined methodology that measures can demonstrate the veracity of both audience conceptions and audience views about the source of their beliefs.

Andsager and White (2007) note that there has been relatively little interest in measuring the accuracy of third-person perceptions. Combining cultivation analysis and related third-person questions provides a method for testing the accuracy of third-person perceptions. This combined methodology also offers insights into the question of why some members of the audience might spend time watching television even though they know it makes them vulnerable to negative effects. Third-person research shows that people generally believe cultivation happens, but they also believe it happens to others and not so much to themselves. This finding is a good example of the general fallacy of third-person perceptions articulated by Tiedge, Silverblatt, Havice, and Rosenfeld (1991), who noted that it is not possible for everyone to be correct in their assessment that others are more influenced than themselves.

Several additional studies making direct connections between cultivation and third-person effects emerged in 2008. Fisher (2008) conducted a qualitative analysis using focus groups and individual interviews to explore college students' beliefs about the effects of television on themselves and others. Participants expressed the belief that media content was too violent and that it often does not depict reality. Participants additionally believed that television portrayals affect the way that others dress and act but do not have an effect on them.

Dworznik (2008) examined compassion fatigue and posttraumatic stress disorder in news professionals working in the field. Surveys of news personnel indicated a third-person effect. News professionals recognized that issues of compassion fatigue and posttraumatic stress were potential problems, but they believed that such conditions would affect others more than themselves. This is an interesting spin on third-person effects. Traditional third-person effects research looks at what the audience believes the effects of media exposure are on themselves and others. Dworznik examined what people *creating* media content believe the effects of that process are on themselves and others. Dworznik connects this approach to cultivation as well. Half of the respondents reported trouble separating their work from personal lives, and 43.5% avoided activities that reminded them of violent stories they covered. Dworznik suggests giving journalists a cultivation scale or mean world index in future research to explore the special case of determining the worldview of media professionals cultivated by creating television.

Hennessey, Bleakley, Busse, and Fishbein (2008) combined elements of cultivation and third-person effects research to explore factors that predict support for fining television stations for portrayals of sex and violence. They found that total exposure to television did not predict beliefs about the level of sex and violence on television, but third-person beliefs that sex and violence on television would lead others (teenagers in this case) to engage in sex and violence did predict support for fining television stations.

Jeffres, Neuendorf, Bracken, and Atkin (2008) proposed that the third-person perception can be used as a tool for mass communication theory integration, and they used agenda-setting and cultivation to explore this possibility. They note that since the third-person perception "…is an 'audience perception' of effects…we can literally insert variables from different effects models/theories into the slot" (p. 476). Jeffres et al. asked cultivation-related third-person perception questions about the most enduring variable that can be cultivated over a long period of time: what people think is important in life. In the area of agenda-setting they asked respondents third-person perception questions about what they think media influence is on themselves and others regarding what topics are important to think about. They also tested voting choice. Jeffres et al. note that research has demonstrated greater media influence in producing cognitive effects than in changing affect, values, or behavior, and they see a parallel distinction between agenda-setting and long-term cultivation; accordingly, they predicted that respondents would demonstrate a greater third-person effect on cultivation-related questions than they would on agenda-setting measures. This hypothesis was based on the premise that respondents would be likely to attribute greater media influence on others than self in shaping core values (cultivation) than they would be in estimating the effect on self and others from a simple cognitive association, such as greater media coverage of an issue and its salience as an important issue (agenda-setting). This was supported. A third-person effect was found in all areas tested, and the third-person perceptual gap for cultivation was greater than it was for agenda-setting.

Since 2008 a few additional published studies have made connections between third-person effects and cultivation, but the connections are made only in passing and are not the focus of the research. It is clear there is more that can be added to this promising area of theory development and empirical investigation.

## Projection, Projective Identification, Splitting, and Communication Theory

Can viewers watch hours of television a day and recognize that this lifestyle is distorting their view of reality? Generally, third-person research suggests, they cannot. Using self-enhancement, ego-defense, or other mechanisms, they shift the weight of media effects onto others.

Believing that others are more affected than oneself by television when the facts say that is not the case (Diefenbach & West, 2007) brings to mind the concept of projection. In fact, projection was cited by Perloff (1999, 2002) as a potential mediating process behind the third-person effect, but this theoretical perspective has been virtually absent from the third-person effects literature. We propose that projection and related phenomena—projective identification and splitting—may provide meta-theoretical explanations offering insights into both cultivation and third-person effects.

A primary impediment to growth in mass communication theory has been that the theories we explore are not grounded, in a Mertonian sense (Blau, 1995). While theoretical perspectives such as agenda-setting or cultivation theory may have ample empirical support, they are not justified through recourse to broader theoretical perspectives, such as an appeal to more general theories like functionalism. This appeal to more abstract theoretical levels for justification, which Merton calls "grounding," is an important aspect of the theory-building process in the positivistic approach to sociology (Zhao, 1996). There is little if any linkage between middle-range theories, such as agenda-setting or cultivation, and grander theories that would better allow researchers to posit larger-scale reasons *why* they observe the effects they see. The application of widely accepted psychological or psychosocial theories to communication research could lead to a substantial cross-fertilization between both the domains of psychosociological study and communication research;

it would also enable research areas such as agenda-setting, third-person research, and cultivation analysis—for too long considered separate domains—to examine the psychosocial underpinnings that launch the causal chains of events leading to observed outcomes. Such formal theoretical efforts are more common now than in the past in sociology and related fields (Willer, 1996), and it may be time for theoreticians to attempt a similar grounding of communication theories.

In the case of cultivation, we might pose the question: What sort of psychological process would explain the mean-world view as well as third-person effects? Are there psychological forces, operating *ab initio*, that cause individuals to identify with television actions and events in such a manner that they become unable, in some sense, to differentiate between reality and media depictions of reality? Do individuals, as some research has posited (Ridout, Grosse, & Appleton, 2008), actually come to change their perceptions of desirable public policy concerning national and international affairs as a result of their perceptions of the world as frightening? And can we relate, in a formal sense, those transformations back to fundamental psychological processes that are well recognized and described in the psychological literature?

The concepts of splitting, projection, and projective identification are primary components of object relations theory, which is a descendant of Freudian theory and one of the primary theoretical modes of psychoanalytic understandings of the current era (Greenberg, 1983). Projection, projective identification, and splitting are useful not only in understanding basic psychological and psychosocial processes but also in the analysis of macro-level social processes.

Freud, particularly in his earliest writing, began a discussion of the manner in which the child, unable to tolerate aspects of its personality that it found distressing, would project those aspects onto others, thus "splitting" the personality (Freud, 1987). These theories were more fully developed by his student, Melanie Klein (Klein, 1948; Sayers, 1987). Klein argued that the task of the mature individual is to integrate those cast-off aspects of the self into a coherent whole, which contains both undesirable and desirable attributes, in order to arrive at an accurate perception of the self (Epstein, 1991; Klein, 1975). Rather than being an exotic process associated with mental disorders, projective identification is currently seen as more common. For example, it is a process that occurs when an individual sees a political candidate about whom they know very little, but they conclude as a result of the candidate's folksy portrayal in a television ad that that candidate is "just like them" (Gordon, 1965).

Projective identification is the initial mode by which the young child psychically interacts with the world, and it is gradually replaced by more mature and functional modes of interaction over time in the psychologically healthy adult. While projective identification is generally reduced as people mature, it does not disappear (Kernberg, 1976). Projective identification is commonplace in everyday face-to-face interactions and more distant, electronically mediated modes of observation (Grotstein, 1981).

What we propose here is the notion that such projection is a primary mechanism by which mass communication effects arise. Individuals form pictures of a world from the media, a world in which they imagine others not as they are (Coelho & Figueiredo, 2003), but rather as if they are themselves, or, perhaps better said, *themselves as others*; and in that imagining of themselves in the place of others, they create perceptions of a scary world just like the one they've seen on television. They see a television show about a murder, imagine the good and acknowledged aspects of themselves as the victim, the bad and cast-off aspects of themselves as the murderer, and believe the world to be a mean and dangerous place. The viewer's acknowledged and potent aspects of psychic self are able to resist the negative effects of sexual content, advertising, stereotypes, and violence. The bad and cast-off aspects of themselves, which they project upon others, are not able to resist the influence of such undesirable messages—and so cultivation occurs at the same time as the third-person effect is demonstrated.

## A Study Integrating Cultivation and Third-Person Effects

The literature exploring the intersection of cultivation and third-person effects is small, but what has been published makes significant strides in advancing our understanding. The survey component of Diefenbach and West (2007) explored both cultivation effects and third-person effects, but the analyses were treated separately and the findings for each area were reported in the aggregate. Delving more deeply into the possible interrelationships between cultivation and third-person effects requires further merging of cultivation and third-person variables in the same analysis. This is the objective of this section of the chapter. A regional random-digit dialed survey of 551 respondents conducted in November 2010 asked questions about television viewing levels, beliefs about the real world, and beliefs about the influence of television on self and others.

Consistent with the body of cultivation research, we predicted that heavier television viewers would be more likely to view the world as a mean and dangerous place. We also expected that amount of television viewing would be related to viewers' estimates of the probability of violent crime victimization in the general population, the probability of personal violent crime victimization, and the percentage of households containing firearms.

Third-person effects were tested by asking respondents to estimate the influence that TV has in telling oneself and others what's important in life. This is the operationalization of cultivation utilized by Jeffres et al. (2008) in their third-person effects study. Consistent with previous research and underlying theoretical perspectives (self-enhancement; ego-defense; projection), we predicted that respondents will demonstrate third-person effects in estimating television's impact on cultivating attitudes about what's important in life.

To test whether or not there is evidence that cultivation and third-person effects are directly linked, we predicted that total television viewing—the independent variable in cultivation analysis—will also predict third-person effects on the Jeffres et al. (2008) third-person, cultivation measures. Previous research has tested the relationship between amount of media exposure and third-person effects, but such research has generally been content specific. Increased exposure to news decreases the third-person effect while exposure to entertainment programming increases the effect (Price, Huang, & Tewksbury, 1997). The relationship between *total* television exposure and third-person effects has not been previously tested in a cultivation context. Shanahan and Morgan (1999) argue that total television exposure is the key independent variable in cultivation analysis, and that genre studies, while valuable for other reasons, do not actually test cultivation. Using theories of ego-defense and projection, we predicted there will be a positive relationship between total television viewing and third-person effects on beliefs about the influence of television on self and others in shaping core values.

We recruited 570 respondents from Western North Carolina to participate in a random-digit dialed telephone survey in November 2010; 551 completed the survey. Phone numbers were created from lists of known working exchange COC+1 prefixes, to which randomly generated three-digit suffixes were affixed. The overall response rate after a suitable respondent was contacted was 37%, roughly comparable to other regional studies in North Carolina.

Respondents were asked how many hours of television they watch per day on a typical weekday and how many hours they watch per day on a typical weekend. These responses were weighted and combined to create a measure of average weekly viewing. Three questions were traditional cultivation measures: "Do you think most people would try to take advantage of you if they got a chance or would they try to be fair?"; "Would you say that most of the time people try to be helpful or that they are mostly just looking out for themselves?"; and "Generally speaking, would you say that most people can be trusted or that you can't be too careful in dealing with people?" Three additional questions were designed to measure beliefs about societal violent crime rates, personal likelihood of violent crime victimization, and the percentage of households with guns. Respondents were asked, "What percentage of Americans do you think are victims of a violent crime each year?"; "What do you feel is your risk of being the victim of a violent crime in the next year?"; and "What percentage of households do you think contain firearms?" The societal violent crime rate and households with firearms were recorded as percentage estimates and personal violent crime risk was recorded on a five-point scale of "not at all likely," "slightly likely," "somewhat likely," "very likely," and "extremely likely."

Respondents were asked a pair of cultivation-related third-person effects questions, which assessed beliefs about television's influence on general values and was adapted from items previously used by Jeffres et al. (2008). The questions in our study were "How much influence would you say television has in telling you personally what's important in life?" and "How much influence would you say television has in telling people what's important in life?" Responses were recorded using a four-point scale of "almost no influence," "a little influence," "considerable influence," and "very much influence."

A few notes are needed on cultivation and third-person survey methodology that are relevant to the present research design. Cultivation scholars caution that when respondents are aware or primed that the survey is about media effects it could contaminate cultivation measures (Shanahan & Morgan, 1999). We asked cultivation perception questions first and asked the third-person effects questions and television exposure questions later in the survey, after a battery of unrelated items. Secondly, question order within third-person effects pairs is not a significant moderator of third-person effects. Self/other and other/self pairings yield similar results (Dupagne, Salwen, & Paul, 1999). In the present study the question order was self/other. A number of control variables were recorded including race, age, sex, political views, income, and days per week of newspaper reading.

## *Results*

The mean age of respondents was 60. The western counties of North Carolina are well known for their retirement communities. As a result of the older population, there is also an over-representation of females (60.7%).

Five of the six cultivation hypotheses were supported. Heavier television viewing was associated with all three mean-world measures. People who watched more television also believed the national crime rate was higher and that more households contained firearms. Each relationship was tested using a multiple regression analysis controlling for race, age, sex, political views, income, and days per week of newspaper reading. The only equivocal cultivation-related finding was the relationship between television viewing and estimates of personal likelihood of violent crime victimization. Heavier television viewers were not more likely to think that they personally will be the victim of a violent crime. Tyler & Cook (1984) note that media affect societal-level risk assessments much more than assessments of personal risk, and previous cultivation research has found that TV is less likely to cultivate a sense of personal risk if respondents live in a relatively safe area, which the survey region is.

Respondents demonstrated a third-person effect when asked about the influence of television in telling self and others "what's important in life." On a four-point scale, respondents attributed over a full point more influence of television to others than they did to themselves; this result was statistically significant. This is consistent with the findings of Jeffres et al. (2008), who first used this operationalization of cultivation-related third-person perceptions. These findings replicate established relationships in cultivation and third-person effects and lay the foundation for testing the integrative hypothesis of the present study.

We predicted that total television exposure would be associated with third person-effects when using the Jeffres et al. (2008) cultivation-related third-person effects questions. This was the case, which indicates that cultivation and third-person effects may be interrelated and interactive. However, as seen in Table 1, heavier television viewing resulted in a *reduced* third-person effect. This is the exact opposite of what we expected to find—which raises the question of "How did that happen?"

As reviewed above, Sun et al. (2008) found that message desirability is the most important moderator in determining the strength and direction of third-person effects. Andsager and White (2007) note that while message desirability is a key moderator, researchers rarely allow participants to define the desirability of the message. When media violence is defined as undesirable and a PSA to promote recycling is defined as desirable, this is usually an assumption of the researcher. This might work well for clear-cut content, but what about asking viewers about the influence of television in telling self and others what's important in life? It appears that mass communication scholars can fall into patterns of projection too. We assumed that survey respondents would recognize that much television content is false, negative, sensationalized, exploitive, can have adverse effects on viewers, and that they would generally think that allowing television to tell them what is important in their lives would not be such a keen idea. That assumption was correct across all respondents. Jeffres et al. (2008) found, and we replicated, that respondents demonstrate third-person effects on this question and attribute more media influence to others than to themselves. What we were not able to do in formulating our expectations, however, was to put ourselves into the mind of the heavy viewer. A post-hoc analysis reveals that heavy television viewers are more likely to think that television has an influence on the *self* in guiding beliefs about what's important in life (see Table 2).

Table 1. Regression of respondent beliefs concerning the differential of perception of influence of television upon others and upon self on television viewing habits and demographic variables

| | b coefficient | t | Significant? |
|---|---|---|---|
| Media use | | | |
| Television hours | -.008 | -2.69 | * |
| Days reading newspaper | -.035 | -1.55 | |
| Demographics | | | |
| Race (r is white) | .235 | 0.91 | |
| Age | .002 | 0.38 | |
| Gender | .202 | 1.61 | |
| Income | .132 | 3.14 | * |
| Political Views | | | |
| Conservative | .050 | 0.90 | |

*"How much influence would you say television has in telling you personally what's important in life?"* and *"How much influence would you say television has in telling people what's important in life?"*

Recorded on a four-point scale, with 4 = "Very much influence" and 1 = "Almost no influence."

$n = 320$; $F = 3.38$; $p = 0.01$; $R^2 = 0.07$. *$p < .05$

What is most interesting, however, is that the third-person effects gap on this question closes among heavy viewers. They not only believe that television shapes their beliefs about what's important in life, they also believe that television does this for others. They see themselves as being much like other viewers in this sense. Heavy television viewers apparently do not see other people who watch television as different and vulnerable, onto whom they project negative media effects, but rather they see other viewers as members of their in-group in a projective, parasocial interaction; people much like themselves, in different places, sharing the same television experience. While heavy viewers believe their ideas about what's important in life are impacted by television in a way that is similar to all viewers, the cultivation component for this same sample shows that heavy viewers live in a perceptual world constructed by television

Table 2. Regression of respondent beliefs concerning the influence of television upon self on television viewing habits and demographic variables

| | b coefficient | t | Significant? |
|---|---|---|---|
| Media use | | | |
| Television hours | .006 | 2.82 | * |
| Days reading newspaper | -.002 | -0.13 | |
| Demographics | | | |
| Race (r is white) | -.537 | -2.69 | * |
| Age | .002 | 0.73 | |
| Gender | -.082 | -0.87 | |
| Income | -.051 | -1.58 | |
| Political Views | | | |
| Conservative | -.061 | -1.43 | |

n = 321; F = 2.74; p = 0.01; $R^2$ = 0.06. *p < .05

that tells them what's important in life is suspicion of others and protecting oneself in a world where crime is high and guns are everywhere.

Although Jeffres et al. (2008) did not expressly say it, their question about television and its influence on telling us what's important in life is a semi-projective one. It is without judgment and without the trappings of asking respondents about blatantly undesirable or desirable content. It is a question into which respondents can insert their own ideas about television—not just a genre or type of content but of all television.

Combining cultivation and the third-person effect does not simply provide a public opinion measure of what people think about cultivation effects. It puts us into the mind of the viewer in a way that other measures cannot. We see that the heavy television viewer does not see the world of television as undesirable. We see also that the heavy television viewer believes the level of impact of television on his or her views of what's important in life will be similar for the self and others. This sounds oddly familiar. Heavy television viewers and beliefs shaped in a way that are similar to others? We consider this finding and can't help but wonder if third-person effects in this respect are conceptually linked to one of the most important concepts in cultivation: mainstreaming. This is just one of many important questions for research in cultivation and third-person effects integration to develop in the future.

### *Summary*

The study described here was designed to integrate cultivation analysis and third-person perceptions and found support for both cultivation and third-person effects. The integrative test examining the relationship between total TV viewing and beliefs about the influence of TV in telling oneself and others what's important in life yielded surprising results. The relationship was significant but in the opposite direction as predicted. Heavy TV viewers did not manifest greater third-person effects, as would be predicted by ego-defense mechanics in response to watching a lot of TV, but rather they apparently do not view total TV viewing as having as much potential to do harm as do other people. Heavier TV viewers were more likely to say that television has a larger impact on telling oneself what's important in life. And heavy TV viewers demonstrated a significantly *smaller* third-person effects gap on the issue tested. They believed that other TV viewers were influenced by television to a degree that is similar to themselves. These findings point to the value of third-person effects measures in expanding our understanding of cultivation, and the third-person effects findings we observed support an important premise of cultivation: that heavy television viewers see the world around them in a way that is different from other people.

## Conclusions

Since it was first tested in 1983, the third-person effect has been shown to be a reliable and stable phenomenon. More recently, scholars have proposed that the third-person effect can provide greater understanding of established mass communication theories. Studies integrating cultivation and third-person effects are few but promising. Third-person effects research does not just tell us what people think about cultivation but can serve as a tool to put us into the mind of the television viewer and offer additional insights into the processes that explain *why* cultivation happens.

Future research integrating cultivation and third-person effects would benefit from attention to moderating variables identified in both cultivation and third-person research (e.g., heuristic and systematic processing; cognitive and affective mechanisms; message content) to explore the interaction of cultivation and third-person effects, and to extend understanding of processes underlying both domains. Additionally, future research (with more diverse samples than the one examined here) can use cultivation analysis to measure the accuracy of self and other assessments in third-person research, and third-person questions can offer insight into beliefs and attitudes of the television viewer.

The third-person effect has been proposed as a potentially valuable tool in mass communication theory integration as well. The third-person effect has been previously demonstrated to be related to agenda-setting and the spiral of silence and has been used to connect agenda-setting and cultivation. These syntheses suggest that traditional theories of mass communication, long considered in isolation, may share overlooked similarities and may be elements of a yet elusive larger model. Projection, for example, is a meta-theoretical perspective that can be applied to both cultivation and third-person effects and may prove a useful tool for mass communication theory in the future. We believe that further integration of existing theories through crossover empirical studies will be the most fruitful route toward grounding mass communication theory in the future. The third-person effect will continue to serve as a valuable tool in mass communication theory integration, and cultivation will undoubtedly serve as a cornerstone of any unified model.

## References

Andsager, J. L., & White, A. (2007). *Self versus others: Media, messages, and the third-person effect.* Mahwah, N.J.: Erlbaum.

Blau, P. M. (1995). A circuitous path to macrostructural theory. *Annual Review of Sociology, 21*, 1–19.

Coelho, N. E., Jr., & Figueiredo, L. C. (2003). Patterns of intersubjectivity in the constitution of subjectivity: Dimension of otherness. *Culture & Psychology, 9*(3), 193–208.

Cohen, J., & Davis, R. G. (1991). Third-person effects and the differential impact in negative political advertising. *Journalism Quarterly, 68*, 680–688.

Cohen, J., Mutz, D., Price, V., & Gunther, A. (1988). Perceived impact of defamation: An experiment on third-person effects. *Public Opinion Quarterly, 52*, 161–173.

Davison, W. P. (1983). The third-person effect in communication. *Public Opinion Quarterly, 47*(1), 1–15.

Diefenbach, D. L., & West, M. D. (2007). Television and attitudes toward mental health issues: Cultivation analysis and the third-person effect. *Journal of Community Psychology, 35*, 181–195.

Dupagne, M., Salwen, M. B., & Paul, B. (1999). Impact of question order on the third-person effect. *International Journal of Public Opinion Research, 11*, 334–345.

Dworznik, G. J. (2008). *The psychology of local news: Compassion fatigue and posttraumatic stress in broadcast reporters, photographers, and live truck engineers.* (Unpublished doctoral dissertation). Kent State University.

Eveland, W. P., & McLeod, D. M. (1999). The effect of social desirability on perceived message media impact: Implications for third-person perceptions. *International Journal of Public Opinion Research, 11*, 315–333.

Eveland, W. P., Nathanson, A. I., Detenber, B. H., & McLeod, D. M. (1999). Rethinking the social distance corollary: Perceived likelihood of exposure and the third-person perception. *Communication Research, 26*, 275–302.

Fisher, S. M. (2008). *Perceptions of programming: Cultivation and third person influences on college students.* (Unpublished masters thesis). University of South Florida.

Freud, S. (1987). The origin and development of psycho-analysis: First and second lectures. *The American Journal of Psychology, 100*(3/4), 472–488.

Gerbner, G. (1970). Cultural indicators: The case of violence in television drama. *The Annals of the American Academy of Political and Social Science, 388*(1), 69–81.

Gerbner, G., & Gross, L. (1976). Living with television: The violence profile. *Journal of Communication, 26*(2), 172–194.

Gordon, R. (1965). The concept of projective identification. *Journal of Analytical Psychology, 10*(2), 127–149.

Greenberg, J. R. (1983). *Object relations in psychoanalytic theory.* Cambridge, MA: Harvard University Press.

Grotstein, J. S. (1981). *Splitting and projective identification: Classical psychoanalysis and its applications.* New York: J. Aronson.

Gunther, A. C. (1991). What we think others think: Cause and consequences of the third-person effect. *Communication Research, 18*, 355–372.

Gunther, A. C. (1995). Overrating the X-rating: Third-person perception and support for censorship of pornography. *Journal of Communication, 45*(1), 27–38.

Gunther, A. C., & Mundy, P. (1993). Biased optimism and the third-person effect. *Journalism Quarterly, 70*, 58–67.

Gunther, A. C., & Thorson, E. (1992). Perceived persuasive effects of product commercials and public service announcements: Third-person effects in new domains. *Communication Research, 19*, 547–596.

Hennessy, M., Bleakley, A., Busse, P., & Fishbein, M. (2008). What is the appropriate regulatory response to wardrobe malfunctions? Fining stations for television sex and violence. *Journal of Broadcasting & Electronic Media, 52*, 387–407.

Hoffner, C., Buchanan, M., Anderson, J. D., Hubbs, L. A., Kamigaki, S. K., Kowalczyk, L.,...Silberg, K. J. (1999). Support for censorship of television violence: The role of the third-person effect and news exposure. *Communication Research, 26*, 726–742.

Hoffner, C., Plotkin, R. S., Buchanan, M., Anderson, J. D., Kamigaki, S. K., Hubbs, L. A.,...Pastorek, A. (2001). The third-person effect in perceptions of the influence of television violence. *Journal of Communication, 51*, 283–299.

Innes, J. M., & Zeitz, H. (1988). The public's view of the impact of mass media: A test of the 'third-person' effect. *European Journal of Social Psychology, 18*, 457–463.

Jeffres, L. W., Neuendorf, K., Bracken, C. C., & Atkin, D. (2008). Integrating theoretical traditions in media effects: Using third-person effects to link agenda-setting and cultivation. *Mass Communication & Society, 11*, 470–491.

Kernberg, O. F. (1976). *Object-relations theory and clinical psychoanalysis: Classical psychoanalysis and its applications.* New York: J. Aronson.

Klein, M. (1948). *Contributions to psycho-analysis, 1921–1945. International psycho-analytical library, no. 34.* London: Hogarth Press.

Klein, M. (1975). *The psycho-analysis of children.* New York: Delacorte Press/S. Lawrence.

Lasorsa, D. L. (1989). Real and perceived effects of "Amerika." *Journalism Quarterly, 66*, 373–378, 529.

Matera, F. R., & Salwen, M. B. (1995). Issue salience and the third-person effect: Perceptions of illegal immigration. *World Communication, 28*(3), 11–27.

Paul, B., Salwen, M. B., & Dupagne, M. (2000). The third-person effect: A meta-analysis of the perceptual hypothesis. *Mass Communication & Society, 3*(1), 57–85.

Perloff, R. M. (1989). Ego-involvement and the third person effect of televised news coverage. *Communication Research, 16*, 236–262.

Perloff, R. M. (1993). Third-person effect research 1983–1992: A review and synthesis. *International Journal of Public Opinion Research, 5*(2), 167–184.

Perloff, R. M. (1999). The third-person effect: A critical review and synthesis. *Media Psychology, 1*, 353–378.

Perloff, R. M. (2002). The third-person effect. In J. Bryant & D. Zillmann (Eds.), *Media effects: Advances in theory and research* (2nd ed., pp. 489–506). Mahwah, NJ: Erlbaum.

Perloff, R. M., Neuendorf, K., Giles, D., Chang, T. K., & Jeffres, L. W. (1992). Perceptions of "Amerika." *Mass Communication Review, 19*, 42–48.

Price, V., Huang, L. N., & Tewksbury, D. (1997). Third-person effects of news coverage: Orientations toward media. *Journalism and Mass Communication Quarterly, 74*, 525–540.

Ridout, T. N., Grosse, A. C., & Appleton, A. M. (2008). News media use and Americans' perceptions of global threat. *British Journal of Political Science, 38*(4), 575–593.

Salwen, M. B., & Dupagne, M. (2001). Third-person perception of television violence: The role of self-perceived knowledge. *Media Psychology, 3*, 211–236.

Sayers, J. (1987). Melanie Klein, psychoanalysis, and feminism. *Feminist Review, (25)*, 23–37.

Scharrer, E. (2002). Third-person perception and television violence: The role of out-group stereotyping in perceptions of susceptibility effects. *Communication Research, 29*, 681–704.

Shanahan, J., & Morgan, M. (1999). *Television and its viewers: Cultivation theory and research.* Cambridge: Cambridge University Press.

Sun, Y., Pan, Z., & Shen, L. (2008). Understanding the third-person perception: Evidence from a meta-analysis. *Journal of Communication, 58*, 280–300.

Tiedge, J. T., Silverblatt, A., Havice, M. J., & Rosenfeld, R. (1991). Discrepancy between perceived first-person and perceived third-person mass media effects. *Journalism Quarterly, 68*, 141–154.

Tyler, T. R., & Cook, F. L. (1984). The mass media and judgments of risk: Distinguishing impact on personal and societal level judgments. *Journal of Personality and Social Psychology, 47*, 693–708.

Willer, D. (1996). The prominence of formal theory in sociology. *Sociological Forum, 11*(2), 319–331.

Willnat, L. (1996). Mass media and political outspokenness in Hong Kong: Linking the third-person effect and the spiral of silence. *International Journal of Public Opinion Research, 8*, 187–211.

Zhao, S. (1996). The beginning of the end or the end of the beginning? The theory construction movement revisited. *Sociological Forum, 11*(2), 305–318.

# 17. Cultivation and the Spiral of Silence

## Theoretical and Empirical Intersections

*James Shanahan & Dietram Scheufele*

Two of the most frequently cited theories of media effects are cultivation and the spiral of silence (Noelle-Neumann, 1993). Surprisingly, though, the theories have not often been considered in relation to each other, even though they do share some important similarities. In this chapter, we point out some of these similarities, and then propose ways to examine the two theories together, empirically.

## Cultivation and the Spiral of Silence: "Powerful" Media

Both cultivation and the spiral of silence emerged around the same time, so they inevitably share some historical roots. Most notably, in the early 1970s both theories outlined a view of social-level media effects that was more "powerful" than what had been advocated by many theorists in the wake of Lazarsfeld et al.'s widely accepted limited effects models (Katz & Lazarsfeld, 1955; Klapper, 1960; Lazarsfeld, Berelson, & Gaudet, 1948). While media effects research was never truly characterized *only* by a fascination with "propaganda" or "magic bullet"-type effects—as some received histories of the early studies argue—the dominant view by the 1950s and 60s was certainly one that minimized supposed media power. Moreover, any adherence to a powerful media view was often characterized as unscientific (e.g., Klapper, 1960). However, neither George Gerbner nor Elisabeth Noelle-Neumann, as theoretical architects, seemed at all discomfited by the possibility that their proposals would be poorly received as going against theoretical orthodoxy.

It is Noelle-Neumann who is usually associated with the idea of a "return" to a powerful mass media, especially due to her 1973 article with that title (Noelle-Neumann, 1973). Somewhat surprisingly, Gerbner's name is less often mentioned with this move, even though cultivation deals very explicitly with the broad, social-level power of mass media. Peter (2004), for instance, lays out the following list of scholars dealing with media power:

> Along with Tichenor, Donohue, and Olien's (1980) study on the knowledge gap hypothesis and McCombs and Shaw's (1972) article on agenda-setting, Noelle-Neumann's (1973) publication is often considered the turning point in the development from the notion of limited effects to the rediscovery of powerful mass media....(p. 144)

Even more surprising is that Gerbner's name did not come up given Noelle-Neumann's (1993) now widely accepted definition of the "powerful effects paradigm." Strong media effects, she argues, are a function of (a) ubiquitous and (b) consonant media coverage. In other words, certain issues are covered in a consistent fashion across different media outlets. Or as Peter recaps: "The basic idea is that, if all media depict and evaluate an issue similarly, citizens hardly have a chance not to be exposed to that information" (2004, p. 145). Both Noelle-Neumann and Peter describe a situation that, of course, is also central to cultivation theory. Gerbner's idea that a message "system" tends to encompass all television viewers to some extent, even light viewers, is quite similar to Noelle-Neumann's ideas about message "consonance" and her related concept of "media tenor." For Noelle-Neumann, the "tenor" is the overall tone or attitude of repeated and frequent media coverage, usually on political issues. As we will see below, it is a concept with many congruencies and parallels to Gerbner's ideas of what heavy television viewers see.

Perhaps the greatest unstated distinction between the research approaches that Peter is describing and cultivation is the fact that cultivation focuses on stories, while the other theories (and spiral of silence to some degree) focus almost exclusively on news. Still, even a cursory examination shows that both Gerbner and Noelle-Neumann are dealing with a conception of mass media as an extremely important institution with significant influence. Since they were putting forth their ideas at around the same time, why are they not linked more often? Especially since they are both still frequently cited and remain among the few multi-level models of media effects, an up-to-date appraisal of their connections and intersections would be of great value.

## Gerbner and Noelle-Neumann: European Scholars using Social Science Methods

First, we do know that Gerbner and Noelle-Neumann were aware of what each other was doing. Gerbner's correspondence[1] contains several exchanges between the two. Noelle-Neumann had an email exchange with Gerbner (in his function as editor of the *Journal of Communication*) about her later-to-become-seminal publication on the spiral of silence in that journal.[2] Noelle-Neumann was also interested in Gerbner's TV violence studies, as she was preparing to play a similar role in consulting about possible German legislation on TV violence. In her most substantive exchange with Gerbner, she commented on one of Gerbner's seminal papers: "…I felt very much in agreement with your statement that instead of studying media effectiveness using individual programs it should be studied for the entire system" (in reference to Gerbner, 1969; Gerbner/Noelle-Neumann correspondence, Sept. 4, 1981). In this brief exchange she highlights perhaps one of the most important similarities of the two theories: Both Gerbner and Noelle-Neumann were interested in mass media as a macro-level social institution. They were less moved by the many and various experimental demonstrations (or lack thereof) of media "effects" (although Noelle-Neumann often drew on some of this experimental research on conformity, as we outline below). For Gerbner, his tendency toward a macro-level understanding of mass media was greatly influenced by various interests that could be subsumed under the idea of "culture" (including humanistic concerns such as folklore and poetry). That is, collective and mass storytelling and reception was his main interest. For Noelle-Neumann, her experiences in the Europe of the 1930s and 1940s could not have failed to have an impact on a macro-level understanding of mass media as a possibly monolithic institution of state power. Even a casual student of Noelle-Neumann will see that she was widely read, as she undergirded her theory with ideas drawn from the major thinkers of the European Enlightenment (Locke, Rousseau, Hobbes, etc.). Her interests were wide, and her work is of value as much for the very skillful weaving of historical strands of thinking about public opinion as it is for any hypothesis testing that was done within its framework. For both Gerbner and Noelle-Neumann, then, there was much more behind the theory than the rather sterile social science "theoretical" summaries that appear in so many articles, then and now.

However, unlike many European scholars who pondered mass media effects in deep philosophical terms, both Gerbner and Noelle-Neumann were willing to subject their ideas to tests using data, particularly using essentially the same techniques that would be used by "positivists," "empiricists," and other scholars using quantitative methods. And again, both Gerbner and Noelle-Neumann understood that *both* content analysis and survey data would be needed to come to a comprehensive understanding of, and convincingly demonstrate, media effects.

Gerbner and Noelle-Neumann carried these influences in different directions (see below), but they both go against the stereotypical view that Europeans would not use empirical methods. Thus, cultivation and spiral of silence in the end become theories that combine the historical and philosophical underpinnings of centuries of European philosophy with modern methods (often seen as American in origin) of data collection and analysis. They both require content analysis and survey data, and they both focus on media from a macro-social perspective.

## The Theories in Relation to Each Other: Propositions and Questions

The spiral of silence, of course, is the idea that peoples' perception of public opinion on an issue influences their willingness to speak out—or rather, to remain silent. When an individual perceives that the majority is against or turning against a position that he or she holds, the individual is more likely to avoid expressing that view. The idea is most famously seen in Noelle-Neumann's "train-test." In a typical survey item, respondents are asked to evaluate whether they would be willing to discuss a controversial issue with a traveling companion (specifically, a stranger in a European-style train compartment) if the stranger is perceived as holding an opinion divergent from one's own. While many of the studies testing the spiral of silence have focused on this phenomenon exclusively (see Glynn, Hayes, & Shanahan, 1997 for a review), there is more to the theory. The first column in Table 1 reviews the complete set of "questions" that Noelle-Neumann says need to be in place to provide a true test of the theory.

A focus simply on narrow mechanisms of conversational avoidance tapped in the train-test portion of the spiral of silence might leave one wondering how this is a theory of media effects at all. Really, the media factor into the theory at the end (question 6). That is, when the media are seen as favoring a particular viewpoint, public opinion is seen as being inevitably swayed toward that view; as more and more people perceive that their opinion on an issue might not be shared, they tend to restrict their expression of it. This is the "spiral" of silence, where the media "tenor" (again, the overall slant or take that the media portray on any given issue) affects people's expression of views, which is in turn again taken up by the media. Noelle-Neumann is very strong on this point:

> Not in a single instance has the process of the spiral of silence run counter to the line taken by the media. The fact that an individual is aware that his opinion is supported by the media is an important factor in determining that person's willingness to speak out. (Noelle-Neumann, 1993, p. 201)

Table 1. Questions and propositions about the spiral of silence and cultivation

| Noelle-Neumann's "Questions" | Shanahan and Jones' (1999) "propositions" about cultivation |
|---|---|
| 1.Using representative surveys, the distribution of public opinion on a given issue should be determined | 1. Institutions of mass communication are controlled by social, cultural and primarily economic elites. |
| 2. The climate of opinion must be assessed, the individual's opinion on "What do most people think"? | 2. Social and economic elites codify messages in their media that serve elite aims |
| 3. How does the public think the issue will develop: Which side will gain strength; which side will lose ground? | 3. Messages in media content can be empirically studied. |
| 4. The willingness to speak out on a particular issue, or the tendency to remain silent, especially in public, should be measured. | 4. Audience members, while perhaps seeking to serve individual needs, participate in a process in which they hear and internalize messages of elites |
| 5. Does the issue in question bear a strong moral or emotional component? Without such a component, there is no pressure of public opinion and therefore no spiral of silence. | 5. Audience members more "committed" to media will have belief structures more consonant with beliefs desired by social elites. |
| 6. What is the position of the media on this issue? Which side do the influential media support? | |

Note:From Noelle-Neumann (1993); see also Scheufele and Moy (2000).

Interestingly, Noelle-Neumann bases much of her theory on social psychology, especially the famous conformity studies of Asch (1956) and others. She apparently had no qualms about using experimental findings where they seemed consistent with her own macro-level views. But the finding that individuals' willingness to express viewpoints is strongly influenced by the social context is given its full sociological impact by connecting it to media. Mass media are seen as the broadest possible influence on the individual's opinion and willingness to express it. Equally importantly, media are an influence on what individuals think about other peoples' beliefs. When media emphasize an issue a certain way, the impact on the individual is seen as almost automatic. In this way, a fundamentally individual and group process (opinion formation and expression) is given meaning in the context of mass communication. Noelle-Neumann's test of the media effect is most often seen by comparing opinion trends to content data over time (which makes it, like cultivation, a multi-level theory of media effects).

Gerbner's approach is different in that it actually starts with the media. This can be seen in the "propositions" about cultivation that were developed by Shanahan and Jones (1999, see the second column in Table 1). As analyzed by Shanahan and Jones, cultivation begins with the proposition that media are controlled by elites (compare to Noelle-Neumann who brings in media at the end of a series of questions that really deal with interpersonal and group processes). For Gerbner, the foundational assumption is therefore more "critical" than Noelle-Neumann's. Also, it would not be a stretch to say that Gerbner was probably more activist in his leanings. Noelle-Neumann was well known for her commercial public opinion research efforts on behalf of the Christian Democratic Union (the main conservative party in Germany), while Gerbner was often cast in an adversarial role against the TV networks and their inherently conservative and commercial bias (he explicitly pursued media activism at the end of his career). Thus, while many have treated cultivation as a fairly simple theory of media effects (using an overly simplified stimulus-response model), in Gerbner's work and that of the Cultural Indicators research team there was always a focus on the *institution* of television (and this is why Gerbner himself insisted that some sort of "institutional process analysis" be part of the research picture).

It is therefore ironic that both Noelle-Neumann and Gerbner saw systemic ideological biases in the media system but in diametrically opposite directions (Scheufele & Moy, 2000). Noelle-Neumann often attributed biases in media coverage to the political leanings of journalists who—as a profession—tend to be significantly to the left of the general population. Gerbner—in contrast—argued that media content bears the imprint of the organizations, and *not the individuals*, who produce it. He held the ownership structures and the commercial imperatives of mass media responsible for messages that promoted a "Mean World Syndrome." He did not share a view of liberal media bias like that perceived by Noelle-Neumann; rather, he saw television "blurring, blending, and bending" the views of viewers toward a more conservative mainstream (see Gerbner et al., 1982).

Nonetheless, there is a lot of overlap among the questions and propositions outlined in both theories. In a way, Noelle-Neumann articulates a process that can be completed by a cultivation model. In questions 1–4, Noelle-Neumann is identifying the key variables for describing the state of public opinion on a given issue. For her theory, it was important to be specific about these variables because so many previous studies had not paid attention to issues of perception, which Noelle-Neumann referred to as the "normative" aspect of public opinion. Much research had simply assumed that public opinion was essentially the accumulation of individual opinions. One of Noelle-Neumann's most important contributions among media theorists, therefore, was to highlight that what we think about what others think—accurately or not—is just as important as what they actually think (Scheufele, Shanahan, & Lee, 2001). Of course, Lippmann (1922) and others made similar observations, albeit less systematically, before her, which she readily acknowledged.

Once she cements her key observation, which is that public opinion is a kind of "social skin" that is very responsive to social pressures, the observation that "media tenor" plays a key role follows very naturally.

Gerbner was less concerned with the individual aspects of the opinion formation process, and it's not clear what he would have said about, for instance, the Asch conformity studies. But the propositions outlined in Table 1, and of course Gerbner's own work, are quite clear that a process of message selection is occurring in television whose main outcome can only be in the end a greater (though not complete and total) convergence of opinion (or feeling, belief, attitude, whatever is being studied by cultivation). Thus, the propositions of cultivation theory, when added serially to those given by Noelle-Neumann, create a mass-level and critically focused extension of the work of spiral of silence theory. In brief, the spiral of silence explains how individuals use their social sense (a "quasi-statistical organ" in Noelle-Neumann's parlance) to understand where they and their opinions fit in the social world; cultivation expands on these observations, identifying media as an elite-driven institution with specific messaging goals, leading to cultivation's conclusions about consonance of messages (Gerbner's "message system") and the resultant homogenization of views (as seen in the "cultivation differential" and the process of mainstreaming).

Thus, while neither Noelle-Neumann nor Gerbner intended their work in any way to be an articulation of what the other was doing, Noelle-Neumann's questions do lead one rather naturally to the propositions of cultivation (and the connection is not without irony, given the political predispositions of the two). Conversely, those beginning with an interest in cultivation can find a meso-level explanation of cultivation effects in the spiral of silence's propositions. To extend this discussion, we look at how the theories meet up on the issue of social control.

### *Social Control*

In an edited volume *Mass Media, Social Control, and Social Change* (Demers & Viswanath, 1999), chapters on cultivation and the spiral of silence appeared next to each other. Noelle-Neumann's chapter (1999) is really a personal history of the idea of powerful media effects. Along the way, she makes a number of comments that are quite consistent with cultivation. Early on, in a connected series of observations, we get the following:

> As a rule, a single communication transported by the mass media is weak, whereas strong media effects are cumulative in nature . . .
>
> . . . the effects are for the most part unconscious, so that direct questions are hardly helpful.
>
> No wonder someone once sarcastically said that much of media effects

> research resembles trying to determine the effect of smoking based on the effects of inhaling the smoke from just one cigarette. (p. 54)

The parallels with cultivation are obvious. Still, Noelle-Neumann was describing her views on media effects generally, not cultivation specifically. Later in the chapter, she cites Gerbner's work as part of the various research strands that were using both content analysis and survey research to establish longer-term and cumulative effects of media. She also highlights the importance of television specifically (pp. 61–63). While her chapter does not explicitly address social control, the connection to a powerful media with specific interests to promote is easily made. Media exert a long-term influence on the structure and valence of opinion. This, in her view, is most readily seen in news content and its effects on political views, but there is no reason why these effects could not be seen in other domains. And cultivation was, of course, starting to investigate these effects in both political and non-political realms.

In Shanahan and Jones' (1999) chapter in the same book, the implications of cultivation for social control are laid out explicitly. Gerbner, as mentioned, was not shy about taking on the media, and it was always clear that he had a very critical view of a storytelling system that was based on having, to paraphrase one of his favorite slogans, "something to sell rather than something to tell." However, the critical ramifications of cultivation were often misunderstood for a variety of reasons. Methodological debates sometimes focused attention on very specific issues such as controlling for spuriousness or subgroup analyses (see Shanahan & Morgan, 1999, for a review). The intensity of these debates often pushed critical questions into the background. Also, the emphasis on cultivation (as opposed to the message system analysis) meant that the complete picture of Cultural Indicators (CI) research was not always seen. Cultivation has often been reduced to simply looking at the statistical relationship between exposure and belief/attitude (and attempts to debunk it); the richer theoretical observations that are laced all through the work of the CI research team are sometimes obscured.

When they are revealed again, the connections with spiral of silence theory are also more easily seen. One point made in the analysis by Shanahan and Jones is that cultivation can be seen from a functionalist perspective. Although functionalism has its critics, Noelle-Neumann was also interested in the functions of media. Thus, compare two arguments, first Shanahan and Jones commenting on why media messages serve elite aims:

> While it has never been shown that media professionals systematically conspire to use violence to serve goals of social control, the cultivation argument was that these messages served the needs of institutions wanting to preserve perceptions

> of the need for authority and power. While individual intentions could not be shown (and the individual intentions may not even exist), cultivation argued that the 'system' required such performance from its mass media. Essentially, a 'functionalist' argument was used to indicate that such messages persist precisely because they tend to perpetuate the systems that depend on them. (Shanahan & Jones, 1999, p. 44)

Noelle-Neumann devotes the entire last chapter of her book (1993) to an examination of manifest and latent functions of mass media. For Noelle-Neumann, the latent function of public opinion (and mass media) was explicitly social control. While public opinion's manifest function was to "form opinion" in a democracy, the more interesting and less-recognized role was to set the boundaries for discourse (see discussion in Noelle-Neumann, 1993, pp. 227–229).

> . . . the concept of 'public opinion as social control' affects *all* members of society. Since participation in the process that threatens isolation and prompts fears of isolation is not voluntary, social control exerts pressure both on the individual, who fears isolation, and on the government—it too will be isolated and eventually toppled without the support of public opinion. (Noelle-Neumann, 1993, p. 228)

While Gerbner would probably have been more likely to see social control operating on publics than on the government, both Gerbner and Noelle-Neumann are describing a system of social control that operates above and apart from just the actors involved. Or, perhaps more accurately, they are describing a system in which no single actor can control outcomes, but in which aims of social control are served by the mass media and other large-scale actors. In Noelle-Neumann's terms, this is a latent function that needs to be unearthed and examined as directly as the manifest functions of democratic opinion formation; in Gerbner's terms this was probably always a manifest function of an explicitly profit-oriented media system. As he frequently noted, in cultivation television was seen as the cultural arm of the industrial order fulfilling a function previously served by religion.

Even given the distinctions in their views of media functions, both are relatively unique among media theorists who used explicitly empirical methods of data collection and analysis. Unlike the tendency of most American researchers to use "positivist" methods to divorce their findings from critical or wider social implications, Gerbner and Noelle-Neumann both saw mass media as playing a critical role (function) in the maintenance of social order and—in Noelle-Neumann's case—social norms, and they were willing to subject these claims to tests that could be examined, replicated, and criticized by both critical and social science-oriented researchers.

Based on these conceptual comparisons, in the remainder of this chapter we explore how cultivation and the spiral of silence can be empirically tested "side by side." Demonstrating the conceptual linkages between the two theories is interesting, but future work to tie them together will need models of data analysis that permit the linked questions to be answered.

## Ideas for Empirical Tests of Cultivation and Spiral of Silence

There are very few empirical tests of cultivation and the spiral of silence "side by side" in the same dataset or in the same study. Perhaps unsurprisingly, for reasons discussed above, students trained in the traditions of either of the two theories have not been inclined to examine their data from the perspective of the "other." But such tests should be relatively easy to accomplish, even if they don't yield results as neat as what might be suggested from the foregoing discussion. And, we believe that many existing datasets are likely to have the minimum set of variables that would be required.

One of the simplest possible models for testing the two theories is shown in Figure 1. The top row of the figure represents a cultivation hypothesis; the bottom is a spiral of silence hypothesis. They are linked (dashed arrow) by an association between estimates of a phenomenon in the real world and estimates of opinion about that phenomenon.

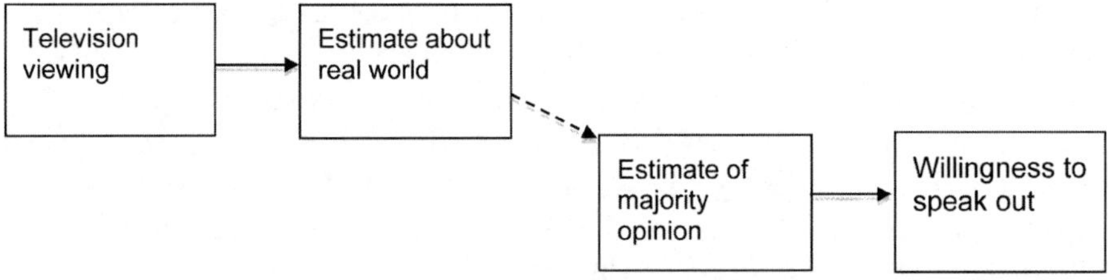


Figure 1. Schematic model linking cultivation and spiral of silence

The hypotheses embodied in the model are as follows:

H1 (the upper level of the figure): Television viewing is associated with estimates about the real world (cultivation).

H2 (the link [dashed arrow] between the upper and lower levels): Estimates of real world phenomena are related to perceptions of the opinion climate (this is related to and derived from the "quasi-statistical sense" of Noelle-Neumann; see pp. 9–16 in Noelle-Neumann, 1993).

H3 (the lower level of the figure): Perception of opinion climate is related to willingness to speak about an issue (the spiral of silence).

To explore how these hypotheses might work with a real issue, we'll look at perceptions about smoking. Noelle-Neumann examined this issue in her book; it has some of the features of being morally "loaded" (which Noelle-Neumann says is necessary for an issue to be subject to opinion spirals), and it has a very public dimension. Perceptions about smoking have changed radically in the past decades, and it's an issue that people can speak about in public. Asking someone not to smoke in a train compartment (the operationalization given by Noelle-Neumann) is something that could have happened to most people up until recently. Thus, as a test issue for the spiral of silence it is a good fit. Similarly, because smoking is portrayed with some regularity on TV, there are natural assumptions that can be made about the cultivation of acceptance of smoking. In the next sections we'll look at some literature related to these hypotheses.

### *Smoking and the Media*

Prior to hypothesizing, all analyses of cultivation or the spiral of silence need to begin with content analysis. What are the media saying about the issue? Concerning smoking, there are numerous studies on which to build. Content analytic studies have been used to show to what extent smoking is prevalent in media content. Particularly after the decision was taken to ban smoking ads on U.S. television in 1970, the rate of appearance of smoking in mass media program content became an important issue. In general, the frequency of the portrayal of smoking in media has decreased since those early days, along with decreasing smoking rates in the population.

Breed and De Foe (1984) found that tobacco use in the media declined (and alcohol use increased) from the 1950s through the early 1980s, with considerably less smoking portrayed in the 1981–82 television season. Examining trends, Cruz and Wallack (1986), in a sample from the fall of 1984, found one smoking act per hour of programming, with more smoking in dramas than situation comedies; two-thirds of smokers were lead characters, with 70 percent cast in strong, enduring roles. Hazan and Glantz (1995), in a sample of network programs from the fall of 1992, found that 24 percent of programs contained at least one tobacco event; 92 percent were pro-tobacco events, while eight percent were anti-smoking messages. They argue that higher rates of smoking occur on television than in real life. However, another study found that on television (in 1998–99):

> One in five episodes (19 percent) portrayed tobacco use. No characters under the age of 18 were shown using tobacco. Eight percent of adult major characters used tobacco. Twenty-three percent of episodes that showed tobacco use expressed negative statements about smoking. Overall, teen viewers were exposed to relatively little tobacco use. These episodes avoided underage tobacco use and presented adult use to a limited extent. (Christenson, Henriksen, & Roberts, 2000, p. 4)

This study also concluded that smoking was portrayed with decreasing frequency on television.

The data tend to confirm the impression that we see smoking *less* on television than in real life. In general, TV characters smoke at a rate *lower than* the real world. Actual smoking rates are in the low 20 percent range, varying by state (Centers for Disease Control, 2000). Thus, from a cultivation standpoint, we would hypothesize that heavy television viewers will *under*estimate the extent to which people smoke in the real world. Thus, based on changes in content patterns over time, while early studies on cultivation and smoking would have tested the hypothesis that television cultivates perceptions that there are more smokers, nowadays we would assume the opposite. At the same time, we should note that heavy viewers are themselves more likely to smoke (Sidney et al., 1996), and this may affect their perceptions beyond what they see on television.

### *Perceptions of Smoking*

A few studies have looked at smoking from an opinion perspective. Kim and Shanahan (2003) found that unfavorable opinion discourages smoking itself. Their study found that the smoking rate is lower in states that have more unfavorable opinion climates. They conclude that "unfavorable public opinion may have been partly responsible for the decrease in the smoking population in this country" (p. 360). The study doesn't directly test Hypothesis 2, but it establishes that opinion climate may have an effect on behavior (which is relevant to Hypothesis 3).

Relatedly, social norms have been considered important in recent work on health prevention communication, but much of this work is not aware of mass communication research dealing with media effects on social norms (and the spiral of silence specifically). For instance, two economists argued that:

> smokers do care about social acceptance. Inconsiderate smoking is assumed to trigger negative emotions on [the] non-smokers' part, and these reactions are stronger the less used non-smokers are to such inconsiderate behavior. Smokers decide whether to be considerate or not by weighing the inconvenience costs of being considerate against the benefits of social acceptance. (Nyborg & Rege, 2003, p. 325)

They were unwittingly stating the key axioms of spiral of silence theory, in which willingness to express opinions publicly is weighed against social costs that might come from majoritarian pressure.

Gunther et al. (2006) found that the media influence smoking as much by influencing perceptions of what *others* think as by influencing the actual perceptions of audience members. Consumers of media process not only the messages, but they form opinions about what others (in this case peers) are likely to think about those messages. This "influence of presumed influence" is an opinion process that depends on active processing of perceptions about smoking; perception of the opinion climate (what others think) is just as much an issue as the actual message received by viewers. While the model of media influence proposed is different than our linked model in Figure 1, there are broad similarities in terms of how opinion processes are conceived.

Working from Figure 1 and the existing research, a test study for the issue of smoking might yield the following hypotheses: media use cultivates perceptions that fewer people smoke (H1), which would then be associated with perceptions that more people are against smoking (H2), which in turn would suggest that people will be more likely to speak out about smoking in public (H3).

### *Revising the Model*

In Hypothesis 1 the media role is clear. Media use is related to perceptions about objective states in the world; this is what some would call "first-order" cultivation. However, media use can also relate to beliefs, attitudes or feelings; this is sometimes known as "second-order" cultivation (see Shrum & Lee, Chapter 8, this volume for a fuller discussion of first- and second-order cultivation). In Figure 2, we give a revised model that includes the possibility of second-order cultivation, within the more complete (combined) cultivation and spiral of silence model. The revised model includes the possibility that messages from television *about* smoking (e.g., smoking is "uncool," smoking is not healthy) matter as much as the frequency with which smoking is shown on TV. From a cultivation standpoint, the *content* of messages about smoking, as much as their simple frequency, can be of importance.

The revised model thus includes the possibility that cultivation can occur with both real world estimates and feelings/attitudes about the issue. However, there is no *a priori* reason why perceptions of real-world frequency must come "before" attitudes. As frequency estimates can affect opinions, so too can attitudes and feelings about smoking influence how prevalent people think smoking is in the real world. For instance, if people see that most television images of smokers are depicting behaviors by villainous or bad characters, they might be likely to lessen their estimates of how much people in the real world (where fewer people are legitimately "bad") smoke. Given these possibilities, a model such as the final one shown in Figure 3 might be best. In this model, television use is seen as being related to *both* real world perceptions and attitudes, which in turn then are related to willingness to speak out. And these perceptions and attitudes (the two dependent variables in the cultivation portion of this model) are related to each other.

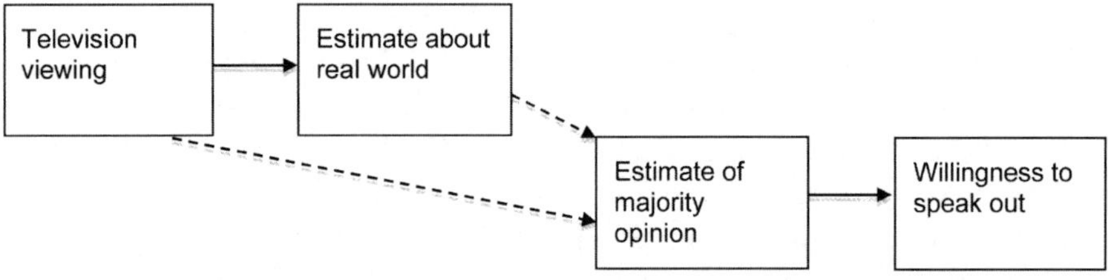


Figure 2. Revised schematic model linking cultivation and spiral of silence

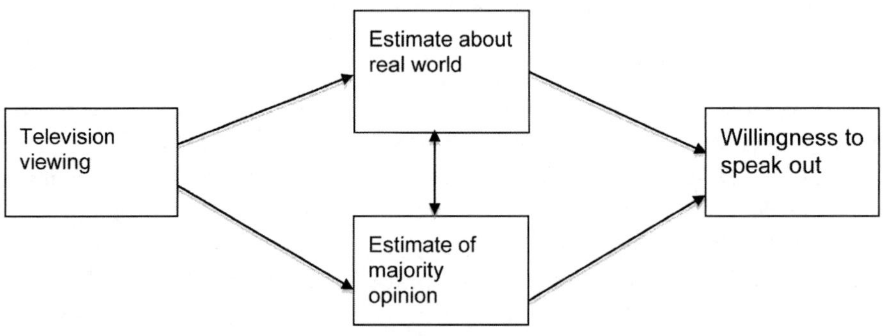


Figure 3. Further revised schematic model linking cultivation and spiral of silence

### *Linking Cultivation and the Spiral of Silence?*

How well do these hypotheses perform in the real world? Of course there are many hundreds of studies on both cultivation and the spiral of silence, but we are not aware of many studies that have directly tested these hypotheses *together*. Noelle-Neumann used the issue of smoking mainly to develop survey measures of the threat experienced from social isolation. Less was said about it as an actual issue that might be undergoing social change. Spiral of silence theory will normally assume that the “media tenor” is an important factor in how people determine where majority opinion is centered. In other words, much like cultivation, the spiral of silence assumes that broad patterns of media content will sooner or later be related to people's views on issues. In this case, as viewers see fewer people smoking in the media, the spiral of silence and cultivation both predict that they will internalize these perceptions into their own beliefs about how prevalent smoking actually is. Once these perceptions are more or less cemented in public opinion, people's attitudes and willingness to speak out about the issue should also change accordingly.

Shanahan and colleagues (Shanahan, Scheufele, Yang, & Hizi, 2004) looked at these issues with a dataset that included both cultivation and spiral of silence measures. The study contained some findings that confirm the model suggested in this chapter, and some that do not. The study examined the issue of proposed regulations on smoking (a smoking ban) as a perception variable and willingness to speak about smoking in a public situation (a restaurant) as a final dependent variable. Both were connected to media use, especially television viewing.

Their questions about perceptions of smoking showed that people think that there is broad support for regulation of smoking and also that most people would be willing to speak up in public about smoking. Consistent with what national public opinion data were showing at the time, the data confirmed that smoking was becoming less socially acceptable.

However, there was a *positive* correlation between television exposure and estimates of smoking in the real world. As in some earlier studies, television viewing was also correlated to smoking itself, so it may be that heavy viewers were simply applying a projective bias to their estimates. In any case, the hypothesis that reduced smoking rates on television would be associated with lowered estimates of smoking prevalence was not supported. Heavy viewers thought that *more* people smoked.

Concerning support for a smoking ban and willingness to speak about smoking in a public situation, personal support for a smoking ban was positively related to willingness to speak out. However, a correlation showed no significant positive relationship between the *perception* of how many people support a smoking ban and willingness to speak out. This runs counter to the spiral of silence explanation of willingness to speak out.

The data showed an interesting interaction between personal support, perception of public support, and willingness to speak out. Those who thought that a majority would support a ban but who did not themselves support such a ban were least willing to speak up, while the other groups all showed relatively higher willingness. Perceptions of majority opinion marked them off from the others who also do not support a ban. This is probably best seen as a group with a "defensive" opinion position.

A final analysis tested whether media use was related to willingness to speak out. The data showed that media use was only *indirectly* related to estimates of public support for smoking legislation as well as to personal support. As noted above, heavy viewers thought that more people smoke; moreover, those who tend to see the world as populated by more smokers are also more likely to see others as supporting antismoking legislation, and they themselves support such legislation.

Those who think that the majority supports smoking legislation are also more likely to support such laws themselves, which in turn positively relates to willingness to speak. This pattern comes closer to a spiral of silence explanation. Thus, perceptions do relate to willingness to speak out, even if there is not a direct relationship (in this case) as proposed by spiral of silence theory. Television exposure makes a positive contribution to willingness to speak out, indirectly through its relation to estimates of public support and personal support.

Summarizing, then, television exposure may be related to images of how many people support smoking legislation (and how many people smoke), which then cultivates willingness (or lack thereof) to speak out. In this one study, heavy viewers think there are more smokers, think more people support a ban, and support a ban themselves, even though they're more likely to smoke. And this pattern tends to encourage willingness to speak up about smoking in a public situation.

## The Future for Cultivation and Spiral of Silence Research

As seen above, simple models don't always yield neat results. With both cultivation and the spiral of silence, real world conditions sometimes turn hypotheses on their heads. But the overall promise for this sort of research is great. As with many of the other chapters in this volume, connecting cultivation to other theories opens up new avenues for both cultivation and the theory to which it is connected. And only with future empirical work will linked models become stronger in their ability to explain opinions on real issues.

Both cultivation and the spiral of silence are often oversimplified. Cultivation sometimes is portrayed as being *only* about perceptions of the frequency of events in the world, but the issue of smoking shows that even simple perceptions of how much people do smoke are sometimes unpredictable. And further, these perceptions are contained within a web of other types of perceptions, especially about what others think.

Similarly, the spiral of silence is often seen as being *only* about the relationships between fear of isolation and willingness to speak out. Noelle-Neumann herself complained about this frequently. But again, as we see from one short example, willingness to speak out about an issue is also contained within a web of associations about what others think and about what we see in the media.

Even given the complexities of real-world data, between the two theories the common concerns with media portrayals and their long-term relationship to our views about the world are striking. Noelle-Neumann thought that media played a vital role in establishing the "climate of opinion." Gerbner thought that television was a key aspect of what we might normally call "culture." In the end, how different are these two concepts? Of course at the operational level they can be very different, but conceptually there is a lot to be shared.

An issue that should be stressed is that both Noelle-Neumann and Gerbner were concerned with a "normative" perspective on public opinion. Noelle-Neumann used this term explicitly, Gerbner less so, but both strands of research look at the media as institutions that make judgments about things in the world. For Noelle-Neumann, media "tenor" is an explicitly positive or negatively valenced concept that tells how us how people are (or should be) thinking about issues. For Gerbner, the "lessons" of something like television violence are similar: They are the cumulative outcome of a stream of messages that is telling us what is "good" and "bad" in the world.

Both Gerbner and Noelle-Neumann, then, are on very similar ground. For this reason, we think that cultivation variables and spiral of silence variables can make sense when used together. And there are other questions to pursue. Does it work to see cultivation as a "critical" extension of spiral of silence? Conversely, is the spiral of silence a social psychological account of how cultivation works, while extending it to the behavioral realm? Obviously more data and theoretical work are needed to answer such questions. Nevertheless, we argue that there is value in exploring these two theories in relation to each other. Because both theories are continuing to be developed (even all these years after they were introduced), we expect the possibilities for the two theories to be articulated with each other to grow in the future.

## Notes

1. Collected at http://www.asc.upenn.edu/Gerbner/Archive.aspx
2. Noelle-Neumann was originally unhappy with cuts that were made to the journal article; later she thought they made the article more accessible. The article (Noelle-Neumann, 1974) has been cited many times since then.

# References


Asch, S. (1956). Studies of independence and conformity: I. A minority of one against a unanimous majority. *Psychological Monographs, 70*(9), 70.

Breed, W., & De Foe, J. R. (1984). Drinking and smoking on television, 1950–1982. *Journal of Public Health Policy, 5*, 257–270.

Centers for Disease Control. (2000). State-specific prevalence of current cigarette smoking among adults, and policies and attitudes about secondhand smoke. *Morbidity and Mortality Weekly Report, 50*(49), 1101–1128.

Christenson, P. G., Henriksen, L., & Roberts, D. F. (2000). *Substance use in popular prime-time television*. Studio City, CA: Mediascope.

Cruz, J., & Wallack, L. (1986). Trends in tobacco use on television. *American Journal of Public Health, 76*, 698–699.

Demers, D., & Viswanath, K. (Eds.) (1999). *Mass media, social control, and social change: A macro-social perspective*. Ames: Iowa State University Press.

Gerbner, G. (1969). Toward 'cultural indicators': The analysis of mass mediated message systems. *AV Communication Review, 17*(2), 137–148.

Gerbner, G., Gross, L., Morgan, M, & Signorielli, N.(1982). Charting the mainstream: Television's contributions to political orientations. *Journal of Communication, 32*(2), 100–127.

Glynn, C., Hayes, A., & Shanahan, J. (1997). Perceived support for one's opinions and willingness to speak out: A meta-analysis of survey studies on the "Spiral of Silence." *The Public Opinion Quarterly, 61*(3), 452–463.

Gunther, A., Bolt, D., Borzekowski, D., Liebhart, J., & Dillard, J. (2006). Presumed influence on peer norms: How mass media indirectly affect adolescent smoking. *Journal of Communication, 56*, 52–68

Hazan, A. R., & Glantz, S. A. (1995). Current trends in tobacco use on prime-time fictional television. *American Journal of Public Health, 85*, 116–117.

Katz, E., & Lazarsfeld, P. (1955). *Personal influence*. New York: The Free Press.

Kim, S., & Shanahan, J. (2003). Stigmatizing smokers: Public sentiment toward cigarette smoking and its relationship to smoking behaviors. *Journal of Health Communication, 8*, 347–367.

Klapper, J. T. (1960). *The effects of mass communication*. New York: Free Press.

Lazarsfeld, P. M., Berelson, B. R., & Gaudet, H. (1948). *The people's choice: How the voter makes up his mind in a presidential campaign* (2nd ed.). New York: Duell, Sloan & Pearce.

Lippmann, W. (1922). *Public opinion*. New York: Macmillan.

McCombs, M., & Shaw, D. (1972). The agenda-setting function of mass media. *Public Opinion Quarterly, 36*(2), 176–187.

Noelle-Neumann, E. (1973). Return to the concept of powerful mass media. *Studies in Broadcasting, 9*, 67–112.

Noelle-Neumann, E. (1974). The spiral of silence: A theory of public opinion. *Journal of Communication, 24*(2), 43–51.

Noelle-Neumann, E. (1993). *The spiral of silence: Public opinion—our social skin*. Chicago: University of Chicago Press.

Noelle-Neumann, E. (1999). The effect of the mass media on opinion formation. In D. Demers & K. Viswanath (Eds.), *Mass media, social control, and social change: A macro-social perspective* (pp. 51–76). Ames: Iowa State University Press.

Nyborg, K., & Rege, M. (2003). On social norms: The evolution of considerate smoking behavior. *Journal of Economic Behavior and Organization, 52*(3), 323–340.

Peter, J. (2004). Our long 'Return to the Concept of Powerful Mass Media'—A cross-national comparative investigation of the effects of consonant media coverage. *International Journal of Public Opinion Research, 16*(2), 144–168.

Scheufele, D. A., & Moy, P. (2000). Twenty-five years of the spiral of silence: A conceptual review and empirical outlook. *International Journal of Public Opinion Research, 12*(1), 3–28.

Scheufele, D. A., Shanahan, J., & Lee, E. (2001). Real talk: Manipulating the dependent variable in spiral of silence research. *Communication Research, 28*(3), 304–324.

Shanahan, J., & Morgan, M. (1999). *Television and its viewers: Cultivation theory and research.* Cambridge: Cambridge University Press.

Shanahan, J., Scheufele, D., Yang, F., & Hizi, S. (2004). Cultivation and spiral of silence effects: The case of smoking. *Mass Communication & Society, 7,* 413–428.

Shanahan, J., & Jones, V. (1999). Cultivation and social control. In D. Demers & K. Viswanath (Eds.), *Mass media, social control, and social change: A macro-social perspective* (pp. 31–50). Ames: Iowa State University Press.

Sidney, S., Sternfeld, B., Haskell, W. L., Jacobs, D. R., Jr., Chesney, M. A., & Hulley, S. B. (1996). Television viewing and cardiovascular risk factors in young adults: The CARDIA study. *Annals of Epidemiology, 6*(2), 154–159.

Tichenor, P., Donohue, G., & Olien, C. (1980). *Community conflict and the press.* Thousand Oaks, CA: Sage.

# 18. Cultivation Analysis and Cultural Studies

## Ritual, Performance, and Media Influence

*Andy Ruddock*

> (James) Carey's seminal work joins central issues in the field and redefines them. It will force the reader to think in new and fruitful ways about such dichotomies as transmission vs. ritual, administrative vs. critical, positivist vs. Marxist, and cultural vs. power-oriented approaches to communication study. An historically inspired treatment of major figures and theories, required reading for the sophisticated scholar. (George Gerbner)

This Gerbner quote, from the jacket of James Carey's *Communication as Culture* (1989), announced an interest in cultural studies on Gerbner's part that many qualitative scholars would find surprising. Carey's renowned ritual model of communication, premised on terms such as "sharing" and "participation" (1989, p. 18), seems at odds with the alienation and passiveness of the "Mean World Syndrome." Yet Gerbner and Carey largely agreed on the nature and purpose of critical media analysis. They concurred that technological, economic, and ideological structures of message systems were more important, politically speaking, than how audiences used media. Their consensus is significant, because the effects message systems have on sharing in social media is a major theme in contemporary cultural studies. Carey thought sharing was a complex phenomenon, involving questions of what gets shared, why it is shared, and what the outcomes of sharing are, and it is here that his interest in message systems intersected with cultivation theory.

These same questions are germane in studies of social media, where it appears to many scholars that message systems still work hegemonically. Carey's thoughts on sharing remain influential, because current studies of media rituals conclude that users often do little to subvert centralized modes of media production and the meanings they tend to make. Media sport is an example, and in this chapter I discuss an online soccer fan community whose activism was characterized by a lack of interest in how digital media have colonized sporting traditions as well as by a marked pleasure in reproducing the same sorts of cultural distinctions around gender that troubled the early violence profilers. Recent unfortunate events in the U.K. have shown that these distinctions are still at play in media sport, meaning that Gerbner's concerns about the gendered politics of corporate media remain strikingly appropriate. Perhaps more importantly, for this collection, the case study discussed here indicates how the conceptual similarities between cultivation theory and ritual theory might carry over into applying cultivation methods to the analysis of online fandom, a domain traditionally seen as lying beyond its scope (see Harris, 1998).

The current significance of a Gerbner/Carey comparison can be appreciated through Couldry's notion of media practice (2004). Media practice reconciles cultivation analysis and ritual theory by framing media use in a manner that makes the idea of the "active audience" redundant. Couldry concurs that media have an independent "reality effect" that he explains in the following way: Although social and media rituals are distinct, they are rarely experienced as such, because media use is so habitual. Couldry defined ritual as "action that is associated with transcendent values" (p. 22); that is, rituals are practices where people live social values. Media practice is what "people [are] doing in relation to media across a range of situations and contexts" (p. 119). In rituals, participants consciously use symbolic practices to express common values. *Media* rituals are "a special type of ritual action, distinguished by a particular type of relation to…media processes" (p. 23). Media practices are the habits that make ritual a common part of daily experience; the need for ritual and the constant availability of media as a way to satisfy it place media at the hub of defining what is social. What this means is that the values offered to audiences by message systems come to life most immediately through the things that people do with media, rather than the political attitudes that emerge later (as in phenomena such as the Mean World Syndrome). Media rituals are a source of what we might call "pre-cultivation," where it is understood that social values live most handily in relation to media. This "pre-cultivation" can be seen when, for example, people travel to media places ("pilgrimage" sites such as New Jersey's *Sopranos* tour; Couldry, 2007) or are shoved before global audiences by live news events (Couldry, 2003). Such events acknowledge media industries as primary definers of the things that matter and surrender to a deeper truth: that it is no longer possible to avoid dealing with media industries.

"Media practice" connects message systems with lived experience because "users" always *respond* to the *fact* of media saturation. There is no media tourism without sacred places of production; ordinary people do not perform for the world before journalists impel them to. Rituals are experiences where the logic of message systems reaches into the everyday; they bring cultural indicators to life as political forces. Whatever the diversity of their motivations and habits, users reinforce the idea that we can trust media industries to tell us what society is like or at least concede that there are no alternative methods for organizing public imagination. People, as Couldry puts it, "act out in formalized ways category differences that reproduce in condensed form the idea...that media are our access to society's centre" (2003, p. 52).

Ritual theory has always agreed that media encourage us to accept how things are. Because of this, ritual theory offers an alternative version of audience studies. Conventionally, cultivation analysis is set at odds with qualitative studies of audience engagement. However, a closer analysis of the history and current practice of ritual studies tells a story of consensus, and this opens new methodological possibilities and research avenues. Research on web-based soccer communities explores them. For example, a study by Rowe, Ruddock, & Hutchins (2010) found that even when fans complained about being exploited by digital media, dissent was constrained by a broader acceptance of online fandom as a natural progression of traditional supporter cultures, even among those who traditionally blamed media for turning the game into a consumer sport.

Couldry's work, like cultivation analysis, continues to be concerned with inequalities in symbolic power. Media practice should level the playing field in making common cultures, but *in* practice it rarely does, and often this is due to users. For Couldry, the things that people do in relation to media generally discriminate between "special" media people, places, and moments and others are deemed unimportant because they are not "of the centre." The lessons that Gerbner thought television taught are now cultivated *and* expressed by habits rather than exposure and attitudes, raising the possibility that action should sit alongside exposure as an independent variable. Media practice shows that the similarities between Carey and Gerbner still matter because within cultural studies many questions about ideological effects have changed little in the shift from "audience" to "user," even when discussing sharing through social media. As an example, I consider how male soccer supporters recreate gender biases when socializing on the web, a typical social concern that the original Violence Profiles would have recognized.

## Sport and Social Media

Studies of digital sport media conceive of sport as a message system where fans are less resistant to the commodification and mediatization of public culture than is often imagined. According to Hutchins and Rowe and (2009), the eventual meanings of digital sport are being defined in battles over rights and revenues within rapidly changing technological and economic structures. Because sport is such an "important aspect of national popular culture" (p. 358), brawls over who profits from media rights are the vanguard of platform conflict, particularly as those who depend on television monies confront online technologies that make it hard to be paid in full. Nevertheless, the fact that fans regularly evade the clutches of pay-per-view services and the like by sharing pirated streams disguises a deeper dynamic: a monetization of sport that is of unprecedented scope. Sharing through social media is determined, in Rowe and Hutchins' view, by the capacity of Web 2.0 for "digital plenitude," and bargaining among sports organizations, television companies, online platforms, and even individual athletes over content rights. Finely graded definitions of proprietary claims are liquidating common public sport cultures that users are free to share. This is a channeling of capacity that mirrors Carey's vision of economic media reality and, of course, Gerbner's thinking on the industrialization of culture. Elsewhere, Rowe describes a "media sports cultural complex," and as we see from his definition, sport is a powerful example of how centralized media production cultivates the sentiment that the mediatization of cultural life is nothing more than common sense:

> By gaining a better knowledge and understanding of how media sports texts are produced and what they might mean, it is possible to learn more about societies in which 'grounded' and 'mediated' experience intermesh in ever more insidious and seemingly seamless ways. (Rowe, 2004, p. 35)

In a study of online soccer fans, Rowe et al. (2010) combined cultivation analysis and ritual theory to describe how users indeed experienced the "intermeshing" between "grounded" and "mediated" as seamless. Digital media let fans enjoy traditional pleasures through communities that principally exist online. Participating in web forums, tweeting comments to presenters during live televised games, contacting after-match call-in radio shows and the like, or providing content for the very media that fans once blamed for turning a truly popular sport into a media spectacle, have all become part of what *real* soccer supporters do. This, we argued, was shown with particular clarity through the online phenomenon *MyFootballClub* and its offshoot *FreeMyFC. MyFootballClub (MFC)* was a website that, combining the thrill of management simulation games with the sociability of online fan forums, offered global users a chance to manage a real soccer club—England's Ebbsfleet United—for a fee. *FreeMyFC* was a dissenting site established by disgruntled members who felt *MFC* had duped its subscribers, never allowing them to become truly involved in decision making. We felt the intriguing thing about the latter site was that its "rebels" accepted key principles of media sovereignty that "authentic" soccer fans had resisted for years. We made this argument by describing both sites as examples of media rituals (where fans expressed the view that soccer affords authentic community experiences that cannot be bought or faked) and analyzing the data with methods inspired by cultivation analysis.

We felt that cultivation methods offer much to studies of how these media cultures work, but equally that these cultures represent new forms of media cultivation that incorporate the rituals of media use. The power model that results reconciles centralization with the indeterminate outcomes of media practices crossing multiple domains. There are four stages that explain how we reached this conclusion. First, I describe what Carey and Gerbner agreed upon. Second, I explain why cultivation analysis now appeals to cultural studies, particularly as research on social media favors the analysis and operation of message systems over the question of how users make content. Third, I explain in more detail how ritual theory has contributed to this compatibility because "media practice" is uninterested in the distinction between active and passive audiences. Finally, I put these ideas to empirical test by asking what is cultivated among online soccer fan communities.

## Carey's Ritual Definition of Communication

Carey defined communication as "a symbolic process whereby reality is produced, maintained, repaired, and transformed" (1989, p. 23).[1] His interest in how communication *ideally* features sharing and participation may seem at odds with cultivation analysis. However, Carey agreed with Gerbner on four crucial things:

1. Media power is about more than persuasion.
2. Media matter because they create and maintain value systems.
3. Industrialized media production limits the range of voices that participate in the creation of reality.
4. The task of the communication scholar is to agitate for industrial reform, because without action on the structure of media industries, inclusive democracy is impossible.

Carey's model set out to clarify how communication in participatory democracy *should* work. But his immediate goal was to show that existing media arrangements *failed* because they operated in a society that celebrated wealth in every artifact it made:

> Because we have seen our cities as the domain of politics and economics, they have become the residence of technology and bureaucracy. Our streets are designed to accommodate the automobile, our sidewalks to facilitate trade, our land and houses to satisfy the economy and the real estate speculator....[R]ecasting our studies of communication in terms of a ritual model is...to give us a way in which to rebuild a model of and for communication of some restorative value in reshaping our common culture. (Carey, 1989, pp. 34–35)

Carey agreed with Gerbner on the idea that the U.S. media had transformed business values into persuasive representations of social reality that audiences largely accepted. He actually held quite a deterministic view of how social meaning was made and shared. To begin, "what is thought about, thought with, and to whom it is expressed" was deduced by "forms of communication technologies [which] affect the constructions placed on experience" (1989, p. 64). Moreover, the harnessing of human sense-making to corporate interest had visibly affected the physical realities of social life, let alone what people thought. Carey believed that the "reality maps" produced by North American mass media directed social and economic practice, creating the need for a cultural intervention because new ways of living had to be imaginable before they could be possible. Unlike Gerbner, his model of cultural power depended on communication structures *and* end-users. Media reality, partial though it was, was real because the public lived it in their daily habits. For Carey, concentrated media power happened *because* of the end user, and "restorative action" on communication systems was necessary *before* ordinary media practices could function democratically. This applies to the idea of media practice, because what is shared depends what it is possible to share.

Ritual theory and cultivation analysis are both concerned with the forces that narrow public discourse. In this, neither regarded distinctions between active and passive audiences as meaningful. Shanahan and Morgan (1999) argue that while audiences may interpret the same content in different ways, these variations have little effect on the general right-of-center gravitational pull exerted by international media industries. Carey's work, a major force in cultural studies, did nothing to contradict this position. Keen as he was to vanquish simple notions of media effects, Carey did not believe in autonomous audiences. Carey described the audience member as an "observer at play"; media-related cultural practices happen under conditions determined by others. Ritual media studies emphasize the communication structures that make action possible, not the actions themselves. From this position, we can speak of people doing things with media without implying that these "things" are unconstrained.

Carey's position is consistent with Couldry's views of media practice. Media rituals need audiences to act them out, but these "performances" are compelled by hegemonic values that have infiltrated ordinary media habits. According to Couldry, media power works because audiences like industrially made distinctions between "special" moments—where public issues are defined through professional symbolic action—and "ordinary" media experiences and places that are deemed private and socially irrelevant. For example, when the public encounters celebrities in nondescript settings, like supermarkets, they enjoy the feeling that they have been temporarily transported into a special, alien world where they do not really belong (Ferris, 2003). This feeling is only possible because of the powerful, intertextual celebrity industry, but in turn that power is never stronger than when it is recognized in how audiences respond in the things that they do. Here public *actions* (which are a productive force that help marshal the boundaries from which media institutions benefit) acknowledge the divisions between media and non-media places, reinforcing common sense beliefs that media hold a privileged place in defining public agendas (Couldry, 2003). Media power is therefore secured when "non-professionals" agree that they play no role in creating and sharing the "maps of reality" that orient public life. The audience is happy enough to participate in media cultures, as long as the manufacturing of those cultures is left to the professionals.

Studies of media practice are relevant to cultivation analysis because the "gauntlet" thrown to the latter today is the observation that "audiences" now routinely "create" and "share" content (Gauntlett, 2007b; Merrin, 2007). This is a descendent of long-expressed reservations about how cultivation analysis understands and "measures" reception and interpretation. Although digital resources let non-professionals perform for other audiences, this is often because users have absorbed the production values of corporate media (Andrejevic, 2008). In this sense, audiences *make* corporate message systems powerful when they do things that, consciously or not, acknowledge the authority of those systems as they evolve with one eye on profit and the other on controlling participation. "Ritual," in the form of media practice, makes the distinction between behaviorist and materialist understandings of media effects that Gerbner (1983) advocated. Ironically, the move from audience to user makes the issue of interpretation less important than it once was to studies of "active" audiences, substantially removing a key barrier between cultivation analysis and cultural studies.

## Cultivation, Cultural Studies, and the Question of Interpretation

The idea of mainstreaming has been dismissed on the grounds that media have no political influence until they are interpreted or used (Newcomb, 1978). However, this is not a unanimous position within cultural studies, and therefore it is important to describe how "interpretation" has been deployed in qualitative studies, and why some researchers now argue that its significance has been overstated. The matter has current relevance, as a marked feature in analyses of social media. Audience interpretation was pivotal to Newcomb's influential "Humanistic Critique" (1978) of cultivation analysis. Newcomb thought Gerbner and Gross's "mean world hypothesis" was unsustainable, since it tied the political outcomes of television violence to the assumption that this violence expressed coherent values that heavy viewers (allegedly) uniformly accepted. It made just as much sense, Newcomb argued, to assume that violence meant all sorts of things to different viewers, and that its ambiguity made it a resource for ordinary political engagement with the public world. Since Jenkins (2006) substantially repeated this point in arguments about the value of popular culture to American teenagers, made to the U.S. Senate in the wake of the Columbine High School shootings, we know that Newcomb's thesis has become authoritative.

For some audience researchers, the methods and assumptions of cultivation analysis provoked suspicion about the politics of the paradigm itself. Gerbner intended to liberate audiences by puncturing the idea that American television worked in the public interest (1983). Ang (1991) countered that his methods and assumptions demonized them instead. Ang argued that cultivation is obsessed with pathologizing rather than understanding heavy viewing, thereby underplaying the complexity of television audiences; cultivation and other empirical researchers, she charged, are:

> driven toward drawing 'fictions' of rigid, reified audience categories [in a way] that forecloses understanding of the concrete practices and experiences of people because those 'fictions' are regarded as reflecting essential viewer identities....Consequently, in a paradoxical leap...it is...the viewers that are...put on trial, not the institutions that provide the programming. (1991, p. 159)

Ang's position echoed across fan studies, which, among other things, deliberately set out to reverse the association between "immersion" and "influence," arguing that in many cases it was the people who spent the most time watching television who were the medium's fiercest critics (Harris, 1998).

Yet recent studies of how "audiences" make media content are less dismissive of the case for cultivation. Gauntlett's work is noteworthy here, since he has been at once a scathing critic of cultivation analysis and a champion of the idea that the rise of the media user has made the term "audience" obsolete (2007a). In his 1998 essay "Ten Things Wrong with the Effects Model," Gauntlett castigated the mean world hypothesis as a "snobbish" and "elitist" notion that could hardly serve democracy since it had no interest in what television viewers had to say about their experiences, in their own terms. He repeated this charge in *Moving Experiences* (2005). However, In *Creative Explorations* (2007a), Gauntlett significantly changed his tune. Gauntlett noted that when asked, audiences do not think that media have much influence on their sense of self. Nevertheless, having examined how people use media narratives and images by asking them to build "identity models" using Lego blocks, he also concluded that identities "will almost inevitably have been affected by the stories and values which we encounter so regularly in popular media," meaning "further research which turns the spotlight back onto people's relationship with media narratives [is] needed" (2007a, p. 195).

The divisions in audience studies circa 1975–95 were therefore strategic devices that challenged future empirical research to be more catholic. Certainly, cultivation analysis has opened itself to the possibility that interpretation and differences between media content may be more important than was first thought (see Bilandzic & Rössler, 2004; Bilandzic & Busselle, Chapter 13, this volume). But cultural studies has made some moves in the opposite direction. Miller, for example, thinks it vital to note the centralizing power of "the most global (but local), communal (yet individual), and time-consuming practice of making meaning in the history of the world" (2010, p. 115). Miller argues that television continues to dominate the cultural and political landscape in ways that have changed little in the post-broadcast age. In the U.S., people spend far more time watching television than they do using the Internet. They still rely on the former during presidential campaigns, and the exponential increase in spending on political advertising has proved a boon for an anything-but-ailing television industry. According to Miller, during prime-time hours, 80% of American families watch together.

Simple empirical facts establish the longevity of television's power. In the face of "labor exploitation, patriarchy, racism, and U.S. neo-imperialism" (Miller, 2010, p. 126), focusing on the significance of audience interpretation, in Miller's reading, mistakenly creates the impression that political structures do not matter if audiences do not acknowledge them. To illustrate, Miller noted how "fanspeak" during televised sporting events is often about advertising. Evidence shows that when fans chat electronically during events like the Super Bowl, they spend a great deal of time discussing commercials. Faced with this evidence, "the idea that audiences using several different communications technologies while watching TV makes them more independent of, for example, commercials is laughable" (2010, p. 126). Miller abandoned the idea that what matters most is how audiences use and interpret media, because there is nothing liberating about knowing that media constantly spin reality in favor of groups who are already powerful if there is nothing one wants to or can do about it.

So another reason for pursuing similarities between ritual and cultivation theory is that many cultural studies scholars agree that the latter provides stimulating accounts of media influence. The core idea that television dramatizes, justifies, and recreates the unequal distribution of political and social power has been widely accepted as an intriguing possibility. Newcomb (1978) recognized the value of using quantitative content analysis to show how 1970s American television violence distorted social reality. Miller (2010) thought the plotting of associations between exposure to televised crime and the endorsement of racist attitudes had made a major contribution to debates on cultural politics. Morley (2006) conceded that peripatetic viewing habits underlined the importance of analyzing narratives and images that cross programs and genres. Couldry, Livingstone, and Markham (2007) referred to mainstreaming—defined as the "media's ideological power to...[mask] diversity and [undermine] dissent" (p. 29)—as a critical concept in explaining media's political effects. Generally, then, many in cultural studies view cultivation analysis as a promising method for investigating how audiences are swayed by media representations. What is more, as ritual studies have started to use its methods, the growth of social media is establishing further grounds for pursuing this trend.

## Message Systems and Public Engagement

Critical scholarship on social media accepts that the logic of the entire message system is more important than the discrete choices that audiences make *within* that system. Napoli (2010) writes that what gets *made* is less important than what gets *shared*, and that the mechanics of message distribution systems is what really counts. Van Dijck (2009) thinks that social media promote greater interdependence between platforms like YouTube and users who provide content that attracts advertising revenue. Andrejevic (2008) portrays cult television fans who contribute to the "snarking" site *Television Without Pity* as willing sources of labor for producers in search of free market research. At any rate, many writing within cultural studies think that the structure of message systems is influential in tying public creativity to profit.

In sum, this literature warns against affording too much significance to creativity. Couldry et al.'s *Media Consumption and Public Engagement* (2007) pursues this theme. The project resembles a hybrid cultivation analysis that deploys qualitative and quantitative methods to show how media limit participation in public life. *Media Consumption and Public Engagement* used panel diaries, interviews, and a large sample survey (of 1000 people in England) and started with the empirical case for disconnection: Evidence showed that levels of participation among today's audiences have been overstated, and that most people, for the most part, continue to peruse content in non-directed ways that do not engage with anything they would recognize as being political (Couldry et al., 2007). Quantitative data also showed low levels of interest in politics and voting among socially marginalized communities, and evidence of a general feeling of disconnection that, surveys suggest, crossed 70% of the voting public. Given this evidence, the authors concluded that it made sense to commence from the hypothesis that media entrench distinctions between those who are already in the political mainstream and others who effectively recognize its presence and power by opting out.

The surveys supported the hypothesis, showing that disengaged people found nothing in media to reconnect them to the political world. Part of the conclusion drew directly on cultivation analysis. Looking at differences between levels of media use and political engagement, Couldry et al. found that heavy television viewers were significantly less likely to feel engaged or to take part in any sort of political action (voting, demonstrating, writing letters to politicians, signing petitions, and the like), were less trusting of the news, were less likely to feel the news spoke about issues that affected them, and were less likely to feel that they could affect the world they saw in media. Rituals were relevant in a negative way. Media habits were no antidote to disaffection in and of themselves. The only people who showed positive correlations between exposure to news and feelings of connection were those who actively sought out particular stories. People who watched the news or read the paper out of habit, or to track celebrities or sport, were no more likely to feel engaged than (relative) non-readers and non-viewers.

Ritualistic use was therefore distinct from notions of creativity or participation. If the political problem is that those who suffer most from the existing distribution of power are also the least likely to become engaged with the world that has created these conditions, then nothing in existing media practices, either in terms of production or consumption, promises an alternative: "Although media consumption is largely constituted by habit...habit itself does not guarantee an interpretive context sufficient to sustain mediated public connection in the long run" (p. 103). Thinking in terms of "effects," the argument Couldry et al. presented was that, most of the time, media practices sustain existing political gaps and end in inertia, because media use affirms the sense that however much they care, there is little that audiences can do about public issues. This is not the same thing as arguing that audiences are apathetic. Many of the people in the diary study cared deeply about international affairs, but lacked the social connections to put their emotions to work. Couldry et al. raised the possibility that this lack of connection is partly explained by media monopolization of leisure time. The conventions and structures of social life and media habits mean that, in effect, audiences grudgingly acknowledge that politics is a spectator sport.

Modern ritual media studies therefore respond to the perception, articulated by Miller (2010), that audience research needs a stronger engagement with the political consequences of living with media habits that continue to exhibit strong centralizing tendencies, inasmuch as they favor the status quo. To show this, its practitioners have adapted ideas and methods also used in cultivation analysis. The following section considers how this can be moved forward into studies of online sport media communities. The study discussed below drew on cultivation in that the underlying theme is how numbers identify cultural patterns showing how online communities accept the organization of social life that sustains the media business. The idea that repetitive aspects of media cultures temper understandings of "resistance," "creativity," and "autonomy" was used to justify the combination of quantitative and qualitative methods. In combination, these methods indicated that *MyFootballClub* and *FreeMyFC* incorporated audience cynicism, anger, enthusiasm, and pleasure within what can be called the "media sport cultural complex." In particular, we noted how digital media subverted traditional soccer fan complaints *about* media. To understand this, we need to explore historical antagonisms between soccer fans and media.

## Soccer Fans: From Performers to Users

Soccer is a model *par excellence* of synthesis between sport and transnational digital media. Since the 1980s, its administrative re-organization has gone hand-in-hand with the development of international cable, satellite, and television systems to create huge global media audiences that pulverize live fans in economic clout. But "live" soccer fans have not simply stood by and watched. Their performances in soccer stadiums are vital to the game's appeal to international television markets (Giulianotti, 1991). These performances have, paradoxically, created a situation that soccer fans object to (the fact that games now matter more as media events than as live ones); they are expressions of group identity (rituals) that take on a knowing intensity because of the presence of television (*media* rituals). As such, intentionally or not, fans of live soccer validate the idea that events take on a heightened importance when they are televised and, in turn, that television makes a distinct contribution to the "specialness" of these events.

This apparent contradiction is nothing of the sort because, as Sandvoss (2003) argues, soccer succeeds as a media event because "sportsbiz" (Rowe, 2007) eschews ideological dogmatism. The business of international televised soccer is rather like the Elizabethan Church Settlement; supporters are free to think as they will, as long as their *actions* are consistent with the smooth operation of the ritual. Pragmatic media soccer cultures mollify a series of contradictory positions. Television is widely blamed for taking the game away from its "true" working class male supporters by privileging the screen spectacle over the live event. This perception has been a deep-seated source of resentment (Rowe et al., 2010; Ruddock, Hutchins, & Rowe, 2010). Certainly, tournaments like the World Cup secure the integration of soccer with television and international commerce. Prior to the 2010 competition in South Africa, live games were widely touted as an elixir for the beer industry, as pubs and breweries welcomed the trade boom that televised games would bring (Footit, 2009). But the success of such media events also depends on their ability to channel traditional supporter rituals through media practices. Soccer fans quickly recognized that the televising of live games also gave unprecedented opportunities to perform for global audiences.

In a telling example, Giulianotti (1991) described how Scotland fans quite consciously acted out carnivalesque identities during televised matches to distinguish themselves to a global audience from English hooligans. Internationally televised soccer tournaments therefore soothe audience "resistance" by giving it a voice, such that fan practices become part of the very spectacle to which they are opposed. In this case, the question of what audiences "do" around media is indeed key, but the relevance of their intentions is questionable. Like loyal Elizabethan clerics, the purveyors of televised soccer agree not to pry into the souls of their audiences, as long as those audiences show up. When they do, the fact that their presence makes the World Cup a media event that supersedes all other forms of sociality for a month for most of the world is indubitable.

The example of soccer helps us think through how industrial and user power work in unison. It expresses ideas that draw on both ritual theory and cultivation analysis, and is ripe for the application of cultivation-like methods. This case becomes stronger by considering how soccer fans relate to other sorts of audiences and thinking through the convergence between ritual and cultivation studies. Despite the antipathy that soccer supporters have historically directed at the media and "armchair supporters" (Ruddock, 2005), studies of soccer fans who build the media events that they also consume have found evidence that their actions are consistent with the logic of changing media forms which "cultivate" the belief that sport and media are indivisible (sport is, for most people, something one does through media), and that transformations in fan experiences through international sport media events are inevitable. In a sense, the literature on soccer fans describes a mainstreaming process, where the practices of global, multimedia operations have infiltrated the values, traditions, and habits of fan communities, partly because they offer those values and pleasures longevity. The *MyFootballClub* case is notable as an instance of this convergence.

## *MyFootballClub* and the Gender Politics of Digital Messages

*MyFootballClub* (http://www.myfootballclub.co.uk/) was founded by former journalist Will Brooks in 2007, and was heralded as "the world's first and only web-community owned football club." Members were charged an annually renewable fee of $70US. Having attracted almost 30,000 subscribers from 91 nations, Brooks bought a controlling interest in Ebbsfleet United, a semi-professional club playing in the fifth tier of the English professional leagues. Early success, capped with an appearance at Wembley Stadium (the "home" of English football), proved difficult to sustain, and by 2009 the ranks had dwindled to just 9000 renewing members, as Ebbsfleet languished near the bottom of their division. Journalists speculated that the allure of *MFC* had disappeared when Brooks, as Chief Operator, failed to purchase a better-known team. However, looking at what members had to say, it also seems that significant numbers resented the fact that *MFC* had never, in their view, delivered on the promise that it would involve subscribers in the daily management of the club and its teams. This led to *FreeMYFC.com*, a website styling itself as "a place for the *MFC* disillusioned," which as of July 2009 had attracted 292 members who wanted a place to vent their feelings about the failings of Brooks's venture, free of charge.

Cast in the language of the present chapter, a study by Hutchins, Rowe, and Ruddock (2009) showed how fan experience is shaped by media practices. Whatever fans do, their actions take place within the industrial and technological shifts that have already mapped the international sport media territory:

> A rapidly expanding digital interactive games industry and culture, the social networking capacity of Web 2.0, and do-it-yourself digital media culture...are creating the conditions for a profound change in sport's sociocultural milieu. (Hutchins et al., 2009, p. 90)

We developed this argument by quantifying fan complaints. Our argument was that the daily rituals of fans are now so heavily mediated that "resistance" to the further advances of media into the sports folk traditions *accepts* the new cultural geography that digital sport media have imposed. This could be seen in the actions of a "dissident" group of *MFC* fans who rebelled against the phenomenon almost as soon as it began.

We purposively sampled this group to test how skeptical soccer fans have accepted that their traditions now run through digital media. We had described how *MFC* deployed a novel strategy in presenting itself as an authentic supporting experience (driven by notions of community, participation, equality, and fairness rather than the imperatives of vertically integrated commerce), which nevertheless relied on a sophisticated media network of management simulation games, iTunes, online television, and the pleasures of fan message boards (Hutchins et al., 2009). The question applied to *FreeMYFC* was therefore how far this "resistant" group went in questioning the general thrust of sport media cultures as opposed to the specifics of *MFC*. What we found was that those devoted to denouncing *MFC* as an elaborate scam were also fascinated by the promises of online fandom, and enjoyed its masculine pleasures.

The study began in our suspicion that men who complain about mediated football are actually quite content within the sport/media complex, since complaining is a pleasurable part of masculine sport fandom. We wondered if we could demonstrate this through statistical associations between complaining and signs of commitment to online fan practices. This lent itself to a cultivation-style project, where we wanted to find out if those who posted the most to *FreeMYFC*. were also most fascinated with the *idea* of online fandom. This hypothesis was not supported, inasmuch as moderate and heavy posters were not significantly different, but quantifying fan responses *did* uncover a range of issues that would benefit from a hybrid ritual/cultivation framework.

We began by simply counting the things that the "rebels" complained about, running crosstabulations to examine the relationship between numbers of posts and types of complaint. Raw figures themselves revealed much. First, there was relatively little evidence that the dissidents were unhappy and still less that their gripes had anything to do with the mediation of sport. It was difficult to find meaningful distinctions between "heavy" and "light" posters because 59% of the 292 members posted *nothing*, and only 14% had written more than 100 times. Among those who did complain, the main objections (26% of the top 100 most popular posts in the "General Chat" area, as defined by number of replies) were that *MFC* had been a financial failure because of the covetous, incompetent Brooks and his accomplices on the Ebbsfleet board who consistently privileged the opinions of "live" supporters over the interests of *MFC's* globally dispersed (audience) majority. The only form of media criticism was of the technical variety, with 1% of the posts writing about web functionality; one way to interpret this is that the dissenters didn't think that *MyFootballClub* was mediated enough. This made sense because, in the previous point, a key complaint seemed to be that *MFC* did not respect its *audience.* Significantly, in the same forum, the second most popular reason for posting, at 16%, was to socialize with other members in comments that had little to do with the ostensible point of the operation. As the board's heaviest poster put it:

> We swear a lot, we make jokes about people's mums...we particularly say the 'C' word a lot about people we definitely don't like, sometimes we even say it about each other....Some of us really push the boundaries and it's not an excuse, it's certainly not even a good excuse but for most...it's cathartic and otherwise generally therapeutic, it's called 'letting off steam'...

This explanation of what *FreeMyFC* was ultimately about seemed significant as an articulation of the gender dynamics uncovered by the "Violence Profiles" (e.g., Gerbner, Gross, Morgan, & Signorielli, 1980), which had concluded that television violence told stories about male power and recreated the idea that it's a man's world. The maintenance of male privilege is also an ongoing issue in soccer and its mediation. According to Nash (2000), the transformation of English soccer stadiums in the 1990s made live games more welcoming to women, Black, and Asian supporters—much to the chagrin of its traditional White male rump. Far from being a part of this "revolution," *FreeMyFC* supported the idea that the political questions to be asked of media cultures have not fundamentally changed, because one motivation for mediated fan practices across "new" media is the preservation of gendered exclusions. Digital media environments afford daily opportunities for men to exercise their masculinity through sport fandom, in distinction to the days when, because sport was a once-a-week live experience, its pleasures were relatively divorced from everyday life (Palmer, 2009). Once again, the mediated cultivation of sport-dependent masculinity draws on the media routines of users. In these routines, it is remarkable that when given the chance to make media, men appear to repeat the sort of content that the Violence Profiles noted in 1970s television. According to Palmer (2009), this is attributable to message systems that let the boys be boys, and a recent example from the U.K. shows why it is worth asking if this is a trend crossing digital platforms. In February 2011, Richard Keys and Andy Gray were suspended from their duties as soccer commentators for Rupert Murdoch's Sky Sports 1, having been recorded making sexist remarks about assistant referee Sian Massey prior to an EPL game. The scandal gathered pace; Gray was fired after footage emerged of the former playing star sexually harassing a female colleague. Keys swiftly resigned but not before more off-camera moments became public; Keys leeringly inquiring as to whether co-presenter Jamie Redknapp had "smashed" a woman with whom he had been linked in the press. Within days, the pair found new employment with Radio TalkSport, a commercial station specializing in male bonhomie. Reviewing their debut, Kelner (2011) thought the key moment was when Keys took a break to promote a brand of floor tile. Where many had expected a mea culpa that was never delivered, the point was that TalkSport was indifferent to the duo's blemished credentials. TalkSport is a niche station catering to a large market of men who worried more about tiling than sexism. This is not to say all men who like tiling or TalkSport are sexist, but it is to say that the sort of attitudes that made Gray and Keys unpalatable to a general audience were irrelevant to a commercial platform that didn't need one. This exemplified how the mechanics of a message system lent itself to exclusionary ideologies, where unreconstructed sexism still works because of how messages are shared and monetized. The important thing to note here is that the message system angle sidesteps issues of public and private and in doing so establishes the importance of quantifying common messages and responses that cross different content. It does not matter whether a sexist remark comes from the mouth of an international broadcaster in an unguarded moment or the keyboard of a fan forum participant; both are afforded by message systems where the realities of distribution protect system, producer, and user alike from the full political fallout of their words.

## Implications for Audience Studies: The Past and the Future

These conclusions are more polemic than empirical; but this makes the case for pursuing relations between cultural studies and cultivation analysis more absorbing. This chapter has argued that cultivation analysis and ritual theory ploughed the same furrow in the 1970s, that cultural studies is increasingly interested in cultivation's conclusions and methods, and that this is now leading to empirical projects that combine methods and ideas from each. Further, studies of what fans do with media, framed in ritual theory, provide accounts of how cultivation happens in changed media environments. Media sport is a fruitful testing ground for these ideas, as something that attracts audience groupings who have moved from being devoutly anti-media to becoming key acolytes in the rituals that underpin media's quotidian powers.

Many future research questions arise. Would this observation be supported through large survey studies with media variables sufficient to support proper analysis of the relationship between time spent being a sport media fan and attitudes toward sport media industries? How do these relationships play across different sports and fan groups? Does the soccer example indicate that today's sport media systems amplify gender biases that effectively discourage women from sharing in these cultures? What other sorts of exclusions come into play, and how are they affected by the economics of digital plenitude? Whatever the differences between cultivation analysis and cultural studies, the development of ritual theory shows that these are questions that are compatible with both.

## Note

1. This quote is taken from Chapter 1 of *Communication as Culture*, and it should be noted that this essay was written in 1975.

## References

Andrejevic, M. (2008). Watching *Television Without Pity*: The productivity of online fans. *Television & New Media, 9*(1), 24–46.
Ang, I. (1991). *Desperately seeking the audience.* London: Routledge.
Bilandzic, H., & Rössler, P. (2004). Life according to television. Implications of genre-specific cultivation effects: The gratification/cultivation model. *Communications, 29*(3), 295–326.
Carey, J. (1989). *Communication as culture.* Boston: Unwin Hyman.
Couldry, N. (2003). *Media rituals: A critical approach.* London: Routledge.
Couldry, N. (2004). Theorising media as practice. *Social Semiotics, 14*(2), 115–132.
Couldry, N. (2007). On the set of *The Sopranos*: Inside a fan's construction of nearness. In J. Gray, C. Sandvoss, & C. L. Harrington (Eds.), *Fandom: Identities and communities in a mediated world* (pp. 139–148). New York: NYU Press.
Couldry, N., Livingstone, S., & Markham, T. (2007). *Media consumption and public engagement: Beyond the assumption of attention.* Basingstoke: Palgrave.
Ferris, K. (2003). Seeing and being seen: The moral order of celebrity. *Journal of Contemporary Ethnography, 33*, 236–64.
Foottit, L. (2009). *World Cup to boost pubs' business.* Retrieved from http://www.morningadvertiser.co.uk/news.ma/article/85311
Gauntlett, D. (1998). Ten things wrong with the effects model. In R. Dickinson, R. Harindranath, & O. Linne (Eds.), *Approaches to Audiences* (pp. 120–130). London: Arnold.
Gauntlett, D. (2005), *Moving experiences: Media effects and beyond.* London: John Libbey.
Gauntlett, D. (2007a). *Creative explorations: New approaches to identities and audiences.* London: Routledge.

Gauntlet, D. (2007b). Media studies 2.0. Retrieved from http://www.theory.org.uk/mediastudies2.htm

Gerbner, G. (1983). The importance of being critical—In one's own fashion. *Journal of Communication, 33*(3), 355–362.

Gerbner, G., Gross, L., Morgan, M., & Signorielli, N. (1980). The "mainstreaming" of America: Violence profile No. 11. *Journal of Communication, 30*(3), 10–29.

Giulianotti, R. (1991). Scotland's tartan army in Italy: The case for the carnivalesque. *Sociological Review, 39,* 503–527.

Harris, C. (1998). A sociology of television fandom. In C. Harris & A. Alexander (Eds.), *Theorizing fandom: Fans, subculture and identity* (pp. 41–53). Cresskill, NJ: Hampton Press.

Hutchins, B., & Rowe, D. (2009). From broadcast rationing to digital plenitude: The changing dynamics of the media sport content economy. *Television & New Media, 10*(4), 354–370.

Hutchins, B., Rowe, D., & Ruddock, A. (2009). "It's Fantasy Football Made Real": Networked media sport, the Internet, and the hybrid reality of MyFootballClub. *Sociology of Sport Journal, 26*(1), 89–106.

Jenkins, H. (2006). *Fans, bloggers, and gamers: Exploring participatory cultures.* New York: NYU Press.

Kelner, M. (2011). Richard Keys' and Andy Gray's *TalkSport* debut: What did you think? Retrieved from http://www.guardian.co.uk/tv-and-radio/tvandradioblog/2011/feb/14/richard-keys-andy-gray-talksport

Merrin, W. (2007). Media studies 2.0. Retrieved from http://mediastudies2point0.blogspot.com

Miller, T. (2010). *Television studies: The basics.* London: Routledge.

Morley, D. (2006). Unanswered questions in audience research. *The Communication Review, 9*(2), 101–121.

Napoli, P. M. (2010). Revisiting "mass communication" and the "work" of the audience in the new media environment. *Media, Culture & Society, 32*(3), 505–516.

Nash, R. (2000). Contestation in modern English professional football. *International Review for the Sociology of Sport, 35,* 465–486.

Newcomb, H. (1978). Assessing the violence profile studies of Gerbner and Gross: A humanistic critique and suggestion. *Communication Research, 5*(3), 264–282.

Palmer, C. (2009). The "grog squad": An ethnography of beer consumption at Australian rules football. In L. Wenner & S. Jackson (Eds.), *Sport, beer, and gender: Promotional culture and contemporary social life* (pp. 225–242). New York: Peter Lang.

Rowe, D. (2007). Sports journalism: Still the toy department of the news media? *Journalism, 8*(4), 385–405.

Rowe, D. (2004). *Sport, culture and the media: The unruly trinity* (2nd ed.). Maidenhead: Open University Press.

Rowe, D., Ruddock, A., & Hutchins, B. (2010). Cultures of complaint: Online fan message boards and networked digital media sport communities. *Convergence: The International Journal of Research into New Media Technologies, 16*(3), 298–315.

Ruddock, A. (2005). Let's kick racism out of football—and the lefties too! *Journal of Sport and Social Issues, 29*(4), 369–385.

Ruddock, A., Hutchins, B., & Rowe, D. (2010). Contradictions in media sport culture: "MyFootballClub" and the reinscription of football supporter traditions through online media. *European Journal of Cultural Studies, 13*(4), 323–339.

Sandvoss, C. (2003). *A game of two halves: Football, television and globalization*. London: Routledge.

Shanahan, J., & Morgan, M. (1999). *Television and its viewers: Cultivation theory and research*. Cambridge: Cambridge University Press.

van Dijck, J. (2009). Users like you? Theorizing agency in user-generated content. *Media, Culture & Society, 31*(1), 41–58.

# *Conclusion*

# 19. Looking Forward, Looking Backward

## Ten Questions about Cultivation

*Michael Morgan, James Shanahan, & Nancy Signorielli*

As the chapters collected here vividly demonstrate, there are many distinct and divergent viewpoints on the theory of cultivation and how cultivation analysis should be done, as well as a tremendous variety of studies connected in some way under the "umbrella" of cultivation—so much so that one might wonder if it is possible to synthesize them all. The last time we anthologized studies of cultivation was in 1990, in *Cultivation Analysis: New Directions in Media Effects Research* (Signorielli & Morgan, 1990), the first book-length examination of cultivation.[1] Topics and trends examined in that volume included psychological processes, new media, pornography, and religion, among others.

Much has taken place in the intervening years. One way to take stock of where cultivation has been—and where it might be going—is to consider "the state of the art" at the time of that 1990 volume. The editors concluded their introductory/overview chapter with a list of "some of the major issues that have evolved from cultivation analysis and which numerous independent investigators are pursuing" (Morgan & Signorielli, 1990, p. 26). At the time, these were thought to be the major research questions and challenges that cultivation analysis would be facing in the near future and beyond. Over 20 years later, we can see how much—or how little—cultivation analysis has developed by revisiting those questions in light of the chapters presented in this book. We now take a look at how much those questions still matter, how many have been answered by the chapters in this volume, how many have been neglected, and what new questions have emerged.

***

First, in speculating about the question "How does cultivation occur," Morgan and Signorielli wondered if research into the psychological processes underlying cultivation would become a more fruitful area of inquiry. At that time it had reached something of a dead end, and beyond 1990 we did not have much hope that research on cognitive processing would offer much of consequence to the overall question of cultivation. Our view was that cultivation was essentially a macro-cultural process occurring in the society at large that did not need to be considered from a cognitive standpoint. Gerbner summarily dismissed work on cognitive processes as irrelevant to the questions he was interested in, arguing that whatever "processes" were involved in cultivation were simply those by which we learn from our environment in general.

Neverthleless, as Hawkins, Pingree, and Adler (1987) argued, no matter how many correlations are found in surveys between amount of viewing and attitudes, identifying the psychological mechanism(s) that underlie cultivation would significantly enhance the internal validity of the theory. Indeed, the work pioneered by L. J. Shrum proved to be highly successful in showing how individuals process the stories of television in ways that are consistent with (and that help explain) what is seen at the macro level. Shrum's frequently cited work is well represented in this volume (see Chapter 8, which pushes his lines of investigation further). While his work shows quite clearly how television can be the source of information people use to make numerical estimates about the world (so-called "first-order" judgments), this chapter shows that his cognitive models now include more hints about people's more general attitudes as well (i.e., "second-order" judgments; and see below for further discussion of first- and second-order cultivation).

The present volume includes a good deal of new material for those interested in how we process the messages and stories of television at a cognitive level. Shrum's work provides solid evidence that heuristic processing (the use of mental shortcuts) is at play when forming judgments of social reality (and that, unless prompted to do so, we do not consider the source of our impressions, and hence do not discount them as coming from television). Building on these insights, Bradley and Matthews (Chapter 11) provide a novel and interesting look at how cognitive processing can be modeled in computer simulations; their results are highly consistent with a heuristic processing explanation of how cultivation occurs. Busselle and Bilandzic (Chapter 9) investigate a related but distinct question: how much realism makes a difference in whether or not programs contribute to cultivation. "Realism" is a slippery term that has been invoked by researchers in many vague and contradictory ways; Busselle and Bilandzic's valuable inquiry provides a clear and systematic explication of the concept, and in the process they illuminate and extend its relevance to cultivation. While many researchers have thought that only programs perceived as "realistic" would have an effect on our beliefs about the world, we can now see that while the answer is not that simple it is also more interesting.

Busselle and Bilandzic argue that the assumption that viewers are more likely to be influenced by content perceived to be "real" needs to be conceptually reversed. They contend that perceived realism is a default condition, contrary to conventional presumptions regarding the "suspension of disbelief." The implications for cultivation are that most content (even fantasy content) carries some stamp of perceived realism; it is not that far-fetched that viewers then carry impressions from TV over to the real world. More interesting may be the cases in which viewers decide that content is *un*real, potentially affecting and disturbing the cultivation processes that depend on viewers' natural assumptions.

Since the question was posed in 1990, we can now say that we know quite a lot about the cognitive mechanisms that explain how cultivation occurs. Still, there is little doubt that the cognitive processes at work in cultivation are ripe for even more investigation. While our volume highlights the major achievements so far, all of the authors dealing with this question discuss new directions in cultivation research that are likely to yield even more fruit.

In their second question, Morgan and Signorielli asked if cultivation research would show different or unexpected results when expanded to more demographic categories and subgroups. One of the early complaints about cultivation was that it was too "macro" in its focus because it examined entire populations. The early research that broke down overall relationships within single subgroups resulted in the phenomenon of mainstreaming, so perhaps it was logical to think that further specification would yield other, even more interesting results. In 1990, variations in subgroup patterns seemed especially important; although conditional patterns such as mainstreaming and resonance appeared in the data with great frequency, the challenge was to try to predict *when* and *for whom* they would occur. As it has turned out, this line of investigation was not one that many scholars have explicitly pursued, although we see it here and there in this volume (and in the larger body of cultivation literature). Subgroup analysis is a standard aspect of cultivation research, but it often has an ad hoc quality to it; little theorizing has been devoted to questions of systematic differential vulnerability across demographic groups. Consequently, those questions remain to be answered.

Interesting findings are seen in Mastro and Tukachinsky's examination of the cultivation of perceptions of minority groups (Chapter 3). Moreover there is still valuable work that can be done on perceptions *by* minorities as well as perceptions *of* minorities. Yet, the exploration of specific patterns of cultivation in diverse subgroups, to determine if certain types of people are consistently more or less "cultivation-prone," has not been a major focus of recent research. Interestingly, this may be due to the fact that our meta-analysis (Shanahan & Morgan, 1999) did not yield many differences by subgroup. Our most notable and consistent finding was that cultivation was stronger for liberals than moderates and conservatives; this is because many cultivation analyses of political issues have found mainstreaming patterns in which subgroups' positions showed "blurring, blending, and bending" toward a conservative view. A similar pattern emerged for those with more education, with mainstreaming in the direction of less educated individuals. While the theory still allows that issues of social identity are important in terms of how they bound television's contributions, empirical work has not continued to put much sustained or systematic effort in this direction. Most studies find clear differences across and among various demographic and other subgroups, and we hope that researchers will put some effort into developing and testing theories about what those differences mean.

Third (and related), Morgan and Signorielli asked whether future research might explore how cultivation was mediated by family or interpersonal relations. Since explorations in subgroups are an ideal way to uncover moderation, the idea that familial co-viewing or interpersonal processes stand "between" television and the viewer was also intriguing, since so much television viewing takes place in a family context (just as so much family interaction takes place in a television viewing context). Some studies in the 1980s looked at how family and peer relationships and patterns of co-viewing mediate cultivation (Rothschild, 1984; Rothschild & Morgan, 1987), and this seemed to be a promising area for future research. Indeed, since that time a fair amount of research has been conducted that looks explicitly at interpersonal discussion in relation to media exposure in areas such as political awareness or political behavior (e.g., McLeod, Scheufele, & Moy, 2001). Not surprisingly, the statistical influence of interpersonal discussion networks often outweighs that of exposure to mass media, a consistent finding in media effects research since the 1940s. Yet, research that actually examines the mediation of *cultivation* through discussion networks is much less frequent, and the role of family viewing patterns has not been given much recent attention in cultivation research. To an extent, this may have something to do with the proliferation of multiset households and the decline of television viewing as an all-family experience. But even if they're not watching together as much, family relationships in general are still likely to moderate cultivation patterns.

While most researchers recognize that mediated, interpersonal, and mediated interpersonal influences are all relevant to cultivation, not much research in the interim has looked directly at these mediations. One exception is

Busselle (2003), who found that parents who watch more crime shows issue more precautionary warnings, and this in turn relates to their children's perceptions of crime frequency. Further, as technologically mediated interpersonal forms have become more relevant (with email, the Internet, social media, texting, etc.), these questions can now be explored in new ways, and we look forward to research that will explore what social interaction via new media means for cultivation. We should also note that mediation itself has become quite an issue in communication research, especially from a methodological standpoint. Hayes (2005), for example, has offered more advanced models and methods for assessing mediation, and these could be of great use in cultivation research.

Fourth, one of the most complex issues identified by Morgan and Signorielli was the differences between first- and second-order effects (referred to then as the "levels" of cultivation). Again, first-order cultivation refers to beliefs about states of the world (often seen as estimates of the frequency of some type of behavior or type of person in the world). Second-order cultivation, on the other hand, is the cultivation of attitudes or feelings *about* the world. The distinction was first put forward by Hawkins and Pingree (1982), who called them "demographic" and "value systems" measures, respectively. Morgan and Signorielli also speculated about whether a third level (behavioral manifestations and consequences of first- and second-order cultivation) would prompt any research.

Initially, the term "second-order" cultivation (with no mention of "first-order" cultivation) was introduced in a 1986 overview of cultivation theory and research by Gerbner, Gross, Morgan, and Signorielli (p. 28). In delineating various "modes" of cultivation analysis, they first noted that many analyses compare a "real-world" statistic with a "TV world" statistic (e.g., the percent of people involved in violence, or the number of people in the population over 65, etc.) Then, they noted that cultivation analysis is not always based on the comparison of "facts" in the world of television and reality, but sometimes on "extrapolations" of those facts. For example, the notion of the "Mean World Syndrome" does not make any reference to or assumptions about how mean people are in the real world. This was referred to (in passing) as a kind of "second-order" cultivation.

Soon, others started using the terms first- and second-order, which led to an interest in whether first-order judgments somehow precede or "lead to" second-order judgments. The Cultural Indicators research group (and others; see Potter, 1991) found that there was no simple link between first- and second-order measures (and other studies using the distinction were not very successful). For these and other reasons, Shanahan and Morgan (1999) reported that Gerbner et al. attempted to "decommission" these terms from the cultivation vocabulary. But other researchers were far less willing to give them up.

For Shrum, the distinction between first- and second-order judgments turned out to be critical to understanding the psychological processes of cultivation. Precisely because they seem to be very different types of judgments that people make (especially in terms of when and how they make them), the concepts of first- and second-order judgments have gained even more traction and have now become well established; clearly, the terms appear in numerous chapters throughout this volume. While the differences are not necessarily those expected when the terms were first coined, it now seems that "first-order" and "second-order" are useful and valid concepts within the lexicon of cultivation, even though (or perhaps because) the simplistic notion that second-order beliefs flow linearly from the cultivation of first-order estimates has been dispelled.

Fifth, Morgan and Signorielli raised the question of the role of personal experience in cultivation, a matter that has received a lot of attention. The most well-known example from the cultivation literature was the role of personal experience in the cultivation of images of violence. Some critics had suggested that those who lived in more violent areas would also be more likely to stay inside their homes and hence watch more television, making the relationship spurious (Doob & Macdonald, 1979). These critiques sparked the development of notions such as "resonance," which argued that heavy viewers whose personal experiences with an issue most matched television's portrayals would actually be markedly higher on measures of a dependent variable (because they get a "double dose" of messages and experiences about that variable). Since those early days, resonance and mainstreaming have been the two most frequently cited elaborations of the basic cultivation finding, although mainstreaming seems to be much more commonly observed in the data. In this vein, Oliver, Bae, Ash, and Chung's review of the literature on television and fear of crime (see Chapter 2) focuses on "assessing individuals' affective and cognitive experiences related to their media exposure" (p. 18). The research reported in their chapter is not unlike that seen across much media effects research: There is a very strong move toward psychological-process examinations, reflecting the cognitive turn across many social sciences. But while these moves strongly implicate the importance of the individual (given their cognitive focus), the actual extent to which they uncover individual experiences is perhaps less noticeable. In many of these studies, individuals are basically seen as sharing cognitive processes that are fundamentally universal, so variance in individual experience is given less importance.

In this regard, Mastro and Tukachinsky's comparison of the resonance and substitution hypotheses is also relevant (Chapter 3). The hypotheses differ in their predictions (with resonance claiming that direct experience can enhance effects and substitution positing greater effects in the *absence* of direct experience), but what they have in common is that both suggest that effects will be more pronounced when first-hand experience does *not* run counter to television's messages and images. In an international context, Hetsroni, Elphariach, Kapuza, and Tsfoni (2007) found that cultivation was stronger when "geographical proximity" (and, therefore, first-hand experience) was low. Bilandzic (2006) frames this issue in terms of "distance" according to subjective "zones of relevance" that activate distinct cognitive mechanisms and processing strategies that also vary differentially for first- and second-order cultivation. Clearly, theorizing about the moderating role of personal experience in cultivation has come a long way since 1990. Yet, the fact that various studies (e.g., Gross & Aday, 2003; Minnebo & Eggermont, 2007) continue to produce conflicting findings on this question confirms the perfunctory maxim that "more research is needed."

Sixth, Morgan and Signorielli asked about the "orientations" of viewers toward television, by which they mainly meant "active" versus "passive" viewing along with issues related to viewer "involvement." Viewer activity has of course been a frequent topic of debate in the media effects literature. Cultivation has often been dismissed as simplistically assuming a passive audience of "cultural dupes." This is, we feel, an overstatement and mis-interpretation of Gerbner's original ideas. While cultivation presumes that viewers do watch television ritualistically, by the clock, and not necessarily in a mindful way, this does not mean that viewers are in a "robotic" state or that all messages somehow magically create effects. Rather, the point of cultivation is that routine exposure to many consistent messages, over time, results in absorption of the main features of those messages by heavy viewers, contributing to the stability of dominant cultural patterns. Viewer activity might actually strengthen the process. So, Morgan and Signorielli called for research to see how viewer "activity" (which can be both a trait and a state variable) might moderate cultivation. Once again, the most important findings come from Shrum's research. Basically (and again, see Chapter 8 for a fuller discussion) cultivation is due to heuristic processing, which implies a relatively less active cognitive state (in the sense of the desire to take cognitive short-cuts) at the time a judgment is made about social reality. Viewers, when prompted to think intensely about an issue, are less likely to show cultivation effects. When experimental participants are prompted to think actively, they very clearly discount sources such as television because it is mostly fictional or in other ways not worthy of informing their judgments about actual reality. This finding is consistent with the arguments originally set forth by Gerbner et al., but of course it is open to revision as cognitively oriented studies proceed.

Moreover, in many ways the entire active/passive question is misleading, at least insofar as it is usually focused on a somewhat false dichotomy of viewers as either very active (always interpreting, viewing critically, searching for unique meanings, etc.) or very passive (never displaying any of these interpretive qualities, constantly victims of television's "magic bullet"); viewers of either type are imaginary. Fortunately, this controversy seems to be fading away. More interesting are ideas such as narrative "transportation," which explores what happens when viewers becoming "lost" and "absorbed" in stories. Is transportation an active or a passive state? Transportation may have both active and passive elements, making the distinction even less relevant. Moreover, as Busselle and Bilandzic note in this volume (Chapter 9, p. 81), "research has shown that higher levels of transportation or absorption in stories positively relate to changes in beliefs and attitudes." Thus, while engaged viewing is a highly active process (viewers don't do much of anything else while they are actively absorbed in stories), it also seems that being "carried away" tends to open viewers up to all sorts of information absorption and outright persuasion that might not otherwise occur. As well, the discussion of mental models by Ewoldsen and Rhodes (Chapter 10) shows that viewers are active in internalizing models that everyone else shares. Thus, we think a good deal of the research discussed in this volume should dispel the idea that cultivation assumes "passive," helpless viewers and should help move beyond the entire distracting active/passive debate. Research on richer concepts such as transportation has been promising so far, and we hope to see more of it.

Still, on this general topic Morgan and Signorielli were also wondering whether viewer "involvement" (a concept often employed in uses and gratifications research) was an intervening "orientation" variable in cultivation. Some people watch a lot of television because they love it, and are devoted fans of their favorite shows and actors. Others watch a lot of television because they have very little else they can do in their lives. It's an open question whether these sorts of different orientations—and differences in the "meaning" of television in people's lives—produce different patterns of cultivation.

Seventh, Morgan and Signorielli highlighted the roles of specific programs and genres in cultivation. There has always been a certain amount of ambiguity (and controversy) about genres within cultivation. The basic, "classic" hypothesis indicates that overall amount of viewing is the only meaningful independent variable of interest. Gerbner felt that different genres of television were not insignificant but that they raised research questions different from those of cultivation. He argued not that there were no differences between different types of programs (much less that their messages were invariant or all the same), but that they have more in common than meets the eye, and that the overall, aggregate *system* of messages across and within all of the genres of television was the critical issue in cultivation; to understand the cultural role of television the institution requires taking account of that overall system of messages. According to Gerbner,

> Even to the extent that viewers feel that they are being selective in favoring or avoiding certain types of programs, the thematic and dramatic elements making up different types and genres of programs are often quite similar. In cultivation analysis we should ignore plot configurations and formal variety as—while perhaps aesthetically and morally satisfying—concealing by their surface novelty the underlying uniformity of the basic 'building blocks' of the television world: thematic structure, interaction patterns, social typing, and fate (success-failure, violence-victimization, etc.) meted out to the different social types. These over-arching elements expose large communities over long periods of time to a coherent structure of conceptions about life and the world. The investigation of this structure is the principal aim of cultivation analysis. (Gerbner, 1990, pp. 255–256)

Plots and formats clearly vary in different genres, but it is the overall patterns of settings, actions, casting, and fate "to which total communities are regularly exposed over long periods of time" that "is most likely to cultivate stable and common conceptions of reality" (Gerbner, 1998, p. 121). As Shanahan and Morgan (1999, p. 28) argued, it is the "bucket, not the drops" that should matter most to the cultivation researcher.

Nevertheless, Gerbner's insistence on overall, undifferentiated amount of viewing always generated much criticism (e.g., Hawkins & Pingree, 1981) and early on, other researchers eagerly explored how exposure to specific genres was related to attitudes. Signorielli and Morgan's (1990) volume contained examinations of pornographic and religious genres, and today, probably more studies that invoke cultivation as their conceptual framework look at exposure to some specific genre(s) than look at overall amount of viewing. In this volume, Bilandzic and Busselle (see Chapter 13) are strong advocates of examining genres, and they reference many studies that have been similarly approving of the concept of genre analysis within cultivation research. Many of these studies have focused on crime genres (which includes local news programming), as exposure to these genres has predicted attitudes about crime. Their research is interesting in that they see genre as simply another important facet of narrative that is consistent with Gerbner's original outlook on cultivation.

All this relates to the question of selective viewing: How much do viewers with "pre-existing" characteristics or traits turn to types of genres that gratify these traits? Morgan and Signorielli's concern, when they raised the question, focused on how much portrayals and images cut across most types of programs; and, at the time, it could be taken for granted that the vast majority of heavy viewers were seeing pretty much the same programming. Of course, we are now dealing with a television environment that has many more channels available, and new genres (such as reality programming) have emerged, which is certain to make genre an ongoing focus for cultivation research.

Similarly, both Scharrer's chapter on gender roles (Chapter 5) and Mastro and Tukachinsky's on race (Chapter 3) show that genres continue to be investigated for their impacts on conceptions about people and for their impacts on specific subgroups. With all of these developments, it's impossible to ignore that television is in many ways becoming more like magazines—divided into all kinds of special interests (cooking, dancing, home renovation, romance, golf, cars, etc.). As Gerbner himself was interested in magazines (Gerbner, 1958) and was known to write about particular programs (Gerbner, 1963, 1991), it is possible that he would now also be more interested in specific types of shows. But surface diversity does not necessarily mean true heterogeneity of message content, both for magazines and television. Thus, for these and other reasons, we expect and hope that researchers will also continue to measure and analyze overall viewing even when assessing cultivation within genres.

This raises the issue of new media environments. Morgan and Signorielli posed two questions (the eighth and ninth in our ongoing list): "How and what do other media cultivate?" and "How will new technologies influence cultivation?" In 1990, before the real rise of the Internet, "other media" meant newspapers, radio, and cinematic film, and "new media" meant devices such as VCRs or cable service. Clearly there has been a dramatic shift in the potential impact of new media. We have dealt with this elsewhere (Morgan & Shanahan, 2010), arguing that the fundamental tenets of cultivation have not changed: Mass-produced commercial storytelling—mostly through television and other "screens"—means that it is still reasonable to look for cultivation, even if those screens are now mobile and if programs can be watched at will. And it is interesting to note that, despite the proliferation of new media, studies on cultivation continue very strongly, just as television viewing itself continues to rise.

Some new media do get research attention, such as video games and social networking, as they should. To the extent that these new media are narrative devices (with video games, at first they weren't but now, much of the time, they are), one may look for cultivation. But, to take another example, there are really no studies on cultivation by the Internet because it is not clear what the consistent "message" of stories would be from that system. When one watches TV programs on the Internet one is still "watching TV," but when one uses the Internet to read email, check a friend's Facebook status, or tweet, something else is happening, something that does not (usually) involve mass-produced stories. Therefore, we didn't see a need within this volume for a chapter devoted exclusively to "new media" and cultivation. We had such a chapter in *Television and its Viewers* (Shanahan & Morgan, 1999), perhaps defensively arguing that cultivation would survive the expected onslaught of attacks from those who were ready to assume that TV would die along with the theories that originated in an outdated era of mass communication research. That day may still come, but it is not here yet. As we have said elsewhere:

> the future paradigmatic status of cultivation and other related theories depends in large part on future developments in media institutions and technologies. The traditional business model of broadcast television may be in peril, but we think it's safe to say that television will remain our primary cultural storyteller for some time to come (Morgan & Shanahan, 2010, p. 351)

The contributions by Hardy (Chapter 6) and Ruddock (Chapter 18) show that key arguments from early cultivation studies remain vital, sometimes in unexpected ways, as new media continue to emerge and evolve. At the same time, the Internet raises a host of as-yet unexamined new issues for cultivation that we hope researchers will take up in the future. Again, does the use of social media moderate cultivation? Early research showed that children who were less integrated into peer groups were more "vulnerable" to cultivation (Rothschild, 1984). Are those who have more online "friends" more integrated into meaningful social networks or are they in some ways more isolated, and how does that affect cultivation? Does the heavy use of fan sites or Twitter feeds devoted to specific programs increase the likelihood of transportation? Does heavy use of the web *per se* moderate cultivation? How does using the web *while* watching television affect the way program content is processed? Does heavy viewing online (or on a DVR) have different implications for cultivation than heavy viewing over the air on a conventional television? On the other hand, Riddle (Chapter 14) shows that it is television viewing across a lifetime that should spur our interest, and her chapter shows how this construct may be measured. Clearly, television will evolve from this point forward, so it behooves researchers to keep their eyes on what *joins* different forms of watching TV (whether it be traditionally, on computers, time-shifted, on cell phones, etc.) as much as what will separate the different forms in the future. These and other questions are waiting for researchers to explore.

This brings us to Morgan and Signorielli's tenth (and final) question, which had to do with comparative cultivation analysis in international environments. At that time, international cultivation was an important and growing issue. Wober (1990), for instance, had argued that his failure to find cultivation in the U.K. meant that the theory did not work; Gerbner et al. (1979) simply ascribed that as being due to differences in the television systems between the U.S. and the U.K. After the early debates, attempts to replicate (or refute) cultivation were carried out in many different countries. Cultivation has now been examined in at least 25 countries around the globe, and such comparative analyses offer a rich perspective on the dynamics of diverse constellations of media messages, cultural systems, and political/commercial controls and constraints.

But what has also occurred since that time is the rapid globalization and commercialization of most television systems around the world. Accompanying this change has been the moves of most other countries toward something like a U.S. commercial model (and with many U.S. and global channels delivered via cable or satellite). So, even while Wober might have found that television in a more paternalistic system such as England's might foster less cultivation of images of violence, the structural differences between the U.S. systems and systems based on public service (as well as many of those under strict state control) have narrowed considerably. More and more countries have gained the ability to produce their own programs in local languages, but audience demand in the commercial environment means that they veer toward tried and true story formats. And while there is far more international exchange of programs, the U.S. still dominates exports. Thus, and not just for issues of violence, the possibilities for cultivation internationally are probably magnifying. Moreover, the tendency for some programs to achieve massive global popularity in diverse local manifestations (e.g., locally produced versions of program types such as *American Idol* and *Big Brother* are huge hits in dozens of countries) raises fascinating issues for cross-cultural comparative analysis.

In this volume, Van den Bulck (Chapter 12) puts international cultivation on a more solid theoretical footing. As the amount of international cultivation work has grown, so has the need to take stock of it in a systematic way. Van den Bulck focuses more on how television affects people when it is not from their own culture (as he has studied so voluminously in his native Belgium). The culture of American TV still reaches far beyond its borders; prisoners in Belgium think they will be read their Miranda rights. For Van den Bulck, many new avenues of investigation are being opened up, with television being seen as something that can be important not only to native populations ("primary cultivation") but also to visitors, immigrants, and those outside of the country where the content was produced. Undoubtedly, the expansion of television channels will mean that more people can be exposed to messages from more systems; as global culture evolves television will with it as well as the possibilities for international cultivation analysis.

Van den Bulck's chapter is also an example of how cultivation research can expand and intersect with other disciplines. There is no reason that how cultivation relates to sociological concepts such as acculturation might not see parallels in fields such as criminology, sexuality, and politics. Clearly, as television evolves, cultivation also needs to evolve to capture new phenomena, but also to make sure that what is invariant and traditional about television (its storytelling capacity) is understood as well.

***

Moving beyond the questions posed over twenty years ago by Morgan and Signorielli (1990), several chapters in the present volume reflect the emerging phenomenon of exploring the intersections of cultivation and other theories of media effects. Hetsroni and Lowenstein, in Chapter 15, examine the similarities and differences between cultivation theory and agenda-setting. They propose a model that combines these two theories in a framework described as a "reality construction process." This multi-step model examines first- and second-order effects in relation to both theories, looking particularly at media consumption habits and how topics are presented in the media in both news and fiction. As the authors note, the model can be applied to virtually any topic, and we hope researchers will put it to the test in the near future.

Diefenbach and West (Chapter 16) explore the relevance of cultivation for research on the third-person effect. They found that the third-person effect can help shed light on the processes involved in cultivation—and vice versa. More specifically, these two theories are seen as being complementary to each other in that cultivation may be used as any other media effect in terms of measuring perceived effects on self and other; unlike many other such effects, combining cultivation with the third-person effect may also say something about the *accuracy* of those perceptions. At the same time, they found that research on the types of questions explored in third-person research may provide "insight into beliefs and attitudes of the television viewer" (p. 344) in some surprising ways.

Similarly, the theoretical and empirical intersections of cultivation theory and the spiral of silence are examined by Shanahan and Scheufele in Chapter 17. They link the two theories in a study focusing on individual attitudes about smoking and willingness to speak up against it in a public setting. Above and beyond the results of this particular study, the chapter shows that these two seemingly disparate theoretical approaches have a great deal in common. Apart from the interesting links that can be developed in an empirical model (some of which are seen in the chapter), the synthesis of two previously disconnected components of a "powerful effects" model is also of interest.

All of the chapters that link cultivation with other theories tend to confirm an observation made by Morgan and Shanahan (2010): Cultivation seems to be evolving from a "theory" more toward something of a "paradigm." As more and more investigators take up the basic threads of the theory, they seek to test subsidiary hypotheses not necessarily suggested by the earlier basic research. And since the theory has been developing since the 1970s, there has been ample time for many new ideas and issues to arise. Certainly the work collected here looks far different (though with many important continuities) from what the original investigators might have envisioned.

Thus, the methods and approaches seen in Ewoldsen and Rhodes (Chapter 10) and Ruddock (Chapter 18) differ greatly from the (relatively) straightforward survey and content analyses that Gerbner and Gross (1976) first laid out for message system and cultivation analysis. Ewoldsen draws from anthropology; Ruddock from cultural studies. While these interdisciplinary influences certainly could be seen as consistent with Gerbner's original outlooks, it's still striking to see how far afield the investigations are now traveling. In some ways these chapters take us beyond what the vast majority of researchers have done with Gerbner's original ideas, though they also are heavily informed by the spirit of his ideas.

We see other promising advances in the methodology of cultivation analysis here as well. Nisbet and Myers (Chapter 4) deploy new multi-level methods to address more exactly some of the questions that Gerbner posed. Using advanced techniques, they may be one of the first to capture the nature of cultivation *in the data*. And in Chapter 7 (Brossard & Dudo), we see more than ongoing research on cultivation of science attitudes. The work provides an agenda for future research development and exemplifies the forward progress that cultivation continues to make in a variety of specialized areas. But it also signals a path for traditional cultivation methods, recognizing that detailed content data, analysis of more complex models, and increased theoretical sophistication will always be a feature of any research that is going to make progress in this area.

We titled this book *Living with Television Now* both to acknowledge the elegant simplicity of the techniques introduced by Gerbner and Gross (1976) and to point out that they are still relevant. The book, then, is a compendium of much that is new, but it is of a piece with what has come before. Television as storyteller, audience as listener, and the relationship between teller and listener are the fundamental components of the outcome that we call "cultivation." The audience is more fragmented than when Gerbner was writing, and the number (and size and quality and mobility) of screens available to us has steadily increased. But the question of the relationship between the stories we tell and the way we see the world (and who gets to tell those stories, and to whom) remains as vital as ever. Gerbner's concept of cultivation has proven to be persistent, resilient, and flexible as times change and technologies emerge and institutions evolve. For the future: stay tuned. . .

## Note

1. Despite the prolific nature of George Gerbner's scholarly output, he never authored a book about cultivation. See Morgan (2002) for an anthology of Gerbner's key writings.

## References

Bilandzic, H. (2006). The perception of distance in the cultivation process: A theoretical consideration of the relationship between television content, processing experience, and perceived distance. *Communication Theory, 16*, 333–355.

Busselle, R. (2003). Television exposure, parents' precautionary warnings, and perceptions of Crime. *Communication Research, 30*, 530–556.

Doob, A., & Macdonald, G. (1979). Television viewing and fear of victimization: Is the relationship causal? *Journal of Personality and Social Psychology, 37*(2), 170–179.

Gerbner, G. (1958). The social anatomy of the romance-confession cover girl. *Journalism Quarterly, 35*, 299–306.

Gerbner, G. (1963). 'Mr. Novak': Young man to watch. *Phi Delta Kappan, 45*(1), 13–19.

Gerbner, G. (1990). Epilogue: Advancing on the path of righteousness (maybe). In N. Signorielli & M. Morgan (Eds.), *Cultivation analysis: New directions in media effects research* (pp. 249–262). Newbury Park, CA: Sage.

Gerbner, G. (1991). The turtles live to ooze again. *AdVice, 1*(3), n.p.

Gerbner, G. (1998). Telling stories, or how do we know what we know? The story of cultural indicators and the cultural environment movement. *Wide Angle, 20*(2), 116–131.

Gerbner, G., & Gross, L. (1976). Living with television: The violence profile. *Journal of Communication, 26*(2), 173–199.

Gerbner, G., Gross, L., Morgan, M., & Signorielli, N. (1979). On Wober's 'Televised Violence and Paranoid Perception: The View from Great Britain.' *Public Opinion Quarterly, 43*(1), 123–124.

Gerbner, G., Gross, L., Morgan, M., & Signorielli, N. (1986). Living with television: The dynamics of the cultivation process. In J. Bryant & D. Zillman (Eds.), *Perspectives on media effects* (pp. 17–40). Hillsdale, NJ: Erlbaum.

Gross, K., & Aday, S. (2003). The scary world in your living room and neighborhood: Using local broadcast news, neighborhood crime rates, and personal experience to test agenda setting and cultivation. *Journal of Communication, 53*(3), 411–426.

Hawkins, R. P., & Pingree, S. (1981). Uniform content and habitual viewing: Unnecessary assumptions in social reality effects. *Human Communication Research, 7*(4), 291–301.

Hawkins, R. P., & Pingree, S. (1982). Television's influence on social reality. In D. Pearl, L. Bouthilet, & J. Lazar (Eds.), *Television and behavior: Ten years of scientific progress and implications for the 80's,* Volume II, Technical Reviews (pp. 224–247). Rockville, MD: NIMH.

Hawkins, R., Pingree, S., & Adler, I. (1987). Searching for cognitive processes in the cultivation effect. *Human Communication Research, 13*(4), 553–577.

Hayes, A. (2005). *Statistical methods for communication science.* Mahwah, NJ: Erlbaum.

Hetsroni, A., Elphariach, H., Kapuza, R., & Tsfoni, B. (2007). Geographical proximity, cultural imperialism, and the cultivation effect. *Communication Monographs, 74*(2), 181–199.

McLeod, J. M., Scheufele, D. A., & Moy, P. (2001). Community, communication, and participation: The role of mass media and interpersonal discussion in local political participation. *Political Communication, 16*(3), 315–336.

Minnebo, J., & Eggermont, S. (2007). Watching the young use illicit drugs: Direct experience, exposure to television and the stereotyping of adolescents' substance use. *Young, 15*, 129–144.

Morgan, M. (Ed.). (2002). *Against the mainstream: The selected works of George Gerbner.* New York: Peter Lang Publishing.

Morgan, M., & Shanahan, J. (2010). The state of cultivation. *Journal of Broadcasting & Electronic Media, 54*(2), 337–355.

Morgan, M., & Signorielli, N. (1990). Cultivation analysis: Conceptualization and methodology. In N. Signorielli & M. Morgan (Eds.), *Cultivation analysis: New directions in media effects research* (pp. 13–34). Newbury Park, CA: Sage.

Potter, W. (1991). Examining cultivation from a psychological perspective: Component subprocesses. *Communication Research, 18*, 77–102.

Rothschild, N. (1984). Small group affiliation as a mediating factor in the cultivation process. In G. R. Melischek, K. E. Rosengren, & J. Stappers (Eds.), *Cultural indicators: An international symposium* (pp. 377–387). Vienna: Verlag der Osterreichischen Akademie der Wissenschaften.

Rothschild, N., & Morgan, M. (1987). Cohesion and control: Relationships with parents as mediators of television. *Journal of Early Adolescence, 7*(3), 299–314.

Shanahan, J., & Morgan, M. (1999). *Television and its viewers: Cultivation theory and research.* Cambridge: Cambridge University Press.

Signorielli, N., & Morgan, M. (Eds.). (1990). *Cultivation analysis: New directions in media effects research.* Newbury Park, CA: Sage.

Wober, J. (1990). Does television cultivate the British? Late 80s evidence. In N. Signorielli & M. Morgan (Eds.), *Cultivation analysis: New directions in media effects research.* (pp. 207–224.). Newbury Park, CA: Sage.

# About the Authors

**Erin Ash** is a doctoral candidate in the College of Communications at Penn State University. Her research is focused on stereotyping in media and cognitive and affective responses to media portrayals of racial groups.

**Keunmin Bae** is a PhD student (ABD) in the College of Communications at Penn State University. His research interests include news media, communication technologies, and media psychology.

**Helena Bilandzic** is a Professor at the University of Augsburg. Her research interests include narrative experience and persuasion, cultivation, media use, and methodology.

**Samuel D. Bradley** is an Associate Professor and chairperson of the Department of Advertising at Texas Tech University. His research interests include psychophysiological responses to and computational modeling of mediated message processing.

**Dominique Brossard** is an Associate Professor in the Department of Life Sciences Communication at the University of Wisconsin-Madison. Her research program focuses on the intersection between science, media and policy, and more particularly public opinion dynamics in the context of controversial scientific innovations, such as biotechnology, stem cell research and nanotechnology.

**Rick Busselle** is an Associate Professor in The Murrow College of Communication at Washington State University. His research focuses on audience members' experiences with stories and how those experiences contribute to the social construction of issues related to poverty and crime.

**Mun-Young Chung** is a doctoral student in the College of Communications at Penn State University. His research interests center on psychological effects of media entertainment in the context of intrapersonal and intercultural communication.

**Don Diefenbach** is an Associate Professor in the Mass Communication Department of the University of North Carolina at Asheville. His research interests include cultivation, media violence, content analysis, and media portrayals of mental health issues.

**Anthony Dudo** is an Assistant Professor in the Department of Advertising and Public Relations at the University of Texas at Austin. His research interests include media coverage, public opinion, and strategic communication related to scientific and environmental issues.

**David R. Ewoldsen** is a Professor in the School of Communication and the Department of Psychology at the Ohio State University. His research interests include media psychology, attitude accessibility, and message processing.

**Larry Gross** is Professor and Director, USC Annenberg School for Communication & Journalism. From 1968 to 2003 he was on the faculty of the Annenberg School at the University of Pennsylvania, where he joined with George Gerbner in creating the Cultural Indicators project.

**Bruce W. Hardy** is an Assistant Professor in the Manship School of Mass Communication and the Department of Political Science at Louisiana State University. His research interests include the effects of political campaigns, political advertising, emergent technologies and society, and the interactive impact of interpersonal communication and media on attitudes and behavior.

**Amir Hetsroni** is an Associate Professor of communication at Ariel University Center in Israel. His research concerning popular TV programming and advertising and its impact has appeared in journals such as *Journal of Communication, Journal of Advertising, Communication Monographs, Sex Roles and Communication Research.*

**Jaehoon Lee** is Assistant Professor of Marketing at the University of Houston-Clear Lake. His research interests include the effects of self-threats on consumer behavior, conspicuous and status consumption, and the antecedents and consequences of materialistic goal pursuit.

**Hila Lowenstein** is a doctoral student of Political Science and Mass Media at Bar Ilan University, Israel. Her research focuses on the role of media in legitimizing enemy leaders as partners for peace. She also studies the effects of television in cultivating worldviews. She teaches the courses Introduction to Media, Television and New Media and Media and Society at Ariel University Center and at The Open University—both in Israel.

**Dana Mastro** is an Associate Professor in the Department of Communication at the University of Arizona. Her research examines the role of media in stereotyping, prejudice, and a variety of intergroup and identity-based outcomes.

**Curtis B. Matthews** is an Assistant Professor of Advertising & Public Relations in the A.Q. Miller School of Journalism and Mass Communications at Kansas State University. His research interests include the online cognitive and emotional processing of television narratives, and the impact storytelling has on memory.

**Michael Morgan** (Ph.D., University of Pennsylvania, 1980) is Professor of Communication at the University of Massachusetts Amherst. He has published many national and international cultivation studies and is the author of *George Gerbner: A Critical Introduction to Media and Communication Theory* (Peter Lang, 2012).

**Teresa Myers** is a Postdoctoral Research at the George Mason University Center for Climate Change Communication. Her research interests focus on media effects and public opinion, often in the context of environmental and political communication.

**Erik C. Nisbet** is an Assistant Professor at the Ohio State University School of Communication. His research interests are political communication, public opinion, and media effects.

**Mary Beth Oliver** is a Professor in the College of Communications at Penn State University. Her research interests focus on entertainment psychology and social cognition and the media.

**Nancy Rhodes** is an Associate Professor in the Department of Communication Studies at Indiana University Purdue University at Indianapolis. Her research interests include social influence processes in health, persuasion, and media psychology.

**Karyn Riddle** is an Assistant Professor in the School of Journalism and Mass Communication at the University of Wisconsin, Madison. Her research interests include the psychology of media effects, especially in the context of violent media content.

**Andy Ruddock** is Senior Lecturer in Communications and Media Studies at Monash University, Australia. His research interests include integrating cultivation and cultural studies, audience research and historical approaches to media and youth.

**Erica Scharrer** is a Professor in the Department of Communication at University of Massachusetts Amherst. She studies media content, media opinion, media effects, and media literacy, especially pertaining to gender and violence.

**Dietram A. Scheufele** holds the John E. Ross Chair in Science Communication at the University of Wisconsin, Madison, and is Co-PI of the Center for Nanotechnology in Society at Arizona State University. He has published over 100 peer-refereed articles, book chapters and monographs dealing with public opinion on emerging technologies and the political effects of mass communication.

**James Shanahan** is a Professor in the College of Communication at Boston University. His research interests include cultivation, cultural indicators and media effects.

**L. J. Shrum** is Professor and Chair of Marketing at the University of Texas at San Antonio. His research interests include the cognitive processes underlying media effects, the multiple roles of the self in consumer judgment, and the causes, consequences, and underlying processes of materialism.

**Nancy Signorielli** is Professor of Communication at the University of Delaware. An original member of the CI team, her research focuses on media content specifically relating to gender and violence and cultivation.

**Riva Tukachinsky** is a Doctoral Candidate in the Department of Communication at the University of Arizona. Her research interests are focused on the psychology of media effects.

**Jan Van den Bulck** is a Professor in the School for Mass Communication Research of the Katholieke Universiteit Leuven, Belgium. His research interests include cultivation, violence effects and health effects of media use.

**Mark D. West** is Professor and Chair of the Mass Communication Department of the University of North Carolina at Asheville. His research interests include cultivation, public sphere theory, content analysis, and public opinion.

# Author Index

# Subject Index